Communist Politics

Communist Politics

A Reader

Edited by

Stephen White
University of Glasgow

and

Daniel Nelson
University of Kentucky

MACMILLAN

First published 1986

Published by
MACMILLAN EDUCATION LTD
Houndmills, Basingstoke, Hampshire RG21 2XS
and London
Companies and representatives
throughout the world

Printed in Hong Kong

British Library Cataloguing in Publication Data
Communist politics: a reader.
1. Comparative government   2. Communist
countries—Politics and government
I. White, Stephen, *1945*– II. Nelson, Daniel N.
320.3'09171'7   JC474
ISBN 0–333–41406–3
ISBN 0–333–41407–1 Pbk

Contents

List of Contributors

Jack Bielasiak, *Indiana University*
Valerie Bunce, *Northwestern University*
Timothy J. Colton, *University of Toronto*
†John M. Echols III, *University of Illinois*
David S. G. Goodman, *University of Newcastle-upon-Tyne*
Alexander J. Groth, *University of California at Davis*
William M. LeoGrande, *American University, Washington DC*
David Lane, *University of Birmingham*
David S. Mason, *Butler University*
John H. Miller, *LaTrobe University*
Daniel N. Nelson, *University of Kentucky*
Michel Oksenberg, *University of Michigan*
David M. Olson, *University of North Carolina, Greensboro*
†Ralph Pervan, *University of Western Australia*
Alex Pravda, *University of Reading*
Tony Saich, *Sinologisch Instituut, University of Leiden*
Maurice D. Simon, *University of North Carolina, Greensboro*
H. Gordon Skilling, *University of Toronto*
Bogdan Szajkowski, *University College, Cardiff*
Michael Waller, *University of Manchester*
Stephen White, *University of Glasgow*

Preface

Comparative communist politics is one of the most rapidly expanding sub-fields of political science. There are at least three reasons, in the mid and late 1980s, why this should be the case. The first concerns the considerable expansion in the number of communist or Marxist-Leninist regimes that has taken place over the past twenty years, or even over the past decade. At the end of the 1950s there were just fourteen generally recognised communist systems, in the USSR, Eastern Europe and Asia. By the early 1960s the Cuban revolution had publicly associated itself with Marxism-Leninism, the first regime in Latin America to do so; and by the mid-1970s communist governments had become established throughout most of South-East Asia, in Kampuchea, Laos and South Vietnam. At the same time a number of radical revolutionary movements, many of them of Marxist-Leninist inspiration and affiliation, came to power in various parts of Africa, Asia and Latin America. There has been some debate about the extent to which such regimes, many of them military, Islamic and of doubtful durability, may be classified as 'communist systems', and in this book we limit ourselves almost exclusively to the 'established' communist regimes – those that publicly identify with Marxism-Leninism, share important political and economic characteristics and are generally recognised as such. The expansion in the number of systems, at both the local and national level, claiming some sort of relationship to Marxism-Leninism is nevertheless a global reality of the 1980s, and it has given a continuous stimulus to the sub-discipline – comparative communism – which seeks to make sense of such developments academically.

A second reason for the expansion of comparative communist politics is the greater wealth of information and data that are now available for the serious student of the subject. Communist regimes have traditionally been among the world's most secretive systems, maintaining a firm and effective domestic censorship and limiting the flow of information both within each country and across its borders. There are obvious advantages in any such arrangement for regimes which are seeking to maintain their power other than through competitive elections and which are also attempting to socialise their populations into new, collectivist norms. At the same time the tight control of information leads to practical difficulties for planners, for party officials and for social scientists, who are expected in these countries to make a positive contribution to the formation of party and state policy; and with the slowdown in economic growth that the communist countries have generally experienced since the 1960s, a lack of information or openness in decision-making also runs the risk of encouraging alienation or even active opposition among the populations by whom any resulting sacrifices must be borne. The 1970s and 1980s have accordingly seen substantial improvements in access to information in most communist countries: in the USSR, for instance, reports of weekly Politburo meetings have been appearing in the press since the end of 1982, and in China a national statistical handbook has been appearing since 1981, together with a profusion of data of all kinds. Even for foreigners access to archives, to government officials, to villages for field studies, or even (in a few cases) to the mass public have all improved greatly, with major consequences for the academic literature on communist politics.

Thirdly, and no less important, the years up to the 1980s have seen important developments in theoretical approaches to the politics of the communist countries. The totalitarian paradigm, which was still dominant in the 1950s, came under increasingly critical scrutiny as the 1960s advanced. In turn a variety of other approaches, from 'modernisation' and 'convergence' to 'bureaucratic politics' and 'corporatism', made their appearance. By the 1980s it was probably fair to say that no alternative orthodoxy had become dominant; rather, a plurality of approaches had become accepted as legitimate or even desirable in relation to a group of political systems which were increasingly recognised to vary from each other and to contain a level of contradiction and complexity which made any single all-embracing formula more of an obstacle than an aid to understanding. Perhaps in consequence, scholarly interest has turned increasingly from 'macro' propositions in relation to communist systems as a whole towards 'micro' studies of more limited questions. Topics such as the role of groups, coalition formation, ethnic nationalism, the nature of associational bodies such as trade unions, the role of the mass media, political recruitment, the work of legislative bodies and regime–citizen relations, and the policy process in particular areas have all attracted a greater degree of attention and have begun to be dealt with in a manner which reflects both a greater concern for developments elsewhere in comparative politics and the improvements that have taken place in terms of access to information over the intervening years. By the late 1980s the study of comparative communist politics had attained, if not a higher level of development, then at least a greater maturity and theoretical awareness, combined with an expanding body of solidly documented individual and more general case studies.

In the chapters that follow we have sought to reflect some of the best of this recent work under five broad headings. The first section, which is limited to a single article, deals in a wide-ranging way with the historical origins of contemporary communism and with its contemporary global presence. The second, on structures of government, examines the formal framework of state politics in the communist countries with particular reference to the role of elections and of legislative bodies. In the third section we turn to the ruling communist parties, which direct this state machinery and which dominate political life in their respective countries; and in the fourth section we consider the variety of pressures, of both an institutional and an informal kind, which influence the parties and through them the pattern of public policy in these countries. Finally, in the fifth section, we consider a number of comparative perspectives upon the politics of the communist-ruled nations, including authors who reach rather different conclusions upon these hotly contested questions. Each of these later sections contains four or five different chapters, the first of which is normally a general or scene-setting paper, followed by others which deal in more detail with the same question in a particular national context. In each case we have sought, so far as possible, to include work published in the 1980s and reflecting current approaches to comparative communist politics. We have also included the work of political scientists who are based on both sides of the Atlantic, and in two cases further afield, in a manner which we hope provides an international as well as a contemporary perspective upon the work that is currently being conducted on the comparative politics of communist systems.

Even in a large book such as this there has been severe pressure upon space, and we have had to leave out many papers that under ideal conditions we would certainly have wished to include. We have, however, been able to find room for 19 separate contributions by some twenty-one different authors, and our selection is we hope a fair representation of some of the best of the work that has recently been appearing in communist politics. Most of the articles that have been included are reprinted at their original length; a few, however, have been shortened slightly, in most cases by the reduction of notes rather than of the text itself. All the articles have also been converted to a name–date style of referencing; a full list of sources, together with some other recent work on communist politics, appears in the bibliography at the end of the book. The transliteration of Russian is based throughout upon the style employed by the journal *Soviet Studies*, and Chinese transliteration is based upon the currently favoured *pinyin* system. In other respects the stylistic conventions of each article have been respected. Almost every article, however, has been partly rewritten and updated for this book, at least in terms of references to subsequent literature; a number of minor errors and misprints have been corrected; and in general, the versions which appear in this collection reflect so far as possible the state of knowledge in their respective subjects as of the mid-1980s. The present texts have in each case been approved by the authors concerned, and appear by permission of author and publisher. The appropriate acknowledgement appears on the first page of each chapter.

In conclusion, we would like to thank the authors of the chapters included in this volume, not simply for their permission to republish, but also for their active assistance with the revised text. Thanks are also due to Steven Kennedy, the publishing editor, for his interest in this project and for his detailed advice at all stages of its preparation. Drafts of edited chapters for this volume were typed by Kim Hayden at the University of Kentucky, and other sections by Elspeth Shaw, Avril Johnstone and Barbara Fisher at the University of Glasgow. Kathie Golden, a PhD student at the University of Kentucky, assisted in the preparation of references for many of the chapters. Therese C. Nelson assisted in proofing much of the text. Their help is appreciated greatly; none of them, of course, bears any responsibility for remaining errors or infelicities. The project as a whole was jointly planned by the two editors, first of all in a walk around Glasgow's Botanic Gardens and later in correspondence, and each was responsible for arranging for the preparation of about half of the edited chapters. The general introduction which follows was written by Daniel Nelson, and this preface and the section introductions by Stephen White; both authors, however, accept full responsibility for all aspects of the volume as a whole, which reflects the need they have felt for some time as teachers of comparative communist politics for an up-to-date and reasonably comprehensive selection of recent papers which could helpfully be recommended to their students. We hope that students and scholars in other universities, and in comparative politics as well as communist studies, will also find it of value.

Stephen White
Daniel Nelson

Introduction: The Comparative Study of Communist Politics

In the March 1967 issue of *Slavic Review* several political scientists whose specialties were principally Soviet politics wrote of the need for, and problems with, the 'comparative' study of communist systems (see Meyer, 1969 and Fleron, 1969, pp. 198–214). The appearance of such a collection of essays, at about the same time as the appearance of H. Gordon Skilling's *The Governments of Communist East Europe* (1966a) and Ghita Ionescu's *The Politics of the European Communist States* (1967), marked a significant change in the study of communist politics – a change that was to reduce substantially our reliance on the concept 'totalitarianism' as the focal point for understanding the USSR or other states ruled by communist parties. Instead of emphasising rigid, dogmatic political environments, as most scholars throughout the post-war period had been doing, social scientists studying communist politics began to probe the complexities of such systems, using the empirical tools increasingly at their disposal. By means of comparisons, scholars also began to test our 'hunches' about how political life operated in communist polities, subjecting commonly accepted propositions about these systems to empirical scrutiny.

Two decades after the transformation of communist studies was begun, it is no longer possible to give students a comprehensive reading list that would encompass most of the field. Nevertheless, the similarities and differences among communist systems form a critical part of students' understanding of any single communist state, or of Marxism and twentieth-century socialist thought, Central and East European history, East–West relations, and so forth. There is, in other words, a need to make available to students a collection of readings about contemporary communist politics from which comparisons can be drawn. Earlier efforts to satisfy such a need, while appropriate a decade ago, are now very outdated (Cohen and Shapiro, 1974; Bertsch and Ganschow, 1976). *Communist Politics: A Reader*, as we have noted in the Preface, is meant to satisfy this need: in other words, to make available a broadly comparative portrait of communist systems based upon research completed principally in the 1980s. This collection of scholarly articles, selected from professional

1

journals and other edited books, is a genuinely international endeavour, drawing upon the literatures of both the British and American scholarly communities, and representing the work of a wide variety of scholars.

Considerable attention, moreover, has been devoted to arranging selections in an understandable sequence, a sequence that integrates into five topics both cross-national and country-specific studies. Because any study of communist states requires an awareness of prior transformations in such systems, we begin with a selection which focuses attention on the recent political history of communism. Whereas the Soviet Union once epitomised communist party states, national cultures and international events have reshaped the environments in which communist leaders rule. At the outset, then, this volume points to the heterogeneous nature of communist systems in the 1980s. Political institutions occupy the second and third sections of this volume, with selections devoted to state organs such as national assemblies and local councils and changes within ruling communist parties. Particularly evident in these chapters about governmental structures and parties are the dynamic elements of communist politics which have yielded a diversity of communisms. No political institution in communist systems is uniform across systems or over time within one polity.

The complexities of communist systems, however, extend well beyond formal institutions. Varying among these states ruled by communist parties, many socioeconomic segments or strata, occupational or professional organisations, and other less well defined 'groups' appear to play a role in the making of public policy. This more recent interpretation of communist politics has been debated among scholars, and a section of this volume is devoted to selections representative of that debate. Such chapters regarding the 'inputs' affecting communist regimes' policy-making are followed by several chapters concerning the distribution of resources within political systems of a 'state socialist' character. Present throughout these final selections are the diverse achievements of communist party governments in the areas of human rights, worker welfare systems, and equality; and comparisons are offered, both with western liberal-democratic regimes, and with the regimes' own stated objectives and values.

Studying the comparative politics of communist systems

These nineteen articles, or any other collection for that matter, can hardly hope to cover every nuance of political life in communist systems. Indeed, these chapters represent, at most, the 'tip of the iceberg' in terms of available literature and research foci. (The lengthy bibliography appended to this volume includes not only the literature cited by the authors of these chapters but also a selection of other recent work in communist politics, and should serve both to indicate the literature available and to provide a basis for essay and research assignments and for further work.) Assigned in conjunction with other texts, however, this collection should help to post a *comparative* perspective on communist politics. The articles that follow contain both simple truths and complex findings about communist politics. Neither, however, would be evident through an intensive study of one communist state alone.

The simple truths of comparative communism are embedded in the diversity, change, paradox, and irony which abound in the politics of such systems. These are not nation-states with identical frameworks of government, 'rules of the game', or political personalities. While they rule in an environment still heavily influenced by the hegemonic power of the Soviet Union, most communist parties have increasingly adapted to domestic circumstances via economic reforms, their treatment of dissent and political self-expression, or divergent foreign policies. What was once presumed to be the constancy of totalitarianism also gives way to another simple truth – namely, the dynamic nature of communist systems. It is easy to presume that, in political environments where organised opposition is banned, the potential for systemic evolution must be nil. But the deaths of leaders (e.g. the deaths of Stalin or Mao) create opportunities for successors to alter substantially the party's policies and its relationship with the people it rules. Moreover, policy initiatives (such as the New Economic Mechanism in Hungary) can transform the regime's image and substance; abandoning rigid central planning has been an important element in the political changes one finds among communist systems.

The simple truth that communist systems are filled with inconsistencies, contradictions and absurdities also becomes apparent from comparative study. Certainly we know that political systems such as the United Kingdom and the United States exhibit many examples of paradoxical behaviour. Laws are passed by legislative bodies that exacerbate the problem they were meant to correct; policies which have disastrous consequences are continued because bureaucrats have vested interests in them; individuals known to be incompetent are advanced into posts of responsibility because of their personal loyalty to a particular politician. The comparative study of communist systems suggests that these conditions of political life are present where Leninist parties rule as well. Indeed, one encounters in communist party states much of the same irrationality of our own democratic polities; to ask *why* an event occurs often reveals a failure to perceive the system's paradoxical and irrational nature. That 'monolithic, totalitarian communism' can be, and often is, at a 'loose end' – unable effectively to coordinate and control all social and political forces – is easily recognised. But a comparative study of communist systems refines such a point, and enables us to identify where such regimes are most inconsistent and contradictory.

Finally, one learns of irony in communist systems. The most poignant of such ironies is that of persistent or even growing inequality in allegedly socialist systems ruled by parties with Marxism at their intellectual core. More than any other modern political philosophy, Marxism is rooted in the value of equality, specifically through an end to economically based classes. Communist parties rationalise both the fact of their rule and the manner in which they effect that rule by arguing that the interests of working people are pursued through the party's hold on power. But the concern of communist regimes has always been, at least from the time of Stalin's first five year plan, extensive growth of the economy much more than a redistribution of wealth among socioeconomic segments and strata. In that very important respect, the performance of communist party governments has never squared well with their ideological roots. And the irony of parties with such ideological origins pursuing extensive growth at the expense of equality becomes dramatic in comparative studies of communist politics.

Complex findings regarding communist party states are also evident in the studies contained in this volume. A few of the chapters principally offer summaries of the field of communist studies. However, the predominant theme of the work included in *Communist Politics: A Reader* is concern with the development, or testing, of hypotheses. Hypotheses – statements regarding the expected relationship between two or more variables – are not always clearly identifiable in these selections. Nevertheless, the task undertaken consistently by these authors is the observation of political phenomena in one or more communist states in order to allow comparison with other communist states. Many chapters in this book focus on one country, and do not explicitly compare findings with other cases. But the questions being asked are always comparable; that is, scholars often utilise 'leads' drawn from one case to investigate similar phenomena in another country.

For example, one will find that Olson and Simon's article provides many details about the Polish national assembly (the Sejm) without explicitly using another communist state's legislative body for comparison. Yet, they not only make occasional references to the USSR, but also consider the broader questions of parliamentary development and institutional change in authoritarian systems generally. Similarly, Oksenberg writes about China alone, but the issues are omnipresent for all students of authoritarian polities. When a charismatic leader dies – such as, in this case, Mao Zedong – what transformations take place in policy-making and implementation? What are the strengths and weaknesses of the new system? And to what extent will it serve the purposes of the new leaders?

One might begin either an analysis of parliamentary institutions or policy-making in communist states with certain expectations. After the death of a charismatic figure, for instance, a widespread turnover of administrative elites might be expected to occur, as might also a swing towards decentralised policy-implementation. The Chinese case allows a 'preliminary test' of that hypothesis. Likewise, the Polish case enables one to test expectations about changing functions of national assemblies or other representative institutions in authoritarian systems. By looking at data regarding the Sejm's activities, one finds considerable evidence regarding the potential for representative assemblies to expand their roles in authoritarian environments. And many other examples could be quoted.

The point of drawing attention to these specific findings from articles in *Communist Politics: A Reader* is not to exaggerate the explanatory power of the social sciences. Rather, one needs to recognise that the purpose of studying communist states is not merely to portray in ever greater detail the 'simple truths' discussed above. We are, instead, engaged in a process of expanding knowledge about political life regardless of the nation-state in which it occurs. While knowledge about Poland, China and other communist countries is vital, we are also interested in issues that transcend particular borders. The communist 'world', then, may be seen as an arena in which to develop or to test broader hypotheses. From the standpoint of British, American or other Western states' foreign policies, we do need much greater levels of knowledge about individual communist states. But we also require an understanding of the kind of topics included in this volume – structural changes in communist governments, the crises and transformations of ruling communist parties, the role of interest groups – especially the military and the working class – on policy-making, and the performance of communist systems in the distribution of resources.

Ultimately, descriptive knowledge of each communist country ought to be tied to an analytical understanding that seeks to explain what we observe. The chapters included in this volume allow greater specificity regarding our descriptive comparisons. After the identification of similarities and differences among communist systems, however, our next endeavour is to seek explanation. Comparison by means of the contributions included in this volume offers students the opportunity to build their own portraits of communist systems – deriving their generalisations from recent empirical research. *Communist Politics: A Reader* also challenges students, and established scholars, to search for explanations that account for such similarities and differences. The following pages should suggest both the complexity, and the rewards, of such an endeavour.

PART I
HISTORICAL ORIGINS

Little sense can be made of communist political systems if we divorce them from their historical past. Communist revolutions have occurred in countries with very different political traditions, cultures, and levels of social and economic development. In complex but important ways, their pre-revolutionary inheritance has continued to play a role in their contemporary politics down to the present time. Soviet political development, for instance, reflects the habits of thought and patterns of behaviour of a country which, for all but a few years in the early twentieth century, has known autocratic rather than liberal or democratic forms of government. Arguably at least, the centralism, relative lack of civil liberties and low levels of autonomous political activism that we observe in the contemporary USSR owes something to this distinctive historical experience – as well as to other factors. The historical experience of China, similarly, has tended to contribute in the modern period to such features of its political life as a defied ruler and a powerful central bureaucracy, modified by a strong local particularism and a tradition of anarchic rebellion. In many of the East European countries, on the other hand, some form of democratic government had become relatively well established before their respective communist revolutions, and western-style civil liberties such as freedom of speech and assembly and religious toleration were better understood if not always respected. Quite apart from their traditions of rule, communist governments also inherited a society, an economy and indeed a geography which placed limits upon their freedom of action and encouraged particular policy options as against others. In turn, the patterns of rule established in the early years of communist rule – of rapid industrialisation under state auspices, and of police terror – have made their own independent contribution to the contemporary politics of the communist nations.

We have included a single paper, but a particularly wide-ranging one, in this first section so as to illustrate the complex interaction between doctrine and practice, between past and present, and between the universal and more nationally-specific features of communist rule. Marxist forms of socialism, Michael Waller and Bogdan Szajkowski argue in this chapter,

7

are not necessarily to be identified with the USSR, the country in which they first became associated with a government in power; Marxism should rather be seen as a body of ideas which has taken different forms in different national contexts, no single form of which in today's world should be seen as more authentic or authoritative than any other.

1

The Communist Movement: from Monolith to Polymorph

MICHAEL WALLER AND BOGDAN SZAJKOWSKI

If spirits can be assigned geographic or cultural characteristics, the spectre of communism which, for Marx, was haunting Europe in 1848 was itself European. It was an emanation of the circumstances of early industrialism in that part of the world where the industrial revolution was taking place. It spoke (or got a variety of mortal voices to speak for it) in European languages about a European predicament.

By the turn of the century the spectre had learned Russian, and, at the periphery of Europe, it was speaking through the mouth and pen of the Russian Lenin about a double predicament: still about that of European industrialism, but also now about the predicament of another world, which was being economically and politically penetrated by the advanced industrial nations, whose military resources were now not only overwhelming, but also more mobile in effecting and ensuring this penetration.

Yet another three-quarters of a century and the spectre is no longer only European, nor is it haunting only Europe. It is, however, despite its linguistic virtuosity and cultural adaptability, Marxist, in a fundamental sense which is spelled out below (see also Harding, 1981; Waller, 1982; Szajkowski, 1982; White, 1983b). Though it speaks still about the same double predicament, the balance has clearly shifted. It was in Chinese that the spectre first spoke unequivocally of the encirclement of the world's cities by the world's countryside.

The imagery of the preceding paragraphs may not appeal to pragmatic readers. It has, however, a certain value for understanding what communism has been about for the last 150 years and also quite simply for understanding what has been happening in the world in the twentieth century. For Marxism has been a *movement*, and movements are like

Reprinted with adaptations from Bogdan Szajkowski (ed.), *Marxist Governments: A World Survey*, vol. 1 (London: Macmillan and New York: St Martin's, 1981) with the permission of the authors and publishers.

spectres in important ways. They can adopt different guises in different places at one and the same time. In a sense they escape the constraints of time and space. A movement carries its past with it into the present, and can perform the apparently mysterious feat of gathering wide cultural divergences into a single stream. Since, however, the age is not one of mysticism (or, in so far as it is, it is so in reaction against a prevailing pragmatism), we must oblige by clothing the spectre in the more acceptable garb of concrete events, concrete social forces, and the pronouncements of real live men and women.

Seen from the vantage point of the present day, the fulcrum around which the history of Marxism as a movement turns is the revolution in Russia in 1917. The discussion which preceded that revolution and the events which succeeded it are worth examining in some detail.

When the Russian Lenin wrote *What is to be Done?* in 1902, he was taking part, and saw himself as taking part, in a debate within the European Marxist parties of the day. This was a debate about the way in which the pursuit of radical change in Europe should be conducted, and it was one which set English Fabians, French 'ministerialists' and German 're-visionists' against those who condemned a gradualist strategy and an obsession with immediate economic goals on the grounds that such concerns distracted the working class from the political goal of a radical reordering of society. Lenin saw this 'revisionist' debate as of relevance to the strategy of a Marxist party operating in Russian circumstances. The practical conclusions which he drew, however, centred on the impediments which were imposed by tsarist absolutism on political organisation *of any kind at all* in Russia. If the view of party organisation which he put forward in 1902 has been seen as Jacobin, this is entirely owing to the fact that he could see that 'broad democracy' and full publicity were ruled out for a Russian party.

The oppressive circumstances of tsarism were somewhat eased as a result of the revolutionary upsurge of 1905. Through the concessions which the Tsar made at the end of that year were shortly to be severely whittled down, the sense of euphoria was sufficient to cause Lenin to acclaim the arrival of an era in which his earlier call for organisation and cohesion could be matched by an appeal for democratic procedures in the Party. It was in those circumstances that the idea of democratic centralism was born, the idea of a dialectical balance between organisational cohesion and democratic procedures. They were circumstances which appeared to draw the situation of the Russian Marxists closer to that of the Western European Marxists. Still, however, Lenin maintained his earlier insistence on the goal of a revolutionary reordering of society.

No political organisation of the day could claim responsibility for the collapse of the tsarist system when that event took place in March 1917. When the Bolsheviks came to power in November of that year, it was at the head of social forces which had imposed themselves autonomously on the scene under the double pressures of external war and internal frustration. The consolidation of the Bolsheviks in power, however, in the ensuing period of civil war and economic collapse, was a different matter. For whilst the Bolsheviks were soon brought to outlaw even their rival revolutionary organisations, democratic centralism, as it had been conceived in 1905, succumbed to the ban on factional activity at the Bolsheviks' Tenth Congress in 1921. It was to start a new life, however, as a formula which validated the highly authoritarian pattern of politics which was in the making.

It was thus not the Bolsheviks who dissolved the tsarist order; but it *was* the Bolsheviks who reconstructed Russia. If the consolidation of the revolution had brought about the authoritarianism which a situation of social dislocation invites, the ensuing task of economic construction from a starting point of economic and cultural disadvantage produced, in fact if not necessarily, a continuation of authoritarian rule. And if to the historian Stalin must appear as a reincarnation of Peter the Great, dragging a backward nation into modernity, it is no less important that this more recent attempt was seen as involving the creation of the material base for the construction of a socialist society.

When, in 1928–9, this drive for economic construction was begun in earnest, with the first five-year plan and the collectivisation of the peasantry, Lenin was already in his mausoleum, and his close comrades of the revolutionary period, in most cases intellectually highly gifted people who had been brought up in the general European discourse on Marxist socialism, were soon to be cut down in the Stalinist purges. The men of the construction drive were people of a different sort: the vast army of cadres, home-grown, the produce of revolution in a country marked by a low level of literacy and of economic and cultural development; the thousand and one Khrushchevs who saw their own image in Stalin.

Before Lenin died, however, two important events had occurred; or, rather, one of them had occurred, whilst the other was an expected event which *failed* to occur. First, the enunciation of the twenty-one principles for acceptance of a party into the Third (Communist) International in 1920 split the socialist Left in Western Europe. The distinction drawn in 1920 between communist parties which adhered to the Comintern and the social-democratic parties which did not do so; the identification of the first set with Soviet policies and indeed with the Bolsheviks' organisational norms; and the concomitant association of the latter set of parties with the reformist views against which Lenin had inveighed in *What is to be Done?* – all these things lived on to become what is still now a familiar part of the furniture of the political life of Western Europe. But the implications of the splitting of the Left in 1920, and, likewise, the implications of affiliation to the Comintern, only became clear when an expected development failed to materialise: the spread of revolution to the nations of Western Europe.

For both Lenin and Trotsky, and for others too, the success of a socialist revolution in Russia was predicated upon the occurrence of revolution in Western Europe; only such an eventuality would enable the Bolsheviks to realise their socialist goals in a way which made sense within the discourse on Marxist socialism as it had been conducted up to that time. The political revolution had been achieved and socialist policies instituted. Russia alone, however, appeared to lack the economic and cultural resources to make the carrying through of those policies practicable.

By 1924 these internationalist hopes were dead. In their place arose the doctrine of socialism in one country. The Bolsheviks were left with the phrase, and the aspiration, of proletarian internationalism and a reality cruelly discrepant with both the phrase and the aspiration, at least in the short term. The phrase, of course, was retained, and the aspiration, in formal terms, upheld. But the pressures, internal and external, which the construction of socialism in one country *and in that particular country* imposed, led to the promotion of national goals and to an emphasis on economic achievement at the expense of a deepening of democracy. It was a process from which the capitalist West benefited through the creation of a visible bogy named communism, through the association of the more radical Western political parties with this bogy, and with the resultant tendency of the less radical socialist parties to steer yet further away from a phenomenon which could easily be presented as involving the redistribution of poverty through strong-arm methods. The process can be seen now to have benefited the Soviet population considerably in material terms, and to have benefited the Soviet Union as a nation state quite massively. But it benefited not at all those who continued to present Marxist goals in terms of the growing-over of a mature capitalist society into socialism, and in terms of the end of alienation and of the control of the producer over his own product.

One thing which the Soviet Union of the Stalinist years had shown the world was a successful method of bringing development to an economically retarded country, of restoring national pride to a disfavoured nation, and of keeping the penetration of the industrialised world at bay. If it was Lenin, relying on the ideas of Hilferding and others, who had given Marxism its theory of imperialism, his Soviet heirs provided at least one set of tools for combating imperialism and for undertaking the task of untying the colonial knot. It is in this sense that the Russian revolution was a major fulcrum in twentieth-century history. It was in its inspiration an outgrowth of European Marxism, but became in its effects a catalyst in the struggle of oppressed nations against their oppressors.

If we exclude the Mongolian People's Republic, which came into being in 1924 and from the start allied itself with the Soviet Union in order to escape Chinese domination, the Soviet Union remained the single bastion of established Marxist socialism until the closing stages of the Second World War. The Comintern parties were pressed into service to support this bastion through all the tergiversations of Soviet foreign policy in the inter-war years. They also adopted the organisational norms of the Communist Party of the Soviet Union, norms which were shaped by the pressures of the period during which the Bolsheviks were securing themselves in power and addressing themselves to the tasks of economic development in a backward country. The West European communist parties thus became doubly estranged from their cultural environment: on the one hand their policies were shaped with primary reference to a foreign nation, whilst on the other hand their procedural norms conflicted with their domestic political cultures. Soviet influence made itself felt even more directly in the accession to power of a number of communist parties in Central and Eastern Europe in the immediate aftermath of the Second World War – in Poland, in Czechoslovakia, in Hungary, in the Soviet part of occupied Germany, in Romania and in Bulgaria.

In the same period, however, communist parties had come to power *without* overt Soviet support in Yugoslavia and Albania. Both these parties set about forming the economic and political structures of the societies over which they now ruled in conformity with the Soviet model, but the fact that these revolutions had taken place autonomously had important implications for the future configuration of what at that time was known as the socialist camp.

Meanwhile, since 1936 the Communist Party of China had been engaged in a contest with both the Chinese Nationalists (the Kuomintang) and Japanese occupying forces. The interest of this long struggle is twofold. First, Mao Tse-tung based his strategy on the *rural* areas of China. The social policies of the communists were applied first in microcosm in the peasant countryside. Spreading thus from the countryside to the cities, the revolution had a populist flavour. Secondly, this populist flavour was strengthened by Mao's concept of the people, the *renmin*, which included the national bourgeoisie but excluded the 'comprador capitalists', whose interests were associated with those of the Japanese and other foreign powers. Thus to the liberation of the peasant from the landlord was joined the liberation of the nation from foreign penetration.

As had the Yugoslavs, the Chinese communists initially set up economic and political structures which were modelled on those of the Soviet Union. Ironically, however, in 1948, the year before the Chinese revolution culminated, the Yugoslav party had been expelled from the Cominform – the international body which between 1947 and 1956 was the organisational expression of the notional socialist camp. This cardinal event, which with the hindsight of history must be seen as marking the logical development from the idea of socialism in one country to that of different national roads to socialism, was offset by the Chinese success and by the fact that the

Chinese and Soviet leaderships were united at that time in their condemnation of Yugoslav 'revisionism'. Nevertheless, expansion of the 'socialist camp' had been accompanied by diversification, and it was this novel element of diversity which was most significant for later developments.

Ten years later the situation was to recur, this time Castro's success in Cuba being followed by the definitive rift between the Soviet and the Chinese communists. Both events were highly significant. In the case of the Cuban revolution, this was because the revolution was spearheaded not by the communist Popular Socialist Party but by Castro's personal following – the Movement of 26 July. The redistributive and cultural policies which Castro instituted on achieving power were indeed revolutionary, and early on a bridge was formed between the Popular Socialist Party and Castro's organisation, but this was first and foremost a nationalist revolution directed against the penetration of Cuba by the 'colossus of the North'. It was not until after the revolution that Castro embraced Marxism-Leninism.

The Sino-Soviet split was important in that it made it clear that the days of monolithic communism were over. The Cominform had been dissolved in 1956, to be replaced by *ad hoc* conferences. Soon, in fact after 1969, *ad hoc* was to become *ad numquam*.

Once again the universe of communist systems had expanded, and once again this expansion had been accompanied by diversification, but this time the resonance of the latter element was far greater than it had been ten years earlier. The Soviet Union was now but one of an increasingly diverse set of communist systems. It continued to benefit from an authority conferred by the 'October' of 1917. It had been the first in the field and it had been established longest. It was, moreover, able to dominate, by force or by blandishments, the majority of the other Marxist-Leninist ruling parties. But it was no longer the model of a society ruled by a Marxist-Leninist party. If it was still an emperor, from now on it was open to any Marxist-Leninist child to claim that the emperor's clothing was deficient.

Up to this point, the occurrence of revolutions involving Marxist-Leninist parties, espousing redistributive policies derived from the tenets of Marxism, and throwing up political and economic structures which seemed to form an identifiable category, had taken place rather gradually, with the important exception of the Eastern European 'revolutions'. The failure of the American involvement in Vietnam, however, was to prove exactly what American strategists had assumed; and the dominoes have since tumbled with bewildering rapidity, not only in South-east Asia, but also in South Yemen and, most recently and strikingly, in Central Africa. The phenomenon is bewildering in particular for those who have to deal with the concepts of socialism, communism, Marxism and Marxism-Leninism. From studying, in the inter-war period, a single example of a Marxist-Leninist party in power, the student of the communist movement now has to deal with the wide spectrum, in terms of culture and economic development, of established regimes on four continents. Nor is this all. The West European communist parties have at last begun to retrace the steps which they have taken since the splitting of the Left in 1920, and have in certain cases gone so far as to expunge the 'Leninism' from Marxism-Leninism. They have, however, been outflanked by the reinvigoration of the radical Marxist Left in the Western industrial societies, and the European debate is in a sense back where it was at the beginning of the century, when revolutionaries confronted reformists in that first revisionist debate.

We shall shortly be turning to the nature of Western comment which the evolution of the communist movement has elicited, and a statement will be made as to what, in the present circumstances, it may mean to call a regime 'Marxist'. First, however, it is worth drawing attention to some of the implications, from the vantage point of the present day, of the evolution of the communist movement as it has been described above. The first of these implications concerns the way in which the term 'ideology' has been used and the way in which it must now be understood.

It should be clear from the foregoing that the fundamental conflict of values in the world as a whole today – a conflict which is older than our century but which was given its present configuration by the revolution in Russia in 1917 – is no longer simply a conflict within the world of West European culture between bourgeois liberal and socialist values (Waller, 1979). It has become a conflict between the developing world and the West, and the developing world has brought onto the battlefield where it has confronted the technological superiority of the West a number of prominent values deriving from the political modalities of cultures which have for centuries been regarded as alien to West European culture, and remain so in their post-revolutionary guise, whatever the debt which they owe to the West European Marx.

The result is that the earlier problem of ideology, in which ideology was seen as a simple conflict between liberal democracy and Marxist socialism, is now beginning to be seen as a much more complex affair. In fact, it comprises a tight knot of problems concerning ideology, culture and language. This lesson is now being learned both by practical political figures and by commentators on communism. For the first, the Euro-communist parties are coming to realise that Soviet political practices are separable from Marxist socialism; for the second, scholars such as Tucker and Meyer have pointed out that the communist systems derive their values, including their political values, as much from their cultural past as from the tenets of Marxism (Meyer, 1972; Tucker, 1973). These advances in our understanding of what has been happening under the label of socialism are valuable; but they also serve to increase our perplexity. For the phenomenon with which we have to deal turns out to be composed of a number of intersecting dimensions. To the two dimensions suggested above – on the one hand the class conflict of industrialising Europe and the ideas which that conflict generated, and on the other the conflict between the West and the developing nations – must be added a third: that provided by cultural dissonance between the various societies of the world, a dissonance which may seem to present us with a series of totally disparate cultures, but which does not in fact do so, since these various conflicts of interest and ideas reinforce each other. There emerges a world of liberal democracy, comprising distinct cultures which, none the less, at a certain level, coalesce; and there is also a world of communism, made up of societies which again exhibit wide cultural variation, but which share a range of values deriving from a refraction of the tenets of Marxism through a shared historical predicament of national disadvantage.

Secondly, the story recounted above has answered the question 'How has the communist movement developed since Marx's days?' If, however, we were to pose a rather different question and ask what, in the most general terms, has been happening in the world in the twentieth century, a rather different perspective would be obtained. For the twentieth century has been one of revolution, yet not of revolution in the industrialised world. The mainstream of the century's upheavals, which have combined political with social revolution, has flowed in the economically less-developed areas of the globe. Since these revolutions have in most cases, and with increasing frequency, brought a Marxist-Leninist party to power, the process has presented the now familiar triad of revolution/national liberation/Marxism-Leninism.

It is illuminating to consider the cases of the revolutions in Mexico and Cuba within the framework which is here being presented. The 'forgotten revolution' in Mexico happened, as it were, before Lenin came along. That revolution in 1910, together with the political forms and processes which it engendered, has much in common with the experience of the communist systems. And yet it lacks an important dimension which has been almost universally shared by upheavals of a similar nature which have occurred since 1917, and which are being reproduced almost annually in Asia and Africa. Even more interesting is the case of Cuba, where the revolution owed little to the ideas of Marxism-Leninism, and indeed was carried through by a force which was independent of the Marxist-Leninist Popular Socialist Party, but then went on to adopt not only the symbols, but also the organisation characteristic of the communist systems. This has been seen as the price paid for Soviet assistance – an argument which carries some force, but which, if carried through, requires us to believe that the Soviet Union has purchased virtually the entire national-liberation movement of the twentieth century. There is no doubt an element of truth in this, but at the same time it is difficult to believe that so many shoppers did not understand the market they have been shopping in.

This view of what has been happening in the twentieth century helps us to get into perspective a series of revolutions and the political forms which emerged from them. And not merely a series of revolutions, but *the mainstream* of twentieth-century revolutions, in which considerations of national liberation and national development have been paramount. The Russian revolution, semi-industrialised though Russia was at the time, may be seen, for present purposes, as the first of these, with the series constantly augmenting itself in Angola, Mozambique, Ethiopia, Benin and elsewhere.

But other things have been happening in the twentieth century which are important for a perspective on the political forms and processes of the communist systems. It will have been noted that the post-war 'revolutions' in Eastern Europe do not fit the pattern outlined above. In fact they form a special case, in which extraneous factors (including such overwhelming factors as the presence of the Soviet Army and proximity to the Soviet Union itself) were present and indeed determinant. But they are special cases for another reason, relevant to the development of the Soviet Union as an industrial giant. If the revolutionary phenomenon described above has predominantly involved the developing countries, the twentieth century has seen, in the more developed parts of the globe, the growth of industrial society into the stage of high technology. This has brought with it new problems of the relationship between the individual and this new pattern of production, the new Leviathan which has preoccupied Huxley, Zamyatin, Orwell, Marcuse and so many others.

But there is no need to refer to fictional works for evidence. If the regulatory power of the state is greater in the Soviet Union than in the Western industrial nations, it is only a matter of a greater distance covered along the same path. The same can be said for the development of planning, of developments in communications and the control of them, and, indeed, all the rest of the convergence thesis, which, like the other models so far suggested to aid our understanding of the communist systems, has its failings but also an irresistible grain of truth.

Looking at the politics of the communist systems from *this* aspect of what has been happening in the twentieth century throws us into an entirely different discourse from that other revolutionary aspect; and what is interesting about communist politics is that both these strands run strong and that they interconnect – indeed, that they are in contradiction with each other.

It is in this interconnection, and in this contradiction, that lie the clues for understanding what is specific to the communist systems. Social revolutions and national liberation movements may throw up elite leaderships, but they are none the less mass affairs, involving a high degree of spontaneity. On the other hand, the organisation of post-industrial society, as we have so far seen it, seeks stability, the dominant image of social health is 'the harmonious functioning of the system', and in the Soviet Union as in the West rewards and prestige go to the technically competent. But it is of course in China that this contradiction has most recently been visible, and it is the Chinese who have endowed the communist movement with the phrase that encapsulates it: red and expert. This phrase has no doubt served many trivial purposes, but it enshrines a basic contradiction which runs through the politics of the communist systems, and indeed, in an indirect way, through the entire communist movement, the bureaucratic tendencies within the communist systems engendering a radical reaction amongst Marxists outside them, a spectre of redness which today is haunting communism.

We can now turn to the history of Western comment on the political forms which the communist movement has presented during its evolution. This history can be usefully seen as comprising three phases. These we shall outline and shall then go on to suggest that today's circumstances of extreme variegation in the communist movement call for a substantial rethinking of the assumptions which have informed these three phases.

The first phase need not detain us long, although it lasted for the considerable period from the establishment of Bolshevik power in the Soviet Union until the 'iron curtain' descended in the aftermath of the Second World War. These were the years of the first reactions to the novel political and economic creature which had been ripped from the womb of old Russia by the Bolshevik midwife. The discussion, in so far as it went beyond memories and eye witness accounts of the revolution and its immediate sequel, was pitched, naturally enough, in terms of the presuppositions about Marxist socialism which preoccupied Western Europe and the English-speaking world at the time of the Russian revolution. The fact that it was at times naive reflects the circumstances. The emerging economic and political forms *were*, after all, novel; they were also, for the first ten years and more, somewhat mobile. By the time they had become less mobile, information had become exceedingly difficult to obtain, and equally difficult to digest. A command of the Russian language was a scarce commodity, and, moreover, the preoccupation with constitutional formalities which marked the political science of the day made it difficult for the few scholars who did interest themselves in the Soviet Union to deal with a political system in which the political processes differed so widely from the formal constitutional structure. Two features of those days are worth noting. First, the form of Marxism in practice which the Soviet Union presented was not taken to be an example *faute de mieux*; it was taken to be the model *par excellence*. Secondly, and more obviously, comment was partisan. The importance of this point is that it suited both apologists and critics to present the Soviet Union as the model *par excellence* of Marxist socialism – the former playing down the more objectionable aspects of Soviet life in order to build up support for the single established bastion of

Marxist socialism, the latter playing them up in order to discredit the whole regrettable exercise.

The beginning of a second phase in the history of studies of communism was marked by the arrival of the first really sophisticated analysis of Soviet political forms. This analysis linked the Stalinist Soviet Union with Hitler's Germany and Mussolini's Italy in a concept of 'totalitarianism'. The theme was articulated in various ways, but the 'six-point syndrome' put forward by Friedrich and Brzezinski is worth citing, since discussion of the totalitarian view has tended to revolve around it. Totalitarianism, for these two scholars, comprised the following six features: (1) an official ideology; (2) a single mass party led typically by one man; (3) a terroristic police system; (4) a monopoly, in the hands of the party, of the means of communication; (5) a similar monopoly of the means of armed combat; (6) central control of the entire economy (Friedrich and Brzezinski, 1965, p. 22).

The historical circumstances in which the totalitarian view arose should be noted. First of all, since it accompanied the onset of the Cold War, there was a strong 'know your enemy' flavour about it. Secondly, the linking of Stalin with Hitler and Mussolini illustrates a further important point: the totalitarian view was analysing a pre-war pattern of politics in a post-war situation. As far as the communist movement as a whole was concerned, the period from 1945 to the middle 1960s – that is, the period during which the totalitarian view held sway – was one of increasing differentiation. It had seen the creation of Marxist-Leninist regimes as far apart, in terms of geography, culture and level of economic development, as China, Czechoslovakia, Yugoslavia and Cuba. The result was that the totalitarian view, whilst historically valid for an earlier period, turned out to be historically vulnerable almost as soon as it had been put forward. For, with all three tyrants – Stalin, Hitler and Mussolini – gone, with the systems created by the last two dismantled, and with the abandoning of terror as a political instrument in the Soviet Union after Stalin's death, the shrunken concept had to be fleshed out *by inference* with recently created communist systems, which did indeed show similarities to the Stalinist Soviet Union, but showed important differences from it too.

A further feature of this second phase in the study of communist politics served to perpetuate the notion that the political system of the Soviet Union provided a norm to which other communist systems had to be related. This was the abrupt upsurge in Soviet and Eastern European studies in the early 1950s. In the case of Britain, it was the armed forces, through their language courses for conscripts, which were chiefly responsible for the establishment of the Russian language and of Soviet studies in the British educational curriculum, and this development was given a further impulse by the Hayter report, which led to a very substantial investment in Soviet and Eastern European studies in institutions of higher learning and research. But Britain was by no means peculiar in this respect (see Cohen, 1985, ch. 1). The rocket which launched the first sputnik also gave a powerful boost, in the whole Western world, to the idea that the Soviet Union was the model *par excellence* of a Marxist-Leninist regime. Moreover, since the political systems of Eastern Europe resembled that of the Soviet Union in most important respects, the model appeared to be a multi-member category and therefore gained in credibility. The Prague Spring was, much later, to show that behind this enforced uniformity – for such it was – lay very different notions of what Marxist socialism involved – a message which had already been made clear by the way in which Yugoslavia, free from Soviet interference, had presented to the world its own highly original contribution.

Finally, despite the association with fascism and nazism, it was a characteristic of this second phase in the history of studies of communist politics that commentators saw the communist systems as *sui generis*, as forming a category which not only used a particular language in self-description, but which also required that a special language be used in analysing them. No way had been found of integrating studies of communist politics into the discourse on comparative politics in the broad. Partisan attitudes again played an important role here: it suited the preferences both of critics and apologists of communism to emphasise the particularity of the communist phenomenon.

For a considerable period the totalitarian view overlapped with other approaches, which were beginning to register the very real diversification which had been taking place within the communist movement. But from the middle 1960s the emergence of a third phase in the study of communist politics was discernible. This phase, which takes us up to the present day, has been marked by a considerable variety in the approaches taken to communist politics. Some of these approaches go so far as to disestablish the communist systems as a distinct subset of the world's political systems. For Kautsky, for example, they are subsumable under the general heading of the politics of development – a view for which the historical sketch presented earlier in this chapter offers considerable support (Kautsky, 1968, 1972, 1973). Most approaches, however, retain the idea that the communist systems do form a subset of the world's political systems, though no longer a homogeneous one. It has come to be recognised that what was originally a peculiarly Soviet product has been adapted by a variety of societies with rich and distinctive political traditions of their own and that to apply to those societies an analysis based exclusively on the Soviet model is not good enough, and more attention has begun to be given to differing traditions and differing political cultures. The result has been a merging of the study of Soviet politics and comparative politics into what is now called 'comparative communism' (see, for instance, Fleron, 1969; Johnson, 1970; Kanet, 1971; Ionescu, 1972; Cohen and Shapiro, 1974; Bunce and Echols, 1979; Bertsch, 1982; White, Gardner and Schopflin, 1982).

This initiative in political science combines what is unique in the various communist systems with the general concepts which were originally developed in the study of Soviet politics. At the same time it is recognised that the Soviet experience gives only partial explanations of the other communist systems and that concepts and techniques developed by comparative politics are applicable to those other systems.

It might appear that, with the emergence of comparative communism, a congruence has at last been achieved between a highly variegated object of study and an appraisal which can cope with variety on a comparative basis. A number of considerations, however, make it difficult to accept so optimistic a conclusion.

First of all, if comparative communism has so far involved a vigorous methodological debate, it is one which rides on top of a literature which is *not* comprehensive in its scope. There is a wealth of studies of individual systems or groups of systems, and of symposia. But even symposia do not meet the demand for *synthesis* which the current situation in the communist world imposes. Meanwhile, single-author works which take a synoptic view of the politics of the communist systems as a whole are so rare as to be almost non-existent (for an important exception see von Beyme, 1982).

This would not matter, and the situation might be expected to correct itself in time, were it not for a second consideration: the tendency to see comparative communism in terms of an extension of the study of Soviet and East European studies (see, for instance, Gélard, 1975). Now, to a certain extent this is quite understandable and unexceptionable. The Soviet Union as noted above was the first in the field; it has been able to influence in one way or another the political forms of most of the other communist systems; the problems of economic and cultural underdevelopment which the majority of the communist systems faced at their inception were faced first by the Soviet Union, and newly emerging regimes usually turn to the Soviet Union not only for political and economic support, but also for an organisational model. All this is true, and must be taken into account.

But other things must today be taken into account as well. Neither historical seniority nor power and blandishments necessarily confer authority or authenticity, and one of the chief features of the communist movement today is that the Soviet Union's authority is under rather substantial attack – from other ruling parties, from non-ruling parties, which traditionally have supported the Soviet Union's policies and imitated its organisational patterns, and from the Trotskyist Left. Further, even where, as in Angola, Vietnam, Cuba and Ethiopia, Soviet influence is particularly strong, the countervailing effects of cultural diversity and local circumstances make it increasingly difficult to make these societies 'fit' a political model which draws overwhelmingly on Soviet experience. Moreover, there is ample evidence from all corners of the communist movement that the majority of the regimes that compose it are themselves not looking for the import of socialist practice from abroad. They aspire to their own original socialism, a socialism that will accord with their own circumstances. Comparative communism has so far been like a boat which originally sailed well and held water. With the passing of time new planks have had to be added here and there to keep the boat seaworthy. But recent events have meant the nailing on of so many hefty new timbers that the discerning shipwright would surely prefer to be given the separate planks and told to make a new boat.

Comparative communism, however, is open to an even graver charge. It has so far presented the student of communist politics with a group of the world's political systems and has invited him to see what these systems have in common in terms of structures and functions. This again is a possible and worthwhile exercise. But is it the *best* way of making sense of the politics of communism? To repeat yet again, we are dealing with a movement, with political organisations which subscribe to a shared cosmology and to a shared set of goals which derive from it. However 'petrified' (Hough, 1972) a given organisation may be at a given time, there is a dynamic in the movement which the scholar neglects at his peril. For one thing, the distinction which is so obvious in Western political science between a ruling party and a non-ruling one is by no means so obvious within the logic of communist politics. In terms of the structures and functions of existing political systems the distinction is capital; in terms of the shared goals and cosmology it is much less substantial. No adequate account can be given of the politics of the communist movement without full and equal consideration not only of the ruling parties as *individual* entities operating in highly differentiated circumstances, but also of the non-ruling parties in all their phenomenal variety – because, however varied, however mutually destructive, they are an essential part of the movement, and moreover they are politically interdependent. That movement, like any other movement, has turned out to be – and annually can be seen more and more to be – Protean. It assumes different forms at different times in different places. It is *polymorphic*. And it is ultimately more important to register this fact than to assume that any single form of it is a model *par excellence*.

The politics of communism ought therefore to be studied at three levels. First, the component organisations (states and parties) ought to be analysed as part of the general discourse on comparative politics in the broad, using the very generalised language which that discourse requires (patterns of participation and elite recruitment, present interests versus future goals, and so on). Secondly, the movement as a whole ought to be analysed in terms of its goals and its cosmology (which means analysing it in its own language, its own semantic system). And, thirdly, each component organisation requires separate investigation of a kind which will reveal its particularities, either as an individual organisation or as a member of a coherent group (the Eurocommunist parties, the Eastern European states, and the like).

These are clearly separate tasks, and yet comparative communism has so far attempted to conflate them. The result is that, with rare exceptions, the first two of these tasks have not yet been satisfactorily tackled. The third, on the other hand, has produced an abundant literature, whilst being the least comparative of the three exercises.

At least thirty regimes in the mid-1980s defined themselves as Marxist-Leninist (Szajkowski, 1985ff). The foregoing should make it plain that we regard these regimes as but a part of the universe of political organisations which make up the communist movement. Moreover *even within this category of ruling parties* the communist movement is marked by variety. What these regimes have in common (and what they have in common both with non-ruling parties which style themselves Marxist-Leninist and with non-ruling parties, such as the Spanish, which have dropped the 'Leninist' element of the title) is that their respective elites maintain that their countries' social, political and economic development is guided by Marxism. All alike profess what they regard as the 'scientific theory' of the laws of the development of human society and human history. This scientific doctrine is claimed by the political leaderships of these countries to consist in the discovery of objective causal relationships; it is used to analyse the contradictions which arise between goals and actuality in the pursuit of a common destiny. The acceptance by ruling parties in these thirty or so countries of this conceptual framework has been the criterion for their inclusion within this category of systems.

At the same time, the fact that they call themselves Marxist-*Leninist* marks their subscription also to a certain view of the relationship between the party and society. It has been argued above that this does indeed make for a family resemblance between all these systems and the Soviet Union, but that this resemblance can be overemphasised, at the cost of concealing the markedly different ways in which this relationship between party and society works out in practice – a point which can be readily exemplified by noting the highly variable role of the military and of religious organisations in these societies.

We are quite aware of the problems of taking self-ascription as the basis for accepting a regime as Marxist, or Marxist-Leninist. We are aware of the important distinction between, for example, China, where a long-established communist party's accession to power was the result of an organic relationship between the party and the masses which matured over time, and Benin, where Marxism-Leninism was rather abruptly embraced by a military government in a state which holds the African record for military *coups d'état*. There is not enough space in this chapter to conduct the full exercise of comparison between these extremely diverse systems. On the other hand self-ascription is not such a bad starting-point for that comparative exercise. First of all, it is clearly better than basing the exercise on models and categories formed in an earlier situation and which by that very fact may not be capable of making sense of new phenomena. Secondly, self-ascription does at least provide an initial hypothesis, even if it does nothing more. Thirdly, however, it does in fact do more than merely provide a hypothesis. A shared rhetoric is an important factor in politics, affecting in particular the legitimacy of leaderships which espouse that rhetoric. And finally, to repeat, communism must be seen as a *movement*, and movements grow by a process of diffusion which involves not only proselytisation but also self-ascription. Calvinism, for example, must be considered a strand of the Christian tradition despite the fact that its self-ascription to the tradition jarred with the views not only of Roman popes but also of those commentators on Christianity whose theoretical constructs had no place for Calvinist notions of salvation.

The novelty of this proposal is that it does not assign authenticity or authority to any single Marxist-Leninist political system. It shows that, depending on a variety of historical, cultural and political factors, the pursuit of goals derived from the tenets of Marxism has produced different political forms at different times and in different places. It also illustrates the rich diversity among these societies, where attempts to achieve a synthesis between goals derived from Marxism, on the one hand, and national realities, on the other, have often meant distinctive approaches and solutions to the problems of social, political and economic development. Furthermore, in discussing these diverse societies one can learn much more about the foundations and meaning of the ideology, development, adaptations and effect of Marxism-Leninism within them. Marxism, as Roger Garaudy points out, has as its universal vocation to be rooted in the culture of every people. An Algerian, Islamic in culture, can arrive at scientific socialism by other roads than those of Hegel, Ricardo or Saint-Simon. He has his own utopian socialism in the carmathian movement, his rationalist and dialectical tradition in Averroes, his forerunner of historical materialism in Ibn Khaldun; and it is upon these traditions that he can graft scientific socialism. This in no way excludes his integrating the heritage of our culture just as we have to integrate his (Garaudy, 1970, pp. 35–6). The conceptual framework of Marxism-Leninism has in fact made possible the construction of socialism in very varied ways along roads proper to local conditions.

PART II
STRUCTURES OF
GOVERNMENT

In the second part of this reader we turn from the historical origins of communist systems and look instead at formal institutional structures. It is, of course, widely accepted that constitutions, elections, legislative bodies and other forms of official state life have generally played a limited if not entirely negligible role in the politics of the communist-ruled countries, and that in the 1980s, as in previous decades, they remain subordinate to the directives and detailed guidance of the ruling communist party authorities. In no communist system, for instance, has a government ever lost power at the polls, and in no communist legislature has an important measure of government policy ever failed to receive a majority of votes (in most cases all such measures have been adopted unanimously). At the same time the communist states have always remained committed at least to the theory of popular sovereignty, expressed through directly elected people's councils or soviets, and by the mid-1980s, if not before, there was some evidence that they were seeking to make use of the potential of such institutions for a variety of instrumental purposes. Elections, for instance, could be allowed to play a greater role in expressing and communicating public sentiment by permitting or even requiring a greater number of candidates to stand than seats available (although so far no direct opposition to communist rule or party policies has ever been permitted in this context). Legislative bodies, similarly, could be employed to convey at least the appearance of genuine debate on matters of public concern, and to provide a means by which the party could arrange for government ministers and other state officials to be held to account for their performance. The development of an elaborate and increasingly effective committee system has so far proved one of the most effective means by which these ends can be accomplished.

In the first of the chapters in this section, Alex Pravda provides a general overview of the nature and function of elections in communist systems,

drawing particularly upon the Soviet, Czech, Polish, Hungarian and Yugoslav experiences from their origins up to the present day. In the two
following chapters Stephen White and David Olson and Maurice Simon
examine in more detail the working of the national legislature in the USSR
and in Poland respectively. In further chapters Ralph Pervan assesses the
distinctive form of self-management, in both the political and economic
spheres, that has functioned in Yugoslavia since the early 1950s, and David
Goodman surveys the changes that have taken place in Chinese state life
under the modernising Dengist leadership since the late 1970s. The 1985
national elections in Hungary, in which 25 seats were won by independent
(but non-dissident) candidates and 45 constituencies required a second
ballot because no candidate had obtained an absolute majority on the first
round, showed the potential of such mechanisms even under communist
party dominance and suggested that electoral and legislative institutions in
the communist nations were still evolving as of the mid and later 1980s.

2

Elections in Communist Party States

ALEX PRAVDA

Elections in communist party states have traditionally been seen in the West as grotesque parodies of liberal democratic originals. As such, they have been described so as to reveal the bogus nature of their democratic pretensions (see, for instance, Carson, 1956, esp. pp. 85–100; MacClosky and Turner, 1960, pp. 324–32; Fainsod, 1963, pp. 381–2). With the decline of the 'totalitarian school' and the advent of a less doctrinaire approach to the study of communist party systems, elections have been given more attention and more complex analysis. For the Soviet Union we now have detailed, largely descriptive accounts of the mechanics of Soviet elections and some analysis of their functions. A considerable body of material deals with the composition of elected representative bodies, and some attempts have been made to use voting as an indicator of political dissent (see for instance Swearer, 1961; Mote, 1965; Churchward, 1966; Clarke, 1967; Gilison, 1968; Jacobs, 1970; Hill, 1972, 1973, 1976a; Friedgut, 1979; Zaslavsky and Brym, 1978, 1983; White, forthcoming). In Eastern Europe, where elections offer a potentially more fruitful field for research, treatment has been piecemeal: only Poland has received anything like detailed coverage (Pelczynski, 1959; Wiatr, 1962; Ptakowski, 1965; Dinka and Skidmore, 1973; Rusinow, 1977; Sakwa and Crouch, 1978. Useful reports and analyses may also be found in the *Situation* and *Background Reports* of Radio Free Europe).

Since no attempt has been made to compare elections in communist party states or systematically to analyse their development, this analysis has the following objections: first, briefly, to survey the background and development of elections to national parliamentary and local government bodies in communist party states; second, to detail a typology of elections

Reprinted with adaptations from Guy Hermet *et al.*, *Elections without Choice* (London: Macmillan and New York: Halsted Press, 1978) with the permission of author and publishers.

in these states; and, third, to examine the main functions performed by these elections and assess the variations in functions between types.

The study focuses upon the degree and kind of the choice of non-choice provided by elections in communist party states. Any attempt to evaluate the democratic or non-democratic nature of these elections is deliberately eschewed. The very different meanings assigned to the concept of democracy in liberal thought and in Marxism-Leninism make use of the term a hindrance rather than an aid to clear analysis. Although the study covers elections in all the communist party states of the Soviet Union and Eastern Europe, constraints of length rule out detailed treatment of elections in all nine states. Evidence is therefore drawn largely from Soviet, Czechoslovak, Polish, Hungarian and Yugoslav elections; between them, they provide good examples of the whole range of elections in communist states.

The background and development of elections in communist party states

The view of elections in Marxist–Leninist ideology is ambivalent. On the one hand they appear to be in a weak and subordinate position. As part of the state superstructure, elections are seen as deriving their real nature from their socio-economic content. Because elections are supposed to reflect the infrastructure, they have constantly to be adjusted in order to keep pace with developments; hence the frequent and often confusing changes in communist electoral laws and regulations. Another factor contributing to the ideological weakness of elections is their notionally temporary nature. As part of a system of representative democracy, elections in their present form are scheduled to be superseded by more advanced direct democratic processes in the course of evolution towards full communism. On the other hand, for the foreseeable future, ideology endows elections with considerable legitimacy. By contrast with the treatment accorded to elections by fascist and Nazi regimes, in communist party states they are lauded as essential channels for expressing popular sovereignty and socialist democracy. As the eschatological elements of the ideology continue to give way to those legitimating the political status quo, so the position of elections becomes more firmly entrenched (see for instance Chkhikvadze, 1972, p. 79; Bezuglov, 1973, pp. 16–18).

General political traditions, however, undermine the position of elections. It is extremely important that none of these countries, except for Czechoslovakia and East Germany, has a historical tradition which endowed elections with a strong authority prior to communist rule. The weakness and deficiencies of the Russian electoral tradition are particularly important. The only elections which took place under the Tsarist regime were to the Duma between the 1905 and 1917 revolutions. Designed to ensure the dominance of the propertied groups, the system divided electors into five *curiae* and heavily favoured the landowning class. Furthermore, the Imperial Duma was indirectly elected through a multi-stage system of assemblies which effectively eliminated all vestiges of lower-class influence. Just as traditional Russian authoritarianism largely shaped the nature of the Soviet regime, so the Tsarist electoral system formed the basis for post-revolutionary elections until the mid-1930s (Emmons, 1983; Vanneman, 1977, ch. 1). The tradition of controlled elections, functioning as instruments to be used by the ruling minority to enhance its power, imbues Soviet elections to this day.

Electoral traditions in Eastern Europe prior to the establishment of communist party states were also weak by Western standards. No country, except Czechoslovakia, enjoyed an unbroken period of free elections affording voters real political choice. Nevertheless, the political tradition of many of these countries was less authoritarian than that of Russia, and the citizens of Poland, Czechoslovakia and what was to become East Germany had some experience of competitive multi-party elections in the inter-war period (McCartney and Palmer, 1962; Rothschild, 1974. On Poland more particularly, see Polonsky, 1972, pp. 60–1, 247–51, 321–3; for Czechoslovakia, see Zinner, 1963, pp. 63–5, 183–6).

The influence of these pre-communist traditions was twofold. First, some of the old structural features were retained in the constitutions of the new People's Democracies, including non-communist parties and proportional representation. Second, the experience, short as it was, of participation in competitive elections affected popular attitudes and expectations and thereby coloured the subsequent development of elections (Skilling, 1966a, pp. 65–6; Brown and Gray, 1979).

The influence of such elements was more than offset by the political structure and style of the communist party states, which built upon and greatly reinforced the authoritarianism characteristic of many of these countries' historical traditions. The concept of the communist party's leading role in society and the operation of democratic centralism have made non-party representative bodies, and elections to them, instruments for the implementation of communist party policy. Any changes in elections are dependent upon changes in the exercise of the party's leading role, and this in turn hinges on developments in the general political situation. One way to approach the whole problem of election development, and its relationship to systematic change, is to outline the main stages through which elections in these states have passed and identify their salient features.

(1) In the 1920s in the Soviet Union and in the late 1940s in Eastern Europe, elections took place in conditions of political struggle; they can be designated 'semi-civil-war elections'. Their nature was shaped by two sets of circumstances. First, in most cases the communist party had taken part

in competitive elections before assuming power, but in none had it succeeded in obtaining a clear majority. Second, the communist parties thus found themselves in power in a hostile political climate, without a basis of popular support or popular legitimacy. From these circumstances stemmed a general anxiety to hold elections which would endow the new regime with the popular legitimacy it lacked. In order to ensure a favourable result in what were at best unsure political conditions, various precautions were taken: those groups most likely to oppose the new regime were disenfranchised, voting was by show of hands, and an element of indirect election was introduced. Opposition parties were so emasculated that the Bloc or Front led by the Communists appeared the only viable choice.

(2) The establishment of firm political control and the execution of fundamental 'socialist' transformations in the social and economic spheres brought about the second stage: Stalinist plebiscitary elections. The defeat of 'class enemies' made safe the introduction of universal suffrage, direct elections at all levels, the secret ballot and all the other trappings associated with free elections in the West. In the Soviet Union, where the new electoral system formed part of the 1936 constitution, these changes were explained as reflecting the new socialist stage of development. Whereas in the period of outright proletarian dictatorship it had been necessary to use elections as an instrument of class power to forge unity, in a basically harmonious socialist society the role of elections was to give unimpeded expression to existing unity. Similar arguments were employed in Eastern Europe, where parallel electoral reforms were accompanied by new constitutions in the early 1950s.

On paper, Stalinist plebiscitary elections were the very model of electoral rectitude. However, their coincidence in time with the highest levels of monolithic Stalinism and hyper-centralisation of the power structure meant that these rules and regulations had little practical impact, and many were customarily violated. Held in a climate of coerced unanimity, these elections approximated very closely to an ideal-type plebiscite, in which all parts of the process, from the selection of candidates to the counting of votes, were bureaucratically manipulated and coordinated to produce the desired result.

(3) The process of de-Stalinisation can be seen as the most important factor operating in the third stage of election development, from the mid-1950s to the mid-1960s. A relaxation of centralisation and a decline in police powers gave somewhat greater control over elections to state, as against party, authorities. More importantly, the new emphasis on socialist legality and constitutionalism reduced the violation of electoral rules and enhanced the standing and role of representative bodies. The decompression of the general political climate and the new stress on active and voluntary popular participation in public life combined with the above to encourage voters to take advantage of their formal electoral rights.

The minimal effect of de-Stalinisation was thus to reduce a little the chasm which had existed between formal electoral rules and election practice. Where, as in Yugoslavia and Poland, de-Stalinisation was transformed into far-reaching reform of systematic proportions, the plebiscitary nature of elections was itself changed qualitatively by the introduction of elements of real choice. It is a token of the political significance of elections that elections offering choices between political parties were seen as one of the most important guarantees against the return of Stalinism.

(4) The current stage of election development, since the mid-1960s, has been characterised by a steady leavening of the plebiscitary lump and a general spread of limited-choice elections. Two sets of changes in the outlook of communist party leaderships have fuelled this process: first, the growing realisation that the achievement of increasingly secularised goals in a highly complex modern society requires considerable decentralisation of decision-making powers and administrative responsibility to non-communist party bodies (this has led, *inter alia*, to the elevation of the role and powers of parliamentary and local government bodies and to a greater emphasis on the need for deputies and councillors of high ability; see Nelson and White, 1982); and, second, the recognition that the most effective way to underpin political stability and maintain economic progress is to provide more institutional opportunities for the expression of different interests within the community, and closer links between the electorate and their representatives.

These changes in thinking have moved election development further away from bureaucratic control and toward greater voter choice, but their impact has varied with political conditions. Where strong concern with the maintenance of very close control over all political processes persists, as in the Soviet Union, Czechoslovakia or Bulgaria, proposals advocating the introduction of elements of choice and competition have remained on paper (Golan, 1971, pp. 185–8; Hill, 1976b).

In other communist party states, such as East Germany, Hungary and Romania, varying elements of electoral choice have been offered to voters. Even in Poland and Yugoslavia, where a degree of choice has long been an established part of elections, measures have been taken to enhance its scope and encourage its utilisation. It is difficult to generalise about regime motivations, but election changes have often been part of a larger package of reforms making the political system more responsive. The introduction of electoral choice has invariably been officially depicted as proof of advances in 'socialist democracy'. This underlines the ever-increasing importance accorded by the regime to representative bodies and to public opinion.

In all instances where choice has been introduced, the communist party's leading role has continued to be beyond electoral challenge. There is no question, even in Yugoslavia, of voters being given a choice between the communist party and an organised opposition. Only in one case, that of the abortive Czechoslovak reform movement of 1968, has a communist party put forward proposals to allow electoral contests involving several parties with differing platforms. And even these proposals stipulated the maintenance of the leading role of the communist party for some considerable time to come (Pelikan, 1972, pp. 234–7).

A typology of elections in communist party states

As a result of the developments outlined above, elections in communist party states vary significantly, even if they do so within the limits imposed by one-party rule. In order to clarify the situation, elections to representative state bodies at all levels have been categorised according to three sets of criteria: (1) the degree of contest permitted, the main factors here being the number of candidates standing for every seat and the scope of programmatic differences in election campaigns; (2) the scope made available for the expression of voters' preferences both at the polls and in the selection process; and (3) the consequences of election results, in terms of the tenure of political power and in terms of policy.

As can be seen from Table 2.1, elections in communist party states at present fall into two main types: plebiscitary elections and limited-choice elections. Because the latter has evolved from the former, and both are set within similarly structured political systems, the two types share many characteristics and in some respects are separated by only slight differences. The number of candidates per seat has been selected as the key distinguishing factor, because of its salience to this study. This is not to imply the existence of a direct correspondence between the number of candidates standing and the degree of electoral choice. Without qualitative differences between candidates, their numbers can be almost meaningless. Furthermore, electoral choice is not restricted to polling day, but can occur at the selection stage. Lastly, any assessment of the degree of choice in these elections must take account of the size and composition of the body of choosers, and of the extent to which they take advantage of the opportunities proffered them. It is not so much the availability of choice as its actual use which ultimately determines political reality.

Plebiscitary elections

In terms of political forms, there seems to be no necessary connection between plebiscitary elections and the existence of the communist party as the only political organisation. In the Soviet Union, which provides the prime example of this type of election, the communist party is in a monopolistic position – i.e. there are no other political parties, and the

TABLE 2.1 *A typology of elections in communist party states*

Type	No. candidates/no. seats	Election platform and campaign	Voting	Selection procedure	Consequences	Current examples
Plebiscitary elections	One candidate per seat	One election platform. High levels of pressure, to ensure unanimity	Direct voting for single-member constituencies. Facilities for secret ballot, but demonstrative voting encouraged; unmarked ballot counted as a positive vote	Usually determined by executive decision; voter choice largely formal except occasionally at lowest levels	None for tenure of power None on national policy; possible minimal consequence for local policy	USSR 1937– Czechoslovakia 1954– Bulgaria 1953– Albania 1954–
Limited-chance elections	More candidates than seats, particularly in local elections	One national election platform; some variation in individual candidates' interpretation	Multi-member constituencies, in-built bias in favour of official candidates; *or*	Greater voter choice and say, especially at local level	None for tenure of power Minimal for national policy, some for local policy	Poland 1957– East Germany 1967–
			single-member constituencies. Greater secret voting; unmarked ballot invalid. Mixture of direct and indirect voting	Considerable legal rights possessed and more influence exerted by voters' meetings, especially at local level		Yugoslavia 1953– Hungary 1967– Romania 1975–

electoral Bloc, uniting the communist party with all social organisations, functions only during elections. On the other hand, Czechoslovakia and Bulgaria combine plebiscitary elections with a political structure incorporating non-communist parties organised in a permanently operating Front in which the communist party has a dominant position. While the presence of such satellite non-communist parties can contribute to the introduction of electoral choice, the way in which the communist party exercises its power is far more important. Plebiscitary elections are most firmly grounded where the communist party behaves in a monopolistic fashion even if structurally it is in a position of hegemony.

Nothing in electoral law prohibits more than one candidate standing for any seat; indeed, provision is often specifically made for such a contingency. The defining characteristic of plebiscitary elections is that this legal possibility is not translated into electoral practice. The standard official justification of the absence of electoral choice has been that there is no political conflict in socialist societies; to insist upon several candidates would be to create disunity where none exists. Moreover, it is claimed that, because the selection process allows the widest possible say to all those who wish to participate, the lack of alternatives on polling day in no way infringes voters' freedom of choice. The anxiety to justify the situation belies a certain defensiveness, which has recently given way to some expression of unease and doubt. Several Soviet academics have pointed out that the established political custom of allowing only one candidate per seat might be doing more harm than good, and that the introduction of an element of electoral choice would probably stimulate popular interest and improve the quality of candidates. To this end, proposals have been put forward advocating the introduction of electoral contest at local levels for a trial period, but there is no evidence that they have been acted upon (Hill, 1976b, p. 486; Medvedev, 1975, p. 144).

The presumption of consensus embodied by the custom of one candidate per seat is reinforced by the election campaign. All candidates stand on the 'unbreakable' platform of the Bloc or Front, which unites all social and political organisations under the leadership of the communist party. Great stress is laid on the fact that all candidates have equal access to campaign facilities, but the legitimate use of such facilities is restricted to those canvassing in favour of those standing; no mention is made of the right to campaign against candidates. Indeed, all campaigning is coordinated and steered by the communist party's agitation and propaganda departments to project the best possible image of party and government achievements and plans. Throughout the three weeks or so of the campaign national policies are lauded and not discussed. At nomination and campaign meetings, criticism is sometimes voiced of the performance of local government bodies and demands are raised about matters such as housing and transport, but national political issues are studiously avoided. Some additional opportunity for discussing local issues is provided by door-to-door canvassing, but the main thrust of these visits is to convey the achievements of the communist party and the government.

Considerable criticism has been voiced in the Soviet Union and Czechoslovakia about the monotony and lack of imagination evident in campaigning, and the call raised for a more varied and sensitive approach. Yet, given the unchanged nature of the ruling purpose of the campaign – to ensure that the entire electorate demonstrates its unanimous support for the Front or Bloc – it is not surprising that blanket mobilisation remains dominant.

The citizen has very little real choice about whether he votes in plebiscitary elections. There is no legal compulsion, but the overwhelming social and organisational pressures to turn out make the difficulties of absenteeism far outweigh the inconvenience of voting. As a result, electoral turn-out since the 1960s has ranged from a 'low' of 99.4 per cent in Czechoslovakia to a 'high' of 100 per cent in Albania. The missing percentile fractions are being steadily eroded and should be ascribed mainly to organisational shortcomings rather than to determined absenteeism.

Voting procedures facilitate the expression of support and discourage dissent. To register a vote in favour of the candidate the elector has merely to place an unmarked ballot paper in the box; those who wish to vote against the candidate have to delete his or her name. As secrecy of the ballot is constitutionally guaranteed, voting booths are provided for this purpose. In the circumstances, however, their use can be interpreted as indicating dissidence. These conditions, in addition to the strong campaign pressures to vote 'demonstratively', result, at least in the Soviet Union, in an estimated 1–5 per cent of the electorate using the booths to cast a 'secret' ballot. Several academic commentators have criticised existing voting procedures for their failure either to assure secrecy or to afford electors the opportunity to express their opinions. It has been suggested that positive marking of the card should be required, encouraging all voters to use the booths (Swearer, 1961, p. 146; Mote, 1965, pp. 77–81; Hill, 1976b, pp. 487–8; see also Piekalkiewicz, 1972, p. 172).

Given existing arrangements, which so strongly militate against the negative vote, it is not surprising that the number of such votes rarely exceeds 0.5 per cent of the total votes cast. These votes appear to be largely protest directed against local policies and performance and against unpopular local candidates; only at village level are they sufficient to bring about the defeat of any candidates – in Soviet elections, approximately one in every 10 000 fails in this way (Gilison, 1968, pp. 820–2; Jacobs, 1970, pp. 70–6).

Electors' rights do not end with a ballot on polling day. The right of recall has long been highlighted as exemplifying the high level of popular control and choice made available in all socialist elections. In the Soviet

Union since the late 1950s, increasing stress has been placed on the voters' right to recall any deputy who has failed in his duties or betrayed his constituents' trust. The organisations nominating a deputy have the right to raise the question, which is then examined by the executive of the representative body of which he is an elected member. If this body decides there is a case, it organises a vote on the matter. Interestingly enough, in the campaign leading up to this vote, canvassing is permitted against as well as for the incumbent. The actual question of recall is usually decided by a show of hands at a local electors' meeting and, if it proves necessary, a by-election is then held. Inbuilt executive filters make it a highly controlled process which restricts actual incidence of recalls to a very small number of cases, involving misdemeanours; recalls do not occur where policy questions are involved.

One of the standard official explanations offered for the absence of choice at the polls is that voters have already exercised their choice in the course of the selection process. Formal selection procedures appear to grant considerable powers of choice to work-place meetings of voters: all nomination proposals have to be submitted to them for approval; and, even after the registration of nominations, further voters' meetings have the right to alter the lists. The entire process is purportedly designed to give the voter the decisive say in determining who stands for elections.

In practice, selection is a far more closed process offering only a limited degree of choice to small groups. As one would expect, the communist party, whose role is glossed over in the formal procedures, exercises a decisive influence over the outcome of selection. It is evident from written accounts, and from the remarkable consistency of the composition of deputies, that central party directives are issued for every election which lay down definite guidelines according to which candidates are to be selected. These guidelines stipulate the overall proportion of candidates in terms of social – occupational status, political and organisational affiliation, age, sex and so forth. Party committees, particularly at the district level, then break down the overall proportions for their own areas and issue appropriate recommendations to other organisations involved in selection, including Front committees. These proportions vary in specificity, and leave the communist party and, in Bulgaria and Czechoslovakia, other organisations, at district and at the lowest levels, with a good deal of discretion in selecting names to fit the bill.

It is within circles of local officials that most of the real selection takes place, accompanied by a good deal of consultation and bargaining. The resulting lists of proposed candidates are then presented to nomination meetings of voters at their places of work. Usually there is little discussion of or challenge to any of the nominees. Nominees are then registered as candidates and duly presented to voters' meetings. These are generally rather tame affairs, at which a few questions are addressed to candidates and electors' instructions are issued. Such instructions or mandates, which are supposed to guide and not totally bind candidates when elected, are often drawn up by local campaign officials and merely formally ratified by the meeting. At the lowest levels in local elections, where issues and individuals are better known, both nomination meetings and those between voters and candidates tend to be more lively and occasionally result in the replacement of official candidates.

The reality of candidate selection thus departs from the avowed principles of broad voter involvement, choice and influence. Several aspects of the process have prompted critical comments and proposals from academic and official platforms.

First, some Soviet academics have underlined the need to strengthen links between nomination and representation, between those who select candidates and those whom the candidate is elected to represent. Under the existing system of nomination at work-places, and elections for territorially based constituencies, such links are often tenuous and, for some voters, non-existent. To solve this problem, some have advocated nomination rights for territorially based voters' meetings and the election of deputies on a mixed territorial – production basis; others favour a return to the pre-1936 Soviet production-based constituencies. On a different tack, but with the same end in view, one writer has proposed that candidates standing for re-election should as a rule do so in their old constituency, rather than be moved elsewhere as at present; they should certainly not, as often happens, be foisted on new voters without the latter's being given some idea of their previous record (Hill, 1976b, pp. 489–92). The contention of all these critics is that, were such proposals enacted, those participating in nomination meetings would have a greater interest in choosing the right candidate, and the capacity to do so.

The second concern is the gap between the voters' formal prerogatives in selection and their use of these rights. Soviet academics and party spokesmen and some Czech local councillors have deplored the general hastiness and superficiality of nomination meetings and the lack of real discussion and questioning of candidates at voters' meetings. The official answer to this is a call for greater activism on the part of the rank and file. Academics, on the other hand, have suggested procedural changes to strengthen the influence of nomination and voters' meetings over selection (Kim, 1965, pp. 180–1; Aimbetov, 1967, pp. 91–2; Klokocka, 1968, p. 249; *Problemy rad narodowych*, 1969, no. 14, p. 77; *Partiinaya zhizn'*, 1973, no. 9, p. 14).

Predictably, none of the Soviet critics sees the passivity of the voters in selection as a direct function of the bureaucratic domination of the process. No attempt had been made to suggest a change in the principle of party 'supervision' over selection. This is deemed to be necessary in order to prevent any 'spontaneity', i.e. uncontrolled grass-roots activity, which is regarded in all communist party states, but particularly in those with plebiscitary elections, as a heinous offence. What is suggested instead is that all nominating organisations consult local activists and voters more fully and take greater care to put forward candidates of the highest calibre who command genuine popular respect and support (Aimbetov, 1967, pp. 91–2; Hill, 1976a, p. 595).

While there is no evidence of any of the specific proposals for structural and procedural change being put into effect, there are signs that steps have been taken in the direction of fuller consultation. In a few cases, official candidates have been withdrawn in favour of those chosen by votes at work-place nomination meetings. Developments along such lines would extend the exercise of selection choice from 'roomfuls of officials' to assembly halls at places of work. Such an extension would not necessarily diminish greatly the level of bureaucratic control, but it would bring the selection process closer to fulfilling its supposed 'primary election' function (Medvedev, 1975, pp. 372–3; for this particular term see Rigby, 1976, p. 260).

Limited-choice elections

As with plebiscitary elections, there is no uniformity of political structure among the states whose elections are of this type. The existence of non-communist parties is not a prerequisite of limited-choice elections: the communist party retains a monopoly of organised political activity in Yugoslavia and Hungary, but these countries offer a greater amount of electoral choice than do other communist states. What distinguishes them from their plebiscitary counterparts is higher levels of political pluralism, stemming in part from a greater social heterogeneity, and in part from a more flexible party attitude toward political expression.

The distinguishing characteristic of this type is the extension of voter choice from the selection stage to the polls. In all these elections it is established practice for there to be more candidates than seats. The degree of electoral contest and choice does, however, vary considerably from country to country.

In East Germany the element of competition and choice is kept to a minimum. The list of candidates for the multi-seat constituencies comprises two groups: the 'seat' candidates (listed first), equal in number to the seats to be filled; and the so-called 'surplus' candidates. The electoral chances of the two groups are very different. In order to become deputies the 'seat' candidates merely have to get a simple majority of the votes cast. On the other hand, the 'surplus' candidates, even if they poll 99 per cent of the vote, have no chance of becoming deputies unless one or more of the 'seat' group fails to get a majority. In the event of there being no such failure, 'surplus' candidates who get 51 per cent or more of the vote become what are called 'substitute' deputies, and can be brought in to fill any vacancies which may arise between elections (Sontheimer and Bleek, 1975, p. 80; Scharf, 1984, pp. 25–6).

The Polish system provides for a far more equal and meaningful contest. As in East Germany, the list is divided into 'seat' candidates and 'surplus' candidates, but in this case the number of votes received is decisive. Those candidates who poll the largest number of votes, over and above a simple majority, become deputies regardless of their status. The success of the 'surplus' candidates is thus not conditional upon the failure of one of their 'seat' counterparts. The latter, however, have one considerable advantage – namely, that an unmarked ballot paper is counted as a vote for the 'seat' candidates alone (Gebert, 1976, p. 115; Sakwa and Crouch, 1978, pp. 410–14).

No such bias is present in the Romanian, Hungarian or Yugoslav systems. In none of these is there any limit to the number of 'surplus' candidates allowed; nor do they suffer any under formal voting handicaps. It is interesting to note that the Hungarian and, especially, the Yugoslav electoral systems also incorporate an important element of indirect election; this might be seen as an inbuilt safeguard against excessive voter influence.

Just as the formal regulations vary, so do the quantitative levels of choice. Yugoslav elections have produced the highest ratio of candidates to seats. In 1967 this ranged from approximately 1.5 to 1 at the national level to 2.5 to 1 in local contests. In Poland the legal surplus of 50 per cent has rarely been fully achieved, though levels have usually not fallen far below a 40 per cent excess of candidates over seats (legislation now provides that, from 1985 onwards, there shall be twice as many candidates as seats available at local and national elections). The only Romanian elections to have offered any real choice, those of 1975, 1980 and 1985, had slightly higher levels, while the Hungarian record makes it numerically less competitive than East Germany (Hungary, like Poland, has however introduced the practice of multiple candidacies on a mandatory basis from 1985 onwards at both the local and national level). The general pattern is that, the lower the level of election, the greater the quantitative choice available. Several factors can be held to account for this. At the local level there is greater involvement and therefore a greater tendency on the part of organisations and groups to insist that their candidates stand for office. Because the political importance of such elections is small, central authorities are also more likely to allow most nominations to go through. At higher levels central controls are more stringent; many seats are held *ex officio* and few candidates are willing to risk defeat by standing in contested constituencies.

Although the excess of candidates over seats is an essential precondition for electoral choice, it is the existence of qualitative differences between the contestants which determines the reality of that choice. The first overall factor limiting the differences between candidates is that they all stand on the same electoral platform, that of the Front or its equivalent, which is based on the programme of the communist party. Repeatedly it is officially emphasised that the choice with which voters are presented is one between personalities and not between policies. Individual candidates may interpret certain aspects of their common programme in slightly different ways, but they all, regardless of political or organisational affiliation, stand for one party line. In practice, such consensus is generally maintained; only in some Yugoslav election contests, notably in 1967 and 1969, have candidates ever questioned the policies embodied in the official election programme (see Rusinow, 1977, pp. 222–4, 229, 243, 261–6, 332). Despite such programmatic unity, it is only in East Germany and Poland, where the electoral system almost guarantees who will be elected, that the electors are given a choice among individuals who hold important political or administrative office. In Hungary, Romania and Yugoslavia, where electoral contests are more equal, officials from the higher or even middle echelons of the party and other organisations almost invariably stand unopposed. Even the Hungarian system of mandatory contest provides leading politicians with the fall-back of running unopposed on a select national list of parliamentary candidates. Officials of lower ranks are sometimes put up in contested seats, but usually only against officials of similar standing. Were communist party officials to stand against rank-and-file candidates and be defeated this would reflect on the party's image, despite official insistence that all differences are merely personal. A similar tendency emerges when one examines the electoral position of the larger 'core' of deputies who seem to enjoy almost permanent elected office. These sitting deputies are generally placed in safe seats, the contested ones being reserved in large part for their 'one-term' colleagues (see, for instance, Hill, 1972).

As far as communist party members as a whole are concerned, it is difficult to discern any definite patterns. They seem to form as large a proportion of competing or 'surplus' candidates as they do of the other categories. This is the result of deliberate party policy. In order to assert its presence and maintain certain set levels of saturation in all representative bodies, the party makes sure that its members stand in what can be identified as unsafe as well as safe situations. Lastly, there is usually very little difference between competing candidates as regards their social – occupational status; at the most, workers stand against foremen or the latter against works engineers. Distinctions between candidates, and thus choice, are narrowed down to differences in individual experience, popularity and ability to carry out what remains a common programme.

The entire election campaign is directed towards underlining the unity of outlook and interest of all candidates, and obscuring the differences separating them. As in plebiscitary elections, campaign effort popularises the positive aspects of past national achievements and future plans. Appeals are made, if in somewhat less strident tones, for the electorate's wholehearted support and unanimous endorsement of the Front platform. The attention given to publicising individual candidates and their views still tends to be very secondary by comparison. Polish surveys show that the majority of voters do not have sufficient knowledge to assess candidates' relative merits (see, for instance, Gostkowski, 1967).

The rules and conventions governing the campaign still explicitly prohibit canvassing against candidates, and even efforts by individuals to win votes for themselves are frowned upon. All candidates are meant to act the same. All have to get exactly the same amount of publicity and press coverage. Even in Yugoslavia, where campaigns have been freer than in other limited-choice elections, attempts to attract support by making promises to promote local interests are condemned as 'demagogy'. Despite such restrictions, competitive electioneering has occasionally occurred. In the Polish elections of 1957 and in Yugoslavia in 1967 and 1969 some contests assumed a combative nature, with candidates playing on local grievances and even running their own campaigns in opposition to the official machine (Pelczynski, 1959, pp. 154–7; Rusinow, 1977, pp. 222–4, 261–6).

Official endeavours to minimise differences between candidates notwithstanding, these elections present voters with some opportunity to express their preferences. In addition to the black-and-white options available in plebiscitary elections – of voting or not voting and of casting a positive or a negative vote – there are further possibilities for choice. In Hungary, Romania and Yugoslavia, many electors have a straight choice from two or more candidates; in East Germany and Poland they can either vote for the 'seat' candidates or for those in the 'surplus' positions on the list, or opt to vote for a mixture of individuals. Voting procedures facilitate the use of these options. Passive voting is still encouraged by the Polish and East German systems, where unmarked ballot papers are counted as votes for the 'seat' candidates. In Hungary and Yugoslavia, however, unmarked ballot papers are considered invalid; this makes it easier to vote secretly without incriminating oneself as an opponent of the regime. Finally, procedures governing the recall of deputies give Hungarian and Yugoslav constituents a greater say than they would enjoy in plebiscitary elections. Grounds for recall are somewhat broader and the control exercised by executive bodies over the whole process is less prohibitive. Yet there is still widespread feeling that recall is under-utilised because it is not sufficiently open to voter influence.

What use does the electorate make of the opportunities offered by limited-choice elections and what preferences do voting figures reveal? Election turn-out tends to be lower and a good deal more volatile than in plebiscitary elections, ranging from a low of about 90 per cent in Yugoslavia to about 96–98 per cent in Poland, Hungary and Romania. The figures reveal the usual pattern of lower turn-out in local elections and in rural areas; consistent regional and nationality group variations; and fluctuations corresponding to changes in policy. The less highly charged election atmosphere and less intensive mobilisation efforts allow for the greater use of absenteeism as a means of registering indifference to or even disagreement with regime policy (this was clearly the case, for instance, in the 1984 local elections in Poland, the first since the emergence of Solidarity and the imposition of martial law; the turnout, according to official sources, was about 75 per cent, or according to Solidarity sources no more than 60 per cent).

A more direct indicator of such disagreement is the number of protest votes, i.e. votes cast against all the candidates standing. The availability of choice does not seem to reduce the number of such votes, though many of those who supported the introduction of an element of choice probably hoped it would. On the contrary, it appears to result in a significant increase. Negative votes constitute 1–2 per cent, and in Yugoslavia up to 7 per cent, of all votes cast. Once again, the slightly more tolerant election climate must be held to account in large part for this phenomenon. Organisational factors, however, are of less importance than in the case of turn-out, and voter apathy does not cloud the political meaning of acts of this kind. It is clear from the Polish and Yugoslav data that negative votes reflect both underlying political antipathies and short-term reactions to changes in political course.

It is difficult for voters to express their political preferences when presented with a straight choice between two or more candidates of equal status standing on the same platform. Even where one of the candidates is known to be officially sponsored, the evidence indicates that voters tend to decide on the basis of candidates' individual qualifications and past record, and not on the basis of their official standing. Although being the unofficial candidate is no handicap, it is not necessarily an advantage either. Those candidates who have successfully stood as independents in Yugoslav elections have achieved their success not because of their contradiction of the communist party line, but because of their promises to promote local interests (Singleton, 1976, p. 147; Rusinow, 1977, pp. 222–4, 261–6).

Polish elections, which demarcate clearly between official ('seat') and unofficial ('surplus') candidates, shed more light on this point. Given the rarity in these states of the opportunity to choose between official and unofficial standpoints, one might expect the 'surplus' candidates to do very well. Yet very few of them are elected and then only at lower levels in local elections. Several factors might be held to account for this. First, the voting system: to get elected, the 'surplus' candidate needs to combine a large personal vote with concentrated voting against one of the 'seat' candidates.

Second, careful selection: this not only excludes most potentially unpopular candidates but also often ensures that popular and able individuals are placed in the 'seat' positions. The voters are therefore not presented with a choice between unsuitable official candidates and able unofficial ones. As a result, only a very small minority of electors, usually in tightly-knit communities, have the knowledge and motivation to vote against a particular 'seat' candidate, let alone for a particular 'surplus' candidate.

While the vast majority of voters do not, therefore, attempt to defeat the official slate, enough vote against the 'seat' candidates to alter substantially from the original listing the order in which they are elected. In this way voters in Poland can make their preferences felt without implying any wholesale rejection of the official election platform. At first sight, these changes in order seem to operate against communists and in favour of candidates from other parties and the unaffiliated. On closer inspection, however, it emerges that the apparent anti-communist party vote is secondary to one directed against office-holders. The functionaries who are usually placed first in the list of 'seat' candidates are often well known and sufficiently unpopular with the electorate to attract a number of negative votes, which result in their demotion to the bottom of the 'seat' group. This seems to be the case whether or not they are members of the communist party. Because the majority of communist candidates hold some kind of office, they poll a lower percentage of votes cast. Although it can be argued that electors do not use their vote against communists *qua* members of the communist party, it is mistaken to claim, as does Wiatr (1959, pp.114, 178–9), that these consistent changes in the order of seat candidates are essentially non-political. By deleting the names of party and government apparatchiks, a small yet significant number of voters do make effective use of the system to voice their political opinions (see Sakwa and Crouch, 1978, pp. 414–22).

The formal stages of selection in many ways parallel those in plebiscitary elections. The right of proposal is universally possessed by social and political organisations, meetings of working people and of electors. In some instances it extends to groups of citizens and even to individuals. By a process of consultation, organisation representatives draw up lists of nominees, and these are submitted to voters' meetings or to conferences of elected voters' delegates. Such meetings or conferences are generally empowered to reject names on the lists and put forward nominees of their own. A vote decides the composition of the list of proposed candidates, which goes to the election or Front committees and is then forwarded to official bodies for registration. Even after this stage, meetings of voters with prospective candidates can alter the final election line-up.

The formal rights of voters' meetings vary considerably. In Poland and East Germany their powers are as nebulous as in plebiscitary systems. While the meetings can change the lists of nominees submitted to them, the election or Front committees are obliged merely to take these views into account. The meetings are seen as no more than sounding-boards to facilitate the consultation of voter opinion. In Yugoslavia and Hungary, these meetings or their equivalents have far more extensive and more closely defined powers. Yugoslav regulations lay down that the decisions of meetings comprising set minimum proportions of voters must be confirmed by the electoral commissions, unless there are strictly legal grounds for their rejection. Hungarian electoral law stipulates that all nominees who receive a third of the votes at electors' meetings must be put forward for registration by the Front committees. In both cases, therefore, the decisions taken at voters' meetings are legally binding and not merely views to be taken into account.

In practice, by far the most important stages of the selection process still take place within the communist party and the main social and political organisations. Although the scope for choice afforded by party guidelines is similar to that in plebiscitary selection, influence is brought to bear by a wider range of opinion. First, the selection procedures within organisations are more open. While the majority of nominations for national level bodies continue to be issued from central executives, all other nominations are decided by conferences of delegates. In Poland, for instance, not only have communist party nomination conferences taken on the character of primaries, but they have also been opened to non-communist activists, who thereby have an opportunity to influence the composition of party nominees. Yugoslavia offers the best instances of nomination lists being drawn up by a process of hard bargaining and trading between delegations from the main social organisations. The communist party still exercises a guiding role but does not always seek to get its own way (see, for instance, Rusinow, 1977, pp. 263–6).

Any attempt to assess the impact of voters' meetings on the lists of nominations produced by the organisation 'primaries' must take into account the differences between selection of candidates for national representative assemblies and selection of candidates for lower-level bodies. In the first category, voters' meetings and conferences seem to leave little impact. In Yugoslavia in 1965 and 1967, for example, voters' meetings put forward a large number of nominees for election to federal office, but many were disallowed on what were often spurious grounds. In Hungary, the reluctance of voters to propose nominations from the floor has combined with the authorities' determination to secure the adoption of their candidates to prevent anything more than occasional changes being made in the lists. When candidates are rejected by these meetings all that usually happens is that a substitute candidate is put forward by the Front – the umbrella body which co-ordinates the main organisations' election activity – and is endorsed by the same or by a second meeting. Only very rarely is a candidate 'spontaneously' proposed from the floor added to the final list.

At local level, voters' meetings and conferences have greater influence. Because controls are less tight and because participants know a good deal about the merits and demerits of each nominee, searching questioning often takes place. As a result, a small yet significant proportion of the names submitted is rejected; in the Polish local elections of 1965, for instance, 4 per cent of village-level candidates were changed in this way. The most common objection raised against these candidates was that they were not locals and would therefore be unlikely to understand and represent constituency interests. The nominations put forward by such meetings show a bias towards locals or towards those who can convince voters of their determination to promote local interests. This criterion appears to far more important than political affiliation, though, in Poland at least, there is some prejudice in favour of candidates who are not members of any party. The alterations made by voters' meetings to the lists of nominations fare differently from country to country. In Yugoslavia, for instance, most of the changes proposed get through to the final lists, while in Poland election committees use their discretionary powers to neutralise much of the meetings' impact.

Functions

As all elections in communist party states exclude the possibility of choice between competing national programmes, it is often assumed that their functions are confined to mobilisation and legitimation of a crude and uniform kind. In point of fact, they perform a range of functions which in many respects resemble those associated with classic Western elections.

Mobilisation

Organised mass activity is a salient feature of public life in all communist party states, involving up to half the adult population. Elections are an important occasion for the mobilisation of the normally passive members of the community. In plebiscitary elections, overwhelming emphasis is placed on achieving extremely high levels of turn-out. Electoral participation is almost exclusively 'stalactite', i.e. the result of organisational pressure from above, including occasional voting by election officials on behalf of absentees. In limited-choice elections, high turn-out is still worked for, but greater priority is accorded to encouraging participation of a more top-down 'stalagmite' nature (for these terms see Nettl, 1967, pp. 271–2). These differences in approach largely account for the differences in turn-out between, to take the two extremes, Albania and Yugoslavia.

Getting voters out is not the only dimension of election mobilisation. Improving disappointing attendance at meetings throughout the election period is also important. Low attendances can present a serious problem where voters' meetings play an important part in selection; in Yugoslavia many nominations have fallen through because of the lack of a quorum at meetings, and at some Polish pre-electoral meetings in 1984 officials are reported to have outnumbered ordinary citizens. Yet it is contradictory for elections stressing voter choice to employ plebiscitary pressures to ensure that choices are made.

Elections provide a unique opportunity for all political and social organisations to collaborate on a national political mobilisation which is in many ways the political equivalent of the launching of a Five Year Plan. Economic issues pervade all campaigns; in Czechoslovakia and Hungary the parliamentary term of office has recently been extended to bring it into line with the period of the economic plan. In Eastern Europe elections are the only occasion at which otherwise semi-moribund Fronts come into effective operation to co-ordinate the activity of the communist party and its partners. More generally, elections test the organisational and propaganda abilities of the various apparatuses and offer an excellent opportunity to activate the mass memberships. Officials carefully monitor all aspects of electoral mobilisation for signs of organisational strength and weaknesses. In both types of election, mobilisation is a demonstration on the largest scale of the regime's political control and organisational effectiveness. While differences between the types are largely ones of degree and emphasis, mobilisation in limited-choice elections is somewhat less dragooned and inflexible.

Political education and socialisation

All these elections are occasions for the intensification of political education and socialisation. Their sheer duration and frequency give them weight. In the Soviet Union, for instance, elections occupy up to two months in three out of every four years. Elections open up a greater variety of channels for political communication. Political information is given even greater media prominence than usual and direct contact with the electorate is made possible, if not always utilised, by meetings at places of work and residence. In addition, agitation points and centres are established and used for political discussion and the distribution of election literature. Finally, canvassing operations are mounted on a massive scale, particularly in plebiscitary elections. Most families are visited at least once in the course of the campaign and given a political-education talk and some opportunity to discuss local problems. It is difficult to assess the impact made by such methods. Very wide coverage is achieved, but much of the campaigning remains perfunctory and usually too much is crammed into the final weeks of the campaign period. Because the flow of political propaganda is continuous, the majority of the population has considerable resistance to indoctrination. In these conditions the concerted use of communications channels during elections probably reduces the credibility of the messages conveyed.

In both types of election, campaign themes are invariably taken from the last party congress or Central Committee session. The election programme of the Bloc or Front and election addresses tend to highlight the work of parliamentary and local government bodies. In local elections considerable effort is made to weave matters of local concern into campaign material. This is particularly the case in some limited-choice elections. In Poland since 1965, election programmes have been formulated for local councils. The introduction of electoral contests has led, in Hungary, Poland and, especially, Yugoslavia, to candidates' expounding their own views of election issues. On rare occasions even national-level elections, as in Yugoslavia in 1967 and 1969, have witnessed public argument and conflict. What has happened more often, however, is that contest has enlivened discussions and helped to make elections into more of a two-way exchange of information and opinion.

Participation in such discussions forms part of the socialisation effect of elections. Attendance at election meetings usually involves between a third and a half of the electorate, if only to a minimal extent, in the campaign and thereby in the whole political process. The act of voting is more significant in socialisation terms, because it constitutes the culmination of elections as civic rituals of participation and commitment. In some plebiscitary elections, Czechoslovakia in 1971 being a case in point, electors are strongly encouraged to vote with their fellow workers, to strengthen the collective ethos which figures so prominently in the ideal political culture. All this underlines the importance of elections as May Day demonstrations writ large.

Very large numbers also participate in elections through working in election commissions and committees, in canvassing groups and at polling stations. More than two million citizens, for instance, were members of electoral commissions in the Soviet national elections of 1984, and about 15 per cent of the adult population are estimated to play some part in the proceedings (Zaslavsky and Brym, 1978, p. 365; *Pravda*, 4 February 1984, p.2). Such active involvement is likely to create some feeling of co-responsibility, even if only as a result of its being ascribed to this group by the non-involved. By far the most far-reaching involvement and socialisation is undergone by those elected to office. The very high rates of turn-over associated in particular with plebiscitary elections – 50 per cent plus is common – exist partly for reasons of socialisation. In the USSR, the soviets are seen as 'schools of ideological and political upbringing', though greater concern with representatives' performance and their links with constituents has prompted calls for a reduction of turn-over. Such concern may account for the lower rate of turn-over – about one-third – in recent Hungarian elections, and for the falling rate in Poland.

The effectiveness of elections as agents of political education and social-isation must be assessed in the context of regime objectives. In the Stalinist stage, the overriding objective was to convey a few simple messages and socialise all into compliant behaviour; convictions were of secondary importance. Plebiscitary elections are still geared to and largely succeed in achieving these objectives. Since the late 1950s, however, the socialisation goals of those states which retain plebiscitary elections have become more complex. They now incorporate some desire to produce participation based on a conviction that elections truly express popular sovereignty. Measured against such aims, plebiscitary elections fail dismally. Levels of information and interest seem to be low; one Soviet survey found that under 10 per cent of electors knew the names of the candidates they had elected (Powell and Shoup, 1970, p. 577). Czech surveys in 1968 revealed enormous discrepancies between the officially propagated image of elec-tions and popular attitudes; in one national poll only 1 per cent of respondents shared the official view that the existing election system was the best system for the 'democratic' expression of the people's will (Pie-kalkiewicz, 1972, p. 175).

Limited-choice elections are better suited to newer socialisation objec-tives and seem to do marginally better in achieving them. Research conducted during the Polish elections of 1958 and 1961 showed increasing levels of information and high levels of interest, even though some of the latter should be discounted as the result of conscious effort to give the 'right' answer. Yet what is worrying from the standpoint of newer socialis-ation objectives is that the polls revealed that under 10 per cent of voters believed in the 'socialist democratic' nature of elections (Gostkowski, 1959, pp. 375–80; 1967, pp. 50–1). Even in Hungary and Yugoslavia, where electoral contest is more equal, 'tolerant cynicism' is widespread and it is unlikely that this will be transformed into active participation without the introduction of some choice of programmes.

Integration

Even in communist party states, which have a whole array of integrating mechanisms at their disposal, elections still perform a useful role. Both types of election enable party leaders to appear as national figures and to appeal to all citizens on a national rather than party-political platform. Election declarations are notable for the care they take to give weight to the achievements and contributions of all groups and for the emphasis they place on their interdependence. Not only are the politically unaffiliated made to feel equal to their communist fellows, but, in addition, attention is paid to those groups distanced from the centre by their geographical, social, ethnic or spiritual location. In Poland and Hungary, for example, party leaders stress the alliance with the Catholic Church. Elections are fought on a platform uniting organisations representing a wide spectrum of interests and identities, and not by the communist party alone.

Integration by way of a public image of unity and equality is accompanied by integration through representation. The main rationale behind the party's guidelines on the composition of candidates is to achieve a balanced and proportional 'mix' of occupational, ethnic and minority groups. The assumption is that the presence of group representatives will assure the identification of all the groups concerned with the election process and the political system as a whole. As the elective offices involved have little political influence, proportional group representation seems a convenient way of furthering integration without jeopardising control. The flaw in this reasoning is that, for such representation to operate effectively, the groups concerned must feel that they are being given a meaningful say in public affairs. Yet, the more meaningful that say becomes, the greater the risk of its undermining a system of integration based on the principles of democratic centralism.

Integration in states with plebiscitary elections is conceived as a top-down process. The role of an elected representative is primarily to ensure local compliance with central directives and not to press local interests. Accordingly, the ideal representative is a respected and exemplary member of his group, and not a local politician. Indeed, while it is stressed that he should do his best to fulfil constituents' mandates, it is made clear that in any conflict precedence must be given to national interests.

This concept of integration through representation has several weaknesses. First, it produces many deputies and councillors unable to cope with the tasks involved; this in turn contributes to constituents' dissatisfaction with representatives (see, for instance, Powell and Shoup, 1970, p. 577). Second, unless candidates enjoy genuine popular support, their ability to perform linkage and integrating functions is weak. Shared social-group membership is not sufficient for popular support. Czechoslovak, Polish and Yugoslav evidence shows that voters tend to put experience and capacity to represent local interests first (*Problemy rad narodowych*, 1969, no. 13, pp. 49, 74; Piekalkiewicz, 1972, p. 179; Rusinow, 1977, pp. 260–6).

The logic of the situation leads to a different concept of integration in many limited-choice elections. By giving voters a greater say in selection and a choice of candidates, these elections move from the principle of group membership ordained from above to a more flexible combination of group membership and popular choice. While the deputy or councillor is still urged to place national interests above local ones, there is greater emphasis on his discretion and on the need to harmonise the two, rather than subordinate one to the other. This approach has the potential to produce integration founded on local identity and involvement, but it carries with it the danger that candidates will campaign on a platform of promoting local interests over and above all others. Though controls remain tight, Yugoslav elections show that greater voter choice can produce representatives who foment rather than stem parochialism, thus weakening integration (Rusinow, 1977, pp. 260–6).

Legitimation

Legitimation is by far the most important function performed by elections in these states. In a strict sense, the leading role of the communist party is beyond questioning by elections. Nevertheless, they legitimate it in at least two ways. First, as a large proportion of candidates are communists – 60 to 70 per cent at national level and 40 to 50 per cent at local level – elections can be paraded as a vote of confidence in the party. Second, elections confer legitimacy on the whole political system, of which the communist party is the core. By voting in favour of candidates standing on a single platform, the electorate is said to be voicing its approval of the performance and plans of the party and government. Electoral success is taken to signify not only agreement with plans but also a firm commitment to work for their implementation. Votes are interpreted as the political equivalent of the pledges given by work-forces to fulfil production targets ahead of schedule. Furthermore, the very high votes received by party and government leaders, all of whom stand in parliamentary elections, are interpreted as popular votes of confidence; they can be seen as fulfilling the leaders' psychological need for mass public support.

By conferring legitimacy, elections also make illegitimate any political alternatives. This is particularly important when a regime's overall legitimacy is in doubt. The Hungarian election of 1958 and the Czechoslovak election of 1971 were held with the express purpose of showing that opposition elements had no popular support and that their attacks upon the regime had no substance. In both cases the 99 per cent plus majorities were heralded as conclusive demonstrations of legitimacy, and arguably this had some impact on the domestic and international front (Vali, 1962, pp. 417–18; Dinka and Skidmore, 1973, p. 413).

Plebiscitary elections provide legitimation by a guaranteed and unanimous demonstration of mass support. Insistence on one candidate per seat is a logical part of a concept of elections as primarily acts of affirmation, and only secondarily procedures whereby individuals are selected for office. The legitimacy provided by plebiscitary elections has several weaknesses. First, it may not stand up under pressure. Events in Poland and Hungary in 1956 and in Czechoslovakia in 1968 revealed the lack of legitimacy of regimes with excellent election records. Second, insistence on extremely high levels of electoral support means that any falling below those norms might be dysfunctional. Lastly, it follows from the principle of one candidate per seat that all votes cast against candidates can be seen as votes against the regime.

The legitimation sought in limited-choice elections is of a somewhat different kind; greater importance is attached to the quality of electoral support. Appeals for unanimous support are frequently but not invariably made, but are couched in different terms; rather than reminding voters of their obligation to register support, they ask for approval of the election programme (Wiatr, 1959, pp. 179, 204; Pelczynski, 1959, pp. 164–5; Kadar, 1971). The introduction of choice between candidates breaks the direct connection between votes against officials and system rejection. But there are also disadvantages. Although all electoral defeats are depicted as reflecting upon only the personal qualities of the candidates concerned, they can negatively affect regime legitimacy because of official insistence on the indivisibility of the election platform. As has been noted, the introduction of choice between candidates increases rather than siphons off the totally negative votes. Finally, the higher status of popularly elected bodies might weaken the legitimacy of those not formed on that basis, namely party bodies.

The contribution made by elections of both types to regime legitimacy is very minor when compared with other factors, particularly economic performance. Yet the official emphasis on popular sovereignty and the long tradition of holding elections has made them necessary rituals the removal of which, to put their importance in minimal terms, would weaken legitimacy. In situations of economic and political flux their legitimating role increases considerably. The postponement of elections in Hungary in 1956 and in Czechoslovakia in 1968, when it was feared that they would have a negative effect on stability, and their advancement in Poland in 1972, when it was thought they would legitimate a new leadership and a new programme, testify to this; so too to the 1984 local and 1985 national elections in the same country, which were intended to legitimate the Jaruzelski leadership domestically and internationally.

Influence on public policy

The policy process in all these states is highly bureaucratic and decisions are largely confined to the upper echelons of the party and government. Nevertheless, the last twenty years have seen a certain opening up of policy-making, creating some very limited scope for the expression of popular attitudes toward policies through electoral barometers.

Nomination meetings and meetings between candidates and constituents provide forums for the expression of voters' opinions on matters of local concern. Even in plebiscitary elections, views are aired at such meetings and in canvassing – on housing, transport and local government performance. The introduction of greater choice stimulates discussion and produces a greater polarisation of opinion, though this still revolves overwhelmingly around local issues. Careful note is taken not only of views expressed at these meetings, but also of complaints and suggestions made to canvassers.

Greater differences between the types of elections emerge from the way in which they communicate public opinion by means of the ballot. In plebiscitary elections the minute levels of absenteeism and votes against are probably of very limited significance to policy-makers. In limited-choice elections, voting reveals a good deal more. In Poland, for instance, patterns of turn-out and negative and selective voting are sufficiently marked to make possible the grouping of regions and cities according to levels of political acceptance. From the policy-makers' standpoint, such data provide some indication or confirmation of the location of conformity and non-conformity. The selection of certain types of candidate reveals something of the attitudes of local voters, and particularly of local activists.

The information derived from campaigns and from voting probably has a very limited effect on local policy; it forms only a small part of a large fund of information which is systematically gathered in all these states by means of sociological surveys as well as by nationwide discussions and organisation reports. Only when election information is corroborated by other sources is it likely to have any policy influence. The most direct impact made by elections has been on electoral policy. The tightening of election regulations in Poland in 1957 and 1960 and their easing in Hungary in 1970 can be attributed in part to the results of preceding elections, as well as to changes in political climate. The introduction of mandatory multiple candidacies in Hungary, similarly, was prompted at least in part by a sharp fall in the number of seats contested in the 1975 and 1980 parliamentary elections. In terms of general policy, however, only in conditions of political flux have elections made any impression. And even in such situations – Poland in 1954, 1957 and 1972, and Czechoslovakia in 1971 – their influence has been indirect. Elections have been treated as showing certain policy tendencies, and have been used by the party leadership to justify their extension. There is no hard evidence to substantiate Wiatr's contention that Polish elections influence the way in which the country is ruled (1962, p. 239).

The potential policy influence of elections is restricted by the small extent to which they affect the composition of representative bodies and by the marginal influence exercised over policy by those bodies. This circumscribed scope for influence has been enlarged, however, by several related developments. First, in both types of election, fulfilment of electors' mandates has improved. Second, as a result of limited-choice elections, the presence of greater numbers of constituency-centred and politically-oriented deputies and councillors increases the likelihood of efforts being made to influence policy. Lastly, the chances of such efforts being successful improve with the growth in policy activity of parliamentary and local government bodies (see Nelson, 1980c, and Nelson and White, 1982).

Conclusions

All the evidence indicates a general movement towards greater choice. Twenty years ago only two European communist states, Yugoslavia and Poland, had limited-choice elections; now five have. Within plebiscitary elections, the scope for voter influence on selection, and for closer links between constituents is growing. Proposals have emerged, at least in the Soviet Union, advocating a transition to limited-choice elections. The likelihood of such a transition depends in part upon the balance of advantages and disadvantages of limited-choice elections. On the plus side, limited choice appears to endow elections with a marginally greater popular interest and credibility. Greater voter say in selection and election tends to produce representatives closer to and better able to serve their constituency. All this can increase the value of the legitimacy conferred by such elections. The list is longer, however, on the minus side. Greater vote and local activist choice means a commensurate loss of central and local executive control and even a certain weakening of party control over the composition of state representative bodies. More importantly, the very existence of electoral choice and contest breaks with the tradition of an indivisible party line. The reality of Hungarian, Polish and especially Yugoslav elections has not always conformed to the official picture of no policy differences or contests. Competition for voters' support has questioned government policy and brought a greater emphasis on local interests. Representatives may be more able, but by the same token they are also more capable of weakening executive control.

At first sight, the minuses seem to outweigh the pluses, yet many of the drawbacks appear formidable only if one assumes a static political system. Over the past twenty years communist party states have evolved in the direction of less rigid central control and greater provision for the regularised expression of interests. Yet such provisions have been insufficient to relieve the mounting pressure under which these regimes have to operate. Partly because of the lack of opportunity to exercise any political choice, there has been an overwhelming concentration on economic choice. The extractive attitude of the mass of the population towards party and government stems in part from its feeling of political powerlessness (see Pravda, 1976, 1982). As material expectations of voters rise faster than the capacity to satisfy them, so these regimes are likely to seek new ways in which to divert these pressures. Hence, for instance, the much publicised recent drives against corruption in the USSR and, more importantly, the growing emphasis placed by Gorbachev and other leaders upon the need to improve communications (*glasnost'*) between the authorities and the public.

Real electoral choice might create some feeling of political efficacy and thus reduce pressure on the centre. Limited-choice elections have failed to do this because they do not go far enough. By attempting to combine electoral choice with a monolithic policy platform, these elections have brought many of the disadvantages of competition without the considerable benefits accruing from the institutional expression of popular choice.

It was this line of reasoning that lay behind the Czechoslovak Communist Party's proposals of 1968, outlining a system which would maintain the leading role of the party but also offer voters a choice of policies. This choice was limited by the stipulation that all candidates had to stand on a National Front platform, ruling out all those advocating non-socialist policies or questioning the party's leading role. Within these bounds, all parties and organisations were to campaign on their own behalf. All were entitled to put up as many candidates as there were seats in the multi-member constituencies; most of these seats were to be allocated by proportional representation to candidates standing on organisation and party platforms, and the rest were to go to those candidates standing as individuals who polled the highest number of votes (Pelikan, 1972, pp. 234–7).

The Czechoslovak scheme is important because it constitutes the only really coherent proposal for communist electoral reform which goes beyond limited choice. Even though the scheme is a logical projection of limited-choice elections, it cannot be put forward as the only possible next stage of development. The scheme emerged in specific political conditions and was meant to serve only for a period of political transition, after which it was hoped that insistence on the leading role of the party would be unnecessary. Subsequent electoral development was to depend on the evolution of the political situation and the political system. This scenario underlines a point of cardinal importance. Elections in all communist party states reflect political realities there: evolution is therefore totally dependent upon the direction of developments within the political system as a whole.

3

The Supreme Soviet and Budgetary Politics in the USSR

STEPHEN WHITE

Compared with its counterparts in other countries the Soviet Union's national legislature, the USSR Supreme Soviet, has generally received little attention from scholars (the only book-length treatment to date is Vanneman, 1977; see also Hough and Fainsod, 1979, ch. 10, White, 1980, and White, 1982). The reasons are not far to seek. The Supreme Soviet meets much less frequently than its counterparts elsewhere; its votes are almost always unanimous; its discussion of government legislation is generally perfunctory and confined to details; and it has yet to ask a Soviet minister to resign. Yet, for all these obvious shortcomings, it has become increasingly apparent in recent years that the Supreme Soviet, like the soviets at lower levels of the state hierarchy, has been assuming greater powers and becoming a less marginal participant in the policy process than it was under Stalin or even Khrushchev. This apparent assumption of authority is evident most clearly in the expansion in the number and powers of the standing commissions attached to each of its chambers, through which, as in most modern legislatures, an increasing proportion of its business is conducted (Lees and Shaw, 1979), but it is apparent in other ways as well. All in all, as one commentator has put it, the Supreme Soviet's meetings and discussions were indeed 'perfunctory' and 'stage-managed' for perhaps the first three decades of its existence (1936–66); but since Stalin, and more particularly since Khrushchev, the Supreme Soviet has made a 'modest – but in terms of past history, impressive – comeback as an institution with more than purely symbolic functions' (Gilison, 1972, p. 50).

In this paper I propose to examine how this apparent assumption of authority has been reflected in the Supreme Soviet's consideration of the annual state budget of the USSR. This is a function of central importance

Reprinted with adaptations from the *British Journal of Political Science*, vol. 12, no. 1 (January 1982) with the permission of author and publisher.

in any polity, especially one in which the state budget accounts for so large a proportion of GNP (about 60 per cent in the late 1970s, according to Shermenev, 1978, p. 25), and yet one which has to date been relatively little explored by scholars. I shall consider, first of all, some of the recent developments in the Supreme Soviet and its activities which are relevant to this process; secondly, the procedure by which the state budget is considered by the Supreme Soviet itself and by its standing commissions; and thirdly, the extent to which the government's financial proposals have been altered by this process of consideration over the post-Stalin period (1954–80). Finally, I shall consider the extent to which these changes provide evidence of the existence of a form of 'budgetary politics' in the USSR, linking the mass public, deputies, the legislature and public spending together in a manner not entirely different from that which may be encountered in the Western liberal democracies, and suggesting in turn that the Supreme Soviet may perhaps be less peripheral to the 'authoritative allocation of values' in the USSR than is commonly supposed.

Recent developments in the USSR Supreme Soviet

The present Soviet Constitution, adopted in 1977, made few changes in the composition and structure of the USSR Supreme Soviet, which had been set up under the previous Constitution in 1936 to replace the All-Union Central Executive Committee as the country's legislature (see Vanneman, 1977, ch. 1). The Supreme Soviet, as before, was to have two chambers with equal powers, the Council of the Union representing the population at large and the Council of Nationalities representing national-territorial areas, and it was to be their joint responsibility, as before, to elect the Soviet government (the Council of Ministers) and the Soviet collective presidency (the Presidium), both of which were to remain formally accountable to it for their actions (for the text and a discussion of the new Constitution, see Sharlet, 1978, Feldbrugge, 1979, and Unger, 1981). The chambers, unlike before, were to be composed of equal numbers of deputies (previously the Council of the Union had enjoyed a slight numerical preponderance), and they were to be elected for a five year period of office (previously deputies had served for four years at a time). The Supreme Soviet continued to be described, however, as the 'highest body of state authority of the USSR' (Art. 108), and its major constitutional powers – the exclusive right to adopt and amend the Constitution, to admit new republics to the USSR, to ratify the state plan and budget, and to pass laws – were essentially unchanged (the only substantial innovation was the introduction, following a nationwide discussion in the summer of 1977, of a procedure for the adoption of laws by a popular vote or referendum; see Sharlet, 1978, pp. 108–9). The Supreme Soviet is conventionally described in the Soviet literature as not simply an effective national legislature but as a body 'a thousand times more democratic than any Western parliament', mainly because of the large numbers of workers and peasants represented within it (see, for instance, Gureyev and Segudin, 1977, ch. 1). It is not, however, a body that is normally taken seriously outside the USSR, and for a number of good reasons.

First, and most obviously, there is no choice of candidate. Although the present electoral law, like its predecessor, prescribes no limit to the number of candidates that may be put forward (*Zakon SSSR o vyborakh*, arts 9 and 38), and although the ballot paper in fact provides ample space for the insertion of the names of other candidates should this at any time be necessary, the right of nomination is reserved for the Communist Party of the Soviet Union or for mass organizations, such as the trade unions, which are effectively controlled by it. The nomination of an oppositional or even alternative approved candidate is in present circumstances inconceivable (an attempt to challenge this monopoly by two independent candidates in 1979 was unsuccessful). No candidates may be proposed by individuals, as is the case, for instance, in Hungary (Toma and Volgyes, 1977, p. 43), and there is no choice from among a number of approved candidates on a single list or even from among a number of different (non-competitive) political parties such as that provided in a number of other communist-ruled states (see White, *et al.*, 1982, tables 3.1 and 4.1).

The election itself places further restrictions upon the articulation of popular preferences. Although voting is in principle voluntary, an army of agitators throughout the country makes sure that turnout is as close to universal as is humanly possible, with ballot boxes being taken to the sick in their beds, to shepherds on remote hillsides, to passengers on long-distance trains and to Soviet ships in foreign waters. Even Soviet cosmonauts in outer space are provided with facilities for telegraphing their vote to earth, although hardly for keeping it secret as the electoral law provides (see Zaslavsky and Brym, 1978; Friedgut, 1979, ch. 2). It is possible to vote against the single approved candidate by crossing his or her name off the ballot paper, but to do so it is normally necessary to make use of the screened-off booth at the side of the polling station and most voters appear to be reluctant to draw attention to themselves in this way. At the local level candidates are occasionally 'defeated' by securing less than 50 per cent of the poll or by failing to secure the participation of at least 50 per cent of the registered electorate. At the national level, however, no candidate appears ever to have been unsuccessful, and the vote in favour of the list of approved candidates in recent years has never been less than 99 per cent (White, 1982, p. 128). If deputies diverge even momentarily from party policy in their subsequent activities, moreover, they can readily be replaced by the mechanism of recall (Article 107 of the Constitution).

The Supreme Soviet to which the deputies are elected, moreover, is a body that meets only twice a year (although further sessions may be specially convened by the Presidium), and in recent years it has met in full session for only about four or five days a year, making it among the world's least frequently convened assemblies (Blondel, 1973, pp. 56–60). Relatively few deputies are able to take part in discussion during its plenary sessions (about thirty or forty in the annual plan and budget debate, for instance), and although amendments are sometimes carried it is unknown for government bills to be defeated or to be challenged in principle. Votes are in all but exceptional circumstances unanimous (three disagreements on procedure in 1938 are recorded by Vanneman, 1977, p. 92, and an involuntary abstention on the unexpected resignation of Malenkov in 1955 by Leonhard, 1965, p. 93); and both chambers of the legislature have similarly been in perfect agreement with each other, no use ever having been made of the complex constitutional mechanism for resolving differences between them. The total volume of legislation enacted by the Supreme Soviet, in comparative terms, is also very low (Herman and Mandel, 1976, pp. 630–7). For perhaps most Western students of Soviet politics the conclusion has followed logically that the USSR Supreme Soviet is a purely ratificatory or 'rubber stamp' legislature, designed to give the appearance of popular approval to policies that have in fact been decided on beforehand by the party leadership, and that its proceedings have more to do with theatre than with politics in the ordinary meaning of the word (see, for instance, Armstrong, 1978, pp. 154–5).

Even those who dissent to some degree from this assessment have little alternative but to accept that it was valid for most of the period up to the 1960s. Since that time, however, the Supreme Soviet as well as soviets at lower levels of the state hierarchy have been making the 'modest comeback' referred to in the introduction and arguably becoming less peripheral to the policy-making process. The powers of deputies at all levels of the system, for instance, have been codified and enlarged in the Law on the Status of the Deputy, adopted in 1972 (*Vedomosti*, 1972, no. 36, art. 347); the powers and competence of soviets at various levels have been clarified and extended in a series of laws dating from 1957 and more particularly from the mid-1960s (Hill, 1983); the Supreme Soviet has gained additional powers in relation to the plan and budget (see the next section); and above all, perhaps, the system of standing commissions attached to each chamber of the Supreme Soviet has been extended and enlarged, particularly since 1966 when the system then existing was thoroughly reformed (Georgadze, 1975, pp. 119–21). In 1938, when the Supreme Soviet held its first session, there were only four standing commissions attached to each chamber of the house, with no more than 7.8 per cent of deputies serving on them. By 1966, however, a total of eleven standing commissions had come into being, and by 1984, as a result of further changes, a total of seventeen standing commissions had been set up in each chamber of the house with

80.7 per cent of deputies serving on them (*Vedomosti*, 1984, no. 16). The development of the system of standing commissions has reasonably been described as 'perhaps the most interesting development with respect to the Supreme Soviet [to have occurred] in recent years' (Hough and Fainsod, 1979, p. 373).

Standing commissions meet more often than the Supreme Soviet itself (about three or four times a year in most cases) and they have an important part to play in perhaps three main respects (see White, 1982, pp. 138–43). First of all, they can initiate legislation or (more usually) consider draft legislation submitted to them for consideration by the Presidium on behalf of the Council of Ministers. The commissions draw upon outside experts and research institutes in this work, and they also consider the comments of the Soviet public, particularly when (as is frequently the case) the legislation is printed in draft form in the newspapers and journals and comments are specifically invited. In the second place, the commissions play an active role in monitoring or checking upon the work of government (*kontrol'*) in matters that relate to their areas of competence, such as the general performance of the ministry or ministries in question, their observance of Soviet legislation and the adequacy of their response to consumer demand. Matters of this kind are usually investigated by a preparatory group (*podgotovitel'naya gruppa*) of commission members in the first instance; they report their findings to a full meeting of the commission at which ministers and relevant officials are usually in attendance, and a series of recommendations is agreed upon with a view to eliminating the shortcomings that have been identified. The length and thoroughness of the initial investigation, the use of outside experts, the support of the Presidium bureaucracy and – not least – the presence on many commissions of leading party notables gives these recommendations an authority they might not otherwise possess (Minagawa, 1979).

The Supreme Soviet and the budgetary process

The third important role that is played by the standing commissions relates to their consideration of the USSR's economic plan and budget. Under the Supreme Soviet's standing orders, adopted in 1979, the national economic plan and budget must be presented to the Supreme Soviet by the Council of Ministers not later than a month before the session of the Supreme Soviet at which they are to be considered. The plan and budget are in turn remitted by the Presidium to the planning-budget and other commissions for preliminary consideration and for the formulation of recommendations on their adoption (*Vedomosti*, 1979, no. 17, art. 272). Under the present Constitution the approval of state plans and budgets of the USSR, and of reports on their implementation, are among the exclusive prerogatives of the USSR Supreme Soviet (Art. 108). The approval of the state budget has in fact always been among the functions of the Supreme Soviet, although in earlier years it was not necessarily submitted in advance of the year to which it was supposed to refer (in 1946 it was submitted as late as mid-October), and during the wartime period it was sometimes not submitted at all. Since 1955, however, the budget has always been submitted in advance of the year to which it is meant to refer, and since 1957 the annual economic plan has been presented for approval as well as the budget (with the exception of a single year, 1958). In addition, since 1971, the Supreme Soviet has considered five year plans as well as annual ones, and since 1978 it has considered the fulfilment of the plan in the current year as well as proposals for the year to come (Shermenev, 1978, ch. 23; Rovinsky, 1978, ch. 10; Shitikov, 1979, pp. 16–25).

The work is evidently taken seriously. In 1978, for instance, the standing commissions set up sixteen preparatory committees to go through the government's plan and budgetary proposals, with about two hundred deputies as members. (The international affairs, mandates and legislative proposals commissions are not normally involved in this work.) The preparatory committees were assisted by about two hundred expert advisers from the State Planning Committee (Gosplan), the Ministry of Finance, the Central Statistical Board and other bodies; they held sixty-five meetings over a three week period, and considered 199 reports from ministries, state committees, councils of ministers of the union republics and other state institutions (Shitikov, 1979, pp. 21–2). The chairmen of the planning-budget commissions then presented the conclusions of the commissions to each chamber of the Supreme Soviet, following the presentation of the government's proposals to a joint session by the Chairman of Gosplan and the Minister of Finance respectively. The commissions, while broadly endorsing the main lines of party and government policy, none the less suggested a number of specific amendments to the original proposals, recommending that budgetary income and expenditure be increased by 138 million roubles respectively so as to cover a number of proposals for additional expenditure. The commissions' amendments were accepted by the Minister of Finance in his speech at the conclusion of the debate, and a promise was made that the additional suggestions made by deputies from the floor of the house would be 'carefully examined'. The government's proposals, as amended, were then passed into law (*Izvestiya*, 1 December 1978, pp. 1–3). These procedures are set out schematically in Figure 3.1.

The political significance of the budgetary process in the USSR has hitherto been considered mainly in relation to the patterns of expenditure that result from these deliberations. Changes in budgetary allocations, for instance, have been related to the turnover rate of republican party first secretaries and to elite turnover more generally (Bunce, 1976, 1979), to regional policy (Echols, 1975, 1979; Bielasiak, 1980a), and to the degree of

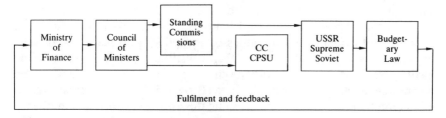

FIGURE 3.1 *The Soviet budgetary process (simplified)*

Source: Based upon Rovinsky, 1978, pp. 121–8.

incrementalism in policy-making in the USSR (Bunce and Echols, 1978). The specifically political factors responsible for changes in spending patterns of this kind, however, are difficult to isolate. Allowance must be made for changes in administrative boundaries, in fiscal organization and accounting practices, in demographic structure, in the location of natural resources and so forth, all of which will tend to modify patterns of budgetary spending quite independently of the political influence of the various interests involved. It is also important to note that, with the increasing emphasis in recent years upon the financing of investment and other policies from the retained profits of enterprises, bank credits and other sources, the state budget has come to account for a declining proportion of public spending and may vary in a manner that does not necessarily correspond to variations in the level of total public support for the area or spending category in question (Shermenev, 1978, pp. 25–6; Hutchings, 1983). The problems of comparability involved have serious implications for research in communist budgetary politics, not all of which have been successfully resolved (see Bahry, 1980; Seroka, 1982).

A more promising approach is to examine the differences between the government's budgetary proposals to the Supreme Soviet and the budgetary laws that are finally adopted over an extended period of time. No problems of equivalence arise between these two sets of figures, which are based in each year upon identical assumptions, and the difference between the two may be taken to reflect whatever influence the Supreme Soviet is able to exert upon the budgetary proposals originally presented to it. The government's proposals, as we have seen, are not normally unaffected by the Supreme Soviet's consideration; they go through an extended and detailed examination by the standing commissions in private as well as through the annual plan and budget debate on the floor of the Supreme Soviet itself, and there is no shortage of opportunities for deputies to use whatever influence they possess in an attempt to bias the allocation of resources towards whatever local or other interests they regard themselves as representing. The discussion of the plan and budget by the commission sub-committees, as Hough has noted, is 'especially likely to be a significant stage' in this process (Hough and Fainsod, 1979, p. 378); and there is a good deal of evidence that deputies do indeed seek to make use of such opportunities to press the claims of their constituents, their republics or the institutions in which they work, both in the formal sessions and in the committee meetings that precede them (Brown, 1979; Fuller, 1980). In the discussion that follows we shall examine this apparent exercise of influence more closely, considering both the degree of change that has been imparted to government budgetary proposals over the period and more particularly the extent to which deputies have redistributed resources as between the various spending categories and union republics.

The data which are necessary for this purpose are fairly readily available from the speeches made to the Supreme Soviet each year by the Minister of Finance and from the budgetary laws that are finally adopted, which incorporate the amendments that have been agreed upon by deputies. Since the object of the exercise is to obtain an impression of broad, long-term changes in expenditure rather than of minor year-to-year fluctuations the data have been grouped into totals for four or five year periods corresponding to the periods for which each successive Supreme Soviet has been elected (these periods are known as convocations (*sozyvy*)). Data for the earliest years of the Supreme Soviet's existence are both incomplete and seriously distorted by the war and by post-war reconstruction. For the period since 1954, however, the relevant information is available for each year from the printed record of Supreme Soviet proceedings, and both total government budgetary proposals and total agreed budgetary allocations have been calculated for each convocation from this time (the fourth convocation, 1954–8) up to the year 1980 (the second year of the tenth convocation, 1979–84). Comparing the data convocation by convocation, we shall first consider the changes that have occurred in government budgetary expenditure by spending category and then secondly the changes in government budgetary expenditure by union republic, with a view to establishing the nature and degree of bias that the Supreme Soviet has imparted to the budgetary proposals it has considered over the whole period.

Changes in budgetary spending by category

The spending categories employed in Soviet budgetary practice are the national economy, which covers expenditure on industry, agriculture, transport, construction, housing and such matters; socio-cultural, which covers expenditure on education, science, cultural amenities, sport, the mass media, the health service, social security and welfare payments; defence, which covers publicly declared expenditure upon the Soviet armed forces; and administration, which covers operational costs of government, the Supreme Soviet itself, the courts and the Procuracy. There is also an unexplained residual which is understood to cover loans and reserves, but which has steadily diminished as a proportion of budgetary expenditure since the 1950s and currently accounts for no more than 4 or 5 per cent of the total (Nove, 1977, pp. 229–37; Shermenev, 1978, part 3). Expenditure is further divided into two categories: that which is channelled through national ministries and is contained in the federal budget (*soyuznyi byudzhet*), and that which is disbursed by republican or lower levels of government and which is contained in the union republican budget (*byudzhety soyuznykh respublik*). An examination of the manner in which the Supreme Soviet has redistributed spending between these various categories has a certain intrinsic interest. More important, perhaps, it may provide evidence of a consistent attempt to increase the allocation of resources on categories of expenditure of obvious public appeal, such as socio-cultural purposes and the republics, rather than on others which may be of less immediate interest to local areas and constituents, such as administration, arms and the economy. What does our evidence suggest on this point?

The data on voted increases in expenditure in terms of these categories are set out in Table 3.1, which indicates both the percentage increase in expenditure voted in each category in each convocation and also the relative magnitude of the increases between one category and another in each convocation. It will be noticed that the largest individual increases occur under the heading of administration, in the eighth convocation (1970–74) and to some extent also in the seventh and ninth convocations (1966–70 and 1974–79). However, the sums involved are relatively small ones (administration generally accounts for no more than about 1 per cent of total spending) and, because of rounding error, they are more subject to 'accidental' fluctuations of this kind than the other major categories of expenditure which account for much larger proportions of the total (in 1979, for instance, the national economy accounted for 54.8 per cent of total budgetary expenditure, socio-cultural items for 33.6 per cent, defence for 6.2 per cent, and administration for 0.9 per cent; *Narkhoz 1979*, pp. 553–4). So far as these other categories of expenditure are concerned perhaps four main conclusions may be drawn.

First of all, it is notable that, at least since the sixth convocation (1958–62), there has been a continuous fall in the relative magnitude of the increase in spending voted for the national economy. Still above average in the 1960s, it dropped steadily throughout the 1970s and in the tenth convocation (1979–80) it recorded no increase at all. Secondly, it is clear that military expenditure, by and large, has not been popular with Soviet legislators; its rate of increase has been below the rate of increase in budgetary spending as a whole in every convocation, although its relative

TABLE 3.1 Changes in budgetary expenditure by category, 1954–80 (percentage increases in expenditure voted by the Supreme Soviet in each category in each convocation, and relative rates of increase (average percentage increase for all categories of expenditure in each convocation = 100))

	IV 1954–8		V 1958–62		VI 1962–6		VII 1966–70		VIII 1970–4		IX 1974–9		X 1979–80	
	% inc.	Index nos	% inc.	Index nos	% inc.	Index nos	% inc.	Index nos	% inc.	Index nos	% inc.	Index nos	% inc.	Index nos
Total expenditure	0.11	100	0.10	100	0.11	100	0.09	100	0.08	100	0.06	100	0.05	100
Economy	0.06	55	0.13	130	0.12	113	0.10	104	0.03	36	0.00	8	0.00	0
Socio-cultural	0.15	128	0.15	151	0.16	149	0.15	162	0.14	164	0.14	244	0.13	270
Defence	0.00	2	0.03	28	0.06	51	0.00	3	0.01	7	0.03	60	0.02	50
Administration	0.06	48	0.05	45	0.11	99	0.16	174	0.71	863	0.11	186	0.04	80
Republican budget	0.22	191	0.32	318	0.23	210	0.21	228	0.16	195	0.12	217	0.11	242

Source: derived from Zasedaniya, 1954–81.

position has improved somewhat in the last two convocations (and the published figures here must obviously be treated with a certain amount of caution). Thirdly and most strikingly, there has been a steady and all but unbroken growth in the relative magnitude of the increases in budgetary expenditure voted for socio-cultural purposes: from about one and a half times the average for all categories of spending during the 1960s, the rate of growth in spending on such purposes is now between two and three times greater than that of budgetary spending as a whole, and is steadily increasing. And fourthly, there has been a comparable if less dramatic tendency for the rate of growth in the union republican budget to exceed the rate of growth in budgetary expenditure as a whole, although the difference has not been increasing as sharply as in the case of socio-cultural expenditure. The rate of growth in the most recent convocation is none the less about two and a half times that of budgetary expenditure as a whole, and it has been increasing in relative terms for at least the last three convocations (since 1970).

We have only limited and somewhat unsatisfactory information about the issues that Soviet constituents bring to the attention of their deputies. We know, however, that they have no shortage of opportunities to make their views known, whether by correspondence or visits to deputies' surgeries, by attending meetings at which deputies report back on their fulfilment of their mandates (*nakazy*), by responding to the opinion polls occasionally commissioned by local soviets, by letters to the press or by approaching the deputy directly at his place of work (see for instance Nudnenko, 1975; Georgadze, 1975, pp. 161–72; Bezuglov, 1978; Hill, 1980, ch. 3). Such information as is available on the state of Soviet public opinion also suggests that it is the categories of spending that have been receiving increases consistently above the average, covering matters such as transport, schooling, the health service and social welfare benefits, that Soviet citizens would ordinarily be most inclined to favour (Connor and Gitelman, 1977, ch. 4; White, 1979, ch. 5; Connor, 1981). In present circumstances it is impossible to specify more precisely the manner in which Soviet citizens bring such concerns to the attention of their deputies and the extent to which deputies in turn are influenced by such considerations in making their annual decisions on budgetary allocations. It seems clear, however, that deputies have at least been acting as if they were aware of such pressures and were influenced by them, and there is at least prima facie evidence of the existence of an embryonic form of 'linkage politics', connecting the mass public, deputies, the Supreme Soviet and the national budget in a manner not unfamiliar to the student of the politics of budgetary spending in political systems elsewhere (see, for instance, Wildavsky, 1975, 1979; Ippolito, 1978; Robinson, 1978; Coombes and Walkland, 1980).

It should perhaps surprise us less than it does to come to a conclusion of this kind. The Soviet system of government, admittedly, does not provide for competitive elections or for the direct challenging of party policy; but the party is itself formally committed to the development of a society of material abundance and popular well-being, and deputies, by pressing for a greater share of additional expenditure to be devoted to particular areas, purposes or institutions, need not necessarily challenge the party's right to determine the ultimate goals of the society by doing so. Indeed, the party has itself initiated a number of the more obviously welfare-related developments that have taken place in public policy over the past decade or so, such as the introduction of a family income supplement scheme in the mid-1970s (Nove, 1977, p. 224) and the allocation of priority to consumer rather than producer goods in both the 1971–5 and 1981–5 five year plans (*Pravda*, 25 November 1971, pp. 1–3, and 2 December 1980, pp. 1–5). In the climate of economic austerity which appears likely to affect the USSR as well as most Western countries during the 1980s there seems no reason for the Soviet authorities not to permit and even encourage such quasi-electoral connections, with a view to giving at least the impression that public opinion is taken regularly into account in the making of legislative decisions and that no effort is spared to maximize budgetary spending on the purposes of most immediate and obvious interest to constituents (see Nelson and White, 1982, ch. 8; Bialer, 1980, ch. 15).

Changes in budgetary spending by union republic

Budgetary expenditure, as we have noted, is also divided into federal and union republican budgets corresponding to the level of government at which the funds concerned will be disbursed. Expenditure totals for each of the fifteen (until 1956, sixteen) union republics are specified separately in the Finance Minister's proposals and also in the final budgetary law, thus permitting a comparable exercise to be performed to discover to what extent, if at all, particular republics have been able to use the leverage they command through their representation in the Supreme Soviet to bias the redistribution of budgetary spending in their favour. The relevant data are set out in Table 3.2, which shows the percentage increase in expenditure voted for each republic in each convocation and also the relative magnitude of each increase in relation to the average increase awarded to all republics in each convocation. (The figures, it should be noted, are again subject to a degree of rounding error and we shall accordingly be concerned here only with substantial and consistent variations in the data, not with minor fluctuations from convocation to convocation.) The figures, as before, have been grouped into four-year or five-year periods corresponding to particular convocations from the fourth (1954–8) up to the second year of the tenth convocation (1979–80).

TABLE 3.2 Changes in budgetary expenditure by union republic, 1954–80 (percentage increases in expenditure voted by the Supreme Soviet for each republic in each convocation, and relative rates of increase (average percentage increase for all republics in each convocation = 100))

	IV 1954–8		V 1958–62		VI 1962–6		VII 1966–70		VIII 1970–4		IX 1974–9†		X 1979–80	
	% inc.	Index nos	% inc.	Index nos	% inc.	Index nos	% inc.	Index nos	% inc.	Index nos	% inc.	Index nos	% inc.	Index nos
All Republics	0.30	100	0.24	100	0.24	100	0.21	100	0.16	100	0.13	100	0.11	100
RSFSR	0.19	65	0.14	60	0.22	91	0.22	105	0.16	100	0.12	90	0.10	93
Ukraine	0.16	54	0.23	94	0.26	106	0.22	108	0.18	111	0.14	102	0.11	102
Belorussia	0.35	118	0.31	127	0.25	104	0.17	82	0.14	87	0.11	81	0.11	98
Uzbekistan	0.53	179	0.23	96	0.24	100	0.19	91	0.13	83	0.12	91	0.10	96
Kazakhstan	0.23	76	0.14	58	0.18	72	0.15	74	0.13	78	0.11	81	0.14	130
Georgia	0.28	94	0.19	80	0.27	109	0.19	92	0.15	94	0.14	109	0.10	96
Azerbaidzhan	0.24	80	0.19	77	0.26	107	0.33	158	0.22	135	0.19	142	0.18	163
Lithuania	0.31	104	0.23	97	0.24	100	0.18	87	0.13	78	0.09	70	0.10	90
Moldavia	0.40	136	0.39	161	0.26	108	0.20	99	0.18	112	0.15	111	0.12	113
Latvia	0.37	123	0.34	141	0.33	137	0.20	99	0.15	95	0.12	87	0.10	92
Kirgizia	0.32	109	0.23	97	0.16	65	0.20	98	0.14	84	0.13	99	0.15	134
Tadzhikistan	0.38	128	0.24	100	0.24	99	0.22	108	0.18	110	0.18	135	0.06	58
Armenia	0.29	98	0.26	107	0.20	84	0.14	67	0.16	98	0.16	120	0.09	79
Turkmenia	0.29	96	0.23	96	0.30	122	0.20	96	0.21	129	0.14	107	0.12	115
Estonia	0.26	88	0.26	108	0.23	95	0.28	136	0.17	104	0.10	75	0.05	43
Karelo-Finnish*	0.15	51	—		—		—		—		—		—	

Source: as for Table 3.1.
* Abolished in 1956.
† Excluding 1974.

The single most striking conclusion to be drawn from these figures is perhaps the negative one that, unlike the pattern that emerged when the redistribution of budgetary spending between categories was considered, there has been no obvious tendency for the reallocation of resources to be biased towards one particular republic rather than another over the period under consideration. No republic appears to have made substantial net gains or losses over the period; with a few exceptions, no republic has fared much better or much worse than the average for all republics in any convocation; and no republic appears to have been consistently gaining or losing in influence from convocation to convocation. Indeed, the data show no tendency even for republics from the same part of the country to gain or lose in common.

The least successful republic, on the evidence of Table 3.2, is clearly Kazakhstan, which has improved its position by less than the average for all republics in every convocation except the most recent (and this despite Brezhnev's close association with the republic and its party first secretary's full membership of the Politburo). The Russian Republic (RSFSR) has also performed rather less well than the average in most convocations, although, accounting as it does for rather more than half of the total republican budget, there can obviously be no wide degree of variation between the two. It may be that the relative under-representation of Russians in the Supreme Soviet, where they account for less than their share of total population and where the Russian Republic is the least well represented on the standing commissions attached to the Council of Nationalities, is in part responsible (see Gaidukov, 1979, p. 143). However, the data reveal no consistent tendency of this or any other kind. In the Caucasus for instance, Georgia and (with one conspicuous exception) Armenia have obtained less than the average increase in expenditure for all republics in most convocations, but Azerbaidzhan, at least since the 1960s, has normally been able to secure a better than average increase in its allocation. In the Baltic area, similarly, Lithuania, Estonia and (until it was abolished) the Karelo-Finnish republic have performed relatively poorly in comparison with most other republics, but Latvia, at least in the earlier convocations, has been rather more successful than the average. The Central Asian republics have been below-average performers in most convocations, but there have been some conspicuous variations between republic and republic and between convocation and convocation; while Moldavia, for reasons that are not immediately apparent, has been consistently the most successful republic in securing above-average increases in its budgetary allocations. Moldavia, Kazakhstan and Azerbaidzhan apart, however, there has been no obvious tendency for particular republics to emerge as 'winners' or 'losers' from this process.

It is less easy to explain why this should be the case. In part, at least, it may owe something to the fact that, under Soviet conditions, a claim may legitimately be advanced on behalf of a particular social group, such as workers in the Far North, pensioners, veterans or students, since claims of this kind cut across ethnic boundaries, involve no necessary antagonism with other social groups and do not necessarily prejudice the party's claim to represent the best interests of the whole society. No such claim can be advanced for a particular ethnic group or republic, however, since this would run counter to Leninist policy on the nationalities. More important, it would also threaten to disturb the precarious equilibrium that has been established in relations between the major Soviet nationalities and republics in the post-war period based upon approximate equality of treatment. All can agree that resources should be shifted from investment to consumption, or from the economy to the health service, education and social benefits. An attempt by any republic or nationality to increase its share of the union republican budget, however, composed as it largely is of allocations for socio-cultural purposes, would inevitably be at the cost of the ability of another republic or major nationality to do likewise. The evidence suggests that no republic has been willing to forgo its proportionate increase in allocations, or has been able to compel other republics to do so, over the period we have been considering (for similar conclusions see Echols, 1979, pp. 368–9, and Bialer, 1980, p. 218).

It appears that the economic commission of the Council of Nationalities, established in 1957 with a membership drawn equally from each of the republics, may for a time have provided a basis upon which claims for additional resources could be formulated upon an explicitly republican or national basis. Khrushchev called for the formation of the commission at the 20th Congress of the CPSU in 1956, supposedly with a view to studying the uneven development of the union republican economies and correcting their disproportionate budgetary allocations (Vanneman, 1977, p. 127); and on at least one occasion, in October 1959, the commission appears to have gone so far as to propose an increase in capital expenditure against the advice of the budget commissions of both chambers, which were seeking a reduction. In the end the economic commission's views prevailed (Churchward, 1975, p. 129). The commission was dissolved in 1966, however, no doubt in part so that it would be more difficult to make claims of this divisive character in future, and its functions were taken over by a series of sectoral commissions whose members did not necessarily represent any particular republic or nationality. Republican or national claims, in other words, have so far as possible been prevented from finding institutional expression within the Supreme Soviet, and changes in budgetary spending have not played a role of any significance in redistributing resources from one republic to another, at least within the period we have been considering. This finding accords with the conclusions of independent investigations into variations in living standards among the union republics, which have shown little tendency to diminish over the same period (McAuley, 1979, ch. 5; Zwick, 1979; Dellenbrant, 1980).

Some conclusions

The purpose of this analysis has been, firstly, to present a method for the examination of the Soviet budgetary process which has not, so far as is known, been previously employed (see however Minagawa, 1975, p. 65), and only secondly to reach substantive conclusions as to the politics of that process over the period considered (1954–80). It must be remembered, in this connection, that what this paper has examined is the USSR state budget rather than public spending as such, which would include bank credits and enterprises' retained profits as well as allocations from the state budget. We have also excluded from our analysis the important but largely opaque process by which enterprises, areas and institutions 'bid' for a favourable plan and budgetary allocation in the first place, a process which must clearly exercise a considerable influence upon the proposals that the Soviet government presents to the Supreme Soviet for its consideration but which does not, as a rule, take place in a sufficiently open manner to permit its systematic investigation. Nor have we considered the politics of budgetary fulfilment, or the tendency for both income and expenditure targets to be slightly but consistently exceeded. Our concern in this paper has been the process, more limited perhaps but at least more amenable to empirical analysis, by which the government's budgetary proposals are considered and to some degree modified by the Supreme Soviet and its standing commissions before they are passed into law. The nature and extent of these modifications, it was suggested, particularly the propensity of legislators to devote a growing relative share of increases in expenditure to the purposes of most immediate and obvious interest to their constituents, provided at least preliminary evidence of an exercise of influence to which the term 'budgetary politics' could reasonably be applied.

It has sometimes been objected that the changes that take place in budgetary proposals are arranged beforehand by the government, and that the 'whole procedure has the versimilitude of an amateur theatrical performance' (Gilison, 1972, pp. 90–1; similarly Fainsod, 1965, p. 384). This seems to me an unduly hasty judgement. No doubt a certain amount of consultation does take place between standing commission members and government departments before the commission's recommendations on the budget are made public, both (as we have seen) to satisfy the commissions' inquiries on a number of factual matters, and also, we may assume, to secure that so far as possible the commissions come forward with proposals for change that are actually realizable. But this does not mean that we can set them aside entirely. It does not account, for instance, for the considerable variations in the rate of increase between one category of spending and another that we have observed, nor does it explain why the government should apparently feel it necessary to grant any increases of this kind in the first place. In fact, the practice in the first, second and third convocations (1938–54) was generally to increase budgetary revenue rather than expenditure, or else to leave both unaltered. Only since 1954 has the Supreme Soviet regularly been permitted to vote an increase in the budgetary proposals it considers; and whether this was because the deputies gained additional leverage over the government at this time or because the government felt it necessary that deputies should appear to have such influence makes little difference in this context (for what it is worth the memoirs of the former Soviet finance minister, A. G. Zverev, do indicate that he and his colleagues 'always expected some kind of "surprises"' from the budgetary commissions on these occasions (1973, p. 174)).

It is less clear that these findings require a more far-reaching modification of the conventional assessment of the USSR Supreme Soviet itself. It remains the case, as we noted at the outset, that it meets infrequently, that it has never rejected government legislative proposals, that it rarely modifies them substantially, and that in all important matters it is subordinate to the authority of the Communist Party to which the majority of its members belong. There are signs, however, that even the formal sessional debates have been becoming somewhat less routine in recent years (see, for instance, Brown, 1979; Fuller, 1980). And it is certainly party policy, as expressed in speeches, resolutions and declarations, that the soviets at all levels should expand their authority further in these ways, so that 'every, I repeat, every Soviet citizen should feel involved in state affairs, that his opinion, his voice will be heard and taken into account in the making of both large and small decisions', as Brezhnev put it in his 1979 electoral address to his constituents (1979, p. 616). These concerns were once again emphasized in Brezhnev's report on behalf of the Central Committee to the 26th Congress of the CPSU in February 1981 (1981, pp. 708–10).

It would be hazardous to predict how such matters will develop further in future decades. It does at least seem clear, however, that a Supreme Soviet which is more active and influential in the manner considered in this paper need not necessarily represent a threat to party dominance. On the contrary, it may help to buttress the regime's legitimacy by giving at least the impression that government decisions and budgetary allocations are not uninfluenced by the various preferences of the Soviet public, and at the same time it can provide a legal basis upon which the party can monitor or exercise *kontrol'* over state and public institutions which formally are not subordinated to it (see Vanneman, 1977, ch. 10; Nelson and White, 1982, ch. 8). In the difficult economic circumstances that appear likely to affect the USSR as well as Western countries in the coming decades, it would be surprising if the Soviet authorities did not feel that these purposes justified at least as prominent a role for the USSR Supreme Soviet in the future as it has enjoyed, on the evidence presented in this article, since at least its reorganization in the mid-1960s.

4

The Institutional Development of a Minimal Parliament: the Case of the Polish Sejm

DAVID M. OLSON AND MAURICE D. SIMON

Examinations of Polish society in the late 1970s (Blazynski, 1979; de Weydenthal, 1979; Simon and Kanet, 1981) depicted a situation in which the intensification of citizen demands for a variety of economic, social and political benefits and rights placed heavy strains on the institutional capacities of the system. Even before Solidarity, pressure from workers and other strata prompted the ruling Polish United Workers' Party (PUWP) repeatedly to issue promises to reform and perfect governing institutions by promoting 'socialist democracy' (Zawadzki, 1980a).

This political context provides the background for our analysis of the institutional development of the Polish Sejm through a decade of significant change in that country's political life. Ostensibly, if there is to be a fuller realisation of socialist democracy, the Sejm as the highest representative legislative body would have a key role to play. Its formally assigned functions – legislation, exercising supervisory control over the government, adopting resolutions, and maintaining links with citizens – are essential to democracy (Zawadzki, 1980b, pp. 66–8). Its constitutional–legal status undoubtedly endows it with political powers and responsibilities of considerable potential. Yet as a legislature operating in a hegemonic party system – even before the military came to dominate – the activeness of the Sejm has been highly dependent upon the role ascribed to it by the ruling PUWP (Ulicki, 1980, pp. 62–105). Thus, its influence within the political system has been 'a barometer of the seriousness with which Poland's

Reprinted with adaptations from Daniel Nelson and Stephen White (eds), *Communist Legislatures in Comparative Perspective* (London: Macmillan and Albany: State University of New York Press, 1982) with the permission of authors and publishers. The primary focus of this chapter is the Sejm prior to the formation of Solidarity in 1980.

communist leadership at any point in time has regarded the need for meaningful participation in the decision making process' (Terry, 1981, p. 28).

The history of the Polish Sejm under the constitution adopted on 22 July 1952 raises serious questions about its capacity to gain institutional influence within the political system. As has been the case with other communist legislatures, the image of the body as either a 'rubber stamp' or as serving primarily symbolic functions has often been applicable (Nelson, 1980a, pp. 161–2). According to our own definition, in comparative terms the Sejm should be classified as a 'minimal parliament' (Mezey, 1979, p. 36; Olson, 1980, pp. 450–2) owing to its relative weakness in relation to the ruling PUWP and the state bureaucracy. Its role in legislative formulation and public critical discussion has been constrained and it has often served to provide endorsement and approval for decisions made elsewhere by the party and/or the government.

Even Polish scholars admit the limitations of the Sejm's past political activities. Four distinct stages have been identified (Ulicki, 1980, pp. 102–4). In the first stage, 1948/49–1955, the Sejm was assigned a minimal role by the PUWP and was subordinate to the Council of State and the Council of Ministers. In the second stage, 1955–9, connected with the revitalisation of political life associated with the 'Polish October' of 1956, there was an assertion of the Sejm's rights and a notable increase in its activities. In the third stage, 1960–70, despite the formal strengthening of the committee system, there was a 'regression' in its functioning. The years 1965–9 are particularly notable in terms of the Sejm's dependency and passivity, evidenced by the perfunctory fashion in which it exercised its legislative and control functions (Ulicki, 1980, pp. 178–80). The fourth (1970–81) period is viewed as the occasion for deepening the role of the Sejm in governance by enlarging its legislative and control prerogatives. Finally, a post-martial law period is still underway. This characterisation of the Sejm as oscillating from passivity to activism and from dependency to limited assertiveness is in agreement with Western analyses (Terry, 1981). The pivotal role of the PUWP in determining the latitude for Sejm activism, then, conforms with our definition of a 'minimal parliament'.

Despite this general classification, the Sejm cannot be dismissed as an insignificant constituent of the Polish political system. Unlike some parliaments in authoritarian systems, the Polish Sejm has maintained a continuous existence, it has retained formal legitimacy as 'the highest organ of state authority' (Article 21 of the Constitution of the Polish People's Republic), and it has provided, on some occasions, a forum for the critical discussion of party and governmental policies. Moreover, as discussed below, it has evolved in terms of its organisational structure and composition of membership, displaying characteristics of adaptability, complexity, coherence, and perhaps also some degree of autonomy, which may be taken as evidence of 'institutionalisation' (Huntington, 1968, pp. 8–32).

Particularly between 1970–1981, one heard a constant verbal commitment to the Sejm. In the aftermath of the 1970 workers' revolts, the then leader of the PUWP, Edward Gierek, pledged at the Eighth Plenum of the Central Committee of the PUWP to foster socialist democracy by strengthening the role of the Sejm in developing legislation and in critically discussing socioeconomic problems (*Nowe Drogi*, special number, 6–7 February 1971, p. 33). At the Sixth and Eighth Congresses of the PUWP, continued attention to enhancing the Sejm was evident (Burda, 1978, p. 46; PUWP, 1980, pp. 41–2).

Has the Sejm, in fact, exhibited institutional development? The evolving capacity of a parliament has been defined as 'the capabilities the legislative system has to perform effectively'; these include the quality of its leadership, the status of its legislators, its intelligence-gathering abilities, its organisational structure and effectiveness, its formal powers, its public support, and its degree of importance in policy-making (Patterson and Wahlke, 1978, p. 286; derived from Fried, 1966, pp. 28–43). Here, we focus first on the level of activity of the Sejm, particularly its consideration of bills and its legislative relationship with the government. Then we examine the composition of the Sejm, which provides information on the status of its legislators, including their potential to represent various group interests affected by legislation. Next we examine the structural elaboration of the Sejm's specialised committee system, which affects its organisational effectiveness in fulfilling assigned tasks. Finally, we offer a preliminary assessment of the relationship between the institutional development of the Sejm and its evolving capacity for influencing policy-making.

Activity of the Sejm

Compared with the world's parliaments, the Sejm meets relatively infrequently and considers a small number of bills (Table 4.1). Excluding the summer recess, the Sejm as a chamber meets about once a month, with most meetings taking one day each. The number of bills considered is much more variable among the sessions than is the frequency of meeting. The number of bills has been highest in the terms immediately following years of political turmoil and change, such as 1956, 1970 and 1976. It is in the reaction to such turmoil that the new leadership of the ruling party vows to increase the activity and meaning of the Sejm.

Highly indicative of the Sejm's changed status within the governmental structures up to 1980 was the dramatic decline in the number of executive decrees. The Stalinist regime of the Sejm's first term ruled by decree, by-passing the parliament. The Sejm had only a rudimentary committee structure, and the parliamentary party clubs were even abolished. Being

TABLE 4.1 *Activity of the Sejm by term*

Activity	I (1952–6)	II (1957–61)	III (1961–5)	IV (1965–9)	V* (1969–72)	VI (1972–6)	VII (1976–80)
1. Meetings	39	59	32	23	18	32	28
2. Days of meetings	39	71	44	40	22	38	NA
3. Laws passed	42	174	93	60	36	103	42
4. Bills not passed	0	4	5	2	2	2	NA
5. Total bills introduced†	42	178	98	62	38	105	NA
6. Executive decrees	106	13	1	1	0	11	4

* Term V was of three years' duration; the others were four years each.
† Surmise; Polish sources are not explicit on this point.

Sources: terms I–IV: Burda (1975) pp. 445, 511 and 512; Term VI: Sejm (1976a) cols 24 and 26 and file of introduced bills in the Sejm Library; Term VII: *Tygodnik Demokratyczny*, 17 February 1980, p. 5.

subordinated to the external central leadership of the party, the Sejm has since been characterised during that period as the 'silent' parliament (Burda, 1978, p. 163).

Our impression from interviews is that the Sejm deputies have a strong sense of their institutional identity. They view themselves, whether party members or not (parties as well as independents are represented within the Sejm), as separate from the ministries and also as separate from the external organs of their respective parties. They have been particularly critical of any perceived effort by a civilian prime minister (before Jaruzelski) to evade the Sejm. This sense of institutional identity and this critical attitude towards the government of the day has manifested itself in several ways. By far the most important development has been the institutionalisation of the committee system, which we discuss below.

Several other developments have also occurred. First, the government, when rushed at times of crisis, has attempted to speed consideration of Sejm bills by evading the committee stage of legislation. Bills have been introduced and adopted on the floor in a single day. In response, the committees have attempted to assert their rightful legislative jurisdiction. Secondly, members have criticised the government for delaying the introduction of planned legislation. As an innovation in the 1970s, a Council on Legislation was created at the cabinet level, to review the schedule of anticipated legislation and to also review the draft of bills. A counterpart committee was created in the Sejm, the Committee on Legislation, with some overlapping membership with the Executive Council. Thus, the Sejm has had an official means of knowing the schedule and content of government legislation. The government, however, has delayed the introduction of planned bills, giving rise to considerable criticism of the government by Sejm deputies and their leadership.

Much of the floor schedule of Sejm activity revolves around the Socio-Economic Plan and Budget. Once a five-year plan is adopted, the annual plans and budgets must be adopted (in December for the coming year) and the government's performance in the implementation of the previous year's plan and budget reviewed (in late spring). This twice-annual schedule sets the cycle for both floor sessions and for the preparatory meetings of the committees. In addition, considerable floor time is given to a review – at times critical – of the government's implementation of previously adopted policies, spanning a number of years.

Nevertheless, as measured by most numerical indicators of activity, the Sejm would be considered a 'minimal' parliament (Olson, 1980, pp. 16–21, 448–53). It is greatly constrained, in particular, by the time allocated for its meetings. Since the Sejm is a relatively large body (460 members) but meets relatively infrequently, the individual deputy is doubly limited in his access to the rostrum. Furthermore, the number of bills considered is relatively small. The Sejm, however, appears to be more active than is the

USSR Supreme Soviet. The Sejm meets more frequently than the Supreme Soviet, and its committee system is more developed than in the latter (White, 1982). Furthermore, the Supreme Soviet is not either regularly or predictably the arena through which legislation is enacted (Little, 1977). Though both the Sejm and the Supreme Soviet are considered 'minimal' parliaments, there are discernible differences between them, indicating the need to develop more refined categories of types of parliaments. Some appear to be more 'minimal' than others.

The Composition of the Sejm

According to Burda (1978, p. 84), the composition of the Polish Sejm is 'shaped under the influence of objective factors' and 'reflects the actual structure of society, as well as the social and political role of different strata of society and social groups'. This statement implies that the composition of the Sejm should change in accordance with the socioeconomic transformation of Poland. However, political considerations constrict the full representation of citizens' interests and group claims in Poland. There is a controlled process of representation (which may involve increasing interest articulation and aggregation) expressed by legislative recruitment patterns.

Parties and Interests

In Poland, deputies to the Sejm are not selected through a competitive process but in 'consent elections' where there is no choice between opposing political parties. Instead, positive and/or negative voting ostensibly indicates acceptance or disapproval of either specific candidates and/or governmental policy (Wiatr, 1978, pp. 203–4). Opposition and dissent are unlikely to appear either during elections or within the Sejm, because the candidate nomination process is dominated by the PUWP. As Burda explicitly states, 'Only citizens holding determined specific political views can cooperate in the conduct of state affairs.' The composition of the Sejm is a 'consequence of the leading role of the Marxist-Leninist Party' (Burda, 1978, p. 85).

Control by the PUWP over which interests and groups can participate in the Sejm places a major limitation on legislative representation. Yet the 'hegemonic' nature of the Polish party system, it is asserted, creates an 'alliance' between three recognised 'cooperating' political parties, the PUWP, the United Peasant Party, and the Democratic Party, and three Catholic political associations (Znak, Pax, and the Christian Social Association), which assures a degree of 'political pluralism'. This political configuration assumes that the cooperating political organisations have the right to attempt to 'shape public opinion by their own propaganda machine' while refraining from seeking to undermine the hegemonic party; in return they 'share governmental and administrative posts at all levels and participate in policy-making, especially in so far as it concerns the groups represented by them' (Wiatr, 1978, pp. 193–4).

The rapid socioeconomic development of Poland during the post-war period has not led to any notable shifts in the strength of these parties and associations within the Sejm. The PUWP, said to represent the working class and collective national interests, held from 62.4 to 52.1 per cent of the deputies' seats in the eight terms from 1952 through 1980; in the 1985 elections it accounted for 53.3 per cent of successful candidates (Zawadzki, 1976, p. 11; *Polityka*, 26 October 1985, p. 6). The United Peasant Party (UPP), composed primarily of citizens from farming communities and intelligentsia of rural background (Lipski, 1978, pp. 25–9), ranged from 25.7 to 21.2 per cent of the total deputy seats, usually holding at the latter percentage. The Democratic Party (DP), whose members come mainly from the intelligentsia, small business and segments of the services sector (Lezenski, 1978, pp. 42–6), had between 8.5 and 5.9 per cent of the seats, with the former percentage most frequently the case. Non-party deputies, some of whom are members of the three Catholic associations, have comprised as much as 13.7 and as little 8.7 per cent of the deputies, the norm being about 11 per cent. Party representation has been rather static, even though the growth of membership for the PUWP between 1960 and 1976 was significantly greater than that of either the UPP or DP (Lutrzykowski and Zemke, 1980, p. 27).

Decisions about the membership of the Sejm are made in the nomination process, not in the election itself. Nominations, in turn, were made through 1980 by the three political parties through the coordinating mechanism of the Front of National Unity. After martial law, the Patriotic Front for National Rebirth (PRON) was given that role, and the earlier 'front' was disbanded. Unfortunately, little information is available about decision-making in this pre-election stage.

Incumbency

The stability in representation of parties and associations within the Sejm does not mean that the parliament has been resistant to change. We have calculated incumbency rates for the fifth, sixth and seventh terms of the Sejm, shown in Table 4.2. The turnover of deputies from the fifth term (1969–72) to the sixth term (1972–6) was relatively high. Most likely as a consequence of the 1970 political crisis in Poland, only 37 per cent of the PUWP deputies were incumbents in 1972, the beginning of the sixth term. The corresponding figures for the UPP, DP and non-Catholic association independents were similar – 39, 36 and 38 per cent respectively. Some 92 per cent of the deputies from the three Catholic associations, however,

TABLE 4.2   *Rates of continuous service, by party, over three terms (percentages)*

Continuous terms served	Workers Party (PUWP) (N = 255)	Peasants Party (UPP) (N = 117)	Democratic Party (DP) (N = 39)	Independents		Total (N = 460)
				Catholic groups (N = 12)	Others (N = 37)	
Fifth (1969–72)	100	100	100	100	100	100
Fifth and sixth (1969–76)	38	32	38	92	32	37
Fifth, sixth and seventh (1969–80)	18	18	18	42	19	18
Sixth (1972–6)	100	100	100	100	100	100
Sixth and seventh (1972–80)	44	45	38	50	35	42

Source: calculated from name lists in *Rocznik Polityczny i Gospodarczy*, 1970–7.

were retained. Fewer than half of the deputies from the sixth term were selected for the seventh term (1976–80) of the Sejm, with incumbents constituting 44 per cent of PUWP deputies, 45 per cent of UPP deputies, 38 per cent of DP deputies, 50 per cent of the Catholic association deputies, and 35 per cent of other independent deputies. Although late 1975 and early 1976 (immediately preceding the election) were somewhat tense periods in Polish politics, no major event such as the ouster of the Gomulka leadership team (in 1970/71) can explain the high turnover of 1976.

Successive incumbency from the fifth through the sixth and on to the seventh term of the Sejm included less than 20 per cent of all deputies, except for the three Catholic associations which kept over 40 per cent of their deputies during this time span. The fact that about 60 per cent of Sejm deputies were legislative novices both in 1972 and 1976 is consistent with the high turnover rates in other communist parliaments (LaPalombara, 1974, p. 152; Little, 1977, p. 32; Seroka, 1979, p. 107). In the Polish case turnover rates have varied, since the first term beginning in 1952, from a low of 38 per cent in 1965 to a high of 82 per cent in 1957. In the Sejm elected in 1980 the incumbency rate rose to 52.6 per cent (*Trybuna Ludu*, 4 April 1980), and it has increased successively in the three most recent terms (the elections of 1972, 1976 and 1980). In the 1985 elections, however, no less than 373 of the successful candidates (81.1 per cent) were first-timers (*Polityka*, 26 October 1985, p. 6).

Demographic Composition

Age   High turnover in the Sejm has not greatly affected the age structure of the body (Table 4.3). For the past eight terms, the Sejm has been occupied primarily by middle-aged legislators. From the third term up to the sixth term there was a consistent rise in the proportion of members aged between 40 and 59, while there was a corresponding drop in the older age-groups. The seventh term witnessed a shift back to an older membership, with 42.2 per cent of the deputies being aged 50 or above; in the eighth term 51.1 per cent of the deputies were aged 50 or above. Since youth under 30 have normally constituted about half of the Polish population in the post-war period, there has been a consistent under-representation of this age category. The high turnover rates, then, do not seem to indicate a marked generational shift in legislative influence.

Sex In contrast to youth, women have made substantial gains in their representation in the Sejm, especially during the 1970s – a trend depicted in Table 4.3. The steady increases in female participation in the Sejm since the fourth term constitutes a political recognition of the important role women play in the socialist labour market, as well as an outcome of their superior educational attainments. It should be noted that the representation of women in the Sejm, as well as in other communist parliaments, surpasses Western democratic membership patterns (LaPalombara, 1974, pp. 143–4). Yet, women are still greatly under-represented in the parliament, and more markedly within the top ranks of the PUWP and the Council of Ministers, where it is extremely rare for women to hold top positions (Fiszman, 1977, p. 317).

Education The available data strongly suggest that educational upgrading of the Sejm is the most important change associated with the recent high turnover of deputies. Table 4.3 shows the marked increase in the educational credentials of legislators since 1969. As of 1976, Sejm deputies were quite a bit more educated than the Polish population generally (*Rocznik Statystyczny 1977*, p. 32). From what we know about the educational attainments of members of the Central Committee of the PUWP, however, the Sejm is not quite as well educated as the party top leadership, 83 per cent of whom had either partial or completed higher educational qualifications in 1971 (Mason, 1977, p. 61).

Rising educational credentials have brought about official disavowals of the need for the Sejm to be statistically representative of the particular classes, strata, or occupational groups in Polish society. In 1965–9, for example, only 11 per cent of the Sejm deputies were workers employed directly in production. During the 1970s worker representation ranged between 16 and 20 per cent of the deputies, well below their actual percentage in the Polish social structure (Gebethner, 1976, p. 32). In 1969, 54 per cent of the deputies were from white collar (mainly administrative) occupations, 6 per cent were managers of state-owned enterprises,, 6 per cent were from other professional occupations, 17 per cent were classified

TABLE 4.3 *Demographic attributes of Sejm deputies, by term (percentages)*

Attributes	I 1952 (N = 425)	II 1957 (N = 459)	III 1961 (N = 460)	IV 1965 (N = 460)	V 1969 (N = 460)	VI 1972 (N = 460)	VII 1976 (N = 460)	VIII 1980 (N = 460)
Age 40–49	40	43	36	37	43	45	38	32
Women	17	4	13	12	13	16	21	23
Higher education	32	40	42	42	46	47	55	59

Sources: *Rocznik Statystyczny, 1977*, Table 1, p. 18, and *Trybuna Ludu*, 4 April 1980, p. 6.

as workers, and 15 per cent were farmers or were engaged in some aspect of agricultural production (LaPalombara, 1974, p. 148). For the 1980 term of the Sejm, about 23 per cent of the deputies were workers or technicians, about 17 per cent were farmers, agricultural specialists or activists of agricultural cooperatives or circles, about 20 per cent were in white collar or professional occupations, and the remaining 40 per cent were activists in various socio-political organisations or holders of government posts (*Trybuna Ludu*, 4 April 1980, p. 6). These educational and occupational trends would seem to indicate that that there has been an increase in the proportion of deputies with administrative/managerial or professional backgrounds since 1970.

Socio-Political Elites   The pattern of legislative recruitment that emerges from available data suggests that the hegemonic party mounted a systematic effort during the 1970s to incorporate professional and elite groups within the Sejm. The maintenance of stable but minority proportions of deputies for the two other recognised parties, the Catholic associations and non-party representatives assured PUWP control over the parliament. The higher turnover of deputies and increasing selection of better-educated administrators and managers may have been intended to encourage greater political communication and participation by competent citizens possessing various interests and opinions – a trend discussed in analyses of elite recruitment in the party (Bielasiak, 1981b). We will return to this theme in the final section of this chapter.

We do not mean to suggest that the Sejm is increasingly composed of highly-educated but politically inexperienced citizens. On the contrary, the body appears to be a veritable who's who of 'establishment' members of Polish politics and society. At present, the Sejm may be more important for who is in it than for what it does. We do not, however, have sufficient time-series data to know whether or not the Sejm is more occupied by notables now than previously. This feature of its composition becomes especially clear when we examine the committee system.

Committee Officers   The 22 committee chairmen in the Seventh Term (1976–80) held a large number of other positions within their respective parties. Within the PUWP, 60 per cent of the 15 committee chairmen were members of the Central Committee of the party, while 73 per cent held other party posts, most of which were full-time salaried positions within the party's administrative offices. Taken together, only two of the 15 chairmen were without either type of party position. This practice is a specific Polish version of a more widespread practice in communist systems (Ionescu, 1967, pp. 60–4; Gripp, 1973, pp. 48–50). Those who held the salaried party jobs present an instance of overlapping specialised membership in that their paid party occupations appear to have had a jurisdiction similar to those of their respective committees. For example, the chairmen of the Sejm committees on Education, Foreign Affairs and the Economy were also ranking officials in the party's departments of Education, Foreign Affairs and the Economy, respectively. Moreover, the chairman of the Sejm committee on Mandates and Rules was an official in the Organisation Department of the PUWP.

It is also noteworthy that 40 per cent of the PUWP committee chairmen were officers of their parliamentary party. A lesser number, 33 per cent, held positions in other types of organisations, such as veterans, youth, or women's groups and local or provincial governmental councils. The same pattern holds for chairmen of the UPP and the DP.

Turnover in Sejm membership is in part a reflection of changes in personnel in the ruling party. All of the Politburo and over half of the PUWP Central Committee were members of the Sejm, as were the 49 provincial first secretaries of the party. As changes occur in these posts, corresponding changes also occur in the Sejm membership. As a result, the Sejm deputies who serve more than two terms tend to be the leading officials of their party organisations and of the government (Ulicki, 1980, pp. 124, 139–40).

Structural elaboration of the committee system

The capacity of a legislature is affected critically by its organisation. A key question related to organisational effectiveness is whether the legislature is 'characterized by procedural and structural complexity responsive to its tasks, functions, and goals' (Patterson and Wahlke, 1978, p. 286). The structural elaboration of the specialised committee system (Little, 1977, pp. 23–4) seems particularly appropriate and useful to analyse because these units have been observed to be quite active in the communist legislative process:

> What is . . . remarkable about the so-called rubber-stamp legislatures of the Communist world is the marked tendency to increase the number of specialised committees . . . From what information we have, these committees are anything but inert bodies; they carry on investigations, often criticize the technical details of legislation, increasingly engage in critical review of legislative proposals from the bureaucracy, and supervise administrative behavior itself (LaPalombara, 1974, p. 129).

Studies of the Sejm (Chrypinski, 1965 and 1966) and of the Supreme Soviet of the USSR (Little, 1971 and 1972; Vanneman, 1977; White, 1982) confirm this observation.

Polish scholars have emphasised the central role of the standing committees in handling the technical details of legislation too complex for the parliamentary body as a whole. The committees are said to provide specialised expertise, increased opportunities for involved discussions, and the best setting for thorough deliberation. Burda (1978, p. 102) contends that these characteristics allow the committees to play a 'momentous role' in legislation; the fact that they are 'an indispensable part of the mechanism of parliamentary work' has resulted in their being called the 'little parliaments'. In common with other parliaments of communist nations, the Sejm meets relatively seldom in full plenary session – usually not more than 10 or 12 days annually (Burda, 1975, p. 511). Thus, the committees assume a special importance, for they are the one available means by which the Sejm can be active and influential.

Number and Size

The number and size of committees indicates the Sejm's potential capacity to deal with the increasingly complex and diverse problems generated by socioeconomic growth (Little, 1977). Table 4.4 shows that various aggregate measures of committee activity have indeed grown. From 7 committees in the early 1950s, the Sejm by 1980 had 22 permanent committees. The maximum size of these committees had grown from 25 to 53 members. The combination of these developments increased the total number of places on the committees from 30 per cent of total Sejm membership to over 150 per cent of the total body. With the exception of the 34 deputies on the Sejm's presidium and in high party office or the Council of Ministers, all deputies belonged to committees in the seventh term. To fill out the available memberships, some deputies served on two committees. The average annual number of committee meetings was about 200, or about 10 meetings annually per committee. In addition, subcommittees were formed within the main committees – about 50 by the early 1980s.

The number of committees is comparable with those in a number of Western parliaments. The frequency of committee meetings, however, is much less than in those countries. Perhaps this low frequency indicates that the main controversies have been resolved within the PUWP and the Council of Ministers. But we also know that most contentious issues within the committees are referred to informal *ad hoc* subcommittees for resolution. The greater the controversy, the greater the reliance on informal subcommittees of this kind. The Sejm, however, does rank higher than the Supreme Soviet of the USSR on these measures of committee activity (cf. White, 1980, pp. 257–8).

Bill Referrals

More direct measures of committee activity include the number of executive decrees and bills referred to committees. The number of bills referred

TABLE 4.4 *Committees in the Sejm, by Sejm term*

Term	1 Number	2 Size	3 Committee memberships Total	4 % of Sejm	5 Meetings Total	6 Av. Yr	7 Subcommittees*
I (1952–6)	7	15–25	130	30.6	247	61.7	NA
II (1957–61)	19	11–40	501	109.6	1203	300.7	NA
III (1961–5)	19	12–50	516	112.2	887	221.7	58
IV (1965–9)	19	17–45	540	117.4	801	200.2	54
V (1969–72)	20	18–47	579	125.9	538	179.3	52
VI (1972–6)	22	15–51	643	139.8	1060	265.0	55
VII (1976–80)	22	19–53	698	151.7	1130	282.5	53

* Permanent subcommittees. In addition, a variety of *ad hoc* subcommittees are also formed.

Sources: Terms I–IV: cols 1–3 and 7, Kedzia (1975) pp. 254, 284 and 299; cols 5 and 6, Burda (1975) p. 512; and Sejm (1976a) Terms VI–VII: Sejm (1976a); Zawadzki, 1980(c) p. 24 (for col. 5, cf. Jarosz and Popkowski, 1980, p. 27); and authors' calculations.

to committees annually is not large by the standards of Western European parliaments.

The most active committee in the number of bills submitted to it and in the frequency of its meetings is usually the Committee on the Economic Plan, Budget, and Finance. In a centrally planned economy, the budget is a far more important document and of wider scope and complexity than in other industrial states. This committee usually takes 25–30 days to consider the annual budget and economic plan. Representatives of administrative agencies and of the chief audit agency, the Supreme Chamber of Control (*NIK*, or *Najwyszej Izby Kontroli*) meet with the full committee and its several subcommittees. The number of these committee meetings to consider adoption of the economic plan and budget proposal ranged from 5 to 10 annually between 1957 and 1967. The maximum number of annual meetings of this committee has been 38 and the least 11 over the 18-year span of 6 terms for which we have data (Burda, 1975, p. 433 and 514 successive issues of the Sejm's *Informacja*).

The variations in the tempo of committee activity would appear to be related to, and also perhaps indicative of, variations in the activity of the Sejm as a whole, which in turn reflects the broader political and governmental context. The Sejm's activity, for example, declined towards the end of the Gomulka period. It increased somewhat at the beginning of the Gierek period, but declined again as the crisis of 1980 approached (Terry, 1981).

Supervision of the State Administration

It has been pointed out that 'perhaps the most dramatic examples of upgrading the investigatory and supervisory functions of legislatures have occurred in the USSR and Eastern Europe' (LaPalombara, 1974, p. 162). Polish scholars argue that administrative supervision by the Sejm 'combines state control and social control'. The main purpose is to ensure that 'administrative activity conforms with the basic line of state policy' (Burda, 1978, p. 162; see also Bierzanek and Gwizdz, 1967; Sokolewicz, 1975, pp. 89–90).

Sejm committees, in order to accomplish this task, largely parallel the structure of administrative agencies. This principle of organisation permits specialisation within the legislature, increasing its capacity to scrutinise the activities of the government's agencies (Herman and Mandel, 1976, p. 471). It also has the long run potential for increasing the legislature's ability to match the government's knowledge on questions of broad policy. It is our impression that the Sejm's committees have been encouraged to examine the suitability and efficiency with which governmental agencies implement policies already adopted by the Sejm, but their effectiveness in doing so is still an open question (see Terry, 1981, for a negative evaluation).

One means of reviewing administrative performance is on-site inspections by *ad hoc* subgroups which have numbered in the hundreds in each of the several Sejm terms. Another means of supervising administrative performance is to issue 'requests' or desiderata to agencies that they undertake specific designated actions (Sokolewicz, 1975, p. 86). Relevant agencies must answer such concrete demands within a month (personal interviews, 1980). Apparently the committees have worked hard at it, for in 1972 their scope was limited by a new rule stipulating that committee-issued requests could be returned to the committee by the Sejm's presidium (Burda, 1975, pp. 308, 439). Agency requests during the sixth and seventh terms of the Sejm (1972–6 and 1976–80) were only one-third the number of those issued in the fourth term (1965–9), but field trips by subcommittees nearly doubled in the sixth and seventh terms compared with the fifth (1969–72).

Beginning with the sixth term of the Sejm in 1972, 'opinions' have also been issued as a means of agency regulation. Opinions are more descriptive and evaluative of the agencies' performances than are desiderata. They argue a case, but the agencies need not reply to the parliamentary committees with precise answers. In fact, the agencies often do reply, but deputies point out that the broad nature of the opinions generate imprecise and vague answers (personal interviews, 1980). During the sixth term of the Sejm, the committees issued 124 opinions; this more than doubled to 280 opinions during the seventh term (Zawadzki, 1980c, p. 24). It is probable that the decline in the use of desiderata during the sixth and seventh terms is linked to the increasing use of opinions.

Legislative Impact

We have only indirect evidence about the actions of the committees on legislation. The extent of change made in the government's proposed bills, according to one study, fits within five categories. The first two categories in Table 4.5 indicate acceptance by the committees of the proposed bills. That rate has fluctuated from one-third in the 1961–5 period to a high of 74 per cent in 1972. The substantive change category has tended to decrease through time. The intermediate category of amendments has fluctuated widely, but has usually been the largest single category. Another indicator of committee legislative activity is the time taken to process bills. Given the infrequent and short floor sessions of the Sejm, most of the lapsed time presumably occurred at the committee stage. Although we have data only up to 1972, the proportion of bills handled within a single week steadily decreased until that year, while the proportion taking over one month steadily increased.

Taking these findings together, we see that the longer the committees work on bills, the more they amend the original texts. Since committees

TABLE 4.5   *Impact of committees on Bills, by Sejm term (percentages)*

Impact	Term of Sejm					
	I (N = 39)	II (N = 161)	III (N = 90)	IV (N = 56)	V (N = 32)	VI* (N = 46)
Fully accept	25.6	19.3	18.9	17.9	25.0	50.0
Accept with editing	15.4	33.5	15.6	25.0	12.5	23.9
Subtotal	(41.0)	(52.8)	(34.5)	(42.9)	(37.5)	(73.9)
Amended	46.2	37.9	64.4	57.1	56.3	23.9
Substantive changes	12.8	8.7	1.1	–	6.3	2.2
Abandoned	–	0.6	–	–	–	–
Total	100.0	100.0	100.0	100.0	100.1	100.0

* Only the first year, 1972.

Source: Burda, 1975, p. 457.

can be bypassed in the consideration of legislation, the bills enacted within a week are mainly those which have been handled entirely on the floor. Such bills are a considerable portion of those which have been accepted without any amendments at all (personal interviews, 1980). In one day in March 1972, for example, sixteen bills were introduced and passed without amendment (Terry, 1981, p. 41). In 1978, of the ten non-budget bills considered, most were in committee three or fewer weeks. One bill, however, on the improvement of the quality of building construction, was completely rewritten, while the others had only a few specific amendments, and correspondingly took fourteen weeks to emerge from committee (Sejm, 1978/9).

As part of the reorganisation of committees in 1972, the new Committee on Legislation was created to review all bills irrespective of the jurisdiction of other committees (Burda, 1978, p. 107). The purpose of this committee is to review the technical and legal draftsmanship of legislation before the bills go to the floor. In its first year, this committee adopted 250 amendments to about 40 bills passed by the Sejm. It also reviewed the 16 bills which bypassed the substantive standing committees (Burda, 1975, p. 456). As a result, it has become one of the most active committees in the Sejm. This committee appears to resemble the Legislative Proposals Committee of the Supreme Soviet, which holds 'jurisdiction over the preparation of the final revision of all draft bills' (Vanneman, 1977, pp. 145–8).

A number of bills have been indicated to us in interviews which, through the 1970s, illustrated the potential for the Sejm to extensively modify and delay government legislation, and to even block it completely. The Labour Code; the proposed legislation on mental health and the reform of primary and secondary education were all prime examples. The legislation on agriculture policy and on retirement pensions for the private farmers (roughly 70 per cent of Polish agriculture is in private hands) heavily involved the Peasant Party as well as the PUWP; their joint consultation over a number of years preceded the introduction of a bill to the Sejm, which then was further delayed and amended in committee. Constitutional revision was a particularly dramatic example of delay, amendment and external opposition, followed even by abstentions on the floor in voting. These and other amendments, delay, and blocking activities have occurred within the committees. Once a bill is released from its committee – invariably with a unanimous report – it is approved at the floor stage (personal interviews, 1980).

None of these issues raised questions of national security, and none concerned the continued hegemony of the Workers' Party – though the proposed constitutional revisions touched upon both issues. Except for this case, the examples of legislation that have been quoted concerned domestic policy. Though the issues skirted the hard questions of foreign policy and internal political (and police) power, the bills raised important issues of public policy. That the Sejm has been an arena in which such issues have been discussed, amended and even blocked indicates that there are varying degrees of policy impact and activity. If the Sejm is 'minimal' in comparative perspective, it has not been inert and completely passive. While the deputies may be selected by a process of 'consent elections' (Wiatr, 1978), the selected deputies do not always give their full consent to the policies proposed by the government and the ruling party.

Party Representation Within the Committee System

Within Western European parliaments, committee memberships and officerships are usually shared among the parties in a strictly proportional ratio. Strict proportionality is not followed in the Sejm. Perhaps the acceptance by all parties and independent deputies of the hegemony of the PUWP makes such a principle less important to the hegemonic and majority PUWP than would occur in a more competitive system.

Committee Memberships

In the 1976–80 parliament (the seventh term), the PUWP's share of committee memberships ranged from a high of 69 per cent to a low of 37 per cent. On 7 of the 22 committees the Workers' Party did not even have a majority, though on all committees it held a plurality. The committees on which its share fell below 50 per cent were those on which other parties – especially the Democrats – and also the independents had their highest share of seats. These were also the committees on which the chairmanships were held by the other two parties. The Peasant Party held a minimum of five seats on every committee. Its share ranged from a low of 14 and 15 per cent (Education and Heavy Industry respectively) to a high of 41 per cent each on the Forestry and Agriculture Committees. As the smallest party, the Democrats' maximum was 15 per cent on the Internal Affairs Committee, but it held at least two or three seats on each committee. Independent deputies were not represented on two committees – National Defence, which has a critical external function, and Mandates and Rules, which has a vital internal function. Their highest proportion of seats was on the Foreign Affairs Committee, which has an important diplomatic purpose, and on the Science Committee, a field with which many of the independents are associated.

This distribution of selective party over-representation indicates a variety of functionalism. The committees particularly relevant to the constituency base of each of the smaller parties were those on which each was over-represented. The same logic applies, at least in part, to the Workers' Party. Its strongest positions were on committees concerned with Heavy Industry, Mining, Foreign Trade, Construction, and Communications. It held the chairmanships of each of these committees as well.

The distribution of party seats on the committees has not been constant over time. In each term, the exact size of each committee changes (they usually grow), and the exact number of seats allocated to each party and to the independents also changes. Over the five terms for which we have data, the Workers' Party's share of seats has usually varied by about 10 per cent on each committee. There is no apparent pattern in these shifts, either through time or among committees (Ulicki, 1980, pp. 144–5). Yet some committees are consistently high, or low, in their proportion of Workers' Party members. The National Defence, Communications and Machine Building Industry Committees, in particular, have been consistently the highest through all the terms in their proportion of PUWP membership. The highest percentage held on any committee in any term has been 78 per cent, held by the PUWP on the Machine Building Industry Committee in the sixth term (1972–6).

At the other extreme, the PUWP share of committee seats fell below 50 per cent, though not invariably, on a total of 7 of the 22 seventh term committees in the Sejm. The committees on which the PUWP consistently held the lowest proportion of seats were Culture and Art, Health and Physical Culture, Education, Labour and Social Affairs, Agriculture, and Foreign Affairs. The PUWP share of the total number of committee memberships has also varied between the sessions, but not in any consistent or dramatic fashion, ranging from a low of 53 per cent in the third term to a high of 65.6 per cent in the fifth term. What has grown steadily, however, is both the total number of committee seats and the number of PUWP seats. Indeed, because of the growth in the former, every party's absolute number of committee seats has expanded. Nevertheless, the PUWP's share has not been either constant or steadily growing (Ulicki, 1980, p. 145).

TABLE 4.6   *Party distribution of Sejm members and chairmen and vice-chairmen of committees, 1976–80 (percentages)*

Position	Workers Party (PUWP)	Peasants Party (UPP)	Democratic Party (DP)	Non-party	Total
Members					
(N = 460)	57	25	8	11	100
Chairmen (N = 22)	68	23	9	0	100
Vice-chairmen					
(N = 78)	49	22	15	14	100

Sources: members: *Rocznik Statystyczny, 1977*, Table 1, p. 18; Chairmen and Vice-chairmen: calculated from Sejm, 1976b.

Committee Officerships

Strict proportionality is not followed in the share of committee chairmanships and vice-chairmanships, any more than with the ordinary memberships. As shown in Table 4.6, the PUWP had a disproportionate share of the chairmanships (though not of vice-chairmanships) in the seventh term. Of the two other parties, the smaller DP was over-represented in the committee offices. The non-party deputies held no chairmanships, but served as vice-chairmen on 11 of the 22 committees. As a result, both the PUWP and the Peasant Party were under-represented in the vice-chairmanships.

In the seventh term (1976–80), the ruling party held the chairmanships of the important committees such as the Economic Plan and Budget, Legislation, and National Defence Committees, but not of the Committee on Internal Affairs and the Judiciary. The DP, representing those in small scale trade, services, as well as professionals, held the chairmanships of two committees of importance to its electoral clientele: Internal Trade, Small Scale Production and Services, and Culture and Art. The UPP held five chairmanships: Agriculture; Forestry; Administration, Regional Economy and Environmental Protection; Internal Affairs and the Administration of Justice; and Health and Physical Culture. All the other committees, having a political significance or dealing with major sectors of the economy, were typically chaired by members of the hegemonic PUWP (Ulicki, 1980, p. 149). The distribution of chairmanships among the three parties is identical in the eighth term (1980–85) to that of the preceding term. Furthermore, none of the committees were chaired by independent deputies.

Taking all committee chairmanships and vice-chairmanships together over a number of terms, we note the steady, if slow, growth in the proportion held by the PUWP (Table 4.7). The under-representation of the ruling Workers Party in each term, we assume from the data for the seventh term (in Table 4.6), occurred in the numerous vice-chairmanships.

TABLE 4.7   *Committee officers by party, by term (percentages)*

Party	Term						
	II	III	IV	V	VI	VII	VIII
PUWP	36.4	43.8	45.3	46.0	49.0	53.0	42.0
UPP	24.2	24.7	25.3	25.0	24.0	22.0	28.0
DP	21.2	19.2	20.0	19.8	17.0	14.0	16.0
Independent	18.2	12.3	9.4	9.2	10.0	11.0	14.0
Total	100.0	100.0	100.0	100.0	100.0	100.0	100.0
N =	66	73	75	76	100	100	79*

* Preliminary and probably incomplete data.
Sources: Terms II–VI: Ulicki, 1980, p. 148; Term VII: calculated from Sejm, (1976b); Term VIII: calculated from *Trybuna Ludu*, 4 April 1980.

Like the committee memberships, the total number of officerships usually grows each term. Unlike the ordinary membership, however, the PUWP has steadily increased its share of the officerships.

Party–Committee Linkages

By all accounts, the committees are the locale within which the work of parliament is accomplished. The more important they are, the more important it is to the parties – especially the ruling party – to monitor and control them. Yet we have been informed that prior to 1980 party discipline was not exerted within the Polish committees, and that agreements and disagreements were expressed across party lines. One source of interparty agreement was apparently a pervasive dissatisfaction with the performance of government ministries. Furthermore the party clubs, which did impose party discipline, did not meet to take a position on legislation until the bills had been reported from the committees and were ready for consideration at a plenary session (Olson, 1982). All of these circumstances could lead to the independence of committee members from their parties, and to the autonomy of the committees from the chamber leadership.

Institutional development and the capacity to influence policy

Our analysis of several central aspects of the Sejm's institutional development suggests there are some important, if somewhat contradictory, trends. On a rhetorical level, we note the intensification of pronouncements that the Sejm has a wider role to play in the governance of a socialist society which appeared through the 1970s and 1980 (Zawadzki, 1980d, p. 8). Nevertheless, the Sejm continues to be dominated by the PUWP and the state bureaucracy. There were, however, several developments through the last decade indicating a growth in the Sejm's capacity to assume a more active if not independent role in the governance of its nation. Its membership improved in qualitative terms, and there were indications of increased activity by its committees, and its administrative supervision and control functions, became quite serious enterprises. We will briefly and selectively review these developments.

The hegemonic PUWP came to recognise the value of a Sejm which shares in the policy process, albeit in a role defined by the party. It has been pointed out repeatedly that the development of socialist democracy is based upon 'the strengthening and perfection of the leading role of the communist party' (Ulicki, 1980, p. 184) and that the evolution of representative institutions will be guided by that party. One deputy noted to us that there are two competing orientations towards the Sejm – a technocratic approach which stresses the Sejm's usefulness in framing and drafting legislation and a second and broader approach which stresses the Sejm's capacity for translating citizen demands into policy and for facilitating critical discussions. The PUWP, and now the military, will decide which approach is to be emphasised.

Levers of influence over the Sejm, particularly in post-martial law Poland, are guarded closely. Most of the decisions regarding the broad legislative agenda are probably determined by the party leadership. Moreover, as we have seen, the PUWP exerts dominance over committee activities in the areas it deems most critical by controlling most chairmanships and vice-chairmanships, through the supervisory activities of the officers of its deputies' club, and by wielding the influence that comes from the high party and governmental expertise and power of its own members. The fact that the PUWP committee officers often occupy top party and governmental positions suggests that their presence in the Sejm constitutes more than symbolic rewards for service; rather, the Sejm positions define additional sets of functions to be performed responsibly and within the ultimate control of the external PUWP. Finally, the PUWP normally emphasises unity and consensus on the floor of the parliament unless it chooses to publicise certain pressing problems and to assign blame as in the case of continued economic ills. In the latter case during the 1970s, deputies of all parties criticised governmental performance and the daily press likewise vented similar criticism. This practice has diminished during and after martial law. Despite sharp debate in the committees, however, this depiction of the Sejm conforms with our initial judgement that it is a 'minimal parliament'.

Another set of institutional developments, however, suggests that the Sejm was making the transition to a 'stable marginal' status prior to martial law (Mezey, 1979, pp. 26–7, 36–43; Olson, 1980, pp. 450–2). Marginal parliaments do not raise questions of basic policy, but can deal with matters of intermediate importance (Blondel, 1973, pp. 104–17). They consider such items as administrative organisation, budgetary allocations, and the effectiveness of policy implementation. Like 'minimal parliaments' they are quite constrained in their ability to initiate discussions of fundamental policy directions and to touch on ideologically and power-sensitive issues. Though minimal parliaments accept governmental legislative proposals, and do so quickly, marginal parliaments can delay and modify such proposals. We even have seen instances in which the Sejm has blocked government initiatives.

The trends in the composition of the Sejm through 1980 were indicative of a move towards 'marginal' status. Despite a reasonable representation of workers and peasants, it became increasingly the domain of highly-educated and rather successful citizens who occupied élite positions in the party – state and professional networks. While the incorporation of such individuals within the parliament could serve a symbolic and legitimation function (Little, 1977, pp. 2–9) and could be utilised to coopt groups and curtail dissent, the presence of capable and knowledgeable deputies in increasing numbers also extends the possibilities for more effective use of the Sejm's real and potential powers. Most deputies, even those who are serving their initial terms, are not political amateurs. Their connections ensure an increasing access to information about the operation of society and government, information that can be utilised in developing or criticising legislation and its implementation. We cannot simply assume that communist party membership and external expertise in party or governmental work denotes servility and suspension of critical faculties. While neither the increasing education nor the higher connections of deputies secure policy-making influence for the Sejm, both characteristics do create a strong basis for attempts to gain greater independence and powers for the body.

The evidence we have presented and the statements of interviewed deputies also suggest that the committee system provided through 1980 a setting for a growing and organised interest articulation and aggregation. One deputy emphasised that constituency demands were intense, diverse, and growing. Moreover, we have seen that the composition of committees is apparently shaped not only by the criterion of expertise but also by a representative principle, with the UPP and DP chairing certain committees closest to their memberships' interests. It is worth re-emphasising that the PUWP even lacked a majority on some committees. During the last decade, growth of committee activity in altering and blocking legislation in accordance with deputies' interpretations of social needs and demands was particularly important. This development indicates that the committees had begun to foster political communication. While there is great confusion about the nature of interest groups and the degree of toleration for their activities (even in conceptual terms) within the Polish political system

(Terry, 1979; 1981, pp. 51–2; Simon, 1980), a constellation of diverse social, economic, and even philosophic views appears to have found expression within the Sejm committees.

Trends in the elaboration of the committee structure point similarly to a more systematic consideration of policy (Popkowski, 1980). The increase in the number and specialisation of committees and subcommittees encouraged a more sophisticated and thorough process of deliberation at least during the period before 1981. The creation of committees paralleling the structure of governmental administrative agencies widened the potential for effective parliamentary oversight.

The marked development of control or oversight functions, taking the form of the review and supervision of administrative agencies, was probably the most significant institutional development we have identified in the Sejm up to 1980. The issuance of desiderata and opinions provided the Sejm with an important set of tools for regulating the governmental bureaucracy (Zawadzki, 1980c). The communist party leadership had been encouraging these activities with the hope of increasing governmental efficiency and responsiveness. We sense that deputies relished the opportunity to lock horns with governmental officials over policy implementation.

> Sometimes the narrow ministry-centered approach of the administrative apparatus is enriched by the supra-ministerial comprehensive view of the Committees. An approach which mainly considers financial resources may be supplemented by a view which accents social needs; a professional approach is expanded to include a consideration of socio-political consequences from the citizen's standpoint . . . The important thing is that this makes possible a more thorough evaluation of the existing situation and of proposed solutions (Zawadzki, 1980d, pp. 9–10).

While we most commonly think of parliaments in their policy-making function (Mezey, 1979), we suggest that the Sejm's most consistent function has been the review and supervision of administrative agencies. These two potential activities of parliaments constitute separate dimensions along which parliaments may be placed. The Polish Sejm appeared to have become the most active legislature in a communist state – because of its developed committee structure – in administrative review and supervision. The Yugoslav Assembly appears to be the most active in the formulation of public policy, principally because of the latitude afforded to it by the Yugoslav League of Communists. The USSR Supreme Soviet, on the other hand, while increasing its activity over time, appears to be less active in these respects than both the Polish and Yugoslav assemblies, while perhaps more active than those of China, Czechoslovakia (since 1969) and Romania.

While the parliaments of Western democratic systems are assumed to be more independent and active than those of communist systems, this general observation may not apply consistently to both of the suggested dimensions along which parliamentary activity may be compared. This judgement may very well be accurate in respect of the policy-making function, but not necessarily in respect of the review and supervision of administrative agencies. It may be, in fact, that the Polish Sejm, until martial law, was more active in this respect than at least some Western parliaments. The British parliament is a case in point: it created a new committee system in 1979 expressly for the purpose of monitoring and scrutinising the work of government ministries. Previously, it had little capacity for such review. That it created a new system of committees for this purpose illustrates the potential possessed by the already existing (but still developing) committee system of the Polish Sejm.

The institutional development of the Polish Sejm presents an example of the evolving capacity of a formally democratic institution in a communist political system. Even before the Solidarity period and martial law, the political dilemmas of the 1970s led the PUWP leadership, with quite a bit of ambivalence and trepidation, to permit the expansion of parliamentary activities. Deputies demonstrated considerable skill in probing the limits of political possibilities available to them under those circumstances. The Sejm's more active role during the events of 1980–81 showed that it can play a considerable and positive role in the governance of Polish society. Its full potential, however, has been and still remains dependent upon the flexibility and self-assurance of the ruling communist party and government.

5

Yugoslavia: Towards Self-Management?

RALPH PERVAN

Introduction

In the communist world and indeed the world as a whole, Yugoslavia has an importance far beyond what one would expect of a country of its size and economic strength. This is due to various interrelated factors most of which derive from Yugoslavia's position, precariously poised between East and West. These factors include the remarkable resistance movement of World War II, the successful defiance by its leaders of Stalin, its leading role in the non-aligned movement and its bold socio-political model known as self-management.

Yugoslav spokesmen claim this model as a major step towards Marx's 'association of free producers', that is, towards a system in which all have a real opportunity to participate as equals in the decisions affecting them in both the workplace and community. As a substitute for directives from the state apparatus, emphasis is given to workers' control within particular economic and communal collectives and to 'self-management agreements' and 'social compacts', which establish mutual rights and responsibilities and which are worked out in negotiations between these separate collectives. Similarly, 'delegation' rather than 'representation' is stressed as a means of reaching such agreements and compacts (as well as determining any laws which may still be necessary) with the aim of ensuring that power remains in the hands of the working people. In short, it is urged that not only has there been a substantial reduction in the role of the state but that, largely through the delegate system, the state has been transformed from something above the working class to the instrument of that class.

Reprinted with adaptations from Leslie Holmes (ed.), *The Withering Away of the State?* (London and Beverly Hills: Sage Publications, 1981) with the permission of the author's executors and publisher.

And what is the role of the Communist Party, or rather, as it is known, the League of Communists of Yugoslavia (LCY)? It is insisted that the dramatic transformation in the role of the state has not been achieved by enlarging the role of the communist organization; on the contrary, the role of the League has been reduced primarily to one of guidance, so paralleling these other changes (see the 'Basic Principles' of the Constitution of the Socialist Federal Republic of Yugoslavia, 1976, and Kardelj, 1978. See also more generally Rusinow, 1977, and Bilandzic, 1978).

The self-management model emphasizes the determination of the rights and responsibilities of individuals and groups through discussion leading towards consensus; it therefore assumes a considerable sense of community and responsibility. However, it is difficult to imagine a country which has more obstacles than Yugoslavia to the development of such attributes.

The chief obstacle is the enormous diversity of its peoples, a diversity born of both its history and geography (see, for instance, Hoffman and Neal, 1962; Vucinich, 1969; Singleton, 1976, 1985). For centuries the region was a battleground between rival religions (most notably Catholic, Orthodox and Islam) and between rival empires. From the beginning of the sixteenth century only the city state of Dubrovnik (at least until 1805) and the tiny, mountainous and barren Montenegro maintained a precarious independence. It was not until 1878 with the decay of the Turkish Empire that Serbia formally won its independence and it was only with the collapse of the Austro-Hungarian Empire in World War I that the last major empire was pushed from the region. The different circumstances and historical experiences of the various groups led to the development of profoundly different and often mutually suspicious and habitually hostile societies. At one extreme, for example, the traditional values stressed 'honour', while at the other, values of hard work and thrift were developed. According to one Yugoslav sociologist, the range and diversity might best be appreciated by imagining a country containing both a Switzerland and a Syria (Pusic, 1976, p. 114) – one is tempted to add 'and just about everything in between'. The experience of generations of foreign control and exploitation, often implemented by soldiers and officials of another south Slav ethnic group, bred a suspicion of outsiders as well as a feeling that government was the enemy to be fought, fooled, bribed or evaded. Conversely, clan, district and, to a lesser extent, ethnic 'connections' became of central importance. These connections, rather than regulations and laws, were the primary means by which one sought to survive and prosper.

It was not until after World War I that the peoples of present-day Yugoslavia were even brought within the same boundary. From the beginning there was bitter dispute especially between the Serbs and the Croats – the Serbs, dominant within the central governmental structures, favoured a greater concentration of power; conversely, the Croatians sought its dispersal. Another dimension to the conflict within Yugoslavia was seen in the activity of the communist party.

These conflicts, some of which grew out of and were stimulated by the desperate economic situation, led to the discarding of the parliamentary system in 1929 and the assumption by the monarch of virtually complete powers. At the same time the name of the state was changed from the Kingdom of the Serbs, Croats and Slovenes to Yugoslavia, and the various south Slav ethnic groups were proclaimed as 'tribes' of the one Yugoslav nation. However, the ethnic problem was not one that could simply be defined away. And despite the harsh measures directed against the communist party and the decimation of its ranks, the party survived to provide the framework on which was built first a guerilla movement and then an army during World War II. The assumption of power by the communists at the end of this war was in large part due to their leadership of this major resistance movement; this sharply distinguished them from the other regimes of Eastern Europe.

During the war almost 11 per cent of the population lost their lives, more than half of them at the hands of their 'fellow Yugoslavs' and this often not in battle but in cold-blooded slaughter (Singleton, 1976, p. 86) – such was the intensity of the political, ethnic and religious hatreds which divided these peoples. The new leaders of Yugoslavia insisted, however, that, despite these events, a new relationship based on the 'brotherhood and unity' of the various ethnic groups had been forged in the Partisan struggle.

The new government quickly set about consolidating its control and embarking on new policies. The first included the removal, often local and spontaneous, of both past and potential rivals (Rusinow, 1977, pp. 14–15). The second meant nothing less than endeavouring to build a modern industrialized society almost overnight through a political and economic system closely modelled on that of the Soviet Union in which the state controlled and regulated almost every aspect of life. There was only one significant exception. No doubt recognizing the danger of alienating that group which had formed the basis of the Partisan movement and which now formed the backbone of the army, police and party, the Yugoslav leaders refrained from the collectivization of agriculture.

All their plans, however, were thrown into confusion by the break in 1948 with Stalin and the consequent expulsion of the 'Tito clique' from the communist fraternity. For some time there had been differences and even tensions between the Yugoslav and Soviet leaders. In particular, the ambitions and pride of the Yugoslav leaders meant that they did not easily accept that they should totally subordinate themselves to Stalin's grand design or stand idly by as the Soviet leadership sought to have its agents infiltrate the major organs of society (Rusinow, 1977, p. 24). The Yugoslav leadership vehemently insisted that this latter action was unnecessary and that it impugned their loyalty to Stalin and the Soviet Union. However, it would be surprising if wounded pride were the only reason for their protestations; Tito at least, with his long experience of Stalin's methods, could not have been unaware of the threat this penetration posed. Nevertheless, while the Yugoslav leaders were prepared to resist on such points, they were devastated when they found themselves suddenly thrown out of the parental home. Their initial reaction was to proclaim their fervent loyalty to Stalin and to urge that the dispute derived merely from misunderstandings. To prove both their loyalty and their ideological integrity they even embarked on a vigorous programme of agricultural collectivization and generally strengthened central controls (Singleton, 1976, p. 120). But to no avail – the breach remained.

To justify the continuation of this breach the Yugoslav leaders then began to criticize the Stalinist system – the model which until very recently they had faithfully followed – and proclaimed a dramatically new model, that of self-management. This model entailed nothing less than the dismantling of those centralized structures. A new and important era in the history of world communism had begun.

The party

In 1920 the Communist Party of Yugoslavia had some 65 000 members and significant electoral support. Shortly afterwards, however, the party began a precipitous decline down to a mere 500 members. Most significant in this decline was its persecution by the government which included the banning of the party, but also of relevance was the factionalism which rent it from within (Moraca *et al.*, 1976, pp. 19–23, 33–7, 60; Rusinow, 1977, p. 7).

The deteriorating domestic and international situation in the late 1930s provided both the opportunity and desire for the new party leadership (headed by Josip Broz) to expand the party's ranks, and by July 1941 membership had grown to 12 000 (Laca, 1977, p. 28). This membership became the nucleus around which the overwhelmingly peasant-based resistance struggle of World War II was organized.

As a means of maintaining and extending control, the party leadership drew an increasing number of these new recruits into the party – by the end of the war the party had grown to just under 150 000. These recruits often appeared to accept the party not so much because of its economic and social policy, but rather because it was the most vigorous opponent of the occupiers and their domestic allies. This new influx, together with the decimation of the ranks of the pre-war communists (only 3000 of the 12 000 survived the war) meant that the party became overwhelmingly a party of the resistance movement, overwhelmingly a party of peasants (Jambrek, 1975, p. 77).

In the immediate post-war period, the party, together with the security forces, was the leadership's principal weapon of control. Many communists found themselves placed at this time in positions which were often beyond their experience, qualifications or even abilities; they received these posts in part because the number of positions was expanding rapidly as the Yugoslav leadership sought to bring about dramatic change, in part because they were adjudged the more reliable in what was still seen as an uncertain political situation and in part because of the time-honoured tradition that to the victor belong the spoils. Concerning this last point it is noteworthy that, in marked contrast to the ascetism which was preached and often observed during the war itself, most of these new office-holders were quick to claim the privileges they deemed appropriate to individuals in such exalted posts. The old, much admired model of the 'gospodin', the gentleman who never deigned to soil his hands, quickly reappeared as the model for the functionaries of the new regime.

Inevitably, as the months passed, as the problems of transforming the economy and society became more apparent and as officials at various levels became increasingly attached to their new life style, revolutionary fervour began to wane. None the less the sudden announcement in 1948 of the split with Stalin came as a stunning blow. For those with the greater commitment to Marxist ideology the dilemma was clearly a serious one. A minority wavered (or threatened to waver) towards the Soviet position and found themselves quickly purged from the party and in many cases imprisoned. The overwhelming majority, however, swung behind Tito, the crucial factor appearing to be opposition to foreign domination.

To strengthen its position in this crisis the leadership made vigorous efforts to boost party membership; hence, despite the expulsion of those members who showed less than complete support of the new party line, membership increased by over 60 per cent in the years 1948–52 (Laca, 1977, p. 29). As had been the case during the war, one suspects that the major motivation for many of these new members, leaving aside personal ambitions, was not so much doctrinal conviction as support for those resisting the external threat. These points concerning the nature of the party membership must be borne in mind when considering later debates concerning the party's role.

As noted, the rift evoked vehement protestations that the breach stemmed from misunderstandings. As time passed, with only a worsening of the dispute and with the Yugoslav leadership retaining its control both within the party and the country, it was no longer sufficient or necessary to maintain that the Soviet leaders had made an unfortunate error; rather, it was necessary to explain how they could persist in this error. Consequently, the Yugoslav leaders began to assert that the Soviet Union under Stalin's domination had distorted the basic tenets of Marxism and had built a system characterized by the growing, rather than declining, power of the state apparatus, and had developed a bureaucracy which stood above the masses in an exploitative relationship. Similarly, the relationship between the Soviet state and the other socialist states was described as being essentially a relationship of exploitation rather than mutual benefit (Zaninovich, 1968, pp. 73–5).

Thus, as they sought to explain and justify the past, the Yugoslav leaders were forced onto a new path. And, with the passage of time, what began as reluctant and nervous steps away from the Stalinist pattern developed into an eloquent elaboration of an alternative model, 'self-management'. It was observed that the term 'management' customarily meant that one man, or group of men, dominated other men; the new system of 'self-management' negated this contradiction as man became both worker and manager. (Incidentally, it is worth noting that recent explanations by Yugoslav spokesmen of the abandonment of the Soviet model play down the rupture with Stalin, presenting it more as a catalyst than a cause (Kardelj, 1977, pp. 77–8).)

The self-management system was presented as crucial to the construction of a truly socialist society; it was asserted that socialism could not be built or imposed from above but rather had to grow from below, from the people themselves, that the state apparatus must be permitted to 'wither' away, and that it was no longer appropriate to have the party as a directing and controlling force (Pasic, 1976, p. 64; Programme, 1977, pp. 117, 121). This must be borne in mind when considering comments of Yugoslav spokesmen regarding the necessity of recognizing the right of each country to determine according to its own particular circumstances its own path towards socialism; it is difficult to avoid the impression that they often seek to imply that one path is smoother and more direct than some they are too diplomatic to name.

To symbolize the changed role of the party from that of direction to guidance, its name was changed from the Communist Party to the League of Communists (1952). Inevitably there was confusion. At one extreme were those who believed that a drastic reduction in the role of the League was imperative, most notably one of Tito's closest associates, Milovan Djilas. However, his colleagues were not prepared to accept his views for a variety of reasons – fear that the level of socialist consciousness within the League and society was too low, that their own positions and privileges might be jeopardized and even that if the League withdrew too precipitously the secret police and army might fill the resultant gap. They dismissed Djilas as a 'pseudo-liberal', who sought to reduce the league to a discussion club with no responsibility to struggle against anti-socialist tendencies and for socialism (Neal, 1958, esp. pp. 47, 49, 64–9).

At the other extreme, a significant number were described as behaving as though the eloquent principles of self-management were mere slogans in a propaganda war.

The principal exponent of this tendency was alleged to be Aleksandar

Rankovic, also a close associate of Tito; indeed, prior to his fall from favour in 1966 he was seen as Tito's right-hand man and probable successor. He was charged with having used his position as organizational secretary of the League and his influence over the secret police to establish an apparatus through which reforms and self-management itself were gravely undermined; by means of massive domestic spying and the spreading of false information he had been able to slant discussions within even top party circles and politically to destroy large numbers of officials and then to replace them with his own supporters – in Tito's words, there was a 'considerable resemblance' between Rankovic's methods and Stalin's. Even his immediate colleagues were subjected to telephone taps and listening devices. Indeed Rankovic may have lost the crucial support of Tito because of the latter's discovery that such devices were apparently being used against himself (Rusinow, 1977, esp. pp. 184–91; Soskic, 1978, p. 105).

The situation within the League was far more complex than the bald presentation of these two positions suggests; both positions continued to exist within the party and often within the same individual. Which one appeared to predominate at a certain time often depended on particular circumstances, both foreign and domestic, and on a variety of factors, some 'principled', some pragmatic and some personal (the importance of some of these factors is elaborated below).

Rankovic's removal provided the opportunity for those leaders at the republican level who had chafed under his domination to strengthen their own positions. It is important to note that it was not merely the so-called liberals in Slovenia and Croatia who spoke out against the Rankovic system, but also the so-called conservatives from the other republics.

Their efforts to strengthen their positions were seen in two broad areas. First, only some 10 per cent of the delegates to the subsequent republican party congresses had previously attended such a congress and only some 31 per cent of the republican central committees retained their positions (Bilandzic, 1978, p. 328). Those brushed aside tended to be older members of the League, often of the Partisan group, who were suspected of being sympathetic to the Rankovic 'firm hand' centralist policies. Second, the League appeared to change into a confederation of separate republican organizations rather than a single body. For example, in contrast to previous practice, members of the central organs of the LCY were elected by the various republican congresses rather than coopted from above, and these central organs were reconstituted on the basis of strict parity of representatives for each republic and 'appropriate' representation for each autonomous province (Bilandzic, 1978, pp. 328–31).

Increasingly, the republican leaders of the League seemed concerned with maintaining their republican base and, increasingly, decisions of the central organs of the League appeared to be the result of negotiations between representatives of separate republican organizations. Arising out of this were the changes in the federal constitution (sketched in the following section) which weakened the power of the central state organs and strengthened those of the several republics. In turn there was the gradual clogging up of the central organs of both the state and League machinery. The new system in effect provided structures in which consensus between the views of the separate parts was to be reached; however, forces had been unleashed and stimulated which made the reaching of consensus increasingly difficult.

Inevitably, the League became far less effective in carrying out its role. The guidance of the League continued to be described as crucial because the socialist consciousness of many was such that they often saw only their immediate interests. It was the task, for example, of communists within a collective to explain how the 'real' interests of the collective could be harmonized with the interests of individuals, other collectives and with the interests of the socialist community as a whole without a detailed and inevitably clumsy central plan. Take the policy of a factory collective concerning scholarships for university students and concerning the employment of graduates; it was the task of communists to point out that the long-term interest of the collective lay, first, in providing scholarships to ensure the availability of appropriately qualified experts, and second, in employing these experts when they had completed their studies. This would improve the factory's productivity and at the same time the interests of the entire socialist community would be advanced by policies which led to the education and employment of experts who were actually needed. As for the students, they could expect the assistance of a particular collective and, at the end of their studies, worthwhile employment (Pervan, 1978, esp. pp. 101, 173). This at least was the theory.

With the gradual relaxation of central controls within the League following Rankovic's removal, League policy became increasingly vague. This may have been inevitable, given the wide range of attitudes and interests of the members; in addition there were no simple solutions to the worsening problems of high inflation, unemployment and uneven regional development. Further, it was apparent that there were some who felt these problems were best left for the market to resolve. This reflected, according to a subsequent judgement of the League leadership, the fact that the League had become more a party of the middle and upper levels of society (bureaucrats, managers and the like), because for the ambitious, League membership remained useful, indeed almost indispensable (Soskic, 1978, pp. 105–6). Many were described as using the influence which came from League membership to obstruct League policies not to their advantage. Thus they might resist the employment of young experts in their collective, fearing the effect on their own careers, or they might urge pricing policies for their collective simply on the basis of what the market would stand (Pervan, 1978, esp. pp. 137–8, 169).

The effect of the changed structures and climate in the post-Rankovic era became most visible and significant in Croatia. In addition to providing greater scope to 'liberal technocrats', the leaders emphasized what they termed the injustices still suffered by their republic, despite the reforms, and the manner in which the implementation of some of the reforms (especially regarding banks) had been to Croatia's disadvantage. This greatly strengthened their position within the republican League organization because it aroused a responsive chord with many in that organization and the community. However, this heightened support in turn became pressure to expand their demands. For example, the leadership in Croatia now began to urge that Croatia should keep the foreign currency it 'earned' through its enormous number of foreign tourists. As has been cogently argued (Rusinow, 1977, pp. 296–7), this would have destroyed a unified Yugoslav market and led to bewildering counter claims. For example, would Croatia be required to pay foreign currency for the food it purchased from other republics for its tourists?

The expression of increasingly strident nationalist views, mass demonstrations, a student strike and so on led to increasing tensions particularly between Serbs and Croats within Croatia and increasing concern even from liberals in other republics that the Croatian leadership might have gone too far. According to Tito there was even the threat of civil war. Eventually the situation was defused, at least for the time being, through a major purge in Croatia in late 1971 (Bilandzic, 1978, pp. 418–23, 426–30).

Not long afterwards the purge was extended to the other republics, most notably Serbia. Here the post-Rankovic leadership had tended towards a more liberal position, in no small part because Serbia, for reasons elaborated in the succeeding section, had found itself doing much better under the economic reforms than had been expected. As was also the case particularly in Croatia and Slovenia, the leaders had allowed substantial scope to the market and thus to 'liberal technocrats'. These leaders were described by some, including most notably Tito himself, as having failed to deal adequately with developments which stemmed from the unchecked operation of market forces, developments which included the stimulation of Serbian nationalism. Justified or not, the clear inference was that these leaders sympathized with and supported these developments and therefore had to be removed. Significantly, so firm was the resistance of the Serbian League that Tito was obliged to use all his prestige and authority to force the resignation of the key figures (Rusinow, 1977, p. 325; Bilandzic, 1978, pp. 423–6, 431–41).

Subsequently, the balance within the top ranks of the League in all regions was shifted toward more conservative and often older cadres and the organization's unity and role was strengthened in several major areas. The dominance of the central leadership was reasserted; the League, as demonstrated by substantial personnel changes in the media, publishing, universities and the like, resumed a major role in appointments; it sought a more direct role in sociopolitical organizations; and it urged greater worker and youth representation at lower and middle levels of the League so as to dilute the influence of 'liberal technocrats' and enhance the possibility of its policies being implemented. In short, according to the distinguished Yugoslav political scientist Dusan Bilandzic, the slogan that the League should not interfere was suppressed and the view that it was responsible for developments in society was renewed (1978, p. 444; see also pp. 442, 443).

The state

Several major obstacles impede the ready understanding of the changing role of the state apparatus in Yugoslavia: the major debates are rarely conducted directly and openly, the principal declarations may in fact mask a very different underlying trend and there is an enormous mass of relevant material – since World War II there have been no less than four different constitutions (the latest of which runs to 406 articles over some 160 pages) as well as several major constitutional amendments. However, one thing is clear in all of these changes – at least until relatively recently, there has been a strong trend towards a diminution of the powers of the central government and state bureaucracies in general.

In the immediate post-war period, economic enterprises functioned merely as branches of government. As noted earlier, it was not until after the rupture with Stalin that changes occurred and most of them were more significant in theory than in practice (Suvar, 1976, p. 464; Bilandzic, 1978, p. 404). For example, legislation in 1950 gave workers the formal right to manage their enterprises, but, since state organs continued to decide production, income and investment, the essentials of the administrative state were preserved (Rusinow, 1977, pp. 58–9).

Nevertheless, a new set of principles had been invoked and it would not be easy to turn back. For example, those who favoured further change, for whatever reason, tended to base their case on self-management, thus forcing their opponents into the untenable position of appearing to be against it.

Efforts to meet the expectations aroused by this new rhetoric, as well as to deal with the burgeoning economic problems, prompted further changes which were proclaimed as enhancing the independence of individual enterprises. The avowed goal was to stimulate greater productivity by providing greater incentives and reducing 'irrational' political controls and at the same time to make self-management more of a reality. But again the changes were much less significant than heralded and the consequences not always what was predicted or expected.

For example, efforts towards the expansion of the role of local authorities often led neither to the more efficient use of resources nor to the expansion of self-management. Factories in various communities would be opened frequently on the basis of overly optimistic or even deliberately misleading presentations and often the approval for such proposals came for political and personal reasons rather than economic. Once established, local pressure coupled with these political and personal links ensured the factory's continued survival through regular financial support from government funds (Rusinow, 1977, pp. 97–8, 128).

On the one hand, the leadership proclaimed the necessity of reducing the drain of these so-called 'political factories' and of expanding self-management rights and responsibilities. On the other hand (and here the influence of Rankovic was of paramount importance), subsidies continued to be provided for these enterprises, and controls, albeit of a different sort, continued to be exercised. The significant consequences therefore were not so much the expansion of self-management as the stimulation of localism and the expansion of Rankovic's authority.

Even at the formal level the change in the position of enterprises was far less than it at first sight appeared. The division within the League leadership meant that a particular proposal providing for substantial change might be agreed to only after it had been qualified virtually out of existence. For example, beginning in 1952, enterprises were relieved of detailed regulation by state organs so that they could independently determine such matters as the type and quantity of production. However, in practice, incentive to change was limited because any increase in revenue would not be their own and any significant loss was usually covered by government subsidy; the apparently decentralized decision making process occurred within a centralized system of collection and disbursement of funds. The reforms of 1958 had similar justification and similar effect (Rusinow, 1977, pp. 63–4 and 103ff; Bilandzic, 1978, esp. pp. 281–2).

In 1961 there were further changes which reduced the role of the state – but almost immediately economic difficulties prompted government intervention, which appeared to herald the imminent return to central controls. A vigorous debate ensued (see Milenkovitch, 1971; Rusinow, 1977, ch. 4; Pervan, 1978, ch. 7). The frequently veiled statements make it difficult to determine the principal positions, but there appeared to be two major camps. Some opposed the reduction of central controls, urging that the economic achievements since the war demonstrated the value of such methods while the current economic difficulties demonstrated their need. In their opinion the market at least unless carefully regulated was an imperfect and dangerous tool. Others however urged that there were basic weaknesses in the methods adopted to date or at least that they were now outmoded. They claimed that political controls led to serious distortion and waste, that long term economic strength required integration into the world economy and that this could not occur while potentially strong industries were drained or neglected while others with minimal prospects continued to be subsidized. As for the current economic difficulties, they only confirmed the need to place the economy on a more realistic footing.

Members of the more conservative group expressed concern that the greater reliance on the market and the consequent encouragement of 'consumerism' would lead to the weakening of socialist values. Others, however, insisted that the present restraints prevented working people from realizing their self-management rights and from enjoying the benefits of their own endeavour. Further, the strength and legitimacy of the system depended to no small degree on its capacity to meet the aspirations of the populace for better living standards; these could only be satisfied by further changes.

Many among the more conservative group appeared concerned that greater emphasis on the market would seriously retard growth in the less developed regions by the destruction of their infant industries in open competition and by the reduction of state investment funds. Continued support for these regions was urged as a demonstration of socialist solidarity. They pointed to the bitterness deriving from the gulf between the richer and poorer regions, a bitterness fuelled by the conviction that the wealth of the more developed regions was to no small extent due to the artificially low prices they paid for raw materials from the less developed regions and the artificially high prices for finished products which they obtained within a protected Yugoslav market. By contrast, members of the more liberal group suggested that effective development of these regions could only flow from rational economic policies and certainly not from policies which bled efficient collectives so as to prop up waste and inefficiency.

As the latter points show, the division was not a simple philosophical one but one overlain with regional and ethnic considerations. To a remarkable degree the divisions within Yugoslavia reflected the cleavage in international politics between 'developed' and 'developing'; it was no coincidence that most of those described as liberals came from the more developed republics of Slovenia and Croatia, nor was it coincidence that most of those described as conservatives tended to come from the less developed regions. However, the battle lines were neither clear nor permanent. Coalitions formed and re-formed as the economic climate changed, as concessions were made or as new possibilities or dangers were seen.

At first in 1962/3 the conservatives seemed to have the upper hand but economic difficulties weakened their confidence and support. The leaders of some of the less developed regions moved closer to the liberal position, in part because of their view that the present system kept them too much under the control of Belgrade and in part by the promise of a special fund to assist the less developed regions (Rusinow, 1977, chs. 4 and 5, esp. pp. 135–7, 166).

This led to decisions which described the market as the decisive factor in economic regulation, which made banks rather than state organs the primary source of investment funds and which brought prices closer to world prices. The role of the central state apparatus was thus substantially reduced; however it still retained responsibility for broad monetary and fiscal policy (Bilandzic, 1978, pp. 310–13).

Almost immediately there were economic difficulties (Bilandzic, pp. 313–19). Some urged this was due to external factors, others that the reforms had gone too far while others seemed to believe that the reforms had been sabotaged, largely by forces led by Rankovic. As noted earlier, his removal gave the various republican leaders the opportunity to root out his actual or potential supporters and to consolidate their own positions; with that came a substantial shift of power within the LCY from the centre to the various republican organizations. In turn there was a dramatic change of the formal structure and rules of the League and of the state apparatus. In part this reflected what the republican leaders managed to win and in part it reflected the desire at the centre to placate the grievances felt within the separate republics and which had grown out of the previous system. Thus the 'sovereignty' of the republics on most subjects was officially conceded and the powers of the federation were limited to what were in general terms described as foreign affairs, defence and steps necessary to preserve a single Yugoslav-wide market and ethnic equality. It was also insisted that there should be equitable representation for all within the federal organs. Thus a collective presidency was established consisting of equal representation from each republic and 'appropriate representation' from the two autonomous provinces. The changes in economic policy which were now implemented substantially boosted production. However, significant problems also resulted, in particular, inflation, unemployment and economic disparities all increased rapidly. In turn this exacerbated or revived the resentments of various groups which had, under the reformed structures of both party and state, greater opportunity for expression (Rusinow, 1977, pp. 284–6).

Most bitterness was expressed in Croatia both within the League and by leaders of outside groups (students and the major Croatian cultural organization) which flourished in the freer atmosphere. They insisted that they were robbed of their rightful share of foreign exchange earnings and complained of the growing might of the central banks based in Belgrade; central government funding had been largely ended but the effect of the reforms was to replace it with funding by banks concentrated in the Serbian capital. These banks became increasingly significant in economic policy-making.

At a more general level fears were expressed concerning broad societal developments now that the role of the state had been greatly diminished and the League as a whole and its members were proving unable and/or unwilling to provide significant guidance. The emphasis in the economy was also entirely on increasing income at both the personal and the collective level. Thus, banks, export-import agencies and those with a near or actual monopoly in a particular product were described as charging virtually what the market would bear and consequently income differentials between collectives soared. Within particular collectives the emphasis was not so much on the development of self-management as on profit, and managers often sought and received a virtual free hand.

Inevitably there were strong resentments at the manner in which some were able to boost their incomes. Particular resentment was directed at banks which were seen as making enormous profits on the money earned by others. However, others retorted that allowing banks to determine investment policies independently of government interference was the best means of encouraging general economic growth (Gerskovic, 1976, p. 104; Bilandzic, 1978, pp. 396–412). The emphasis on profit, income and consumerism together with the encouragement of small scale private business heightened concern regarding the future of socialism; in the words of the frequently-heard quip, Yugoslavia was demonstrating the possibility of the peaceful transition from socialism to capitalism.

Confusion, uncertainty and resentments were rife, all of which help explain the points made earlier concerning how the decisionmaking process at the federal level was virtually stalemated, how different interests came to be expressed, how nationalism was described as having become a major problem and how ultimately Tito decided on a purge of leaders, especially in Croatia and Serbia.

In the aftermath of these expulsions and demotions, greater attention was given to the so-called 'workers' amendments' to the Constitution made in 1971; hitherto, they had virtually been ignored because of the focus on the amendments relating to the federation. The amendments had the avowed aim of providing workers with a real opportunity to control their own affairs; for example, large enterprises were to be broken down into smaller, self-contained entities called Basic Organizations of Associated Labour. The decisions of particular collectives regarding the allocation of funds for personal incomes, social services and investment, regarding prices and the like were to be decided according to criteria set by 'self-management agreements' and 'social compacts', which were voluntarily entered into by the various organizations. Further, public services were to be provided not by state organs but by 'self-managing communities of interest'. These bodies would bring together delegates from collectives which provided a particular service and delegates from those collectives which benefited from that service. The assembled delegates would decide, for example, what the education system was to furnish within the commune and decide the support to be provided by the various work organizations (Kardelj, 1978, esp. pp. 141–65).

As noted earlier, of fundamental significance was the insistence that all these agreements and compacts (as well as any laws, which might still be necessary) were made by 'delegates'; bourgeois representative democracy was specifically rejected as being outmoded and undemocratic. According to the theory of the delegate system, a topic was discussed and a position reached at each level; delegates were then obliged to present this position at the next level and then, after the matter was decided among the assembled delegates, to report back to their collectives (Kardelj, pp. 18, 155).

It seems that a major aim of implementing this reform was to provide some means of restraining 'liberal technocrats' without dramatically increasing the role of state organs. Each collective would be obliged to observe limits set in negotiations with delegates from other collectives; adequate worker representation in these delegations was also emphasized, such delegates being seen as more responsive to guidance by the League; further, because of their direct and real links with other groups, workers would be less easily manipulated by liberal technocrats within their own collectives and more readily kept under League control. The need to justify their policies in negotiation with other collectives, particularly since many of the delegates were at the same time members of a League in which discipline had been significantly tightened, was seen as an effective means of ensuring that the separate collectives were more successfully restrained than in the past.

The avowed aim remained to keep the role of the state to a minimum; however, that minimum was now seen as substantially greater than had been the case in the near past. Thus the most recent Constitution emphasizes the broad right and responsibility of the state to act as a guardian of socialism – for example, to intervene, 'if serious harm has been caused to social interests' (Constitution, art. 130). In explaining this reversal of what was a consistent trend it was urged that previously the major threat to self-management came from bureaucratic forces, hence reducing the power of the state was the progressive course. However, this reduction of state power opened the way for liberal technocrats who then became the principal danger so in this situation the withering of the state was the reactionary course (Pasic, 1976, p. 67; Bilandzic, 1978, pp. 452–3; Popovic, 1978, p. 166) and, of course, the development of the delegate system was described as transforming the contemporary state into the instrument of the working people.

Conclusions

Of all the countries of the communist bloc, Yugoslavia stands out as the one which has made the most radical change in its basic political system. Almost overnight the party which had seemed more Stalinist than Stalin's own became the bitterest critic of the centralized Soviet model and almost overnight a dramatically new model emphasizing participation, not only as the right of all working people but also as essential to the construction of socialism, was proclaimed. According to the party's principal theoretician, Edvard Kardelj, 'No state, no system and no political party can bring a man happiness'. Rather, the opportunity must be provided for individuals and groups to voice their own interests and to determine their rights and obligations in discussion and negotiation within particular collectives and between collectives (1978, p. 17). In this system the role of the state is substantially reduced and the nature of the state fundamentally transformed to ensure it does not stand above the working people. Similarly the League is described as having been alerted from something above society (in the manner of the traditional single-party) to an organization which is an integral part of society, guiding and inspiring, but also learning and adapting according to circumstances which include the views of the working people themselves (Kardelj, 1978, pp. 212–13; Popovic, 1978, p. 163).

Clearly this is a most ambitious model – it requires substantial basic agreement and a degree of interest and participation far above that of our own. It is especially ambitious when one has regard for the traditions and cultures as well as the circumstances of contemporary Yugoslavia. Those being asked to decide complex economic and social policy often have limited knowledge of urban, industrial society, most of them being scarcely one step removed from a traditional, insular peasant background. (In 1948, two-thirds of the active population were engaged in agriculture and in 1953 four-fifths had not even completed primary school.) One suspects that most of those who have flocked to the cities since the war (reducing those engaged in agriculture to 31 per cent of the total by 1977) are preoccupied with coping with the massive dislocation in their personal lives (*Samoupravni*, 1978, p. 100). In addition there are the bitter ethnic rivalries (compounded by the growing assertiveness among the Moslem minorities, which constitute at least 16 per cent of the total population), low and uneven economic development coupled with high and growing expectations, a low level of socialist consciousness and commitment in the community and the League itself, a strong commitment to private interests and personal connections and the seriousness and complexity of many of the current economic problems.

Prior to 1966 the most overt consequences of such factors appeared to be held in check by the controls largely organized by Tito's close associate, Aleksandar Rankovic. Indeed, it might be claimed that despite profound formal changes many aspects of the 'bureaucratic' system were preserved (Suvar, 1976, p. 464; Bilandzic, 1978, p. 404). Rankovic's deposal opened the way for significant changes, providing substantially greater opportunity for the expression of particular demands. However this greater freedom only revealed how deep and irreconcilable many of the cleavages were.

Since the early 1970s the leadership, while vigorously proclaiming the further evolution of self-management, has clearly sought to tighten controls so as to eliminate what it termed these nationalist and liberal-technocratic excesses. The methods include increasing the representation of youth and workers within all sociopolitical bodies, strengthening the role of the state and tightening discipline within and enhancing the role of the League. In this vein it is important to note that Kardelj, in the same work in which he lauded the rights of individuals and groups to pursue their own interests and spoke of the need for the League to revise its policies 'when the prevailing social consciousness is still not ready to accept them', insisted on the continued need for 'special repressive measures' against the forces of 'bourgeois and technocratic-bureaucratic counter-revolution' (1978, p. 117). In simple terms, this means that 'anti-socialist' ideas and developments cannot be permitted. The critical question is who determines what is, or is not, 'anti-socialist'? Here there can be no doubt that the leadership of the League insists that it alone has the final say.

The leadership has significant problems. The effort to restrain 'liberal-technocrats' and enhance the influence of the League leadership through an expanded role for youth and workers in delegations and in the League may have but limited success. It is clear that workers are still greatly under-represented in delegations and further that they appear overwhelmed by the volume and complexity of materials they are expected to master outside their normal working hours. As for increased worker and youth representation within the League it is clear that this is frequently secured through 'campaign methods'. By implication, the members chosen in this way are unlikely to have the qualities or desire to play the role avowedly expected of them. Second, these new inexperienced members make up an enormous proportion of the League membership; of the membership in late 1977 some 40 per cent had joined in the previous four years. Just over 30 per cent of the new members were 'workers' bringing the percentage of workers in the total League to just under 30 per cent (*Statisticki*, 1978, pp. 12, 36). It may be that the leadership will be obliged to endeavour to devise policies at the top and then endeavour to force their implementation. The dilution of the existing membership with youth and workers who can be expected to be more amenable to League 'guidance' may, at least, make the latter a little easier by reducing the prospect of open resistance.

However, as the outline of the current problems suggests, it will not be easy in the post-Tito era to decide policies for the entire country despite, indeed partly because of, the elaborate structures providing for balanced representation of the various regions and ethnic groups and the system of annual rotation in League and state positions. These methods, designed to allay suspicions and fears (although presented primarily as a means of preventing the re-emergence of 'bureaucratism'), only demonstrate how strong such feelings are. Further, there is the problem of tightening controls without jeopardizing vital Western economic support, without arousing substantial domestic opposition and without making a mockery of what is fundamental to the regime's claim to legitimacy, the system of self-management. It would be a mistake, however, to overlook the support for the recent, tighter policies; many citizens appeared concerned at the trends of the recent past, not necessarily because of a strong commitment to the system, but often because of a fear that any substantial change is likely to be for the worse.

6

State Reforms in the People's Republic of China since 1976: a Historical Perspective

DAVID S. G. GOODMAN

Since the death of Mao Zedong in 1976, and particularly since the first session of the 5th National People's Congress (NPC) in early 1978, the leadership of the Chinese Communist Party (CCP) has implemented various political reforms in the People's Republic of China (PRC). The explicit context of reform has been a reaction to the political practices and policies pursued during the period of the Cultural Revolution, 1966–76. In particular, state reforms have been presented as the means to encourage a revitalised and autonomous (but by no means independent) structure of government, and a return to the political status quo of the early 1960s. Some commentators have regarded the word as the deed, arguing, moreover, that the PRC has returned to the orthodox 'Leninist–Stalinist' model it had adopted during the early 1950s, and which exists in other communist party states (see, for instance, Walker, 1980, p. 12). It is, of course, too soon to assess what the actual impact of state reforms will be, as opposed to their intention, not least since many have only just been implemented and it is reasonable to assume that more reforms are on the way. However, it is possible, by considering recent reforms not only in their immediate context but also from a wider historical perspective to assess the limits of their possible significance. Specifically, it is possible to consider further the claims that those reforms may lead to the state's relative autonomy, a return to the administrative and political framework of the early 1960s, and even a return to the 'organisational orthodoxy' of the Soviet Union and Eastern Europe.

Although the concept of 'the state' is clearly open to a variety of

Reprinted with adaptations from Neil Harding (ed.), *The State in Socialist Society* (London: Macmillan and Albany: State University of New York Press, 1984) with the permission of author and publishers.

interpretations, Western political studies of the PRC have tended to regard the state in the very specific and limited sense of government organisation, the state *apparat*. In that definition, the terminology employed within the PRC has to a large extent been adopted. When applied to the PRC itself that terminology differentiates relatively clearly between, on the one hand, the state, and on the other, party, nation, and the more general political (or social) system. In general, it is only when the PRC is considered in comparative perspective, or in description of other polities that the state is less clearly or more widely defined. The conceptualisation of the state in the PRC as government is reflected in two commonly used terms. The first and more abstract is *guojia*, usually translated as 'the state', which entails the organised strength of centralised and united political power, and stresses its coercive functions. For example, a recent political encyclopaedia provides as its examples of the state's most important institutions 'the armed forces, police, law courts, and prisons' (*Cihai*, 1978, p. 60; see Goodman, 1984, for a full documentation of these and other points). The second is *zhengfu*, usually translated as either 'government' or 'administration', which refers to the administrative units of the state's organisation, from the central to the basic level. Somewhat paradoxically, the notion of the state *apparat* in the PRC is even narrower than it is more generally conceived, for it does not include the People's Liberation Army (PLA). As Schurmann, among others, has pointed out, the CCP has viewed the PRC's political system since 1949 as comprising three major hierarchies, namely the CCP, the PLA, and the state (1968, pp. 532, 557ff). It is the last of those three that is the focus here. First, the context and nature of state reforms will be outlined. Thereafter, the limits of their potential significance will be considered through an examination of party–state relations since 1949; a comparison of the state structure before the Cultural Revolution and since 1976; and a discussion of the peculiarities of the PRC as a communist party state.

The context of reform

With respect to the state *apparat* recent reforms have had two stated aims. One has been the desire to promote 'socialist democracy and legality' as opposed to the 'autocracy, bureaucracy, love of privileges, the patriarchal style of work, and petty-bourgeois individualism' that is now said to have existed during the period of the Cultural Revolution from 1966 to 1976. That decade is now virtually written off as a period of 'feudal fascism' for which the 'Gang of Four' are held responsible. Curiously, from any Marxist perspective, that appellation is presented with little discussion of the relation between base and superstructure or the prevailing mode of production. In general, it has been described as 'feudal' because there were no laws, the rule of an emperor (in effect), no courts, arbitrary arrest and torture.

The specific criticisms of a leading party theoretician, Li Honglin, in 1979 are particularly interesting. He pointed out that the NPC had not met often enough; and that as a 'democracy' the system, far from being socialist, did not even measure up to that of capitalist democracies. Moreover, Li criticised not only the Cultural Revolution's decade as feudal, but also by implication included the years 1958–1961, thereby obliquely attacking Mao since all those years are clearly recognisable as times of his ascendancy. Two years later, the CCP was more openly hostile to both Mao and the Cultural Revolution. The 'Resolution on Certain Questions in the history of our Party since the establishment of the PRC' was adopted by the 6th plenum of the 11th central committee of the CCP in June 1981. It criticised Mao generally for his personal arbitrariness, held him responsible for the evolution of the Cultural Revolution, and regarded that decade as an almost unqualified disaster. Though the resolution recognised Mao's contribution to the Chinese revolution, it criticised his political activities, particularly after 1958, and drew a distinction between the ideology that bears his name (Mao Zedong Thought) and his personal activities to such an extent that it explicitly condemned Mao for having contravened Mao Zedong Thought during the Cultural Revolution (Goodman, 1981b, p. 518; for the full text, see *Resolution*, 1981).

The second expressed aim of state reforms has been the need for economic revival, recognised in the campaign to achieve the 'Four Modernisations' – that is, of industry, agriculture, science and technology, and national defence. Though the slogan of the 'Four Modernisations' and its general content had first been coined in the early 1960s and even supported by Lin Biao in his foreword to Mao's 'Little Red Book', during the mid-1970s it became associated with those opposed to the economic policies of the Cultural Revolution. Although the extent of economic problems during the 1970s has only become apparent, at least partially, since 1976, by all accounts the economic situation during the Cultural Revolution was certainly not as healthy as had been claimed at that time (see, for instance, Eberstadt, 1979). In the summer of 1975 a series of policy documents was drafted as the first stage in a programme for economic revival and the achievement of the 'Four Modernisations' by the end of the century. Though they fell foul of the intraleadership conflicts of 1975–6 and were removed from the political agenda along with Deng Xiaoping in April 1976, they reemerged and were enlarged after Mao's death and the arrest of the 'Gang of Four'. In essence the economic policies of the Cultural Revolution have been criticised for 'placing politics in command' too much, not 'paying attention to economic laws', and for a lack of adequate economic planning.

State reforms since 1976

Diagnosis of the PRC's economic, political, and administrative problems has led to changes throughout the state *apparat*. The re-orientation of economic perspectives since 1976 has resulted in an expansion of the state's central organisational framework – that is, the ministries and commissions directly under the State Council, whose ministers are members of that body; the introduction of a new system of economic administration; and the creation of new co-ordinative planning units. In 1975–6 there had been 25 ministries, but as of 1 April 1981 there were 38. With two notable exceptions, that expansion has resulted directly from the renewed concern with administration of the economy. The exceptions are the re-establishment of Ministries of Justice and Civil Affairs, which are undoubtedly an integral part of the programme to promote 'socialist legality'. However, perhaps of greatest significance, seven new commissions (there had only been four during 1975–6) have been established for the explicit purpose of co-ordinating economic activities across ministries. At the basic level, economic enterprises formerly under the close direction of local government have been encouraged to experiment with a greater degree of freedom in their management and administrative procedures. Flexibility has been the keyword in planning, purchasing, distribution and pricing policies. At the regional level, the six large economic coordinative regions (each covering several provincial-level units) that existed in the late 1950s and early 1960s have been re-established. As before, it would appear that their intended function is to attempt regional (as opposed to provincial) economic self-sufficiency, while maintaining both continued and centrally directed economic growth.

From an administrative perspective the post-1976 critique of current ills and the Cultural Revolution has been directed at the overconcentration, both institutionally and associationally, of functions and powers within the politico-administrative system; and at previous policies on cadres, their appointment and terms of office. Putative reforms have included the restructuring of local (that is, non-central) government, and the adoption of new policies towards cadres. A major administrative problem facing the PRC increasingly during the 1970s was the guaranteed employment and lack of compulsory retirement for cadres. The results have included not only the emergence of a significant gerontocracy and the lack of an adequately traincd administrative successor generation (particularly given the relative youth of cadres on attaining power in 1949), but also considerable overmanning. As one complainant described the general behaviour of cadres in a letter to the *People's Daily*: 'With tea to drink and fags to puff, The daily paper's work enough!' Though noises have been made to end cadres' guaranteed employment, little has so far emerged. On the other hand, Deng Xiaoping and several other elderly vice premiers led the way and resigned their official positions in the state *apparat* at the third session of the 5th NPC in 1980 in order to encourage other older cadres to do likewise, and the cases of those who have followed received considerable publicity (see, for instance, *Beijing Review*, 1980, no. 46, p. 20).

The restructuring of local government has been a necessary consequence of the rejection of the Cultural Revolution. At its very start the Cultural Revolution involved, outside the centre, the dismantling of the previous organisational frameworks of both party and state, and their replacement by what at that time was described as 'the brand new proletarian organ of power', the revolutionary committee. Though the functions of the revolutionary committees (which originally replaced every administrative unit from the basic to the provincial level) changed considerably during the 1970s, they were originally conceived as joint agencies of party and state. Despite the recreation of a party *apparat* at local levels after 1969, the lack of differentiation between party and state characterised the period of their existence. In addition, despite the revolutionary committee's claim to be 'representative' there would appear not to have been any pretence of election. Thus, for example, after 1965 and until 1977 no people's congresses were convened to elect or approve people's governments at the various levels of local government, as they had been before the Cultural Revolution. Between 1977 and 1980, however, the pre-Cultural Revolution structure of local government was re-established at all administrative levels. People's congresses were re-convened and have continued to hold approximately annual sessions. That has followed the practice of the 5th NPC, elected in 1978, for although a 4th NPC had been elected in 1975, it had not (unlike its pre-Cultural Revolution predecessors) held annual sessions. Local people's congresses have elected permanent standing committees (as representative bodies) and people's governments (the executive branch of the state *apparat* at each level). In line with the new principles of clearly differentiating between the roles both of institutions and of individuals and of not over concentrating functions and powers, an attempt has been made to minimise the overlap between people's congresses and people's government. For example, at provincial level, no individual holds a leadership position on both the standing committee of the people's congress and in the people's government, and that would appear to be generally the case at lower administrative levels.

The concern with promoting 'socialist democracy and legality' and the consequent state reforms have perhaps received the greatest publicity within the PRC. The legal system, in particular, has been refurbished. As previously noted, ministries of justice and of civil affairs have been reestablished; the law courts have been regularised, and to be a lawyer has once again become respectable. Moreover, the attempt to codify and regularise the PRC's laws has been started, with several new major laws, notably the Criminal Code, Marriage Law, and Electoral Law, drafted and implemented. The emphasis has been on a 'socialist rule of law' (contrasted to the tyranny of the decade of the Cultural Revolution) and on 'equality before the law', despite the apparent paradox that similar sentences were prescribed for Yao Wenyuan (one of the 'Gang of Four') and Wei Jingsheng (a leading radical dissident of Beijing's Democracy Movement during 1978–9). Though the trial of the 'Gang of Four' was a clear symbol of both emphases they have also been pursued in other ways. For example, the state has prosecuted officials for corruption and held cadres responsible for apparent mistakes, even of delegated responsibility. Thus, Wang Shouxin, manager of a county fuel company was imprisoned after having been found guilty of misappropriating approximately £160 000, and Song Zhenming, Minister of the Petroleum Industry, was dismissed following the capsizing of an oil-rig in the Bohai Gulf.

Regularisation, accountability and responsibility have been the keynotes of political reforms in the state *apparat*. A completely new Electoral Law was adopted in 1979, quite apart from a revised state constitution in 1978 and 1982. The new Electoral Law provides for competitive elections on the grounds that competition 'would prevent officials becoming "masters of society"', a constant complaint during the late 1970s. In principle there are to be more candidates than places to be filled in any election, and there are even regulations covering the numbers of candidates. For direct elections the number of candidates should be 50–100 per cent above the number of places to be filled; in indirect elections, 20–50 per cent higher. The Electoral Law also stresses the accountability of cadres to their electorates, and provides for the possibility of recall meetings and elections. Finally, the new law provides for direct elections, not only at the basic level as before, but also (in a new departure for the PRC) in county elections. Since its national adoption, the new law would appear to have been implemented, at least formally (see, for instance, *Beijing Review*, 1980, no. 8, p. 11). Moreover, considerable emphasis has been placed on the 'democratic' implementation of not only the Electoral Law but all the reforms in the state structure. Thus, for example, 'by-elections' (*buquexuanju*), as had occurred during the 1950s but not thereafter, have once again been held; and elections have been declared null and void on the grounds that there had been undue outside interference, notably from the CCP. For similar reasons great stress has been laid on the need for regular sessions of people's congresses at all levels, *inter alia* to receive and approve government work reports, plans and budgets. Though that practice had generally occurred before the Cultural Revolution, it had not thereafter until late 1977. Since then, however, people's congresses have met on a more regular basis and their published proceedings have included government work reports, plans and budgets. All in all, then, the long-term aims of reforms in the state *apparat* since 1976 have been its revitalisation: to create a separate and functioning structure of government, capable of fulfilling the tasks allotted to it by the CCP.

It is interesting that the revival of concern with the state *apparat* has been reflected in recent attempts to establish political science as an academic field of study in the PRC. Though other aspects of Western political studies are, and have been for some time, studied under other academic subject headings (for example, philosophy, political economy and history), the state has not been a focus for academic work or political science studied more generally since 1949. However, in May 1980, steps were taken to establish the study of political science within institutes of higher education and research. The inaugural meeting of the Chinese Political Science Society proclaimed (perhaps somewhat optimistically by Western standards):

> Political science is an independent basic branch of learning in the social sciences. However, since the founding of the People's Republic, political science has not been given the importance it merits . . . As a result, there is insufficient research on such important theories and practical questions in political science as 'the institution of the state', 'the organization of governments', 'the functions of legislative, executive and judicial organs and their mutual relations', or 'the cadre system'. The lesson is profound.

Party and state

Viewed in isolation, the potential of any government organisation, let alone the whole state *apparat*, may clearly be exaggerated. However, almost by definition, in a communist party state it is the state *apparat*'s relationship with the communist party that is of key significance. Ever since the establishment of the PRC, except for a brief period during 1967–8 when its position was ambiguous, the CCP has held to the theoretical position that the party makes policy but the state implements it. If nothing else, that distinction between two parallel hierarchies preserves the party's vanguard role. In a speech in 1952, the veteran communist Dong Biwu emphasised that 'The CCP should issue general directives to the government administration but the party does not directly conduct the affairs of the state.'

However, ever since 1949 the distinction has proved difficult and sometimes impossible to maintain in practice. Speaking in 1951, Gao Gang, the then chairman of the State Planning Commission, complained bitterly that cadres were not maintaining any distinction between party and state and concluded, 'We must understand that party organs should not and cannot replace state organs.' If anything, the party's tendency to subsume the state *apparat* has increased with time. For example, in 1957 the Tangqi *xian* (country) CCP committee (in Zhejiang province) stated that, 'At present the phenomenon of replacing the government with the party is tending toward becoming a tradition', and criticised the situation that had arisen when 'A meeting of *hsiang* [village] magistrates recently summoned for the purposes of discussing work on grain was monopolised by the Department of Trade and Finance of the *hsien* [County Party] committee.' During the Great Leap Forward and early 1960s, as Barnett (1967, p. 429) indicates, there was a recurring tendency for the CCP

> to go far beyond acting as director and supervisor of other political organizations, and has constantly encroached upon government admi-nistration as such. In short, on many occasions and in many fields the party has not simply supervized the running of things but has tended to step in and run them itself.

Explanations of the tendency for the CCP to subsume the state *apparat* vary from the cultural to the institutional and political. A cultural explana-tion is provided by Pye in his research into Chinese political culture. He has argued that in the PRC political power is not only undifferentiated and indivisible, but also that it has a tendency to drift towards its nominal location (1980, pp. 120ff). Though to a certain extent such findings would imply that within the state *apparat* political power would come to be concentrated in the hands of leading cadres, they also suggest an explana-tion for the party's over-dominance.

The maintenance of the distinction between party and state has not been aided by the attitude of CCP itself. Even before the Cultural Revolution several of the CCP's practical policies created ambiguities. Though the overlap between the leadership of party and state organisations before 1966 was not as complete as it became in the following decade, none the less it was considerable. At every level of the politico-administrative system the majority of leading state cadres were also leading party cadres. It was not just that there were exceptionally few non-CCP members in leadership positions within the state *apparat* (particularly after 1954), or that most leading state cadres were party members, but that taken as a whole there was considerable similarity between the top decision-makers in the party and state organisations at each level. Though the leading cadre in one *apparat* at any given level more often than not was not the leading cadre in another *apparat*, they were extremely likely to have been a leading cadre in the other *apparats*. Thus, for example, before 1966 it was almost a rule that a provincial governor (the leading cadre in the state *apparat*) was also the second secretary of the party committee in the same province.

Though it is clearly possible for an individual to wear two or more hats, it is also reasonable to assume that when it occurs on as large a scale as in the PRC before 1966 considerable confusion ensues, at least occasionally. However, that is as nothing compared with some of the institutional reforms implemented by the CCP, in terms of blurring the distinction between party and state. Two of considerable significance were the decentralisation measures of 1957–8 and the introduction of the rural people's communes in 1958. Conceived as administrative decentralisation within the state *apparat*, the 1957–8 measures were designed to increase local flexibility and initiative. Several of the central economic ministries were closed down and their functions devolved to provincial level. However, an essential concomitant of the decentralisation of state functions was that the provincial party committees were directed to act as co-ordinating committees for all state activities within the province. The contribution of the rural people's commune to blurring the distinction between party and state was even simpler. Right from its inception in 1958 the rural people's commune was conceived as the basic-level unit jointly of party and state (Schurmann, 1968, pp. 487ff).

It would of course be easy to overestimate the extent to which the party subsumed the state before 1966. However, it would appear that outside the centre the distinction between party and state often existed more on paper than in reality. In that context the changes introduced during the Cultural Revolution, and particularly by the institution of the revolutionary committee in its early stages, can be seen more as a natural development from earlier practices than as a radical break with the past. In that context too, it would seem likely that it will take more than rhetoric to ensure that the more recent reforms of the state *apparat* result in a clear and continuing distinction being maintained between party and state. Certainly the evidence from provincial people's congresses held in early 1980 and early 1981 would seem to suggest that either in formulation or in implementation the party–state distinction remains confused in many respects (for a further discussion see Goodman, 1985).

Before and after the cultural revolution

As already noted, the officially stated context of all reforms and not just those concerning the state's organisation, has been the reaction against the Cultural Revolution. To quote Hu Yaobang, when General Secretary of the CCP (Hu became Party Chairman in June 1981):

> the decade between 1966 and 1976 of the so-called great cultural revolution was a period of catastrophe. There was nothing correct nor positive about these ten years. The whole thing was negative. Tremendous damage was done to our economy, culture, education, political thinking and party organization. The only positive factor, if we may call it that, is that we have learnt some lessons from the mistakes made during this decade.

The apparent implication of Hu's statement, and indeed those of other national leaders during recent years, is that reforms are intended to restore the status quo of the early 1960s, now regarded as a 'golden age' in the PRC's development. Thus in an important speech delivered in January 1980, Deng Xiaoping rejected not only any other more radical solutions to the PRC's problems but also those practices implemented during the 1950s. Instead, he emphasised the strength of the PRC during the early 1960s – 'Under the united leadership of the CCP, we quickly overcame the grave difficulties of 1959, 1960 and 1961. It is worth recalling that.' Certainly, the resolution adopted at the sixth plenum of the 11th central committee of the CCP in June 1981 contained a similar judgement on the respective merits of the periods of the Cultural Revolution and the early 1960s. Finally, the impression of a return to the early 1960s has been reinforced by the large-scale rehabilitation, sometimes even posthumously, of those who had been leading cadres at that time but who were attacked and removed from office during the Cultural Revolution.

However, even on a very superficial analysis it is clear that recent reforms in the structure and operations of the state do not obviously represent a return to the early 1960s. Though it is undoubtedly true that there are similarities between the intentions of the reforms recently adopted and the first half of the 1960s, there are also significant differences. Though there had formally been a judicial and legal system in the period immediately before 1966, it had largely been in disgrace following the 'Hundred Flowers Movement' of May 1957, and could hardly be regarded as a lively part of the state *apparat*. Similarly, though people's congresses existed between the Great Leap Forward and the Cultural Revolution, they met infrequently (often without even annual sessions) and in considerable secrecy. Except for the NPC, no government work reports, budgets and plans were published, and even at national level such statements were couched in very general terms. Indeed, from 1961 to 1977 there was almost no official publication of economic statistics and similar detailed information.

Certain aspects of the new Electoral Law, similarly, have no precedents before 1966. For example, previously, even elections to the county people's congress had been indirect rather than direct; and though there had been no regulation concerning the number of candidates for each place to be filled, it had not been the usual practice for there to be more candidates than places. Again, though the seven so-called 'Democratic parties' (that is, those accepting the CCP's leadership after 1949, and, in the party's theory, representing 'non-antagonistic' classes other than the working class and peasantry) formally participated in the state's organisation during the early 1960s – for example, Zhou Jianren (Lu Xun's brother and a biologist of international standing) was Governor of Zhejiang province – in fact they too were criticised in the wake of the 'Hundred Flowers Movement' and their involvement decreased thereafter. However, as part of the recent reforms, not only have the 'Democratic parties' been revived as organisations, but for the first time since the early 1950s they have started to recruit new members. Finally, the introduction of a certain amount of economic decentralisation to enterprise level is a completely new departure. Although that had been under discussion during the mid-1950s and provided for in the first draft of the Second Five Year Plan, in fact it was never implemented. In its place, as already noted, administrative decentralisation to the provincial level was introduced during 1957–8.

The significance of those differences to the situation as it existed immediately before the Cultural Revolution is that it suggests more of a return to the mid-1950s than to the first half of the 1960s. Before 1958 the state was a more functioning organisation, even given the limits imposed by the CCP's direction and involvement, than it was later to become. At all levels, people's congresses had met regularly and more openly, receiving government work reports, plans and budgets. Moreover, there had been a functioning judicial and legal system; and the 'Democratic parties' could be considered active, if restrained, political organisations. However, the real relevance of the mid-1950s to the more recent reforms is that the earlier period was one of debate and discussion. Between the second session of the 1st NPC in the summer of 1955 and the third plenum of the 8th central committee in the autumn of 1957, the CCP decided to abandon the Soviet model of development and debated its replacement. Though that debate was primarily concerned with economic development, it necessarily entailed discussion of the state's organisation. Thus, a major topic of discussion was the extent and form of decentralisation (for a general account see MacFarquhar, 1974). In the wider debate, reforms were proposed and adopted, though never implemented after 1957, that in many ways are the direct ancestors of the reforms promoted since 1976. For example, Chen Yun, probably the most important architect of economic policy since 1976, first outlined his programme for economic development during 1956. One of his proposals was for decentralisation, not just administratively to provincial level, but also economically to the basic level, in both industry and agriculture (Schurmann, 1968, p. 86). It is interesting to note that though Zhao Ziyang, the current premier, has received considerable publicity for his experimental implementation of economic decentralisation to the basic level in Sichuan when he was that province's first party secretary after 1975, that reform had been promoted not only by Chen Yun but also by Li Jingquan, one of Zhao's predecessors in Sichuan, during 1956.

More important still are the reasons for the non-implementation after 1957 of the reforms agreed in 1956. Before 1976, it was fashionable for Western academic scholarship to argue that the severity of the economic crisis that became apparent in the second half of 1957 enabled Mao to persuade the rest of the national leadership to adopt his programme for economic development (as later enshrined in the Great Leap Forward), rather than the more gradual (and probably more realistic) Second Five Year Plan (see, for instance, MacFarquhar, 1974, pp. 293ff). However, since 1976, with the re-evaluation of PRC history both inside and outside China, considerably greater emphasis has been placed on Mao's role in abrogating organisational and political norms. Thus, for example, Teiwes has argued that it was during 1955–7, that Mao changed the rules of politics within both the CCP and the PRC in general. In his view, the post-1976 reaction to the Cultural Revolution, and its subsequent reforms, are in fact a reaction to the process initiated by Mao during the mid-1950s (1979, pp. 601ff). It is a view shared by at least some of the current leadership of the PRC, in substance if not in rhetoric. Though it is the 'pernicious influence of Lin Biao and the Gang of Four' that is held responsible for the emergence of 'feudal fascism' in general, that phenomenon is not limited to the decade of the Cultural Revolution. As previously noted, Li Honglin has traced the origins of 'feudal fascism' back to the Great Leap Forward in 1958, and, by implication, Mao's personal intervention. Nor is he alone in appearing to take that stance against Mao's disrespect for organisational and political norms. A conference organised in early 1979 by the CCP Propaganda Department shortly after the decisive third plenum of the 11th Central Committee concluded that Mao had been guilty of 'left adventurism' after 1957. It is a conclusion that seems to have gained wide support. For example, Lu Dingyi, in a 1979 article to the memory of Zhou Enlai, criticised Mao's behaviour at the Lushan Plenum of 1959; and the leading economist Xue Muqiao, in a major speech in the same year to a conference organised by the State Economic Commission, took Mao to task for insisting on the pursuit of his policies no matter what, pointing out that a 'leftist' error was not necessarily the best antidote for a 'rightist' deviation, for in the final analysis it was still an error. Though there can be little doubt that Mao's post-1976 critics disagreed with the contents of his policies, they disliked his methods even more.

Two reasons may be suggested for the CCP's reluctance to 'reverse the verdict' on the whole of the period since 1957, and its apparent continued insistence on a return to the status quo of the early 1960s. The first is the question of legitimacy. Deng Xiaoping, and other national leaders, have repeatedly stressed that a 'crisis of faith' in the regime by the population has become manifest and must be resolved. In a real sense Mao can be seen as both the cause of that 'crisis' (through the Cultural Revolution) and its solution (as author of the regime's ideology). Thus the resolution of the sixth plenum of the 11th central committee of the CCP, as has already been noted, deliberately created a distinction between Mao Zedong Thought and Mao's political activities. If somewhat cynically, clumsily, and in a not altogether convincing manner, that resolution does attempt to differentiate between criticism of Mao and criticism of the Cultural Revolution. However, criticism of the 1950s would necessarily challenge any basis for the newly refurbished Mao Zedong Thought. It is for that reason that the 'spirit of the 8th party congress' (of 1956) has been re-invoked and heavily publicised in the approach to the 12th national party congress in 1982. The historical irony of that situation is that whereas the CCP's new state constitution claims 'Marxism–Leninism, Mao Zedong Thought' as its guiding ideology, that of 1956 omitted any reference to the latter. The second reason, which may perhaps be related to the first, is that there may well be a divide within the national leadership. Clearly there are those, particularly among the economic planners – for example, Xue Muqiao and Sun Yefang – who regard the policies pursued from 1957 to 1977 with extreme disfavour. On the other hand, there are those, like Deng Xiaoping, who for various reasons at least publicly have a more positive attitude towards Mao and the policies of the late 1950s. In other words, it seems possible that the leadership is united only in its opposition, and not in its prognosis, and so the rhetoric of politics reflects their lowest common denominator.

The PRC and the Soviet model

The argument that recent state reforms in the PRC represent a return to the 'organisational orthodoxy' of the Soviet Union and Eastern Europe seems rather unconvincing, not least because it is difficult to ascertain when, if ever, the PRC had conformed to such an orthodoxy. Though the PRC adopted a Soviet model for its development during the early 1950s, it is largely a myth that it subsequently implanted the Soviet Union's organisational forms *in toto*, or that those which were adopted remained permanently. It is certainly true that during the first four years of the First Five Year Plan (1952–7) the PRC's economic administration was highly centralised and the central ministries dominant in the state *apparat*. However, an over-simplistic model of a communist party state as a centralised political system in which the party hierarchy parallels the state *apparat* has never really been an appropriate description of the PRC. As far as its state *apparat* is concerned the PRC's lack of conformity is revealed through even a brief consideration of its non-central government, and the relationships between the state and other hierarchies.

An obvious but non the less important determinant of government and politics in the PRC has been its guerilla heritage from before 1949. Both before and after the Long March (1934–6) the communist movement had established base areas not only for military purposes but also in order to create rural soviets. However, the requirements of guerilla warfare meant that the communist movement's cadres had to be soldier, administrator, political leader, as well as peasant. For long periods the CCP was in effect the Red Army (the PLA's forerunner) and vice versa. The lack of differentiation between the party and administrative hierarchies in the base areas, and between cadres' roles in the CCP and local governments, undoubtedly helps to explain why the maintenance of a party–state distinction has proved so difficult since 1949. Those who came to power at all levels of the politico-administrative system in 1949 had been trained in and emerged from the guerilla tradition. In 1949 the PRC's cadres were relatively young, and to a large extent the generation that came to power then have remained in office ever since. Though it might be reasonable to assume that the technicalities of state administration after 1949 would have created greater role differentiation, that was to a certain extent counter-balanced by the success of Mao's appeal to revive the guerilla heritage (the 'Yanan tradition'), an integral part of his vision for the PRC's future development from the mid-1950s on.

Moreover, just as the guerilla heritage had influenced party–state relations, so too has it affected party–state–military relations. As already noted, the PRC has described itself as comprising three major hierarchies, one of which has been the PLA. Ever since 1949, except for a brief period during 1955–7, the PLA has played an active role in civilian politics. At times, such as between 1949 and 1952 and during 1967–71, the PLA *qua* organisation has been institutionally involved in the state's administration. Throughout, PLA cadres (that is, currently serving PLA cadres, and regardless of the not insignificant fact that most post-1949 cadres of any description had a military background) have held civilian positions in both party and state. Conversely, party and state cadres have held positions in the PLA. Thus, for example, since the mid-1950s it has been common practice for the posts of party secretaries (CCP) and political commissars (PLA) in any one province (each province is also a military district) to be held by the same individuals. Although the extent of PLA involvement in civilian affairs has varied over time, largely as a result of changes in the CCP's general line, none the less it has remained considerable. Even during the period since 1976, when role differentiation has been emphasised, the by now traditional relationship between military and civilian has been retained. Thus, for example, as of April 1978, 10 per cent of provincial party secretaries and almost 11 per cent of provincial leading cadres in the state *apparat* were also currently-serving PLA cadres.

A further effect of the CCP's guerilla heritage has been an appreciation of the need for considerable local flexibility in implementing policy, which to some extent has countered the over-centralisation usually associated with the 'Soviet model'. Before 1949 each communist base area operated more or less independently, and on occasion had to in order to survive. Though attempting to maintain political and ideological unity through rectification campaigns, the CCP also recognised the need for a high degree of local flexibility. In the early 1940s, the CCP adopted the administrative principle of 'Do the best according to local conditions' for the implementation of central policies and directives. Since 1949, that administrative principle has quite explicitly been retained. Generally, in any campaign, the centre lays down the broad outlines for policy implementation but leaves the concrete arrangements to the localities. It is even possible for some areas either to fail or to be excused from implementating policies on the grounds that 'local conditions are not suitable at present'. Thus, for example, during the early 1950s when land reform was national policy, those areas inhabited by non-Chinese peoples were largely exempted from the campaign since it was claimed that other social reforms (such as the abolition of slavery) were of a higher priority.

Finally, the applicability of an over-centralised 'Soviet model' to the PRC is brought into question by the roles of the regional and provincial levels of administration since 1949. From 1949 to 1952, the PRC was administered to a large extent by the six regional military and administrative committees whose boundaries largely resulted from the PLA's pattern of final conquest, with each region having been occupied by one of the PLA's Field Armies. Each region covered several provinces; its government involved CCP, state, and PLA cadres, as well as leading local notables sympathetic to the CCP without actually being members; and its responsibilities were wideranging. In 1952 a major attempt to establish central economic ministries was launched, and military involvement in regional administration decreased. None the less, until 1954 the region remained as a counter-balance to centralisation. Though it is true that the state *apparat* was at its most centralised immediately after 1952 with the introduction of the administrative principle of 'vertical rule', that changed in and after 1956. Discussions at the third session of the NPC in the summer, and at the 8th national CCP congress in September 1956, revealed the near-unanimous criticism that the system was too inflexible and centralised. Two reforms followed. First of all, at the regional level economic co-ordinative areas were established. Though little is known about their specific activities it is certain that they existed until 1961, and probable that their functions were taken over by the regional party bureaux that operated from 1961 to the Cultural Revolution. More important were the adoption of the administrative principle of 'dual rule' and of the decentralisation of the functions of many of the central economic ministries, both of which resulted in the enhanced importance of the provincial level. Whereas previously within the state *apparat* each unit at any level had been subordinated solely to the unit at the immediately superior level within the same organisation (the former had, in other words, been the branch agency of the latter), 'dual rule' additionally subordinated each unit to the party committee at the same level. Decentralisation reduced the number of central economic ministries, devolved many of their functions to the provincial level, and transformed the provincial party committee into a co-ordinating committee for state as well as party activities. Though equivalent in many ways to centralisation at the provincial level, central ministries have since had to share authority with provincial administration.

Final observations

There can be little doubt that the intention of recent state reforms in the PRC is for radical change. However, unless it is assumed that the PRC's past experience is completely irrelevant to its future, the impact of those reforms is likely to be more limited than may at first sight seem apparent. Those reforms have officially been presented as a reaction to the Cultural Revolution. Here it has been suggested that in interpreting the possible results of those reforms it is their wider historical context that is of greater importance. Rather than concentrating on recent reforms as a reaction to the Cultural Revolution, it is perhaps more useful to see them as a reaction to Mao-dominated politics from the mid-1950s up to his death. As has been noted here and elsewhere (Goodman, 1980, 1981a), it is easy to over-emphasise the organisational and associational changes wrought by the Cultural Revolution. Without for a minute wishing to minimise the dramatic impact of some aspects of the Cultural Revolution (particularly during 1966–9), it is none the less possible to argue that the political changes it invoked were not as revolutionary as is often claimed, and were in many ways a development of practices pursued (by at least some members of the national leadership) since the mid-1950s. In that context, the apparent resurrection of the state *apparat* becomes the re-assertion of the CCP as an organisation in its own right. Mao bent and broke the rules of organisational behaviour, and after his death the CCP is attempting to regularise its own internal politics and its leadership of the state and society in general. Deng Xiaoping, in a report to the Politburo during August 1980 (which first became available outside the PRC in April 1981) concerning the reforms in party and state leadership, was relatively explicit: for example,

> From the Tsunyi Conference to the period of socialist reformation, both the Central Committee of the Party and Comrade Mao Tse-tung paid greater attention to the practice of collective leadership and democratic centralism . . . It is a pity that these good traditions have not been sustained, nor were they developed into a strict and perfect system . . . After . . . [1958 and 1959] democratic life in the Party and the state gradually became abnormal. This gave rise to the patriarchial phenomena characterized by one man speaking for all, the deciding of

important questions by an individual, the personality cult, the riding of an individual on the organization, etc. . . . without thorough elimination of this patriarchal work style, there can be no intra-party democracy or socialist democracy to speak of.

Having outlined the reforms under consideration, Deng concluded:

> To change the leadership system of the party and state is not aimed at weakening the party's leadership or slackening the party's discipline; on the contrary, it is for upholding and strengthening the Party's leadership as well as discipline . . . The core of the four principles to which we must hold fast is the party's leadership. The problem is that the Party must be skilled in leadership.

The parallel with the revival of 'party life' in the Soviet Union following Stalin's death is too obvious to avoid. Whether, despite the PRC's peculiarities as a communist party state, such parallels can be taken further is a task for the future.

PART III
THE RULING PARTIES

There can be little dispute about the centrality of a ruling communist party to a political system of the Marxist-Leninist type. Indeed, the presence of such a party has been taken, by the communist authorities as well as by outside observers, to be virtually the defining characteristic of such a system. The ruling party may be called a communist (as in the USSR and China) or a united or socialist workers' party (as in Poland and Hungary respectively); it may hold power by itself (as in the USSR, China, Yugoslavia, Albania and elsewhere), or it may permit other parties to contest elections within a joint umbrella organisation variously called a national or people's front (as, for instance, in Bulgaria, Czechoslovakia and the GDR). In none of the communist-ruled countries, however, is a genuinely oppositional party, or even a genuinely oppositional candidate, permitted to stand for office; other parties, if they exist, have a limited or negligible role within the political system and generally exist for purely historical or propagandistic reasons. Within the ruling party itself power is typically highly centralised, thanks to the operation of two important principles: the doctrine of democratic centralism, which provides for the electibility and accountability of office-holders but also for majority rule and the subordination of lower bodies to those above them, and the 'ban on factions', first introduced in the Soviet party in 1921, which prohibits the formation of organised groups in opposition to or even in support of the central party leadership. In turn the ruling party is supposed to play a 'leading role' within its society, guiding or directing all aspects of public life through its control over appointments (the *nomenklatura* system), through its caucuses of activists in all elected bodies, and through the supervision of state and public affairs by its full-time central apparatus.

The first chapter in this section, by John H. Miller, examines in detail the structure and role of the oldest and most influential ruling party, the Communist Party of the Soviet Union, devoting particular attention to the changing composition of the party's mass membership and leading personnel. The second chapter, by David S. Mason, examines the rather more troubled history of the Polish United Workers' Party in the early 1980s, and shows the effect upon the party of the formation of Solidarity and of other changes in Polish public life up to and beyond the imposition of military rule in 1981. The revival in the fortunes of the Cuban Communist Party in the late 1970s is the subject of William M. LeoGrande's chapter; and this section concludes with a consideration by Tony Saich of the changes in the structure and functioning of the Chinese Communist Party since the death of Mao Zedong in 1976. Although important similarities are readily apparent, the varied performance of ruling parties in each of these different national contexts suggests that the nature of party dominance may be powerfully affected by the particular circumstances of the country within which it is exercised.

7

The Soviet Communist Party: Trends and Problems

JOHN H. MILLER

The management of the party in society

It makes sense to picture Soviet leaders as convinced and thoroughgoing Hobbesians, so persuaded of the precariousness of social cohesion and so appalled at the prospect of social breakdown as to rate the absolute position of the sovereign as a supreme value in politics. They are Hobbesians, moreover, not Machiavellians, because they seek the bulwark against social breakdown in an institutional arrangement, the Communist Party of the Soviet Union, and not in the personal qualities of the sovereign. If we imagine Soviet leaders proceeding from a serious conviction of the actual superiority of one-party (absolute) government over other forms, we find a great many of the familiar but characteristic features of Soviet politics, ideological, stylistic and institutional, taking their place in a coherent pattern.

First, it directs our attention away from the prevalent assumption that the essence of Marxist-Leninist ideology is to be sought in principles, priorities, ideals determining policy content or governmental output. Following that line one becomes enmeshed in the attempt to disentangle 'sincere' beliefs from tactics and public relations. Yet, at the same time, commonsense and elementary testing suggest that there *are* principles of government, which, in simple and unambiguous sense, the Soviet leaders hold dear and act upon; and they suggest further that these principles lie in the field not of policy content, but of *social organisation and management*. They are beliefs, in fact, about how organised society holds, or is held, together, and they bear such familiar labels as 'party supremacy', the 'vanguard role of the party', 'democratic centralism', the ban on faction in

Reprinted with adaptations from Archie Brown and Michael Kaser (eds), *Soviet Policy for the 1980s* (London: Macmillan and Bloomington: Indiana University Press, 1982), with the permission of the author and publishers.

the party. It is perfectly reasonable to treat these as the active, operative aspects of ideology for the Soviet leadership, and to suspend judgement on the question of how these aspects relate to the rest of the ideological corpus.

Second, such stylistic features of Soviet politics as the intense (and utterly non-Marxist) concern with security, control and social order; the publicity given to political participation, but participation only in the implementation, not in the making of policy; the acknowledgement of interest-diversity combined with the lack of institutional form for its public expression, and hence the tendency for political communication to develop along personalist and clientelist lines; the half-heartedness of arrangements for the public arbitration of political disputes: all these are features that should be expected of politics conducted by, and within, a single and sovereign political organisation.

Institutionally the key elements of the party's position in society are also entailed in a thorough and radical application of the principle of one-party government. Crucial to the maintenance of the party's pre-eminent 'vanguard' role in society are: (i) the licensing of other, 'non-party' organisations and meetings (Khazikov, 1964, pp. 111–12); (ii) the centralised control by party officials of all staffing, party and non-party, under the so-called *nomenklatura* system (Harasymiw, 1969); (iii) the penetration of other organisations and meetings by party members and the obligation of the latter to meet separately as a group (*Ustav*, paras 68 and 34); (iv) the control of communications by means of standardised curricula and censorship of the media (Matthews, 1974, pp. 71–3; see also *Ustav*, paras 34, 42(b), 45 and 49).

Some of these procedures underpinning the party's vanguard position in society have to be worked by comparatively junior party officials, or by ordinary party members. So the maintenance of the party's position is linked closely with the maintenance of internal discipline and cohesiveness among party members. In fact the institutions for promoting the latter (listed below) often bear a strong resemblance to the institutions for maintaining the party's social position, allotting to party officials a role within the party analogous to the role of the party within society.

(1)   The ban on groups with a distinct, organised platform within the party, the shorthand for which is 'factionalism' (Matthews, 1974, pp. 149–51; for the contemporary version, see *Ustav*, Preamble and para. 26). Although the original ban was on organised platforms (many of which are familiar by name from the 1918–21 period), its effect in practice would seem to have been to inhibit the ordinary party member from canvassing or lobbying for a position before meetings, and hence to hand over the dominant role in policy-planning and the steering of decisions to party officials, part of whose job it is to draft

policy (including policy alternatives and 'contingency' plans) and to organise its formal acceptance.

(2) The doctrine known as 'democratic centralism' (*Ustav*, para. 19). This amounts in practice to the centralised, heirarchical management of party appointments and party communications, with permanent officials, not meetings, processing the important documents at all levels. It is, however, a doctrine of 'informed centralism': a positive effort is made to collect social information from all walks of life supplementary to that supplied by the state bureaucratic networks (*Ustav*, paras 2(g), 42(f), 60).

(3) The careful regulation of admission to the party through a system of fourfold checks: references from party members of at least five years' standing; approval by a party meeting usually at one's place of work; approval by party officials at the next highest administrative level; and a period of a year's probation (*Ustav*, paras 4, 5, 14–16).

On the basis of all the above, a working definition of the CPSU might be: 'the One Political Organisation, into which the maximum of society's decision-makers, and the maximum of communications to and from them are drawn'. Simply to state this as a claim made concerning a society of 270 million people is to invite the thought that there must be an immense investment in the promotion, maintenance and protection of such a role in society. Let us call the staff in charge of this sector of party tasks the party 'managers' as distinct from the party leaders. It is reasonable to assume that the party managers have thought seriously, have accumulated and evaluated experience, and formulated rules and practices governing their work, and that we should see rules and practices being applied as the party responds to the challenges of the 1980s. Unfortunately, documentation of these guidelines for the post-Stalin period is sparse, and so the next stages of this argument have to be deductive.

First, it is entailed in the role that the party claims for itself in society that party membership will include certain types of people:

(1) All (or virtually all) persons who take, or interpret, decisions at any level in society, plus those who might be needed to replace them, and a substantial proportion of those who influence or communicate decisions. This will give the party a commanding presence, inter alia, among people who appoint or supervise the work of others; communicators in the media and education; the armed forces, police and security; and people in a position to affect economic output (see Rigby, 1968, ch. 14).

(2) A second, much larger group whose function is to permeate all walks of ordinary, non-party life, to gather and report information, to mobilise local opinion and lead local activity, and to verify performance (*Ustav*, paras 2, 68).

Party members in the first of these groups would number not less than two million, and those in the second group about twelve million. The second group are important. Their information-gathering and local leadership are functions that have to be performed by someone in society; if not by party members, then by some other group or groups who could thereby encroach upon party supremacy. And their qualifications and attributes as party members matter, if they are to do their job reliably, and serve as a field for recruitment into the first group.

Thus far, functional imperatives seem to suggest a surprisingly large party presence in society, a good deal larger, for instance, than the proportion of people with tertiary degrees in Britain. The party managers are certainly aware that too exclusive or selective an admissions policy carries with it the risk of losing touch with social groupings or swings in the popular mood and, perhaps more importantly, the risk of driving talented and articulate persons into independent collective action, perhaps organised, perhaps oppositionist. The rise of dissidence since the mid-1960s must have reinforced this belief.

On the other hand, it is abundantly clear that the notion of the party as a vanguard is perceived as setting upper limits to the party's presence in society. If there were unrestricted entry into the party, it would sink from its position of the 'leading and guiding force of Soviet society' (*Ustav*, Preamble, and USSR Constitution, art. 6) to being the place where all social interests are pooled and aggregated, a sort of forum for collective bargaining. The warning that 'numerical growth is not an end in itself' and that neglect of this 'spreads dissension in the (party) ranks' (*zasoryayut eë ryady*) is sounded clearly in an important Central Committee decree of July 1965, one which signalled the end to a period of rapid expansion in party membership (*Partiinaya zhizn'* [hereafter *P.zh.*], 1965, no. 15, pp. 23–5). Similar diagnoses were apparently made three years later about the way in which Czechoslovak party membership had been managed (Wightman and Brown, 1975, p. 413). It sounds very much therefore as if the party managers regard admission into the party as a matter of striking a delicate balance, between, on the one hand, the maximum engagement of society's influentials (with the concomitant risk of devaluation of its vanguard role) and, on the other hand, maintenance of admission standards (which could foster an isolated elitism). Thus it is likely that the party managers have a working notion of the optimum size of the party presence, in society as a whole, and perhaps also in particular social groups; in the latter case the optimum figure would vary with the group's political importance. The principal hypothesis of this chapter is that it will be policy to achieve and maintain an optimum party presence in society, and in individual social groups, particularly groups which can affect decisions, output or the public mood.

All the signs are that, with small exceptions, the party managers believe they have achieved this optimum, and that their current task is to maintain equilibrium. This might seem a routine and unimportant task, but it is almost certainly not so; rapid social change, some planned and some not amenable to planning, and in particular social change affecting some groups more than others, has an immediate effect on people's understanding of their eligibility for party membership, or on the party managers' perceptions of the optimum party presence. So there arises what has been termed the 'dilemma of party growth' (Hammer, 1971).

Suppose that group X – an example of such a group would be the holders of tertiary degrees – had undergone above average growth in size or in eligibility for party membership, the latter being gauged from past practice. The party managers can then choose one of three alternative policies for party recruitment from group X:

(1) They can maintain what they see as optimum party 'saturation' of society as a whole, but allow an increase in party admissions among group X. If this group is sizeable the consequence will sooner or later be a reduction in party admissions somewhere else in society.
(2) They can maintain current admission levels both in society and in group X. This carries with it the risk of disaffection in group X, particularly if those turned away from the party are articulate or have alternative foci of loyalty.
(3) They can concede increased recruitment in group X, and in other groups as well, so that overall party saturation increases. This was the course pursued under Krushchev and repudiated by the Brezhnev leadership, seemingly because of the damage it could cause to the party's vanguard status.

As a problem for the 1980s the party managers may expect to encounter the dilemma of party growth among certain socio-economic groups as education and economic complexity increases; or among regional and ethnic groups in consequence of demographic trends.

If there is competition for admission to party membership – and all the signs are that this is the case in most parts of the USSR – then the word 'optimum' will have to be interpreted in a qualitative as well as a quantitative sense. People should be let into the party because an efficient purpose is thought to be served by this, rather than for such formal or routine reasons as that it goes with the job or runs in the family. To the precautions against the party losing touch through underrepresentation in certain areas of society must be added precautions against those representatives becoming insensitive because they are too old, or have come to take their social and political position as a matter of right. These, too, are problems that a party in its seventh decade of sole power might be expected to encounter.

Party Membership In The 1970s And 1980s: Data And Trends

Total party presence in society

Table 7.1 reveals the rapid – one might almost say heedless – way in which the party expanded its ranks when N. S. Khrushchev was first secretary. If growth rates of that period had continued, there would now be 28 million persons (one in every six adults) in the party! Instead the growth rate was halved by the new leadership, and the public signal for this seems to have been the Central Committee decree of August 1965 mentioned above. The growth rate was halved again in the 1971–76 period. Examination of regional growth rates (of which more below) shows that they may vary quite considerably from the national figure; but whatever their absolute level, these growth rates were also generally halved around 1966 and again in 1971. This suggests the thought that party admissions targets were handed down for the five-year inter-congress periods (that they were five-year plans, in fact), and that they took the form of directives to halve current net growth rates. In the latter part of the 1970s party growth rates have risen again somewhat, possible reasons for which will be touched on below.

The size of the party's presence among those eligible to join is most conveniently worked out as a percentage of those aged 20 or above in the population. Table 7.1 shows how this 'party saturation rate' (PSR) increased dramatically during the Khrushchev administration, and then only very slowly during the 1970s. Table 7.3 shows that the party saturation of the employed population has also risen slowly during the Brezhnev period, from 10.5 per cent to about 11 per cent. At the most recent party congresses in the Union Republics mention was made by more than one party first secretary of the fact that the local party now included one in ten

TABLE 7.1   *CPSU growth and saturation of USSR adult population*

	Party (members and candidates)	Growth over five-year period %	Adult population (aged 20 and above)	Percentage of adults in party (PSR*)
1956	7 173 521	—	(125 885 000)	5.7
1961	9 275 826	+29.3	(135 246 000)	6.9
1966	12 357 308	33.2	(144 165 000)	8.6
1971	14 372 563	16.3	(152 281 000)	9.4
1976	15 638 891	8.8	(165 767 000)	9.4
1981	17 430 413	11.5	(178 874 000)	9.7

Figures in brackets are estimates.
* Party saturation rate.

Sources: *P.zh.* 21/77, p. 21 and 14/18, p. 17; *Itogi . . . 1970*, vol. II, pp. 12–13; *Naselenie SSSR . . .*, pp. 69 and 141; *Narkhoz, SSSR 1975*, pp. 40 and 43.

of the employed population (*kazhdyi desyatyi rabotayushchii*) (Shcherbitsky, 1971; Rashidov, 1971). Is it possible that they were referring to the fulfilment of a target, and that 10 per cent of the employed population is the optimum party saturation figure aimed at by the party managers? As a target it would have the great advantage that it could be monitored where most party admissions occur – at the workplace; knowledge of demographic trends would not be required.

Party membership by education and occupation

For an understanding of the way in which the socio-economic composition of the CPSU is changing, Tables 7.2 and 7.3 need to be read in conjunction with each other. From Table 7.2 one of the most important of recent social developments is at once apparent: holders of tertiary qualifications have more than doubled in 14 years, and persons with the completed secondary qualification called 'secondary specialist' have increased nearly as fast. And the party managers' response to this is equally clear: they have adopted the first of the strategies foreshadowed above, admitting tertiary graduates into the party at a rate almost commensurate with their output in society, and far outpacing overall party growth rates. So graduates have increased in 14 years from 16.5 per cent to 28 per cent of the party, and party saturation of the poorly educated – already low – is declining. The change is massive and rapid; as Unger has pointed out (1977, p. 313), annual increases in tertiary qualifications in the party – many acquired by people in the party, of course – were the equivalent of 80 per cent of overall party growth in the early 1970s. That figure seems to have slackened off in the late 1970s, because all-round party growth has increased; in terms of the above analysis, because an element of strategy (3), the Khrushchevian one, has been introduced. But the basic picture of the increasing dominance of the party, and especially of entrants to the party, by the highly qualified till stands.

Table 7.3 presents two puzzling features at first sight, one of which is resolved in part by the trends derived from Table 7.2. First, the party has presented it as a matter of urgency for many years that the working-class element in its membership be increased. If this has been successful, why is it not reflected in an increased share in the party by workers in 'material production'? The answer to this is, in part, that such an increase has been masked by the other, less publicised, drive to maintain party saturation among the educated. When the latter slackened slightly, in the late 1970s, a tendency for material production to reassert its position can just be detected.

The second puzzle about Table 7.3 is as follows. Party saturation of different sectors of the economy has not changed dramatically, in the way that education statistics have, and such increases as have occurred – in

TABLE 7.2   *Party membership and levels of education*

| | People with completed tertiary qualifications | | PSR | % of |
	in the population	in the party		whole party
1967	(6 674 000)	2 097 055	31.4	16.5
1970	8 261 541	(2 618 000)	31.7	18.7
1973	(10 040 000)	3 209 605	32.0	21.7
1977	(13 019 000)	4 008 986	30.8	25.1
1979	14 826 000	(4 424 000)	29.8	26.5
1981	(16 400 000?)	4 881 877	29.8?	28.0

| | People with secondary specialist qualifications | | PSR | % of |
	in the population	in the party		whole party
1967	(11 603 000)	2 574 162	22.2	20.3
1970	13 420 241	(2 937 000)	21.9	21.0
1973	(16 162 000)	3 351 395	20.7	22.6
1977	(20 707 000)	3 915 346	18.9	24.5
1979	23 439 000	(4 129 000)	17.6	24.7
1981	(25 900 000?)	4 355 000	16.8	25.0

| | People with primary, incomplete secondary or secondary general education | | PSR | % of |
	in the population	in the party		whole party
1967	(118 489 000)	7 686 931	6.5	60.6
1970	128 405 693	(8 017 000)	6.2	57.2
1973	(135 821 000)	7 931 538	5.8	53.5
1977	(146 378 000)	7 689 795	5.3	48.1
1979	151 960 000	(7 746 000)	5.1	46.3
1981	(156 900 000?)	7 802 000	5.0	44.8

Figures in brackets by interpolation or extrapolation.

Sources: *Itogi . . . 1970*, vol. III, pp. 6–7; *Vestnik statistiki* 6/80, p. 41; *P.zh.* 14/73, pp. 16–17; 21/77, pp. 29–30; 14/81, p. 17.

construction and agriculture – and such decreases – in administration, science, education and health, transport and communications – are not such as to suggest particular recruitment among the skilled and qualified. But it must be remembered that these are data about sectors of the economy; *within* these sectors we have only the sketchiest idea about the distribution of skill or income. The fact that Table 7.3 reflects virtually none of the immense changes revealed by Table 7.2 suggests that these have been changes *within* individual economic sectors.

Table 7.4, which concerns party members in white-collar employment (*sluzhashchie po rodu zanyatii*) throws light on the situation, even though we do not know the absolute numbers of white-collar employees involved.

TABLE 7.3 *Employment of communists in branches of the economy*

Party members and candidates employed in:	1967			1977			1981		
	No.	PSR	% of whole party	No.	PSR	% of whole party	No.	PSR	% of whole party
I *Material production*									
Industry	3 195 718	11.0	25.2	3 968 712	11.2	24.8	(6 697 000)	10.9	38.4
Construction	666 380	8.7	5.3	1 069 939	9.8	6.7			
Transport	838 019	11.2	6.6	947 612	9.9	5.9			
Communications	(112 000)	10.0	0.9	(125 000)	7.9	0.8			
Collective farms	1 330 316	7.3	10.5	1 371 435	9.5	8.6	(1 427 000)	11.0	8.2
State farms	1 006 096	10.7	7.9	1 273 194	11.6	8.0	(1 413 000)	12.0	8.1
Trade, catering and supply	(464 000)	7.1	3.7	(568 000)	6.2	3.6			
Miscellaneous	(122 000)	6.9	1.0	(133 000)	7.4	0.8	(820 000)	7.0	4.7
Subtotal	(7 735 000)	9.5	61.0	(9 457 000)	10.1	59.1	(10 357 000)	10.6	59.4
II *Non-material branches of the economy*									
Science, education, health and culture	(1 741 000)	12.0	13.7	(2 145 000)	10.7	13.4	(2 275 000)	10.3	13.1
Administration	(939 000)	47.4	7.4	(1 098 000)	38.3	6.9	(1 229 000)	38.0	7.1
Housing and services	139 386	5.2	1.1	222 014	5.5	1.4	(269 000)	5.7	1.5
Subtotal	(2 817 000)	14.7	22.2	(3 463 000)	12.9	21.7	(3 773 000)	12.6	21.6
Total Communists employed in the national economy:	(10 552 000)	10.5	83.2	(12 920 000)	10.7	80.8	(14 130 000)	11.0	81.1
Communists not employed in the national economy:	(2 132 000)	?	16.8	(3 074 000)	?	19.2	(3 300 000)	?	18.9
Total party personnel	12 684 133			15 994 476			17 430 413		

Figures in brackets by calculation.

Sources: *P.zh.*, 21/77, pp. 33–5; 14/81, pp. 19–20; *Narkhoz 1967*, pp. 492, 648–9; *1977*, pp. 276, 378; *1979*, pp. 290, 387–8.

It is clear that party membership has increased among two particular groups of white-collar employees: supervisory personnel (*rukovoditeli*) and the technically qualified. Whatever absolute number we attribute to the total of white-collar Communists in Table 7.4, the number of them in routine clerical occupations, and also in the politically innocuous sectors of trade, catering and supply, has stayed static, or, quite possibly, fallen. That is, within all economic sectors, recruitment has been concentrated in the decision-making, supervisory and specialist grades and has ignored the less senior and the less qualified. This can be seen as an attempt to

TABLE 7.4   *Distribution of communists in white-collar employment*

Of all Communists in white-collar employment:	1967 %	1977 %	1981 %
Heads of institutions, organisations and their structural subdivisions at county level or higher:	4.7	5.5	
Heads and deputy heads of economic enterprises:	3.2	3.6	9.4
Engineers and technical personnel, agricultural specialists:	34.9	40.4	42.0
Employees in science, education, health, literature and art:	23.6	24.2	23.4
Subtotal	66.4	73.7	74.8
Employees in trade, catering and supply:	5.5	4.3	4.1
Unspecified white-collar employees:	28.1	22.0	21.1
Subtotal	33.6	26.3	25.2
Grand total	100.0	100.0	100.0

Source: *P. zh.*, 21/77, p. 28; 14/81, p. 17.

maximise the efficiency of the party presence (see above p. 140) and to serve notice to rank-and-file white-collar employees (who in Stalin's time would have had high expectations of entry into the party) that white-collar status (or parentage?) is no longer enough. To have increased the selectivity of party admissions along these lines without significant effects on party saturation by economic sector has arguably been an operation requiring care and skill.

Class and social mobility of communists

It was noted above that we do not know how many Communists are in white-collar occupations. We do, of course, possess the standard Soviet threefold class breakdown – into workers, peasants, or employees (*sluzhashchie*) – of party members by what is termed their 'social position' (*sotsial'noe polozhenie*), that is their class affiliation at the time of joining the party, which must amount to a classification, typically, of their first job, or that of their parents, if they are not yet in employment. Extracts from such data are given in the top left quarter of Table 7.5. It has been taken for granted for a long time that these statistics of the social 'position' underestimate the proportion of Communists actually in white-collar employment; the discrepancies between the social position data and the education statistics in Table 7.2, for instance, seem insoluble, unless we make that assumption. That is, it has been taken for granted that there is significant mobility of party members out of the worker and peasant classes into the white-collar, 'employee' class during – and connected with – their party membership.

It now seems possible to put an approximate figure to this mobility, using regional statistics, that have become available recently, which distribute party members both by social position and by class of current employment. Table 7.5 shows the sums of these data for 15 regional party organisations comprising about a quarter of the total membership (see Miller, 1982, p. 32 n. 43). A fairly regular picture emerges from the regional statistics: that 10 or 11 per cent of employed Communists are persons of worker or peasant social position who have moved into white-collar employment. Transposed into national terms, it is likely that about 56 per cent of employed Communists (or seven and a quarter million) were in white-collar occupations in the 1970s, and about 20 per cent of *these* were recruits from the other two classes. This last figure would seem to be rising very slowly.

Reducing the number of employees by social position and increasing the number of workers has, as noted above, figured large in party public relations during the 1970s. Clearly, one way to preserve both the social profile of the party and high party saturation of the administrative grades is to give preference in party recruitment to upwardly mobile workers and peasants, the sort who seem good prospects for qualifications and promotion. Like this, the party managers can evade, in a technical sense, the charge of blurring the party's 'proletarian social profile' (Unger, 1977, pp. 314–15), though increasingly the party's proletarians are the skilled and upwardly mobile working class. The policy has a further advantage. If one wanted to work against notions that party membership was the automatic

TABLE 7.5   *Communists by class background, original and current*

All communists		By social position Workers and peasants	Employees	Employed Communists Total	Employees
I *Party as a whole*					
1967	12 684 133	6 868 423	5 815 710	(10 552 000)	(6 000 000?)
		(54.1%)	(45.9%)	(83%)	(57%)
1977	15 994 476	8 895 280	7 099 196	(12 920 000)	(7 250 000?)
		(55.6%)	(44.4%)	(81%)	(56%)
1981	17 430 413	9 792 935	7 637 478	(14 130 000)	(7 750 000?)
		(56.2%)	(43.8%)	(81%)	(55%)
II *15 Regional organisations*					
mid-1960s	3 122 430	1 669 075	1 453 355	2 738 077	1 570 837
		(53.5%)	(46.6%)	(87.7%)	(57.4%)
mid-1970s	4 098 214	2 267 954	1 830 260	3 553 385	2 001 349
		(55.3%)	(44.7%)	(86.7%)	(56.3%)

Sources: *P. zh.* 21/77, pp. 21, 28; 14/81, p. 16 plus Miller, 1982, p. 32 n. 43.

perquisite of a desk job, or to reduce tendencies for son to follow father in party membership, one might introduce a substantial proportion of recruits from worker and peasant backgrounds into the market for senior positions and, at the same time, cut back the admission of routine clerical workers into the party. This would be to spell out that there is now more competition for party membership in white-collar occupations. The party managers would seem to be observing one of the oldest rules of survival for a ruling group, the maintenance of channels of recruitment into it. Whether, of course, they are doing *enough* to counteract other tendencies towards the formation of a hereditary ruling group is a different matter, one much less capable of investigation.

Ethnic composition of the party

Table 7.6 shows how CPSU membership has grown over the years 1971–1981 in the non-Russian Union Republics of the USSR. Two things are to be noted from this table. First, the parties in the non-Russian republics (with one exception) keep up a growth rate higher than that of the RSFSR or the USSR mean. This has been so since the death of Stalin, and can be accounted for either by the higher population growth rates of southern republics, or the later incorporation of western republics into the Union, so that the corresponding party organisations have had to catch up with 'normal' levels of party saturation. In the case of the southern republics, where 'native' adolescents have been reaching adulthood, and formal eligibility for party membership, twice as fast as in Russia proper, the party managers must have faced another form of the 'dilemma of party growth'. They could have tried to keep pace with the surge in potential recruits, risking a lowering of entry standards and, possibly, pressure against local European minorities, who are disproportionately urbanised and disproportionately represented in white-collar jobs. Alternatively, admission standards could have been maintained, leading to a fall in the already low party saturation levels of the non-European population, with the risk that communism might come to be identified increasingly with Europeans, and the native elites pushed towards the Islamic revival.

Uzbekistan provides the best documentation on this issue. Party growth rates have been about 3 per cent per annum (as compared with an all-Union mean of 2 per cent), and it would seem that this growth has been concentrated on the non-European population, such that, though party saturation in Uzbekistan is almost certainly down, it has fallen only marginally among Uzbeks, and faster among Europeans. In other words, greater efforts (or responsiveness) are being devoted to the party recruitment of non-Europeans. And a side-effect of this would seem to be that education levels in the Uzbekistan party are falling – in contrast to the all-Union trend (see Miller, 1982, p. 32 n. 46).

TABLE 7.6   *Party membership in the Union Republics, 1971–81*

Party (members plus candidates) in:

	1971	PSR	Growth	1976	Growth	1981
Ukraine	2 386 789	7.5	+10.0%	2 625 808	+11.7%	2 933 564
Belorussia	434 527	7.7	16.5	506 229	17.6	595 311
Uzbekistan	428 507	7.6	13.8	487 507	16.6	568 243
Kazakhstan	575 439	8.3	14.2	657 141	11.0	729 498
Georgia	296 375	10.3	7.4	318 371	10.1	350 435
Azerbaidzhan	258 549	10.6	11.3	287 823	14.8	330 319
Lithuania	122 469	5.9	18.9	145 557	17.4	170 935
Moldavia	115 164	5.5	17.5	135 303	21.1	163 902
Latvia	127 753	7.5	12.2	143 305	12.5	161 264
Kirghizia	104 632	7.1	4.9	109 746	15.2	126 402
Tadzhikistan	86 491	6.5	11.8	96 716	12.7	108 974
Armenia	130 353	10.1	9.7	142 959	15.2	164 738
Turkmenistan	69 862	6.9	11.5	77 910	20.1	93 556
Estonia	73 168	7.6	15.2	84 250	16.2	97 923
Remainder	9 162 485	?	7.2	9 819 266	10.3	10 835 349
USSR	14 372 563	9.4	8.8	15 638 891	11.5	17 430 413

Sources: entries concerning the Union Republics in *Ezhegodnik*, 1971 and 1976; *P. zh.* 14/81, p. 14.

The second conclusion to be drawn from Table 7.6 is that party growth rates in the Union Republics show considerable variation among themselves, only some of which is readily explicable. That Uzbekistan and Turkmenistan (with their higher population growth rates) and Belorussia (with its record industrial growth rate) should also show rapid party increase is plausible; that Kazakhstan should move from above average to below average party growth during the 1970s, that Kirghizia should move strikingly in the opposite direction, and that Georgia should show the slowest growth rates of all republics since 1956 is less obvious. Mary McAuley (1980) has recently marshalled evidence suggesting that republican central committees may have a considerable measure of responsibility for the planning of their local party membership (whether those plans succeed or fail!) and her approach is probably the most sensible one to the figures in Table 7.6. One is left, though, with the lingering suspicion that Georgia was instructed centrally after 1953 to lower its 'profile' in the all-Union party; it is difficult to see how its low party growth rates can have been the outcome of any perceived interest within Georgia itself.

The Union Republics are not, of course, ethnically homogeneous, so that trends discerned in Table 7.6 may be quite different from trends affecting ethnic groups *sensu stricto*. Table 7.7, which simplifies the available data on the latter, reveals some curious developments. Russians still have a disproportionate share in party membership compared with their

TABLE 7.7   *Share in party membership of major Soviet nationalities*

% share of party taken by	1961	1967	1977	1981
Russians	65.9	61.9	60.5	60.0
Other titular nationalities				
Ukrainians, Belorussians, Moldavians	18.6	19.3	20.1	20.3
Transcaucasians	4.7	4.5	4.7	4.8
Central Asians	4.1	4.3	5.0	5.3
Balts	1.1	1.3	1.4	1.5
Subtotal	28.5	29.4	31.2	31.8
Non-titular nationalities	5.6	8.8	8.3	8.2
Total	100.0	100.0	100.0	100.0

Sources: calculated from *P. zh.* 1/62, p. 49; 19/67, pp. 14–15; 21/77, p. 31; 14/81, p. 18.

share in the population (a little over 52 per cent); this share is declining, but not so rapidly in the 1970s as it did in the late Khrushchev period. For reasons noted immediately above, the share in party membership of the non-Russian 'titular' nationalities – that is, those nationalities which give their name to a Union Republic – continues to increase. But it should be noted that it is their share of total party membership that is increasing, not their party saturation, which may well be falling among the titular nationalities of the southern republics.

This expansion in party membership among the non-Russian titular nationalities, combined with a tendency among Russians (however caused) to cling to their dominant position in the party, has occurred at the same time as a general cutting back in party growth. Table 7.7 suggests how this feat was achieved. The share in party membership of nationalities not associated with Union Republics – the largest of these being the Tatars, Jews, Germans and Chuvash – is falling, and their party saturation is probably virtually static. Whether this sluggishness in the recruitment to the party of 'non-titular' nationalities is to be attributed to someone's plan, or to their own reluctance to join, strength is added to McAuley's argument that some aspects of party recruitment are being controlled at republican level. Titular nationalities appear to be at an advantage in party admissions; and, by the same token, minorities at a disadvantage.

The largest local minority in republics outside the RSFSR is often the Russian one, and it has, of course, been normal in the post-Stalin period for these Russians to have a larger share in the local party than would be warranted on population grounds, and for this share to be declining. But there are odd divergences from this pattern. In Belorussia and the Ukraine, for instance, the Russian share in net increase during the 1970s is well above their share in the population. In Georgia, Azerbaidzhan, Kazakhstan and Uzbekistan, it is below that share, and declining. And in the first two of these republics the decline in party recruitment of Russians has been accompanied by a substantial emigration of Russians (Miller, 1982, p. 33 nn. 50–2). It is difficult not to invoke anti-Russian tension in part explanation of this and, if this is correct, it is highly interesting that party membership should provide us with an early signal of such developments.

What is striking about trends in the ethnic composition of the CPSU is how varied they are. There would seem to be no underlying pattern to them, and in some cases – such as the sharp decline in Russian admissions in four southern republics – things may be taking place that are unwelcome in Moscow. There seems to be something of a contrast between the party's handling of socio-economic features of its membership, and of ethnic ones; the former certainly present problems but the response to them seems to be a deliberate and coherent one; the response to ethnic pressure does not.

Internal migration and party membership

Table 7.8 reveals an important trend in party membership which has received little attention. Four northern provinces of the RSFSR in which agriculture – and poor agriculture at that – is an important source of employment are contrasted against four urbanised and industrialised provinces. Massive emigration, since confirmed by the results of the 1979 census, stands out as a feature of the former type of province.

TABLE 7.8   *Impact of rural depopulation on party membership*

Province	1966		1976	
	Party (full members)	Population	Party (full members)	Population
Kirov	80 000	1 775 000	96 000	1 662 000
Kostroma	55 000	870 000	66 000	802 000
Novgorod	42 500	724 000	60 000	719 000
Vologda	70 000	1 308 000	87 000	1 286 000
Subtotal	247 500	4 677 000	309 000	4 469 000
% increase			+24.9%	−4.4%
Gor'ky	197 500	3 668 000	234 000	3 658 000
Kuibyshev	155 000	2 559 000	207 000	3 043 000
Saratov	155 000	2 386 000	192 000	2 522 000
Volgograd	150 000	2 163 000	180 000	2 434 000
Subtotal	657 500	10 758 000	813 000	11 657 000
% increase			+23.7%	+8.4%
Approx. % increase for RSFSR	—	—	+21.6%	+6.4%

Sources: *XXIII S"ezd KPSS: stenograficheskii otchet*, vol. II, pp. 389–607; *XXV S"ezd KPSS: sten. otch.*, vol. II, pp. 329–596; *Narkhoz* 1965 and 1975.

It is reasonable to assume that this migration has been disproportionately one of young, adult, rural males, and that urbanised provinces like
Gor'ky or Kuibyshev have been beneficiaries of this migration. Party
growth, on the other hand, is about the same in each group of provinces,
and not very different from the overall RSFSR level; that is, admissions
into the party have proceeded at a standard rate irrespective of demographic trends, and it looks suspiciously as if the plans for these admissions
have been based on data about the party organisation, not about the
population, something that was hinted at above. Although our ignorance
of age distribution makes accurate measurement difficult, it is virtually
certain that the party saturation of adults in rural provinces undergoing
depopulation has risen very fast, whereas that of urbanised areas, the
recipients of immigrants, has been sluggish. On p. 144 above, it was argued
that the party managers have made serious efforts to hold steady party
saturation in some white-collar occupations. No such efforts are in evidence among the agricultural workers of North Russia – perhaps because
they *are* agricultural workers, or perhaps because they are also disproportionately female.

Women in the party

The proportion of party members and candidates who are women has
increased from 19.7 per cent in 1957 to 26.5 per cent in 1981, but the latter
figure still entails an adult party saturation rate of only about 4.7 per cent
among females, and 16.1 per cent among males. Not unnaturally, therefore, increasing or high levels of female party membership are presented as
matters of importance and success. The 1977 source lists twenty provinces
where women are 30–40 per cent of party membership, and one, Ivanovo,
where the figure is 43 per cent (*P.zh.*, 1977, no. 21, pp. 26, 32–3). At the
same time, in many southern parts of the USSR, the proportion of women
in the party is below or just above 20 per cent and has remained virtually
unchanged since the mid-1950s. This tends to suggest that, if there has
been a plan to boost female membership, it may not have been an entirely
successful one. The provinces which show the highest female participation
in the party are (with one exception) all provinces where there is a high
component of light industry (Ivanovo, the Baltic republics) or agricultural
provinces to the north and west of Moscow, from which there has been
high emigration. Although it is difficult to prove, it seems likely that in
both cases we have to deal with a workforce which is disproportionately
female. If this is correct, high rates of female party membership can be
accounted for satisfactorily by postulating that party recruitment plans are
plans for the *employed* population (as was suggested above, p. 141); there is
no need to postulate specific targets for female admissions.

Female membership of *obkomy* and *raykomy* is only slightly lower than
that for the party as a whole (*P.zh.*, 1977, no. 21, pp. 26, 32–3). It is well

known, of course, that women hold only an insignificant number of the most senior party positions, amounting to 3.8 per cent of the members and candidates of the 1981 all-Union Central Committee, and being unrepresented among *obkom* first secretaries; in this, however, the party leadership corresponds to senior positions in Soviet life generally.

Problems of party membership in the 1980s

The detailed examination of the composition of the 'outer', non-official, circle of party members has pointed up two trends which are likely to become more pronounced in the 1980s, and suggested one provisional conclusion about the party's arrangements for handling problems. First, the educated and the qualified are increasingly becoming the typical CPSU members, and the party presence among the poorly educated is falling. Risks are entailed in the withdrawal of the party presence from any area of society, and it would seem to be in recognition of such risks that the party is now making admission more difficult for many white-collar employees.

Second, an increasing proportion of the party are non-Russians and non-Slavs; and legitimately so, given the demographic trends of the last 30 years (quite apart from the much older Russian preponderance in the party). Yet side-by-side with this trend, party saturation among many non-Slav groups is falling, and in some overwhelmingly Russian regions, that of the local population is rising fast. It might easily be that party saturation of groups is a better indicator of popular perceptions within and towards such groups than the absolute share of party membership they provide. In addition, the share in party membership of the 'non-titular' ethnic groups, and of some Russian minority groups outside Russia, is falling, with just a hint that community tensions may be linked with this.

Finally, the most plausible hypothesis concerning the mechanism for controlling the party's presence in society is that primary party organisations are set admission targets based on the size of their existing organisation and the nature of their workforce. Such targets would be easy to plan, to implement and to monitor. Admission targets planned on the basis of the workforce and implemented mainly at the workplace could explain why the socio-economic aspects of the party presence in society appear to be managed in a smoother and more regular manner than do its ethnic aspects.

Trends among officialdom

The nature and significance of nomenklatura

The suggestion was raised above (p. 139) that the party managers need to maintain not only an optimum presence in society, but also an efficient and responsive presence. With the latter phrase we are shifting attention to that inner circle of party members who hold society's most responsible and influential positions, and who may be labelled, very loosely, 'officialdom'. Only a fraction of the posts they hold are party posts, of course, but they have in common the fact that party membership is a prerequisite for holding these posts, and that they are all on the *nomenklatura* of a party committee at some level.

The word *nomenklatura* requires some clarification. Strictly and in origin it denotes a list or register of posts, occupancy of which must be ratified by a particular person or group. In this sense most people employed in organisations in any society would be said, in Soviet parlance, to be on someone's *nomenklatura*. There are two things which are distinctive about Soviet staffing practices. First, a very high proportion of posts, and the most senior at that, are ratified not by administrative superiors in the organisation (a Ministry, for example) where the posts are located, but by a *party* committee at a superior administrative level. It is this party control of *nomenklatura*, not the supervision of staffing establishments as such, that is so important for the position of the party in society. Second, the party *nomenklatura* extends to posts in the everyday workplace – factory, farm and office – and in this way, the party has achieved a deeper and more comprehensive penetration of society than any previous rulers of Russia.

The present author disagrees fundamentally, therefore, with a recent development in academic shorthand, that of deeming 'the' *nomenklatura* to be equivalent to 'the' ruling class (see for instance Voslensky, 1984). It is true that this usage reflects colloquial developments in more than one Slavonic language. To adopt the colloquial usage as a technical term, however, obscures two important points about Soviet politics: that the party *nomenklatura* is more important than all others combined; and that it includes positions at *rayon* level which, by no stretch of imagination can be called 'ruling class' positions. There may well be an identifiable group in Soviet society whose internal cohesion and disproportionate access to power would earn them the label 'ruling class'; if so, they would be a subset of, not identical with, those on party *nomenklatury*, let alone those on every *nomenklatura* (see Nove, 1975).

The number of persons on party *nomenklatury* (*nomenklaturnye*) would seem to be in the region of two million or more (Harasymiw, 1977). It is an immense number. The attempt to centralise and co-ordinate the principles whereby two million posts are filled is a powerful illustration of the 'Hobbesian' urgency with which the party has approached the problem of government effectiveness. But the *nomenklatura* system has now been in operation since the 1930s, and it would be reasonable to ask whether it has not evolved. *A priori* such evolution could have proceeded in either – or indeed both – of two directions.

First, the centralised nature of the system may have weakened. It is an inherent problem of centralised government that it cannot get enough detailed, undistorted information about local situations, and there is thus systemic pressure to delegate to the man on the spot who is in a position to know. The staffing equivalent of this is pressure to hire, other things being equal, local men to handle local problems and to let them represent their localities in dealings with the centre. If this is acceded to, centralised and co-ordinated staffing practices are eroded, to be replaced by a network of diverse patronage systems.

Second, central insistence on the necessity for centrally organised staffing may have won through, but with the side-effect of reinforcing bonds of common group interest and identity among *nomenklaturnye*. We have already seen that it is colloquial usage to perceive *nomenklaturnye* as a class, that is, to suggest that the children of *nomenklaturnye* are likely to succeed them in that sort of job. Another common allegation is that *nomenklatura* status, once acquired, is not easily lost, that it is a tenured status in fact (see, for instance, Nove, 1975, p. 618).

The fact that the last two paragraphs have touched on some of the most basic and well-known critiques of the Soviet system should prepare one for the fact that research progress on the issues involved is difficult and inconclusive. All the publicly available evidence is that the social characteristics of officialdom under Brezhnev were extraordinarily stable. Such trends as we can detect can be said to illuminate the broad lines of critique but they certainly do not falsify or confirm them. Two relevant issues will be examined, the appointment of local personnel to local posts, the rejuvenation of officialdom, and the balance of interests within the new Central Committee.

Nomenklatura and local appointments

Centralised staffing principles will be of particular usefulness – and face their hardest testing – in provincial areas of the multiethnic USSR. Of the four institutional controls for the maintenance of party supremacy listed on p. 136 above, three could easily become less effective in areas of homogeneous subculture where local officials and ordinary citizens shared differences from central policy. The fourth control is the centralised party *nomenklatura*; from the perspective of the centre it might seem imperative that at least some officials be brought into a provincial locality from the outside, and the party *nomenklatura* would be a mechanism for ensuring this.

This expectation is borne out when staffing in the provinces is examined, but the presence of non-locals is less obtrusive and more discriminating than might be imagined, and in one important respect it is declining.

The situation is clearest in the non-Russian Union Republics. A majority of senior positions and, in particular, publicly visible ones are held by 'natives' of the Union Republic in question, but virtually reserved for outsiders are either a small number of key, and usually inconspicuous posts, or a presence among the top half-dozen officials in a given policy sector (see Miller, 1977; Hodnett, 1978). These outsiders are almost always Russians (or Russianised Slavs) and a significant proportion of them are secondments direct from Moscow, often from the all-Union Central Committee *apparat*. Movement from one provincial post to another across republican boundaries is very rare, for natives and Russians alike (Miller, 1983). The most important change over time that can be detected is that the above rules became more standard under Brezhnev than they were under Khrushchev.

In the RSFSR a preliminary investigation (Miller, 1983) suggests that the proportion of outsiders – as measured by promotions across province lines – is *lower* than it is in the other Union Republics, and that it decreased under Brezhnev; more careers are made locally and a longer proportion of careers are spent locally. This seems to have been in fulfilment of an undertaking given by Brezhnev (*XXIV S"ezd*, I, p. 124).

The broad interpretation would seem to be that the party managers do not seek to use *nomenklatura* procedures to prevent the identification of officials with local interest and the development of experienced regional lobbies, and perhaps more may be heard of these during the 1980s. Central controls are instead, first, on the accumulation of comparative experience of different kinds of regional problem (with the exception of a specialised group of officials based on Moscow); and second, the monitoring of regional interest group activity by these seconded specialists and, in the case of the RSFSR, this second control has been considerably scaled down. The workings of the *nomenklatura* system would seem to be considerably less interventionist than they were under Stalin or Khrushchev, in part because of local pressure against such interventions. However, there are no signs hitherto of diverse staffing practices growing up in the regions; the centre would seem to be accepting local recommendations more than formerly in making its appointments, but not to have waived its right of veto.

Voting members of the new central committee

It has been laid down in the Party Rules since 1966 that the full members of the Central Committee elect the General Secretary; on two occasions (July 1957 and October 1964) this vote would seem to have been more than a formality. So in proposing the membership of the new, March 1981 Central Committee, the party managers were drawing up a list of people who would vote on the succession to L. I. Brezhnev, and who *might* play a decisive role in this. It is relevant, therefore, to see whether any trends in the background or interests of this electorate can be discerned. Of the two most obvious indicators of such interests, occupation and clientele, the

TABLE 7.9 *Occupational representation among 1976 and 1981 central committee members*

	1976			1981		
	All-Union	**RSFSR**	**Other republics**	**All Union**	**RSFSR**	**Other republics**
Party apparatus	18	65	37	30	67	41
Government apparatus	65	11	7	71	9	5
Supreme Soviets	3	1	5	3	1	5
Military	17	1	2	17	4	1
Security and law	4	—	—	7	—	—
Foreign affairs	17	—	—	16	—	—
Academy, media and writers	10	2	2	11	2	2
Trade unions	3	—	—	5	—	—
Economic management	—	4	—	—	3	—
Workers and peasants	—	7	3	—	12	4
Others	3	—	—	3	—	—
	140	91	56	163	98	58
Total		287			319	

Notes: Government apparatus means, above all, Ministers, but includes a few chairmen of *ispolkomy*; Security and law covers the KGB, the MVD, the Procuracy and Supreme Court; Others are voluntary organisations and the Komsomol. Commanders of military districts are classified under RSFSR or Other Republics; military commanders abroad and ambassadors are included in the all-Union figures.

latter is exceedingly difficult to process and will not be attempted here (for an example of such an inquiry see Willerton, 1979). Table 7.9 shows changes in the current occupation of Central Committee members, and in the locality or administrative level where they work.

Table 7.9 shows interesting, but slight increases in percentage terms in the representation of security and of workers and peasants in the Central Committee, and slight decreases in the representation of Councils of Ministers, Supreme Soviets and diplomacy. But the significant change is the increase in the representation of the all-Union Central Committee *apparat* from 18 to 30 persons (or from 6.3 per cent to 9.4 per cent). Thus, the Central Committee members who can be formally associated with the all-Union rather than lower levels of administration have risen from just under to more than half of the total membership.

Another way of looking at the same trend is as follows. The majority of Central Committee members appear to get their membership *ex officio*; the party managers influence, through the party *nomenklatura*, who is appointed to senior positions, but have rather less short-term control over the balance of these senior positions on the Central Committee. They can, however, modify this balance of power by increasing the size of the Committee. There are 89 persons among the 319 Central Committee members in 1981 who were not members in March 1976; of these 89, 44 are new incumbents of posts whose former occupants were members in 1976; and 45 have jobs which did not carry this status in 1976. Of these 45, 9 hold positions in the Central Committee *apparat*, 9 in the all-Union Council of Ministers, 3 are from the military, 3 from the KGB and two are institute directors associated with foreign policy (G. A. Arbatov and N. N. Inozemtsev); on the other hand only 8 are regional party secretaries and 11 are workers (9 from outside Moscow). Thus the majority of the net additions to the Central Committee, and the most effective of them, are likely to be defenders of all-Union as opposed to regional interests, and the most important effect of the expansion of Central Committee membership would seem to be a proportional cutback in regional representation. Indeed, an attempt to curb the influence at the centre of regional lobbies might well have been the purpose behind this expansion.

The foregoing survey of trends in party membership and among party officials in the 1970s and early 1980s has revealed little that is dramatic, still less evidence of failure to come to grips with problems. Perhaps ethnicity and regionalism come closest to falling into that latter category. The most sensible interpretation to be put on developments is that, in so far as matters can be managed, the party managers have handled them with caution, deliberation and strategy; and that they have also shown considerable acceptance of evolutionary change in both party and society. This may sound an unremarkable conclusion, but it is one remarkably close to the platform on which the Brezhnev administration came to power in October 1964.

8

The Polish Party in Crisis, 1980–82

DAVID S. MASON

During the early 1980s the Polish United Workers' Party suffered a major crisis, the most substantial crisis of any communist party in any communist party state. The disintegration of the party was at least partly responsible for both the development of Solidarity in the summer of 1980 and the imposition of martial law in December 1981. The lack of trust in the party and its authoritarian and unrepresentative character led the workers to demand an institution more responsive to their own needs. But the growth of Solidarity during 1981 and the continuing disintegration and fragmentation of the party led the military to preempt the leading role of the party by imposing martial law at the end of that year.

The collapse of the party in 1980 and 1981 was due to a number of factors (Bielasiak, 1983, pp. 10–25). The party leadership had to bear the burden of the economic failures of the late 1970s and the consequent decline in the standard of living. The party itself had grown rapidly in size during that period, even though the influence of ordinary party members and local party organizations declined in the face of increasing tendencies towards centralization in the second half of the decade. This development led to problems of morale even within the party and to the growth of horizontal barriers between the membership and its leaders. The population at large was increasingly annoyed and disgusted with the failure of the party to improve the economic situation and to allow a more honest and open discussion of Poland's problems. The dissatisfaction was compounded by the widespread perception that the elite was increasingly looking after its own interests only and that benefits and privileges were accruing only to those in power.

By the spring of 1981, however, the 'renewal' movement that was sweeping the country had begun to penetrate the party, leading it to

Reprinted with adaptations from *Slavic Review*, vol. 40, no. 1 (spring 1984) with the permission of author and publisher.

embark on housecleaning and reforms of its own. Much of this initiative came from the rank and file of the party, while there was some resistance on the part of the leadership. The changes that did occur were extensive enough to worry the Soviet party leadership, which issued a number of warnings to its Polish counterpart. As the party became less hierarchical and less disciplined, as party members continued to join Solidarity, and as Solidarity continued to mount its challenge to the centralized Polish political system, the regime apparently feared a total collapse of the party – a collapse creating a vacuum that only Solidarity or the army could fill.

In this chapter I shall examine membership and policies of the party during 1980–82, the attitudes of the public towards the party and its role in society, and the opinions of party members themselves. Survey research conducted by Polish institutions during this period, or conducted earlier and distributed during 1980–82, furnishes much of the data on which this study is based. Some of the material is remarkably candid and provides an unusually detailed picture of the membership, attitudes, and role of a ruling communist party.

A major and long-term problem for the Polish United Workers' Party, as for all ruling communist parties, is that of maintaining the elite and leading role of the party while simultaneously keeping the party reasonably representative of the population (Hammer, 1971). For the Polish party it has been particularly difficult to limit the proportion of white-collar workers, who have normally dominated both membership rolls and leadership positions. In 1974, for example, 'mental workers' made up 42 per cent of the party membership but only 22 per cent of the work-force. While 49 per cent of all engineers, 45 per cent of technicians, and 70 per cent of blue-collar workers were members of the workers' party. Furthermore, representation of blue-collar workers in other institutions, including workers' councils, was also weak. A Polish sociologist noted in 1975:

> The degree of organization and social activization of workers is quite low, relative both to the postulated model of the working class in socialist society and to the size and economic role of that class (Drazkiewicz, 1975, p. 21).

The problem posed by the lack of institutionalized mechanisms for the expression of workers' grievances was once again dramatized in the riots of the summer of 1976. One of the responses of the regime to these events was a sustained campaign to increase the number of workers and young people in the party. Party membership rolls expanded at an unprecedented rate in the late 1970s (Mason, 1982a). By the end of 1979, members and candidates of the party constituted almost 12 per cent of the adult population and over 20 per cent of those employed in the socialized sector of the economy. These percentages were the highest in the history of the party.

The large membership tended to jeopardize the party's elite image and 'leading role', but the expansion had increased the representation of young people, women, and blue-collar workers in the ranks of the party, making it as representative in these categories as it had ever been. Blue-collar workers, for example, constituted 46.2 per cent of the party in 1979, compared with 41.8 per cent in 1975 (*Zycie Partii*, February 1980).

Despite these improvements, the party was still highly unrepresentative of the population in several respects. While more blue-collar workers had joined the party, this group was still not well represented in leadership positions. Even though blue-collar workers constituted almost half of the party membership, they held only 10 per cent of the central party leadership positions, and only 3 per cent of the discussants at Central Committee plenary sessions came from their ranks (Kolankiewicz, 1982, p. 59). Peasants made up about one-third of the work-force but less than 10 per cent of the party membership. This fact was of less interest to urban residents than the perception – largely based on fact – that the party was dominated by highly educated white-collar workers with high incomes. Official party statistics showed that 12 per cent of party members had a higher education, compared with just 7 per cent of the work force. But a sample of working males in the city of Łodz showed that 30 per cent of party members had a higher education compared with 11 per cent of non-members. In fact, over half of those with a complete higher education were party members (Łodz Survey, 1980). While the party considered it important to attract the 'best' people to the organization, including the best educated, the less well-educated blue-collar workers were irritated by this kind of differentiation.

The expansion and diversification of the party did not solve the problems of credibility and representation for the regime. If anything, the image of the party as being made up of 'opportunists' was reinforced in the late 1970s. Furthermore, the failure of the regime to allow decentralization of power and decision-making even within the party was an obstacle to people's confidence in the party and detrimental to morale within the organization. Public assessment of the party remained highly negative.

The party had never been very popular in Poland, but the lack of confidence in the organization was not publicly affirmed until spring 1981, when the press briefly referred to an official public opinion poll on confidence in institutions (Osrodek Badania Opinii Publiczne, May 1981). This very low level of support for the 'leading' organization was derived from a number of complaints Poles had about the party and about those in power. They included the widespread feeling that those in policy making and managerial positions were incompetent, that they abused their power by attaching extravagant privileges to their positions, that the party and the elite closed off access to decision-making for people who were not members of the party and ruled by compulsion rather than consensus, and that the party had forsaken its own stated ideals of socialism and egalitarianism. These were wide-ranging issues that called into question the role of the party in Polish society.

The sense that the party and its leadership were incompetent was not always as strong as it had become by 1980. During the first half of the 1970s, for example, there were some positive evaluations of the Gierek leadership. An official poll from 1975 showed that almost 85 per cent of the people believed that 'in the last several years society had confidence in the leadership of the country' (Sufin, 1981, p. 21). Over 90 per cent of this sample believed the developments in the country since 1970 had been 'quick', and the most frequently mentioned reason for these developments was 'the new leadership of the party and the country'. Even taking into consideration the official nature of this poll and the atmosphere in which it was conducted, the results are markedly different from answers to similar questions in 1981, which showed 30 per cent or fewer expressing trust in the government and the party (Mason, 1983a). This decline in confidence in the late 1970s was due in large part to the decline in the economy and the standard of living during that period and to the simultaneous burgeoning of Poland's foreign debt. Many Poles wondered where the money had gone and assumed that it had been either wasted or appropriated by the elite , an assumption that contributed to the widespread belief that the economic and political leadership was incompetent. A poll conducted among a small (330) sample of men in Warsaw in the summer of 1979, for example, showed that only 20 per cent thought 'ability' played a decisive role in helping people reach high positions in Polish society. As the researchers pointed out, a similar question asked in the United States showed 70 per cent assigning a decisive role to ability (Gadomska, 1981, pp. 19–21).

The popular perception of incompetence in the leadership of the party and the country was aggravated by the widespread belief that the elite was unjustly benefiting from its positions of power. The issue of privilege has always been a sensitive one in Poland, a society that values highly the principle of egalitarianism. Unequal distribution of wealth and power is seen as contradictory to the basic principles of socialist society. This issue has always been discussed in Poland, though largely in private. In the period between 1979 and 1981, however, it was treated more directly and openly in both the official and the unofficial press. The result was an increase in popular frustration.

In the unofficial 'Report on the State of the Republic' by the 'Experience and the Future' study group, the issues which most clearly stood out in their description of society were 'the social structure, its hierarchical character, anti-egalitarian tendencies, and the emergence of a system of privileges that conflicts with the sense of social justice so deeply rooted, thanks to socialist ideology, in our society' (*Poland Today*, 1981, p. 57). There was a widespread perception in Polish society at the end of the 1970s that social inequalities had increased over the past decade. But as one analyst of official public opinion data pointed out, 'the present egalitarianism' was directed not so much against differences in earnings as 'mainly against the economic position and life style of the leadership apparatus'. Most people, he pointed out, believe

> it is unfair that high positions are linked with privileges and they demand that incomes be reduced, and that the availability of goods in short supply, such as housing and automobiles, access to special shops, private clubs, clinics, and so forth, for persons in high positions be restricted (Kurczewski, 1981, p. 9).

All of these issues and complaints were to become strong elements in the appeal of Solidarity and its program. The preliminary program for Solidarity, drawn up by a group of advisers for the organization in the spring of 1981, demanded that restrictions be placed on the privileges of the elite and that the costs of economic recovery and reform be borne 'particularly by people enjoying privileges linked with the exercise of power' (*Glos Pracy*, 14 April 1981). The restrictions on privileges were especially directed at those in 'the power apparatus' and included limitations on apartments, offices, automobiles, and special health services. The Solidarity program also would have required the elite to disclose the presence of other income and property.

It should be emphasized here that the concern over privilege was not directed at the party membership at large but rather at those in positions of power. Considerable concern with elite privilege existed even within the party. A party report on letters addressed to the Central Committee by rank-and-file party members mentioned numerous letters advocating 'the liquidation of commercial stores and other special stores' and 'stores in the militia, the army and the committees of the PUWP' (Sufin, 1981, p. 221). The reference to the committees of the party suggests that there was concern with privilege not just in the central bureaucracy but at lower levels as well. Here, as elsewhere, we see that Polish society in 1980–81 was divided not so much between party members and non-members but rather between those in positions of power (at all levels) and the rest of the people, whether party members or not.

While the issues of competence and privilege were sensitive and inflammatory ones, questions about the role of the PUWP in Polish society were potentially much more dangerous and destabilizing. The issues raised in this context included overcentralization of power and lack of democracy within the party and the excessive control and dominance of the party in societal decision-making. These kinds of criticisms were voiced both by the public and by rank-and-file party members during 1980 and 1981. Kurczewski's analysis of an official poll by the Center for Public Opinion

Research of Polish Radio and Television in 1980 concluded that the leadership should be rotated and 'the principles of selection and promotion be democratized' within the party (Kurczewski, 1981). The 'Experience and the Future' group also argued in favor of limiting the terms of office of the top leadership levels of the party (*Poland Today*, 1981, p. 173).

Perhaps the most systematic criticism of party organization and leadership came from within the party. The suggestion most frequently made in letters to the Central Committee was that the terms of office for party leaders should be limited. But the writers also called for more information within the party, secret elections, changes in party nominating procedures, and open sessions of the Central Committee and lower level committees (Sufin, 1981, pp. 209–30). These criticisms were accompanied by complaints about the increasing centralization of power in the hands of members of the central party apparatus. Centralization took two forms: the arrogation of decision-making authority by the party from the state and other institutions, and the concentration of power within the party from the periphery to the center. A Polish sociologist pointed out that this 'absurd' process of centralization had reduced the significance of local party committees 'almost to zero' in the late 1970s (Tarkowski, 1983, pp. 23–76). Solidarity asserted in its program that the method of governing based on the domination of the central party–state institutions 'had led the country to ruin' (*Tygodnik Solidarnosc*, 16 October 1981).

Many of these issues were summed up in a set of recommendations issued to the Central Committee of the party by a group of experts attached to the party's Institute of the Basic Problems of Marxism-Leninism. The report, delivered in October 1980, defined the main characteristic of the crisis as a lack of confidence in the governing of society and suggested a number of changes, including decentralization of state and party authority, greater intra-party democracy and egalitarianism, the widening of 'social participation' in decision-making and increased autonomy for other institutions, and an improvement of the electoral procedures of the party, including the nomination of two candidates for each leadership position (Sufin, 1981). As will be seen below, many of these changes were made during 1981.

These criticisms and recommendations reflected a deeper sense that the population had little opportunity to voice its opinions or participate in decision-making. The popular feeling of alienation from politics had increased dramatically during the late 1970s. In 1976 only 41 per cent of a sample of males in the city of Łodz cited the degree of 'participation in governing' as a source of tension and conflict in society. By 1980, 80 per cent cited this factor (Łodz Survey, 1980). Solidarity's preliminary program hammered at the idea that the loss of democratic institutions was the root cause of the crisis: 'The bureaucratic system of governing the state and managing the economy has helped establish a closed group of rulers who are not subject to control by the governed' ('Directions of the Operations of Solidarity', 1981).

The popular frustration with the role of the party and the centralization of power was especially apparent in two national surveys conducted by the Academy of Sciences at the end of 1980 and the end of 1981, entitled *Polacy '80* and *Polacy '81*. In the *Polacy '80* survey, over 92 per cent agreed with the proposition that there should be 'increased control of society over the authorities'. That this was not to be accomplished through the party was evident from the response to another question about 'strengthening the role of the party in the administration of power'. In 1980 only 33 per cent agreed with this proposition and 56 per cent disagreed; by the end of 1981 only 20 per cent favored strengthening the party. When the question was reversed in 1981 – whether the role of the party should be limited – 60 per cent favored the idea, while only 20 per cent opposed it. Even 46 per cent of party members favored limiting the role of the party (*Polacy '81*).

In trying to determine the types of authority relationships desired by the population, the researchers for *Polacy '81* asked if the respondents favored a centralized or a decentralized system, with or without the party playing a leading role. Although there was a considerable division on both issues, by far the largest proportion of respondents favored a decentralized system without a leading role for the party and 'based on the participation of various social forces', as the statement was phrased. There was stronger support for a decentralized system (44.4 per cent) than for a centralized one (32.8 per cent). But the really astounding result of this question concerned the leading role of the party. Only 24.5 per cent favored such a role, while a clear majority (52.7 per cent) opted for a system without a leading role for the party (*Polacy '81*). This result testifies to the thorough disillusionment of Polish society with the PUWP. In Poland, as in all communist states, the leading role of the party has been the *sine qua non* of the political system. This principle is incorporated in the Polish Constitution and even in the Gdansk Agreements of 1980. It was the basis on which the Soviet Union intervened in Hungary in 1956 and in Czechoslovakia in 1968. Yet by the end of 1981 the Polish party was so discredited that the majority of Poles was apparently willing to revise that fundamental component of the political system.

Frustration with the PUWP did not, however, translate into a wish to constitute any new political parties. In the *Polacy '81* survey only 25 per cent favored constituting some 'new political parties besides the PUWP, the Social Democratic Party and the United Peasant Party' (these are the two satellite parties of the PUWP, which are allied with the PUWP in the Front of National Unity and which have some seats in the Polish parliament but exert little independent political influence). Opposition to the creation of a new political party was fairly uniform across the political spectrum. Some 76 per cent of party members were opposed to the idea (although 24 per cent favored it!), as were 69 per cent of Solidarity members. There was also little support for the proposition that Solidarity should create a political party to operate alongside the union. Only 20 per cent of the overall sample and 23 per cent of Solidarity members favored this idea.

The population thus did not favor the elimination of the PUWP, or even its replacement by other parties. It wanted a more pluralistic society, in which 'society exercises more control over the authorities' and in which there is more room for political participation and political maneuver by other groups, including the existing non-communist parties and the trade unions. As Solidarity's program put it: 'The state must serve man, and not rule over him; the state organization must serve society and should not be identified with a single political party' (*Program NSZZ Solidarnosc*). Poles opposed the monopolistic control of power by the party, not the party itself.

These increasingly vigorous and open challenges to the party could not help but affect the members of that besieged organization. Between August 1980 and December 1981, there were unprecedented changes in party membership and party leadership. Between the end of 1980 and the end of 1981, over 400 000 members left the party. This was by far the largest number of defections in one year in the history of the party, and, with 13 per cent of the total party membership, the largest percentage decline except for the year 1958. In February 1982 the official press admitted that the party had lost almost a half million members since July 1981. It is evident that most of those who left were blue-collar workers, since the working-class component of the party had declined from 46.2 per cent at the end of 1979 to 42.7 per cent in early 1982 (*Rzeczpospolita*, 9 February 1982).

. Many of those who left the party joined Solidarity, but there were probably even more party members who stayed in the party *and* joined Solidarity. Estimates of the number of party members in Solidarity range up to 1.7 million of the party's three million members (*Christian Science Monitor*, 28 January 1981). This figure is probably too high. In two separate survey research polls at the end of 1980, 35 per cent of party members admitted to membership in Solidarity (*Polacy '80*; Łodz Survey, 1980). This is a remarkably high percentage in itself, however, and is close to the percentage of the general population in Solidarity (37 per cent). An even greater number of party members supported Solidarity, even if they did not join the organization. In the *Polacy '80* survey, 45 per cent of party members expressed 'decisive support' for the activities of Solidarity. Dual membership in Solidarity and the party was especially prevalent among skilled blue- and white-collar workers, as is apparent from Table 8.1.

TABLE 8.1 *Party members in Solidarity, by occupational groups (percentage)*

Occupational groups	Percent in Solidarity among:	
	Party members	Non-members
Specialists with higher education and leadership cadre	55.0	69.5
Middle cadre and specialists	64.7	71.8
Office workers and administration	33.3	61.2
Skilled workers	76.0	77.6
Farmers and farm workers	15.8	20.0

Source: *Polacy '81*.

As the table shows, three-quarters of all skilled workers, party members and non-members alike, belonged to Solidarity at the end of 1981. There were also extremely high rates of Solidarity membership among specialists and the 'leadership cadre', including most party members in these categories.

There are several possible explanations of why so many party members, particularly those in prestige and leadership positions, joined Solidarity. First of all, the appeal of Solidarity was so widespread that it cut across the lines of the 'establishment' to include many supporters of the regime. Most rank-and-file party members supported the existence and goals of Solidarity and may have seen in it a potential means to loosen the hierarchical controls within the party. As Solidarity adviser Jadwiga Staniszkis has pointed out, the antihierarchical, anti-institutional and egalitarian attitudes of Solidarity found support in the party as well and fostered genuine common interests between the 'renewal' movement in the party and the membership of Solidarity (Staniszkis, 1981, p. 229).

Second, it might be expected that party members would be attracted to Solidarity simply because of their political activism. Party members are joiners and activists and are more likely to have definite opinions on public issues. Solidarity provided a new channel for their activities, and a more productive one. That PUWP members played an active and leading role in Solidarity is evident from data on party membership among the factory commissions of Solidarity. In five of the six regions (*wojewodstwos*) for which membership was reported, party members constituted at least 20 per cent of the Solidarity factory commissions (*Information Biuletynu MKZ, NSZZ Solidarnosc*, 30 January 1981). This overlapping membership of Solidarity and the party extended to the very top of the political system: at the Ninth Congress of the party in July 1981, 20 per cent of the delegates were also Solidarity members.

The changes in the party also affected the professional apparatus. In the eighteen months after August 1980, 53 per cent of party workers, the professional staff of the organization, left the party 'for various reasons'. In the preliminary elections leading up to the Ninth Congress, there was 'an almost complete turnover in the leadership cadre of the party'. Eighty per cent of the regional party committees were new, as were 65 per cent of the village, town, and factory committees and 50 per cent of the first secretaries of the primary party organizations (*Rzeczpospolita*, 25 February 1982). Many of these newly elected local leaders were young people, often with short party membership records.

The turnover in the professional ranks was bound to affect the leadership as well. When the party congress elected a new Central Committee in July, 91 per cent of the winners were new to the position. Of the fifteen Politburo members elected at the congress, only four were holdovers. This was the most rapid and thorough change in the party leadership of any Communist party state. It reflected fundamental changes and strains within the organization and had both positive and negative consequences. The 'renewal' and rejuvenation of the party raised the possibility of changes in policy as well, and perhaps of a more accommodating stance towards Solidarity. But it also caused concern and fear in the Soviet Union that the Polish party might be losing its 'leading role'.

The PUWP made substantial efforts to clean house during 1981 and to join the 'renewal' that was occurring throughout Polish society. These efforts included crackdowns on corruption and illegality within the party, restrictions on privileges, provisions for more openness within the organization, and reforms in party election rules. However, the desire for renewal was not unanimous. In the provincial, enterprise, university, and military party conferences, nominations would be made by special electoral commissions. But a crucial difference in the new rules was that there could be an unlimited number of nominations from the floor of the conferences and that the voting would be by secret ballot. In the past, the maximum number of nominations permitted from the floor was 15 per cent of the available seats. The 'provisional' electoral rules adopted in December 1980 had allowed for 50 per cent, but in response to widespread criticism the limitation was dropped altogether. Furthermore, the provision for unlimited nominations had already been adopted by some regional and local party organizations.

Another major accommodation the party had made was in its attitude towards religious believers within party ranks. Officially the 'scientific' and atheistic worldview of a Marxist-Leninist party was inconsistent with religious belief. In practice, that inconsistency has been overlooked in a society that is overwhelmingly Catholic. By 1981 even most party members professed to be believers (80 per cent) and 27 per cent called themselves 'practicing' Catholics (*Polacy '80*). The party finally recognized this fact officially when the program of the Ninth Party Congress acknowledged that 'religious believers can join the party if they wish to and be politically active in keeping with its program' (Stefanowski, 1982). This stand was reaffirmed, though modified somewhat, in an article on 'Believers in the Party' in *Zycie Partii* (2 September 1981). The article asserted that the PUWP was primarily a political party and not connected with people's world view (a remarkable statement in itself). Believers could join the party, and the party recognized religion as a private matter. But the party should strive to change the world view of religious members in the direction of materialism.

These changes in party policy were criticized both inside and outside the country. In May 1981 a party 'discussion forum' in Katowice adopted a declaration accusing the Kania leadership of having lost its 'ideological and political compass in the struggle for socialism . . . under the pressure of alien ideological influences, supported by right-wing opportunism and liberalism of the bourgeois type'. The statement expressed alarm over increased tendencies within the party of 'Trotskyite-Zionist views, nationalism, agrarianism, clericalism and anti-Sovietism' (*Sztandar Młodych*, 29–30 May 1981). It was not clear how large this group was, or even who was in it, and the declaration was rejected by official party bodies. But the fact that the statement appeared in an official publication suggested that these conservative views had at least some support.

Conservative elements in the party received support from a powerful outside voice in early June 1981 when Soviet party leader Brezhnev addressed a sharply worded letter to the members of the Polish Central Committee, criticizing the party leadership for its 'constant concessions' and its inability to cope with 'counterrevolutionary forces' within Polish society (*Nowi Drogi*, July 1981, pp. 29–32). Brezhnev also expressed concern about the upcoming Polish party congress and the failure of the party leadership to defend its 'experienced cadre' in the preparatory electoral conferences. He asserted that the Soviet Union was the only guarantor of Poland's sovereignty and reminded the party of its responsibility to the entire socialist community for the preservation of party rule. The language of the letter was pointedly similar to that of messages conveyed to the Czechoslovak leadership in the spring of 1968. The letter must have encouraged conservatives at the Central Committee plenum a few days later, where there were appeals for the Politburo to show some 'muscle' against the forces of counter-revolution and Solidarity's 'march toward power'. In his speech to the plenum, Kania said that the accusations in Brezhnev's letter were 'fully justified' and pledged efforts to meet the criticisms while maintaining the commitment to socialist renewal (Radio Free Europe Research, 19 June 1981).

By 1981 there were no major differences in outlook between members of the PUWP and the rest of society. Most of the views of society reflected in public opinion polls were similar to those held by members of the party. Table 8.2, drawn from the *Polacy '81* survey, shows the responses to selected questions by party members and non-members. On some of the

TABLE 8.2   *Public opinion of party members and non-members on major issues in 1981 (percentage)*

Issue	Party members	Non-members
Support guaranteeing Solidarity access to mass media	79.8	93.5
Support limiting the role of the party in the administration of power	46.0	62.0
Support for the development of private agriculture	56.2	74.9
Oppose temporary increase in the powers of the militia and the security forces	53.5	64.5

Source: *Polacy '81.*

major issues of 1981, a majority of party members agreed with the majority view of non-members. It is clear from these data that party members by no means followed a hard line on these issues. Eighty per cent favored access to radio and television for Solidarity, and almost half of all party members even favored limiting the role of the party in Polish society!

A remarkable degree of support by party members for the actions and programs of Solidarity is evident in other issues, too. Only 21 per cent of party members 'decisively opposed' strikes as a form of protest (compared with 13 per cent of non-members). When asked about participation in acts of protest, party members more frequently admitted to such acts (21.6 per cent) than did the overall sample (18.4 per cent). When asked who was responsible for the governmental and political crisis, party members rarely blamed Solidarity (see Table 8.3), even though they were also less likely than non-members to assign primary responsibility to the government. Furthermore, they overwhelmingly opposed hard-line emergency measures to cope with the crisis at the end of 1981 (*Polacy '81*).

TABLE 8.3   *Opinion on responsibility for crisis, by party membership (percentage)*

Who's responsible?	Party members	Non-members
Government	25.5	41.7
Solidarity	8.7	2.4
Both	47.1	38.9
Someone else	4.4	6.1
Difficult to say	14.6	10.9

Source: *Polacy '81.*

If earlier there had been a division between party membership and society, this division largely disappeared by the middle of 1981. The division became one between society, including most party members, on the one hand, and the state and party leadership on the other. Many party members had joined Solidarity, and most of them sympathized with its goals. As Alain Touraine's groups concluded from their interviews with Solidarity activists, 'ordinary members of the Party are closer to members of Solidarity than they are to their own leaders' (Touraine, 1983, p. 59). The party had joined the process of renewal, but the process was being blocked at the top.

In the course of 1981 the authorities became increasingly isolated even from the party membership. In October Kania was replaced as first party secretary by Premier General Jaruzelski, marking a further diminution of authority for the party. Even Lech Wałesa recognized the dangers posed by the weakening of the party. In an interview with Western reporters just before the imposition of martial law, he pledged to help the party if it started to discredit itself or collapse:

> There are no other realities here. We cannot overthrow the party. We cannot take the power away from it. We have to preserve it. At the same time, tame it and let it eat with us, so that it will relish what we create (*Washington Post*, 10 January 1982).

But it was too late even for Wałesa to help the party. In the face of accelerating demands from Solidarity and the accelerating disintegration of the party, Jaruzelski was faced with considerable pressure from hard-liners in the bureaucracy. There is even some speculation that party bureaucrats attempted to seize power in March and again in December. According to a Western observer, 'the day before martial law was imposed, Jaruzelski sent the entire apparatus of the Polish Central Committee into the provinces, trapping them there in order to prevent a concerted response' (Spielman, 1982–83, p. 32). Jaruzelski claimed that the army had taken control to reestablish order and stability and to prevent the total collapse of the party which he said was threatened with 'physical liquidation'. In the months following the imposition of martial law, the regime made efforts to restore the legitimacy and reputation of the party. There were extensive purges of party functionaries at all levels in an apparent effort to 'trim both wings' of the party. According to Jaruzelski, the changes in the party cadres in the two months after martial law were the most extensive in the history of the party (*Rzeczpospolita*, 25 February 1982). The party was also trying to attract back many of those members who had turned in their party cards after August 1980. But these efforts faced a contrary tendency: tens of thousands of party members who had stayed in the organization during the Solidarity era turned in their cards in protest of the imposition of martial law. Membership continued to decline during 1982.

The role of the party in Polish society was another issue that elicited live and open debate during 1982. In a discussion of the relationship between the unions and the party, *Trybuna Ludu* (the party daily) declared that 'it is the party, or rather political parties, and not the trade union movement, which are the instruments representing the interests of various classes and nation-wide interests' (*Trybuna Ludu*, 19 February 1982). But by the spring the line had softened somewhat, partially perhaps because of the regime's lack of success in resuscitating the party. In discussions about the creation of a 'Front of National Understanding' (*Front Porozumienia Narodowego*), which was presumably to play a political role, it was stressed that the front should include people who were not members of the party and even those who 'do not like socialism' (*Zycie Warszawy*, 6 April 1982). The front 'should enable all social organizations in favor of the political and social system in Poland to participate in political decision making' (*Zycie Warszawy*, 14 April 1982). Despite this rhetoric, the martial law regime was unsuccessful in transforming the party, the front, or any other official organizations into legitimate representative bodies. By the end of 1982, the regime still faced a dilemma. Martial law was suspended and formal power returned to the party and state offices. But the reputation and membership of the party remained at low levels. By imposing martial law, the army had provided a crutch to the injured party. But the party was still not able to walk without at least leaning on the army.

The events of 1980 and 1981 marked a fundamental turning point both for Poland and the other European communist states. For the first time in the post-war history of this region, virtually the entire population united to demand a qualitative transformation of the system. Most basic was the demand for a broadening of the base for participation in economic and political decision-making and for restrictions on the decision-making prerogatives of the party elite. Support for this demand was widespread even among the party membership which also suffered from the centralization of power.

The need for political decentralization in the communist states and the benefits of such decentralization have long been recognized by Western political scientists. As David Lane has put it, 'the rigid centralised political system devised to implement rapid industrialisation now becomes redundant when its major task has been completed. It comes into conflict with participant-oriented groups' (Lane, 1976, p. 81). By 1981 the imperative for such change was being openly discussed in the Polish press: 'In a word, an escape from the crisis demands changes in the political system, changes of a qualitative character, such that the system would rely not on methods of compulsion, but on methods which in effect lead to the desired integration of society' (Morawski, 1981, p. 6). Poland was moving from a 'subject political culture' to a 'participant' one. Solidarity was the main vehicle for this movement, and the central party bureaucracy was the main obstacle. While many elective party posts fell into the hands of reformers during 1981, the central administrative staff – largely appointed – remained intact. This group was the most threatened by the challenges posed by Solidarity. In retreat, the central party organization relied increasingly on power to maintain its position. In the past the party had been able to derive some legitimacy from socialist ideology. As the ideological legitimacy of the party waned, power became the overriding motivation for the bureaucracy, further exacerbating the tensions between the rulers and the ruled. The elite increasingly depended on 'exclusionary closure' to maintain itself (Parkin, 1979). But in doing so it became further removed and alienated from society.

Solidarity tried – unsuccessfully – to reform the Polish political system from the 'outside'. In order to reform the system, it was necessary to penetrate and reform the party. There was considerable success in this regard; many party members joined Solidarity or sympathized with it. The grass roots of the party initiated significant changes in the rules, structure, membership, and leadership of the organization. Even the central party leadership tried to adapt to the new environment by encouraging initiatives, democratization, and decentralization at the lower levels. But by the end of 1981, the process of renewal was caught on the horns of a dilemma: the reform was too slow for many members of Solidarity and too fast for the party bureaucracy (and the Soviet leadership). Many members of Solidarity believed that the union was making too many compromises and that the only way to move ahead was to continue the pressure on party and government (Mason, 1982b). This group constituted only about a third of the membership (and leadership) of Solidarity, but it was a vocal minority. The regime targeted its criticisms on these 'radicals' and identified them as the dominant force within the movement. The appeals of this group for new elections to the Sejm and a referendum on the party triggered the declaration of martial law.

Many Poles were equally dissatisfied with the pace of change within the party. 'For Poles of the 1970s, the present party would have been the realization of their most ardent aspirations', but for Poles in late 1981, 'the party is still not democratic enough, not sufficiently humble, too sure of itself, too ready to usurp power and therefore untrustworthy' (Szczpiorski, 1982, p. 146). The party had undergone the most substantial changes in its history, indeed in the history of any communist party. Yet the population remained critical of its concentration of power and privilege.

The party bureaucracy saw its position as dire, and this perception was reinforced by the continuing demands of the more radical Solidarity supporters. The regime – in contrast to Solidarity – defined renewal as 'a process of social adjustment articulated and implemented "from above"' (Bielasiak, 1984). But this concept conflicted with what was happening both in society and in the party itself, where most of the changes were generated from below. The party leadership was put in an unusual and uncomfortable position: for the first time in its history, the PUWP was not the primary agent for initiating social and economic reforms. At the same time, the Soviet leadership was issuing dark warnings about the necessity of maintaining the leading role of the party. The imposition of martial law probably reflected a combination of two interests among the elite: to maintain itself in power and to avoid the possibility of Soviet intervention.

During 1981 the Polish United Workers' Party had attempted to adapt to the renewal that was sweeping the country. It became less hierarchical, more representative, more democratic, and more reformist. It effected significant changes in its own membership, leadership, organization, and processes. But the party, like Solidarity, exceeded the boundaries of the possible in the Poland of 1981. The changes that occurred in the party threatened its 'leading role', the *sine qua non* of communist rule in Eastern Europe. While most party members were willing to adapt the party to Solidarity's Poland, much of the entrenched party and government bureaucracy was not. And those elements found powerful support both within the country and without. Contrary to the expectations of most Poles, the democratization of the party was not a sufficient guarantee of the process of renewal.

9

The Communist Party of Cuba since the First Congress

WILLIAM M. LEOGRANDE

The main concern of the Communist Party of Cuba (PCC) in recent years has been to lead and supervise the implementation of the resolutions adopted at its First Congress in 1975. Those resolutions cover a broad range of political, social, and economic issues, so that a full account of the party's work over the past five years would require a complete survey of Cuba's domestic and foreign policies during that period. The very breadth of the PCC's work agenda in the latter half of the 1970s indicates how much the role of the party in Cuba has evolved over the past decade (*Bohemia*, 25 May 1979, pp. 58–65). Such responsibilities demonstrate a continuation of the process of strengthening the party begun in the early 1970s. The first half of the decade involved rapid expansion of the PCC's membership and major reorganizations of its apparatus aimed at creating an institution capable of playing the 'leading role' in Cuban politics. The years since the First Congress have been marked by more measured growth and the final completion of the party's organizational framework and operational procedures. This second phase of the PCC's post-1970 evolution has been aimed at consolidating the party's leading role, both by extending its influence among the masses and by establishing the party's political hegemony over the island's other political institutions, particularly the administrative bureaucracy.

The First Congress of the Communist Party of Cuba

The First Party Congress was a milestone in this process. Through it, the party set basic policy principles (the Programmatic Platform); detailed specific policy in a wide variety of areas (the Theses and Resolutions); and

Reprinted with adaptations from the *Journal of Latin American Studies*, vol. 12, no. 2 (November 1980) with the permission of author and publisher.

codified the essential organizational framework and operating principles of the party itself (the Party Statutes). While it is true that all these documents were drafted by the party's top leadership long before the Congress convened (Dominguez, 1978, pp. 330–1) and that their adoption by the Congress was a virtual certainty, it would be a mistake to evaluate the significance of the Congress simply on the basis of the meeting itself. The process of preparing for the Congress was, in a very real sense, as important as the final event.

In the first place, drafting the basic documents for the Congress necessitated fundamental policy reviews by the national leadership in virtually every issue area. The scope of this review was probably unprecedented; certainly nothing like it had been undertaken since 1970. Then, in the months prior to the Congress, all its basic documents were submitted for mass discussion not only by the party's membership but by the whole population. In addition to yielding some amendments to the documents under discussion (Raul Castro, 1976, pp. 5–15), the discussion process served a number of other important political functions. It constituted a test of the party apparatus's ability to mount a major organizational effort and to mobilize mass participation. In addition, the discussion of a broad spectrum of basic policies *under the auspices of the party* demonstrated to the population in a direct and practical way the party's assumption of the 'leading role' in politics. Thus it served an important legitimating function and should be understood as a key event in the process of shifting regime legitimacy from a charismatic to an institutional basis. Finally, the discussion process provided the entire party apparatus from the grass roots upward with basic political orientation on key policies, their rationale, and their overall context. Students of organizational behavior will recognize the importance of such orientation in light of the frequency with which policy is distorted by subordinates' failures to comprehend the intent of policy initiatives (Simon, 1976; Halperin, 1974, pp. 239–42). The seriousness attributed to such orientation by the Cubans is evidenced by the fact that the main content of party ideological work in the five years since the Congress has been to continue studying the Congress's theses and resolutions.

The Congress itself can be understood as the culmination of the preparatory process. It brought together 3116 delegates, cadres from all levels and sectors of the apparatus as well as grass roots members, for discussions and explanations of new policies, of the PCC's new role in the political system, and of the party's new internal procedures. It was the ultimate orientation session for key cadres and militants from across the nation (*Verde Olivo*, no. 2, 1976, pp. 28–33). After the Congress, the delegates returned to their various posts, presumably with a deeper understanding of policy in all these fields. The importance of such an event for the party's cohesion and internal co-ordination should not be underestimated.

The PCC at the Base: Size, Composition, and Coverage

The party's gravest problem during the 1960s was the weakness of its apparatus and, consequentially, its inability to play the leading role in Cuban politics. The PCC's ability to mobilize the masses, or even its own infrastructure, was seriously limited. Its ability to exercise leadership over other political institutions and to prevail in the inevitable bureaucratic clashes which arose was virtually nil (see, for instance, LeoGrande, 1978a, pp. 201–18).

The party's weakness during the 1960s derived from a number of specific and related deficiencies: (1) the extremely small size of the party; (2) the limited coverage of the population afforded by the party's meager apparatus; (3) a persistent shortage of competent cadres owing to the low educational level of the party membership; and (4) a serious lack of internal organization and co-ordination both within and between party organs.

When the institutionalization of the revolution began in 1970, the party was one of the first institutions affected. In fact the process of expanding the size of the party actually began before the institutionalization process. In mid-1969 a campaign of 'construction and growth' was initiated in order to expand overall party membership and to increase the number of party cells, or nuclei (Hart, 1969, pp. 3–4). The policy of expanding the party's size was continued throughout the early 1970s as a key element of the overall campaign to strengthen the PCC. On the eve of the First Congress, party membership stood at 202 807, nearly four times the 1969 membership of 55 000 (Fidel Castro, 1976, p. 234).

The number of party nuclei increased by at least a factor of 3 and their average size increased by nearly 50 per cent from 7.4 members per nuclei in the mid-1960s to 10.6 in 1974 (LeoGrande, 1978b). The First Congress mandated continued expansion of the party's ranks, and, though no official data on party membership have been made available since 1975, the Central Committee's 1979 balance sheet of accomplishments since the Congress indicates that the party has continued to grow in size, albeit at a slower rate than during the first half of the decade (Resolucion del VIII Pleno del Comite Central, 1979, pp. 63–4). Most estimates place current PCC membership at over 400 000 in the early 1980s.

The PCC apparatus's coverage of society (and hence its ability to provide political orientation to the masses and to mobilize them) is closely related to its size. In the mid-1960s, the PCC had nuclei in only about 16 per cent of the island's work-places. Though it was organized in the larger work centers, data from the 1966 Industrial Efficiency Plan suggests that less than half the Cuban working class was employed in places that had a party organization. Even in places where it existed, the party comprised only about 3.8 per cent of the labor force. By 1975, the party's expansion had improved this situation considerably. Nearly half the nation's work centers (that is, nearly all the large and medium sized work centers) had party nuclei, giving the PCC immediate access to the vast majority to the working class (LeoGrande, 1978b, p. 13).

Despite these improvements, the extension of the party apparatus was still thinnest among the blue collar workers (Table 9.1), who remained the sector of the working class (as opposed to small farmers) most under-represented in the party relative to their proportion of the labor force. In 1975, only 4.4 per cent of workers directly engaged in production or services were PCC members, only a small improvement over the late 1960s figure of 3.8 per cent in areas where the party was organized.

This issue of the 'social composition' of the party received more attention than any other in the Congress thesis on inner party life, which concluded that the number of workers in the party and the extension of the party apparatus in key sectors of production were both inadequate. Interestingly, this problem was due primarily to promotion patterns within the party rather than to the pattern of membership recruitment. The vast majority of party members came out of a working class or peasant background, but the persistent shortage of cadres during the 1960s meant that many people who entered the party as workers were quickly promoted to leadership positions. This was still the case in 1975. Data for the first half of

TABLE 9.1　*Occupational distribution of PCC membership, 1975*

	Occupation as a % of total work-force	PCC members as % of total PCC	PCC members as % of total occupational group
Workers in material production and services*	65.0	35.9	4.4
Small Farmers	9.7	1.8	1.5
Administrative workers †	4.7	4.1	6.9
Professional and technical workers	11.7	9.2	6.2
Administrative leaders ⎫ Political leaders ⎭	7.7	⎧ 33.4 ⎫ ⎩ 8.7 ⎭	43.1
Others ‡	1.2	6.9	45.3
	100.0	100.0	7.9

* Industrial production, agriculture, and construction.
† Clerical
‡ The very high percentage of PCC members in this occupational group suggests that it includes part of the military, most probably just the lower ranks, since the entire PCC apparatus in the armed forces constitutes about 19 per cent (not 6.9 per cent) of the Party membership.

Source: 'Sobre la vida interna del Partido', in *Tesis y Resoluciones*, 1976, pp. 13–54.

that year shows that even though workers constituted a higher percentage of new party recruits than of existing members, the percentage of workers actually fell owing to the movement of party members into other occupational groups (Sobre la vida interna del Partido, 1976, pp. 17–28).

The thesis on inner party life mandated a 'significant increase' by the Second Congress in the proportion of party members working directly in production and services. This is to be accomplished not by quotas but by giving priority to strengthening the party and Union of Young Communists in these sectors, and by regulating the promotion of members from these sectors to other occupational groups (Sobre la vida interna del Partido, 1976, pp. 17–28).

The thesis was careful to add that an increase in the proportion of workers in the party was in no way contradictory with the high proportion of administrative and political leaders in the party. As Table 9.1 indicates, such leaders are greatly over-represented in the party's ranks, and are the single occupational group with the highest percentage of PCC members (43.1 per cent). This is not surprising since party members who hold key posts in other institutions are one of the party's principal means of exercising political leadership over those institutions. Indeed, it is somewhat surprising that more than half the island's full-time administrative and political leaders are *not* party members, and the situation with regard to administrative (i.e., government) leaders is substantially worse. Unfortunately, the data necessary to calculate separately the party's coverage of administrative and political leaders are not available. However, based on rough estimates which disaggregate the leadership category into political leaders, military-administrative leaders (i.e., officers), and civilian leaders, I estimate that only about 36 per cent of Cuba's administrative leadership belongs to the PCC. While the reliability of this figure is admittedly low, it suggests that party discipline by itself is not a sufficient mechanism for exercising party leadership over the administrative bureaucracy.

It seems likely that the party leadership would want to improve the party's coverage of administrative leaders, hence strengthening the party's leading role *vis-à-vis* the government. Such a policy, however, runs headlong into the policy of improving the proportion of workers in the party *by restricting the promotion of party members into administrative posts*. The eventual solution to both problems is, of course, continued increases in the overall size of the PCC, but in the short run these two objectives *are* potentially in conflict. This may account for the apparent difficulty the party leadership has encountered since the First Congress in spelling out precisely how the thesis on social composition is to be implemented. The issue has been discussed at two different Central Committee plenaries, apparently without resolution (*Granma Weekly Review*, 25 December 1977). Nevertheless, the resolution of the 8th Central Committee Plenary notes improvement in the party's social composition since 1975 (*Granma*

TABLE 9.2   *Occupational distribution of PCC membership, 1975 and 1979**

	PCC members as % of total PCC	
	1975	1979
Workers in material production and services†	35.9	44.6
Small farmers	9.2	13.5
Administrative workers ‡	4.1	4.8
Professional and technical workers	8.7	4.8
Administrative leaders	33.4	26.2
Political leaders	1.8	1.3
Others	6.9	4.8
	100.0	100.0

* Unfortunately, since no figure is available for total PCC membership in 1979, we cannot calculate for 1979 figures comparable with those in Table 9.1.
† Industrial production, agriculture, and construction.
‡ Clerical.
Sources: 'Sobre la vida interna del Partido,' in *Tesis y Resoluciones*, 1976, pp. 13–54; Isidro Gomez, 'El Partido Comunista de Cuba,' Conferencia presentada en el Seminario del Instituto de Estudios Cubanos, Washington, DC, 1979.

Weekly Review, 31 December 1979). Workers in material production have risen from 35.9 per cent of PCC members in 1975 to 44.6 per cent in 1979 (Table 9.2).

The policy of expanding the number of workers in the PCC was motivated largely by a concern over the party's ability to orient and mobilize workers in key sectors of production. A similar concern over the PCC's relationship to Cuba's female population produced a policy mandate to increase the number of women in the party so that by the Second Congress women would comprise a proportion of the PCC equivalent to their participation in the labor force (Sobre la vida interna del Partido, 1976, pp. 28–9). In fact, this policy was only part of a much wider concern over the role of women in Cuban society, and particularly in politics (Sobre el pleno ejercicio de la igualdad de la mujer, 1976).

From the party's inception in 1962, women have been grossly under-represented in its ranks (Table 9.3) and its leadership bodies. In part, this was due to the relatively small number of women in the labor force and the fact that, until 1975, the PCC was organized exclusively at work centers. However, during the 1960s, as the percentage of women in the labor force gradually grew, their proportion of the PCC's membership actually fell by nearly a third. As the party expanded rapidly in the early 1970s the proportion of women members recovered somewhat, but by 1975 it still had not surpassed the level of the early 1960s. The first really substantial gains for women in the PCC appear to have come out of the party elections prior to the Congress (Table 9.4), which raised female representation among party cadres by a factor of about four (Fidel Castro, 1976, p. 236),

TABLE 9.3 *Women as a proportion of PCC membership, 1962–75*

	As % of PCC members		As % of PCC members
1962	15.48	1972	12.00
1963	13.24	1973	13.00
1964	10.86	1974	12.80
—		1975	13.23
1967	10.00(—)	—	
—		1979	17.50

Sources: *Cuba Socialista* December 1962; April 1963; April 1964; *World Marxist Review*, March 1974; *Granma Weekly Review*, 8 December 1974; 4 January 1976; Jorge I. Dominguez, *Cuba: Order and Revolution* (Cambridge: Harvard University Press, 1978) p. 324; Isidro Gomez, 'El Partido Comunista de Cuba', Conferencia presentada en el Seminario del Instituto de Estudios Cubanos, Washington, DC, 1979.

TABLE 9.4 *Women as a proportion of PCC cadres, 1975*

	Nuclei (%)	Municipal (%)	Regional (%)	Provincial (%)	National (%)	Overall (%)
Pre-election	n.a.	2.9	4.10	6.3	5.50	5–6
Post-election	17	13(+)	13(+)	13	8.9	n.a.

Source: Sobre el pleno ejercicio de la igualdad de la mujer (La Habana: Departamento de Orientacion Revolucionaria, 1976).

thus making the proportion of women among party leaders approximately equal to the proportion of women party members. Since 1975, the proportion of PCC members who are women has continued to increase slowly, so that by 1979 they constituted 17.5 per cent of total membership. This increase is due primarily to the fact that new party members now reflect more closely the sexual composition of the labor force. In the first half of 1975, 22 per cent of new party members and candidates were women. At the same time women constituted 29 per cent of the UJC, which has become an increasingly important access route to PCC membership (Sobre la vida interna del Partido, 1976, pp. 28–9).

The PCC's organizational problems were aggravated in the 1960s by the persistent shortage and poor educational level of party cadres. The general shortage of qualified personnel generated intense competition among various institutions for the talents of the few skilled people who were available. For a time, the state bureaucracy regularly hired away the party's best cadres, until Fidel himself called a halt to such 'piracy' (Castro, 1963, pp. 1–32).

Table 9.5 summarizes how the educational level of party members has evolved since 1967. While, on the one hand, the improvement has been striking, the majority of party members still have, at best, a sixth grade

TABLE 9.5   *Educational level of PCC membership, 1967–75*

	1967 (%)	1968 (%)	1969 (%)	1970 (%)	1971 (%)	1972 (%)	1973 (%)	1974 (%)	1975 (%)
Below 6th grade	44.2	38.4	34.9	33.6	31.0	28.9	25.9	19.5	18.1
6th grade	36.2	42.2	44.0	44.6	46.0	46.7	47.6	44.7	42.2
Basic secondary	11.9	10.1	11.9	12.1	13.0	14.0	15.0	22.4	25.7
Intermediate	4.8	5.7	6.3	6.9	7.0	7.5	8.4	9.9	10.2
Higher	2.9	3.6	2.9	2.8	3.0	2.9	3.1	3.5	3.8
	100.0	100.0	100.0	100.0	100.0	100.0	100.0	100.0	100.0

Source: Sobre la vida interna del Partido', in *Tesis y Resoluciones*; Isidro Gomez, 'El Partido Comunista de Cuba', Conferencia presentada en el Seminario del Instituto de Estudios Cubanos, Washington, DC, 1979.

education. Not surprisingly, the Congress mandated continued emphasis on improving the educational level of the party membership, setting completion of the eighth grade by a majority of members as the goal for the end of the first five-year plan (Sobre la vida interna del Partido, 1976, pp. 33–8).

During the years from 1970 to 1975, the PCC's principal goal at the base was to expand rapidly its membership in order to increase the party's capacity to lead and mobilize the masses. Though it was still the smallest ruling communist party (on a per capita basis) in 1975, the PCC had, nevertheless, succeeded in expanding its membership fourfold. It had attained at least the minimum operational size necessary to carry out its political work with the masses. The growth of the party has continued since the First Congress, though at a slower rate. Greater attention is now being paid to the extension of the party's infrastructure among specific groups (i.e., production workers and women) where the PCC has historically been the weakest. The present emphasis on improving the educational level of party members is by no means new, and reflects the PCC's continuing concern over the shortage of competent cadres.

The Party Apparatus Since 1975

The PCC labored under a variety of organizational handicaps in the 1960s, most of them directly traceable to the party's low level of institutionalization. It had no written rules and regulations to govern the operation of party organs or their relationship to other institutions; party bodies met sporadically if at all; and there was little internal co-ordination and control (Hart, 1966, pp. 2–3; 1969, pp. 10–11; Machado, 1969, p. 5; LeoGrande, 1978b, pp. 13–16).

Most of these problems were addressed during the early 1970s. Evaluation meetings were convened at various levels of the party apparatus in order to evaluate past work, adopt plans for future work, and elect delegates to evaluation meetings at the next highest level of the party. Once the information provided by the evaluation process had been analyzed, the next step was the full scale reorganization of the party apparatus in 1972. The most important results included the establishment of a routine reporting system from lower to higher party bodies, something which had not existed previously; a specific delineation of the PCC's relationship to the administrative apparatus and the mass organizations; the beginning of regularly scheduled meetings of PCC organs; and the reorganization of the national Secretariat, and the expansion of its membership from 7 to 11 members to facilitate a wider division of responsibilities.

The process of preparing for the First Congress provided a fairly rigorous field test of the new apparatus, and the Congress itself provided the party with its first set of statutes. With most of its organizational problems thus resolved, the Congress resolution on inner party life pays little attention to explicitly organizational issues (Sobre la vida interna del Partido, 1976).

In the years since the First Congress, there have been few organizational changes in the party's sub-national apparatus. It was, of course, restructured in 1976 to correspond to the new politico-administrative division of the island, but this was certainly not unanticipated and probably caused a minimum of disruption in organizational operations. In December 1977, the Central Committee adopted a set of specific regulations for municipal and provincial bodies, thus systematizing their operations even more.

The most significant organizational changes in the party since the First Congress have occurred at the national level. The Central Committee has begun to meet regularly and its role in the overall political process has become more clearly defined; the Central Committee's auxiliary apparatus has continued to expand and a party control commission has finally been created; and there have been some important personnel shifts in both the Central Committee and in its Secretariat.

The Central Committee has met regularly since the First Congress, holding a plenary every six months. The character of Central Committee deliberations is largely unknown since Cuban press reports of the proceedings have been exceedingly brief. None of the plenaries, however, has been longer than a day, and several have lasted only a single afternoon. If press reports of the actions taken at these plenaries are reasonably complete, they have been devoted largely to internal party matters (Table 9.6). Of the twenty-two issues we know to have been considered by the Central Committee, eight have involved the election of personnel to central party organs, three have concerned the rules and regulations governing the operations of party organs, and on two different occasions the Central Committee has taken up the question of the PCC's social composition. The

TABLE 9.6   *Central Committee Plenary Meetings, 1976–9*

1st Plenary	Election of the Political Bureau
22 December 1975	Election of the Secretariat
2nd Plenary	Approval of report on international events
25 July 1976	Approval of proposals on composition of cadres
3rd Plenary	Analysis of the work of the National Assembly
30 November 1976	Election of President and Vice-President of National Committee of Control and Revision (CNCR)
	Addition of Jose Machado to the Secretariat
4th Plenary	Addition of Arnaldo Milian to the Secretariat
19 June 1977	
5th Plenary	Approval of national economic plan and state
25 December 1977	budget
	Discussion of social composition of PCC
	Approval of regulations for Provincial and Municipal PCC Committees
	Addition of Raul Valdes Vivo to Secretariat
6th Plenary	Adoption of Resolution on the 11th World Youth
2 June 1978	Festival
	Approval of regulations for the Central Committee, Political Bureau, Secretariat, and auxiliary apparatus
	Approval of regulation for the National Committee for Control and Revision (CNCR)
	Election of CNCR members
	Report on the international situation
	Approval of the Report of the Political Bureau on work of 1977
7th Plenary	Approval of national economic plan and state
31 December 1978	budget
	Discussion of Political Bureau plan to improve Party's social composition
	Removal of Raul Garcia Pelaez from Secretariat
8th Plenary	Adoption of Resolution reviewing work since
4 May 1979	the First Congress

Sources: 'Cronica Abreviada del Primer Congreso', *Verde Olivo*, no. 2 (1976) pp. 28–33; 'Plenos del Comite Central', *Verde Olivo*, no. 2 (1977) p. 25; '4th Plenary of the Central Committee', *Granma Weekly Review*, 19 June 1977 p. 1; 'Central Committee of Cuba Holds 5th Plenary Meeting', *Granma Weekly Review*, 25 December 1977, p. 1; 'Communist Party of Cuba Holds 6th Plenary Meeting', *Granma Weekly Review*, 11 June 1978, p. 1; 'Central Committee of Communist Party of Cuba Holds 7th Plenum', *Granma Weekly Review*, 31 December 1978, p. 1.

Central Committee has also heard two reports on foreign policy and has approved two annual economic plans and state budgets.

Up until the 8th Plenary, the short duration of Central Committee plenaries and the prevalence of unanimous votes suggested that these semi-annual meetings did little more than provide *pro forma* ratifications of prior decisions by the Political Bureau and Secretariat. While we do not know how often the Central Committee modified proposals brought before it, the only issue that appears to have been at all controversial was the question of the party's social composition (because of the frequency with which it was discussed). Since the Committee was not apparently considering many issues outside the realm of internal party affairs, the Central Committee's role in the policy process remained obscure.

The work of the 8th Plenary has clarified matters considerably. At that meeting, the Central Committee adopted a resolution evaluating the progress made since the First Congress in virtually all areas of endeavor (Resolucion del VII Pleno del Comite Central, 1979). Comprehensive in its scope, the resolution noted a wide variety of shortcomings and recommended a number of solutions. No doubt the resolution was drafted prior to the plenary and presented to it for consideration, though once again we do not know how intensely the resolution was discussed at the Central Committee meeting. Its promulgation is, nevertheless, an important milestone in the development of the party. It marks the first time, as far as we know, that the Central Committee has ever considered an overall evaluation of the 'state of the revolution', and the resulting document suggests that such evaluations are to be an annual event.

The resolution of the 8th Plenary is by far the most important document to be considered by the Central Committee since the First Congress and is thus far the only one to be released publicly. It now appears that the role of the Central Committee is to act as the principal forum through which the top leadership of the party (the Political Bureau and Secretariat) establishes and disseminates party policy to the 'second echelon' leadership directing both other political institutions and the sub-national party apparatus. In the course of carrying out their other leadership responsibilities, most Central Committee members become familiar with the state of affairs in their own policy areas. The Central Committee, however, provides them with an opportunity to trade experiences with leaders in other policy areas and to gauge how their own work fits into the wider agenda of problems and priorities. Though this overall agenda is no doubt set in large measure by the PCC's top leadership, Central Committee meetings may also provide an opportunity for second echelon leaders to offer some modifications of it. Thus the Central Committee seems to be emerging, for the first time, as the principal locus of intra-elite communication and co-ordination and the principal mechanism for the dissemination of party orientation to the nation's political and administrative leaders.

One of the clearest indications of the PCC's development since the 1960s has been the evolution of the Central Committee's auxiliary apparatus which provides staff support for the party's central organs by investigating and clarifying policy options in various policy areas. Certain key bureaux also perform line as well as staff functions by acting as liaisons between central party organs and other institutions in the political system.

The PCC's predecessor, the United Party of the Socialist Revolution (PURS), had only two commissions attached to its National Directorate:

TABLE 9.7   *PCC Central Committee apparatus, 1965–79*

I. Organizational Apparatus of the 1965 Central Committee
   1. Organizational Secretary
   2. Revolutionary Armed Forces and State Security Commission
   3. Commission on Economy
   4. Commission on Constitutional Studies
   5. Commission on Education
   6. Commission on Foreign Relations
   7. Commission on Revolutionary Orientation
   8. Labor Commission (1966)
   9. Commission on Legal Studies (1969)
   10. Commission on Construction (1970)
   11. Commission on Transportation and Communication (1970)
   12. Commission on the Sugar Harvest (1970)
   13. Commission on Consumer Goods and General Services (1970)
   14. Commission on Internal Education (1970)
   15. Commission of Servicing Central Organizations (1970)
   16. Commission on Social Work (1970)

II. Organizational Apparatus of the 1975 Central Committee
   1. Department of Organization
   2. Military Department
   3. Department of Economy
   4. General Affairs Department
   5. Department of Science, Educational and Culture
   6. General Department of Foreign Affairs
   7. Department of Revolutionary Orientation
   8. Department of Basic Industry
   9. Agriculture-Livestock Department
   10. Department of Construction
   11. Department of Communications and Transportation
   12. Department for the Sugar Sector
   13. Department of Consumer Goods and Domestic Commerce
   14. Department in Charge of the Formation of Cadres
   15. America Department
   16. Department for State and Judicial Organs
   17. Mass Organizations Department
   18. Party Control and Revisions Commission

Sources: US Central Intelligence Agency, *Directory of Cuban Officials: A Reference Aid* (Washington, DC, CIA, 1979). This document is publicly available through the Documents (DOCEX) Project of the Library of Congress.

an Organization Commission and a Labor Commission (*Cuba Socialista*, April 1962, pp. 136–7). When the PCC was inaugurated in 1965, the number of Central Committee commissions rose to seven (Table 9.7), all of them headed by Central Committee members. It was not until 1970 that commissions were created to oversee various sectors of the economy.

When the party apparatus was reorganized in 1972–3, the commissions were replaced by departments. While most of the new departments corresponded functionally to the commissions which they replaced the reorganization improved the staffing of the system. Since the First Party Congress the departmental system has continued to expand, so that it is now nearly as elaborate as the system attached to the Central Committee of the Soviet Communist Party.

Unlike the commissions which preceded them, few of the PCC's departments are headed by Central Committee members, thus relieving those members (all of whom have important responsibilities elsewhere) of the burden of directing what is essentially a system of staff agencies. There are, however, several exceptions to this. The Military Department, which acts at least in part as a line agency (liaison both between the Central Committee and the armed forces, and between the Central Committee and the party apparatus in the military) has Central Committee members as both its Chief and Deputy Chief. Similarly, the Mass Organizations Department, which acts as the PCC's liaison with the mass organizations, is also headed by a CC member. Among the staff agencies, both the departments dealing with foreign policy are headed by members of the Central Committee (the General Department of Foreign Affairs, and the America Department). Finally, the newest CC department, the Department of General Affairs, is headed by Central Committee member Secundino Guerro who worked previously on organizational affairs under Organizational Secretary Armando Hart. While the precise function of this department is unknown, it appears to be similar to the General Department of the CPSU Central Committee, whose function is essentially to co-ordinate the work of other Central Committee departments and channel the results to the central party organs. The creation of such an agency in Cuba underlines the extent to which the national apparatus of the PCC has evolved both in size and complexity.

At present, the PCC's departmental system consists of eighteen agencies, eight of which deal with economic issues and five of which deal with internal party matters (Table 9.8). In the early 1970s, the functional boundaries of the economic departments paralleled the sectoral division of responsibilities in the Executive Committee of the Council of Ministers.

TABLE 9.8   *Functional scope of Central Committee apparatus, 1965–79*

	Number of agencies		
	1965 (N=7)	1973 (N=17)	1979 (N=18)
Functional area			
Economy and services	2	8	8
Foreign affairs	1	1	2
Liaison with other institutions	1	3	3
Internal PCC	2	4	5
Other	1*	1†	0

* Commission on Constitutional Studies
† Department on Social Work
Sources: as for Table 9.6.

Since 1975, however, the economic departments have become slightly more functionally differentiated than the sectoral division in the government, though the functional boundaries of the departments rarely cross-cut those of the government.

The increase since 1970 in the number of agencies concerned with internal party affairs is yet another indication of the PCC's increasing organizational coherence and capacity. Because they deal with the party itself, these agencies have administrative as well as staff responsibilities; thus, for instance, the Department in Charge of the Formation of Cadres conducts, co-ordinates and supervises programs aimed at improving the educational level of party members, and the Department of Revolutionary Orientation conducts agitation and propaganda activities (first and foremost for party members, but also for the population as a whole). One of the most significant developments with regard to the strengthening of the PCC was the First Congress resolution on the formation of party cadres, which recommended the creation of a *nomenklatura* system of registering party cadres to improve personnel decisions. Such a decision would probably improve not only the efficiency and effectiveness of personnel policy, but, if the USSR is any indication, it would also tend to reinforce central control in the PCC apparatus as well.

The newest Central Committee agency is the National Control and Revision Committee whose primary function is to 'call members and candidates of the party to account' either for infractions of PCC regulations or, in cases of party members holding posts in other institutions, for their failure to carry out properly their responsibilities in those other institutions (Machado, 1978, p. 4). Thus the Control and Revision Committee is not only a mechanism for ensuring party unity and discipline, but also for supervising the work of party members in non-party posts. If the party's leadership role is exerted principally through party members working in other institutions, then this new agency provides a means for holding those party members accountable for putting party leadership into practice. It also provides, potentially at least, yet another mechanism to maintain party hegemony over the administrative bureaucracy.

Changes in the composition of the Central Committee since 1975 have been small relative to the shifts observed prior to the First Congress (see LeoGrande, 1978c). On the one hand, this stability reflects the incremental character of changes in the PCC since 1975 in contrast to the major structural reorganization and rapid growth which characterized the first half of the decade and culminated in the First Congress. Nevertheless, even the incremental changes of the past three years reflect institutional realignments since the Congress, as well as confirming some of the trends in elite composition which emerged in the early 1970s.

Virtually all the changes in Central Committee composition over the past three years are due to the circulation of Central Committee members

TABLE 9.9 *Institutional representation in the Central Committee of the Communist Party of Cuba, 1975–9*

	1975 (*N*=124) %	1979 (*N*=123) %	Net increase (decrease) %
Party apparatus	29.0	25.2	(3.8)
National	14.5	14.6	0.1*
Subnational	14.5	10.6	(3.9)
Government apparatus	28.2	32.5	4.3
Economic	12.9	11.4	(1.5)
Diplomatic	8.1	8.1	—
OPP	—	5.7	5.7
Other	7.3	7.3	—
Military/Police	29.8	27.6	(2.2)
Regular military	26.6	22.8	(3.8)
PCC-FAR, INT	3.2	4.9	1.7
Mass organizations	7.3	7.3	—
Scientific/cultural	4.8	4.9	0.1*
Unknown	0.8	2.4	1.6
	99.9	99.9	

* Statistical artefact.
Sources: William M. LeoGrande, 'Continuity and Change in the Cuban Political Elite', *Cuban Studies* 8, no. 2 (July 1978) pp. 1–31 for 1975 data; US Central Intelligence Agency, *Directory of Cuban Officials: A Reference Aid* (Washington, DC, CIA, 1979) for 1979 data.

between posts. There have been only three changes in the membership of the CC itself: in 1977 Juan Marinello and Felipe Torres died, and in 1978 Vilma Salinas was added to the Central Committee as an alternate member. Thus the Central Committee is presently composed of 110 full members and 13 alternates. Table 9.9 compares the institutional affiliations of Central Committee members in 1979 to their affiliations after the First Congress.

While the changes are small, they are nevertheless instructive as to how institutional interrelations have evolved since the First Congress. The PCC apparatus is now represented by 5 fewer members than it was previously (a decline of 3.8 per cent from 1975). The government, on the other hand, has gained 5 seats, increasing its representation by 4.3 per cent. Superficially, it might appear that the government has gained influence at the expense of the party, but a closer examination suggests an alternative explanation. In 1975, members of the CC who worked in the government were all part of the administrative apparatus. In 1979, we must distinguish between administrators and government officials working in the Organs of People's Power. In doing so, we discover that the administrative apparatus actually holds *fewer* seats in the Central Committee today than it did in 1979; all the 'government's' gains have come about as a result of OPP. If the OPP, as a political apparatus, assists the PCC in asserting political control over the administrative bureaucracy, then the increased representation of 'government' personnel in the Central Committee due to the creation of OPP should not be seen as a relative loss of influence for the party.

Even the absolute decline in the number of posts held by the party apparatus can be seen in a similar light if we examine the pattern of circulation which produced these changes. Of the eight individuals who left the PCC apparatus for posts in other institutions, seven entered the government (three at the ministerial level). Among these were some of the most competent of the party's national leaders: Isidoro Malmierca (Minister of Foreign Relations), Humberto Perez (President, JUCEPLAN), and Armando Hart (Minister of Culture). Their vacated posts in the national apparatus were then filled internally by the promotion of sub-national PCC leaders (e.g., Jose Machado, Arnaldo Milian, and Rene de los Santos). Thus the representation of the PCC national apparatus in the Central Committee remained constant, with the sub-national apparatus bearing the full brunt of the reduction in the party apparatus's overall representation. This pattern of circulation suggests not so much a loss of PCC influence as an attempt by the party to strengthen its influence over the government by posting some of its best national cadres to key government posts. Such an interpretation is strengthened by the net loss of representation suffered by the administrative apparatus.

Changes in the military's representation on the CC confirm the trend towards reduced military influence evidenced at the First Congress (Leo-Grande, 1978c). In the 1975 Central Committee, members of the armed forces held only 29.8 per cent of the seats, a sharp decline from their 57.0 per cent share of the 1965 Central Committee. By 1979 the military had lost three more seats, reducing its proportion of the CC membership to 27.6 per cent. Equally significant, however, has been the growth in representation of military officers who hold party posts within the military (i.e., are assigned either to the Political Directorates of the Ministry of the Revolutionary Armed Forces and Ministry of the Interior, or the Military Department of the CC). Thus, there are five fewer regular officers in the CC in 1979 than there were in 1975, a decline of 3.8 per cent. This suggests that the military's new foreign policy mission in Africa has arrested neither its declining influence *vis-à-vis* the party, nor the PCC's attempt to exert greater party control over the military through the party apparatus in the armed forces (see LeoGrande, 1978d).

In short, the changes in the party apparatus since the First Congress suggest that the basic trends established during the early 1970s have persisted. The party has strengthened its own internal organizational capacity (as illustrated by the creation of the Control and Revision Committee and the expansion of the Central Committee's auxiliary apparatus) while at the same time consolidating its leadership position *vis-à-vis* other institutions. With regard to the latter, nothing in the past four years has been as important as the creation of the Organs of People's Power.

The most comprehensive discussion of the relationship between the party and OPP was provided by Raul Castro when the Matanzas experiment was just beginning (Raul Castro, 1974, pp. 2–5). He noted that PCC directives were binding only for party members, not for non-party people and certainly not for non-party institutions such as OPP. Thus the party could not 'hand down decisions' to state organs, nor should it undertake 'any manner of reprisals' against non-party OPP officials who disagreed with PCC recommendations. The PCC's only method for exerting influence over state organs and their officials was to be the party's ability to 'convince and persuade'.

The ongoing, operational relationship between the PCC and OPP mandated by the First Party Congress was as follows:

The party must guide, promote and control the work of State organs, control the policy for the promotion and training of cadres, and perfect the mechanism of the state; but the party should never replace the state in the exercise of its powers and functions (Sobre los organos del poder popular, 1976).

In practice, this means that party organs are expected to make 'suggestions, proposals, and recommendations', to 'counsel and guide' OPP, but they cannot issue directives to state organs even if the party discovers that state organs are not complying with existing laws. If such non-compliance cannot be remedied in consultations between the PCC and OPP, the party organ in question can only raise the issue with higher party authorities who then take it up in consultation with higher state authorities (Raul Castro, 1974).

Several mechanisms for exerting PCC influence in OPP exist, the most important of which is the presence of PCC members in the Municipal, Provincial, and National OPP assemblies (Table 9.10). Since party directives are binding for party members, those who sit in OPP assemblies are obligated not only to follow those directives but also to convince non-members of the correctness of the party's position. The large number of PCC members at all levels of OPP assures that the party's position will almost invariably prevail.

At the national level, for example, the possibility that the National Assembly might reject a proposal supported by the PCC is almost inconceivable. Indeed, such an event would constitute a profound political crisis. Not only is the Council of State composed almost entirely of PCC Central Committee members (including the entire Political Bureau) but the membership of the National Assembly itself is 91.7 per cent party members

TABLE 9.10   *Communist representation in the organs of people's power*

	Municipal candidates (%)	Municipal delegates (%)	Regional delegates (%)	Provincial delegates (%)	National deputies (%)
Matanzas, 1974					
PCC	n.a.	46.1	60.3	65.3	—
UJC*	n.a.	13.1	14.4	12.0	—
National, 1976					
PCC	56.0	58.8	—⎫	80(est.)†	91.7
UJC	14.4	16.4	—⎭		5.0

* Union of Young Communists.
† Estimate based on incomplete data.

Sources: Fidel Castro, 'Speech on the 21st anniversary of the attack on Moncada barracks', *Granma Weekly Review*, 4 August 1974, pp. 2–6; Partido Comunista de Cuba, *Informe sobre el desarrollo del trabajo de constitucion de los Organos del Poder Popular* (La Habana, Comite Central del PCC, 1976); 'National Assembly of People's Power Set Up', *Granma Weekly Review*, 12 December 1976, p. 4; Jorge I. Dominguez, *Cuba: Order and Revolution* (Cambridge: Harvard University Press, 1978) pp. 286–91.

(including 74 members of the Central Committee). For the National Assembly to reject a PCC-supported proposal would require that over 200 party members violate party discipline by voting against the proposal. This could only happen if the party itself was no irreconcilably divided that normal party procedures were incapable of resolving the dispute. Yet even in this unlikely scenario, we would not really have a case of the National Assembly overruling the party. Rather, it would be one faction prevailing within the PCC apparatus, and an opposing faction prevailing in the National Assembly.

The reason for the predominance of PCC members in the OPP Assemblies varies from one level of OPP to another. At the municipal level, it is probably because party members are more likely than non-members to be well known and well regarded in their communities. PCC members are selected from nominees ('exemplary workers') elected at the work-place by their co-workers. Thus PCC members tend to be politically active and well regarded by their neighbors, and also the most likely to be nominated as OPP candidates. In the Provincial and National Assemblies, the large contingents of PCC members result from the party's control of the special commissions that propose the slates of candidates for seats in those bodies.

Finally, the political hegemony of the PCC is guaranteed by the *de facto* structure of the Cuban decision-making process. Every important proposal is reviewed by the party's Political Bureau. Critical issues, such as the decision to dispatch combat troops to Ethiopia, are decided by the Political Bureau itself rather than by any state agency (Fidel Castro, 1978, pp. 1–5). Less urgent but no less important proposals, such as the national economic plan and state budget, are not only reviewed by the Political Bureau but are also routed to the party Central Committee for approval before being taken up in the National Assembly. More routine proposals are reviewed simply by the Political Bureau itself which then forwards them, on one occasion with a proposed amendment, to the National Assembly for final action (*Granma Weekly Review*, 24 July 1977, pp. 1, 9). The party, particularly the Political Bureau, occupies a veto point in Cuba's decision-making process between drafting of laws (normally by the administrative apparatus) and their adoption by the National Assembly.

As the system of People's Power evolves, its independence *vis-à-vis* the PCC will not be measured by the degree to which OPP take positions contrary to the party's, but rather by the degree to which the party refrains from the sort of direct interference in state affairs that characterized the late 1960s. The Organs of People's Power were never intended to be above the influence and leadership of the PCC, and of course they are not. The extent to which OPP constitutes a real center of decision-making rather than mere formalism will depend upon its ability to operate effectively within the context of party hegemony rather than against it.

Conclusion

With regard to the PCC, the institutionalization of the revolution has involved a dual process: internal strengthening of the party, giving it the organizational capacity to play the leading role in Cuban politics; and the assertion of party hegemony, that is to say, *political* hegemony over Cuba's other political institutions, most especially the administrative bureaucracy.

The first phase of this process lasted from 1970 to 1975 and was characterized by rapid and fundamental changes in the size and organization of the PCC. Since the First Congress, growth has been slower and more specifically aimed at key sectors. There have been no major reorganizations of internal party operations since 1975, but the process of systematizing and perfecting internal procedures has continued.

Though problems remain – especially regarding the party's composition and educational level – the advances made since 1970 have been extraordinary. As the Cuban revolution enters its third decade, it has for the first time in the revolution's history a party organization fully capable of directing its future course.

10

Party-building since Mao: A Question of Style?

TONY SAICH

Introduction

Perhaps the most enduring and damaging legacy of the Cultural Revolution decade (1966–76) is the loss of the Communist Party's prestige. The sponsored attacks on the party which ushered in the Cultural Revolution, the ensuing twists and turns of political line promoted by the party, the alleged disappearance of intra-party democracy and the exposes of the corrupt practices of some party officials have damaged the party's prestige and 'aroused indignation' (see Saich, 1984, for a full documentation of these and other points). The current view promoted by the Chinese authorities appears to be that what is at fault is not so much the policies but the way those policies have been decided and implemented. The need to build democracy and socialist legality has been a key theme for the present leadership. Since the arrest of the 'Gang of Four' the Chinese press has been littered with articles discussing party workstyle. Following a meeting of the Central Commission for Inspecting Discipline in early 1982, the campaign to rectify workstyle was stepped up. The seriousness of this problem to the Chinese was indicated in a *Red Flag* article of March 1982. The article stated that although five years had passed since the 'smashing' of the 'Gang of Four', party workstyle had not fundamentally improved. Following Chen Yun's lead this problem was described as a 'life and death question for the whole party'. Both Hu Yaobang and Deng Xiaoping, in their speeches to the 12th Party Congress (September 1982), listed the need to rectify party workstyle as one of the four main tasks.

The emphasis on criticism of workstyle and not structures is reinforced by the public reassessment of Mao Zedong. Although great criticism has

Reprinted with adaptations from *World Development*, vol. 11, no. 8 (August 1983) with the permission of author and publisher.

been levelled against Mao's economic policies and his 'erroneous' views on class struggle in socialist society, it could well be argued that, for the present leadership, Mao's greatest fault lay not so much with what he did but with the way in which he did it. In this sense Mao's 'crime' was that he destroyed the 'rules of the game' which he, himself, had helped draw up. The result was that genuine discussion within the party was destroyed as politics became increasingly personalised.

Such a line of argument is enticing. To be sure, the authoritarian political practice of the 'Gang of Four' contrasted strikingly with their espoused democratic principles. However an excessive concentration on workstyle tends to blind one to major changes which have taken and are taking place. First, there appears to be a realisation by some party members that a concentration on workstyle without making structural changes would be a waste of time. Some of the problems of workstyle are endemic to a system where power is so hierarchically arranged and where 'security of tenure' and access to restricted materials and goods gives unlimited opportunity for corruption and patronage. The notion implied by the concentration on workstyle is that the problem is primarily one of attitude, not one of structure. However, past experience not only from China but also from Eastern Europe and the Soviet Union shows that the problems inherent in a system where power is so unequally distributed cannot be overcome simply by ensuring that those within the system think in the proper way and adopt the correct workstyle. Some in the party do recognise the need for structural reform. Indeed the Constitution adopted at the 12th Party Congress takes some tentative steps towards structural reform, although clearly they are not as far-reaching as some would have liked. Also, the sterner measures introduced in March 1982 to combat corruption suggest a more widespread lack of confidence in the approach offered. As of March of that year, corrupt cadres were given the choice of 'owning up now' and receiving seven years imprisonment or waiting to be found out and then being taken out and shot!

Secondly, an excessive concentration on workstyle can obscure the change which has taken place in the role of the party in the Chinese system. The development strategy promoted in earnest since the 3rd Plenum (December 1978) calls for quite a different kind of party than that which existed immediately prior to the arrest of the 'Gang of Four' or, for that matter, to that which existed during the years 1977–8. The current focus on economic modernisation and the exclusion of any 'serious' class struggle from Chinese society requires a different party to preside over the system than the mobilisational party of either the 'Gang of Four' or Hua Guofeng.

The main part of this paper will address itself to the party which has evolved since the 3rd Plenum. It is hoped that the discussion will also highlight different views within the party about what kind of a party it should be and what its correct relationship with state and society should be.

In part, these views are related to differing approaches to development but, as with the study of all things Chinese, a neat division cannot be made.

Party rebuilding before the Third Plenum

Before considering the more recent developments it is instructive to consider briefly differing conceptions of the party since the attacks launched on it in the mid- to late 1960s. Such a consideration not only shows the diverse range of views about the party and its role but also prevents the later discussion from appearing in a vacuum. Although the changes in the post-Mao era appear to have occurred swiftly some of the trends had already been set in motion from the early 1970s. The inability of the Cultural Revolution to find alternative forms of organisation which could gain legitimacy meant that some kind of a party would be in power. The question remained of what kind of a party?

The attack on the party at the start of the Cultural Revolution should have laid to rest the approach of studying the Chinese Communist Party as a monolithic entity. Indeed, the severity of the attacks led some authors to speculate whether the party would continue to provide the institutional core for political leadership. For a while it appeared as if the future of the party as an institution was being called into question. Even though the 'radical' alternative of the commune was rejected it appeared that, from the party's point of view, at worst it would be replaced by the new 'organ of power' – the revolutionary committee – or, at best, it would share power thus losing its uniquely dominant role. Certainly its leadership role had been shattered. There was no possibility that, in Schurmann's words, all members would at any time 'act in a unified fashion throughout the society to carry out policy determined by the top leadership' (1968, p. 107).

Yet, when it came to the crunch Mao was too much of a Leninist to reject outright the concept of party leadership. When confronted with the alternative of the commune as set up in Shanghai, Mao rejected it and claimed that 'communes are too weak when it comes to suppressing counter-revolution'. In fact the revolutionary committees set up in early 1967 implied the future reorganisation of new and independent party committees. Notices published by the Heilongjiang and Guizhou Revolutionary Committees looked forward to the re-establishment of provincial party committees and regarded the jurisdiction of the revolutionary committee over party affairs as a purely temporary measure. Certainly, with the convocation of the 9th Party Congress (1969) it was clear to all that the party would return.

This intended return of the party brought to the forefront of Chinese politics a number of important organisational questions. First, what kind of a party should it be? Second, what should the correct relationship be between the party and other institutions – particularly the revolutionary committee and the People's Liberation Army? Third, where should the new revolutionary cadres come from? Before considering these it is worth outlining those ideas of Mao's which are relevant to the programme of party-building.

Like most people Mao was better at knowing what he did not want than at knowing what he did want. Little of Mao's time seems to have been devoted to working out the precise organisational arrangements which would follow the destruction of the Cultural Revolution. Perhaps like the straw sandals of Hunan they were to shape themselves in the making. In large part it was up to others to put the flesh on the bones which Mao provided, an undertaking which, as later history has shown, was dangerous for those involved.

As was noted above, in the final analysis Mao was unwilling totally to reject leadership by some kind of elite over Chinese society. Hence the suggestions of the Shengwulian to create a system based on the commune were rejected, as were those of Chen Boda who favoured the continuation of the party as it had been in the radical phase of the Cultural Revolution. For Mao leadership was necessary but those people in leadership positions were the object of suspicion. In particular Mao thought that there was a tendency for leaders to divorce themselves from the masses, with disastrous results for the masses. As a consequence leaders were to maintain contact with the masses through, for example, the participation of cadres in labour and by giving the masses the opportunity to supervise and criticise their leaders. Thus, within the party, institutional controls such as the Commissions for Inspecting Discipline were not considered necessary. Cadres would be kept on the 'straight and narrow' by the vigilance of the masses and by their closer integration with the masses. Naturally this also implied a suspicion of the hierarchical structure of the party because it could lead to a divorce of leaders from the led and a pursuit of self-interest. This thread of ideas reaches its fruition with Mao's notion that this could provide part of the basis for the emergence of a new class.

In practical terms this concern was reflected in Party and State Constitutions adopted during the 1970s. The Party Constitutions adopted by the 10th and 11th Party Congresses both contained a stipulation enabling individuals to bypass the normal chain of democratic centralism. Party members were given the right to appeal to the Party Chairman himself (Articles 5 and 12, respectively). The State Constitution adopted by the 5th National People's Congress in 1978 actually gave citizens the right to 'speak out freely, air their views fully, hold great debates and write big-character posters' (Article 45). The growing stress, particularly from 1979, on the restoration of internal monitoring of the party and the adoption of institutionalised channels of participation for the masses has meant that such references have been dropped from the new Party and State Constitutions of 1982.

Another important and related aspect of Mao's ideas was that of the relationship of the party to other organisations and institutions in society. Without doubt Mao saw the party as the most important institution. However, as Schram has shown, the party for Mao was one instrument among many, it was not something unique which, in itself, was the embodiment of legitimacy (1969, p. 11). The party was seen as a means towards an end, a view which gave rise to the possibility that other organisations might be equally effective as the means. The practical consequence of this has been that other institutions gain in importance. The 'Gang of Four' have been criticised for their promotion of non-party organisations as a challenge to party power. In part this can be interpreted as an expedient given their weakness in the party, but also it derives from Mao's ambivalence over the role of the party and its relationship to other institutions. This ambivalence over the superiority of the party and the subordination of mass organisations to it, combined with a suspicion of party leadership, made the operationalisation of the system extremely difficult.

Two other aspects of Mao's thought must be mentioned: his view of class struggle, and his approach to development strategy. While building socialism it was important for Mao that not only the end be borne in mind but also that the means of achieving that end be carefully scrutinised. The party was not only to promote production but was also to ensure that a 'new class' did not come to power in the process. Revolutionary struggle and the struggle for production was inseparable and in the last analysis class struggle was the more important. As Andors has stated, although economic development and technical transformation were seen by Mao as a vital part of building socialism, unless this was accompanied by a struggle to revolutionise production relations 'not only would the transformation of the economy and technology ultimately be limited by the forms these had assumed under capitalism, but also the attempt to revolutionise consciousness or ideology would not succeed' (1980, p. 46). The party, then, has a major role in ensuring political and ideological correctness. Also, Mao's faith in the masses meant that a greater role could be attributed to them as a part of the development strategy. In the Great Leap Forward, although the party was to be in control of the movement, the movement was based on the premise that the enthusiasm of the masses could be harnessed and used for economic growth and industrialization. Such an approach calls for a different type of party than one which relies on experts and carefully prepared plans.

It was left to others to find the required organisational forms. One problem which arose during this search was that of legitimacy, a problem which has persisted. At the start of the Cultural Revolution the massive attacks on the party meant that its legitimacy was eroded and legitimacy was transferred to the supreme leader. Although the extremes of the cult of personality were rejected, as was the form of party organisation proposed by Chen Boda to support it, the problem remains in the post-Mao years. The 'Gang of Four' sought to devise new organisational forms which could combine more traditional Leninist concepts with those thrown up by the Cultural Revolution. They did not seek to abandon Leninism, and as White has commented the 'Gang of Four' failed to 'make a break with the structural and normative logic of the Leninist form of state socialism'. White writes that they used hierarchical means to bring equality, authoritarian means to bring democracy, and the invocation of obedience to encourage initiative (G. White, 1982, p. 6). The models experimented with failed to gain legitimacy. This, combined with their suspicion of the party and lack of support within its top leadership, meant that they all too readily fell back on the invocation of Mao's name as a source of legitimacy. The breakdown of the party's authority and the inability to revive it or to produce a substitute created an excessively leader-oriented source of legitimacy.

Despite Hua Guofeng's policy differences with the 'Gang of Four' he, too, was presented with the problem of securing legitimacy. The problem remained of institutionalising what he perceived to be the Maoist legacy. In terms of development strategy he favoured an approach similar to that of the Great Leap Forward. This approach was to be based on mobilisation but was to be conducted with the party firmly in command. In early 1978 at the 5th National People's Congress, Hua unveiled the economic plans for the future. The basis was the 1976–85 Ten-Year Plan which set forward a series of ambitious targets. The plan bore resemblances to Mao's Twelve-Year Plan of the mid-1950s which had preceded the Great Leap Forward and the rhetoric began to mirror that which accompanied the Great Leap. In fact, the slogan of the Great Leap of 'going all out, aiming high to achieve greater, faster, better and more economical results in building socialism' was included in the General Programme of the Party Constitution adopted by the 11th Party Congress in 1977. Noticeably it is absent from the Constitution adopted by the 12th Party Congress in 1982. Hua appears to have wanted to create a 'Great Leap type of party' – one which was sufficiently flexible and able to use a mobilisational style of politics. However, again the problem of creating legitimacy remained. While trying to restore party prestige Hua also resorted to the adulation of Mao as the source of legitimacy while at the same time creating his own cult of personality.

Most of the 1970s saw an attempt to institutionalize and operationalise a system which did not reject the fundamentals of Leninism but at the same time incorporated the innovative and new organisational principles of the

Cultural Revolution. This is reflected in the Party Constitutions of 1973 and 1977. Although there was a steady erosion of the new and a greater preponderance of the old both Constitutions sought to strike a balance. Consequently, one sees traditional Leninist concepts such as democratic centralism and the need for party discipline alongside emphasis on the rebellious nature of the Cultural Revolution as summed up in the phrase 'going against the tide is a Marxist principle'. The Constitution adopted by the 11th Party Congress reflected the drive to revive traditional Leninism at the expense of innovation introduced during the Cultural Revolution, but not all was thrown overboard. A favourable attitude to the Cultural Revolution was maintained and Hua pointed out that many such political revolutions would be necessary in the future. Although the disciplinary role of the masses was limited they were still expected to 'keep an eye' on the party.

Party rebuilding since the 3rd Plenum

Following the 3rd Plenum of the 11th Central Committee (December 1978) a faster and more fundamental change has taken place. For our purposes the Plenum was important in two respects. First, despite the Plenum's exhortations to forget about the past and look to the future, decisions made at the Plenum led to a selectively detailed review of the thirty years of the history of the People's Republic. From the point of view of party rebuilding the 'reversals of verdict' on two particular people were of great significance. The restoration of Peng Dehuai's good name paved the way for criticisms of the breakdown of traditional party norms while the reversal of the verdict on Liu Shaoqi aided the reconstruction of those norms. Secondly, the Plenum put China firmly on a new economic path to achieve the goal of the four modernisations. The Great Leap style mobilisation strategy was replaced by the more cautious programmes for economic growth favoured by people such as Chen Yun and Xue Muqiao. Although the trend had been visible for a long time the need was clearly for a more predictable party capable of being an efficient organisational decision-making body.

The Plenum marked the subordination of all other work to that of achieving the four modernisations. The Plenum contended that class struggle was no longer the principal contradiction in Chinese society and *Beijing Review* stated that 'the fundamental change in the class situation in our country is the objective basis for the shift in focus of our party's work to socialist modernization'. Political work was being seen increasingly in terms of its ability to increase production. The slogan continually put forward was that of 'less empty talk'. This was used to criticise previous campaigns and political objectives. Also politics and economics were being separated into distinct entities. This was combined with the notion that economic work should 'grasp the Laws of Economic Development'.

Economics and the struggle for production are now clearly in command with immediate consequences for the party. Party work is now to serve and help bring about the realisation of the four modernisations. Correspondingly, political and ideological work decline in importance. Consequently, the role of the party as guardian in these realms diminishes. The role of the party and its superiority as interpreter of the ideology are still affirmed but it is difficult, in practice, to see what this means other than removing the 'ideological driftwood' which is seen as an impediment to economic work. The new stress on production guided by 'experts' and conducted in an orderly fashion without the unrestrained participation of the masses has meant that party organisations are now required to be efficient planning institutions, predictable, but not inflexible, in their actions and with a discernible and hierarchical chain of command. As Young has pointed out, what is now required of the integrative functions of the party is to provide a 'competent administration' rather than to discover and implement a 'correct' political direction (1980, p. 82).

Internal party organisation

Criticisms of the party have concentrated on bad workstyle and only belatedly have structural problems been approached. While criticizing the 'Gang of Four' for their arbitrary methods it is conveniently forgotten that the post-Mao leadership came to power through an act totally outside of the established principles – members of the highest party body were arrested without consulting the Politburo.

The criticism and re-examination of the past have led to the identification of two different problems as the source of faulty workstyle: problems of bureaucratism and problems of remaining vestiges of feudalism. The term bureaucracy in this derogative sense covers a multitude of sins ranging from the swollen and overstaffed offices to the criticism of cadres who are said to have 'divorced themselves from the masses'. As early as August 1980 Deng Xiaoping identified this as a major problem when he told the Politburo that:

Bureaucratism is a great problem that exists in the political life of our party and state . . . Both in our domestic affairs and our international dealings, all this has reached an absolutely intolerable state.

By March 1982 Wang Renzhong was moved to lament that investigation had shown that not a single province could be found which was free from graft, embezzlement and other faults.

The continued existence of feudalism is seen to arise not only as a result of 'hangovers' from the past, such as attitudes towards authority, but also because the 'Gang of Four' promoted 'feudal fascism'. One major concern of this thrust of the criticism is the excessive power which such an approach gives to one person. Deification of Mao clearly has not been eradicated. Those who adhered too closely to the principles laid down by Mao were denounced as the 'Whatever' faction. Later, during the campaign to criticise 'leftism' which preceded the 6th Plenum (June 1981) the criticism was extended to include Hua Guofeng.

However, the extent of criticism of the past has varied considerably. Leaders such as Hua Guofeng and Ye Jianying, for example, have continually sought to moderate criticism of Mao and to stem the flood of exposes of Mao's 'mistakes'. Hua in his pronouncements has sought to narrow the focus of those under criticism. Criticisms of Mao undermine Hua's legitimacy to rule as Mao's personally chosen successor, while a broadening of those to be criticised would chip away at his own supporters. At the other extreme within the party there have been the criticisms of those such as Li Honglin. In March 1979, Li made a scathing attack on the legacy of the Cultural Revolution and he clearly indicated that the source of these faults was the dominance of the individual in the Chinese political system. Li implies that the years of the late 1950s also suffered from the same problem. Clearly these were years when policy formulation was dominated by Mao. Other party members have been less harsh. Li Xiannian, for example, has pointed out that although, in retrospect, the faults of the Great Leap Forward are apparent, the decision to launch the movement was made by the party and not by an individual. Dominating the middle ground have been the shifting views of Deng Xiaoping. He has sought to steer a path avoiding the excesses of criticism and the whitewashing of the mistakes committed by Mao. This approach informed the 'Resolution on Party History' adopted by the 6th Plenum (1981). On the question of Mao the 'Resolution' condemns him for his mistakes but makes it clear that the mistakes were those of a 'great proletarian revolutionary' whose errors were secondary to his great revolutionary achievements.

To right the past wrongs and to suit the demands of the new modernisation programme a number of institutions and policies have been revived or created. For the most part these reflect Deng Xiaoping's desire to return to a 'conventional way of doing things'. Measures have been introduced to deal with both workstyle and some of the more obvious structural problems, such as the abolition of the lifetime tenure of cadres. The reforms being experimented with do not in any way threaten the stability and integrity of the party and represent an attempt to modify the excesses of traditional Leninism. Challenges to the right of the party to rule based on its none too good 'track record' during the Cultural Revolution decade are rejected with statements to the effect that although the 'Gang of Four' used the party to implement their 'disastrous' policies, it was the party which set things to right. Reforms, then, will be carried out by the party itself. Forces outside of the party, such as those unleashed during the Cultural Revolution, will not be mobilised. To revitalise the leadership and to restore party prestige, party discipline has been re-emphasised. Discipline and good behaviour are to be reinforced by administrative control mechanisms and definitively not by mass supervision.

Within the party the correct functioning of principles such as democratic centralism and collective leadership are seen as vital. The Constitution adopted by the 12th Party Congress contains a more detailed outline of the principles of democratic centralism than was previously the case. While stressing the subordination of minority to majority and lower levels to higher levels, the Constitution also states that higher party organisations should pay constant attention to the lower organisations and rank-and-file party members. In terms of the right of party members to criticise, the stress is on this being carried out in an orderly fashion. Party members, if they disagree with decisions or policies, are still accorded the right to take their views to higher levels including the Central Committee, but not to the Chairperson (the post having been abolished). The Constitution stresses, like the 11th but unlike the 10th, that while this process is taking place party members must 'resolutely carry out the decision or policy while it is in force'. Also, it is stated that any criticism of other members or organisations should be 'well-grounded' (for the full text, see Simons and White, 1984).

If recent practice seems to have stressed the centralist component more than the democratic one, democracy is still seen as important not just for the party but for society as a whole. However, within the party, two restraints are placed on democracy. It is limited to those who do not challenge the fundamentals of the party line and it is not to be seen as an end in itself – it, too, must serve the goal of the four modernisations. To date, two groups have been identified to which the rights of democratic expression do not extend. First, there are those who are said to have misinterpreted the degree of freedom possible and who have promoted 'so-called democracy'. Second, there are those who have been denounced as the 'Whateverists'. The existence of democracy in the party is vital both for internal communication and to link the party with state and society. This will provide the party leadership with the necessary information to frame the general policy guidelines to suit the changing conditions.

The new Constitution also shows concern for the need for collective leadership and the avoidance of personal rule. This relationship of leader to the party has been a continual problem. The problem reached its height during the heyday of the Cultural Revolution when, for many, the authority of the party was replaced by the authority of the individual. The present leadership have tried through a series of measures to bring to bear formal and informal controls over the top political leaders.

The 'Guiding Principles for Inner-Political Life' adopted in 1980 criticised the 'unprincipled glorification of leaders'. The 'Principles' stated that publicity for leading members should be factual and while no museums are to be built for the living 'not too many' are to be built for the dead. The move against the glorification of the leader was set in motion by the now deposed Chairman, Hua Guofeng, in December 1978. Hua, at a Central Work Conference, stated '. . . when the local authorities and various units send reports to the Central Committee for its views, then reports should not be addressed to Chairman Hua and the Central Committee . . . Do not call me the wise leader, just call me comrade'. Such modesty and recognition of his past faults were not enough, however, to save him his job.

In September 1980, Li Honglin wrote a more systematic condemnation of the 'incorrect' relationship between the leader and the led. Li criticised the personality cult of the Cultural Revolution, which he said was only necessary in a feudal society. In a sideswipe at Hua Guofeng, Li suggested that the cult had continued for a while even after 1976. For Li the consequence of the cult was that the leader could not be criticised, a tendency which he traced from the treatment of Peng Dehuai in 1959. While not all the leadership would necessarily support the severity of Li's judgements they do seem to accept the need to play down the role of the individual and to institutionalise collective leadership. Measures have been introduced to reduce the adulation of national leaders and also to prevent individuals from holding too many posts concurrently. The Resolution on Establishing the Secretariat of the Central Committee explicitly stated that the Secretariat would apply the 'system of collective leadership and division of work with individual responsibility'.

When listing the principles of democratic centralism the system of collective leadership with individual responsibility was reaffirmed and 'all forms of personality cult' were expressly forbidden. The abolition of the post of Chairperson is seen as a further check on the abuse of the system by individuals. Hu Qiaomu, who presided over the drafting of the new Constitution, when commenting on the change outlined the difference between a General Secretary and a Chairperson:

He (the General Secretary) is responsible for convening the meetings of the Political Bureau and its Standing Committee and presides over the work of the Secretariat. Obviously, convening and presiding are different roles. Such an organisational system will help prevent the recurrence of over-concentration of personal power and arbitrariness of a single person. Experiences of our own and other countries' organisations show that when a party has both a Chairman and a General Secretary, often one position is merely nominal. Therefore, it is unnecessary to have these two positions simultaneously. Moreover, there is no reason for the posts of the Chairman and the General Secretary to be held by one person.

Hu may well be right but the 'foreign experience' of the Soviet Union under Stalin shows that the existence of the post of General Secretary is quite compatible with 'overconcentration of personal power' and arbitrary rule.

The restrictions on individuals acting beyond the scope of party policy are dealt with in Article 16 of the Constitution. The views must be on behalf of the party organisation and the contents must have been referred to that organisation first or have been referred to the next higher party organisation for instructions. Party members, no matter what their position, cannot make decisions on major issues by themselves and cannot place themselves above the party organisation.

However, for the system to work effectively responsibility rests on a well-trained and responsive cadre force. Not surprisingly measures have been introduced to remedy the problems with cadres and their work. However, Deng Xiaoping's and his supporters' attempts to reform the cadre system and improve their quality has met with stiff opposition. Following a speech of Deng's in January 1980, the press has stressed the importance of training cadres and has reiterated Mao's statement that 'after the political line has been fixed cadres become the decisive factor'.

Cadres are not only to undergo the education programme for all party members but have their own specific materials to study and contemplate. The Central Commission for Inspecting Discipline drew up a fifteen-point code of behaviour instructing cadres that they should not act like high officials and overbearing bureaucrats, seek personal gain, become idealistic, act arbitrarily or abuse their power. The new Party Constitution set a number of requirements above those expected of ordinary members. In addition to covering the kind of abuses mentioned above the requirements call on cadres to correctly implement the party's line, principles and policies; fight resolutely against hostile forces and combat all erroneous tendencies inside and outside the party.

The new Party Constitution also calls for 'genuine efforts to make the ranks of the cadres more revolutionary, younger in average age, better educated and more professionally competent'. The attempts to replace the older cadres with little formal training by younger, better qualified cadres has met stiff opposition and it was not until late 1981–early 1982 that the policy was pursued in earnest. However, as early as April 1980 *Red Flag* pointed out the poor quality of cadres. The article pointed out that few cadres were really proficient in professional work, that many were laypeople and that some of these people were in leading positions at the provincial level making final decisions. Later in the year the *People's Daily* pointed out the 'evils' which stem from the life-long tenure of cadres:

Personnel in leading posts tend to be senile . . . it is difficult for talented and erudite people to be recruited to leading bodies and get experience . . . the system does not encourage people to work hard but muddle along . . . nepotism replaces appointment on merit . . . power tends to become highly concentrated until ultimately all powers of the party and state are wielded by one person alone.

In particular there was resentment that 'excessive stress' was placed on formal educational training which would, of course, discriminate against many of the incumbent cadres. The reaction caused Deng to moderate his policy and by the end of 1980 and early 1981 a more flexible application of age and educational requirements was promised and incumbent cadres were promised retraining opportunities and the possibility of training their successors.

Clearly regulations were needed to persuade cadres to retire voluntarily. Given the power and privileged access to scarce goods that leading party positions provide this is hardly surprising. In March 1982, the *People's Daily* informed veteran cadres that their 'glorious and sacred duty' was to retire! This, it was stated, was the greatest contribution that one could make in one's old age. Recognising that such an appeal might not be enough by itself, it was also made clear that financial incentives were available for those who did retire. It is hoped that ending the life-long tenure of cadres, in both party and state, will make cadres more account-able. This, in turn, should make cadres more responsive to both party and the masses and more liable to dismissal should they be found guilty of corruption or incompetence.

The new Party Constitution tackles this problem but not as thoroughly as was originally intended. It contains stipulations that cadres, whether elected or appointed, are not entitled to lifelong tenure, and that they can be transferred from or relieved of their posts. However, the Constitution contains no stipulations strictly limiting the terms of office. An earlier draft which was circulated contained greater details concerning both the period of tenure and the average age limit of cadres. Hu Qiaomu stated that 'after repeated discussions' strict limits on the term of office would not be set. The reason he gave was for the need to retain some veteran cadres with experience and high prestige to ensure 'stability and maturity' of leader-ship. In practice, it seems to be a concession to the large number of cadres who feared their imminent removal from office.

To help with the problem of relieving cadres of their posts while still making use of their expertise, advisory commissions are to be set up at and above the provincial level. It is intended that the members of these commissions will act as political assistants and consultants. Whether this becomes a genuine reform or whether it is a short-term measure to open up avenues for promotion only time will tell. It is difficult to see what the real change would be, apart from the name, if all the oldest party members simply became advisers. The immediate effect of creating these advisory commissions has been to increase the number of people attending plenary sessions of the Central Committee. The 7th Plenum of the 11th Central Committee (August 1982) was attended by a total of 318 people (297 Committee members and alternates and 21 observers), while the 1st Plenum of the 12th Central Committee was attended by 631 people (347 Committee members and alternates and 284 observers). This 100 per cent increase does not bode well for a regime committed to reducing bureaucracy. Also, this can only give more ammunition to those who believe that the Central Committee is not an important decision-making body in the party.

However, the creation of the Central Advisory Commission has provided some places for new members on the Central Committee. Of the 172 Central Advisory Commission members 49 were on the 11th Central Committee (Deng Xiaoping is still on the 12th) and 14 were alternates. This provided some of the places for the 211 newly elected committee members and alternates. However, the vast majority of new places was provided by the purge of members and alternates from the 11th Central Committee. Of the new members 140 are said to be less than 60 with a youngest age of 38. The new Committee and its alternate members also reflects the drive to recruit more specialised personnel to leadership positions. Specialised personnel is said to have increased from 2.7 per cent at the 11th to 17 per cent at the 12th Central Committee.

In company with this 'righting of wrongs' and, to a large extent, preceding it, a number of pre-Cultural Revolution institutions have been revived. As we mentioned, the Secretariat has been revived as a collective leadership body to handle the day-to-day work of the party. This is seen by the Chinese to be a function of the shift of focus of the work to modernisation. Concentration on this objective is said to have produced a greater complexity of work. In theory the Politburo and its Standing Committee are freed to concentrate on taking important decisions on national and international issues with the Secretariat becoming the party's administrative heart. In practice, the Secretariat is placed in an extremely powerful position as it supervises the regional party organs and the functional departments of the party, departments which, in theory, should be responsible directly to the Central Committee and the Politburo.

To overcome the impediments of bureaucratism and faulty workstyle a system of internal party control has been resurrected, the linchpin of which is the Commissions for Inspecting Discipline. This reflects a more institutionalised method for dealing with discipline, replacing the more arbitrary methods which operated during the Cultural Revolution. The Central Commission for Inspecting Discipline was set up by the 3rd Plenum and has been charged with the resurrection of rules and regulations which the party feels have been flouted since the late 1950s. Among its most important activities in this respect have been the publication of the aforementioned 'Guiding Principles' and the draft of the educational materials for party cadres, providing the findings for the posthumous rehabilitation of Liu Shaoqi, and the recreation of a discipline and control system throughout the party.

Also, party schools have been revived to provide party members with a proper education in the way that they should behave and the way in which the party should be run. The influx of new party members during the years 1966–76 is said to be a major cause of the faulty workstyle of the party. *Red Flag* claims that the party ranks expanded by 100 per cent during the Cultural Revolution decade. Because this was a time of 'abnormality' in party life, many of these new members are said to be unfamiliar with traditional party procedures and hence unqualified to be party members. Consequently, a programme of education has been launched to instil in members the 'basis knowledge of the party, its rules, discipline, fine traditions and style of work'. In fact, similar criticisms are made of the basic political knowledge of cadres. According to an article in the mid-June 1982 issue of *Red Flag*, statistics from some provinces showed that 80 per cent of cadres had no systematic and basic knowledge of Marxism. The article called for those between the ages of 30 and 50 to receive special attention in the training programmes given in the party and cadre schools.

Presumably, those who do not come up to the required standards will be expelled from the party. In fact, in August 1982 the *People's Daily* called for 'degenerate elements' to be expelled. Also, Hu Yaobang, in his report to the 12th Party Congress, when talking of the three-year party rectification to begin in the second half of 1983, mentioned that all party members would be required to re-register at the end of this period. He explicitly stated that 'those who still fail to meet the requirements for membership after education shall be expelled from the party or asked to withdraw from it'. Chen Yun, among others, indicated that three categories of people would not be welcome in the future: first, people who rose to prominence in the Cultural Revolution by following the 'Gang of Four' in rebellion; second, people who were seriously factionalist in their ideas; and third, people who indulged in beating, smashing and looting.

Finally, the rehabilitation of Liu Shaoqi by the 5th Plenum (February 1980) was a significant event in terms of the restoration of the norms which had governed party life in the mid-1950s. His rehabilitation has facilitated the republication and discussion of his major works and theories concerning party organisation and how to conduct party life. It is expected that a reading of works such as 'How to be a Good Communist' (1939) and 'On Inner-Party Struggle' (1941) will give party members a clearer understanding of their rights and duties and how debate within the party should be conducted. The most notable feature of these writings is their preoccupation with organization. Such an emphasis obviously finds more sympathy with a leadership committed to the present approach to development. It helps the attempts to build a more professionalised, traditionally Leninist-style party aiding the transformation of the party into an instrument to achieve the four modernisations. The present leadership clearly have a preference for a leadership style associated with Liu than with Mao. As Dittmer has shown, while Liu's style was formal and routinised, Mao's was episodic and provocative; while Liu called meetings, drew up agendas etc., Mao would short-circuit the system, often presenting the leadership with a *fait accompli*; and while Liu's institutional strategy of policy formulation resulted in extremely detailed directives, Mao's directives by contrast were schematic to avoid inflexibility (1974, pp. 185–6). Now, spontaneous action by the masses, albeit often loosely orchestrated, has been replaced by tight organisation and central leadership and a reliance on the ingenuity of the masses is replaced by a reliance on the professional skills of the technical and managerial elite.

Party–state relations

Like other communist party-states, China can be studied in terms of the classic duality of the party and the state and their interrelationship. In theory, the party devises policy and provides political leadership while the state implements and administers the policy. In this section two aspects of recent policy in this area will be considered: first, the attempts to make a clear distinction between party and state; and second, the consequences of the current resolution of the debate on the decentralisation of economic decision-making.

In all communist party-states the distinction between party and state is blurred and in China this distinction has been the least clear. In China there has existed confusion about the division of responsibility between policy formulation and implementation. On occasions, this overlap of party and state has led to the party actually implementing policy. Normally this is condemned, but during the Cultural Revolution it appeared to be positively encouraged. For example, at the beginning of the Cultural Revolution the organs of party and state, at the non-central levels, were identical. Following the attacks on the old party and state organs in 1966 they were replaced by the revolutionary committee which, for a while at least, combined party and state functions in one body. The rebuilding of the party from 1969 following the total collapse of the distinction between party and state caused a persistent confusion over the division of responsibilities between party committees and revolutionary committees. Throughout the early 1970s the press stressed the need for the party committees to strengthen their leadership over the revolutionary committees, emphasising that the party should make the major decisions and that the revolutionary committee must 'consciously accept the party committee's leadership in exercising power and carrying out its work'. This problem was not helped by the fact that the leadership personnel of the two committees were often identical and party committees in some factories were criticised for handling such trivial matters as family disputes and water temperatures in bath-houses. The concurrent holding of posts was even more noticeable at the centre of the system. For example, until mid-1980 all the Vice-Premiers of the State Council were high-ranking members of the Central Committee and Politburo.

This penetration of party into the state and its control of the state sector are reflected in both the 'more radical' State Constitution of 1975 and the 'less radical' one of 1978. While Article 3 of the two Constitutions states that 'all power in the People's Republic of China belongs to the people', Article 2 indicates that the real power lies with the party. In both Constitutions the Article states that the party is 'the core of leadership of the whole Chinese people' and that the working-class exercises leadership over the state through the party – its vanguard.

The post-Mao leadership has attempted to recreate the distinction between party and state which is supposed to exist under 'socialism'. This attempt has gone beyond paying mere lip-service to the distinction as appeared to be the case in the immediate post-Mao years to actually trying to give the theoretical distinction some substance in practice. Direct administration by the party has been criticised and it has been pointed out that the party's responsibility for leadership should never have meant direct control. Apart from the theoretical reasons for maintaining party and state as separate organs there are also practical ones. As Schurmann pointed out, the more an organisation becomes a 'command-issuing body' the more it must 'grapple with the concrete technicalities of command'. This would lead to increasing bureaucratism and inflexibility thus thwarting the party's ability to innovate and adjust to changing circumstances (1968, p. 111). Also, the new development strategy relies heavily on the experts to implement it and this necessitates a weakening of the party's grip over both state and society and, especially in the economic sphere, the relaxation of state over society. Finally, by distancing itself from the day-to-day running of the system, the party can seek to avoid the blame for economic failings. These can more readily be blamed on faulty implementation etc. Particularly at the level of the enterprise this can be important. Management can be held responsible for failings and thus be dismissed if necessary while, in theory, the party could remain intact.

The dangers in such a course are evident. A corporatist structure could begin to emerge with other powerful groups in state and society challenging party dominance. The reliance on groups such as the economic planners must afford them increased power. The solution for the party in this situation, as much of Eastern European experience has shown, is to recruit these groups into the party to maintain control over the state. However, as White points out, this imports their 'autonomous power and distinct interests' thus, in turn, exerting pressure on the direction of public policy (G. White, 1983, p. 40).

The first problem the post-Mao leadership tackled was to try to resolve the continuing confusion between the revolutionary committee and the party committee. The State Constitution adopted in 1978 stressed the purely administrative function of the revolutionary committee, referring to it as the executive rather than the permanent organ of the people's congress at the corresponding level and as the local people's government at the various levels. The committee's ubiquity was curtailed by restricting it only to levels of government. The second session of the 5th National People's Congress went even further than this and abolished them altogether. Peng Zhen in making the, by then, largely symbolic announcement stated that the posts of governors, mayors etc. would be restored.

The next problem tackled was that of cadres holding both top party and state posts, which blurred the distinction between party and state work. At the 3rd session of the 5th National People's Congress (August–September 1980) Hua Guofeng announced that the common practice of the same person holding the leading party and state posts at provincial level was to come to an end. According to Hua, the objective of this was to prevent the 'over-concentration of power and the holding of too many posts concurrently by one person'. Its aim was to 'effectively and clearly separate party work from government work'. Earlier, in July 1980, it was announced that the highest posts in the party and state would again be held by different people – as had been the case up until Mao's death. Hua Guofeng, while remaining Chairman of the party, 'handed over' the post of Premier to Zhao Ziyang.

This freeing of the state from the grip of the party is also reflected in the 1982 State Constitution. This version reverts back to the similar one of 1954 when the power of the party was hidden in the Constitution. The Article of the 1975 and 1978 Constitutions which referred to the party as the 'core of leadership' has been dropped, as has the claim that it is the citizens' duty to support the party (Article 26, 1975; Article 56, 1978). Now citizens are said to have the duty to 'abide by the Constitution and the law'. Direct party control is further weakened by dropping the provision that the party and its Chairperson lead and command the PLA (Article 15, 1975; Article 19, 1978) and also by renouncing the stipulation that the Premier be recommended by the party's Central Committee (Article 17, 1975; Article 22, 1978). In fact the emphasis on constitutionalism appears to go beyond even that of 1954. Mention of party control now only appears in the Preamble where its leading role is acknowledged (*Constitution of the People's Republic of China*, 1983, p. 5).

The period since the death of Mao has seen the revival of the debate over the decentralization of economic decision-making. As Schurmann has shown, in the debates of the 1950s two main options were put forward.

Either powers could be devolved to the provinces (Decentralisation 1) or they could be devolved to the units of production (Decentralisation 2) (1968, pp. 196–9). Both options have consequences for the party's role in economic affairs and both options have been experimented with since Mao's death.

Initial policy was along the lines of Schurmann's Decentralisation 1. As has been noted, Hua Guofeng sought a 'Great Leap' approach to development with the emphasis on social mobilisation rather than on material incentives. This approach was to take place with the party firmly in command and as a consequence greater powers accrued to the provincial party apparatus and the party committees in the unit of production. Provincial government and particularly party committees through their unique coordinating role dominated the process. The individual production units, by contrast, had very little autonomy. As had happened before, this approach was accompanied by announcements that economic zones should be set up for cooperation. Again mention was made in the Chinese press of establishing economic systems in the six big regions. An article by the State Planning Commission on the first anniversary of Mao's death stated that these would have 'their own special features, operate independently, cooperate with one another and ensure a fairly balanced growth of agriculture, light industry and heavy industry'.

More recent policy has produced an emphasis on greater autonomy for the units of production. Such an approach makes the use of material, rather than moral, incentives as a stimulus to development easier. Clearly this approach, too, has consequences for the party's role. Increasingly since the 3rd Plenum we have seen the dominance of the ideas of Chen Yun in the economic field. The role of the market is emphasised along with that of material incentives, and power in decision-making has been shifted from provincial party committees and party committees in production units to the ministries and enterprise managers. The party is forced into a situation where production units, or their managers, can exert considerable pressure on it. The powers of the enterprise party committee will inevitably become limited. Similarly, in the countryside the party's control can be challenged. At present, rural policy favours the wealthier peasants and this should, in turn, increase their power to challenge the party's authority at the basic levels, a problem which will be returned to later.

Party and society

The renewed stress on the four modernisations has revived parallels with other periods when the demands of the economy have required the relaxation of the party's grip over society. As with its relationship with the state, the party is trying to redefine its position *vis-à-vis* society. To encourage the greater supply of information by experts to the party less interference is to be tolerated in specialised areas by the party. Reference is no longer made to the overall leadership of the party over the seven sectors in Chinese society and the State Constitution does not refer to the party as the 'core of leadership of the whole people'. Yet, clearly overall leadership is to be maintained as is encapsulated in the emphasis on the adherence to the 'Four Fundamental Principles'. In an interview a 'leading comrade' of the Central Committee's Organisation Department implicitly criticised past practice by stating that leadership must not be exercised by issuing orders or by using mandatory administrative means. According to the interviewee, the future leadership role of the party is to be exercised in three ways. First, party leading organs are to formulate and implement the correct line, principles and policies. Second, at the different levels the party is to coordinate the relations: the different fields ensuring harmony in achieving the prescribed goals. Third, party members themselves are to set shining examples for others to follow (*Beijing Review*, 1982, no. 28, p. 17).

Similarly, as with other periods of 'liberalisation', differences of opinion have been expressed concerning just how far the party can and should relax its grip. White has pointed out that there is a large area of contention between the notion that the party cannot monopolise everything and the insistence that, as Deng Xiaoping put it, 'without party leadership . . . there would be no force able to lead the four modernisations' (G. White, 1983, pp. 34–7). The party is caught in the contradiction of trying to keep intellectuals loyal to the basic tenets of Marxism—Leninism, thus requiring a fairly strict ideological orthodoxy while, at the same time, encouraging intellectuals to utilise their skills to promote the four modernisations, thus requiring a certain creativity.

One of the major criticisms of the 'Gang of Four' has been the charge that they promoted the mass organisations under their control as a direct challenge to communist party rule. As we have seen, it was not their, or Mao's intention to replace the party by other organisations, but they did have a suspicion of the party which opened the way to criticisms of their diluting the party's leading role. History has shown that the party does not tolerate the emergence of other bodies to challenge its rule. The present leadership has tried to restore the effective leadership of the party while at the same time not negating the contributions that the masses can make to the modernisation programme. This desire is reflected in the current view of the mass line. As Young points out, the current stress on the strengthening of party leadership is seen to be entirely consistent with the mass line concept as the direction in which the masses are heading can only be the correct one if the party is pointing the way (1980, p. 67). The mass line becomes, in fact, another cog in the wheel for reaching the four modernisations, by helping to solve problems encountered on the road. This approach is reflected in the revival of organisations for the masses such as the trade unions, the Youth League and the Women's Federation which fell into disfavour during the Cultural Revolution. These organisations are now expected to provide the link between society and the party.

The policy of relaxation, and its fluctuations, are seen most clearly with respect to policies concerning intellectuals. To provide their 'expert' advice this sector of society must be given certain freedoms and sureties to ensure their support. Despite recent retrenchments, intellectuals in many fields have enjoyed a freedom unparalleled since 1949. A number of 'forbidden zones' have been entered and it has been stated that 'without democracy, there can be no science' and that 'science and culture cannot develop without free discussion'. Intellectual work and achievements are no longer downgraded and the vital role which intellectuals play in the modernisation process has been stressed. Of the 340 model workers at the December 1979 National Model Workers' Conference, 160 were intellectuals. Their status has been improved by the restoration of academic titles and all intellectuals are to have their work and living conditions improved. Most importantly, intellectuals are now defined as a part of the working class – a long way from the 'stinking ninth category' as they were designated during the Cultural Revolution. This means that in future when reeducation for an intellectual is considered necessary, it will be dealt with in the same manner as other contradictions among the people. When Bai Hua was being criticised for his script 'Bitter Love', Chinese leaders were at pains to point out that the Cultural Revolution methods of criticism would not be used. In fact, at the same time as he was being criticised for 'Bitter Love', he received an award for another of his works.

As has been noted, differences exist within the party concerning the degree of freedom permissible. Leaders such as Deng Xiaoping and Hu Yaobang, while stressing the need for party supremacy, seem to have supported greater freedom for intellectuals. Others in the party have clearly sought to reassert tighter party control. They, as in other periods, have been able to use the anti-party sentiments and criticisms voiced in both the official and unofficial media to push through a crackdown on the extremes of freedom tolerated. During the period of greater freedom, views were expressed which desired greater freedom, and, in some cases, total freedom from party control. Liu Binyan put forward a writer's defence of the right to criticise the party when he wrote that 'when literature mirrors what is undesirable in life, the mirror itself is not to blame; instead, disagreeable things in real life should be spotted and wiped out. An ugly person cannot be turned into a beauty simply by smashing the mirror.' Clearly, there are still those who would prefer to smash the mirror.

The changes in development strategy have also had a significant impact on the kind of person whom the party wants to recruit from society. Although the Chinese Communist Party is one of the most exclusive communist parties in the world, recruitment of party members has always been flexible. Since the fall of the 'Gang of Four' and more particularly since the 3rd Plenum, the emphasis of recruitment policy has been on cadres, intellectuals and those who possess technical skills. This has brought into the party those with the high-level of technical skills to help with the programme of economic modernisation. These groups of people are over-represented in recent recruitment when taken as a percentage of society as a whole. In 1979, Guizhou Province recruited 1916 intellectuals to be party members. Similarly, in other provinces emphasis has been on the recruitment of intellectuals and professionals. For example, in Shaanxi in 1981, 36.3 per cent of new party members were intellectuals and professionals while in the same time Henan recruited 4366 intellectuals. From Beijing there is evidence to suggest that recruitment of intellectuals is increasing. In 1979, it was stated that 15 per cent (2600) of the new recruits that year were intellectuals. In 1982, it was stated that from 1979 to 1982, 20 per cent of the new recruits were intellectuals. This same report mentions that most of the new recruits were outstanding factory, scientific, research and teaching workers or labour heroes. The stress on recruiting professionals and technicians is reinforced by statistics from Shandong Province which show that of recent party recruits, 20.9 per cent were specialists and technicians.

However, problems have been encountered in recruitment. The relaxation of the party's grip over the basic economic units could produce a reluctance of the part of the masses to join the party. For example, in the countryside, if the privileged access to goods etc. that party membership gives is undermined and rivalled by other avenues for accumulating wealth, people may decide the gains of party membership do not outweigh those that can be found elsewhere. Also, peasants and workers may feel that the stress on the model behaviour of party members may prevent them from benefiting fully from current policies. Hu Yaobang in his report to the 12th Party Congress pointed out the 'grave situation' of the fewer party members on the 'production front' and how this had 'weakened the direct link between the party and the industrial workers'. When referring to the situation in the countryside Hu stated:

> in a number of rural areas . . . some party members are interested only in their own productive activities and neglect the interests of the party and the masses, and some party branches have relinquished leadership among the masses.

It seems probable that the stress from mid-1982 on the need to 'consolidate primary party organisations' was inspired not only because of the problem of the 'poor quality' of Cultural Revolution recruits but also because of the weakening of the party's grip over the economic sector.

Unless a satisfactory *modus vivendi* is found the party could find itself increasingly 'squeezed out' at the basic level by rival powerful groups.

Concluding remarks

In this final section it is the intention to outline the differing views which exist concerning the party in the Chinese political system. I do not intend to look at views expressed by those writers in the Democracy Movement who proposed a multi-party system primarily because there is no chance of such a view being realised in the foreseeable future.

Four main views can be discerned, but they are not entirely distinct and it would perhaps be better to think of them as points along a continuum. Indeed, Deng Xiaoping appears to have given support to proponents of more than one view since his return, in the same way as the oscillating Mao did during the early years of the Cultural Revolution. The two ends of the continuum are dealt with first and then the two views which appear to occupy the centre and around which future policies will probably revolve.

First, there is the view of the party which was dominant in the immediate post-Mao years. This view retains certain features from the Cultural Revolution years along with the ambiguities and was designed to complement the optimistic proposals of the new 'Great Leap' strategy for economic development. Most of those associated with this type of view have been removed from power during the campaign against the 'Whateverists' and the campaign to eliminate 'Leftism'. Those who share these views and who have not been removed from power have had their power eclipsed. Essentially, this view proposed the continuance of the party as a vehicle of mobilisation to conduct mass campaigns, both economic and political, to achieve the ambitious targets set. While the party was to be firmly in command, the masses were to exercise a monitoring function over abuses by party members. Such a view was liable to allow suspicion of the party to remain while failing to create organisations with legitimacy. It was too dependent on the more 'radical' aspects of Mao's legacy and the creation of a new personality cult around Hua to resist the policy shifts to the new economic programme. Defence of Mao's legacy and opposition to the current economic strategy and the 'open-door' policy has found powerful support in the army. Just before the 12th Party Congress convened in 1982, the *Liberation Army Daily* published an article which was critical of the current 'relaxation' in the ideological sphere and argued for the use of class viewpoint to explain things happening in social, material and spiritual life. The article accused 'certain leaders in China's theoretical, art and literary and press circles of taking the lead in supporting and propagating the erroneous viewpoints of bourgeois liberalizations'. Following the Congress, an editorial was published in the *Liberation Army Daily* retracting the article claiming that it ran counter to the principles of the 12th Party Congress and propagated a 'Leftist' viewpoint while opposing 'bourgeois liberalization'. It was also announced that the PLA's Political Commissar, Wei Guoqing, had been replaced by Yu Qiuli.

The second view is that which has been denounced as reflecting 'bourgeois individualism'. In this speech to members of the Central Propaganda Department in July 1981, Deng announced that liberalism as well as 'leftist' tendencies should be opposed. Deng said that the core of this view was the rejection of the party's leadership, a theme which was picked up by the *People's Daily* which described the trend as a 'wrong and dangerous tendency'. The *Guangming Daily* stressed the importance of, and need to study, Mao's article 'Combat Liberalism' and reiterated that there should be no 'unprincipled peace' between proletarian and non-proletarian ideology. This criticism has been most noticeable in the field of art and literature where the party has sought to reassert stronger control. People such as Bai Hua and Ye Wenfu have been criticised and Hu Yaobang has called on Zhou Yang to compile a book dealing with the basic Marxist theories on art and literature for students and amateur writers.

While it would be wrong to think that most of the people who have been criticised under the umbrella of 'bourgeois liberalism' reject the dominant position of the party it is true that they seek a relationship with society different from that which the top party leadership are willing to accept. They want to see a greater weakening of control by the party over society, the opening up of other channels of communication for the masses and a system of supervision and defence of citizens' rights centred on a viable legal system. Thus, the resurrection of the legal system and a greater emphasis on constitutionalism are fundamental to this approach. The law is vital to protect the rights of citizens and to prevent arbitrary suppression should 'another "Gang of Four"' gain party power. It is felt that if the Constitution had been properly upheld then the 'Gang of Four' would not have been able to proceed as they did. Also important to this view is the role of elections not just to prevent people such as the 'Gang of Four' coming to power but also to give citizens greater control over both party and state machinery. Proponents of this view are suspicious of the party's capability to act as society's control over the state and its coercive apparatus without greater supervision. The political participation of the masses is not to be restricted simply to channelling useful views into the party but should help control access to positions of power. To this extent it does challenge the view that the party has an exclusive claim to leadership over the masses. People's rights and interests, it is said, should also be protected by the Constitution supported by the legal system and not just by the party.

The two views which appear dominant at the moment could be termed the traditional and the pragmatic. The traditional view is that which seeks to operate the party and its relationship to society predicated on orthodox

Leninist lines. There can be no suggestion of a relaxation of party control and supporters seek continually to institutionalise party dominance. Such a view provides stability and assurances as well as status for party cadres and ordinary members. However, at the same time, the view provides an institutional basis for the corruption and stifling of initiative which has been so heavily criticised in recent years. The reasons for this are the hierarchical structure of power and the lack of a genuine system of accountability. Measures adopted to cure problems within the party are designed in such a way as to make sure that the party's dominant position is in no way challenged. As a consequence, the proponents of this view focus criticism on the way in which cadres behave. The cure will come about by making cadres think correctly rather than by making the necessary structural changes which could help cure the problem at the source. Such an approach is, as Schram has referred to it, a 'dead end' (1981, p. 83).

The term 'pragmatic' is used for the fourth view because those who take this approach are willing to introduce reforms which, while not in any way challenging party supremacy, help meet the objective of the four modernisations. Proponents seek to introduce a flexibility into the party which will prevent apathy and the stifling of innovation from ruining the modernisation programme. The necessity for experts and intellectuals is fully recognised as is the need to give these people a greater degree of freedom as a prerequisite for their contribution to the new policies. These people must be given greater guarantees that they will not be punished tomorrow for what they say today. This leads not only to a greater tolerance of 'dissent' but also to a support for the protection of people's rights by the legal system upholding the Constitution. Genuine elections are seen as important not just for allowing mass participation in the decision-making process but also to ensure that those in leadership positions have the support of their constituencies. Finally, some structural reforms are supported to do away with corruption and inefficiency.

As recent history and the past history of the mid-1950s and early 1960s or has shown, this is a difficult position to maintain. Essentially, the view confronts the classic dilemma of democratic centralism – how much democracy and how much centralism? This position comes under pressure from both sides. Some people push for greater democracy, while others use the 'excessive' criticisms put forward to demand a return to tighter party control. It seems that some party leaders were able to use the criticisms made by both official and unofficial media writers to force Deng to accept a tighter party control over society. For the foreseeable future, the role of the party will oscillate between these latter two views.

Finally, the question in the title must be addressed. It is hoped that this article has shown that although in part the changes in the party since the death of Mao have related to a change of workstyle, considerably more than this has taken place. The institutions now in operation and the views on the role of the party represent a dramatic shift away from those of the early and mid-1970s. In major part these changes can only be understood in relation to the change in political direction and economic policy pursued in earnest since the 3rd Plenum. Whether the present institutions and codes of conduct can provide the necessary flexibility to promote the new development strategy and to contain arguments about future directions or whether they will disintegrate once major differences of opinion surface remains to be seen.

PART IV
GROUPS AND THE POLICY PROCESS

Until relatively recently it was often regarded as inappropriate to speak of a 'policy process' or of the role of groups in political systems of the communist type. In terms of the totalitarian paradigm, which was dominant in scholarly circles until the early 1960s, communist systems were properly to be seen as 'directed societies' in which the party authorities, their actions in turn derived from ideological prescriptions, set out the main lines of public policy and then ensured support for it by means of the coercive apparatus. Even in the later Stalinist period this was often a misleading characterisation, obscuring in particular the role of factions within the party leadership and of ministerial, institutional, academic and other interests outside it. In the contemporary period the 'directed society' paradigm is even less adequate. Communist leaderships, clearly, remain exceptionally powerful in relations to the societies over which they rule: they control the electoral process, they dominate the mass media, and in the last resort, through their control of employment and the courts, they can deprive persistent critics of their livelihood or even of their liberty. At the same time the party leaderships may be divided, the ideology may offer no clear guidance, specialist advice may be expensive to set aside, and the consequences of ignoring strongly held public sentiment may be too serious to disregard. The period since the 1960s, accordingly, has generally seen an expanded role in communist political systems for groups, institutions and sometimes individuals outside the ranks of the party leadership.

There are various means by which such influence may be brought to bear. Direct advice, for instance, may be offered on policy-relevant matters, contributions in the general or specialist press may play a role, and conference or seminars may bring together academic specialists and party and state officials responsible for the areas in question. For the mass public the writing of letters to party, state and to the press represents an additional means of attempting to influence public policy. The role of groups in the policy process, however, will vary from country to country and from issue to issue. Broadly speaking, in more developed and 'established' communist systems the role of groups is likely to be greater; and more public, specialist and institutional influence is likely to be possible upon matters of social and economic policy than on foreign policy and defence. Some interests will also be more powerful than others: organised bodies such as trade unions and the military, for instance, which have regularised access to the decision-making process, will normally be more influential than loosely-knit coalitions of environmentalists or reformers. It was, however, a spontaneous workers' movement that brought down the regime itself, in Poland in 1980–81; and in general careful study is required in every case to establish the precise constellation of interests that is involved.

The five contributions to this section consider these matters further from a variety of viewpoints. In the first chapter H. Gordon Skilling, a pioneering student of these questions, reflects upon the developments that have taken place in the study of groups in communist politics since the appearance of his important symposium *Interest Groups in Soviet Politics* (co-edited with Franklyn Griffiths) in 1971. The following chapter, by Timothy J. Colton, examines the role of one particularly important institutional interest in the USSR, the armed forces. The two following chapters examine the contribution of broader social forces, particularly the industrial working class, to the political process in Poland (Jack Bielasiak) and Romania (Daniel Nelson) respectively. The final chapter in this section, by Michel Oksenberg, considers the pattern of policy-making, and particularly the functioning of the governmental bureaucracy, in China in the early 1980s.

11

Interest Groups and Communist Politics Revisited

H. GORDON SKILLING

More than fifteen years have passed since the outline of an interest group approach to communist politics appeared in *World Politics*, and more than a decade has elapsed since the publication of a volume devoted to a fuller elaboration of this theme in its Soviet context (Skilling, 1966b; Skilling and Griffiths, 1971). Since then, according to Jerry Hough's generous judgement, 'Soviet studies have been dominated by the discussion of interest groups and pluralism', and most major research in this field has 'focused in one way or another on the input side of the Soviet political system' (Hough, 1983, p. 37). David Garson, by contrast, wrote of 'a flutter of group analyses of Soviet politics' and predicted that the interest would soon wane as it had with respect to interest groups in political science generally (Garson, 1978, p. 153).

Although it is too early to estimate the lasting impact of this approach, it is perhaps appropriate to attempt some evaluation of its effect on Soviet studies at this stage. *Interest Groups in Soviet Politics* initially struck a responsive chord among many students of Soviet and communist politics, and stimulated a number of studies that employed some version of interest group analysis. The book was translated into German, and two volumes devoted to group interests in Soviet politics were subsequently published in that language (Skilling and Griffiths, 1971; Meissner and Brunner, 1975; Nolte, 1979).

On the other hand, the approach was later subjected to severe criticism, largely negative in character (Janos, 1970, pp. 437–50; Odom, 1976a; McGrath and McInnis, 1976). The critics assumed that interest groups were incompatible with totalitarian, authoritarian, or neo-Marxist models of communist society, or at least very difficult to reconcile with them. No new empirical evidence was submitted, however, and the data offered by

Reprinted with adaptations from *World Politics*, vol. 36, no. 1 (October 1983) with the permission of author and publisher.

the contributors to the Skilling–Griffiths volume or by other scholars were passed over in silence. The emphasis of the criticisms tended to rest upon the uniqueness of Soviet politics and the futility of comparing it with other political systems. In most cases it also tended to focus on the Soviet Union to the virtual exclusion of other communist systems. A much more positive and discriminating critic (A. H. Brown), while not fully accepting the concept of interest groups, sought to integrate the study of 'groups', and Soviet studies in general, into the general study of politics (Brown, 1974).

Students of comparative politics failed to acquaint themselves with the findings of research on interest groups in the Soviet context or to incorporate these in the discipline as a whole. David Garson, for instance, in *Group Theories of Politics*, referred to our volume only once, and interpreted it inaccurately at that (Garson, 1978, pp. 153–4). Other scholars writing on interest groups or group theory ignored the Soviet or other communist cases almost entirely (Greenstone, 1975; Salisbury, 1975). Hough has noted that the fifteen years of scholarly work on the input side of Soviet politics did not have much impact on the views of the Western public, which retained 'the old image of an all-powerful state, directing society . . .' (Hough, 1983, p. 58).

Hough himself, however, made a sustained effort to integrate the field of Soviet studies into the general discipline of political science, eventually publishing his essays on this theme in a single volume. In it he expressed the opinion that statements to the effect that 'there are no interest groups in the Soviet Union, despite the obvious correspondence of Soviet political phenomena to Arthur Bentley's and David Truman's definitions of interest groups' are not 'worth prolonged and serious discussion' (Hough, 1977, p. 8). In his revision of the classic text by Merle Fainsod, Hough treated the interest group (and the factional conflict) approaches as 'a valuable supplement to other models' and maintained that they 'should not be considered controversial'. Although Soviet officials and scholars did not use the term 'interest group' (or 'faction'), the Soviet system, in Hough's view, 'unquestionably . . . features political behavior which corresponds to western definition of those terms'. The ministries, and other Soviet institutions, 'certainly are interest groups by the classical definition of such groups: "any group that, on the basis of one or more shared attitudes, makes certain claims upon other groups in the society for the establishment, maintenance, or enhancement of forms of behavior that are implied by the shared attitudes" ' (Hough, 1979, pp. 528–9). Hough advanced his own version of the group approach, 'institutional pluralism', as a deliberate break with the 'directed society model', and employed it extensively in his empirical studies of the Brezhnev period (Hough, 1977, pp. 10–14).

Lawrence Whetten, in a recently published guide to research on comparative communism, summed up the evidence for the presence of interest groups in the Soviet system (although – strangely, in view of the comparative purpose of his book – he does not refer to other communist systems):

> There appears to be little doubt that interest groups exist in some form in the Soviet system. The task is to identify them correctly, determine their structure, scope and composition, and to ascertain their methods of interest formulation and articulation.

He grasped the meaning of interest groups as used in our book better than many other readers:

> These are not interest groups in the Western sense with shared characteristics, but rather they are identifiable through common attitudes and claims. These associations are not formal organizations but loose informal clusterings that articulate distinctive interests . . . (Whetten, 1976, p. 24).

Interest group theory

The reluctance of some scholars to accept the validity of a group approach to Soviet politics derives in part from the controversies surrounding interest group theory in Western political science. In the long and tortuous history of group theory, one version has followed another, with successive phases of criticism or condemnation and defense. Bentley's classic, which appeared in 1908, was ignored by political scientists for almost two decades. Meanwhile, the importance of groups in politics was recognized by many distinguished scholars, such as Charles A. Beard and Harold J. Laski,. and later by E. Pendleton Herring. The 'golden era' of interest group theory was in the 1950s, after the re-publication of Bentley's work in 1949 and the revival of his ideas by David Truman in his influential volume, *The Governmental Process* (Bentley, 1949; Truman, 1951). A few years later, Robert Dahl reformulated group theory in his version of pluralism. By the 1960s and 1970s, however, successive waves of criticism of both Truman and Dahl brought about what Garson called the disintegration of group theory – at the very time, be it noted, of the publication of *Interest Groups in Soviet Politics* (Garson, 1978).

It is not appropriate to review here even briefly the substance of the critiques of American group theory and pluralism. Much of the discussion had little or no relevance to the very different conditions of Soviet politics. The group approach, even at the height of its influence, was not dominant in American political science – which, as time passed, became more and more fragmented into various schools of political interpretation (Garson,

1978, p. 177). In view, however, of the successive appearance of various versions of the group approach over a period of at least eighty years, it can hardly be said that this model has not been a vital and dynamic element of political science. In spite of the proliferation of other theories of politics, group theory has not lost its relevance and utility as a tool for explaining and analyzing certain aspects of the political system (Greenstone, 1975, p. 300).

David Truman, in the introduction to *The Governmental Process*, made a statement that is relevant to the controversy surrounding the application of his ideas to Soviet politics. As Andrew Janos has reminded us, Truman spoke of formulating, not a group theory of politics, but rather a theory of groups in politics (Truman, 1951, pp. xxii–xxviii; Janos, 1970, p. 19). Some ten years after the original publication, Truman restated this *caveat*, denying that his work was a general group theory of politics, and describing it as an attempt 'to examine interest groups and their role in the formal institutions of government in order to provide an adequate basis for evaluating their significance in the American political process' (cited in Garson, 1978, p. 103). His critics, according to Garson, having distorted the group approach as a general model of politics, were the more easily able to condemn it as having failed to fulfill the latter purpose (Garson, 1978, p. 112).

Similarly, with respect to the group approach in the study of Soviet politics, we expressly stated that this approach did not offer a complete model of the Soviet political system or of the process of decision-making in that system, a reservation that was often ignored by the critics. We might paraphrase Truman's statement to say that the book advanced a theory of groups in Soviet politics, not a group theory of Soviet politics. Interest groups were not asserted to be the most significant feature of the Soviet polity, still less was policy considered an automatic product of group pressures, as some have argued. Nor was the importance of state (and party) authority in policy making denied or minimized. Our approach sought to focus attention and encourage research on a previously neglected aspect of Soviet politics (Skilling and Griffiths, 1971, pp. 44–5, 335, 413).

Interest groups and models – totalitarian and authoritarian

Another obstacle to understanding, and accepting, the group approach to Soviet politics has been the relationship some have attempted to establish between it and various theoretical models of the Soviet system. Garson, for instance, found strength in the group approach because it appeared to be compatible with virtually any model of the political process (Garson, 1978, p. 71). Others, however, such as Odom, in explicitly reviving the model of totalitarianism, ruled out the possibility of interest groups. Andrew Janos posited a more or less black-and-white distinction between authoritarianism and pluralism, and concluded that authentic groups could not be identified in the former category. And, as we shall see below, still others linked the group approach with pluralist, bureaucratic, or corporatist models.

Juan Linz, a prominent scholar in the field of comparative politics, distinguished totalitarian from authoritarian systems: he described the former as having 'a monistic but not monolithic center of power', and asserted that 'whatever pluralism of institutions or groups exists derives its legitimacy from that center, [and] is largely mediated by it' (Linz, 1975, p. 191). In contrasting authoritarian regimes and democratic ones, he maintained that the former are characterized by a certain 'limited pluralism', sometimes confined to strictly political groups, but sometimes extended to include 'interest groups' which are 'not created by or dependent on the state' and 'which influence the political process one way or another'. Some authoritarian regimes, he noted, may even institutionalize such groups and encourage their emergence, although ultimately it is the rulers who 'define which groups they will allow to exist and under what conditions' (Linz, 1975, pp. 265–6).

The protagonists of the group approach did not rule out a strictly limited form of group activity even under the Stalinist system, which I have described as 'quasi-totalitarian' (Skilling, 1970, pp. 222–3; Skilling and Griffiths, 1971, pp. 399–400). Jerry Hough, in his revision of Fainsod's work, cited that author as having recognized that 'behind the monolithic facade of totalitarianism, the plural pressures of professional bureaucratic power continued to find dynamic expression' (Hough, 1977, p. 12; 1979, pp. 187, 529). Alexander Shtromas, a legal scholar in the USSR who is now an émigré, has gone further; he argued that interest groups could, and did, exist under totalitarian regimes such as the Soviet Union's. Totalitarianism was incompatible, he admitted, with 'independent or autonomously functioning organizations adequately representing different interest groups', but this did not exclude certain group activities.

> Hence, in every totalitarian system, interest groups undoubtedly exist; they only function under specific circumstances and in peculiar forms but otherwise act similarly to their counterparts in authoritarian . . . and even pluralistic [polyarchic] systems.

Recalling his own experience, he asserted that his former place of work the *advokatura*, was able to function as 'a typical interest group' because Stalin concentrated on major issues (Shtromas, 1981, p. 68).

In my own view, it is more appropriate to describe the present Soviet regime as authoritarian than as totalitarian. In an earlier essay, I characterized all communist systems as 'authoritarian'; according to the degree and kind of interest group activity permitted or encouraged, they fell into different categories. These ranged from the 'quasi-totalitarian' (in which groups are severely curbed) and 'consultative authoritarian' (in which bureaucratic and professional groups are brought into the decision-making process by the authorities), through 'quasi-pluralistic authoritarian' regimes (in which groups, although not fully legitimate, are allowed to present distinctive views on their own initiative), to 'democratizing and pluralistic authoritarian' regimes (in which groups are substantially independent and even institutionalized, and play a significant role in policy making, although still functioning within an authoritarian framework) (Skilling, 1970, pp. 222–8; cf. Lowenthal, 1974, pp. 337–8, 344–5, 356; Linz, 1975, pp. 245, 277, 336–47). Thus, interest groups are compatible with an authoritarian system – although subject, in varying degrees, to curbs and restrictions imposed by that power (Skilling, 1980, pp. 84–5).

Interest groups and pluralism

Pluralism and interest groups have been closely linked in Western political science (Salisbury, 1975, pp. 172–3). Harold Laski, the father of 'classical pluralism', inveighed against absolute sovereignty (in his day, the counterpart of the totalitarian model), and expounded the rights of groups of citizens *vis-à-vis* the state. Robert Dahl's concept of pluralism emphasized the fragmentation of state power rather than the influence of private groups, but represented yet another version of group theory (Garson, 1978, pp. 18–20, 120–1). It is not surprising, therefore, that Western critics of pluralism often made interest group analysis the target of their attacks.

In my view, communist systems are *not* pluralist according to traditional standards, however varied. The presence of informal interest groups admittedly introduced a pluralist element into communist politics but, as already noted, does not erase the authoritarian character of such systems. In the Soviet political process, the activity of interest groups constitutes at best 'a low and primitive form of pluralism'; it remains a 'qualified' pluralism even in the 'quasi-pluralistic' or 'democratizing and pluralistic' stages of communist authoritarianism in Eastern Europe (Skilling, 1980, p. 85).

Efforts to distinguish the interest groups approach from a pluralist theory of Soviet and communist politics were on the whole unsuccessful. The critics, in spite of frequent protestations on our part, persisted in equating the two approaches and condemning both of them. The distinction became more difficult to sustain than ever when a scholar as positive to the idea of interest groups as Jerry Hough began to use terms such as 'bureaucratic' or 'institutional pluralism'. As early as 1973, Hough suggested a bureaucratic model of Soviet politics, arguing that the bureaucracy of Western political science presupposed not a centralized command-giving hierarchy, but rather an organization characterized by a 'coalition of individuals, some of them organized into sub-coalitions' (Hough, 1977, p. 61). He had already coined the term 'institutional pluralism' to describe a system that is 'somewhere in between authoritarianism and classical pluralism'. According to this view, the Soviet political process takes place within an official framework of institutions and is characterized by a multiplicity of interests, 'a conflict among a complex set of crosscutting and shifting alliances of persons with divergent interests', with the political leaders serving as 'mediators or brokers' (Hough, 1972, pp. 28–9; 1977, p. 23). He added the *caveat*, however, that at most the Soviet Union was moving *towards* this model of institutional pluralism, which was not to be equated with the pluralist model of the contemporary West or with classical pluralism; in fact, it was not likely to move towards the latter (Hough, 1972, pp. 29, 42; 1977, pp. 24, 43–4. See also Ehrlich, 1982, pp. 204, 206).

Bureaucratic pluralism

Hough was not alone in proposing a bureaucratic model of Soviet politics (cf. Kelley, 1977). At a conference of the International Political Science Association in Moscow, in 1979, Darrell P. Hammer employed the term 'bureaucratic pluralism' to describe the Soviet system as one made up predominantly of 'different and conflicting bureaucratic interests, with the ministries and the party apparatus acting as the chief interest groups'. In his words,

A bureaucracy which functions as an interest group will be a complex organization (most typically a ministry) which is a permanently established institution, structurally separate from the political leadership. It is subordinate to the leadership, but it provides services which the regime finds valuable. . . . The interests of the organization, as perceived by its leading officials, can be called 'bureaucratic interests' (Hammer, 1979, p. 17).

This position was not unlike the one taken by a Soviet scholar, B. M. Lazarev (cited by Hammer), who openly discussed the conflicts between the general interests of the state as a whole and the interests of different republics and administrative-territorial entities, branches of the national economy, economic organizations and enterprises, and also referred to personal interests. He saw the task of the party as one of bringing these conflicting interests into harmony, and, in case of collision, to assure the priority of 'integral interests' over departmental, and of general state interests over local ones. Lazarev also noted that persons employed in the organs of administration had 'personal and group interests which can foster or hinder the appropriate fulfillment of this or that function or competence' (Lazarev, 1971, pp. 86, 93; Hammer, 1979, p. 10).

In distinguishing the 'bureaucratic model' from the group approach, Hammer correctly described the latter as dealing with 'inchoate groupings, lacking in organization', although he inexplicably (and mistakenly) suggested that it excluded bureaucratic organizations from its purview. On the other hand, he minimized the role of 'informal, non-associational groups', and ignored the fact that these might exist within bureaucratic organs as well as elsewhere. His analysis placed the emphasis almost entirely on administrative organs and inter-agency conflicts; he thus reduced group politics purely to its state and party components, and neglected the activity of professional and occupational categories, such as scientists and writers. Similarly, Hough's concept of 'institutional pluralism', as he himself has admitted, gave the impression that only institutions could be actors in the political arena. He suggested an alternative term, 'institutionalized pluralization', which, however, did not succeed in removing the ambiguity of his approach. On the other hand, he did emphasize the fact that the individual is also important in Soviet politics – referring, for example, to scholars and educators who are not state employees but who nevertheless work within 'official channels' (Hough, 1977, p. 24; 1979, p. 547).

Interest groups and corporatism

During the 1970s, still another model – that of corporatism – was proposed by two American scholars as a better vehicle for interpreting the Soviet system under Brezhnev than 'institutional pluralism' or 'pluralism' of any kind (Bunce and Echols, 1980). Western political science has in fact long regarded pluralism and corporatism as alternative versions of interest group theory sometimes sharply opposed, sometimes associated with each other (Garson, 1978, p. 47). More recently, the two approaches have again been examined as alternative forms of organizing interests and providing for their representation in the body politics (Berger, 1981; Burke, 1982; Black and Burke, 1983, pp. 393–425).

Philippe Schmitter, an influential exponent of the corporatist model, advanced it as 'a distinctive modern system of interest representation' and applied it to political systems as different as Portugal and Sweden (Schmitter, 1974, 1977). According to Schmitter, corporatism is a system of interest representation in which the constituent units (the interest groups) are compulsory, non-competitive, and hierarchically organized categories which have been given a representational monopoly by the state in return for control over their articulation of demands. He distinguished this system from pluralism, in which the units are voluntary, competitive, and non-hierarchical; are not controlled by the state; and do not exercise a monopoly of representation (Schmitter, 1974, pp. 93–4, 96, 104; see also Bunce and Echols, 1980).

Schmitter argued that the principal difference between corporatism and pluralism lies in the role of the state *vis-à-vis* the interest groups. He smudged this distinction, however, by his attempt to differentiate two types of corporatism – 'societal' and 'state' – depending on the degree of state intervention and on whether this intervention is voluntarily accepted or imposed. Societal corporatism is considered to be characteristic of a number of Western European democratic states and, in an emergent way, of Canada and the United States, where interest groups are in some measure officially incorporated in the state system, but on a voluntary basis. State corporatism, on the other hand, is exemplified by such states as Portugal, Spain, Brazil, and Chile, as well as by defunct systems such as Fascist Italy and Nazi Germany, where the process of incorporation was coercive. Oddly enough, Schmitter did not include the Soviet Union in either of the two categories, but treated it as a 'monist' model – defined as a system of interest representation in which the units are created by a single party and are granted a representational role within the party and *vis-à-vis* the state in exchange for certain controls over their activity. This conception, which seems difficult to distinguish from state corporatism, was not further analyzed and was omitted from the later article.

In spite of these ambiguities, Bunce and Echols found that the corporatist model – characterized as it is by an active role of the state in decision-making – fits the Soviet system under Brezhnev better than the pluralist model. It is, they wrote, 'a system of participation and cooperation among major elements in the polity, society, and economy, enforced and coordinated by the state [or the party]. . . .' The state 'works with groups to make public policy and does not, as in the pluralist model, simply act as a passive broker, mediating interests; interest groups are not the autonomous, independent actors they are in pluralism. . . .' (Bunce and Echols, 1980, pp. 18, 4). The latter assertion is, of course, a far cry from pluralism anywhere; it is a travesty of the group approach. The position of the authors is rendered all the more confusing by the fact that they described the Soviet system as a mixture of both societal and state corporatism.

Jerry Hough has admitted that there are disadvantages in the pluralist model, and that the corporatist model represents in some ways an advance in analyzing Soviet politics.

It does get away from any suggestion of totally autonomous groups or of equality of opportunity for all groups. Its emphasis on the activist role of governmental agencies and officials is a useful reminder of a fact well-known to pluralists, but played down in their imagery. It does emphasize an important aspect of modern government – the attempt to manage the economy in order to produce sustained economic growth (Hough, 1983, p. 55).

In the same paper, Hough pointed out that proponents of the pluralist approach had recognized the active role of the state and had never assumed the existence of voluntary associations in the Soviet Union; they were talking about '"interests" represented by or embodied in governmental agencies and a "group struggle" that had to take place within a tightly-structured and restrictive framework'. He observed that corporatism, too, had its disadvantages, including the ambiguity of its two variants and the difficulty of distinguishing its societal version from pluralism. Moreover, the corporatist model tended to overemphasize the role of the state and to ignore the latter's internal divisions. Its use would create the danger of a return to the 'directed society model', or even the totalitarian model, and might lead to the neglect of the societal autonomy and the political debate characteristic of current Soviet politics. In any case, Hough observed, in a warning relevant to much of our previous discussion, there was a risk in the use of models of any kind, since their ambiguity created misunderstanding and often produced sterile debate in place of scholarly research (Hough, 1983).

There is another drawback to the adoption of the corporatist model. As employed by Bunce and Echols, it includes within its purview the bureaucratic institutions of state and party, and thus overlaps confusingly with the bureaucratic or institutional models of Hammer and Hough; like them, it places undue emphasis on the bureaucratic side of group politics. Strictly speaking, corporatism in its original Western sense refers to non-state interest organizations such as trade unions, which are incorporated in the state structure on either a voluntary or a compulsory basis. Most advocates of the corporatist model, however, have conducted little or no empirical research on Soviet mass organizations, and have not attempted to fit them into either the societal or state models of corporatism as applied to the Soviet Union.

Some scholars, such as Cyril Black, writing about 'organizational participation' in tsarist and Soviet Russia from an explicitly corporatist perspective, have concluded that 'corporatist interests are much more systematically consulted' in the Soviet system than in the tsarist (Black, 1982, p. 9). Robert Dahl, writing from a pluralistic standpoint, coined still another term, 'organizational pluralism', to describe the growing influence of interest organizations as a result of the liberalization of hegemonic regimes (Dahl, 1980, p. 27). Other authors have been more cautious in assessing the importance of such organizations, contending that in the Soviet Union they have continued to be primarily transmission belts, and that they have developed a certain independence as articulators of particular interests only in Eastern Europe, especially in Poland, Hungary, Yugoslavia and, in 1968, Czechoslovakia (Furtak, 1974, pp. 779–92, 790–1).

In a well-documented study of Soviet trade unions, Blair Ruble, while not using a corporatist model, concluded that they are 'significant institutions'; he maintained that, in spite of the authority of the party and the supremacy of the central trade union bodies, the unions, at least at the lower factory level, engaged in 'considerable activity having a favorable influence on the lives of Soviet workers' (Ruble, 1981, p. 140). Apart from this, it has yet to be demonstrated that organized interest groups, at least in the USSR and other countries of 'real socialism', play a role which is comparable even to that of informal and non-organized interest groups, or which is sufficient to justify their treatment as elements of a corporatist system.

The increasing importance of 'specialists' in Soviet decision-making has been presented as further evidence of the corporatist character of the Soviet polity. According to Bunce and Echols, for instance, there has been a growing rationality of policy and planning as the party has made use of specialists within its own ranks, and as outside specialists are regularly consulted by policy makers (Bunce and Echols, 1980, pp. 9–12). Without employing a corporatist approach, Tatjana Kirstein documented the substantial role of such 'outsiders' (*Aussenstehenden*) acting in an advisory capacity to the party, the state administration, and the Supreme Soviet. Still other scholars, such as Peter Solomon, Thane Gustafson, and John Lowenhardt, have substantiated the growing role, and the considerable influence, of outside specialists in Soviet decision-making, but have treated them as evidence not of interest group activity or of pluralism or corporatism, but of increased 'participation' in the Soviet system (Solomon, 1978; Gustafson, 1981; Lowenhardt, 1981).

Some case studies

Concrete empirical research has been much more fruitful in advancing the study of interest groups than wrangling over relevant models; it has been most productive when not entangled with one model or another. As we suggested in *Interest Groups in Soviet Politics* (p. 408), the examination of specific issues of public policy has afforded insight into the actual role of interest groups and into the nature of the policy-making process in general. These efforts to test the hypothesis of the interest group approach deserve at least brief mention (cf. Brown, 1974, pp. 73–4, 85–6).

One, by Theodore H. Friedgut, examined the role of interest groups in the reform of machine tractor stations (MTS) in 1958. Although recognizing the 'limiting nature of the Soviet framework of politics' and 'the broader context of institutional and technical environments', Friedgut concluded that the collective farm chairmen formed 'a functional group expressing a common consciousness of needs', and were able to use official channels, such as journals, conferences, and institutes, for articulating and aggregating their interests. United on some issues and divided on others, the *kolkhoz* chairmen were able in some cases to achieve the satisfaction of their demands, but they were not able to gain the establishment of an autonomous *kolkhoz* union. The MTS tractor drivers and mechanics, too, acted as 'an organized pressure group to defend their work conditions. . . .' The case study, Friedgut concluded, 'contains all the classic elements of interest group activity' (Friedgut, 1976, pp. 524–47).

In another study, Donald R. Kelley analyzed the role of interest groups in environmental policy making in the USSR, taking as his subject the case of pollution control in Lake Baikal. He identified three categories of groups involved: (1) industrial and commercial lobbies, including government ministries and agencies concerned with the manufacture of products; (2) state-related environmental protection agencies, such as the Ministry of Public Health; and (3) semi-official public conservation organizations and informal, *ad hoc* coalitions of environmentalists – the latter best described, he noted, as 'opinion groups'. 'There can be no question', Kelley concluded, 'that non-institutionalized, ad hoc environmental lobbies, working in concert with state environmental protection agencies, played an important role in securing more stringent protection of Lake Baikal'. Although it was an uphill battle, it was significant that these 'environmental lobbies, working without the benefit of an organizational base of operations or high-ranking political allies, were able to have any impact at all'. He argued that the Lake Baikal case demonstrated 'the importance of a non-institutionalized or at best semi-institutionalized environmental lobby' which was able to force the recognition of an issue and also to counteract the resistance of bureaucratic inertia and vested interests within the bureaucracy (Kelley, 1976, pp. 570–89).

In an earlier article, Kelley had examined two other cases of Soviet decision-making – the decentralization of industrial management in 1957 and the reform of education of 1958. In each case, he used a content analysis of several hundred articles published in newspapers and journals by individuals belonging to certain groups. He concluded that the influence of certain specialized interest groups (educators in one case, industrial managers in the other) varied according to the political sensitivity of the issues involved. The educators were able to affect the outcome significantly with respect to higher education, and to a lesser degree in regard to secondary schools. By contrast, the managerial elite were unable to prevent the abolition of ministries, as they had desired; but they were not completely without influence on less sensitive and technical aspects of the reform. Further, the intelligentsia were successful in preserving the research institutes of the Academy of Sciences (Kelley, 1972, pp. 860–88).

More recently, Howard Biddulph, in a paper presented in 1982 to the annual meeting of the Canadian Political Science Association, focused his attention on the articulation of territorial interests at CPSU congresses. Examining the speeches of regional party secretaries at the 23rd, 24th, 25th and 26th Congresses, Biddulph demonstrated what he called 'institutional-ized interest articulation' in the form of the defense of the territorial interests of their respective regions by the secretaries. Admittedly, the influence of these speeches on policy – i.e., on the content of the budget ultimately approved – appeared to be minimal, though some effect could be detected. Biddulph deliberately spoke only of 'interests', and avoided the term 'groups', but his data seemed to suggest the existence of regional interests on behalf of which the secretary was speaking, and of a group of regional secretaries who sometimes expressed similar demands (Biddulph, 1983; cf. Hough in Skilling and Griffiths, 1971, pp. 65–6).

The role of specialists in Soviet decision-making

As a kind of outgrowth of the interest group approach and of case studies such as the foregoing, other scholars have been encouraged to engage in a search for 'participation', especially of technical specialists, in the wider context of Soviet decision-making. Peter Solomon examined the role of outside specialists in a number of case studies of policy making in the field of criminology (Solomon, 1978). Thane Gustafson studied the role of technical experts and advisers in several cases of agricultural and environ-mental policy during the Brezhnev period (Gustafson, 1981). John Lowen-hardt brought together nine earlier case studies of policy making under Khrushchev, and added a detailed inquiry into the reorganization of the Academy of Sciences between 1954 and 1961 (Lowenhardt, 1981). And at a workshop on Soviet policy making, held in California in 1980, a number of scholars embarked on a comparative investigation of that subject, which would examine studies of policy issues in various fields and during different periods (Workshop on Soviet Policymaking, University of California, 1980).

Without offering a new model of the Soviet system or even a comprehen-sive picture of policy making, studies such as these attempted a fuller and more systematic analysis of the process – including its successive phases of initiating issues, building an agenda, making decisions, and implementing them – in a number of spheres of public life and at successive stages of Soviet politics from Stalin to Brezhnev. They considered the role of the several actors involved in each case – political leaders, institutions (official and non-official), individual specialists, interest groups, and so forth. These studies left far behind the concept of a political system in which total power is exercised centrally from the topmost pinnacle and in which there are no inputs from below by a variety of actors in conflict with each other. The authors concluded that there was meaningful participation by outside specialists even during the Stalin period, and that this participation expanded and improved in quality, and was to some extent institutionalized, under Khrushchev and Brezhnev. Not surprisingly, their work showed that interest groups are but one of the many elements involved in policy making; they are not necessarily decisive, and may sometimes be marginal in their impact. This research also confirmed that the participation of specialists is hampered and sometimes blocked by other factors, in particular the power of political leaders and authoritative organs of government and the party.

Studies such as these – as Solomon remarked about his own work – may be regarded as falling 'within the interest group tradition' in the sense that they 'deal with participation and influence in the policy making process' (Solomon, 1978, p. 13). He himself deliberately avoided the use of the term 'interest group' and focused on individual specialists, thus skirting the controversial issue whether the specialists constituted interest groups. Gustafson (1981) also concentrated on individual technical specialists and discounted the role of groups. Lowenhardt, although focusing not on the group but on the decision, did examine the part played by groups. He distinguished 'three types of political groups with differing degrees of "groupness" ': interest groups, opinion groups, and policy coalitions. Apparently equating 'interest groups' with entire occupational categories, he discerned 'different opinion groups that may exist within one and the same interest group', and described policy coalitions as 'composed of representatives of different interest and opinion groups". The process of decision-making involved, in his view, not only groups, but also institutions (formally constituted state and party organizations) and individuals (prominent scientists, writers and other intellectuals) (Lowenhardt, 1981, pp. 6, 25, 26).

Lowenhardt's case studies certainly support the generalization that the party is not monolithic and does not have a monopoly of power in the decision-making process. Influence is shared by many other actors, such as political leaders, individuals, institutions, and groups. His conclusions are, however, confusing and somewhat contradictory. None of the studies, he declared categorically, provided 'evidence of a group or institution in Soviet politics qualifying and behaving as an interest group'. 'Therefore the concept of interest group seems to be of limited use in the study of Soviet decision making.' Yet at the same time, Lowenhardt noted the existence of opinion groups and policy coalitions, and in his own case study assigned influence to these groupings (1981, pp. 86, 184–5). His analysis, if not his conclusions, does not seem too far removed from that of *Interest Groups in Soviet Politics*, where emphasis was placed on the role of 'opinion groups' (within the broader occupational or professional groups) and of alliances of such groups with each other across occupational lines. Nor is it remote from Franklyn Griffiths' tendency analysis, which examined 'sets of *individuals* who share common attitudes' and presumably act in concert (Skilling and Griffiths, 1971, pp. 24–7, 384–7; cf. Hoffmann and Laird, 1982, ch. 6).

Interest group studies in Germany

The fact that *Interest Groups in Soviet Politics* was translated into German suggests a concern with this theme in Austria and Germany. Two other books later addressed themselves to group interests in Soviet politics, but were less successful in demonstrating interest group activity. The first, a collection of essays edited by Boris Meissner and Georg Brunner, examined the role of 'group interests in the Soviet decision-making process' (Meissner and Brunner, 1975). As the editors explained, these studies expressly deal with group interests, and not with interest groups, since the mass organizations in the Soviet Union cannot be compared with Western organized interest groups (p. 7). The editors referred to 'unorganized large social groups', especially the high-ranking bureaucracy and the army, and to a lesser degree the technical-economic intelligentsia (scholars, writers, and artists). They noted that these groupings are not united; each is divided into 'individual partial groups of an institutional and professional kind'. The Kremlin must take account of the interests of these large groups and even the 'unarticulated interests' of workers and peasants, although these groups have no possibility of exerting any influence (pp. 53–4, 7–8). In individual chapters, the contributors examined the role of specialists, the military, enterprise directors and technical cadres, the agricultural population and the workers, as well as scholars, scientists, and writers, but they did not offer empirical evidence that any of these act as interest groups; neither did they document the assumed influence of the military, managers, scholars, and writers.

In the second book, Hans-Heinrich Nolte drawing extensively on Western interest group literature, presented an original and provocative analysis of group interests in the formulation of Soviet foreign policy (Nolte, 1979). Accepting the idea of 'participation of groups outside the party apparatus' (p. 47), Nolte identified what he called 'indirect groups', i.e., groups whose members do not personally know each other, but 'act together in a relevant manner' (p. 42). These include older groups based on nationality and religion as well as newer ones based on occupation (pp. 54, 58). He found that the Soviet system does not differ from parliamentary systems in having 'no group interests', although the group conflict takes place within the framework of the party's hegemony (pp. 123, 132–3). Nolte conducted a content analysis of major Soviet newspapers and journals on the issues of Germany and peaceful coexistence, not on a quantitative basis, but through a qualitative comparison of major articles. He concluded that important differences of opinion are openly or indirectly expressed (Chapters III and IV). In particular, he identified 'an interest group coalition friendly to *detente*' and one 'hostile to *detente*', as well as a party–army–arms industry complex. He admitted, however, that it was not clear how group conflicts worked in concrete cases (p. 68).

Robert Furtak, in an article on 'interest pluralism', set forth a comparative analysis of 'the rise, legitimization and organization of particular interests' in the Soviet Union and Eastern Europe (Furtak, 1974). He noted the recognition by communist theory of the existence of interest conflicts and even groups, and the rise of institutionalized articulation of group interests in certain countries. In view of the part played by societal organizations and professional groupings, and by movements for the defense of religious and nationality interests, he concluded that the totalitarian model had limited explanatory value; but because of the continuing preponderance of the party, he did not think the Western pluralist model was applicable. In suggesting a continuum between totalitarianism and pluralism, he divided the East European states into three categories. The first, and largest, consisted of the Soviet Union, the German Democratic Republic, Czechoslovakia (until 1968), Romania, Bulgaria, and Albania, where the mass organizations remained transmission belts. The second group included Poland and Hungary, where professional organizations had attained a certain independence, and where the Church, in Poland, enjoyed far-reaching independence. Only Yugoslavia fell into the third category, with its self-management system, the trade unions, and the national republics all serving as institutions of interest representation.

Groups in tsarist Russia

Discussion by historians of the role of interest groups in tsarist Russia is not without relevance to our analysis, especially since some critics of the group approach have referred to Russian political culture, and in particular to the 'tradition of positively rejecting interest groups', to support the argument that even a limited pluralism was hardly likely to develop in the contemporary USSR (Odom, 1976a). In contrast to this view, Cyril Black, in a brief but suggestive essay, drew attention to the action, in Russia between 1861 and 1917, of 'interest groups', which he defined as 'associations of individuals with a common sense of values, one of whose main purposes is to influence government policy along lines favorable to their concerns'. He referred to landowners, Moscow entrepreneurs, national and religious minorities, workers and peasants, and even treated political parties as 'interest groups in disguise'. These groups were regularly consulted in the drafting of legislation, and often took the initiative for change. After 1905, some of them formed 'organized pressure groups which sought to influence government policy in support of their diverse interests' (Black, 1980, pp. 2, 6).

Richard Wortman described the efforts of the nobility and the merchants to further their interests in post-reform Russia, but noted the obstacles to their success in the dominant political culture. The supremacy of the tsar and the imperial bureaucracy, which 'provided the framework for the expression of the interests of the social groups', frustrated most of their efforts. The autocracy asserted the dominant interest of the state against the interests of the nobility and the merchants. Spokesmen of the latter groups were so bound to the autocracy that 'loyalty to authority superseded loyalty to group interest' – a comment that seems strikingly applicable to the frequent subordination of group interests to party policy in contemporary Soviet Russia (Wortman, 1980, pp. 3, 11).

Cyril Black developed this theme further in his later paper on the role of interest groups in policy formation from 1861 to the present (Black, 1982). Black was struck by the continuity between tsarist and Soviet Russia (p. 7); he observed 'an active and growing interchange between the central government and the estates and other interests' in the period from 1861 to 1917 (p. 3), and stated that 'Soviet society now tends to be seen as comprising a plurality of institutions with varied strengths and interests' with which the central authorities are obliged to interact (p. 6). His paper concluded on the controversial note that 'the representation of interests in public policy is a great deal more extensive, systematic, and complex in the 1980s than it was in the late 1960s, or in the early 1900s' (Black, 1982, p. 7).

Other communist systems

More directly relevant to our subject is the place of interest groups in other communist states. In a symposium on pluralism in communist systems, Sarah Terry presented 'A Case for a "Group" Approach to Polish Politics', urging its cautious and selective application, at least as 'a secondary or supplementary approach'. Granting that the groups identifiable in Poland do not, strictly speaking, meet the minimal criteria of interest groups in Western pluralist societies, Terry contended that 'one cannot adequately explain the political situation in Poland' after 1976 'without taking into account the very real influence of significant sectors of Polish society', such as the Church, the intellectuals, the workers, and the peasants (Terry, 1979, p. 29). In addition to this limited 'quasi-group activity', she identified the Polish Sociological Association, and its Warsaw branch in particular, as a 'bona fide group' – a coherent organization not only capable of articulating its own interests, but also of serving as a forum for open discussion of policy issues. Terry also noted that Polish scholars perceive the group approach as relevant and applicable to their political system. For instance, in presenting an argument for a better system of 'interest articulation',

Krzysztof Jasiewicz, a sociologist, explicitly used Western interest group theory as a tool for analyzing the Polish political system (Terry, 1979, pp. 33–4; see also Brown, 1966; Skilling, 1968).

Terry, writing in 1977, referred to this quasi-group activity as having at most a 'negative influence', but described the process of group formation as a dynamic one (pp. 30, 34). She could not foresee the blossoming of authentic interest groups and their immense impact on politics and public policy several years later. During 1980 and 1981, with the rise of the independent trade union Solidarity, there emerged in Poland a system of group activity which went far beyond anything that had developed in the Soviet Union and which approached the pluralistic process of a democratic society – although limits to this activity and to its success were set by the continued hegemony of the communist party as well as by the pressures emanating from the Soviet Union.

These pluralizing tendencies in Poland resembled 'the explosion of group activity' in Czechoslovakia during the Prague Spring of 1968, which I have analyzed in *Czechoslovakia's Interrupted Revolution*. In that case, writers, journalists, scholars, scientists, workers, farmers, the churches and various nationalities, as well as other interest groups based on sex, generation, profession, or simply the pursuit of common goals, sprang into action and transformed the political scene. Within each of these groups, these were significant divergencies of interest and attitude, reflecting underlying economic and social diversity and a wide spectrum of varying opinions (Skilling, 1976, pp. 563, 611).

These two cases of 'democratizing and pluralistic authoritarianism', as I have called them, not to mention similar examples in Poland and Hungary in 1956 or the comparable events in Croatia in 1971, threw a shaft of light on the role of interest groups in 'normal' times. When a communist system experiences such a breakthrough to relative freedom, the 'proto-interest groups' that have led a shadowy existence beneath the surface and could express themselves only in rudimentary forms, take on real flesh and blood in the new setting: restraints are removed or lessened and a genuine interest group society begins to emerge. This situation hints at the wide range of unsatisfied interests that existed earlier and appeared, at best, only as the tip of an iceberg of suppressed reality.

Dissent and interest groups

A new and significant form of interest articulation emerged in the Soviet Union in the mid-1960s and in Poland and Czechoslovakia in the mid-1970s in the form of movements for the defense of human rights and independent cultural and scholarly activities. Dissent, or dissidence, as it came to be called, had hardly existed at the time of the publication of *Interest Groups in Soviet Politics*; it is still neglected or played down in interest group analysis. This kind of activity represents a genuine pluralism of ideas and opinions, expressed openly, without censorship, in *samizdat* articles, journals, and books. Although such groups operate under the difficult conditions of constant police harassment, they approximate in some ways interest associations in democratic societies. They are 'less orthodox' and 'less legitimate' than other forms of interest group activity, but paradoxically, they are 'more organized and institutionalized' (Skilling, 1980, p. 87). In the Soviet Union, organized groups – such as the Helsinki monitoring committees, the committee on the abuse of psychiatry, and nationality and religious movements – were formed for the defense of specific or more general interests. In Poland, in the late 1970s, dissident movements – KOR, ROPCiO, many newspapers, the Flying University, and so forth – were even more numerous and active than in the USSR. They helped to prepare the way for the outburst of intense group activity during the period of Solidarity in 1980–81. There was similar dissident activity in Czechoslovakia (Charter 77), and on a smaller scale in other communist countries (Skilling, 1981).

Alexander Shtromas has analyzed dissent as a form of interest group activity (Shtromas, 1981, pp. 74–7, 104). The totalitarian model of Soviet society does not exclude, in his opinion, 'certain interest groups who are able to influence the political decision-makers by trying to present the interests of a group as those of the decision-makers themselves' (p. 68). This 'intra-structural dissent' consists of the pursuit of constructive political, social, economic, or cultural goals by advancing ideas and proposals, or making practical initiatives and experiments (pp. 75, 77). Shtromas described the 'professionals' as 'one of the most important interest-groups in the Soviet Union' (p. 104); he included in this category not only those specialists who are officially brought into the policy-making process as consultants, but also those who take the initiative in making 'constructive demands for essential changes in the system of the country's management' (pp. 74–7).

Shtromas included in the category of 'intra-structural dissent' those whom he called 'moral dissenters' – i.e., 'people motivated by more general moral, philosophical, political and cultural ideas and commitments', pursuing goals of change in the civic realm, and in nationality and religious life (pp. 79–82). Such groups also belong, he noted, in the category of 'extra-structural dissent' – i.e., 'the independent activities of individuals and groups outside the framework controllable by the authorities' and 'directly undermining, challenging, or criticizing the regime and its current and long-term policies . . .' (p. 82). While it is normally concealed, this dissent often becomes overt, and the dissenters, through no desire of their own, move from intra-structural to extra-structural dissidence, as, for instance, in the cases of Solzhenitsyn and Sakharov. Although overt dissent constitutes only a tiny fraction of dissent as a whole, it is important, in Shtromas's opinion, in expressing the views of most Soviet citizens and encouraging others to follow their example (pp. 86–7).

Conclusion

The interest group approach did not succeed in one of its purposes – namely, to contribute to a more comprehensive general theory of group politics (Skilling and Griffiths, 1971, p. 23). As already noted, the results of research on Soviet interest groups were not incorporated in comparative political analysis. The fact that specialists in Soviet studies drew various models from political science and applied them to the Soviet system impeded rather than facilitated a better understanding of that system and the role of interest groups in it. The totalitarian model, and even the authoritarian one (as interpreted by the critics), which excluded, almost by definition, the very possibility of interest groups, naturally discouraged concrete research on this theme. The bureaucratic and institutional models, by focusing on official structures, distracted attention from looser, non-organized professional and other groupings. The pluralist and corporatist models implied a greater participation by interest groups and social organizations than was warranted.

On the other hand, empirical research conducted during the past decade or so has demonstrated the utility of an interest group approach in analyzing the politics of the USSR, not only under Khrushchev and Brezhnev, but also under Stalin, as well as in tsarist Russia. It showed itself to be even more useful in interpreting the politics of East European communist countries, and proved helpful in the study of the dissident movements in those countries and in the Soviet Union. This research, while not neglecting the role of the official authoritative organs of state and party, confirmed, to the satisfaction of many, that interest groups contributed important inputs to the process of decision making. Other scholars, while not employing the interest group concept, established the significance of participation and the influence of specialists. Together, these studies corroborated the assumption that the Soviet system has indeed been 'operating differently than under Stalin' (Skilling and Griffiths, 1971, p. 44).

The term 'interest groups' remained somewhat ambiguous and was given a variety of meanings. It was used to refer to state institutions, such as entire ministries or government departments and agencies; to the party as a whole or its component parts; to non-official bodies such as the Academy of Sciences or its institutes; to non-state societal or mass organizations, such as the trade unions; to outside specialists in specific disciplines; to dissidents and opposition groups; and to broader social groups, such as collective farmers. More discriminating research demonstrated the need to differentiate between the common interests of such groups in their entirety and the partial interests of 'opinion groups' within the same category. Interest groups ought not to be identified with the whole group unless a common attitude of all members could be established empirically. It was the 'opinion groups', or coalitions of such groups (in Griffiths' words, the 'tendencies of articulation'), that were the crucial barometer of interest group activity (Skilling and Griffiths, 1971, p. 336). This concept, it would seem, offered a basis for treating specialists as a group whenever a similarity of opinions and a common set of demands could be established.

Later research confirmed our hypothesis that the Soviet system, regardless of the changes in its mode of operation that had been introduced or tolerated by Khrushchev, remained much the same in its essential features:

> The making of policy remains highly centralized and authoritarian, with great power resting in the hands of a few at the top, and with groups usually playing a secondary and subordinate role . . . Top Soviet leaders are often at one and the same time articulators and aggregators of group interests, as well as the final rule-makers, and may often be in a position to impose policies upon the groups rather than be forced by the groups to follow certain policies (Skilling and Griffiths, 1971, p. 45).

Even under Krushchev, changes had been limited, slow, and erratic; in some measure, they were reversed under Brezhnev. Groups were in the main informal and not institutionalized, and were still officially regarded as illegitimate. Significant activity was confined to elite groups such as the specialists; larger social groups, for instance workers or nationalities, played little or no role in policy making. If this interest group activity was described as 'incipient pluralism', it does not mean that the system had become pluralist in any meaningful sense of the word (Skilling and Griffiths, 1971, pp. 44, 399, 401–5).

Interest group activity has differed greatly in various communist countries. It was substantial in Poland, Hungary, and Czechoslovakia at certain times, and rose to an unprecedented and qualitatively different level in Czechoslovakia and Poland during periods of radical reform. As noted above, this efflorescence of group politics of a quasi-pluralistic kind revealed the hitherto concealed wealth of unsatisfied interests and the potential for radical interest articulation. The weak and informal process of group activity in the Soviet Union appeared, by contrast, embryonic and undeveloped, capable of giving only limited and inadequate expression to the basic interests of the population. The Polish and Czechoslovak experience provided at least a hint of what *might* occur in the USSR if groups such as workers and peasants, the nationalities, and religious believers had an opportunity to voice their opinions and defend their interests freely.

The study of dissidence raises still more intriguing and controversial questions. Many scholars would challenge the link postulated by Alexander Shtromas between the attitudes and claims of the dissidents and the attitudes of the population at large, or even of the less radical and more orthodox critics (Shtromas, 1979, pp. 221, 237–9, 272–3). The dissenters operate on the margin of Soviet political life and do not necessarily embody broader public opinions and wishes. Nevertheless, it is likely that the voices of the dissidents reveal, at least in some degree, tendencies of opinion that are hidden in mainstream politics or only expressed in Aesopian language in normal interest group activity. In Poland, where the dissent movement was greater in scope and enjoyed wide popular support, there could be no doubt that it articulated unsatisfied group interests and unexpressed opinions, and that it helped to pave the way for the more radical and uninhibited pluralism of the Solidarity period.

The reaction of the Soviet regime towards the Czechoslovak and Polish reform movements and towards its own dissidents tells us a great deal about the real nature of Soviet power. The use of military coercion and police violence in these cases indicates how determined Moscow was to curtail genuine articulation of interests in the neighboring countries and to prevent any comparable development in the USSR. The Soviet regime, it is clear, remained adamantly opposed to any degree of genuine pluralization at home or abroad.

The future of group activity is as difficult to foresee now as it was in 1970 (Skilling and Griffiths, 1971, pp. 404–5). Certainly there was not then, and there is not now, any likelihood of an early advance to a more pluralistic society in the Soviet Union or elsewhere in Eastern Europe (Skilling, 1970, pp. 230, 234). On the contrary, genuine group activity has suffered another severe setback. The establishment of military rule in Poland, like the invasion of Czechoslovakia in 1968, terminated the outburst of group activism and the birthpangs of a genuine pluralism, and also eliminated even the relatively modest group and dissent activity that preceded more radical strivings for reform. In turn, this repression discouraged pluralizing tendencies in Hungary and solidified the rigid authoritarianism of Romania. Yuri Andropov, elected party leader of the USSR in 1982 with the support of the coercive forces of the police and army, was hardly likely to permit a revival of group activity in Eastern Europe or of dissent in the Soviet Union. It remains to be seen whether his successors will tolerate even the modest degree of group activity that was permitted or encouraged by his predecessors.

12

The Impact of the Military on Soviet Society

TIMOTHY J. COLTON

'The Army is a part of Soviet society and is nurtured by it not only materially but spiritually. In the Army are reflected all those socioeconomic and ideological-political processes taking place in society' (Sheliag, *et al.*, 1972, p. 3). In these words a major Soviet text clearly states the first lesson a Western observer grasps about the military – that it must be understood as a part of the whole Soviet social and political system. While it has many of the universal characteristics of military organizations (and of all bureaucracies), its molding by unique and often paradoxical circumstances must never be forgotten. It is the largest peacetime army in history yet the leader who presided over its founding had opposed standing military forces until weeks before coming to power, and six decades later his writings are cited to support indefinite accumulation of military 'might'. The army is subject to strict civilian control (as official pronouncements never tire in declaring) yet the country's foremost civilian recently arranged to acquire, in his seventieth year, the military rank of marshal. The army uses the latest in nuclear and electronic technology yet the press routinely describes shortages of fresh fruit, footwear, and shower facilities in military garrisons.

The purpose of this chapter is to explore the military's effect on the overall social and political order by which it so obviously has been shaped, and in particular its effects on those aspects of society that influence foreign policy. This is a question of clear and present significance, both for our overall understanding of Soviet reality and for the formulation of Western foreign policies. The last decade has seen not only a general increase in Western interests in Soviet military affairs but also an introduction into journalistic, academic, and government discussion of themes reminiscent of the notion of 'Red militarism' that flourished between the wars.

Reprinted with adaptations from Seweryn Bialer (ed.), *The Domestic Context of Soviet Foreign Policy* (Boulder, Col.: Westview Press and London: Croom Helm, 1981) with the permission of author and publishers.

The military and society: Western views

In the past Western scholars have tended to be more interested in the substance of Soviet military policy than in political and social processes in which the army is involved. Inasmuch as such processes have been analyzed, the dominant concern has been with relations between the military and the ruling Communist party and the overwhelming consensus has been that these relations are basically adversarial. The military's quest for autonomy is said to clash with party desires for complete hegemony over all potential rivals, thereby resulting in deep-seated and irresolvable conflict. In the words of Roman Kolkowicz, 'The relationship between the Communist Party and the Soviet military is essentially conflict-prone and thus presents a perennial threat to the political stability of the Soviet state' (Kolkowicz, 1967, p. 11). This antagonism is thought to be resolved in the party's favor principally through bureaucratic control mechanisms (the most important of which is the party's apparatus within the military, the main political administration), but even these controls do not prevent aspects of the conflict from surfacing.

This interpretation has recently been seriously questioned by some scholars. In an ambitious and widely read essay published in 1973, William Odom argued that 'value congruence rather than conflict' characterized army–party relations, and he drew attention to linkages between the two institutions and to symbiotic aspects of their relationship (Odom, 1973, pp. 12–26). The present author has found the original model to be particularly misleading when applied to the behavior of the military party apparatus, whose officials have tended, contrary to earlier predictions, to function on most political issues as allies rather than adversaries of military commanders. Rarely does one see sharp lines drawn between an army seeking autonomy and a party wishing to maximize control, or between the military command and the political organs tied to the civilian leadership. Rather, consensus and cleavage normally cut across institutional boundaries and involve coalitions primarily based on location and including *both* military commanders and party officials (Colton, 1976, 1977).

Such a pattern of horizontal linkages between party officials and specialized elites, far from being unique, probably applies to many other particularized groups and issue-areas. For example, in the field of industrial management managers and party workers are in basic agreement on overall goals, and on individual questions most conflicts 'arise between one group of industrial and party officials who support one project and another group of industrial and party officials who support another project' (Hough, 1969, p. 265).

The question that Odom has raised in his more recent work is whether the specific tendency towards civil-military 'congruence' and interpenetration is found with regard to issues *other* than specialized military ones. In a

1976 article Odom points to what he calls 'the militarization of Soviet society'. Concentrating on civil defense, basic military training, and para-military programs since 1967, he draws a picture of a society in which military values and institutions increasingly permeate all aspects of life. Odom's views about exactly *who* is managing the militarization process are somewhat unclear. At times he speaks in general terms of the regime as a whole 'organizing the civil society to support the military', and implies that it is soldiers themselves – the professional military establishment, as organized in the Ministry of Defense – who are appropriating an even greater role (Odom, 1976b).

We have then an approach that – particularly in versions lacking the subtlety of Odom's – conceives of the military's social impact in terms almost diametrically opposed to traditional ones. Kolkowicz's army exerts a sharply limited impact on Soviet society as a whole, its influence being circumscribed by the party's controls and tendency to 'regard any incre-ment in the military's prerogatives and authority as its own loss and therefore as a challenge' (Kolkowicz, 1967, p. 105). In Odom's conception, on the other hand, soldiers and their values, with party encouragement, are acquiring more influence.

This chapter will present somewhat of a middle course. It will concur with Odom that military and civilian elites share certain fundamental objectives and interests as well as commitments to major defense prog-rams. However, it will also strive towards greater specificity in identifying issues on which the military affects policy outcomes and the means by which this influence is exerted. The army's impact on society will be examined in terms of three major roles – agent, educator, and claimant – and tentative conclusions will be drawn regarding trends in its overall influence and implications for foreign policy.

The military as agent

The most important role Soviet military officers play is that of administra-tive agents of civilian politicians. This is the dominant image of the military in the rudimentary Soviet theory on civil–military relations. 'The Soviet commander', according to the leading text on military strategy, 'is the representative of the party and people. He carries out their will and implements party policy in the forces' (Sokolovsky, 1968, p. 445). The line of vertical subordination (extending from party leadership through the successive command and staff layers of the Ministry of Defense) is an obvious and straightforward one.

Perhaps less obvious is what the agent role implies for the military's effect on Soviet society. First, it means that officers exercise a great deal of delegated authority over the lives of a large number of subordinates, including the several million young men (most of them aged eighteen to twenty) serving as conscript soldiers and sailors. One half of all Soviet youths undergo compulsory military service, a proportion that has been considerably higher in the past and will probably increase in the future. For several years their work, social, and even sleep habits are regulated by officers whose orders are, as military regulations state crisply, law (*zakon*) for their subordinates. Under officers' direction they operate a vast and intricate system of activity that includes an enormous store of fighting equipment and most of the facilities needed to train, police, clothe, house, feed, transport, heal, clean, counsel, and entertain the men who make the equipment work (*Tyl i snabzhenie Sovetskikh vooruzhennykh sil*, 1973, No. 4, pp. 52–3).

The vast majority of the officers who exercise this authority are members of the party or Komsomol (this is especially true in troop command posts and almost universally at ranks of major and above), and the military hierarchy is saturated with a network of appointed and voluntary party agencies. Yet this has never made the army anything other than an organization whose prime purpose is to prepare for, wage, and win armed conflict. Even the military party organs' activity has for most of their history been tailored to military purposes. Soviet officers are soldiers of the party, but they are soldiers none the less. They leave their imprint upon their temporary charges as surely as do their counterparts in other armies.

Not only has the party delegated to the military a mission and the authority to perform it, it has also assigned consummate importance to that function. In the belief that defense is, as Stalin said, 'the primary task for us' (Stalin, Vol. 10, 1949, p. 85) the regime has created an innovative and productive infrastructure for the military effort – a military–industrial complex, to use the phrase the Soviets often apply to other countries. This system, undoubtedly 'the most privileged segment' of the economy (Spielman, 1976, p. 52), is best seen as registering the impact of military *goals* – as defined by a basically civilian leadership – rather than of the military *establishment*. But the requirements of their administrative mission do bring Soviet officers into contact with numerous other segments of society and of the governmental system.

For instance, military officials, usually in quite specialized agencies, participate as administrators in several areas of mainly civilian jurisdiction into which they have been allowed to extend their efforts to augment military capabilities. Several issue-areas stand out. In the field of construction, the military has long participated in extramilitary projects on a major scale, partly to enhance its own capacity and partly to compensate for civilian deficiencies. Soldiers (usually specially drafted construction troops) build telephone lines, housing, office and other public building, and irrigation facilities (*Krasnaya Zvezda*, 23 November 1976, p. 2). In the area of transport, too, construction has been a major activity. Since 1945 specialized railroad troops have laid about a thousand kilometers of track a year and have built hundreds of bridges and other structures; they are currently responsible for the eastern sector of the massive Baikal–Amur Railroad project (*Tyl i snabzhenie Sovetskikh vooruzhennykh sil*, 1968, No. 9, p. 9). All facets of military and civilian transport were tightly integrated during World War II, and even in peacetime complex arrangements exist to coordinate use of rail lines, airports, canals, harbors, and other facilities.

Officers also seek to secure specific contributions to their delegated mission from a number of civilian organizations, a fact that implies some military participation in realms of decision entrusted primarily to civilians. The ties with the other parts of the military–industrial complex (scientific institutes, defense production ministries, planning bodies) are often mentioned in Western research. There has been rather less heed paid to collaboration concerning civil defense, civil aviation, maritime navigation, and diplomatic representation abroad. Almost nothing has been written about how the army deals at several levels with civilians providing it with routine goods and services. Its headquarters negotiate agreements with the Ministry of Agriculture (for use of farmland), the Ministry of Oil Refining and Petrochemical Industry (for fuel and lubricants), food-processing ministries, and the Ministry of Trade, Ministry of Light Industry, and other consumer goods producers (for supply of clothing, consumer durables, and other items). At the local level, housing is sometimes leased from civilian authorities, contacts are made with party and government authorities during disaster relief operations and harvest campaigns, conscription call-ups entail close communication with local health and school officials, and annual contracts are made with republican and local agencies for supply of perishable foods, leisure and sporting equipment, household appliances and chemicals, and a range of other commodities.

The military as educator

Implicit in its role as the regime's principal agent in military policy is the army's role as educator. Any peacetime army is essentially an educational organization, teaching citizens how to apply violence in the interests of the state. Yet the role of educator is so important in Soviet military theory and practice and so central to any discussion of the military's impact on society that it merits separate consideration.

Much of the education that occurs within the Soviet military would be familiar to conscripts in other armies: the drill, technical instruction, field exercises, and the like. What is striking about Soviet military training is its deliberate interweaving with a system of ideological and moral upbringing (*vospitanie*). Since the Civil War, Soviet theorists have argued that the training of the good soldier is inseparable from the forming of the good citizen and that wars are won by the side that can field the soldier 'who is able in the most difficult of conditions to maintain his high moral spirit and will to victory' (*Izvestiya*, 9 August 1964, p. 3). To this end all servicemen are constantly bombarded with political information and exhortation, most of it administered by the political organs. Each man attends four hours a week of obligatory political classes and an additional hour of 'political information'. About 80 per cent of all troops are members of the Komsomol (70 per cent are already members when conscripted), and a much smaller proportion are party members (*Krasnaya Zvezda*, 25 April 1974, p. 3). Cultural and recreational activity (supervised by the political organs) is also laden with ideological content.

It is thus readily understandable that the army is referred to as a 'school of Communism', an arena for political socialization as well as specialized military training. Indeed, in the first several decades of Soviet rule the military was frequently heralded as the country's single most important vehicle for this purpose. Stalin described it as 'the sole . . . point of assembly where people from various provinces and regions come together, study, and are schooled in political life' (Stalin, 1949, p. 205). Thousands of servicemen, especially from rural areas, received their first exposure to party ideas (not to mention mass organization and machine technology) in the interwar Red Army. The subsequent growth of the regime's systems of public education and communication has outdated any claim to preeminence, but political training in the military remains an important thread in the overall weave, 'continuing the process of Communist education . . . begun in the family, school, and productive process' (*Krasnaya Zvezda*, 9 May 1973, p. 2). Because soldiers have already been familiarized with the regime's basic values, the emphasis is now on reinforcing and maintaining the desired attitudes against 'nihilism and skepticism' (*Morskoi Sbornik*, 1969, No. 8, p. 6).

During the last decade there has been an upsurge of official interest in military service – in all its aspects – as an inculcator of civic virtue. One now finds statements that the army provides 'particularly favorable circumstances for organizing the entire business of upbringing'. At the Twenty-fifth Party Congress in 1976, Leonid Brezhnev's only reference to the military was in precisely this connection:

In speaking about educational work, comrades, it is impossible not to dwell on the enormous role which the Soviet Army plays in this matter. Young men arrive in the soldierly family with no experience in the school of life. But they return from the Army already people who have gone through the school of tenacity and discipline, who have acquired technical and professional knowledge and political training (*XXV S"ezd Kommunisticheskoi Partii Sovetskogo Soyuza: Stenograficheskii otchet*, Vol. 1, 1976, p. 101).

Two educational goals are now receiving emphasis. One is the development of such individual lines of character as 'tenacity and discipline', which military and party leaders alike often see as lacking in the generation born after 1945. The other reflects what may be an even deeper source of anxiety – the goal of solidarity among the Soviet Union's many nationalities. The army is clearly designed as an integrating and Russianizing institution. Russian is the sole language of instruction and command and facility in it is a prerequisite for admission to officers' schools. There is an 'attempt to reinforce in every soldier the awareness of belonging to a single socialist Motherland, to a great international army' (*Tyl i snabzhenie Sovetskikh vooruzhennykh sil*, 1972, No. 10, p. 13). Political officers operate 'circles for the study of the Russian language' in some units, and they are urged to combat 'elements of national conceit and harmful habits of seeing a national basis for every disagreement or personal insult' (*Kommunist vooruzhennykh sil*, No. 3, 1970, p. 24). This struggle will no doubt become more important as it becomes necessary to conscript larger numbers of non-Russians (particularly Central Asians) in future years.

The development of the last decade that has most caught the eye of foreign observers has been the perceptible increase in military and military-related education *outside* the army. This growth has occurred in three areas.

First, the revised military service law of 1967, while reducing active duty for most conscripts by one year, required all predraft-age youths to undergo basic military training (*nachal'naya voennaya podgotovka*) at their places of study or work. Introduced in stages from 1968 to the mid-1970s, the system placed military instructors (*voennye rukovoditeli*) – most of them reserve or retired officers – in secondary and vocational schools and major production enterprises. The two-year, 140-hour program covers military regulations, use of light weapons, drill, and a technical military specialty (usually operation of a vehicle). Since the early 1970s many post-secondary students (who normally receive draft deferments) have been required to attend courses in new military faculties. They ultimately are given reserve commissions and are thus liable to later call-up. In addition, the preinduction and other programs of DOSAAF (the Voluntary Society for Assistance of the Army, Air Force, and Navy) have continued to expand, particularly in the area of technical specialties. DOSAAF's capital expenditures increased by almost 60 per cent between 1972 and 1976, and by 1977 it was claiming a membership of 80 million – two-thirds of the entire adult population (Goldhammer, 1975; Odom, 1976b; *Krasnaya Zvezda*, 23 January 1977, p. 2).

A second area of growth has been the civil defense program, which has acquired greater visibility and perhaps a higher degree of coordination. Civil defense themes have been more prominent in the mass media and in specialized publications, and since 1971 they have been included in curricula for all second- and fifth-grade pupils. The program of instruction in factories and of the workplaces was standardized in 1972 (at twenty hours of non-working time a year for each employee), and both large-scale exercises and specialized courses for officials have become more common (*Sovetskaya Belorussiya*, 18 October 1972, p. 3).

Third, the regime has placed greater emphasis on the general 'military-patriotic education' of the population, particularly the young. The commemoration of past martial exploits, especially the 'Great Patriotic War' of 1941–5, reached a crescendo with the celebration of the thirtieth anniversary of victory in 1975. In the five years of 1972–6, 80 major war monuments were unveiled; from 1974 to 1976, more than 500 books and 300 serialized novels and short stories on the war were published in Russian alone (*Krasnaya Zvezda*, 7 April 1977, p. 2). Perhaps the major innovation has been in terms of participatory and organized forms of inculcation for young people. These various activities include 'red pathfinders' clubs, which mount excursions to monuments and battlefields; groups of 'young friends' of the army and navy; and military-patriotic 'schools' and 'universities' (most of them attached to elementary or secondary schools or to DOSAAF clubs). Most ambitious have been the two 'military-sports games' organized by the major youth federations – *Zarnitsa* (Summer Lightning) for Young Pioneers (aged 10 to 15), claiming 16 million participants by 1972; and the Komsomol's *Orlenok* (Eaglet), established only in 1972 and, as of 1976, claiming 8 million participants in their later teens (*Sovetsky Patriot*, 29 April 1977, p. 2).

In terms of sheer ambition and energy, all of these programs warrant further attention from Western scholars. But would such attention establish that Soviet society is being 'militarized' and in particular that the power of the military itself is growing? Here a number of cautions are in order.

To begin, one should be careful not to overstate the innovativeness of some of this activity. Preinduction training in the schools does mark a major change (although one accompanied by another change – shorter terms for conscripts – which markedly reduces the exposure of most young men to active military service). Civil defense, on the other hand, dates in its current form from 1961 and, indeed, grew out of a local air defense network established in 1932; the 1972 directive on workplace instruction did not necessarily imply an increased effort, merely a set of minimum standards (*Sovetskaya Belorussiya*, 2 April 1972, p. 3). DOSAAF, too, has a long history (its predecessors were founded in the 1920s). And military-patriotic propaganda and education are by no means a recent creation. If 80 monuments were built between 1972 and 1976, in 1966 there were already 675 military monuments and memorials in the Ural Military District alone (an area in which no land battles were fought during World War II) (*Izvestiya*, 5 May 1966, p. 3). The entire military-patriotic program is fundamentally backward-looking, an attempt to foster by deliberate government effort feelings that for earlier generations emerged more spontaneously from experience. Even tributes to the plethora of war novels protest that authors are now more likely to slight martial themes than in the past.

In the second place, it should be realized that many of the measures reviewed here have complex objectives, and that at least some are essentially used to shape civilian society in accordance with the preferences of civilian leaders and in ways that go beyond merely heightening military capability. This is especially true of military-patriotic education, in which several kinds of values that have long been important to the civilian elite – discipline, nationalism, and respect for past achievements – are at the very heart of the process. It is certainly significant that the regime has chosen the army and the military idiom as the focus for the effort, but it is true none the less that broader civilian purposes prevail. Nationalism is heavily stressed in the program, particularly in non-Russian republics (where it is often referred to as 'internationalist' as well as military-patriotic). The appeal to the accomplishments and heroes of the past is an omnipresent theme (to the point that a story can refer to long-dead revolutionaries and soldiers as 'standing invisibly' in a Komsomol honor guard at a monument) (*Krasnaya Zvezda*, 21 August 1976, p. 4). Here, too, the ideals being promoted far transcend the military realm.

A third pitfall to avoid is confusion of the objectives and exertions of the programs with their actual impact on society. Militarizing government programs do not necessarily mean a militarized society, any more than a 'war on poverty' in the United States automatically implies greater equality.

Quantitative descriptions of the programs should be treated with great care. It is useful to know that 85 000 young people a year took part in the red pathfinders movement in Turkmenistan in 1971–2; that 2000 children and teenagers attended summer military-sports camps in Latvia in 1972 and 16 000 were enrolled in military-patriotic schools in Belorussia in 1973; or that in the summer of 1975, 30 000 students from Dnepropetrovsk oblast visited local monuments and another 8000 went on excursions to four 'hero cities' (*Turkmenskaya iskra*, 26 May 1973, p. 3; *Sovetskaya Latviya*, 17 May 1973, p. 2). What none of these figures indicates (and what Western analysts rarely seek out) is the ratio of participants to eligible populations. The 1970 census makes clear that in these cases the participants amounted, respectively, to 17.6, 0.6, 0.9, 7.5, and 2.0 per cent of the relevant populations (aged ten to nineteen) – proportions that imply far less substantial impact than the absolute numbers might intimate at first glance.

Even where quantitative saturation is indisputably high (as with DO-SAAF and the Zarnitsa and Orlenok games, which between them involve half of the ten-to-nineteen-year-olds), no analysis can refrain from raising questions about program quality and effect. While this is not the place for detailed examination, it should be noted that no serious Soviet discussion of the programs fails to pose such questions.

Basic military training is a partial exception here, at least in the secondary schools; despite construction and other problems, it seems to have produced the desired effect. None the less, even a favorable Soviet overview must conclude that the program 'suffices only to acquaint students with the general structure of [a military] machine, with its most important features and basic operating principles. To put it briefly . . . students acquire elementary knowledge and habits concerning only a single military-technical specialty' (*Sovetskii Patriot*, 31 March 1974, p. 4). Soviet evaluations of non-school programs are often much less positive. Reviews of civil defense preparations refer to 'formalism and vulgarization' and remark on officials 'who "forget" about civil defense, justifying this by their preoccupation with production affairs'; reports about both basic training and civil defense mention 'indifference' in building and maintaining basic facilities; a speech on war novels scores their 'primitiveness' and facile moralizing; and stories tell of participants in military-patriotic projects being assembled from predetermined lists (*po spisku*) (*Sovetskaya Moldaviya*, 15 August 1972, p. 2; *Krasnaya Zvezda*, 28 March 1976, p. 2). The bloated DOSAAF network has been excoriated for similar sins for decades, and this evidence is reinforced by the private testimony of present and former Soviet citizens and the obvious absurdity of some of DOSAAF's self-appraisals (*Krasnaya Zvezda*, 26 January 1977, p. 1). If Zarnitsa and Orlenok seem to be more efficacious, it is probably because they are firmly rooted in the schools; most competitions take place on school grounds (under Pioneer and Komsomol auspices), and only a small proportion of competitors seem to participate in the regional and national games in midsummer.

The fourth and final qualification regarding these programs has to do with their relation to the power of the military itself. Militarizing programs – even a militarizing society – may go hand in hand with greater political power for the professional military, but in the Soviet Union under Brezhnev there is little evidence that they have.

Basic military training, to take the first area, is formally a responsibility of civilian ministries of education, all of which have departments for that purpose. Military instructors are appointed and dismissed by local education departments on recommendation of the school director and with the consent of the local military commissariat. They are paid by the schools and responsible to their directors. In 1972, after receiving letters from several military instructors recommending that they be subordinated to military commissariats rather than to civilian school authorities, the deputy minister of education in charge of the national program dismissed the suggestions as being 'so obviously [mistaken] as hardly to warrant comment'. The deputy minister went on to observe: 'The school must not be transformed into the likeness of a troop subunit. The Soviet school has its own regulations and educational traditions, which the military instructor is obliged to observe' (*Sovetsky Patriot*, 16 August 1972, p. 3).

DOSAAF, which plays a substantial role in several military-related areas, is not under the immediate control of the army. It finances its own operations – with considerable difficulty, as many accounts clearly show – from membership dues, lotteries, charges for sports events, and a variety of recreation services. Military officials do not seem to be involved in DOSAAF's perennial campaigns to persuade local authorities to implement the vague guidelines on assistance to the organization's construction efforts (*Sovetsky Patriot*, 16 August 1972, p. 3).

The fact that civil defense has a uniformed national chief (*nachal'nik*) – currently General of the Army Aleksandr T. Altunin, who has since 1972 also been a deputy defense minister – seems to imply more concerted penetration of civilian society by the military. Yet one should be careful about inferring the 'dominant administrative role of the Ministry of Defense' (Odom, 1976b, p. 47) from Altunin's dual appointment (his predecessor had similar status from 1961 to 1964) or on any other grounds. At republican and local levels, the civil defense chief is invariably the civilian chairman of the relevant council of ministers or municipal council. While most administrative responsibility probably lies with their full-time chiefs of staff, who are professional officers, the fact that civilians remain formally in charge is noteworthy and underlines the regime's intention to keep implementation of the program at least partly in non-military hands. Official pronouncements refer to civil defense as being 'under the leadership of the [local] Party and Soviet organs' and describe 'constant attention' to it on the part of local party executives (*Krasnaya Zvezda*, 16 November 1975, p. 1). No such statement would ever be made about operations within army jurisdiction, which are essentially outside the purview of local politicians. At the plant level, the chief of civil defense is the enterprise director and the part-time chief of staff is one of the director's line subordinates, often an engineer and sometimes a man with minor military experience. All formations within the enterprise are created by order of the director, and they are explicitly characterized as non-militarized (*nevoenizirovannye*) groups. A number of other civilian organizations participate in civil defense planning and exercises – including the Komsomol, Red Cross, railroads, medical and sanitation services, electrical and gas utilities, sports organizations, and territorial planning agencies – and the evidence suggests that whatever coordination is imposed comes from civilian authorities rather than from the military (*Krasnaya Zvezda*, 28 March 1976, p. 2).

A similar situation applies to military-patriotic education. Active and retired military officers, political organs, and occasionally military units are involved in program implementation, but planning is subject to local party control (*Krasnaya Zvezda*, 6 May 1976, p. 1). The Komsomol is actively involved (all its committees have departments for sport and mass defense work), as are the Pioneers, sports organizations, trade unions, ministries and departments of culture, *Znanie* (the mass information organization), school administrators, and the Academy of Pedagogical Sciences. At best, the military is a partner in a program dominated by civilians and using military values to achieve largely civilian ends.

The military as claimant

Besides participating in (and often monopolizing) political decisions within the military establishment, Soviet officers also take part in a variety of decisions together with civilian politicians and administrators. In doing so, they often put forward claims for recognition and resources in much the same manner as bureaucratic officials elsewhere in the Soviet system.

Clearly their main resource with national leaders is their status as specialists and experts worthy of consultation. Even Stalin, when confronted by specialized military decisions, 'repeatedly asked, "What does the General Staff think?" or, "Has the General Staff examine this question?" And the General Staff always gave its opinion' (Shtemenko, 1968, p. 116). Since the early 1960s official statements have been much more explicit than before in referring to consultation as routine: 'Before deciding one way or the other on questions of military development, the Party Central Committee and Politburo carefully study the state of affairs in the Army and Navy and consult with the high command and the most important specialists of the Armed Forces' (*Partiino-politicheskaya rabota v Sovetskikh vooruzhennykh silakh*, 1974, p. 103).

Consultation is formalized to some extent through military membership in bodies such as the Council of Ministers, the Defense Council (a collegium for discussing military policy, currently chaired by the General Secretary), and the Military-Industrial Commission, which deals with defense production. The military is also represented on the formal decision-making organs of the party. The thirty military members and candidates on the 1976 Central Committee (7 per cent of the total) made up by far the largest contingent from any bureaucratic constituency. At the peak level, most Politburos prior to 1955 contained one non-professional defense administrator (Trotsky, Frunze, Voroshilov, Bulganin). Since then there have been two experiments to seat a defense minister who was also a professional soldier (Georgii Zhukov in 1956–7 and Andrei Grechko in the three years before his death in April 1976). Grechko's successor, Dmitrii F. Ustinov (a civilian Politburo member who spent almost his entire career dealing with defense production, ultimately as party secretary), marked at least a temporary reversion to the pre-1955 pattern and shows that the professional military can in no way view a Politburo seat as an institutional entitlement. Military officers sit on lower-level party organs as well. As of the early 1970s individual officers belonged to seven of fourteen republican bureaus, an average of eight sat on republican central committees, and there was substantial representation at the local level.

Less formalized channels are probably of equal importance (as is true for all bureaucratic claimants in Soviet politics). Marshal Grechko, for example, is said to have attended Politburo discussions on military matters even before his elevation to that body (Garthoff, 1975, p. 29), and war memoirs depict similar informal interaction. Some officers seem to have benefited from personal connections with civilian politicians based on friendship and common experience (Grechko is said to have had such a relationship with Brezhnev). One can also assume the existence of less personalized linkages with civilians involved in defense research and production. As in most consultative relationships, there has been no sharp line drawn between advice solicited by civilians and prodding at the military's own initiative. Khrushchev may have grumbled in his memoirs about military 'pressure' or even 'intimidation' of the party leadership, but there is no evidence he sought to prevent soldiers from speaking their minds on military issues. 'I don't reproach the military for that – they're only doing their job' (Talbott, 1976, p. 540).

The Soviet military is denied some of the bargaining resources available to its counterpart in the United States. In particular, the structural primacy of the party executive has precluded the direct appeals to an independent legislature encountered in the United States. None the less, some structural factors clearly work in the Soviet officers' favor. Special weight is lent to their counsel by the fact that their expertise is not widely shared outside the military establishment. Notwithstanding party, KGB, and defense industry involvement in some aspects of military affairs (and the evident growth of military competence in several civilian research institutes over the last decade), the Soviet officer corps does seem to control far more of the information relevant to its mission than do armies in Western societies. The Soviet system does not contain the major non-military sources of military information found in US politics – there is no equivalent to the Central Intelligence Agency or to private consulting firms such as the RAND Corporation.

Officers' status as claimants on the leadership is also reinforced by the high degree of instability and danger that civilians have perceived as inhering in the international milieu, the environment in which military decisions take effect. The tendency of Soviet leaders to resolve uncertainty in foreign policy on the side of safety has clearly made them more receptive to military advice than to that of most other expert groups. Khrushchev's remarks to President Eisenhower in 1959 display this receptivity as well:

Some people from our military department come and say, "Comrade Khrushchev, look at this! The Americans are developing such and such a system. We could develop the same system, but it would cost such and such." I tell them there's no money; it's all been allotted already. So they say, "If we don't get the money we need and if there's a war, then the enemy will have superiority over us." So we discuss it some more, and I end up giving them the money they ask for. (Talbott, 1976, p. 572)

Such high-level consultations on foreign policy issues are, of course, closed to foreign social scientists (for the period since 1945, at least). So are most of the bureaucratic channels at all levels through which influence on civilians is exerted. Much more readily observable are the public discussions in which army officials participate. Officers are subject to the same constraints as other citizens (for instance, in relation to criticism of Stalin) and to special restrictions in the cause of secrecy. Still, one finds a remarkably wide range of military-related concerns and anxieties aired in public: the status of the army and its mission, specific questions on military policy (such as the relative weight given to different branches of the military), the quality of civilian goods and services, and others. In approaching these public articulations, and less open ones as well, several general points should be kept in mind.

The first is that the military does not claim to be a monolithic or isolated organization. Military participation is specialized according to issue and actor (logistics officers are most concerned with relations with the railroads, political officers with military-patriotic education, and so on). Officers are not necessarily coordinated or unanimous in their preferences and may in fact differ among themselves in major ways. And whatever the range of military opinion, the likelihood is that important aspects of military positions will find support from at least some civilians and not offer a frontal challenge to civilian party leaders or to the interests of the regime as a whole. It is clear, for example, that Khrushchev's force reduction proposals in 1960 were opposed by a wide range of civilian party and state officials as well as by the military high command (and the military party organs).

Precisely such a pattern of ongoing discussion has been visible in this decade of relations with the West regarding the desirability and preferred modes of *detente*. Most military spokesmen share the ambivalence that infuses almost all official pronouncements about the 'relaxation of tensions'. While valuing its contribution to Soviet security (they have had virtually nothing to say about the presumed benefits of increased trade and technological exchange), they are anxious about possible Western second thoughts and wary of the long-term effects of relaxation of vigilance on the Soviet population – particularly on the youth.

Undoubtedly it is the latter train of thought that has been emphasized in public military statements. Soviet soldiers have had to make no apologies for the fact that, as Marshal Grechko said, 'For us military men it is impossible to forget' the experience and dangers of war (*Krasnaya zvezda*, 9 January 1976, p. 21). Military officers have been most forthright in arguing the hazards of failing to extract reciprocal concessions from the West, especially on arms control issues: 'A unilateral slackening in the USSR's defense power might call forth sharp changes in the policy of the ruling circles of the imperialist states. . . . Life dictates the necessity of unflagging concern for strengthening . . . the military power of the Soviet Union' (*Kommunist vooruzhennykh sil*, No. 16, August 1972, p. 16). It is interesting that some of the most outspoken declarations about the possible pitfalls of *detente* have come from the Main Political Administration (MPA), a component of the military establishment whose central task is to interpret and enforce party policy in the military realm. MPA chief Aleksei A. Epishev has repeatedly warned against imperialism's 'aggressive nature': 'In a situation where imperialism, in its efforts to regain its lost initiative, has become even more aggressive and adventuristic, Lenin's words about the need to keep our Army "fully ready for battle and increase its military potential" are particularly appropriate' (*Pravda*, 25 March 1971, p. 2). Such sentiments were echoed by Ustinov, his civilian background notwithstanding (*Pravda*, 23 February 1977, p. 2). They are, moreover, sentiments that resonate in many civilian quarters (as is surely the case for corresponding viewpoints in the United States).

In considering the military as a claimant in politics it is also important to understand that in the majority of cases the target of military advice and pressure is not the national party leadership at all, but other organizations or groups whose cooperation is necessary for some specific purpose. For instance, the Ministry of Defense and the MPA have repeatedly urged artists and their professional unions to do more work on martial themes. The latest illustration of concerted pressure occured in April 1977, when General Epishev addressed a hall full of cultural dignitaries (including officials of the Ministry of Culture, the editor of *Literaturnaya gazeta*, and leaders of the writers', composers', filmmakers', and sculptors', unions), demanding more attention to 'soldierly labor, which is just as necessary to society as that of the worker or peasant' (*Krasnaya zvezda*, 7 April 1977, p. 2). Quite frequently, at least on routine service issues, it is local officials who are the targets of military efforts. A bottleneck or disagreement may mean that officers will 'turn for a decision to the corresponding Party and soviet organs' (*Tyl i snabzhenie Sovetskikh vooruzhennykh sil*, 1973, No. 7, p. 63). Public criticisms are many and varied, with officers pressing, for instance, for improved housing and nursery facilities for military families, better treatment of reserve officers and veterans (particularly now that many World War II veterans have reached pension age), more attention to civil defense and paramilitary programs, or more investment priority for local factories producing materials for military construction units.

The final point to be made here is that military claims, for all their complexity, essentially relate to areas of policy in which the army's institutional interests are directly engaged. Soviet leaders have been assiduous in restricting soldiers' participation in administration and politics to questions relating in some way to their professional function and immediate interests. Stalin's conviction that 'the military should occupy themselves with their own business and not discuss things that do not concern them' (quoted in Yakir and Geller, 1963, pp. 111–12) has been retained by his successors. In a way the list of issues on which the military does not play a major role as agent or claimant – including questions of internal order and rural development, to mention two areas where the Chinese military is much more active – is as impressive as the set of issues in which the army's role is significant. Soviet officers have displayed no tendency to expand their participation into new problem areas and some have even declined minor opportunities to do so. For instance, the construction of military retail outlets is often not coordinated with that of civilian stores because 'military clients and construction agencies do not maintain close working contacts with local executive committees' (*Tyl i snabzhenie Sovetskikh vooruzhennykh sil*, 1973, No. 7, p. 62). Some military trade executives 'do not meet their local suppliers for years on end' and fail to obtain delivery of goods already contracted for due to the fact that they 'do not insist on having their orders filled' (ibid.).

Trends and implications

The crucial prerequisite for careful examination of the military's impact on Soviet society and politics is the acceptance of the fact that this impact is complex – complex in its determinants, modes, and consequences. It is surely incorrect to reduce the military's role to that of anxious adversary of the party leadership. Yet it would also be dangerous to accept some of the more simplistic notions (particularly those broadcast by Western journalists and Western generals) about pervasive military influence or about a militarizing or militarized Soviet society.

The army's impact did not change qualitatively during the Brezhnev era. The prospects for qualitative change are not to be dismissed out of hand yet they will depend essentially on developments outside the military establishment, developments that are extremely difficult to forecast. Any outright disintegration of the political system will inevitably bring the military to center stage, as has happened in other societies. The post-Brezhnev era offers the potential for military involvement in the selection of civilian leaders, but that potential will be realized only if civilians fail to observe the restraint in appealing to military assistance that they have exercised in the past. Short of such dramatic developments, the most likely stimulator of a change in the military impact in the next decade is the emerging labor shortage. This dilemma may force the regime in the 1980s to contemplate ways of fusing military training, civilian education, and economic production that have not been seriously entertained since the 1920s (*New York Times*, 17 April 1977, p. 8). If past experience is any guide, changes in this or any other area will be incremental and considered. Inroads on civilian authority are likely to come, as Bruce Russett has written of the US military, 'not [from] a sudden take-over by . . . soldiers but [from] slow accretions in the scope of military influence in the "normal" political system' (Russett, 1970, p. 181).

What do the military's impact and possible changes in it imply for foreign policy? Clearly the weight of military goals and the availability of military instruments in Soviet policy are major data for consideration in the West. Yet in both cases these basically reflect the same factor that has been the main determinant of the impact of the military itself on Soviet society – the values and objectives of Soviet *civilians*. The army is an important focus for political socialization, but this is principally due to civilian acceptance of many of the ideals it embodies. The military–industrial complex is a major constituency in Soviet politics, but largely because non-soldiers have made it one. And if the counsel of generals is heard with respect in Moscow, it is primarily because civilian leaders take seriously the goals that officers pursue. In the 1980s, as in the 1920s when Mikhail Frunze summarized this symmetry in perceptions, Soviet soldiers and civilians seem to agree: 'The stronger and more powerful [the army] is, and the more it is a threat to our enemies, then the more our interests will be served' (Frunze, 1925, p. 365).

13

Inequalities and the Politicization of the Polish Working Class

JACK BIELASIAK

One of the most important features of the 1980 workers' movement in Poland was its emphasis on egalitarianism. The need for social equality and social justice was predominant in the list of demands issued by the striking workers of Gdansk and Szczecin. The workers' demands for equality, however, went beyond economic security and social welfare guarantees to include the demand for free trade unions independent of the communist party and of enterprises (*New York Times*, 29 August 1980; Staniszkis, 1981, pp. 204–31; Tymowski, 1981). This call stemmed from a growing realization that the permanence of economic and social gains obtained during the summer of 1980 strikes could be assured only through re-arrangements within the political system (Pravda, 1982; Bielasiak, 1984). In addition to the establishment of independent, self-governing trade unions, the workers also demanded freedom of speech and open media as a means of rectifying a closed political system that stifled workers' participation in factory and community affairs. The end of economic and social inequality therefore became tied directly to the elimination of discrimination in political participation.

The roots of the egalitarian spirit of the summer of 1980 lay in the increasing awareness on the part of the Polish population that the prior decade witnessed strong social and economic differences. Surveys of Polish citizens during the 1970s revealed their concern with inequitable wages and social injustices and pointed to a growing uneasiness about the expanding socio-economic distance between the diverse social strata (Kurczewski, 1981; Nowak, 1981). While the perception of inequality was justified by the increasing discrepancies in economic and social benefits, the sentiment of injustice was aggravated by the decline in the standard of living of the

Reprinted with adaptations from Daniel N. Nelson (ed.), *Communism and the Politics of Inequalities* (Lexington, Mass.: Lexington Books, 1983) with the permission of author and publisher.

entire society in the late 1970s in comparison with the early years of the decade.

The strategy of the Gierek regime after it came to power in December 1970 was based on the leadership's assessment of the 1970 workers' demonstrations, which were viewed as a direct result of economic dissatisfaction. In order to alleviate the social tensions evident in Polish society, the Gierek program sought to improve the living conditions of the population by rapid economic growth to be attained through increased investments in industry and a higher standard of living through wage increments and a freeze on prices (Fallenbuchl, 1977). The strategy was in fact a materialist conception of socialism, seeking to establish support for the regime by improving the social welfare of the Polish people. Alongside this economic program the Gierek policy called for consolidation and centralization of political power as instruments in the implementation of the 'second Poland's' modernization (Bielasiak, 1983). The concentration of political authority in the highest echelons of the communist party was justified as necessary for the success of the economic drive, which in turn was to resolve the nation's problems and fulfill society's needs.

The combination of economic and political strategies pursued by the Gierek regime, however, had grave consequences for the stability of Poland. The materialist approach to the building of socialism called for incentives for the rising strata of technocrats and bureaucrats, thereby relegating egalitarian values of socialism into the background. Just as materialism penetrated the entire society, so the bureaucratic caste increasingly identified success with the accumulation of its own powers and privileges. As long as the economic miracle of the early 1970s sustained growth for all groups in society, the regime was able to obtain legitimacy by relying on improved economic welfare. None the less the policy of both industrial and consumption growth could not be maintained in the face of domestic over-investment and worldwide recession (Mason, 1983b). By the mid-1970s the initial Gierek strategy of greater material distribution throughout society had to be curtailed, and what had begun as a device to obtain popular support turned rapidly to a cause of societal dissatisfaction. Unable to maintain its commitments of material benefits to all, and in the face of strong resistance on the part of the bureaucracy against the curtailment of its new found privileges, the government began to neglect workers' interests as consumers.

The regime's attempts to lower living standards of the working class by raising prices while continuing the privileges of the political and managerial elites led to the growing conviction that inequalities were expanding rapidly to the detriment of industrial workers. The perception was further enhanced by another consequence of Gierek's initial strategy of political centralization, which contributed significantly to the isolation of the party and government leadership from popular sentiments and prevented working class inputs into centers of decision-making. The consequences of this political failure are well known: attempts to restructure prices of consumer goods in June 1976 and July 1980 met immediately with the workers' protests. In both cases the actions of laborers were motivated by a sense of injustice, which found root in the view that the working class was bearing the burden of economic failure while the elite continued to enjoy its privileges. The rebellion in the factories, shipyards, and mines of Poland began as an attempt to prevent this inequality and ended up as a movement for the restoration of economic equality and social justice.

The demands of the workers' movement were thus a reflection of the economic, social, and political inequalities present in the Poland of the 1970s and the workers' perceptions of these maldistributions. The positions of the labor class in 1980 can therefore be understood only within the context of the economic resources available to different strata of the Polish population, the social opportunities present for the various groups, and their access to participation in policy formulation throughout the 1970s.

Economic inequalities

Economic factors were most directly responsible for the sociopolitical dissatisfaction of the Polish working class at the end of the 1970s, with the July 1980 price increase unleashing widespread labor protests and strikes. In conditions of increasing scarcity and inflation, wages became an important determinant of material welfare that made social differences even more visible.

The temporal decline in the socioeconomic well-being of the workers served to reinforce their subjective assessment of inequalities in Polish society (Malanowski, 1981, pp. 26–45, 111–58). Working class perceptions particularly were affected by the rising expectations of Gierek's early economic miracle and the ensuant propaganda of success, which depicted a society experiencing greater material advances. In the first five years of Gierek's rule (1970–75), nominal wages far outstripped living costs, resulting in an average yearly increase in real earnings of 7.1 per cent. But, as Table 13.1 indicates, the next four years (1976–9) witnessed both an increase in costs of living and a decline in nominal wages. This last trend is a reflection of deliberate government policies aimed at halting the economic deterioration by curbing consumer demand, thus lowering wage increments. The result of the combination of lower pay and greater inflation was a marked decline in yearly average increase in real wages during the 1976–9 period. The drop from 7.1 to 1.3 per cent in the increase of real wages between the two halves of the decade reveals the rapid decline in the population's economic welfare. The falling standard in actual living conditions was exacerbated by the prior rising expectations produced

TABLE 13.1   *Wages and living costs*

Year	Nominal wages	Living costs	Real wages
Percentage change from previous year			
1971	5.5	−0.2	5.7
1972	6.4	0.0	6.4
1973	11.5	2.6	8.7
1974	13.8	6.8	6.6
1975	11.8	3.0	8.5
1976	8.8	4.7	3.9
1977	7.3	4.9	2.3
1978	5.8	8.7	−2.9
1979	8.8	6.7	2.0
Average yearly increase			
1970–75	9.8	2.4	7.1
1976–9	7.7	6.2	1.3

Source: adapted from Wieseaw Krencik, 'Tempo wzrostu a rozpietosc plac w latach 1970–1979', *Gospodarka Planowa*, No. 4 (April 1980) p. 203, Table 1.

by the 'second-Poland' policy, resulting in subjective feelings of relative deprivation.

That the regime's failure to deliver continued prosperity strongly affected the perceptions of Polish citizens regarding living conditions is evident from public opinion surveys. Public evaluation of material well-being declined substantially in the post-1976 period, with those judging the living situation as very difficult or rather difficult increasing from 43 per cent of respondents in 1976 to 72 per cent in 1980, while those describing the material supply situation as bad jumped from 36 per cent to 91 per cent in the 1974–80 period. The negative economic assessment had an obvious impact on the overall evaluation of the previous year, with a substantial shift from a good to a bad response occurring after 1976 so that at no time during that entire period did a majority of Polish citizens assess the prior year as good.

More important for our purposes is that the subjective evaluation of living conditions was unequally distributed among different occupational and income strata of the Polish society. A survey of living conditions among a representative national sample revealed that while most individuals felt that, between 1970 and 1978, their family's economic standard had risen at least somewhat, it was the intelligentsia and the higher income groups that attained the largest gains while workers and low-income groups fared the worst (Beskid, 1979, 1980; Kabaj, 1980). In a similar survey of the 164 largest Polish enterprises (Table 13.2) employees self-identified their living levels, with the vast majority of workers (65 per cent) stating that their standard was at the minimum or basic levels and only 33 per cent at the sufficiency or highest levels. Clearly while the worsening economic

TABLE 13.2   *Self-identification of living standards (percentage of responses)*

	Workers	Intelligentsia
Minimal level	23.6	9.6
Basic level	41.0	37.0
Sufficiency level	26.5	36.6
High level	6.6	12.7

Source: Zbigniew Sufin, 'Społeczne uwarunkowania i konsekwencje kryzysu', *Nowe Drogi*, No. 12 (December 1980), pp. 71–2.

conditions negatively affected the majority of the Polish population, it was the working class and in particular the lower income groups within it that evaluated their situation in the most pessimistic terms.

Data for income distribution in the 1970s tend to support the perceptions of growing differentials in Polish society. Extensive analyses of wage structure and per capita household income revealed that inequality tended to follow the overall pattern of the Polish economy, with a more equal dispersion associated with the years of material prosperity (Danecki, 1978; Krencik, 1980; Flakierski, 1981; Pohorille, 1982). The distribution of wages and salaries in the socialized sector thus became more equal for manual and non-manual workers in the early 1970s, a trend that was once again reversed in mid-decade (Table 13.3). Inequality of earnings grew in the subsequent period to the point that in 1978 it had once again reached the 1967 level.

Working class sensitivity to inequalities heightened notwithstanding a decline in the wage gap between manual and non-manual workers, a difference amounting to 6 per cent between the two groups' median income in 1967 and 3 per cent in 1978 (Flakierski, 1981, p. 138). Other factors tended to override this *rapprochement* between manual and non-manual earnings, however. For example, the income of the technical-engineering stratum continued to be substantially above that of the blue-collar em-

TABLE 13.3   *Distribution of wages and salaries*

	$P_{90} : P_{10}$ ratio			Minimum wage as percentage of average wage
	Total	Manual	Non-manual	
1967	3.14	3.23	3.12	42
1970	2.98	3.31	2.98	40
1972	2.83	2.86	2.78	n.a.
1973	2.95	2.68	2.41	n.a.
1976	3.11	3.14	2.97	33
1978	3.13	3.22	2.93	34

Source: adapted from Henryk Flakierski, 'Economic Reform and Income Distribution in Poland: The Negative Evidence', *Cambridge Journal of Economics*, vol. 5 (1981) p. 139, Table 1.

ployees. Similarly, the dispersion of wages was higher among the manual workers than white-collar employees, a ratio amounting in 1978 to 3.2 and 2.9 respectively (Table 13.3). In fact, one of the most striking aspects of income differentiation in the 1970s was that intrasectoral dispersion within branches of the economy increased while the relative difference between the economic sectors tended to decline. The consequence was that the increase in inequality at the end of the decade within the industry, construction, transportation, trade, and other sectors were more pronounced than for the economy as a whole (Flakierski, 1981, pp. 138–42). Such higher inequality within sectors increased the workers' sensitivity to wage inequalities. The acuteness of such sentiments is evident in a poll by Osrodek Badania Opinii Publiczej of January 1981 when 86 per cent of respondents judged wage differences to be too high, while only 4 per cent thought them to be as they should be and another 4 per cent deemed them too small (Osrodek Badania Opinii Publicznej i Studiow Progromowych Survey, No. 2, 1981).

The perceptions of inequality were further reinforced in that the dispersion of wages created particularly severe inequalities between the high and low extremes of income, which again were felt more by manual than non-manual earners. The 1970s witnessed the emergence of a substantial stratum with high income, while at the other end of the scale a large group of households (21 per cent) was at or below the social minimum (Pohorille, 1982, pp. 164–5). The lowest income groups in Poland fared particularly badly, as is evident from the statistic measuring the minimum wage as a percentage of the average pay. Despite increases in the former, the gap between the two became wider: in 1970 the minimum equaled 40 per cent of the average earning, but by 1978 it had declined to 34 per cent (Table 13.3). Furthermore, in the latter year, more than half of the employees in the socialized economy earned less than the average salary (Flakierski, 1981, p. 144).

Other evidence as well points to the growing inequality of society, reflected primarily in the growing gap between the extremes of income dispersion. For example, the ratio between the highest and lowest wages increased in the 1970s until it reached 11 : 1 in 1978. In conditions where all wages rose rapidly, this meant that the differences in absolute income became even greater during the decade. Because of the higher cost of living, it also signified that people with relatively lower incomes were placed under extreme hardship. Data on per capita household income demonstrate this difficulty very strongly. In large part due to demographic features, since large families tend to bring down the standard of living of even relatively high earners, in 1976 46 per cent of the families with three children and 77 per cent of the families with four children had a per capita income below the social minimum (Flakierski, 1981, pp. 144–8; Pohorille, 1982, pp. 164–5). Given the fact that larger families tend to be found in greater proportion among the working class than white-collar strata, this meant that the living conditions of industrial labor lagged further behind the administrative elite, despite the closing in income that occurred between the manual and non-manual employees.

It is not surprising that, given such circumstances, strong sentiments among workers favored wage restructuring. In a survey of steelmill employees, the overwhelming preference among blue-collar workers was in favor of decreasing the salaries of highest earners or increasing the wages of lowest earners (Table 13.4). Fifty-four per cent of the unskilled workers and 63 per cent of the skilled laborers held such a position, in contrast to 44 per cent of the foremen and 31 per cent of the production directors. Other opinion polls substantiated the view that a vast majority of the population focused on wages as a predominant factor responsible for discrepancies in the standard of living. Already in 1975, 91 per cent of respondents in a survey concerning social divisions felt that differences among people in Poland were due 'strongly' to variations in earnings or wealth, while those attributing the cause of such differences to education amounted to 76 per cent, 77 per cent to differences in managerial and non-managerial positions, and 66 per cent to divisions between manual and non-manual workers (Nowak, 1979; 1981, p. 50). Even in 1980, when the country was undergoing severe economic dislocations and social tensions, the *Polacy*

TABLE 13.4 *Opinions of wage differences by occupation (percentage of responses)*

	Production directors	Technical personnel	Foremen	Skilled workers	Unskilled workers
Increase wage differences	—	2.4	0.9	1.4	1.6
Retain wage differences	56.8	34.1	28.7	15.7	19.6
Regroup wage levels among occupations	11.7	14.6	25.7	17.9	22.9
Decrease high wages or increase low wages	15.6	14.6	19.8	27.8	34.4
Decrease highest wages and increase lowest wages	15.6	34.1	24.7	35.7	19.6
Opinions on range of income					
Increase range of wages	13.7	2.4	6.9	1.4	1.7
Decrease range of wages	19.6	24.4	21.6	42.1	36.7

Source: adapted from Boguslaw Blachnicki, *Pracownicy Przemyslu Wobec Egalitaryzmu* (Wrocław: Ossolineum, 1979) p. 111, Table 24, and p. 99, Table 18.

'*80* survey based on a national sample found that a primary issue of concern centered around changes in wages: among the responses 70 per cent said they definitely favored limiting the salaries of highest earners, while 49 per cent had a similar response towards guaranteeing equal income to all citizens (*Polacy '80*, p. 106).

The strong concern with the structure of wages expressed in all these polls demonstrates without doubt that the increasing inequalities in Poland throughout the 1970s translated into a major social problem. Moreover, the perceptions of inequality were most acute among the working class and low-income groups. An OBOP poll conducted in early 1981, for example, noted that among several severe problems prevalent in the nation, equality of income distribution was mentioned by 42 per cent of unskilled workers, 36 per cent of skilled workers, 34 per cent of white-collar employees without higher education, and 16 per cent of white-collar employees with higher education (Osrodek Badania Opinii Publicznej i Studiow Progra-mowych Survey, No. 10, 1981). In the wake of these sentiments, it is not surprising that blue-collar workers favored most consistently some reme-dial action regarding the structure of salaries and wages. This is clearly evident from data in Table 13.4, where skilled (42 per cent) and unskilled (37 per cent) workers in a steelmill supported to a significantly greater extent a decrease in wage spread than did foremen (22 per cent), tech-nicians (24 per cent), and directors (20 per cent). A similar national sample in *Polacy '80* found that skilled and unskilled workers favored a wage increment only to low earners in a greater proportion than did clerical employees and specialists (*Polacy '80*, p. 82).

The consistent support for wage reform evident among the Polish population during the second half of the 1970s found strong expression during the work stoppages of July and August 1980. Specifically the workers in striking factories and shipyards were concerned with the estab-lishment of a more egalitarian social structure and sought to attain this goal by demanding restrictions on the privileges of the political and administra-tive elite and wage increments to the low-income groups, notably poor workers, large families and pensioners (Tymowski, 1981; Staniszkis, 1981).

Social differences

Changes in the level and dispersion of income are insufficient measures of well-being in Polish society, for social benefits and privileges derived from elite status substantially affected the living standards of the diverse social groups in the 1970s. In fact, as in the case of earnings, social benefits became an especially critical influence on the perceptions of inequality during the growing scarcity environment of the late 1970s.

The importance of social benefits in socialist societies is derived from the position that social policy is to perform a redistributive function, serving as a corrective to earning differences by improving the living conditions of the poorer strata through the provision of social services. In view of such official pronouncements, the normal expectations of the population are likely to be that expenditures in the social consumption fund are to serve the promotion of a more egalitarian distribution of goods and services by providing better social security, education, health care, or housing to low-income groups (Szubert, 1979). Such expectations, however, were largely disappointed in the Poland of the 1970s.

In the first place, Gierek's economic program was unable to sustain throughout the decade a multifaceted growth in industrial investment, consumption and social welfare. In the initial boom years, the government was able to proceed with the building of the second Poland by providing significant fiscal inputs (financed in large part by Western credits) into industrial development and, as a means of stimulating productivity, into the wage fund and social services. However, as the economy began to deteriorate in the mid-1970s, shortfalls began to be evident and the policy of growth across all three investment areas had to be curtailed. In an attempt to salvage the economy, the emphasis on industrial growth created a squeeze on the wage fund and social benefits. One consequence was to defer wage equalization so that pay differentials would serve as incentives for productivity. At the same time as income inequalities increased in the second half of the 1970s, the resources available for social welfare provisions also declined, so that the latter benefits could not be employed to counterbalance the growing earnings' dispersion. This trend is clearly visible from budgetary data in Table 13.5, which indicates that from 1974 on the percentage of government expenditures for social welfare declined (with the exception of housing).

None the less, since investments for the entire economy were being downgraded, the share of personal income derived from social benefits did not decline but was fairly stable throughout this period. Both social transfers in cash and in kind benefits derived from participation in collective consumption services remained steady at around 9 and 11 per cent, respectively, of each individual's per capita income (Table 13.5). That the portion of total income derived from social benefits remained steady at about 20 per cent must be placed in the context of a positive correlation between personal income and gains from social welfare provisions (Pohorille, 1982, p. 169), meaning that the latter could not be used as a policy regulator to equalize differences in salaries and wages.

The evidence on the relation between these two components of income therefore calls into question the alleged redistributive function of social benefits. Ivan Szelenyi argued some time ago that the opposite effect is prevalent in socialist economies and that inequalities are due largely to the administrative allocation of goods and services to the wealthier sectors of

TABLE 13.5 *Social benefits: expenditures and per capita income*

	Percentage of budget expenditures on				Percentage of social benefits in		
	Social security	Health	Housing	Education	Income transfer	Collective consumption	Benefit ratio: highest to lowest per capita
1970	4.4	7.1	15.6	7.5	9.0	10.8	134.9
1971	5.1	7.0	15.4	8.0	9.4	11.4	n.a.
1972	5.2	7.3	13.9	8.2	9.1	11.6	n.a.
1973	5.1	7.8	13.3	8.5	8.9	11.5	123.6
1974	4.8	7.1	12.3	7.4	8.9	10.7	113.8
1975	5.2	6.8	13.1	7.2	8.4	10.7	126.5
1976	4.3	6.7	14.2	7.0	8.6	11.1	127.0
1977	4.4	6.6	16.0	6.7	9.0	11.0	n.a.
1978	n.a.	6.4	17.4	6.4	9.6	11.1	188.0

Source: David S. Mason 'Policy Dilemmas and the Polish Leadership', *Journal of Politics*, vol. 45 (1983) p. 402, Table 1, and p. 403, Table 2, and Henryk Flakierski, 'Economic Reform and Income Distribution: the Negative Evidence', *Cambridge Journal of Economics*, vol 5 (1981) p. 155, Table 4, and p. 156, Table 10.

society (Szelenyi, 1978). The case of Poland under Gierek certainly supports that argument, for the data on collective consumption among social strata indicates a maldistribution in favor of the high income groups. In 1975, for instance, the per capita value of social benefits was 40 per cent higher in the uppermost income bracket than in the lowest, and the correlation held throughout the earnings' scale so that the larger the income the better value obtained from social services (Pohorille, 1982, pp. 154–5). This linkage was true in virtually all areas of social welfare, with true disparities being especially significant in such critical benefits as health, housing, social security, and education. Moreover, the empirical trend shows a definite increase in the inequality of social welfare distribution over time during the second half of Gierek's rule. For example, the cash social benefits obtained by the highest income bracket in comparison with the lowest one were 14 per cent higher in 1974, 27 per cent in 1976 and 88 per cent in 1978 (Table 13.5). The poorer groups were thus falling much further behind their more affluent counterparts. At the same time, it should be remembered, wages too were becoming further dispersed among the social strata.

The inevitable conclusion from the distribution and trend of social provisions in Poland during the late 1970s is that welfare benefits did not serve as a means to equalize real incomes. As a result of the better benefits obtained by higher income and white-collar groups, social inequality was more significant with welfare provisions than without them. That the working class was well aware of the impact that social benefits had on Polish society is evident from the August 1980 demands that not only wage but also social welfare policies be changed in favor of the poor.

The inequality present in the distribution of income and welfare aggravated considerably the differences in consumption among the social groups. In particular during the last years of the Gierek period a polarization in the standard of living occurred, when the amenities enjoyed as a result of higher earnings became much more visible and were further compounded by other privileges derived from positions of power. The consequence was the emergence of a conspicuous consumption style that advertised openly the privileged status of the political and administrative elite (Nowak, 1981, p. 51; Smolar, 1981). The initial impetus for this *nouveau riche* living came from the government's program, which sought to reward strategic elites for their contribution to Gierek's economic policy. Ultimately this meant that conspicuous consumption became the mark of a successful career in the party or state apparatus (Misztal and Misztal, 1982, p. 10).

The benefits derived from positions of power were multivaried and touched all areas of socioeconomic activity (Czabanski, 1981; Smolar, 1981). Besides the higher salaries already available to most officials, they supplemented that pay through various income increments. Administrative personnel, for example, enjoyed special tax exemptions, family allowances, and honoraria, as well as work bonuses that provided a greater share of enterprise earnings to managers than industrial workers. Perhaps the most flagrant attempt at the institutionalization of social privileges for the political elite was the pension decree of October 1972 which provided no limits on retirement benefits and extended their beneficiaries to members outside the immediate family. Other instances of abuse of power also prevailed in the areas of housing, education, services, and justice. For example, in a nation with one of the worst housing records in Europe, one of the preferred perks of the elite was private villas and vacation homes, when families of non-manual employees already had better access to more spacious and better equipped housing than families of manual laborers. In the educational field, the point system that was designed to give preferential entry into universities to working class and peasant origin applicants was offset by the practice of ministerial and rectorial reserved places that went to the privileged. The latter also enjoyed access to scarce resources in the form of yellow curtain shops, foreign travel, exclusive health and holiday centers, as well as immunity from certain legal requirements, for example the R-ki exempting holders from traffic regulations, or the by-passing of construction codes by the elite.

These and many other benefits were the manifestation of power abuses that provided the elite with goods and services that would otherwise be unavailable to them. The privileges were obtained because of connections, gifts, misappropriation of public funds, and other practices that permeated and corrupted the entire society. As scarcities developed and corruption of power became glaring in the 1970s, the sense of relative deprivation among the working class was bound to be affected by the contrast between their material shortages and the elite's conspicuous consumption. Under the circumstances, feelings of frustration and anger at the arbitrary privileges and economic abuses were likely to surface.

This was especially so in view of the decline in social mobility for individuals of working class or peasant background. The pattern of the 1970s meant a significant decrease in intergenerational advancement (Connor, 1977; Bluszkowski, 1979, pp. 135–64). This translated into pessimism about personal opportunity, particularly as the prospects for working class individuals to ascend to low-level management positions diminished considerably in the late Gierek years (Woodall, 1981, pp. 47–8). Of course the discontent at the lack of opportunity for rising above blue-collar status was felt most intensely among young workers. The percentage of young workers under thirty was 35 per cent in 1976, and most significantly it was highest in the metal, steelwork, and transportation sectors (about 40 per cent in each; Gilejko, 1979, p. 270), where militance was most evident in the summer of 1980. The fact that young workers were most likely to maintain their class position must be juxtaposed with the increasing level of education of that youth, which produced higher expectations. The aspirations for social mobility, however, were blocked by the growing ossification of the Polish social structure. Their subjective assessment on the question of equality and social justice is evident from a national opinion poll conducted in 1980. Eighty-five per cent of the respondents judged that inequalities in Polish society were very large or rather large, while in regard to trends over the last ten years 67 per cent saw an increase in inequality but only 6 per cent a decrease. Most striking is the ranking of positive values: 90 per cent mentioned equality and justice, above law and order (82 per cent), freedom of expression (71 per cent) or information on authorities (61 per cent). Clearly then, the frustrations born in mobility blockage were uppermost in the minds of the working class – 85 per cent of that social group declaring the existence of inequalities (Osrodek, Survey No. 27, 1980).

The combination of social immobility and the demonstration of conspicuous consumption by the elite strata in the late 1970s proved to be an explosive problem. Increasingly cut off from advancement in the social structure, the working class realized it could never enjoy the social privileges available to the political-administrative apparatus. Rather, with the growing economic problems, industrial labor was faced increasingly with an environment of material scarcity. The authorities warned of further austerity measures and demanded the absorption of shortages by blue-collar workers (*Trybuna Ludu*, 12 February 1980; Bielasiak, 1980b, pp. 24–31). In the face of the lack of individual opportunity, of blatant abuse of power by the political elite, and of shrinking economic benefits, the workers' only recourse appeared to be collective action to reverse the trend of events. The militant aspect of that action was forced upon the laboring class by the lack of political channels to express their discontent and seek redress.

Political representation

Popular perceptions of the inadequacy of representative and participatory institutions were grounded in the development strategy initiated by Gierek in the post-December 1970 reevaluation of regime–society relations. A concentration of political authority within the party and government organizations was accomplished through a series of reforms in the early 1970s, in effect providing the Gierek leadership with greater control over national politics (Bielasiak, 1983). One of the fundamental steps in this process was an extensive administrative reform between 1973 and 1975 which limited the political capabilities of the local and regional administrative units in favor of central party authorities.

A similar step involved the party organizations of the 164 largest enterprises, which were placed directly under the supervision of the Central Committee staff. While the proclaimed goal was to facilitate the exchange of information between industrial workers and the leadership to prevent renewed outbursts of labor discontent, the practical effect was to facilitate control of the major enterprises by the central party authorities. These administrative measures were enhanced by an expansion of the regime's supervision over the activities of public and state institutions. A major step in that direction was taken through the extension of the *nomenklatura* list to cover a wide range of social, educational, economic, and political positions to better control all aspects of people's lives (Lowit, 1979, pp. 450–65). Other efforts involved the restraint of public organizations by centralizing their operation under the strict guidance of the party. Of particular relevance to the working class was the creation of the Ministry of Labor, Wages, and Social Affairs, leading to a considerable concentration of policy formulation over issues of employment, wages, and work conditions. The shift signified a major devolution of the prerogatives of the trade unions in individual enterprises, further alienating blue-collar workers from institutions that were to function as representatives of working class interests.

The accumulation of power by the regime must be contrasted with the rhetoric of participation emanating from the authorities (Bielasiak, 1981a, 1982). As a response to the growing assertiveness of the workers, as evident by the December 1970 and June 1976 unrest, the Gierek leadership sought to create the impression that the political center was paying attention to the interests of industrial labor by providing new channels for popular inputs into policy deliberations. The aim was to increase the workers' sense of political participation by exhorting such virtues of social democracy as leadership-mass consultation, the proletarian representativeness of social institutions, and workers' self-management. In reality these participatory mechanisms afforded only pro forma participation opportunities to the working class, while the content of policy deliberations continued to be determined by the party elite. While the government's emphasis on mass participation consisted primarily of gestures, it none the less introduced greater participatory expectations among the blue-collar stratum. It is in the wake of the gap between the premise of political involvement and the reality of workers' influence on decision-making that political inequalities in the polity and the work-place emerged as a critical issue in the consciousness of the workers.

Evidence of differences in the political activism of the various social strata touches upon both political and economic participatory institutions. For example, one of the major efforts of the Gierek administration involved an alteration of the Polish United Workers' Party's (PUWP's) membership in favor of industrial workers (Bielasiak, 1981a, pp. 88–93). The action had as its basis an affirmative action program that sought to include a greater number of manual laborers in the communist party in the hope of fostering working class support for the party's policies. Indeed, after a prolonged period when workers made up 40 per cent of the total and white-collar groups about 44 per cent, the trend was reversed in 1976. From then on, the blue-collar component in the party increased steadily, so that by 1979 workers accounted for 46.2 per cent of PUWP members while the white-collar share had decreased to 33 per cent. What appears to be at first a major shift favoring working class involvement in party politics is mitigated by other developments that testify to the continued under-representation of industrial labor in the PUWP and the party's failure to provide the workers with political and economic opportunities.

In the first place the recruitment pattern reflected a continued dispropor-tionate selection of members from white-collar groups, accounting for much higher saturation levels of the latter in comparison with the working class. At the end of the 1970s about 17 per cent of all manual laborers were in the ranks of the PUWP, but the equivalent figure for the technocratic elite was close to 40 per cent and for the professional strata above 50 per cent (Triska and Gati, 1981, pp. 52 and 150). This disparity in the share of the various social groups belonging to the PUWP was a reflection of the leadership's continued need to concentrate on infusing the party with well-educated and skilled personnel capable of managing a modern society and the regime's economic program. Another aspect limiting the effectiveness of workers' involvement in the PUWP was the much higher attrition rate of blue-collar members as compared with their white-collar equivalents. The demands of activism, study, and responsibility were much more difficult to satisfy for the industrial laborer than the administrative employee, resulting in a greater reluctance to be active among workers than the non-manual groups. The consequence was that many more workers resigned or were purged from party rolls than members of other social groups. To compensate for this different retention rate, workers made up a disproportionately higher percentage of new recruits. In effect the working class membership of the PUWP was subject to a revolving door phenomenon that signified lower stability in party affiliation, there-fore limiting the influence of workers in party affairs.

This high membership turnover was of course in itself a reflection of industrial labor's dissatisfaction with the party's representation of blue-collar interests. The differences in saturation and attrition levels between the manual and non-manual sections of the party also had the effect of diminishing the mobility opportunities of the industrial workforce *vis-à-vis* the other strata. The stress on education and expertise as a requirement of Gierek's economic maneuver favored the white-collar population, who were then able to use party membership and political activism for social and economic advancement. In contrast, the lesser qualifications of working-class members considerably diminished their opportunity for upward occupational mobility in the late 1970s. The attraction of party membership thus declined, helping to account for the high attrition rate among workers. As a result of all these factors the party organization not only failed to represent labor's interests but ceased to function as a vehicle for individual workers' advancement.

The ineffectiveness of political participation as a channel for working class interests became especially evident in June 1976, when the government's attempted price increase met with the immediate opposition of the industrial labor force. The government's failure to gauge worker sentiments only strengthened the masses' perception that official political involvement could not be used to advance their interests. The consequence was a general decline between 1975 and 1978, evident from a public opinion survey, of citizens' participation in a variety of sociopolitical organizations, including production conferences, trade unions and workers' councils (Ostrowski and Sufin, 1979, pp. 161–3).

Despite the downturn in political activism, the Gierek leadership paid little attention to a genuine reinvigoration of participatory and representative organs in the polity and the workplace. Instead it chose to revitalize the system through economic tinkering in the form of a new economic maneuver that left untouched the political arrangements and succeeded only in further alienating the work-force from the political authorities.

The perpetuation and even intensification of political inequalities in the late 1970s is especially visible at the enterprise level, where sociopolitical and economic activity varied substantially among the various sections of the work-force. The extent of workers' participation in factory organizations and policy discussions was substantially lower than that of other strata in the enterprise hierarchy. For example, a survey of thirty workers' self-government conferences in the mining industry showed that, of those taking part in discussion of issues, 22 per cent were blue-collar and 78 per cent were white-collar employees (Stefanowski, 1977, Report No. 160; Gajda, *et al.*, 1977, pp. 95–118). The impact of workers' opinions on policy content is thus likely to be less significant than that of the administrative and technical personnel, a conclusion supported by evidence concerning the scope of participation. An examination of workforce activities by occupational groups in the 164 largest enterprises revealed that in 1979 the engineering-technical strata overwhelmingly dominated all forms of activity not only in production but also in sociopolitical and workers' self-management institutions (Table 13.6), despite an apparent willingness by the majority of the workers to be active in decisions affecting work conditions (Sarapata, 1979, p. 126). Moreover, in the critical area of preparation for self-management conferences and meetings of trade union and political organizations the workers were also substantially underrepresented: only 13 per cent of industrial employees took such action, as opposed to 24 per cent of office workers and 38 per cent of the technical

TABLE 13.6 *Political activism by occupation (percentage)*

Enterprise activities	Engineering technical	Workers	Office employees
Issue presentation to superiors	66.7	36.6	35.0
Issue presentation to sociopolitical organs	56.0	n.a.	35.7
Participation with comment at meetings	54.4	33.1	24.6
Preparation of materials for meetings	37.7	12.8	24.5
Election to sociopolitical organs	47.8	27.6	34.7

Source: Zbigniew Sufin, 'Społeczne uwarunkowania i konsekwencje kryzysu', *Nowe Drogi*, No. 12 (December 1980) p. 76.

personnel. Similar proportions were evident in regard to the fulfillment of elected functions in those sociopolitical organs, signifying that executive and administrative roles were also dominated by the white-collar employees. In the face of these findings, there is no doubt that workers' participation in enterprise activities was essentially nominal.

The inequalities in enterprise activism among the occupational strata severely limited the working class' ability to use participation in sociopolitical organizations as a channel for the defense of their interests. The result was that industrial workers attached little value to participatory opportunities in both the work-place and the community, and instead increasingly perceived trade unions, self-management organs and party organizations as vehicles of management control.

Worsening relations between enterprise authorities and the workers were in large part due to the economic downturn in the second half of the Gierek decade. A principal consequence of the crisis was to strengthen the regime's reliance on a technocratic solution to the problems of industry, involving increased material incentives to management as an attempt to foster productivity. On the one hand this increased labor's dependence on administrative performance as a source of bonuses and social welfare, leading to substantial differences over distribution policies. On the other hand, it transformed further the trade-union and self-management organs into vehicles for the stimulation of production, to the detriment of the representative functions of these organizations (Woodall, 1981, pp. 48–53). Instead of acting in defense of workers' interests, their domination by white-collar personnel effectively turned the unions and councils into tools of management.

The workers' inability to foster their interests was aggravated at the same time by the bureaucracy's growing determination to safeguard the socioeconomic privileges attained during the first part of Gierek's rule.

This involved a defense of the status quo that resisted any institutional transformations to open up the political process or to provide the blue-collar stratum with a more significant voice in the determination of enterprise policies. Of course, this attitude was reinforced by the political practices of the Gierek regime, which also opposed a devolution of political power from the *apparat* to the masses. The working class' inability to express their interests through the official institutions, much less to influence the content of economic and political decisions by means of political participation, forced them to develop alternative forms of activism to insure the satisfaction of their demands (Pravda, 1982, pp. 176–7). The alternatives increasingly involved actions such as collective demonstrations in the form of work stoppages. These informal methods of representing workers' interests *vis-à-vis* management and political authorities widened the gap between the official system of workers' representation and industrial labor, instead channeling the workers' activism into more radical attempts to influence enterprise policies. The culmination of these efforts was the formation, from 1977 on, of a movement seeking to establish independent trade unions free of the party's tutelage. This movement burst into the forefront of Polish politics in the wake of the summer 1980 strikes – a spontaneous expression of workers' discontent with the government's economic policies.

Inequalities, politicization, solidarity

The activism of the Polish working class in 1980 was rooted in the linkage between governmental policies, economic decline, and the resultant inequalities in society. The Gierek regime's inability to sustain a program of economic growth throughout the 1970s curtailed increased material compensation for all social groups. The ensuing retrenchment contributed to a disproportionate relative deprivation of the working class, which suffered a rapid decline in income growth at a time when the privileges of the political and managerial elites were maintained. As a consequence the inequalities in income and social welfare benefits became more pronounced and, in turn, strongly affected workers' perceptions. The conspicuous consumption advertising the privileged status of the elite was contrasted with the worsening living standards of manual labor. By the late 1970s the workers' subjective assessment of socioeconomic inequalities between the diverse social strata increased significantly, making the issue of social differences the most critical problem in the consciousness of the masses.

The perceptions of an inequitable socioeconomic distribution among social groups was aggravated by a growing rigidity of the social structure. In this context the mobility prospects for the average worker declined significantly and contributed to the view that industrial labor was permanently cut off from the privileges of the elite, instead facing increasing material scarcity. In the face of entrenched privilege and power, the only resource for the alleviation of blue-collar frustrations appeared to be collective efforts for the redress of workers' grievances.

The politicization of the Polish working class stemmed from its failure to obtain economic and social justice through official representative channels. The unresponsiveness of enterprise and social institutions to the demands of industrial workers increased their consciousness of the maldistribution of political power in Polish society. Inequalities in political influence of the different social strata became more critical in the face of shrinking economic resources, as the domination of enterprise organizations by white-collar employees precluded redress of the unequal income and welfare benefits. The failure to resolve the redistributive issue led to the accentuation of social tensions among the manual and non-manual groups, a conflict that could not be alleviated to the satisfaction of the working class because of the inequities in political participation. The reality of workers' lack of influence in the industrial and community settings resulted in the rejection of the representative structures by the labor class, who sought instead to alter the distribution of political power in society by extra-systemic actions. These efforts took the form of informal collective pressures for the satisfaction of blue-collar demands that strengthened alternative mechanisms of interest representation and simultaneously mobilized the workforce to challenge the official structures of power.

The solidarity of the working class in the summer of 1980 was in turn the product of the workers' experience towards the end of Gierek's rule, and especially of the socioeconomic and political inequalities of the previous decade. The egalitarian, antihierarchical nature of the labor movement was immediately evident in the organization of the striking workers and in presentation of their grievances to the government (Staniszkis, 1981; Mason, 1984). The demands for socioeconomic justice and political equality formulated in the striking factories and shipyards were primarily a reflection of labor's frustrations in the 1970s. The original demands of the interfactory strike committee (MKS) in Gdansk and Szczecin and the points of agreement between the MKS and the government in the 31 August accords are ample evidence of the workers' desire to rectify the social imbalances in Poland (*Protokoly*, 1980). Moreover during the process of negotiations with the authorities and the mobilization of increased popular support, the movement's goals expanded from an attack upon the socioeconomic and political structures to the formulation of an egalitarian sociopolitical program.

The goal of equality was most evident in the call for economic redistribution emanating from the shipyards of the Baltic coast. The long-term dissatisfaction with income distribution was reflected in the attempt to rationalize the wage system by providing increments to all workers but channeling a greater proportional share to the poorer labor strata. The concern and solidarity with the poorest elements of Polish society were also visible in demands for improvements in the social welfare system: the establishment of a social minimum, allowances to large families, and increased aid to pensioners were all part of the Gdansk agreements. The resentment of conspicuous consumption by the power elite found a prominent place in the workers' grievances through their demands for the abolition of the special privileges of the political and administrative apparatus. Together all these issues formed the most numerous set of demands; by means of economic improvements for the working class, redistribution of social welfare benefits, and the limitation of privileges, they sought to create a more egalitarian and just society.

At the same time the experience of industrial labor with existing structures of political participation and representation made the striking workers well aware of the need for institutional change as a guarantee of their socioeconomic gains. The previous inability of blue-collar workers to use trade-union, self-management, and party structures to present their interests meant that alternative forms of representation had to be created. Without such new institutions the workers were condemned to extrasystemic, illegal actions as the only device for the formulation of their demands. The need for more permanent and acceptable mechanisms of representation gave rise to the most radical demand of the movement: the creation of independent, self-governing trade unions that would be concerned exclusively with the defense of workers' interests. The organization of a trade union outside the existing sociopolitical structure was meant to remove it from the influence of the white-collar statum, providing instead a genuine voice to the working class. In turn the functioning of an independent organization as the true representative of labor depended on the availability of adequate information and the possibility of free expression. Trade unionism thus required the advocacy of civil liberties and a pluralism of ideas, turning the nascent workers' movement into a social force for economic and political reform. The previous experiences of the working class had made it well aware that economic changes could be guaranteed only through the democratization of the work-place.

14

Worker–Party Conflict in Romania

DANIEL N. NELSON

Conflict between workers and ruling communist parties offers a compelling irony to Western observers. Where Marx envisioned a harmony of interests and a unity of purpose between the proletariat and its vanguard party, there is suspicion and antagonism. Most dramatically witnessed in the Polish strikes of August 1980, such conflict is implicit in high levels of job dissatisfaction, in workforce instability, and in low productivity throughout Eastern Europe and the USSR. Romania, despite efforts of its communist leadership to identify the country with states at an earlier stage of socioeconomic development than that of many of its communist neighbors, has not been spared.

Before examining some data and observations concerning the operation of such conflictual processes in Romania, it is useful to consider some general propositions about political dynamics in communist systems. The model of dynamic linkages in communist politics discussed briefly below not only helps to shed light on Romanian developments but may also assist in developing explanations, both across countries and across time in a single country, for worker–party conflict and broader processes of change in communist systems. The latter task, however, is beyond the scope of this essay.

The dialectics of developed socialism

Communist parties allege that they rule to guide their societies to the realization of Marxist ideals of higher living standards, equalized incomes and opportunities, and expanded channels for public participation in economic and political decision-making. Despite significant economic and

Reprinted with adaptations from *Problems of Communism*, vol. 30, no. 1 (September–October 1981) with the permission of author and publisher.

social transformations, however, the socialist states of the USSR and Eastern Europe remain far from the utopian goal of communism. To explain this contradiction, Soviet ideologists began in the late 1960s to speak in terms of 'developed socialism' (Evans, 1977), and their counterparts in Eastern Europe soon adopted the same term (Evans, 1977, pp. 425–6; Zimmerman, 1978, p. 8). This concept depicted the current situation – characterized by economic growth, greater socioeconomic complexity and capacity, and wider 'participation' by all social strata – as a significant intermediate stage on the path to communism. Since in this stage (as in earlier ones) the Leninist parties retain a monopoly on the creation of political structures, on the definition of processes, and on policy-making (Nelson, 1981a), the 'participation' offered has been largely of a 'mobilized' nature (Aspaturian, 1980).

Soviet and East European leaders would have one believe that 'developed socialism' is a natural stage in the orderly socioeconomic and political advance of society, an essentially conflict-free transition managed by the communist regimes. Such a position ignores several considerations.

The first is the dialectical, contradictory nature of broad social transformations (Black, 1966, p. 27; Holt and Turner, 1966, p. 329; Huntington, 1968). Communist polities have brought conflict as they promoted growth, and competition as they distributed resources. The very processes of modernization and industrialization pursued by communist parties have required a proliferation of organizations, institutions, occupations, and types of training. Such socioeconomic complexity has been found in non-communist cases to be a correlate of changes in 'political socialization patterns' – that is, 'greater proportions of citizens have those politically relevant life experiences which lead to attitudes such as political efficacy, sense of duty, etc.' As part of these broad social transformations, one can expect the emergence of differing opinions, viewpoints, values, and interpretations – and there is nothing to suggest that communist states are immune from the emergence of comparable phenomena (Nie, *et al.*, 1969).

Marxists expect that the elimination of private ownership will diminish the economic motives for differing interests and that diverse concerns and priorities related to occupational, ethnic, or other distinctions will be addressed and harmonized in the party and the mass organizations under party control. Instead, occupational diversification, a rise in educational levels, and increases in living standards are associated with pluralization of priorities, opinions, and values. Such pluralism conflicts with the goal of party hegemony and seeks participatory outlets.

'Developed socialism' also fails to account for the contradictions between socialism as a political philosophy and the political practice of communist rule. Socialism emphasizes equal distribution of power and wealth. However, Leninist parties and their centralized planning mechanisms for development concentrate access to power in the hands of a few elites.

Finally, the connotations of stable and institutionalized 'development' in the concept of 'developed socialism' are confronted by the conflictual implications of the very dialectics upon which socialism is based. In behavioral terms, this may mean that citizens will look to conflict as a route to structural change rather than place their hopes on controlled evolutionary change under the party.

'Developed socialism', then, incorporates the antitheses of party hegemony (pluralism), of concentration of power and wealth (equality), and of stability (conflict). Thus, as communist rulers plan for further 'progress' on the path from socialism to communism, the dynamic linkages inherent in 'developed socialism' can be expected to present them repeatedly with issues critical to their political control.

One can envisage four possible responses by party leaders to these dialectical phenomena. They can

(1) Oppose change with coercive measures;
(2) Mitigate the challenge of change through minor structural and procedural adjustments by which they try to manage conflict;
(3) Accept change, but attempt to retain the party's leading role;
(4) Endorse change, with the party joining a broad coalition favoring systemic transformation.

There will be a mix of various of these options employed in any state at any given point in time because party leaders are uncertain about the most advantageous path by which to retain political control. And over time, any single system is also likely to exhibit diverse party reactions owing to changes in leadership personnel or exogenous factors (e.g., Soviet threats).

However, I would argue, nothing the communist parties can do – short of renouncing development as a goal – will halt the dialectics of developed socialism. Pluralization can be constrained, without overt coercion by the exercise of control over information, by the application of various socialization techniques and by manipulation of reward structures. All such responses have their own costs, if only in terms of impeding growth or efficiency, and none eliminates the underlying dynamics. Regimes may delay the participatory momentum that tends to flow from pluralization of society. But should these constraints prove insufficient, such regimes would then face strong pressures to digest such structural innovations as a formal opposition, an uncensored press, secret ballots in elections, and independent trade unions – pressures particularly evident in Poland in 1980–81.

Worker–party conflict is an important component of this dialectical process. (One could trace similar conflictual relations between the party and other socioeconomic, ethnic, or regional groups in communist societies. In theory, one could then analyze all such relationships and eventually develop a composite picture of society–party conflict for whole polities, but that would be a mammoth undertaking.) In each of the political issues raised by 'developed socialism' – be it party hegemony versus pluralism, concentration of wealth versus equality, or stability versus conflict – one can find evidence of industrial labor's dissent from the rule of Leninist political parties.

In communist systems, the issue upon which worker–party conflict focuses will vary because, quite obviously, their workforces are not identical in terms of skills, education, trade-union history, material expectations, or a number of other background variables. We find, for example, that the dialectics of Polish 'developed socialism' had by 1980–81 led to worker–party conflict over the issue of stability versus conflict – that is, the workers would no longer accept the political status quo and were willing to engage in conflict to obtain structural change. Romania seems to be at an earlier point in the dynamic chain. By and large, its industrial labor force is just beginning to question party hegemony, broadly expressing its dissatisfaction through opinions that diverge from accepted priorities of the Romanian Communist Party (*Partidul Comunist Roman* – PCR). Conflictual behavior – such as the 1977 strike in the Jiu Valley or the more limited work stoppage at the '23 August' enterprise in Bucharest during 1980 – is still the exception.

The particular configuration of worker–party conflict in Romania doubtless reflects the country's different level and pace of development. Bucharest has for the present eschewed the label of a 'developed socialist state', and the PCR views the country as in an earlier stage of rapid modernization or 'multilateral development' (Ceausescu, 1969, pp. 13–15). The year 1990 has been set as the target date for Romania's arrival among the ranks of 'developed' socialist states (Programme of the Romanian Communist Party for the Building of the Multilaterally Developed Society, 1975).

The PCR's preferred depiction of Romania as a 'developing' rather than a 'developed' socialist system has domestic and international advantages. For one, there is greater rationale for sacrifice by citizens in a 'developing' environment than at an allegedly higher socioeconomic stage. In effect, the quest for a higher level of civilization is so noble and undefined that it tends to give the PCR what amounts to a domestic *carte blanche*. Internationally, Romania's 'developing' status has gained it membership of the Group of 77 and permanent observer status since 1976 at meetings of the non-aligned movement. It also differentiates Romania from the USSR in ideological terms, helps Bucharest resist increases in its Warsaw Treaty defense obligations, and justifies maintenance of more intense extra-bloc trade ties than other East European states.

There is, too, considerable objective truth in Romania's protestations. As one member of the Romanian Academy of Social and Political Sciences wrote in 1972:

Romania still shows a great discrepancy when compared to the economically developed countries, as regards the level of national income, the per capita output of some main products, her economic pattern, the level of labor productivity, of foreign trade, etc. When compared to other countries, the Romanian economy shows features typical of the developing countries. . . . In 1970, the gross national product of per head of population was within the limits registered in certain developing countries which are acknowledged to belong to this category, for it amounted to about 50 per cent of the per capita gross national product of Mexico, Argentina, and Brazil. . . . Some 50 per cent of the working population is employed in agriculture, and the per capita yield . . . is approximately half the figure obtained in the developed countries (Rausser, 1972, p. 195).

However, the PCR's decision to pursue the 'impetuous' development of the forces of production – i.e., industrialization of the forces of production – i.e., industrialization and agricultural modernization – under the firm control of the party (Ceausescu, 1972, p. 98) exhibits many of the contradictory elements characteristic of 'developed socialism'. One may, indeed, ask whether Romania's policies do not contain within them the embryo of the PCR's own antithesis. In seeking widespread systemic changes such as industrialization, urbanization, expansion of literacy, and mechanization of agriculture, is the Romanian party unleashing forces contradictory to total party control? Let us examine this question from the specific perspective of worker–party conflict in Romania.

Changes and pluralism in Romania

The Romanian Communist Party's political decision to transform its agricultural economy and largely peasant society into an industrial and urban system wrought rapid and fundamental socioeconomic change in the 1960s and 1970s. A few data should suffice to demonstrate the point.

Romania's economic growth through the 1960s and 1970s was among the highest in communist Europe as well as in the world. From 1970 up to 1975, for example, the mean annual growth rate of GNP per capita was 8.7 per cent, which exceeded the growth rates of other East European economies by a comfortable margin (see Table 14.1) (Jackson, 1981, p. 276). This growth was reflected in great increases in industrial production; in social terms, Romania has experienced a dramatic movement of population to urban areas, an improvement of medical care, a lowering of infant mortality, a lengthening of life expectancy and expansion of enrollment in higher education (see Table 14.2).

Notwithstanding mounting hard-currency debt, trade imbalances, and

TABLE 14.1 *Romanian economic growth in comparative perspective, 1970–75 (average annual rate of growth, in per cent)*

	1971–5 industrial output (constant prices)	1970–5 GNP per capita (constant prices)
Bulgaria	9.0	7.1
Czechoslovakia	6.7	4.4
East Germany	6.3	4.8
Hungary	6.3	4.1
Poland	10.5	6.8
Romania	13.0	8.7

Source: industrial output for 1971–5 from *Kraje RWPG, 1960–1975* (Countries of CMEA, 1960–1975), Warsaw, Glowny Urzad Statystyczny, 1976, p. 48; GNP data from US Central Intelligence Agency, *Research Aid: Handbook of Economic Statistics*, Washington, DC, 1976; and T. P. Alton, 'Economic Growth and Resource Allocation in Eastern Europe', US Congress, Joint Economic Committee, *Reorientation and Commercial Relations of the Economies of Eastern Europe*, Washington, DC, US Government Printing Office, 1974.

labor-based difficulties, the PCR has pledged to persevere in its drive towards Romania's achievement of the status of a developed socialist state by 1990. This entails heavy demands on worker productivity, a very high rate of investment, and a deferral of major consumption gains (Jackson and Happel, 1977, p. 275).

Nicolae Ceausescu's regime is 'risking' not only financial resources but also political capital in striving to achieve developed status by 1990. The fusion of socioeconomic transformation and political changes connoted by the party's use of 'developing socialism' means that the PCR expects that such dynamic processes will occur within the bounds of its political control. But attainment of the egalitarian goals of socialism seems distant in Romania, and the participatory promise of socialist democracy is yet to be implemented. Therefore, the PCR's goals are out of step with the principal expectations of developed socialism, and the path towards structural change becomes potentially destabilizing for the communist government in Romania.

Romania today remains distant from such instability. Nevertheless, as the parochialism of pre-1950 (or even, perhaps, pre-1960) Romania has waned under the impact of developmental policies, indicators of pluralism have, indeed, surfaced. These 'outcroppings' of challenge to party hegemony are observable among many groups – artists, intellectuals, ethnic minorities, and even within the Romanian military and intelligence establishments. Among workers, however, the PCR has found its most consistent challenge. In tracing the emergence of pluralism in developing Romania, one optimally would either examine data relating to the same individuals across time or use sampling techniques at several points in time. Unfortunately, these techniques have not been available to the outside observer of Romania (Nelson, 1981c, pp. 436–43). However, a variety of

TABLE 14.2   *Socioeconomic indicators for Romania, 1950–79*

	1950	1960	1970	1971	1979*
	Social indicators				
Urban population as percent of total population	25.4	32.1	40.8	48.7	
Hospital beds per 1000 inhabitants	4.2	7.3	8.3		9.4
Infant mortality (deaths under 1 year per 1000 live births)	116.7	74.6	49.4		31.6
Life expectancy at birth (male and female combined)	63.2	66.0	68.5		69.8
Percent of population enrolled in higher education	0.3	0.4	0.7[†]		0.9
	Economic indicators				
Industrial employment as percent of total employed	12.0	15.1		24.7	34.7
Agricultural employment as percent of total employed	74.1	65.4		46.4	30.7
Percent share of industry in national income	44.0	44.1	60.3		58.5
Percent of roads modernized (i.e., paved)	4.8[‡]	6.7[§]		15.1	19.6
Electrical energy produced (kwh per capita)	129.5	415.7		1927.4	2945.0
Motor vehicle production (all kinds)	None	12 123		74 360	128 847
Radios produced	40 000	167 000		484 000	757 000
Television sets produced	None	15 000		300 071	574 000
Refrigerators produced	None	10 548		191 619	446 000

* July 1, estimated.
[†] For academic year 1971–72.
[‡] As of 1956.
[§] As of 1959.

Sources: *Anuarul Statistic al Republicii Romania* (Statistical Yearbook of the Republic of Romania) for 1972, 1979, and 1980, Bucharest, Directia Centrala de Statistica, 1972, 1979, 1980; *Demographic and Statistical Yearbook of the UN for 1950–79*, New York, NY, United Nations, 1950–79.

more limited data sources enable us to assemble a picture of nascent pluralization.

One set of data relates to the spread of the use of electronic information media and the diversifying impact of this development on public attitudes. We know from Romanian sources, for example, that the reliance on television for news among workers has increased as the usage of such media has spread (Firuta, 1978, pp. 75–81). As long ago as 1970, Romania's citizens were found to rely more on television than on other media for knowledge about events of national importance (Nelson, 1981c, p. 444). As the Romanian population becomes more educated, more mobile, and more diverse occupationally, the wider and more rapid dissemination of information may pave the way for a broader range of interpretations by individuals regarding their social, economic, and political circumstances. Although we have few direct measures of attitudes in communist states, Romanian research published in 1978 suggests that, notwithstanding propaganda and misinformation employed by the regime, citizens in a public sample evaluated events reported by mass media in ways quite distinct from that observable in an 'elite' sample (Campeanu, 1978, pp. 97–9). The party's control over media content, then, does not appear to have assured a uniformity of interpretations in an environment of increasing socioeconomic diversity and complexity (Campeanu, 1979, pp. 82–6).

Other forms of data reveal not only typical societal 'growing pains', but also a lack of uniformity and control in Romania's transformation. In part, these reflect rising expectations: for example, only 8.6 per cent of peasant children interviewed in the early 1970s were interested in remaining in rural areas (Mihu and Lascus, 1973, p. 38). In urban areas, where most industrial labor resides, hooliganism (or 'antisocial behavior') and interpersonal violence were on the rise (Damian and Dobrescu, 1974, p. 339), and citizens disagreed regarding how to react to these phenomena (Preda and Vida, 1975, pp. 322–30). Such indices are not conclusive, but they suggest that the complexity of socioeconomic life encourages people in all walks of life to think in terms of a less narrow spectrum, and to be less deferential to elites and to tradition or laws.

Worker perspectives

More specifically, Romania's path towards developed socialism has already generated considerable working-class disenchantment with material and political conditions. A Romanian survey of more than 6000 young workers (aged 14 to 30) conducted in the early 1970s provided strong symptomatic evidence of conflictual processes under way. Half of those interviewed wanted to change jobs, and almost a fourth had already shifted jobs at least once. Young workers, dissatisfied with a system in which few incentives existed (and hence in which there were few opportunities to better their economic situation) argued that their productivity could be increased most effectively by improving the 'co-interest system', i.e., by making stronger the connection between pay and productivity (Badina and Mamali, 1973, p. 66). A plurality of workers of all age groups and 58 per cent of those aged 40–49 that were questioned in another survey were dissatisfied with pay (Sirbu, 1977, p. 37). Overall job dissatisfaction – focusing on the material aspects of employment – and the resulting low productivity and high turnover of the work-force are severe and persistent problems along Romania's path to developed socialism.

Worker complaints do not focus on the PCR's goal of 'development' (how could one favor stagnation?). Instead, they emphasize the inequitable distribution of resources within the country and the workers' inability to find quality consumer products on which to spend their rising wages. Few circumstances motivate discontent more than being called upon to defer realization of material or other values when there is not equal sharing in the sacrifice, and particularly when the beneficiaries of this state of affairs, in this case the ruling communist elite, are on record as ideologically favoring equalization of the distribution of wealth. Although the label of 'developing socialism' might aid the PCR in justifying sacrifices on the part of the citizenry, the same classification tends to harm the party's legitimacy when the sacrifices are perceived as inequitably shared.

To workers, the most evident inequalities are those perceived at the work-place and at one's residence. The Romanian worker has found that a disproportionate share of the material sacrifices required for the sake of development and modernization falls on the shoulders of industrial labor (Radu-Radulescu, 1977, pp. 118–19; Weintraub, 1973, pp. 104–5). Moreover, poor services and severe housing problems negate images of urban life held by millions of erstwhile peasants who are now first-generation factory labor (Lisandru, 1973, p. 72; Jackson and Happel, 1977, pp. 450–1).

There is considerable evidence, admittedly somewhat impressionistic, to support allegations of socioeconomic inequalities at the work-place and within urban areas in Romania. For example, a hierarchy of wages within factories creates a 3:1 ratio between the base pay of lower management personnel and that of line workers. The median wage for an unskilled manual factory worker hovered around 2000 lei a month (about US $180) in the early 1980s whereas the director of a factory's quality control then received in the vicinity of 6000 lei (author's estimate based upon 1979 discussions in Romania).

But salary is only a partial indicator of socioeconomic differences. Privilege and access are the key concepts for understanding social inequalities in communist systems (Matthews, 1978). Party membership in the factory unlocks some doors for some workers, but it is the upper reaches of party elites at local levels that have privileged access to superior housing, goods, and services, which are worth far more than salary increments (Nelson, 1980b, pp. 96–7). The resulting status differences are implicit in the special sections of county capitals and Bucharest that are recognized as elite enclaves, or in the chauffeur-driven limousines – often a Mercedes-Benz – in which the privileged ride.

Perhaps the persisting inequalities of distribution would be more easily accepted were Romania to have a large surplus of labor. But Romania's workforce is expanding very slowly, and there are signs of labor shortages in the late 1980s and beyond, given current demographic trends (*Era*

Socialista, 3 June 1979). In a market economy, the combination of increased demand for labor and a slow growth of the workforce would likely generate a substantial rise in living standards for factory labor. But in Romania, Ceausescu – faced with a threatening neighbor (the USSR), increasingly uncertain energy supplies, and many other international variables – continues to exhort Romanian laborers to defer material gratification:

> Our people are fully conscious of the fact that their welfare and happiness exclusively depend on the work they perform. . . . That is why they carry out with perfect conviction the party's policy for developing the economy at a fast tempo, for devoting a substantial percentage of the national revenue to accumulation, . . . to increasing and modernizing the country's productive forces, being perfectly conscious it is only this that can ensure the welfare and happiness of our entire nation, an ever brighter future for all our people (Tismeau and Zaharia, 1977, p. 90).

As workers observe the consumer societies of neighboring Yugoslavia and Hungary, however, such appeals are likely to decrease in effectiveness.

Romania's industrial labor force also has political grievances. The workers' distinctive priorities, opinions, and interpretations in the political realm are, of course, not evidenced in forms familiar to Western experience – e.g., legislative lobbying by independent trade unions, or support for competitive parties. Instead, it is in the area of work-place governance that the political concerns of workers can be observed and, to some degree, measured. Of particular interest are worker attitudes towards general assemblies of enterprises, and especially the executive organs of such assemblies, called 'workers' councils' (*Consiliile Oamenilor Muncii –* COM).

These structures, offered by a 1971 statute as the organizational basis for worker participation, have merely perpetuated the domination of the work-place by a 'politically reliable, somewhat older, predominantly non-worker cohort' – i.e., the 'same cast of characters' who head party, state, and mass organizations at the local level (Nelson, 1981d, p. 15). As a result of the non-representative aura that surrounds the COM, the councils and general assemblies receive minimal interest from production-line workers, whatever their ages, industries, or other attributes and affiliations. Party cadres control the agendas of meetings (Sirbu, 1977, p. 43). Members elected to workers' councils are not well known to employees and are rarely consulted by workers when a problem arises at the work-place (Petrescu, 1977, p. 79). Such indicators led me to conclude in a previous study that 'workers do not identify with or rely upon these councils or the system of self-management to represent their interests' (Nelson, 1981d,

p. 18). In sum, the COM seem to lack credibility as a genuine participatory mechanism and thus do not serve to mitigate the dynamics of political change or to close the widening gap between worker and party.

The mixture of coercive measures and minor structural and procedural modifications characteristic of PCR policy towards workers since the early 1970s remained clearly in place up to the end of the decade. The Jiu Valley miners' uprising in August 1977, for example, was met with both the movement of troops into the region and a 1978 campaign for workers' self-management (*autoconducerea*) which ostensibly reinvigorated the COM mechanism (Staar, 1978, p. 60). However, the effort by Romania's workers in 1979 to form a free trade union suggested the persistence of disaffection from the party, and the regime's harsh response showed the PCR's continued rejection of pluralistic voices (Goma, 1979). The 12th PCR Congress, in November 1979, did little to reduce the cause of worker discontent: it delayed further the reduction of the work week and offered only modest pay increases while demanding ever greater productivity.

Thus, there is every reason to believe that new outcroppings of pluralism will challenge PCR hegemony in the 1980s. The Romanian leadership can be expected to apply more coercion and procedural adjustments, but will likely need to turn to other policies if the PCR hopes to control the pluralization of Romanian politics into the 1990s. Toleration or even acceptance of dynamic processes within the society might, for a time, give the PCR greater political control. Such tolerance might be symbolized by continued party emphasis on workers' self-management or by extending the practice of having more than one candidate stand in elections for seats in local people's councils and in the Grand National Assembly (Romania's national legislature).

That such a preemptive strategy may, in fact, be contemplated is suggested by Ceausescu's June 1981 speech to the Second Congress of the Councils of Working People in Industry, Transportation, Finance, and Trade, in which he proposed that Romania replace the concept of proletarian dictatorship with that of a 'workers' democracy' (Radio Free Europe Research, 8 July 1981, pp. 2–3). This manipulation of theoretical concepts is designed to serve both an international aim (the distinguishing of Romania from Soviet orthodoxy) and a domestic need (retention by the party of a role as political 'balance' amid the dialectics of developing socialism). It appears that PCR leaders have recognized that the party must soon 'shift its weight', as it were, to confront other issues which dialectical processes uncover.

This said, we should not expect Romania in the 1980s to become pluralistic in the sense that Poland did during the 1970s – as evidenced in the emergence of KOR (the Committee for Defense of the Workers), ROPCiO (Movement for the Defense of Human and Civil Rights), a strongly politicized Church, and numerous underground publications.

Nevertheless, there appears enough circumstantial evidence to suggest that the dynamics of Romanian political life are changing, that the PCR is cognizant of such change, and that the mix of its reactions to political dynamics will also be in flux.

Because data are fragmentary, the risks of drawing conclusions about the Romanian case, whether over time or in a comparative vein, are considerable. Nevertheless, Romania's experience demonstrates that the quest for developed socialism not only brings industrialization, urbanization, and other indicators of increased socioeconomic complexity, but also generates diverse opinions, viewpoints, values, and interpretations. Rule by the PCR, while ending private ownership, has eliminated neither inequalities nor other bases for differing interests. Instead, among Romanian workers there is a willingness to air material grievances and a rejection of sanctioned channels for involvement in work-place governance. Although Romania is far from replicating the volatile conditions of Polish society, we see in this state emerging signs of worker discontent and a restive society.

While Poland and Romania are each quite distinct cases, and neither is necessarily typical of communist systems, governments in both countries have had to respond to similar conflictual undercurrents of change. This would suggest that the model of 'developed socialism' – the limited and careful modernization of society under party suzerainty – in which European communist leaders have invested much political capital is flawed. Inherent in developed socialism are the seeds of conflict and social forces that weaken party authority, i.e., the antitheses of political control by the party. Some analysts have suggested that 'developed socialism' was offered by Brezhnev and others as an effort to 'contain and manage certain kinds of conflict while . . . providing greater space for limited reform' (Kelley, 1979). If so, the party leaders were wrong in believing that the mere conceptualization of dialectical processes could halt them.

Worker–party conflict in Eastern Europe is occurring against the backdrop of much wider and ongoing processes of change in the societies involved. The nascent grievances of Romanian labor are but one manifestation of what I have termed the dialectics of developed socialism. Worker–party conflict is not, then, a contagion to be isolated and eradicated before it spreads, because it is indigenous, fueled by the contradictions evident in every communist party-state.

15

Economic Policy-Making in China

MICHEL OKSENBERG

In the five years following Mao's death and the arrest of his principal surviving supporters who helped launch and wage the Cultural Revolution a major effort was made to reform the Chinese policy process at the higher levels, especially in the economic realm. This chapter focuses on questions regarding economic policy-making in that initial five-year period after Mao's death. To what extent and in what direction did economic policy-making evolve from 1976 to 1981? What of the Maoist system remained by 1981? Further, what are the strengths and deficiencies of the new system? Does the policy process in the economic realm seem capable of directing the substantive economic reforms which the leaders have in mind?

The policy process upon Mao's death

Analysts of Chinese politics disagree over the extent to which the Chinese policy process on the eve of the Cultural Revolution was rooted in institutions or in individuals. Some argue that the system was somewhat regularized and based on widely-shared and understood norms (Schurmann, 1966). Others claim the system was highly personalized and revolved either around Mao or reflected the power of competing factions (Chang, 1978; Pye, 1981). Others suggest that on the eve of the Cultural Revolution power was partly vested in institutions, but that the trend was towards, faction-based, personalized politics (Teiwes, 1979).

No matter what the view of the policy process on the eve of the Cultural Revolution, however, a greater consensus exists among Chinese and Western observers about the consequences of the subsequent ten tumultuous years and about the essential nature of the Chinese polity at the time of

Reprinted with adaptations from the *China Quarterly*, no. 90 (June 1982) with the permission of author and publisher.

Mao's death. The near anarchy of the Cultural Revolution of 1966–9, the traumatic Lin Biao affair of 1970–72, and then the unbridled succession struggle among several competing factions (1973–6) had led to considerable political decay. Power clearly was vested more in people than in institutions. Further, the amount of power which a political system possesses is not absolute; it can grow or diminish. The Chinese political system at the apex had much less power – less capacity to elicit compliance – than it had in 1966.

To be sure, the policy process was not devoid of rules and norms upon Mao's death nor did the struggle for power occur without serious reference to substantive issues. But as of mid-1976, the structure for power and the policy process did seem to be characterized by several principal features.

First, the process remained vulnerable to the capricious intervention of one aged man, Mao Zedong, acting on his idiosyncratic impulses. Indeed, Mao had helped structure the system so that it would be responsive to him.

Secondly, competing factional groupings, some in power, others on the sidelines, and yet others under arrest, sought access to Mao, and if obtained, sought to control and manipulate the Chairman. They struggled to achieve dominance over the personnel system; the apparatus governing allocation of material goods, energy, and capital; the propaganda network; and the coercive apparatus of the military and the public security forces. Different factional groupings at the apex had their distinctive sources of power, based in different organizational hierarchies. Jiang Qing and her associates could draw upon support in the propaganda apparatus and a portion of the military, e.g. the 37th Army (Dittmer, 1978). Hua Guofeng, Wang Dongxing, and Ji Dengqui seem to have had particular strength in the public security forces. The sidelined Deng Xiaoping had supporters among some of the military, in the economic apparatus, and in the organizational apparatus administering personnel. Chen Yun, Bo Yibo, and many others still under house arrest had latent but powerful ties with the economic apparatus and the organizational apparatus.

Thirdly, chains or networks of personnel linked leaders in Beijing to provinces, counties and even basic level units (*danwei*). The cement holding these networks together was the Chinese concept of *guan-xi*, meaning a relationship or an interconnection. A sense of loyalty, mutual obligation, and, given the atmosphere of the times, shared vulnerability bound clusters of people together. A high-level official in Beijing was, in effect, the patron – the family head – of many clients, who in turn were patrons of lower-level clients. Loyalties at any one moment could, of course, be felt towards more than one patron or towards competing clients and an official could move from one network to another. Perhaps it is more accurate therefore to speak of shifting constellations of officials in the capital, the provinces, and the lower levels, linked informally through *guanxi* and formally through bureaucratic ties.

Fourthly, factions in Beijing were not linked equally to all parts of the country. Rather, some factions had more intimate connections with certain cities, provinces, and lower levels, while other factions had their strength in different regions. Clearly Jiang Qing had nourished a strong cluster of support within the Shanghai municipal apparatus, and apparently had sought to root her supporters in Baoting, Hangzhou, and Shenyang as well. Hua Guofeng and his associates apparently had strong links with the Hunan, Shaanxi, and Hobei party apparatus. Deng Xiaoping continued to have latent strength in the south-west.

Fifthly, evaluation of domestic policy choices was not rooted in careful analysis of the alternatives or in use of reliable national statistical information. As we will discuss below, reliable statistics were simply not available on most social and many economic matters.

Finally, bureaucracies in the capital were reeling from the relentless campaigns which had engulfed them for a decade. Few agencies had been exempt from not only the initial terror imposed by marauding Red Guards in 1966–9 but also such subsequent campaigns as 'Struggle, Criticism, and Transformation', 'One Hit, Three Anti's', 'Criticism of Lin, Criticism of Confucius', and 'Criticize Bourgeois Rights'. A significant number of cadres in most agencies were in 7 May Cadre Schools. Another portion, while still listed on the table of organization, were in humiliating circumstances, forced to reside in 'cow sheds' and assigned to menial tasks. These were the former leaders of the unit who had been identified as 'capitalist roaders'. Gradually, beginning in 1973, these officials began to return to other units as rehabilitated officials.

Thus, as of 1976, most national agencies responsible for identifying issues demanding decision by the leaders, for shaping the choices for the leaders, and for implementing decisions were in varying degrees of chaos and paralysis. The typical unit in the party or government consisted mostly of officials who had survived the Cultural Revolution and its aftermath together. Memories of previous injustices and of lost battles were stored, to be acted upon when the opportunity presented itself. Personal animosities had accumulated for a decade, and the malcontents frequently remained in their units, unable to transfer elsewhere. Tensions within units were high. The level of trust among officials within a unit tended to be low. The ability to explore ideas and share information without fear of retribution was limited to one's most intimate and reliable friends, since the sharing of suspect ideas placed one's friends in an exposed position. Rather than breeding cohesiveness, in short, the external pressures had pulverized bureaucratic units (*dan-wei*) into warring factions and isolated, cautious individuals. Factions within each unit were linked to a different external network of personal ties.

The rationale of Mao's policy process

The system as of 1976 was not totally irrational nor meant just to suit the power needs of Mao or his factional backers. China's post-1976 leadership has wished to convey the impression of total chaos partly because that is the image they have of what they seized and inherited and partly because, as good politicians anywhere, by darkening the past they enhance their own performance.

Mao did not consider economic interdependence among regions and a regular, national system of personnel management as the most efficacious means of preserving China's unity. Instead, he relied upon coercion and the propagation of a single ideology as his principal instruments for integrating the heterogeneous nation. To be sure, the central economic agencies retained a role in redistributing resources from the more developed to the less developed regions of the country, a process which may have reduced inter-province tensions and promoted unity (Lardy, 1978).

At the core, however, Mao was a revolutionary and a totalitarian ruler. He believed the only way to transform China was rapidly, violently, comprehensively; its elites and institutions would have to undergo continual transformation. China's problems were so vast that efforts to attain peaceful, gradual change would be lost in the morass of bureaucracy. In his view, to transform China required vision and extraordinary confidence that a politically involved Chinese populace – given no respite to cultivate individually-determined pursuits – could overcome their common plight of poverty and weakness. To unleash the masses in all their fury required leaders capable of interacting directly with the various forces in society unmediated by intervening bureaucracies. Mao saw institutions such as the party, government, or army as having little intrinsic value. They were to be used instrumentally, as divisions in war, their credibility and authority expended in his larger efforts to make China a strong, prosperous, socialist China.

The structural goals of Deng Xiaoping

By the Third Plenum of the 11th Central Committee in December 1978 other visions of rule guided China, principally those of Vice-Premier Deng Xiaoping, but those of Chen Yun and Li Xiannian as well. To oversimplify, if Mao was committed to revolutionary change, Deng in the late 1970s was committed to reform. If Mao was a totalitarian ruler, Deng was authoritarian. If Mao believed in a dialectical path of development, Deng sought to chart a steady, persistent course. Having personally experienced, indeed suffered, the agony of the violence and turmoil of the late 1960s and early 1970s and then again in 1976, Deng returned to office in mid-1977 convinced that Mao's processes of change had failed China, and that perhaps twenty years of massive sacrifices had been wasted.

So, instead of seeking a unified China primarily through coercion and propaganda, he encouraged unity through increased economic interdependence, through reliance on effective, planned allocation of material goods and capital, and through a regularized promotion and personnel management system. The immediate bureaucratic beneficiaries of this emphasis were the economic agencies – the State Planning Commission, the Ministry of Finance, the People's Bank of China – and the Organization Department of the CCP. The losers were the Propaganda Department of the CCP, the Ministry of Public Security, and the military. Propaganda billboards once containing Mao's sayings were turned into advertisements for various merchandise. Tens of thousands left the labour camps of the public security system and hundreds of thousands lost their 'labels' and ceased being under daily public security supervision. The military lost many of their privileges and suffered a reduced budget. Abandoning Mao's totalitarian demand of the positive involvement of all in politics, Deng was willing to permit individuals to withdraw from politics, to pursue their particular interests, in the form of hobbies or careers, or to create works of art, as long as these did not indicate opposition to the rule of the party.

Deng's assessment in early 1978, at least, was that the major impediment to China's development was lack of an economic infrastructure. If only the steel mills, coal-mines, oil wells, hydroelectric projects, and railway lines could be swiftly put in place, China would take off. Here is where the West could be of help. But by late 1978 and increasingly in 1979, Deng concluded that infrastructure economic projects were not enough. Structural changes, institutional reform, had to occur, or else the plants would be badly managed. So, in 1979 and into 1980, Deng and his associates focused on reform of industrial management, on changes in the wage system with provision of bonuses, on the introduction of legal codes, on elections of local officials, and on revitalization of representative assemblies. It was a stimulating era, though with more rhetoric than action.

Deng envisaged the restoration of bureaucracy and saw the need for regularity and predictability. The pledge of the era was: no more campaigns, no more Maoist dialectics between periods of mobilization and of stability. The goal was steady rule through professional bureaucracy, untainted by corruption and personal ties. To guard against bureaucratism in the perjorative sense, Deng reestablished the disciplinary Control Commissions within the party as they existed in the 1950s and again during the post-Great Leap recovery. He sought more vigorous monitoring of the bureaucracy through elected congresses. He encouraged open petitioning over accumulated grievances, permitting the assembly of petitioners at the main gate of the Zhongnanhai from many parts of China in mid-1979 and sponsored the Democracy Wall in late 1978 and the spring of 1979. He assigned close aides to high positions in the newspaper world with a mandate to undertake investigative journalism. He saw expansion of the market-place as a further check on bureaucratic slothfulness. There was even discussion in those heady days of 1979 about establishing a bicameral legislative system, with the invigorated minor democractic parties playing a serious political role in the revitalized Chinese People's Political Consultative Conference.

First with his encouragement, then toleration, then acquiescence, and finally against his increasing impatience as the activities began to harm his political position, the intellectual ferment in 1979 over how to monitor China's inevitable bureaucracy joined the other great moments in modern Chinese history when politically engaged youths and intellectuals wrestled with the same set of problems. After Deng had used the ferment to weaken several key opponents in the Politburo, by mid-1979, concerned with the implications for stability and the party's primacy, he joined in a crackdown on the 'Democratic movement'. In 1980, elections to some local assemblies in which communist candidates suffered defeats saw new challenges to party authority which exceeded Deng's patience. Thus, by late 1980, Deng had tested several methods to foster a responsive bureaucracy, but none had proven satisfactory.

Deng's major immediate objective domestically was to improve the standard of living of the populace. He and his associates also envisaged a more lively, diversified cultural life than the narrow range of theatre, literature, and movies offered in Mao's last years. In short, Deng staked his popular standing on improving the immediate material and cultural quality of life in China, with promises for a more abundant tomorrow. Mao had avoided basing his legitimacy on such tangible promises and, except for 1955 and 1958, tried to avoid arousing expectations about a more abundant life in the near future.

This interpretation of Deng's guiding vision generates a number of key questions. Were Deng and his associates successfully within five years after Mao's death in resuscitating the political system from the ravages of the Cultural Revolution? Indeed, what are the principal features of the Chinese policy process in the Deng 'era'? How much had it evolved by the early 1980s from the Maoist system? Has power become lodged in institutions more than in individuals? Are decisions at least partially based on empirical assessments of reality, or do decisions still reflect the untutored biases of the leader? Perhaps more importantly, do the structures of the power and policy process seem congruent with the demands of reform? That is, do the institutions in the capital seem capable of sustaining a program of economic, cultural, and social change as sweeping as the leaders envisage?

What I propose to do in the sections below is to summarize the broad impressions of bureaucratic practices in the economic realm I gained from five months of interviews in 1981 during which time I visited over 20 economic agencies, the Finance and Agriculture Ministries and other locations. Here I will confine my comments to the arena of agricultural policy since the Third Plenum. I will then return to the themes raised in the introductory sections of this article, offering some tentative observations about the extent to which the Cultural Revolution system has in fact yielded to a more institutionalized policy process.

The top leaders in economic affairs

The top leadership was divided between those Politburo members such as Deng Xiaoping, Chen Yun, and Li Xiannian, who charted the broad economic strategy, and several key Secretariat members and the premier and several vice-premiers, who managed the economy on a day-to-day basis. In the summer of 1981, these principal operators were the Premier, Zhao Ziyang, and Vice Premiers Yao Yilin, Gu Mu, Bo Yibo, and Wan Li. Presumably not coincidentally, these same individuals were also members of the party Secretariat. Hu Yaobang assumed a special interest in agricultural policy in light of the party's role in setting rural social and organizational policy. During the summer of 1981, I did not gain the impression that Yu Qiuli or Kang Shien were playing active roles or that the Energy Commission was fully staffed and had curved out a major role for itself. A similar division of labour existed in foreign policy, where Deng Xiaoping, Zhao Ziyang, and Li Xiannian formed the Politburo cluster responsible for charting strategy in foreign policy, while Ji Pengfei headed the State Council group with operational responsibilities in foreign policy. Vice-Premiers Huang Hua, Gu Mu, and Geng Biao were among the other members of this cluster.

The premier and vice-premiers in charge of the economy were members of the Standing Committee of the State Council, a group which met once a week, usually on Friday afternoon, both to discuss broad policy issues and to resolve particular problems. The agenda for the meeting was set by the State Council Staff Office. The secretaries general (*mi-shu zhang*) of the State Council played a key role in preparing and circulating the documents for the meeting. These documents provided the background for the discussion. If the issue was a large policy issue, then the relevant information may have included statistics generated by the State Statistical Bureau, reports from the field as to how particular units had coped with the problem at hand, and policy analysis prepared either by one of the research offices within the State Council or a research institution within the Chinese Academy of Social Sciences. The search was for consensus, and, in the absence of agreement, the decision on a difficult issue was often postponed.

The premier and vice-premiers had their own special responsibilities. Yao Yilin headed the State Planning Commission, Gu Mu, the Foreign Investment Commission, Bo Yibo, the Machine Building Commission, and Wan Li, the Agricultural Commission. In addition, each vice-premier had a large number of ministries, commissions, and general administrations for which he was responsible. (All together, as of mid-1980, 93 separate agencies were listed under the State Council; see *China Almanac*, 1980.) Put another way, every State Council agency considered one of the vice-premiers, or in some cases, one of the State Council secretaries general, to be its responsible official. In the economic realm, these agencies were clustered according to the commission which the vice premier headed. Thus, Bo Yibo not only chaired the Machine Building Commission, but he was considered the vice-premier with special responsibility for the eight machine building ministries and the Ministry of Agricultural Machinery. Gu Mu's responsibilities extended to the Capital Construction Commission, the head of which (Han Guang) was not a vice-premier. Since Wan Li was the ranking vice-premier who acted in Premier Zhao's absence, his responsibilities extended beyond the economic realm. As a result of his heading the all-important Planning Commission, and also perhaps because of his close ties to Chen Yun, Yao Yilin seemed particularly to carry great weight.

The premier and vice-premiers had very small personal staffs, only two or three personal secretaries or administrative assistants. These aides arranged their schedules and ordered their flow of paper. They did not provide policy advice. The premier and vice-premiers turned to three places to secure the policy support they needed. First, they drew on a common staff within the State Council bureaucracy in the Zhongnanhai [party and state leadership] complex. Within that bureaucracy were economic specialists. Secondly, although they spent little time at their various Commission headquarters, turning over the day-to-day running of the Commission to the ranking vice-commissioner, the vice-premiers sought to turn the Commissons they headed into their instrument for shaping policy. For example, if Bo Yibo or Wan Li wished to pursue an issue or cultivate a successful example of the policy either was advocating, they could use the resources at their Commission to advance their ideas. Thirdly, they could task a researcher at one of the CASS institutes to undertake a policy study, the terms of reference set through consultations between the premier or vice-premier, the institute directors, and the designated head of the research team.

Large numbers of inter-agency and inter-provincial disputes cascaded upon the State Council. In fact, a major structural weakness of the Chinese bureaucracy was the inadequate means for resolving inter-agency disputes. The State Planning Commission (SPC) did act as a filter. The SPC became embroiled in and sought to resolve many such disputes, since they frequently involved either efforts to alter the plan in mid-course or instances of non-fulfillment of or compliance with the plan. If the dispute involved ministries within the jurisdiction of a single commission, then the pertinent commission made an effort to reconcile the differences. But since commissions did not possess line authority over the ministries, the latter were able to reject commission recommendations and plead their case before the State Council Standing Committee and its economic cluster. The minister appeared personally to plead his case. To be sure, such appeals carried inherent risk, since the vice-premier whose commission recommended a remedy sat on the State Council Standing Committee and out-ranked the petitioning minister. Nevertheless, I sensed that the vice-premiers were overburdened by various inter-agency disputes, and much negotiation was necessary to resolve them – disputes which were principally fostered by the reforms themselves.

With the vice-premiers heavily immersed in energizing the bureaucracy and settling disputes, it was no wonder that they turned to brain trusters and trouble shooters to assist them. Though they were not in the limelight, such people as Du Runsheng in agriculture or Ma Hong in industry played crucial roles in assisting the vice-premiers. They had multiple hats, holding a variety of posts in the commissions, the State Council apparatus, and the CASS research institutes. They had all the necessary security clearances and saw the minutes of those high level meetings which they did not attend. They were encouraged to comment on policy deliberations and proposed solutions to specific problems. Moreover, because other officials knew that these officials enjoyed the confidence of particular top officials, their influence was very great, though contingent upon the power of their particular supporters and the success of the programmes they were implementing.

The premier and vice-premiers not only met frequently and commented on draft documents and directives that circulated among them; they were in frequent telephone contact and often reconciled differences among their bureaucracies by telephone. This proved vexing to their aides, since the top officials frequently had different interpretations of the agreement and therefore summarized the conversation differently to their secretaries and subordinates. The staff personnel of the two top officials then had to piece together the likely agreement, or obliged their superiors to address the matter again. (This and many other phenomena we are describing are of course ubiquitous bureaucratic phenomena, as familiar to the White House as to the Zhongnanhai.)

While the economic vice-premiers had distinctive responsibilities, they also shared in and had to concur in many decisions. In a very real sense, many of the most important policies were collective decisions, requiring a high degree of consensus. On some specific decisions, in fact, many agencies had to concur. Responsibilities were sufficiently shared and overlapping that decision-making was a collective process. No one figure, not even Deng Xiaoping, was so dominant that he could unilaterally circumvent the process and impose his will.

The commissions, ministries, and general administrations

Most of the principal national economic agencies were located in the western portion of Beijing, just to the east and north of the Diaoyutai Guest House complex. A few, such as water conservancy and, I believe, agriculture, were in the south-west portion of town. Some others – commerce, foreign trade, and the All China Supply and Marketing Coop – were strung out on Changan Jieh. Walls and fences encircled their compounds. The agencies were located in multi-storied, concrete or brick buildings, the architecture ranging from vintage Stalinist at the high end (e.g., capital construction) to the more drab. Soldiers guarded the entryways in the seemingly languid Chinese fashion, but unauthorized visitors rarely escaped their eye. The halls were dank and ill-lit. The weather thoroughly penetrated the buildings; summer heat, winter cold, spring dust. Beds occupied many offices, to be used for naps or perhaps by workers who found it more convenient to remain in the compound.

Ministry buses transported some of the officials from the agency residential blocks to agency headquarters. A fleet of chauffeured agency cars was at the disposal of higher-level officials. The agency typically ran a canteen where the employees ate lunch and frequently other meals as well. It operated a bathhouse, where a good portion of the employees took their showers or baths. It provided a day-care center, and occasionally offered other facilities as well. The agency disbursed coupons for hard-to-obtain consumer durables and tickets to cultural and sporting events.

In most bureaucracies, about 50 per cent of the employees performed support or logistic tasks; the remainder were the clerks, secretaries, and administrators. The physical setting and the diverse services agencies performed for their employees were not necessarily conducive to crisp, efficient execution of administrative responsibilities. In discussing Chinese bureaucracy, one must never forget that one is analyzing organization in a Soviet-style economy, in a developing country, and in the Chinese cultural environment.

The typical number of administrative cadres in a ministry or commission seemed to hover around 500, with a range from 300 to nearly 1000. These figures were deceptively low, however, since the number did not include officials seconded to the ministry from the provinces who were included in provincial manpower ceilings or others in ancillary service agencies.

Typically, commission vice-chairmen or vice-ministers divided their responsibilities, each supervising one or more bureaux. The general office was the operational command, the central staff for the agency. It maintained the seal, arranged for the circulation of documents within the agency, and issued documents in the name of the agency. In most agencies, a weekly staff meeting of bureau chiefs was held to coordinate work within the agency and develop a coherent agency position *vis-à-vis* other agencies when that was appropriate. The general office managed the agenda and documents for this meeting, though bureau chiefs could put an item on the agenda on request.

The commissions, many of which were established in the post-Third Plenum era, were not recreations of the former functional State Council Staff Offices (*ban-gong-shi*) of the pre-Cultural Revolution era. Those offices had line authority or a leadership relationship (*ling-dao guan-xi*) over a cluster of ministries. The commissions of the early 1980s served a co-ordinating role in their functional sphere; they helped set policy. They balanced the plan among ministries in their sector before the plan went to the Planning Commission. But they could not command the ministries. They only had a professional or business relationship (*yeh-wu guan-xi*) to the ministries. The SPC clearly was the first among equals, the commission with the broadest mandate: to formulate and supervise implementation of the annual and five-year plans. The SPC, in some respects, served the function of the Office of Management and Budget in the US government.

The importance of the bureau level

The interviews in these agencies did yield several important, though tentative impressions. They concern the strength of the bureau level in the Chinese system, the extent of informal, horizontal communications among bureaux, the differences in power among agencies, and the inadequate information on which to plan. As in the American executive branch, the bureau was the basic building block of the Chinese bureaucracy. Ministries came and went; bureaux remained, shuffled from one conglomerate to another as ministries merged and split. Only during the Cultural Revolution, when entire ministry-level units were quite literally abolished, did many bureaux cease to exist. To understand Chinese bureaucratic practice and to identify the key operational figures, therefore, required penetrating to the bureau level: who the chiefs were, with whom they were connected, what precise programmes they implemented.

The overwhelming first impression I obtained of the bureau chiefs is that they were knowledgeable, experienced, articulate bureaucrats. They seemed to be imbued with their agency's mission, eager to defend it, reluctant to alter it, and aware of the many shoals around which they must steer. Typically, they were in their early fifties, and had served in their area of expertise (though not the same bureau) for 25 years, from the mid-1950s, with a four to ten-year enforced absence under varying degrees of duress during the Cultural Revolution. They understood the logic of current practices so clearly that one could sense their keen ability to identify why those practices should not be altered or reformed. They also were circumspect, capable of obfuscating an issue when that seemed appropriate. They conveyed the impression of understanding that knowledge is power. A major research focus in the years ahead should be on the role of the bureau in Chinese bureaucratic practices.

Horizontal communications

Clusters of bureaux in different commissions and ministries had very similar functions. For example, the SPC, the Capital Construction Commission, the Ministry of Finance, and the Material Supply General Administration all had energy bureaux (*ran-liao chu*), while the various energy ministries (coal, petroleum, hydroelectric power) had planning and capital construction bureaux. Greater informal communications existed among these overlapping bureaux than current conventional wisdom would have it or than I had previously thought, at least during the planning process. Indeed, the State Planning Commission deliberately staffed its bureaux with personnel from bureaux in other agencies with similar responsibilities, so that the SPC bureaux had personal connections with other agencies. This personnel practice is similar to the Office of Management and Budget (OMB) in the American government, where officers are drawn from throughout the US government to facilitate inter-agency understanding. In the implementation of policy, however, when tasks had been subdivided and given to action or line agencies, the level of voluntary consultation and co-ordination seemed somewhat less.

Organizational ideologies

A stronger impression I gained was that each agency had its own 'organizational ideology', its own sense of mission and purpose. On only a very few occasions did I leave an interview doubting that were it not for that agency, the Chinese economy would collapse, that this agency played an indispensable role in maintenance of the economy, be it setting prices, allocating labour, designing and approving capital construction projects, setting the budget, or making the plans. My informants were impressive in delineating the extent of their 'system' (*xi-tung*) nationwide.

While agencies tended to be expansive in identifying their personnel, the tendency was to be quite precise about their mission. Words and concepts had particular, precise meanings in the context of the specific bureaucracy, and to understand the official, one had to assume his particular purposes and analytical categories, that is, his particular organizational ideology. Heretofore, in analysis of ideology in China, the focus has been on the unifying ideology enunciated by Mao Zedong and the party (Schurmann, 1966). My limited exposure to Chinese bureaucrats, albeit at a time when propagation of a single, cohesive, coherent set of beliefs was not intense and pervasive, suggested Western analysts should pay more attention to the particular ideologies or values and perspectives propagated within each bureaucratic system (Lampton, 1977). An interplay occurs within the minds of 20 million civil servants between the party ideology, one function of which is to establish a national orthodoxy, and the particularist ideology propagated within each organization, one function of which is to elicit commitment to the organization's distinctive mission. How officials reconcile, compartmentalize, or integrate the two while retaining their own individuality is little understood, but seems to be an important subject for research.

Variations Among Agencies

A final and related impression is that in spite of their structural uniformities and somewhat common policy processes, commissions and ministries varied a great deal as well, and not just because of their function. Formally, for example, all commissions were of equal rank and had a similar professional relationship *vis-à-vis* the ministries. In reality, some came closer to a line relationship than others. For example, Agriculture and Foreign Currency Control had more discernible authority than, say, the Economic Commission. Moreover, even formally, several had distinctive qualities. Agriculture, for example, considered itself jointly responsible to the State Council and the party Secretariat because of the party's role in agriculture. No other commission exhibited as intimate a relationship with the Secretariat. Planning, as noted before, was first among equals, with responsibilities that embraced all other commissions. Export-Import and Foreign Currency Control were separate bodies on the organizational chart but in reality their composition was exactly the same, the identical organization with two names.

More important than the formal were the intangible differences among agencies in China. As in any country, they differed in *elan* and apparent efficacy. Clearly, agencies suffered unevenly during the Cultural Revolution and began their recoveries at different times. The sense I obtained in the course of my summer's research and residence in China also was of momentum and surges: some agencies gaining in power, such as Planning, Agriculture, Finance, and the banks, while others, such as Economics or Capital Construction, were bearing the brunt of the reforms, reorganization, and retrenchment. Yet others felt stymied, eager to launch important programmes but unable to do so.

The single most important factor which the middle level bureaucrats implied determined their fate was the political strength and interest of the premier or vice-premier responsible for their agency. The importance of the links between an agency and the high-level official responsible for it meant all attuned bureaucrats were intense 'Pekingologists', closely charting how their man was doing in the party pecking order. The situation was reminiscent of Washington in the Nixon, Carter, and Reagan administrations, where many at State, Defence, and the NSC staff all too often first read the *Washington Post* and the *New York Times* to see how their boss had fared yesterday against his rivals and in the eyes of the President and how the President had fared in the eyes of the press. In both capitals, the power of a middle level bureaucrat was intertwined with that of his boss and protector, though in China the relationship seemed more intimate.

But its personal connections were not the only source of an agency's strength. Its financial resources were also important. Agencies that presided over revenue-producing enterprises spoke with greater authority than agencies that ran chronic deficits. The latter were known as 'red' (*chih*) agencies. The Ministries of Public Health and of Grain, for example, were considered to be 'red' agencies. This did not mean 'red' agencies were destined to lose when their views conflicted with those of revenue-producing agencies; they just laboured under a handicap.

Capacity to plan

One other facet of the policy process merits elucidation, its low capacity to plan accurately or to develop accurate, long-term forecasts. Several factors accounted for this. Agriculture, which still accounted for a substantial portion of annual GNP, remained vulnerable to the weather. As the economy became involved in international trade, uncertainties about exports and worldwide inflation marginally affected the economy.

But a more decisive factor limiting the capacity of the leaders to develop accurate plans was inadequate, unreliable statistics on many aspects of the economy. The statistical network was still recovering from the damage of the Cultural Revolution. On the eve of the Cultural Revolution, the professional manpower ceiling of the State Statistical Bureau central office was roughly 400. At its nadir, when made into a section in the Planning Commission, it had 13 or 14 personnel. After 1971, it expanded to 40, its number at Mao's death. Its ceiling in the summer of 1981 was approaching 350, with plans to return to its pre-Cultural Revolution number. However, since no statisticians were trained in Chinese universities in the previous fifteen years, the Central Bureau was unable to fill its available slots, and its actual manpower was about 280. This group was expected to direct and monitor the activities of the statisticians in the ministries, provinces, and basic level units. They were struggling valiantly with the challenge, but were not yet fully on top of the problem. In such professional areas as sampling techniques, questionnaire construction, and sophisticated techniques of data control and analysis, recent advances in the west dependent on the computer were just beginning to be acquired.

Without an extensive capacity to generate its own data, the Statistical Bureau was dependent on the figures supplied to it by the central ministries and the provinces, both of which aggregated statistics from lower levels. But within the line agencies, there was an awareness of the softness of some of the data. Indeed, it was not unusual for an entire agency or set of agencies to propagate figures which all knew to be inaccurate. This situation provides the context for understanding the slogan, 'seek truth from facts'. In many ways, the Cultural Revolution greatly intensified an existing propensity, to put it bluntly, to lie. When survival was at stake, lying was justifiable. It then became a way of life in the bureaucracy, the easy way to escape responsibility. The slogan takes on real meaning in that context.

Opinions differed over the inadequacy of statistics. The Statistical Bureau itself, while quick to admit its problems, believed its figures provided an adequate guide to key economic trends. The bureau believed the special weekly and monthly reports it prepared for high-level officials provided sufficient warning, for example, of an overheated economy and of excessive capital construction by early 1980, indeed by 1979. According to many statistical and planning officials, the problem was that the top officials paid insufficient attention to the warning signals. They were reluctant to confront the need for retrenchment, and kept hoping for an easy solution, such as an increase in oil exports.

But policy makers had a different perspective. They believed that they presided over a society reluctant to 'seek truth from facts' and that the statistics supplied to them were frequently quite unreliable. Important decisions accordingly could not be based exclusively on quantitative data. If the statistics pointed to a problem, the leaders were prone then to rely on dispatching specially organized investigation teams to local levels and on making their own trips around the country as the best sources for understanding the problem in depth. Draft directives for solving problems could then be tested in a few locales and discussed nationwide, with the feedback altering the directive. This sequence, of course, exhibited marked continuity with the preferred processes for generating information in the Maoist era (Oksenberg, 1974).

Another reason for a low capacity to plan well was the shortage of design and engineering personnel. Interviews at the Capital Construction Commission (CCC) underscored the importance of this deficiency. In essence, as far as this Commission was concerned, Five-Year Plans were a compilation of capital projects which the Planning Commission had approved to be launched in the coming five years. A Five-Year Plan did not identify priorities or establish a developmental sequence among the projects, however, and at the time of inclusion of a project in the Five-Year Plan, the CCC had only undertaken preliminary design work to establish its feasibility. Not infrequently, the political leaders decided to move a project from the Five-Year Plan list to the annual plan before all the survey and design work had been completed. The impatience of the leaders was understandable, because the design personnel, aware of the inadequacies but reluctant to admit their doubts, were slow to draw their work to a close. Yet, repeatedly, major, unforeseen difficulties were encountered once a project was launched.

A third factor explaining Beijing's inability to plan accurately was the imperfect mechanisms of control available to the central government. Plans and orders could be issued, but they were not necessarily obeyed. The cumulative effect of myriad lower level units diverting resources to unauthorized projects could be significant, as was the case in the excess of capital construction in 1979 and 1980. The decentralization measures of 1979 intensified this problem.

For all these reasons, many officials believed China really did not have a capacity to develop reliable Five-Year Plans. Indeed, without a complex econometric model of the economy, many Chinese planners questioned their ability to make accurate, alternative projections one year into the future based on differing assumptions and different policies. Essentially, annual plans were linear projections of the previous year's trends.

Decisions on agricultural policy

Thus far, our presentation has been static, a portrayal of bureaucratic structures and attributes in Beijing as of the summer of 1981.

Here we shall examine briefly the evolution of policy in one area to see whether Deng's criteria are being met. Because of its centrality to the reforms, agricultural policy seems to merit special scrutiny. Agricultural policy since Mao's death can be divided into two stages. From early 1977 through mid-1979, the policy was to encourage growth of agricultural production through substantial increase in procurement prices, through mechanization and modernization of agriculture financed by the brigade and team levels with their higher incomes, and through some adjustments in state-allocated cropping patterns. The major decision of the first stage was the December 1978 Central Committee directive to increase the procurement price of quota grains by an average of 20 per cent, above quota grain by 50 per cent, and of cotton by 30 per cent (*Ren-min Shouce*, 1979). This decision was then followed by numerous implementational decisions in 1979, the net result of which was to increase dramatically state expenditures on agriculture. In particular, the Ministry of Finance and the provinces began to spend well over a billion *yuan* a year subsidizing grain supplies in urban areas, helping to account for the 1980 and 1981 state budget deficits.

Another essential portion of the December 1978 decision was to expand production and to lower the state sales price of agricultural equipment and other modern agricultural inputs. The increased funds flowing to brigades and teams were to be used to purchase the machinery, fertilizer, pesticides, and so on for a rapid technological transformation of agriculture. By mid-1979, however, it was becoming clear the top officials in charge of agriculture – Premier Hua Guofeng was the official responsible for agriculture – had miscalculated. Production of agricultural equipment could not be expanded rapidly, nor could prices be dropped rapidly. It had been assumed that the price of raw materials used in the agricultural machinery industry (fuel, metals, plastics) would remain constant; in fact, they were increased. It had been assumed management efficiency would improve rapidly with the elimination of the 'gang of four' and their followers; in fact, the problems in industrial management were deeper than that. It had been assumed profit margins in the agricultural machinery industries could be reduced; in fact, the managers resisted the pressure since their performance henceforth was going to be evaluated in part on the basis of their profit margins. Bu autumn 1979, it was clear massive state investments in agriculture and its rapid technological transformation and mechanization were not feasible. Other ways had to be found to sustain agricultural growth.

Thus, a second stage in post-Mao rural policies, ascendant from late 1979 on, was to sustain growth through massive restructuring of peasant incentives and through increased reliance on prices and market forces to determine cropping patterns rather than production quotas. The shorthand slogan for these policies was the 'responsibility system' (*ziren chih*). The principal decisions embodied in the policy were first, to permit and encourage assigning of responsibility for production on specific plots of land to households, individuals, or small groups (a preliminary decision in this direction was made in late 1979; it was then formalized in late 1980 in *zhong-fa* 75; see *Ren-min Shou-ce*, 1979, pp. 37–45 and *Ban-yue-tan*, 1981, no. 8, pp. 4–22); secondly, to expand the free market significantly (a decision made in late 1980); and thirdly, a decision to push expansion of private plots to 15 per cent of cultivated acreage (a decision of spring 1981, in *zhong-fa* 13). The top officials responsible for these policies were Zhao Ziyang and Wan Li. They envisaged major organizational changes in the Chinese countryside, perhaps the most sweeping changes since the mid and late 1950s.

The full implications of these changes were only beginning to be felt by the summer of 1981. Among them were increased yields and significant changes in cropping patterns. While grain yields were up, sown acreage in grain had decreased. Increased acreage was devoted to such cash crops as cotton, hemp, soy beans, peanuts, vegetables, and fruit. Hog production had soared to the point where the state lockers had more butchered hogs than could be sold at current retail prices for pork. Peasant income had increased in many regions, generating inflationary pressures in the country and expansion of peasant housing at the cost of cultivated acreage. The vitality of the free market had led to deserted state vegetable stores, with an accompanying loss of state revenue. With decentralization of production management, the number of required brigade and team cadres was reduced, and some returned to production. The rise in peasant income, coupled with reduction in benefits available to families of PLA members and curtailment of career opportunities available to veterans, meant that for the first time since the introduction of the draft the PLA was finding it difficult to meet its induction quotas in some counties. Some communes were offering wage supplements to those youths who volunteered for the service. All of these consequences of the post-Third Plenum policies, some of them unanticipated at least in terms of their extent, were thought to be manageable.

But as of the summer of 1981, officials at both the local and national levels were less certain how they would handle other implications of the new policies. The assignment of land according to the number of individuals in a family undercut the family planning programme. Incentives were in effect being offered to have larger families. Further, now that income was directly related to productivity and hard work earned reward, the excess of labour during most seasons in the countryside had become particularly evident. That is, under the rural wage systems of the 1970s, the available work was divided among the available labourers. Underemployment was somewhat similarly divided. Under the new system, the industrious peasants threaten to crowd out the less active. For this and other reasons, income disparities were widening in the country, and several thoughtful Chinese quietly shared their concern that the social security system – the 'safety net' – which the previous policies provided was being dangerously eroded. Relatedly, because grain was easily available for purchase on the urban free market at prices only slightly above the state price, illegal peasant migration to cities was becoming somewhat more difficult to monitor. No longer was the *hu-k'ou* or travel permit necessary in order to purchase grain.

Finally, some Chinese did wonder whether the 'responsibility system' marked an abandonment of collectivist agriculture, though my own impression was that this concern was premature. State control and the collectivist features of agriculture still outweighed the individualistic dimensions of the new system. None the less, the important point was that doubters existed among officialdom. In sum, by summer 1981, major reforms had taken place in agriculture which had increased income and stimulated production. But they had also initiated changes, the full ramifications of which were not yet certain, and which could prove to be profound.

Without tracing here in further detail the rationale, implementation, and evolution of each set of agricultural policies, several general observations can be made about the decisional process which produced these major policies.

Both the increase in agricultural procurement prices and the introduction of the responsibility system involved a weighing of alternatives and the building of a consensus. The policy process bore little resemblance to Mao's personal decision of 31 July 1955 to accelerate the pace of collectivization, his August 1958 call for communes, or his September 1962 curtailment of free markets, private plots, and assignment of responsibility to the households (for an analysis of these decisions see Chang, 1978). Post-Mao agricultural decisions were not capricious choices swiftly enforced through campaigns and/or purges.

In the case of the increase in procurement prices, the leaders weighed three options: a 15 per cent increase, a 20 per cent increase in two stages, or a 20 per cent increase in one stage. Different agencies took different positions. The Ministry of Grain was inclined towards the lower figure, while Agriculture supported a rapid increase, initially advocating a 25 per cent increase. A broad coalition supported the increase, not just for the reasons outlined above but because they saw it as a way to increase peasant income rapidly. The process of implementing the decision entailed extensive consultations and meetings with provincial officials and involved bargaining among different bureaucracies to allocate the rewards and costs of the procurement price increase.

The introduction of the responsibility system was also protracted, involving experimentation by Zhao Ziyang in Sichuan and Wan Li in Anhui in 1978–9 before their transfer to Beijing at the end of 1979. In retrospect, of course, one wonders whether their experiments had been encouraged by some among the central authorities, such as Deng Xiaoping, in anticipation of a national effort to move in that direction. In any case, soon after their arrival in the capital, they assumed jurisdiction over agriculture and asked the pertinent institutes in the Chinese Academy of Social Sciences to prepare a report on the responsibility system. Meanwhile, they conducted their own investigation of the agricultural situation in several regions, especially in the north-east, on the North China plain, and in the lower Yangtze. Moreover, the party encouraged widespread experimentation in various forms of wage remuneration and of the responsibility system throughout China. Nor was the effort without precedent. They harkened back to the early 1960s, when somewhat similar reforms had been attempted in Anhui, Honan, and Guangdong (where Zhao Ziyang was then located). Indeed, the agricultural system the leaders were envisaging may have had its origins even earlier. A revival of the memory of Deng Zihui, head of the Party Rural Work Department from its inception in 1953 and the chief agricultural official in the mid-1950s, points in that direction. Deng was an acknowledged opponent of the Great Leap Forward and a supporter of moderate policies in agriculture. Several people in the Agricultural Commission in the summer of 1981 had served with him in an earlier period and wrote articles commemorating him (*Nong-cun gong-zuo tung-xun*, 1981, no. 6, pp. 2–5).

If both the procurement price increase and the introduction of the responsibility system were not the product of hasty decision-making, they none the less were intimately connected with the policy preferences of particular individuals who rose and fell with the policies. Further, the institutional arrangements altered as policy changed. A seamless web connected top officials, their policies, and the institutions for implementing them. It was not clear which came first, and whether institutions and policies would survive their promoters.

Finally, this superficial review of agricultural policy since the death of Mao reveals that the full range of consequences of both the 1977–8 and 1979–81 policies were not foreseen at the time of their adoption. In neither case were the full budgetary implications fully understood, nor indeed was the Ministry of Finance intimately involved in the deliberations from the outset. The budgetary process was seen as essentially derivative of the policy and the planning process. In both instances, bold decisions were made in recognition of the fact that new problems would arise, but it was judged that those problems would be preferable to the foreseeable, calamitous problems that would ensue if no decisive measures were undertaken. Yet in both instances, unanticipated consequences of these policies and the implications of decisions taken in other realms without reference to agriculture posed severe challenges to the durability of the policies. At least within agriculture and in the economic sphere, Deng and his associates had succeeded, at least temporarily, in fashioning a disjointed, incremental, bureaucratic policy process, and they were reaping both its benefits and its costs.

Conclusion

Perhaps the best way to summarize our findings is to recall some of the principal features of the Maoist system and of the goals of Deng and his associates, and thereby to assess what had changed and what progress Deng had made in restructuring the policy process.

Most noteworthy, the process seemed less vulnerable to the intervention of one man. At least in the economic realm, decisions were shared. To be sure, Deng Xiaoping and Chen Yun had engineered major innovations in economic policy, relying on Zhao Ziyang and the vice-premiers to shape and implement the programme. But it was a protracted process, involving widespread consultation and modification in the face of opposition.

Factions may have continued to exist in the Politburo, but unlike the situation in Mao's last years, whatever strife existed was somewhat contained. The economic realm was insulated or cushioned from the other functional sectors. The system resembled that of the mid-1950s and the early 1960s, in short, in which a rational division of labour existed among the top officials, and those in one sector, e.g., the top propagandists or military personnel, did not constantly seek to intrude in economic affairs.

Rule through bureaucracy had also returned. Professionalism was officially esteemed. Campaigns had ceased as a major mode of policy implementation. Ideology and coercion were less intrusive instruments of rule, and the economic sector bore a greater burden for integrating the nation and motivating the populace. Decisions were somewhat more based on empirical evaluations of alternatives. In all these respects, the Maoist system had been altered by mid-1981, and the goals enunciated by Deng, Chen Yun, and others in 1978 had been at least temporarily attained.

At the same time, continuities also existed. The document system, the Central Work Conferences, the role of investigations – all hallmarks of Mao's policy process – remained. Several major problems arising from legacies of the Maoist era, from Chinese culture and from a Stalinist economic system, also remained. To a considerable extent, power remained vested in individuals rather than institutions. One sensed that changes in the top leadership could easily produce changes in structure and policy at the top. Personal relations – *guan-xi* – remained at the heart of the system. In addition, because this leadership group relied on bureaucracy, ensuring the responsiveness of bureaucracy to the leaders and the populace was a major issue for which the leaders had no evident solution. Separate organizational ideologies flourished. Inter-agency conflict was rife. The leaders had the capacity to decide upon, to enunciate and embark on policies of reform, but their capacity to sustain the effort was limited.

Clearly, much had changed since 1976, but one sensed that if the vision which Deng and his associates had for establishing an institutionalized policy process capable of directing sustained reform was to be achieved, much more would have to change in the years ahead.

Postscript

The above article was written in January 1982. Since that time, Premier Zhao Ziyang has announced a major restructuring of the State Council

(New China News Agency, 8 March 1982, K1–K7). Among its principal intended features are these:

(1) The abolition of the Capital Construction, Agriculture, Energy and Foreign Investment Commissions.
(2) The merger of the existing 98 ministries, commissions, agencies and offices under the State Council into 52 bodies.
(3) The reduction of State Council staff personnel from 49 000 to 32 000.
(4) The reduction of vice-premiers to two (Wan Li and Yao Yilin).
(5) The reduction of vice-ministers in each agency to two from four. (In summer 1982, many departments had eight to 10 vice-ministers.) Ministers under normal conditions are not to exceed 65 years of age, and the age limit for vice-ministers and bureau chiefs should not be over 60.
(6) All officials in leading bodies who rose to power by 'rebellion' in the Cultural Revolution, who followed Lin Biao or Jiang Qing, or who in recent years seriously violated laws and discipline, will be dismissed.

These changes are accompanied by a crackdown on corruption within the bureaucracy.

The changes in personnel and structure seek to remedy many of the problems noted in this paper: overlapping jurisdictions, bureaucratic slothfulness and empire building. The retirement of elderly officials and removal of Cultural Revolution beneficiaries theoretically will reduce some of the rancor and incompetence within the bureaucracy and ease the emergence of better educated technicians capable of administering the modernization program.

The changes also reallocate authority among the top officials. Based on interview data, the vice-premiers who lost commissions – especially Gu Mu, Yu Qiuli and Bo Yibo – have a less active role to play, while the head of the amalgamated foreign trade bureaucracy, Vice-Premier Chen Muhua, and the head of the expanded State Economic Commission (SEC), Yuan Baohua, have significantly expanded responsibilities. Indeed, the personnel shifts are likely to be more important than the structural changes, as Premier Zhao now has the opportunity to elevate officials in whom he has personal confidence.

Moreover, the structural changes may be less striking than they initially appear. Some simply mark a return to the structure of the mid-1970s, such as the re-emergence of a single, strong foreign trade bureaucracy or of a single commission, the SEC, in charge of implementing the annual plan. This part of the restructuring, in a sense, entails an abandonment of a four-year effort to elaborate a more complex, specialized structure because of the problems of co-ordination which had arisen.

Other reforms confirm or make explicit what had existed previously. For example, the Ministry of Grain, the Ministry of Commerce (MOC), and the All-China Supply and Marketing Cooperative (ACSMC), now merged, by summer 1981 had arrived at complex arrangements to reduce their common administrative chore of purchasing commodities in the country-side. In some areas, the MOC purchased goods for which the ACSMC was responsible, while in other areas, the MOC had no basic level units but turned over its acquisition tasks to the ACSMC. In another example, Premier Zhao gave prominence to the role of the new State Council Standing Committee and its members, each of whom would be responsible for specific bureaucratic sectors. The members of the Standing Committee, Zhao stated, would have roughly the same ranks as the current vice-premiers. This structure greatly resembles the summer 1981 arrangement described above.

None the less, the restructuring and personnel changes do seem to be a next logical step in the recovery from the Cultural Revolution and its aftermath. If implemented successfully, lines of authority within the bureaucracy may be more clearly delineated and more competent, dedicated officials may be implementing policy. It will be some time, however, before the full impact of the changes can be assessed.

PART V
POLICY OUTCOMES AND
COMPARATIVE
PERSPECTIVES

The previous chapters of this book have focused primarily upon the politics of individual communist nations, and to some extent also upon comparisons across a number of communist nations. There is of course no substitute for the detailed, empirical examination of particular instances in particular national contexts, and such studies have deliberately been given their due weight in the pages of *Communist Politics: A Reader*. Many of them are in fact informed by a concern for more general issues, and shed light upon such questions in addition to dealing with the topic with which they are principally concerned. A second level of analysis has also been represented in the earlier pages of this book, that which compares the political process across a number of communist nations in terms of what has generally been known as 'comparative communism'. Most of the first chapters in each section of this book have been concerned with such cross-communist comparisons, and many of the same issues have been touched upon in other chapters. Again, comparisons of this kind are necessary in order to establish what is general and what is unique among the communist nations. Are they, for instance, uniform in their relative lack of civil liberties and their lack of group autonomy? Are they, however, also uniform in their relatively high levels of social equality, working-class political participation and rapid rates of economic growth? As the previous chapters of this book will have demonstrated, both propositions require considerable qualification in respect both of country and of period of time; but both, perhaps, also have a certain measure of validity.

There is, however, a third level of analysis that remains to be performed: that across communist and non-communist nations, in order to establish what is general to political systems of all kinds and what is unique to communist nations as a particular sub-group of such systems. For instance, is a high degree of centralised state power a universal, encountered in

315

virtually all political systems, or is it something unique to the communist states? Is a relative lack of popular influence upon government, again, unique to such systems, or is it widely encountered at least outside the liberal-democratic West? Or, to take another line of approach, is a relatively high level of social equality associated with level of development (the more economically developed, the more socially equitable), rather than with communism as such? Are relatively high rates of economic growth a feature of communism as such, or simply of states that are 'catching up' from a much lower starting point? In all these matters it is impossible to establish the relative importance of communism as such unless we widen our analysis to include non-communist as well as communist nations, ideally comparing communist nations with a 'matched pair' of non-communist nations which share as many similarities as possible other than their form of rule. Yet here again there are formidable difficulties. The data we require, for instance, may be unavailable, misleading or non-comparable; unique historical and cultural factors may have to be allowed for; and the relevant comparators may not be easy to select – for instance, should communist nations be compared as a group with all non-communist nations, or with the Western liberal democracies (which are generally much more prosperous), or only with those non-communist states that have a similar GNP per capita?

Issues of this kind are taken further in the chapters included in this final section, which is devoted to policy outcomes across communist and non-communist systems and to the conclusions that may be drawn from such comparisons. The first chapter, by Valerie Bunce and John M. Echols III, argues for a reorientation of communist politics from area-based work to a more general comparative politics incorporating non-communist as well as communist nations. The following chapter, by David Lane, examines one particular but important and highly controversial issue, human rights, within such a comparative perspective. The next chapter, by Alexander J. Groth, considers worker welfare – retirement pensions, disability benefits and so forth – in communist and an economically comparable group of non-communist nations, and the final chapter, by John M. Echols III, examines a number of other issues – such as regional equality and female earnings and political participation – across selected communist and non-communist nations. The contribution of communism as such emerges rather differently from these two studies; in turn it suggests the need for a great deal of further work of this kind, designed to explore the 'differences that make a differences' among the varied nations of the contemporary international systems.

16

From Soviet Studies to Comparative Politics: the Unfinished Revolution

VALERIE BUNCE AND JOHN M. ECHOLS III

In the 1950s, political scientists in the United States became increasingly interested in *comparative* analyses of political systems. In large part, this trend reflected a belief that political science should not stop at the American borders – other nations after all could provide interesting and important contrasts to the American variant of politics. However, the attractiveness of comparative politics also had to do with its methodology. Comparative approaches offered scholars an opportunity to expand both the variables they could study and the controls they could build into their research designs. Thus, the appeal of comparative politics was that it would put an end to ethnocentric and unsystematic approaches to the study of political institutions and behaviour (Almond, 1966; Almond and Powell, 1966; Merritt, 1970, pp. 3–23).

Unfortunately, the flaws of the older studies were all too often recapitulated in their successors – many of the so-called comparative analyses turned out themselves to be parochial and unscientific. In the name of comparative politics, scholars tended to continue their analyses of only one country, with the difference being simply that the United States was not the particular system under examination. Area scholars called themselves comparativists, but this was generally not an accurate characterization. Thus, the optimism of the 1950s gave way to the conclusion in the following decade that, for the most part, the comparative revolution had been an abortive venture; the revolution had been betrayed (LaPalombara, 1968; Sartori, 1970; Lijphart, 1971).

Reprinted with adaptations from *Soviet Studies*, vol. 31, no. 1 (January 1979) with the permission of authors and publisher.

While these changes circulated throughout the entire discipline of comparative politics in the 1960s, they were perhaps most strident in the field of Soviet studies. Many scholars agreed with the argument, as expressed by Alfred Meyer, that:

> Political scientists in the West have failed, by and large, to apply to the communist world the rich store of concepts developed for the comparative study of political systems . . . and . . . the concepts that have been used have been applied in ways that are objectionable. If, as it is sometimes maintained, our discipline tends to be provincial or ethnocentric in its methods, this tendency has been most pronounced, perhaps, in the study of communist systems (Meyer, 1969, p. 188).

In the decade since these *samokritika* symposia appeared, however, Soviet area specialists have come a long way towards combining comparative methodology and communist politics. Today, it is no longer necessary to defend the use of behavioural approaches and comparative concepts; indeed, these have crept into the works of even the most traditional area scholars (Rigby, 1972; Oliver, 1973). The real point of contention in the area of Soviet studies now is not whether we *should* use more systematic techniques but, rather, *which* of these techniques are more helpful and reliable. In this sense, the comparative revolution is finally taking place. The calls for more systematic, empirical research have begun at last to be answered.

The evolution of Soviet domestic policy analyses from an area focus into a genuine subset of comparative politics will be the subject of much of this chapter. If one theme may be cited to capture this trend, it would be that both the study of Soviet politics and the very nature of the Soviet polity have become much more complex since the Stalin era and the ascendancy of the totalitarian model. Just as the scope of analysis and the range of testable hypotheses have expanded, so the inferences drawn about the Soviet system have become more complicated and less assured over the past decade. Blanket prónouncements about the power of the Soviet leadership, the role of the masses, and even the effectiveness of the regime are less common today, and certainly more tentative, than they were in the 1960s.

To argue, as we will, that Soviet scholarship is moving in the correct direction does not mean that we fully accept the position that where the field has gone is precisely where it should be. After reviewing the direction Soviet studies has taken, we will suggest where research should be directed in the future. In some cases, this involves extrapolating trends from present efforts, and in others it would constitute basically new directions. However, in either case we will argue that the comparative revolution has still not gone far enough in Soviet studies.

The rise and fall of the totalitarian model

The major contribution of scholarly research on the Soviet Union in the immediate post-World War II era was the development of the totalitarian model (Friedrich and Brzezinski, 1965; Brzezinski, 1967). Whether constructed to characterize Soviet politics, Nazi Germany, or, more generally, a stage in the development of economically advanced authoritarian states, the model was the dominant paradigm employed by scholars in the 1950s to interpret Soviet politics. In laying out the characteristics of the totalitarian state, the model emphasized the total control of the system from the very top (Friedrich and Brzezinski, 1965, pp. 21–27; Welsh, 1973). To understand the Soviet system, then, one focused upon the principal elites and, most importantly (if a succession crisis was not occurring), the *vozhd'*, or supreme leader. In this sense, the totalitarian model made the study of Soviet politics a rather simple affair; there was, after all, only one ring in the circus. However, there remained a crucial problem, and that was that the ring was not very well illuminated – the Soviet political scene 'displayed . . . a bare stage set which must be furnished out of clues and props in the memory and imagination of the observer'. Thus, while the focus was seen to be narrow, the data base, it was argued, was meagre.

By the late 1950s and early 1960s, however, both of these propositions – the paucity of data and the emphasis on the leadership stratum – came under some fire, and in turn the validity of the totalitarian model was questioned. The catalyst in all this was not an American scholar publishing a pathbreaking piece, but rather Nikita Khrushchev who, in opening up the Soviet system, challenged many of our notions about 'closed societies' (Long, 1966) and the overwhelmingly dominant role played by the First Secretary (Linden, 1966; Hough, 1973). Specialists began to offer alternative models which emphasized a host of new features in the Soviet system – new in some cases to the system itself, and in others merely to the community of Soviet scholars.

Unfortunately, this response to the dismantling of the totalitarian model evolved in large part into an effort to construct a new straitjacket. Model-building was too ingrained a habit to be discarded simply because a particular edifice had fallen. Scholars felt that there had to be a way to summarize the Soviet system. Some altered the totalitarian model to meet only the most obvious shortcomings; thus was born the 'directed society' (Meyer, 1965; Fischer, 1968; Kassof, 1969; Rigby, 1969; Azrael, 1970). Others tried to describe the Soviet system as one variant in the process of political development – the mobilization model was particularly popular (Tucker, 1961; Kautsky, 1962; Apter, 1965; Moore, 1967; Huntington, 1968; Dallin and Breslauer, 1970). Many observed the changes in the Soviet polity – the pluralization in particular – and viewed them as part of a trend, and an inevitable trend at that, in an industrializing society. It was argued that imperatives of development (such as the growing complexity of the society and the need for technological advances) compelled the system to open up (Gitelman, 1970; Bauman, 1971; Griffiths, 1971; Gitelman, 1972; Hough, 1975; Jowitt, 1975). While some felt that the Soviet Union was not responding to these 'imperatives' but rather petrifying under a regime of greyish clerks (Brzezinski, 1969; Gitelman, 1972), most scholars saw signs of some change, at least, in response to these new demands (Hough, 1973; Rakowska-Harmstone, 1976).

The 'change to change' (Taubman, 1974; Korbonski, 1977), however, ran into the realization by the start of the 1970s that these postulated trends were not necessarily inherent in the Soviet system. Announced or predicted reforms simply were not being carried out. The Czech invasion was particularly effective in serving notice that the Soviet leaders felt that there were limits on how much a communist system should change. Concurrently, there has not been much evidence to support the petrification argument – the forecast of an endless downward spiral of elite efficiency and system performance. As William Taubman has summarized:

> In the years since Khrushchev's ouster, the Soviet political system has neither transformed itself, nor, it would seem, degenerated. Leadership succession has been neither dramatic nor traumatic; rule by oligarchy had lasted longer than expected, then appeared to erode to the benefit of Leonid Brezhnev without the anticipated turmoil. Nor, conventional wisdom to the contrary, has leadership by 'clerks' produced stagnation – unless stagnation is defined as the absence of transformation (1974, pp. 379–80).

Just as the totalitarian model had over-simplified reality by ignoring the possibility of change, then, too many of its successors made the equally serious mistake of assuming unremitting change.

The response to these deficiencies, however, was not Hegelian; scholars did not opt for synthesizing the various models into a new one which allowed for some change and some stability (Kelley, 1974; Bruce and Clawson, 1977). Instead, as their counterparts in some other areas of comparative politics had been doing, they dropped the model-building and instead focused their attention on what is popularly called the 'middle-range' level of analysis; i.e., studies that encompass an easily identifiable, narrowly focused aspect of the political system, and that involve the use of more systematic approaches. It was argued that such middle-range findings were needed before a parsimonious and relatively accurate model of the Soviet system could be constructed. Future models would be built inductively, not deductively.

In essence, this was what the calls in the late 1960s for a behavioural revolution were all about – to encourage Soviet area scholars to use a variety of approaches, levels of analysis, and concepts drawn from the general discipline of political science in order to examine specific aspects, and not the entirety of what was seen as an increasingly complex political system. There was, however, some disagreement among scholars as to how ripe communist studies were for such a revolution. On the one side, Paul Shoup, for example, contended that the prospects for an empirical approach were indeed bright; while

> we lack convenient typologies and unifying concepts for communist systems, we are on sound ground in treating these systems as distinctive . . . amenable to model building and other forms of comparative research. Not being bound in any way by 'ideal types' or evolutionary models, we are free to assemble building blocks of data applicable to a wide variety of situations (both past and present) and to encourage the broadest possible utilization of new and existing comparative techniques (Shoup, 1971, p. 82).

This optimism, however, was not shared by some other scholars. D. Richard Little, for one, contended that the theoretical and empirical base was still too meagre to support a quantitative breakthrough:

> The overriding fact about the behavioural approach is that it requires large amounts of accurate and quantifiable data. The contrary fact about the communist field is the paucity of such data. It is true that the quantity and quality of data being made available by Soviet and East European governments are improving rapidly . . . [but] more data have been forthcoming in recent years than communist area specialists have been able, conceptually and theoretically, to absorb . . . [Even] when we focus not on our conceptual tools, but on the kinds of substantive questions we would like to be able to answer, . . . the picture is bleak (Little, 1969, p. 101).

In Little's view, then, the call for a revolution was premature – communist studies had to remain for the most part wedded to its own concepts and methodologies.

Recent trends in research on the Soviet Union

Since those projections were made, a veritable avalanche of middle-range, systematic, often quantitative studies have appeared. Most of these – contrary to what Little suggested – seem to have found an adequate base in both theory and data. If sheer numbers are any measure of impact, then it can safely be concluded that the behavioural revolution in communist studies is here to stay.

Whether the approaches involve copies of techniques from the Western literature, or innovations designed to meet peculiar needs of the area (see, for instance, Stewart *et al.*, 1972), the important point is that we are beginning to build a body (or, more properly, several bodies) of systematic findings concerning the operation of the Soviet political system. As in any scholarly discipline, certain areas have received a great deal of treatment, while others are relatively ignored. This reflects, among other things, scholarly perceptions about the importance of the issue, data availability, and whether the topic is currently 'in' the field. Thus, we know a good deal more than we did ten years ago about decision-making and the role of various actors in the Soviet system (Stewart, 1969; Kelley, 1972, 1974, 1976; Bruce and Clawson, 1977), the composition of the elite at varying levels and in different bodies in the Soviet polity (Fleron, 1969; Blackwell, 1973; Moses, 1974; Hough, 1976; Unger, 1977), the treatment and politics of the various regions and nationalities (Hodnett and Ogareff, 1973; Moses, 1974; Silver, 1974a, 1974b; Echols, 1975; Bielasiak, 1980a), social, economic and political change (Lowenthal, 1970; Connor, 1975; Lapidus, 1976), dissent (Tokes, 1975), political culture (Tucker, 1973; Jowitt, 1974; White, 1979), and the role of the masses in general (Oliver, 1969; Hough, 1976; Little, 1976; Rigby, 1976) and of women in particular (Lennon, 1971; Jancar, 1974b; Lapidus, 1977) within the Soviet system.

However, this leaves a number of gaps in our knowledge. We still know very little, for instance, about the formation of the political agenda in the Soviet Union, and how various actors and elements in the system interact to re-order the items on that agenda. We also do not have a clear sense of how elites are socialized into their political roles – what exactly is the impact of factors such as ambition, professionalism, party versus state experience, generational cohort, inter-elite conflict, or the structure of political opportunities and risks on the values, attitudes, and decision rules of the Soviet leadership? To note just one more example, we could do with much more systematic investigation into issues related to policy innovation and implementation. While we are beginning to understand the process by which, and the reasons why, elites make either marginal or major adjustments in the status quo, there is still a great deal that needs to be examined and explained in this area. These innovations – of whatever magnitude they are – can be greatly altered in the implementation process. We have numerous anecdotal pieces that will attest to that – what we need now are more rigorous, generalizable, and especially comparative analyses of the gap between policy pronouncements and their implementation. Is the infamous Soviet bureaucracy more out of control than its counterparts in the West – in which type of system is bureaucracy most responsive to the political leadership? Thus, despite the plethora of recent studies, there are still a number of major topics – what we have presented certainly does not exhaust the possibilities – that have been neglected in current research efforts.

However, even if we focus attention on those areas where extensive research has been conducted, we can still point to a number of problems that exist in many of these studies – the revolutionary intent is not always matched by the methodology. For one thing, there are numerous difficulties that are often involved in employing aggregate data, which are usually the quantitative foundation for these studies (Bunce and Echols, 1975). In addition, scholars still tend to oversimplify politics in a manner we would not dream of when analyzing American or Western European systems. Moreover, we still too readily employ a narrow set of untested hypotheses and causal interpretations as though they were the only alternatives available (Pressman and Wildavsky, 1973; Headey, 1974; Chapman, 1977). We should also point out that Western biases continues to creep into many of our studies, distorting our hypotheses and interpretations (Pirages, 1969; Millar, 1977).

From comparative communism to comparative politics

Perhaps the most important problem, however, is the persistent failure genuinely to make the comparative leap. The calls several years ago for the behavioural revolution were not simply looking for quantitative analyses and some concept borrowing from the research on Western polities, but also to *join* Western and communist studies. The best way to do this is to engage in explicitly comparative *East–West* analyses (Brzezinski and Huntington, 1963; Parkin, 1971; Hollander, 1973; Bunce, 1976; Hough, 1977). At best, we have seen some comparisons of communist systems (and the Soviet Union is often not included even in these) (Triska and Johnson, 1975; Shoup, 1975). While those comparisons are quite interesting, the scope needs to be expanded. There are two ways to evaluate a political system – against an ideal or against another working polity. For too long, the Soviet Union has been judged against some ideal communist society. That, of course, is a legitimate undertaking, holding them to their claims. At some point, however, it becomes tiresome to reiterate simply that the Soviet Union has failed to reach an ideal. It would instead be very interesting to know more precisely how the USSR compares with the working alternatives in the West. By doing this, we would expand the political world (and its variables) that we are working with, and at the same time set more realistic parameters on our evaluations of Soviet politics. We would no longer be able to assert, for example, the ossification of the Soviet elite, without comparing turnover data of that elite with data from Western nations (Nagle, 1977). The capriciousness involved in many interpretations of findings on the Soviet Union would be replaced by more solidy-based, comparative standards.

To engage in this breadth of comparative research would not necessarily require difficult theoretical breakthroughs (Sartori, 1970). We could begin simply by mining the classic, and too little used comparative study by Zbigniew Brzezinski and Samuel Huntington, *Political Power: USA/USSR* – there are dozens of provocative and testable hypotheses in that book alone. They obviously do not exhaust the possibilities, but they do provide one good source.

Evaluating Soviet politics

In the discussion above, we implied something that may seem controversial to some scholars, and that is that we are in the business of evaluating the Soviet system. Supposedly, this violates the canons of the modern, systematic, approaches. We should be trying, some would argue, to understand and explain, and not to pass judgements. Our response is that, in the process of comprehension and explanation, it is virtually impossible to avoid making judgements. We cannot write in a vacuum about how the Soviet system works; we need some standards, some criteria for judgement. Too often, standards of assessment are ignored, leaving us with nothing upon which to anchor our explanations.

Perhaps it is the fear of reverting to Cold War style comparisons of the United States and the Soviet Union that provoke a reaction against evaluation. But what was wrong with those was not the use of comparisons in general, but rather that most of the comparisons drew upon data employed merely to confirm the preconception of the comparativist. One hopes that we are beyond that now, and that scholars can approach the subject with a sufficient degree of objectivity. If so, some very interesting work can be done.

This is especially true for studies of the *outputs* of the Soviet system. For a long time, scholars have shied away from that side of the Soviet policy progress, leaving it to the more popular writers to describe – invariably unfavourably – how Soviet people live and what the government does *to* its citizens (Smith, 1976). Scholars focused instead on the operation of the political system, the *inputs* into the decision-making process, and how that process worked. At best, they examined the actual policies produced by the system only in order to obtain clues from the outputs about the policy process (Armstrong, 1969). More recently, however, the academic community has become interested in the policies of the system as indicators of what the Soviet polity is providing for its people. But we are still a long way from enjoying good *comparative* assessments of the outputs – what they are, and how they are produced in the Soviet Union relative to nations in the West. Economists have been well ahead of political scientists on this point (Pryor, 1968; Wiles and Markowski, 1971; Bergson, 1974); they have been concerned for a long while with evaluating, though with varying degrees of success, the efficiency, effectiveness and impact of the operation of the Soviet economic system, and how it compares with alternative economic mechanisms. Political scientists have a good way to go to catch up, and it is to be hoped that this is a direction many will take in the future.

Conclusion – after all this, we still need grand theory

Many pages ago, we seemed to dismiss grand models of the Soviet system as anachronistic, inaccurate, and wasteful of scholarly resources. While we agree with those assessments, we wish to conclude by contending that there is still room for broad theories of the Soviet political system. There is a very important admonition, however, and that is that these theories should primarily involve the use of inductive and not deductive reasoning. We should not focus our efforts on building models based on one, or a few, central assumptions about the Soviet political system. Rather, we should be building models that are based on the findings drawn from the competent, middle-range literature.

The desire for the latter type of model reflects the need, which everyone can endorse, to stop occasionally and take stock of where we are – to examine the forest, or at least a substantial part of it (one does not have to explain the entire system in order to aggregate usefully a body of middle-range findings). It is easy to become overwhelmed by a continuing stream of 'findings'. Good studies, of course, attempt to place their findings in a larger context. However, the context they refer to is often one or two steps removed from what could be fruitfully employed. The theorizer and the think-piece, then, should not become extinct in Soviet studies; the behavioural revolution can never extend that far. For the theorizer to survive, however, his or her work must be grounded whenever possible on the empirical base that has been laid. When that requirement is met, large theories can play a very useful role in understanding and evaluating the Soviet polity.

What we are recommending, then, is that Soviet studies in the future combine the 'big issues' debated in the 1950s and early 1960s with the more systematic methodologies developed in the current era. In this way we can avoid blanket assertions – a problem in the 1950s – and trivial topics – a criticism of behavioural research. In their place, we can pose important issues in an empirical framework and begin to build inductive models of the Soviet and of other Soviet-type political systems.

17

Human Rights under State Socialism

DAVID LANE

I

Many critics, both liberal and Marxist, argue that the Western concept of rights is not (or should not be) applicable to the Soviet Union and other socialist societies. There are three distinct types of criticism. First, that the doctrine of Marxism–Leninism is alien to the concept of human rights. Second, that individual rights are not defended because of the monistic structure of society. Only pluralist society, it is argued, can secure rights for certain values (religious, ethnic); a monistic state abrogates individual and group rights. Furthermore, the totalitarian nature of Soviet-type society weakens the independence of the individual from the state. Third, that the Russian heritage of orthodoxy and absolutism has continued into the modern period and provides no political supports to Western concepts of rights.

The first type of criticism is voiced by a school of thinkers within socialism who wish to jettison the liberal notions of human rights. Such socialists argue that traditional political rights are predicated on a capitalist society distinguished by possessive competitive individualism. Such rights as have developed under capitalism are based on the assumption that there are conflicts of interest between rights-holders and other members of society; this is at variance with the socialist ideal of community. A conflict of interests 'presumed in the practice of rights could not arise [under socialism] and socialism . . . must involve not the revision but the abandonment of rights along with the institution of the state and its laws (Campbell, 1983, p. 7). In so far then as the state, acting on behalf of the

---

Reprinted with adaptations from *Political Studies*, vol. 32, no. 3 (September 1984) with the permission of author and publisher.

working class, passes laws to protect and to enhance the interests of the working class, claims of individuals against the state are inimical to the interests of the working class and hence to the interests of society as a whole. This school would argue that 'individual' rights have their intellectual and political foundation in a bourgeois conception of society. Socialist society is based on a philosophy of fulfilling human need, not individual rights. Ruth A. Putnam argues that rights involve laws which require a state which for socialists is an 'instrument of class repression'. The legal codes in which rights are embedded are anathema to socialists – 'Rights are the prized possessions of alienated persons' (1976, p. 106). This line of approach is endorsed further by writers such as Steven Lukes and Lezlek Kolakowski who assert that Marxism (and particularly Marxism–Leninism) as a doctrine is alien to the concept of human rights (1981; 1983, pp. 6–7).

On the other hand, other contemporary writers, developing a more humanistic Marxism, and correctly in my view, have argued that human rights are an essential component of socialism. Shingo Shibata (1975), Agnes Heller (1979) and Tom Campbell (1983) regard human rights as means to meet human needs; under socialism such rights are extended in form. While it is certainly true that the doctrine of inherent natural rights was regarded as being part of the democratic or bourgeois revolution, it would be incorrect to regard Marx and all of his followers to be indifferent to rights. It forecloses the issue to dismiss 'many peripheral variants of Marxism and to set aside all the intricate questions as to what may or may not be included in the list of human rights, to what extent their implementation depends on contingent historical conditions, etc.' (Kolakowski, 1983, p. 1). The fact that Marx regarded human rights as emancipation of people in a social and economic sense does not imply the absence of rights under socialism in a legal and political one. Marxism has a humanistic human rights tradition as well as an authoritarian one (Kamenka and Tay, 1980, pp. 50–1). Marx and Lenin were opposed to sham rights which characterised capitalism and which favoured the bourgeoisie. But this does not entail opposition to human rights as such. Political rights are a necessary complement to other social and economic rights and it is incorrect to regard Marxism as a philosophy indifferent to human rights (cf. Pollis and Schwab, 1979, p. 15). Marxism pays respect to individualistic human rights as part of the development of modern society; socialist rights should build on and extend such rights, rather than negate them. This is recognised even by the present leaders of the Soviet Union: 'Just as socialism is unthinkable without human rights and freedoms, the genuine rights and freedoms of man are inconceivable without socialism' (Chernenko, 1981, p. 202).

Writers who deny the validity of rights under socialism adopt an ahistorical and abstract position. In an 'ideal' communist society there would be no 'state' in the sense of a ruling class stratum, but present day societies are far away from such abstract formulations. One must also bear in mind the role of government as an administrative institution providing services and fulfilling public objectives. As officials may abuse their powers, the courts are needed to assert the prerogatives of citizens over misguided or wrongful actions by officials. A state of alienation or estrangement is likely to be caused by deprivation of human rights (to work, housing, education, participation, privacy) rather than the possession of them (cf. Putnam, 1976, p. 106). Lenin objected to the ways that capitalism undermined democracy and insisted that democracy was a necessary condition for socialism. It is a one-sided interpretation of Lenin which considers him to be indifferent or hostile to the rights won by the masses under bourgeois democracy. In seeking to explain the denial of human rights to many people by the actions of the Soviet and other governments, such critics have come to make such actions a principle of socialist action rather than a violation of socialist legality. Similarly, the argument is also utilised by opponents of existing socialist states to label and condemn them as opposed to the concept of rights.

Such violations provide the basis for the second set of criticisms of rights under socialism. A sympathetic commentator on the USSR, Alice Erh-Soon Tay, regards the repression of Stalin's rule as being 'based on sustained and systematic disregard of law and any respect for human dignity or human rights' (Kamenka and Tay, 1978, p. 109). Such violations are not regarded as aberrations or exceptions but are generalized into a critique of socialist states. As Campbell has put it, they are conceived to illustrate that there is

> something inherently antithetical between socialist theory and respect for individual rights. It may be no accident that governments expressing "collectivist" doctrines appear to place less weight on freedom of speech, freedom of movement, and the right to take part in the selection of political authorities than those nations which regard themselves as liberal democracies (1983, p. 2).

Raymond Williams has a similar position:

> There was a real if not inevitable progression from a mainline version of the dictatorship of the proletariat through the control of the vanguard party to the Stalinist regime which in its ultimate development was an outrage to everything that the socialist tradition and indeed the best of the Bolshevik tradition has stood for (1975, p. 233).

Western writers cite in support of this viewpoint the suppression of dissent. Contemporary dissenters in the Soviet Union are harassed by the police, independence of thought is denied and foreign travel, writing and residence are restricted. Chalidze and other dissidents have pointed to the ways that fundamental freedoms of speech, communication, person, association and movement are curtailed (see, for instance, Chalidze, 1974;

Feldbrugge, 1975; Tokes, 1975; Reddaway, 1983). But condemnation of the USSR must be tempered by the realisation that human rights in all societies are infringed. The United States has used civil rights as an agency of its foreign policy to condemn the Soviet Union (Lazreg, 1979).

One must also consider whether the Western concept of human rights is not an ethnocentric one and whether the Soviet Union in some way compensates for the infringement of individual political rights against the state by the implementation of social ones. The denial of some rights to 'dissidents' may not apply to other rights or other citizens. Deprivation of the political right to found a business enterprise and to trade on the market does not infringe the economic right of labourers to receive a just wage or the social right to permanent employment. It will be argued below, however, that the denial of some political rights cannot be defended in terms of human emancipation. Additionally, one must discuss whether the infractions of human rights in the Soviet Union are likely to be a permanent feature of state socialist society or have been associated with the peculiar evolution of the Soviet state, associated with its traditional culture.

The application to socialist states and particularly to the USSR of the doctrines of 'human rights', as understood in the West and as expressed in the UN Declaration of Human Rights, has been questioned by cultural comparativists and they constitute the third approach mentioned above. Pollis and Schwab write:

> only in the Western capitalist states with a shared historical development and a common philosophic tradition does the concept of individual rights against and prior to the state exist. And only in these countries are political and civil rights implemented to a greater or lesser extent. Most non-Western states, frequently for a combination of cultural and ideological reasons and because of policy priorities set by the demands of economic development do not emphasise or attend to political and civil rights. On the other hand, socialist states seem to place greater emphasis on and have a better record with regard to economic rights than do Western democratic societies (1979, p. xiii. See also below, pp. 339–40).

Such writers, like those socialists who identify opposing liberal rights claims with bourgeois society, emphasise the interrelationship and interdependence between particular sets of human rights doctrines and the social, political and economic structures in which they are embedded. Hence human rights have a particularistic rather than a universalistic relevance. Philosophies of human rights adopted by Western states may be appropriate for them in respect of their concern with the rights of private property and to the rights to security which may be given to the individual in a pluralist society. They have their roots in the 'particular experience of England, France and the United States' (Pollis and Schwab, p. 4). These may be contrasted with socialist societies in which economic, welfare and distributive rights are given more priority. The conceptual classification between individualistic and collectivist types of rights, which will be taken up later, may be summarised as follows.

Individualistic	*Collectivist*
Rights are possessed by individuals.	Rights are held by groups or classes.
Rights are determined prior to, and opposed to, the state.	Rights are defined by, and activated through, the state.
Rights are enforced through individual claims against the state.	Rights are enforced through administrative action.
Rights are observed through absence of interference by individuals and institutions.	Rights are achieved through positive actions by institutions and the state.

The comparativist approach, however, is not merely concerned with the conceptual differences outlined above, but seeks the origin of different approaches to rights in the traditional values, practices, and the ideographic features of specific societies. Many of the practices of the Soviet Union, it is pointed out, derive from an autocratic state in which Orthodoxy prevailed – rather than from Marxist political theory. Both the state structure of pre-1917 Russia and the traditions of the Orthodox Church gave no role to *individual* political rights. Individualism was a creed bound up with the Renaissance and Reformation, which had little influence on Tsarist Russia. Such ideas did not penetrate because of the isolation of Russia from Europe due to its size and inhospitable land mass. The integrative structures of Russia were more communal than individualistic. The traditional Russian *mir* or *obshchina* (commune) was essentially a collectivist body. The village assembly had powers of collective ownership of property given to it under the terms of the Emancipation of the Serfs in 1861. The Russian serf, from being bound to the land, became bound to the commune. The American negro, by contrast, from being owned by one master was given his or her individual freedom. In the field of law and civil rights, Henn-Jüri Uibopuu has drawn attention to the '*nichevo*-mentality' (it 'doesn't matter' outlook). This attitude entails 'few or almost no objections to administrative discretion or shortcomings'. This attitude, he points out, 'can be regarded as a heritage from Tsarist times, and . . . makes possible the Soviet form of administrative practice, with such outstanding characteristics as the uncertainty of the *locus standi* of the individual in the administrative procedure. This special feature of Soviet administration . . . can also be regarded as a result of the Soviet approach to human rights which involves an overestimation of society (*obshchestven-nost'*) in general, at the cost of both the individual human being and human dignity. The fact that the individual lacks legal remedies in almost all cases of administrative process demonstrates further the Tsarist influence' (1979, p. 25).

If one can talk of a general *weltanschauung*, comparativists would depict Russians as being collectivist and affective, as accepting authority, and as having a group rather than an individual identity.

In my opinion, comparativists, such as Pollis and Schwab, take too deterministic a position. They ignore the heterogeneity of the Soviet political culture and the important role given by many Russian Marxists to conceptions of individual human and democratic rights. But this traditional background has undoubtedly influenced the evolution of the Soviet state. There was a symbiosis between traditional values and practices and those of the ideology guiding the Soviet state. The Soviet leaders had developmental goals (Lane, 1974). Priority was given to the provision of employment and also the fulfilment of life needs – for food, shelter, health and education. Marxists often point to the fact that bourgeois freedoms of the person, of speech, of association and of the press cannot be fulfilled under capitalism because of the limitations imposed by the bourgeois freedom of property ownership. The political leadership of the Soviet Union and other socialist states has tended to neglect such freedoms and has identified other goals (of economic development and social needs) as being of greater importance. The political rulers have been more concerned with industrialisation, security and defence, and socialist norms of individual rights have been neglected and often infringed. There has been an unresolved tension between the salience of individual and collectivist rights.

Arguments, encountered above, claiming that rights are either inappropriate or even harmful to the integrity of a 'socialist society' may be refuted on two counts. First, these arguments are often posed in terms of an abstract socialist society. The countries of Eastern Europe are not socialist in such an ideal sense: they have a state apparatus and considerable inadequacies in terms of the level of productive forces. At best they are transitional social formations. Second, rights-claims need not be restricted to the model of possessive competitive individualism associated with capitalism. Social and economic rights defined in the constitutions of state socialist societies have a corollary in the duties of agents of the state to provide certain facilities. Rights-claims by individuals, then, in existing societies may have the form of claims on officers of the state to implement rights of individuals. Officials may misuse their powers and they may be inert. Furthermore, interests in the political system (for instance of a bureaucratic kind) may not be responsive to the legitimate rights-claims of citizens. Such claims do not imply antagonistic relations between state and citizen and are therefore quite legitimate under socialism and in a social formation between capitalism and communism.

II

Moving from Western conceptualisations about human rights under social-ism to the study of rights in existing socialist states, one must emphasise the latent tension, mentioned above, between individual rights and class or collective rights.

In the Soviet Union and other state socialist societies the normative approach to rights may be studied in the context of the dominant ideology, and particularly in the constitutions of these countries. In this respect we are concerned with what the political leadership of the dominant ruling class defines as legitimate rights. The extent to which these rights are implemented, or enjoyed by citizens, is a matter for empirical study and also for political and social analysis – one needs to understand what conception of rights underlies constitutional provision. This not only limits what the rulers may *legitimately* do, but also is a basis of demands by those persons or groups whose rights have been infringed. We have now to consider what rights the regime defines as legitimate, the extent to which they are not fulfilled and the ways in which they differ from liberal conceptions of rights.

The Bolsheviks were aware that the October revolution should follow the pattern of the French with its own declaration of rights. Sverdlov, at the opening of the Constituent Assembly on 18 January 1918, said: 'just as in the days of the French bourgeois revolution . . . there was proclaimed a Declaration of Rights of Man and of the Citizen . . . so today our Russian Socialist Revolution should likewise make its declaration . . .' (cited in Bunyan and Fisher, 1934, p. 372). One might extend Habermas's corres-pondence between the rights of the American colonialists legitimating their independence from the British Empire, and those of the French revolutionaries after the overthrow of the *ancien régime* (Habermas, 1974, p. 87), to the rights of the Bolsheviks legitimating the abolition of tsarism and the power of the working class expressed through the Communist Party.

The Declaration of the Rights of the Toiling and Exploited Peoples (Bunyan and Fisher, 1934, pp. 372–4) has set the tone for Soviet declara-tions of rights. It did not, unlike other documents on rights, specify any rights of citizens against the state. It was a declaration of policy; it emphasised the role of class struggle in securing rights for the labouring classes (that is, peasants and workers).

In the first Constitution of the RSFSR, published on 3 July 1918, the general principles of rights were articulated. These shared certain senti-ments in common with the lists of rights declared as objectives in the American and French Revolutions. They included the 'equality of all citizens before the law, irrespective of race or nationality' (Art. 22); the repression of national minorities or any attempts 'in any way to limit their rights' (Art. 22) were illegal. The working classes were given 'effective liberty of opinion', in the promotion of which were transferred to the workers and peasants 'all the technical and material resources necessary for the publication of newspapers, pamphlets, books, and other printed matter'. Their 'unobstructed circulation throughout the country' was guaranteed (Art. 14). The workers were ensured 'complete freedom of meeting' (Art. 15) and 'full liberty of association' (Art. 16). To ensure '. . . effective access to education, the RSFSR sets before itself the task of providing for the workers and poorer peasants a complete, universal and free education' (Art. 17). In addition, it reiterated the obligation on all citizens to work, the duty to perform military service and to defend the Republic. Workers and peasants resident in Russia were given the right of citizenship of the Republic; and persecuted foreigners were given the right of asylum (for the full text, see Rothstein, 1923, and Unger, 1981).

These rights, which were framed in terms of social classes rather than individuals, have to be seen in the context of the Marxist notion of class war, and in relation to the political formation of the dictatorship of the proletariat. As Article 9 of the Constitution put it:

> The principal object of the constitution of the RSFSR [which is designed] for the present transition period, consists in the establishment (in the form of a strong Soviet Government) of the dictatorship of the urban and rural workers combined with the poorest peasantry to secure the complete suppression of the bourgeoisie, the abolition of the exploitation of man by man and the establishment of socialism, under which neither class divisions nor state coercion arising therefrom will any longer remain.

Leaving aside for one moment the fulfilment of the rights promised in the Constitution, the question arises how these provisions differ from constitutional rights proclaimed in the West.

First, rights in state socialist countries have been defined collectively rather than individually. In the seventeenth and eighteenth century, rights were conceived to inhere in persons, in individuals. These included freedom of the person, the right to political consultation through Parliament, freedom of conscience, and also important economic rights for the individual to own property and conduct economic enterprise unconstrained by the government. Broadly, such rights were secured by the English Revolution from 1640 to 1688, and the French in 1789; they were extended to America in 1776 and continued in the decolonisation process of the twentieth century.

The Russian Revolution was a catalyst in the development of social and economic rights. This, of course, extended claims of social rights advocated by other socialist and pre-socialist thinkers, such as Tom Paine (see particularly Part II of his *Rights of Man*, published in 1792). Explicit rights to work, to social security, and to education have been proclaimed. In the economic sector individual rights to enterprise and to ownership of property were abolished; freedom from economic exploitation (in a Marxist sense of the production of exchange values) and rights to employment have been decreed; government ownership, control, and planning of the economy have been introduced. In addition, the individualist and 'market' conception of political rights expressed through competition of political parties and interest groups has been replaced by the idea of a collective political interest articulated by one political party.

From the earliest days of the Revolution, the emancipation of men and women and the development of their human rights were regarded as being dependent on the interests of the working class, as expressed through the Communist Party and as activated by the government. In contrast to Western states, where rights are expressed as inalienable attributes of individuals and are claims which the state cannot (or cannot lightly) override, human rights in the Soviet Union have been bound up with what the state can (or should) do to liberate the working class. In terms of the earlier discussion, needs were met by economic planning and social development rather than by the articulation of individual demands.

A second difference is that political rights in the West have been based on the notion of the equality of citizenship (for men if not for women). Inequalities of condition have been regarded by thinkers such as Locke, Rousseau and Mill as 'artificial' creations of men, having no legitimacy in the state of nature. For de Tocqueville, for instance, the history of Western Europe from the year 1270 was 'the gradual development of equality of conditions . . .' (1960, p. 6). Equality of political rights for men was achieved in the eighteenth century revolutions. In Russia some such sentiments were expressed by liberal opponents of the autocracy, but the dominant political tradition up to 1917 was one of formal inequality of rights: people's status before the law was based on their rank or estate.

Uniquely among European countries, Russia did not experience an era of individual rights. The Tsarist autocracy was never broken by a liberal-democratic movement: individual freedoms of combination or of expression were never achieved; there were restraints on individual ownership of land, on enterprise and on geographical mobility; and religious toleration was not secured (the brief liberal interlude between February and October 1917 can hardly be compared with the long maturation of rights in Western countries such as England). The law classified people's rights in terms of their estate – not as possessions of any individual. The legal estates were abolished in Russia only in November 1917, and members of different economic classes even after this had different rights. Workers and peasants were recruited into the army. Constitutional rights were given to workers and employees, peasants and labouring Cossacks; businessmen, the clergy and 'those who employ others for the sake of profit', however, did not enjoy civil rights and were placed in the same category as criminals and those with disorders of the mind (Articles 64, 65).

Since the Russian Revolution, the content of rights claims in the West and in the USSR has changed. The 'rights' extolled by thinkers of the eighteenth and nineteenth centuries were largely *political* rights. These have been extended during the twentieth century: *de facto* and increasingly *de jure* rights in Western states have covered social and economic matters. There has also been the recognition of group (particularly ethnic and gender) rights in addition to individual ones. Positive government action now is widely accepted in the West as a means to achieve individual and group rights of a social and economic kind. Despite the developments here which have occurred since the Second World War, there is still a strong residual belief that rights are about individual freedoms and that the government has a supportive, though essentially a limited, role in promoting rights. This view finds legitimation in the critique of Cranston (1967) that the new social and economic rights are quite different in quality from the 'inalienable' traditional political rights.

In the Soviet Union the approach to and emphasis on rights is different. The state (party and government) has played a dominant role in defining and implementing rights. Obligations and duties of the state to the citizen are specified and effectively limit individual action. (Planning secures the right of full employment but the absence of a market and the abolition of private property eliminates the rights of individual production and trade.) The Soviet state has always played a greater role in defining and implementing rights. Eighteenth and nineteenth century European thinkers articulated rights of individuals as individuals. Rights have been defined in post-1917 Russia *by* the government, not as claims *on* the government.

The emphasis on the duty of the individual to the state has greater salience in the USSR than in the West. Duties in the 1936 Constitution are defined in Article 12: 'Work in the USSR is a duty, a matter of honour, for every able-bodied citizen. He who does not work shall not eat' (for the full text, see Unger, 1981). Articles 131, 132, 133 and 134 instruct all citizens to 'strengthen public-socialist property, to regard it as the source of the wealth and power of the fatherland, of the health and happiness, the prosperity and culture of the working people . . . military service is the duty of all citizens.' It is the duty of citizens to 'safeguard and fortify public socialist property as the sacred and inviolable foundation of the Soviet system . . .' (Art. 131). Unlike in Western liberal conceptions of rights where individuals are seen as having rights *qua* individuals to life and happiness, in the Soviet Union, these rights are limited by the present incumbents of political power when they are deemed to conflict with the state's role of safeguarding the collective interest.

The priority given to 'the interests of the state or society' over the interests of individuals is also repeated in the 1977 Constitution. Article 39 says: 'Enjoyment by citizens of their rights and freedoms must not be to the detriment of the interests of society or the state, or infringe the rights of other citizens.' Article 59 states: 'Citizens' exercise of their rights and freedoms is inseparable from the performance of their duties and obligations. Citizens of the USSR are obliged to observe the Constitution of the USSR and Soviet laws, comply with the standards of socialist conduct, and uphold the honour and dignity of Soviet citizenship.' And Article 62 requires that 'Citizens of the USSR are obliged to safeguard the interests of the Soviet state, and to enhance its power and prestige' (for the full text, see Unger, 1981). The difference from Western liberal states is not just in the recognition of the limits of the individuals' rights. In no society are human rights absolute: homicide laws in Western states, for instance, limit the right to life, as does anti-terrorism legislation in respect of freedom of association. In state socialist society, however, not only are there far fewer restraints on the state's power to restrict individual rights, but the state, through the 'leading role' of the party, may effectively define which individual rights are deemed to conflict with the state's interests. In practice it is almost impossible to challenge the state's definition of illegitimate activity (see, for instance, Luryi, 1982, pp. 65–8).

Soviet constitutional developments have also recognised individual rights. There is now less prominence given to class struggle and to the class basis of human emancipation and much more to individual rights. The scope of social and economic rights has also been extended. The Constitutions of 1936 and 1977 explicitly define a wide range of 'fundamental rights and duties of citizens' (*Constitution of the USSR* 1936, head to Article CXVII). It should be borne in mind that we are dealing here with normative rights, not empirically effective rights. The intention of the 1977 Constitution is to extend and 'strengthen the legal position of the individual' (Kudryavtsev, 1978, p. 13). There is much greater concern in the 1977 Constitution with law and legality: in 1936 there were only 12 such references, in 1977 there were 70 (Kudryatvsev, 1978, p. 10). In the 1936 Constitution, rights are defined in Articles 118 to 129. In the 1977 Constitution, chapters 6 and 7 (Articles 33 to 69) include statements on the 'equality of citizens' rights' and 'the basic rights, freedoms and duties of citizens'. These rights are comprehensive and are undoubtedly now wider in scope than comparable lists to be found in the constitutions of liberal-democratic states. The formal statements or rights are summarised in Chart 17.1, which is divided into economic, social and political rights.

Rights, however, have to be seen in a political context. Rights are claims on resources and values, and the definition and fulfilment of rights have to do with the distribution of power in society. The *individual* articulation of rights is circumscribed by the *collectivist* control claimed by the Communist Party. Article 6 of the Constitution declares:

CHART 17.1

1936 Constitution *Economic:*	*1977 Constitution* *Economic:*
Right to work, to 'guaranteed employment'. Right to own, as personal property, income and savings derived from work, to own a dwelling house and supplementary husbandry, articles of household and articles of personal use and convenience. Right to inherit personal property.	Socialist system ensures enlargement of the rights . . . and continuous improvement of living standards. Rights to work, to choice of trade or profession.
Social:	*Social:*
Right to rest and leisure, seven-hour day, annual vacations with pay, maintenance in old age, sickness or disability. Education – free in all schools, in the native language.	Right to housing. Right to education, including teaching in native language. Right to cultural benefits. Right to freedom of scientific, technical and artistic work. Rights of authors, inventors and innovators protected. Right to leisure and rest, working week of 41 hours, paid holidays, extension of social service and sport. Health protection. Maintenance in old age, sickness or disability.
Political:	*Political:*
Rights of women on an equal footing with men 'in all spheres of economic, cultural, government, political and social activity'. Freedom of conscience, freedom of religious worship and freedom of anti-religious propaganda. Freedom of speech, press, assembly, street processions and demonstrations. The right to unite in mass organisations. Right of inviolability of the person, of the homes of citizens and the privacy of correspondence. Right of asylum to foreign citizens. Right to vote in elections, to nominate candidates through mass organisations and societies.	Equality before law. Men and women have equal rights. Equality of rights of different races and nationalities. Equality of rights of all citizens. Right to participation in management and administration of the state, to vote and be elected to Soviets, to submit proposals to state bodies, to criticise shortcomings. Freedom of speech, press, assembly, meetings, street processions and demonstrations. Right to asylum. Right to associate in public organisations. The right to profess any religion, to conduct religious worship. Inviolability of the person, of the home. Right of privacy, of correspondence, telephone conversations and telegraphic communications. Right to protection by state bodies. Right to complain against actions of officials, state bodies and public bodies.

The leading and guiding force of Soviet society and the nucleus of its political system, of all state organisations and public organisations, is the Communist Party of the Soviet Union. The CPSU exists for the people and serves the people.

The Communist Party, armed with Marxism–Leninism, determines the general perspective of the foreign policy of the USSR, directs the great constructive work of the Soviet people, and imparts a planned, systematic and theoretically sustained character to their struggle for the victory of communism.

Similar sentiments may be found in the constitutions of other socialist states (see Simons, 1980). That of the People's Republic of Poland, for instance, recognises the new class structure of the 'socialist state' (Art. 1), the leading class of which is the working class and the 'leading political force' of which is the Polish United Workers' Party (Art. 3). The Constitution also proclaims a multitude of rights, similar to those decreed in the Soviet Constitution (see Articles 16–19). It mentions, in distinction, however, the right to 'inherit land, buildings and other means of production belonging to peasants, craftsmen and home workers' (Art. 17). The Constitution also calls for a policy of 'friendship and cooperation with the USSR and other socialist states' (Art. 6).

Though group rights (for women, blacks) are increasingly recognised in Western liberal states, the individual is the unit in which rights claims are expressed. Under state socialism, the communist party (or analogous parties) is defined as the legitimate interpreter of the interests of the working class. In many cases, the role of the state acting (theoretically) on behalf of the working class comes into conflict with individuals who claim to be wronged by the (erroneous) policies or the (harmful) actions of officials of the state. A fundamental tenet of Leninism, as developed in the USSR, is at issue here: claims for individual rights against the state may be interpreted as weakening party hegemony which in turn enfeebles the class character of the state – and its role in defining the path to socialism. Assertions of individual rights against the state – the essence of rights in liberal democracy – can be conflated into attacks on the state. This gives rise to a major dilemma of individual rights under state socialism. While the state, in building socialism, claims to enhance individual rights, demands for individual rights may weaken the state's organising capacity. The role of the party, as developed in the USSR, is likely to be a major impediment to the legitimacy of rights claims by individuals as practised in Western liberal states.

III

Civil rights, as they developed under Marxism–Leninism, were associated with class rule, with developmental goals entailing the implementation of the 'new' social and economic rights (of literacy, employment, education, health care) rather than political rights of the individual: indeed, individual political rights have been abrogated. The greater recognition of individual rights is limited by the Leninist conception of the party (as noted above) as an aggregator of collective rights. There is here a fundamental conflict concerning the units in which rights claims are conceived.

The lack of fulfilment of rights in the past history of the USSR has to be seen in the context of an unstable international political environment (civil and foreign wars) and with the absence of many of the preconditions for the evolution of certain rights. Elements of Marxist theory which are alien to bourgeois society (e.g. bourgeois class rights) were fused with traditional values and led to the imposition of a political system which placed little, if any, emphasis on individual human rights. This process is an episode in the evolution of the Soviet state and should not be conceived of as endemic to socialism. The extent and methods of the abrogation of individual rights under Stalin cannot be justified *ex post facto* even in terms of 'nation-building' and economic growth (see for example Medvedev, 1979; Cohen, 1977; and more generally Lane, 1981). One should not gloss over, in the name of development, the unjustifiable breaches of civil rights, and the wrongdoings of the leadership and administration.

Richard P. Claude has pointed to some of the prerequisites for the implementation of human rights. To ensure constitutional limits on government, a 'universalistic' and 'secularized ideology of the rightful bases of political authority' is necessary; for civil liberties an ideological requisite is 'acceptance of public–private person distinction in politico-economic discourse' (Claude, 1976, p. 40). The Soviet Union has had none of these ideological underpinnings. Following the upheaval of revolution, civil war, the Second World War and the Cold War, there has been the absence of a secure legal system and there has been no generalised 'support for a nonarbitrary, rationalised system of justice' (Claude, 1976). S. M. Lipset and Richard P. Claude have pointed to the conditions for a western-type democratic society. They include: an open class system, economic wealth, an egalitarian value system, a capitalist economy, widespread literacy, and high participation in voluntary organisations (Lipset, 1963, pp. 74–5; Claude, 1976). Pre-revolutionary Russia had none of these preconditions; the Soviet Union until relatively recently has had few of them and this list is still not fulfilled. Also, foreign powers were (and are) regarded by the Soviet leaders as threats to their internal security.

A comparative methodology emphasises the correspondence between values and other forms of social organisation. In doing so it is ethically neutral. This is a very useful antidote to the ethnocentrism of many rights' advocates who ignore the social, political, and economic setting in which human rights are located. But it lacks a dynamic. One has no clues as to whether, or how far, human rights *should be* implemented. There is in comparativist models both an explanation of the absence of human rights in a given society, and an apology for that absence. With this kind of approach, it is impossible to come to any conclusions about what sort of human rights are possible or desirable.

With the consolidation of the revolutions in property relationships and the maturation of policies of economic development pursued in socialist states, the economic, social and ideological prerequisites for the implementation of human rights come into being. Despite considerable methodological difficulties involved in measuring the relationship between economic development and human rights, Hans Park (1980, esp. pp. 91–2) has shown that the physical quality of life (economic rights) is positively associated with levels of gross national product in both advanced capitalist countries ($N = 31$) and Marxist–Leninist ones ($N = 12$): in fact rather more so in the latter than the former (having an index of 0.77 compared with 0.64). In more concrete terms, if rights are measured in terms of welfare, then income is relatively more equally distributed in state socialist societies than in capitalist ones (see, for instance, Wiles and Markowski, 1971, esp. p. 344). A problem here, which is entailed by the notion of a correspondence between rights and duties, is that if one's duty to labour is not performed then rights to benefits are thereby diminished. Hence social security payments (to the aged, disabled, or single-parent families) may leave many citizens in need (see George and Manning, 1980, esp. pp. 44–63). However, the absence of private capital in socialist countries gives the state a greater role in distributing resources than under capitalism and accounts for the higher association quoted by Park between physical quality of life and gross national product.

A similar case may be made concerning the rights of employment. Socialist countries as a whole have very high levels of employment in paid labour. There is little doubt among Western economists that the right to employment has been secured in socialist states, although perhaps at some cost in terms of wage levels (see, for instance, Ellman, 1984). Taking women as an index, in the early 1980s the Soviet Union had 86 per cent of the appropriate female age groups in full-time paid employment; the corresponding figure is 35 per cent in West Germany and 43 per cent in Britain. Moreover in the latter countries 28 per cent and 41 per cent respectively of employed women were part-timers (Oakley, 1981, p. 160). Women, however, are still concentrated in industries such as teaching, health and services; their incomes are lower than men's and they do not have equal access to posts of authority (Lane, 1982, pp. 74–81).

In the capitalist countries there is a direct quantitative relationship between level of physical quality of life and political rights (0.6); the index is positive, but much lower (0.2), for the Marxist–Leninist countries (Park, 1980). Problems here are that 'political rights' are taken from liberal practices (e.g. multiple party choice) and the indexes do not show changes through time. Most qualitative studies have in fact shown that demands for political rights are growing in Marxist–Leninist states with the maturation of these societies (Coates, 1975, p. 6; see also Kowalewski, 1980). One might hypothesise that as 'modernisation' grows, so will individual and group claims for rights.

The recent history of the Soviet Union and some of the socialist states of Eastern Europe illustrates that political subcultures are being created which are coming into conflict with the more traditional ones. Here is a dynamic or contradiction in these societies. The traditional pattern of legitimacy, of the ideology of Stalinism, of central direction and control is being challenged by what Weber called the legal-rational. This involves a greater role being played by the legal system, by civil liberties and civil rights (see Rigby, 1980, esp. pp. 11–12). Soviet legal theory has changed significantly since the death of Stalin and has paralleled the conception of an all-people's state and developed socialism (*zrely* or *razvitoi sotsializm*). In a speech first published in 1959, the former Soviet president M. I. Kalinin called for strengthening the rights of workers, collective farmers and enterprises (Smith, 1982, p. 87). Since the mid-1960s Soviet lawyers have called for the formulation of a 'socialist conception of rights' and for a 'concept of the rights of the individual' (Brunner, 1982, p. 37). This is part of a tendency initiated by Khrushchev for greater regard to be paid to socialist legality, and it has led to 'a considerable upgrading of basic rights in Soviet legal theory' (Brunner, 1982, p. 37). As noted above, this is reflected by a greater concern for rights in the Constitution.

The reason for great emphasis on legal norms is the growing differentiation of society. Its advanced complexity, together with a more urban and educated population, calls for a system of integration through exchange between various institutions and groups (see, for instance, Zabigailo, 1978, p. 74). Such exchanges, however, involve greater autonomy and 'rights-claims', on the one side, and a decline in the hegemony of the state apparatus, on the other. The scientific and cultural intelligentsia (of whom Sakharov and Medvedev are 'dissident' representatives) are a major force in this movement. The ideology of Marxism–Leninism may be utilised, at a normative level, to endorse and legitimise such claims. The values underpinning socialist states – at least under conditions of 'developed socialism' – provide a basis for claims to be made by aggrieved citizens and groups in defence of their rights. The salience of such values, however, has to be studied in the context of the evolution of particular individual states and their political cultures. One may contrast Poland and the USSR in this respect.

In Poland, the rise of the Solidarity movement epitomises Polish claims for rights. It has widened and generalised the aspirations of other rights groups – the Workers' Defence Committee, and human rights committees. Solidarity was a mass movement embracing workers, intellectuals and peasants, including communists, non-communists and anti-communists. Prior to the inception of military rule in December 1981, the rights to free assembly and collective bargaining had *de facto* been conceded by the government, and claims for the right of 'free speech and press' and access to the radio and TV had been partly achieved (US Congress, *Country Reports*, 1982, p. 834). Solidarity campaigned publicly for the implementation of a wide range of rights: for the Church, for limitation of censorship and for the fulfilment of many other social rights, such as housing and health care. All these demands were in correspondence with rights defined in the Constitution. Concessions were obtained from the Polish government: not only were Solidarity and Rural Solidarity given official recognition, but the law on censorship, passed in July 1981, weakened central control over the media and excluded many items from it (e.g. textbooks, academic theses, Catholic Church publications, labour organisations' internal publications) (US Congress, *Country Reports*, 1982, p. 839).

In the Soviet Union, on the other hand, there has been no such widespread civil rights movement. It is well known that a number of explicitly human rights groups have been founded: notably, the Initiative Group for the Defence of Human Rights in the USSR, the Human Rights Committee and the Moscow Branch of Amnesty International (see Kowalewski, 1980, pp. 5–29). These groups advocate to various degrees the rights incorporated in the UN Universal Declaration of Human Rights; they are particularly concerned with freedom of the press, freedom of movement (both within and outside the USSR) and with the rights of various nationalities and religions. The movement, while qualitatively important, has been relatively isolated and on a very small scale. On admittedly inadequate data, Kowalewski estimates that the number of groups demonstrating rose from 6 in 1965 to 12 in 1976 (Kowalewski, 1980, p. 18). The movement is largely intellectual in composition, and there is no involvement by rank and file communists (Kowalewski, 1980, p. 19). Similarly, the recent movement for workers' rights has had little support and has had only a small impact. The Association of Free Trade Unions of Workers in the Soviet Union (AFTU) was founded in 1979. Its Charter defines membership to be open to 'any worker or employee whose rights and interests have been violated by administrative, governmental, party, or judicial agencies' (Karatnycky, 1980, p. 97). AFTU activists were quickly apprehended: some were arrested and others sent to psychiatric hospitals (Luryi, 1982, p. 58). AFTU was followed by the Free Interprofessional Association of Workers (SMOT). Its leaders were harassed and arrested, and a similar fate has befallen other 'rights' groups which have been set up in opposition to the authorities. It is difficult to gauge just how much support exists for these independent unions. But compared to Poland they are insignificant.

In Poland, the formal organisation of labour has many parallels with the USSR: unions have a similar role and ideology to their Soviet counterparts, and the ideology of socialism promises work, income, and a rising standard of living. In most other respects Polish labour-state relations and the Soviet diverge. While strikes are very rare and 'free trade unions' are marginal in the USSR, Poland has witnessed in the past 15 years profound worker upheavals. In 1945–8, 1956, 1962, 1970 and 1980, workers at the place of production have voiced dissatisfaction with the administration and official trade unions, and in those years well organised strikes have taken place (see Triska and Gati, 1981, and Staniszkis, 1979). In November 1980 the Independent Free Trade Union, Solidarity, was officially registered in Warsaw. This followed a period of bitter confrontation between such unions and the government. The demands of Solidarity included the right to form trade unions, the right to strike, and the right to effective freedom of media and speech (Staniszkis, 1981). The Independent Free Trade Union movement had effectively challenged the government and secured a constitutional position. This was short-lived. With the declaration of martial law in December 1981, the unions were disbanded and their leaders imprisoned.

The comparison between Poland and the USSR is impressive. Poland has had a history of greater assertiveness of rights against the government than in the USSR. Why is this the case?

CHART 17.2   *Legitimacy of state*

	Weak	Weak (Spain)	Strong USSR
Intermediate group	Weak	(Spain)	USSR
cohesion	Strong	Poland	(USA)

The context in which rights may be articulated may be analysed in terms of the legitimacy of the state and the strength of group cohesion (see Chart 17.2). By 'legitimacy' I refer here to sentiments of loyalty to the regime, to diffuse psychological orientations or supports. In the USSR legitimacy is strong: the Soviet state was secured by revolution, has fought and won a civil war and a world war. The 'mobilisation regime' was a peculiar mixture of industrial and social goals, traditional and charismatic authority (stemming from Tsarist Russia) and the evolving doctrine of Marxism-Leninism (cf. Rigby, 1982). In Poland, the state was created out of war and is associated with imposed Soviet rule. The Communist Party (PUWP), which has been the driving force and legitimating instrument of the Soviet mobilisation system, has not had widespread and deep support in Poland. The state has been weak. Poland has never had a strong charismatic leader comparable to the Tsar or Stalin. Traditional values manifested in nationalism and the Church have always been powerful. The economic crises of the 1970s and early 1980s further weakened its viability.

The 'rights' which people may seek to articulate must be related to the strength of group cohesion because the expression of rights requires political organization. In the USSR, intermediate groups are weak: the Church has little popular following; and the peasants are effectively contained in collective farms. In areas where national and religious intermediate groups are stronger, outside the Russian heartland, there is greater support for Western notions of individual rights. The Western based 'Soviet Area Audience and Opinion Unit' has found that Soviet citizens from the Baltic and Transcaucasian Republics 'are more favourably disposed to *samizdat* than people from other areas of the USSR'. People from these two areas, uniquely to the USSR, had 'positive views on the aspirations of the Polish strikers outnumbering those with negative views, and . . . these were the only areas to show positive scores' (Teague, 1983, pp. 5–6). In another similar study conducted in the USSR, positive attitudes to the Solidarity movement were recorded by only 23 per cent of Russians interviewed ($N = 487$), by 84 per cent of Jews ($N = 76$), and by 93 per cent of Baltic nationalities ($N = 14$); in terms of social background, positive responses were recorded by 21 per cent of workers ($N = 163$), 51 per cent of the 'humanitarian intelligentsia' ($N = 117$), 33 per cent of engineering-technical personnel ($N = 135$) and 8 per cent of leaders (*rukovoditeli*) ($N = 26$) (Puklov, 1981, p. 250). In Poland, intermediate groups – particularly the Church and the intelligentsia – have a long history as independent forces continuing the traditions of the Polish nation. The manual working class has evolved with a trade union movement in opposition to authority, and the peasantry successfully resisted collectivisation. Poland has a tradition of pluralism – if not of democratic government. Poland has always been greatly affected by European developments: it has had strong links with its neighbours Germany and Scandinavia. Its massive emigration between the wars has in turn strengthened personal ties with Western Europe and the United States. Russia, in contrast, has no tradition of pluralism and has always been more isolated geographically and intellectually from the West. As illustrated in Chart 17.2, the USSR has a strong state legitimacy and weak intermediate group cohesion. In Poland, the situation is reversed.

IV

The dynamic of human rights in the USSR is to be found in 'within system' changes rather than in the dissident movement. This is due not only to public sentiments, but to the power of the Soviet state. Rights claims articulated specifically against the state do not succeed. If individual rights are to be extended and secured they can only be achieved within – rather than against – existing institutions and procedures. In Poland, the state has been unable to meet the economistic expectations of the population and has remained illegitimate; rights have been perceived to be claims on the state. The Solidarity movement in Poland, the political reform movement associated with Dubcek in Czechoslovakia in 1968, the emergence of 'dissident' groups in the USSR, together with a tendency since Khrushchev towards greater legality by the political elites, and the claims of the 1977 Constitution, all point in different ways to the evolution of claims for civil rights under state socialism. It is true that the reform movement led to invasion, that Solidarity was crushed, that the dissident movement has witnessed many infringements of rights. The significance of these developments is that they are indicative of claims on the guardians of political power, of assertions by individual and group interests which the authorities ignore at the cost of political stability and social solidarity. These tendencies seem to me to indicate that civil rights are by no means a dead issue either in Marxism or in the politics of the socialist states. They are, however, only the sharp end of rights-claims. In a less dramatic and less publicised form in the West, individual civil rights may be given greater recognition by process of law, by an awareness of the rights-claims of citizens requiring the officers of state to perform their constitutional duty. It is in the evolution of a more rational legal system which explicitly recognises the duties of the state to meet rights, and the role of the individual in claiming them, that the realisation of human rights is likely to be achieved in the USSR. The articulation of such rights, however, lacks support in the traditional Russian political culture.

If I may speculate as to further developments, I would anticipate developments in Poland leading to further representation and incorporation of interests within the state to strengthen its legitimacy. In the Soviet Union, demands for the implementation of rights are likely to originate from interests already (weakly) established – regional/republican, professional, trade union, and party. With the greater maturation of the society, and given relative international security, interest-demands are likely to increase. Such demands in the assertion of 'rights' claims cannot be easily resolved in the fashion of an economic and political market exchange with the state, as in the West. The greater role of planning and of the government differentiates socialist societies from capitalist ones. Rights claims should not be limited to the particular experience and model of Western capitalist states: this is an ethnocentric and mistaken approach. In both the Soviet Union and Poland, legitimacy is sought by the party to define whose and which rights are fulfilled. This is a cardinal assumption on which the political system is organised and creates a fundamental dilemma for individual rights claims.

18

Worker Welfare Systems in Marxist-Leninist States: a Comparative Perspective

A. J. GROTH

Introduction

How significant are political regime characteristics for the determination of social welfare policies in the modern world? There has been considerable uncertainty in Western literature on social welfare with respect to the significance of 'politics' for welfare policy. In some cases, that significance has been discounted; in some, it has been treated rather ambiguously; and in some, it has been given considerable weight. Differences in findings appear to have been greatly influenced by the different conceptualizations of the research problem, i.e. what precisely was to be examined and how. On occasion, researchers have succumbed to the temptation to draw rather sweeping conclusions from patently limited empirical analyses. Thus, for example, Harold L. Wilensky in his widely cited study, *The Welfare State and Equality: Structural and Ideological Roots of Public Expenditures* (1975), concluded that 'Over the long pull, economic level is the root cause of welfare-state development . . .' (p. 47). Even Wilensky, however, took somewhat divergent positions on the impact of 'ideology' (pp. 42–3) and of political 'organization' (pp. 65–6) on welfare expenditures. He viewed the former as nil and the latter as, in fact, 'significant.'

In his earlier *Welfare Policy and Industrialization in Europe, America and Russia* (1971), Gaston Rimlinger argued that substantial social welfare programmes were compatible with different types of polity or economy. Thus, he observed that 'the need for a highly organized form of income protection increases as a society becomes more industrialized and urban-

Reprinted with adapations from *Coexistence*, vol. 19, no. 1 (April 1982) with the permission of author and publisher.

ized and this need is independent of the nature of the socio-economic order' (p. 334). He concluded that most of the countries spending in excess of 5 per cent of their GNP on social security were highly developed countries (ibid.).

In 1967, Henry Aaron took the view that 'the stage of economic development alone cannot explain why in the initiation of social security [programmes] both Portugal and the United States lagged behind Germany by fifty years' (see Eckstein, 1967, p. 17). Simultaneously, however, he attributed the generosity and cost of such programmes most significantly to chronology: the length of time that they had been in effect in any particular country. Contrary to Rimlinger, Aaron found that the 'very wealthy countries spend proportionately less on social security' (Eckstein, 1967, p.44). Taking note of the relatively 'narrow' and 'limited' American welfare programmes (Eckstein, p. 44), Aaron did not account for the obvious discrepancy between the very high level of economic development in the United States on the one hand, and the relatively low level of welfare development on the other. More recently, a number of scholars have suggested that much greater significance should be attached to political factors in the shaping of welfare policies among the nations (see, for instance, Leifried 1978; Castles and McKinlay, 1979; Leichter, 1979; Koff, 1980; Elling, 1980. Earlier work on the significance of 'political' versus 'environmental' factors in the making of public policy includes Cutright, 1965; Dye, 1966; Pryor, 1968; Cnudde and McCrone, 1969; Fry and Winters, 1970; Sullivan, 1972; King, 1973).

Hypothesis

The hypothesis of this study is that, holding the level of economic development constant, Marxist–Leninist states are likely to provide more substantial welfare benefits to industrial workers than world states generally. This hypothesis is predicated, in part, on the assumption that the ideology of Marxism–Leninism invests the working class with a particular, positive significance. Broadly speaking, the workers are seen as the backbone of the Marxist–Leninist revolution and social transformation: the most advanced, progressive, and revolutionary social class of the contemporary epoch.

The working class is seen as the principal base of support in the development of the newly emergent socialist states toward more advanced forms of socialism and communism. This 'development' involves heavy emphasis on industrial, technological, and scientific-cultural growth and change. It is aimed at the creation of conditions of material abundance, social self-discipline, and a transformation of the bourgeois-feudal class relations inherited from the pre-revolutionary society (see, for instance,

Wilcyznksi, 1972; Deber, 1980). In more immediate and instrumental terms, the working class sustains the efforts of its vanguard, the Marxist–Leninist ruling party. Ideologically, it may be viewed as the single most significant popular source for the party's 'shock troops' of revolution and social transformation. Thus, while the support of various, different, social classes (such as the peasantry or portions of the lower middle class) may be needed at various stages for the processes of political and social change advanced by the party, working class support is generally its most critical and unchanging requirement.

In the authoritative words of V. I. Lenin (1932, pp. 28–9):

> Only the proletariat – by virtue of its economic role in large scale production – is capable of leading *all* the toiling and exploited masses, who are exploited, oppressed, crushed by the bourgeoisie not less, and often more than the proletariat, but who are incapable of carrying on the struggle for their freedom independently.
> The doctrine of the class struggle . . . leads inevitably to the recognition of the *political rule* of the proletariat, of its dictatorship, i.e., of a power shared with none and relying directly upon the armed force of the masses.

And further:

> By educating a worker's party, Marxism educates the vanguard of the proletariat, capable of assuming power and of leading the whole people to Socialism, of directing and organizing the new order, of being the teacher, guide and leader of all the toiling and exploited in the task of building up their social life without the bourgeoisie and against the bourgeoisie.

The assumption here is not only that the workers are a particularly 'envalued' group in Marxist–Leninist ideology, but also that the political machinery of the Marxist–Leninist states safeguards the distribution of values in favour of 'workers'. Obviously not all social groups, including for example the self-employed, landowners, or former entrepreneurs, can be said to enjoy either the ideological value assigned to the 'working class' by Marxism–Leninism, or an equally favoured position of power in the Marxist states. Thus, welfare programmes for the non-industrial, non-worker sectors may indeed, as some authors have suggested, be considerably more austere and modest than the worker programmes (see, for instance, Madison, 1968, pp. 52, 62, 217, 218–19; also Groth, 1971, pp. 167–71).

Obviously under this assumption, a Wilensky-type indicator – total share of the GNP devoted to welfare programme – is certain *not* to reflect the full measure of welfare effort in any particular social sector among a group of countries.

Analysis

The method used here is to compare worker pensions and benefits in states belonging to a self-designated category, i.e., those led by Marxist–Leninist parties, with pensions and benefits offered to workers in a non-socialist 'comparison group'. The assumption is that the relative generosity of programmes can only be judged in relation to at least roughly equivalent total economic capabilities. The 'comparison-group', based on U.S.A.C.D.A. estimates, includes all states whose GNP per capita ranged in 1975 between the lowest ranking Marxist–Leninist member, the PRC, and the highest, Czechoslovakia. It thus includes a band of 59 states ranging from Italy at one extreme to Honduras at the other (for the full list, see Groth, 1982, pp. 49–50). Eleven Marxist–Leninist states are included in the study. Lack of adequate information prevented the inclusion of Mongolia, North Korea, and Vietnam.

The study focuses on two principal questions. First, how do the *minimal* provisions of worker pensions or benefits available in the 'socialist world' compare with the equivalent provisions in the comparison group? In other words, to what extent are the minimal provisions found anywhere among eleven socialist states matched by the 'comparison states'? Second, how do *averaged minimal* provisions of pension and benefits in the two sets of states compare with one another?

The chapter covers several kinds of benefits available to workers. These include benefits available to those who have sustained injury or become disabled at work, and may be ultimately returned to full or partial employment. It also includes permanent disability benefits, as well as the provision of medical care, family allowances, and maternity leaves. Finally, it examines certain aspects of retirement programmes and the question of direct costs borne by workers for the delivery of the available benefits.

Data

The principal source of information on the pension and welfare programmes available in the several countries in 1975 is *Social Security Programs Throughout the World, 1975*, published by the US Department of Health, Education and Welfare Social Security Administration (Washington: US Government Printing Office, December 1975).

There are five categories of welfare programmes surveyed by the HEW studies. These are: (1) old age, invalidity and death benefits; (2) sickness and maternity benefits; (3) work injury benefits; (4) unemployment compensation; and (5) family allowances.

The data of the HEW survey are based on legislation, implementing decrees and regulations in effect at the time of the study. One may legitimately raise questions about how such measures have been actually carried out by the administrative agencies of the various countries. The assumption of this chapter is to accord equal 'face-to-face' validity to all national programmes. It is readily acknowledged that this method may well understate the achievements of some states and overstate the shortcomings of others. The comparisons presented may, therefore, be more like rough approximations rather than mirror images of social conditions. It should also be noted that this study does not address the full scope of various benefits and conditions of workers' welfare programmes, clearly a subject of great complexity. What is presented here is a comparative account of but several major features of social insurance and welfare programmes in a number of countries in effect at the beginning of 1975 (see Tables 18.1 and 18.2). In many cases the information available is sketchy, or equivocal, from the perspective of a researcher who might wish to use rigorously quantitative methods of comparison. There are gaps and often some imprecise formulation of benefits and costs, and these must be borne in mind in subsequent analysis.

Findings

(a) *Temporary disability*. With respect to temporary disability, the lowest level of compensation among the socialist states was 60 per cent of the regular working wage, and a cash ceiling of 108 marks a day, paid in Czechoslovakia (1 mark = 8 US ¢ in 1975). It may be noted parenthetically that the minimum of the *poorest* Marxist state was actually 100 per cent of the regular wage – in the PRC. No other socialist state imposed a cash ceiling on temporary disability. Within the comparison group, however, 23 of 59 states (39 per cent) either imposed cash limits on amounts of temporary disability, or set the compensation below 60 per cent of the regular wage. These states included Algeria, Barbados, Taiwan, Costa Rica, Cyprus, Greece, Guinea, Iran, Iraq, Ireland, Ivory Coast, Jamaica, Jordan, Portugal, Philippines, Tunisia, Turkey, and Uruguay.

In terms of *averaged* minimal compensation available (where the information allows for comparison) the socialist countries substantially exceeded the 'comparison' group with 86.8 per cent of regular earnings, as opposed to only 68.3 per cent for the 'comparison states.'

(b) *Permanent disability*. Unlike the comparison group, all socialist states recognized the 'pension principle' for disabled workers. In the comparison group, 13 states (22 per cent) confined their social obligation to

TABLE 18.1 *Worker welfare programmes: Marxist-Leninist states, 1975*

Country	GNP/Cap.	Urban pop. (%)	Electrical energy per cap. (kWh)	Pop./bed	Pop./phys.	Min. Temporary Disab. Pension as % reg. wage	Min. Permanent Disab. Pension as % reg. wage	Charge for Med. Services to workers
Albania	536	34	0.72	150	800	95	80	None
Bulgaria	2263	59	3.16	118	476	90	55	None
Cuba	683	60	0.65	233	1153	70	55	None
Czechoslovakia	3655	67	4.02	99	432	60	60	None
GDR	3639	75	5.07	92	557	90	67	None
Hungary	2400	50	1.95	120	459	65	60	None
Poland	2438	54	2.87	129	592	100	90	None
Romania	2202	43	2.53	110	805	85	95	None
USSR	3629	60	4.11	86	363	100	90	None
Yugoslavia	1564	39	1.85	169	849	100	35	None*
PRC	318	24	n.a.	n.a.	n.a.	100	60	None†
Average	$2121	51.4	2.69 (10)	1/123.3 (10)	1/604.6 (10)	86.8	60.0	None

* Some regional variations in services.
† Hospital board paid only up to 80 per cent.

TABLE 18.1 (Contd.)

Country	Time limit on free med. services to workers	Family allowances	Length (days) paid maternity leave	Maternity pay as % wage	Age of eligible old age pensioners M	Age of eligible old age pensioners F	% of wage contr. to sick/mat. benefit	% of wage contr. to disab. pensions	% contr. to old age pension
Albania	None	Yes	84	75.0	60	55	None	None	None
Bulgaria	None	Yes	165	100.0	60	55	None	None	None
Cuba	None	Yes	84	100.0	60	55	None	None	None
Czechoslovakia	None	Yes	182	90.0	60	57	None	None	None
GDR	None	Yes	126	100.0	60	60	None	None	10.0
Hungary	None	Yes	140	100.0	60	55	None	None	3.0–10.0
Poland	None	Yes	112	100.0	60	60	None	None	1.2– 3.0
Romania	None	Yes	112	85.0	60	55	None	None	2.0
USSR	None	Yes	112	66.7	60	55	None	None	None
Yugoslavia	None	Yes	105	100.0	60	55	None	None	Up to 13.0
PRC	None	Yes	56	100.0	60	55	None	None	None
Average	None	All	106.5	92.4	60.8	55.8	None	None	5/11 Req W Contr.

Sources: as for Table 18.2.

injured workers to the payment of a basically one time lump sum benefit.

The lowest permanent disability pension in the socialist world was 55 per cent of regular earnings (Bulgaria and Cuba). This minimum was not matched by 26 of the 59 comparison states (44 per cent), either because of lower minimal rates, or because of lump sum compensation, or because absolute cash limits were placed on pensions paid to disabled workers. Such states included Algeria, Argentina, Barbados, Costa Rica, Dominican Republic, Taiwan, Cyprus, Gabon, Iran, Iraq, Ireland, Italy, Jamaica, Jordan, Philippines, Singapore, South Africa, Trinidad and Tobago, Thailand and Tunisia. In one case, Costa Rica, a ten year limit applied to disability pensions.

As for minimal average compensation in the two sets of states, the percentage of wage paid in permanent disability pensions calculable among 33 comparison states (56 per cent) was 75.8 per cent of the regular wage. This was a considerably higher figure than the 60.0 per cent of the wage averaged by all the Marxist–Leninist states. It may be pointed out, however, that in this case the Marxist–Leninist average was singularly anomalous because of the unusually low minimum of Yugoslavia's permanent disability pension: 35 per cent. Excluding Yugoslavia, the remaining 10 Marxist–Leninist states average 71.2 per cent of regular compensation, varying between a low of 55 per cent in Bulgaria and Cuba and a high of 95 per cent in Romania.

Taking into account free medical care benefits (see section (c)), it would appear that the programmes available to disabled workers in most of the Marxist–Leninist states were matched by only a very few of the comparison states.

(c) *Medical coverage.* With the exception of Yugoslavia, the socialist countries operated on the twin principles of (1) exacting no charge for medical services (as distinguished from, to be sure, the cost of medicines in at least some cases); and (2) placing no time limits on the duration of medical care connected with work-related sickness, injury, and maternity care. Among the comparison countries, however, the great majority either limited the duration of free medical treatment or required fees from the recipients. Such states included Brazil, Chile, Costa Rica, Iran, Ireland, Italy, Lebanon, Nicaragua, Panama, Peru, Portugal, Singapore, Spain, Turkey and Venezuela. Only 10 of the 59 comparison states (16.9 per cent) clearly conformed to the socialist pattern of completely free and unlimited medical care in connection with worker injury, sickness and maternity care treatment. These states included Argentina, Italy, Taiwan, Cyprus, Mexico, and Colombia. Seventeen comparison states, i.e. 29.0 per cent, offered no medical service benefits to their workers of any kind. Among the remaining comparison states, 19 (32.2 per cent) offered services for payment, and 13 (22.0 per cent) offered free medical services but imposed a time limit on the availability of such services.

A measure, however imperfect, of the quality of medical care available to workers in the socialist countries may be inferred from the following relationships. Ten of the eleven Marxist states averaged 130.0 persons per hospital bed in 1974, with the Soviet Union at 86 and Cuba at 233. (The PRC data were unavailable.) The comparison states averaged slightly over 440 persons per hospital bed (not counting Malaysia, where the ratio was 3392 persons per each hospital bed). Ten of eleven socialist states provided one physician for every 650 persons in the population. (PRC data were again unavailable.) The comparison group, however, claimed only one physician for each 2930 persons.

Somewhat less complete information indicates that the socialist states also maintained substantially, even drastically, higher ratios of dentists and nurses to population than did the most economically advanced members of the comparison group. Illustratively, the USSR provided one dentist for each of its 2524 inhabitants. Venezuela provided one for each 4066; Spain one for each 9833; South Africa one for each 13 722 persons; and Ireland one for each 4697. Aggregating the populations and dentists of all the socialist states, apart from Albania, Cuba and PRC (whose data were not available), an average emerged of one dentist for each 2750 persons in the population, well excess of the achievements of some of the most economically advanced members of the comparison group (see Table 18.2).

A calculation of the available nursing personnel in Bulgaria, Cuba, Czechoslovakia, Poland, Romania, Yugoslavia and the USSR yields analogous comparisons. The socialist states had a ratio of one nurse to 276 persons. This compared with only one nurse for 466 persons in South Africa; 508 in Venezuela; 6363 in Greece; 822 in Portugal; and 2192 persons per nurse in Iran. (See also life expectancy comparisons in section (f).)

(d) *Family allowances.* All eleven Marxist states provided some form of allowances to persons with children. Cuba provided such payments only for children of 'conscripted workers', China to persons with 'low incomes'. In the other cases the payments were related to number of children in the family: if there was more than one child in the home (Hungary); or if the child or children were under 15 or 16 (e.g., Bulgaria, GDR); with additional eligibility for older children who were also 'students' (Czechoslovakia, GDR;); or if there were several young children in the home (USSR). In contrast, however 31 of the 59 comparison states (i.e. 52.4 per cent) offered no family allowances or subsidies of any kind. These states included Barbados, Taiwan, Costa Rica, Cyprus, Iran, Jamaica, Nicaragua, Panama, Peru, Singapore, South Africa (to Africans), Syria, Trinidad and Tobago, Turkey and Venezuela.

(e) *Maternity benefits*: (1) *Pay scales.* Among the most generous provision in the socialist welfare systems were maternity benefits for working mothers. The principle of paid maternity leaves was recognized by only 47

TABLE 18.2 *Worker welfare programmes among the wealthiest states in comparison group, 1975*

Country	GNP/Cap.	Urban pop. %	Electrical energy per cap (kwh)	Pop./bed	Pop./physician	Min. temporary disab. pension as % reg. wage	Min. permanent disab. pension as % reg. wage	Charge for med. services to workers
Italy	3014	53	2.76	95	502	60.0	Cash limit	No
Gabon	2861	32	n.a.	98	5208	66.7*	100.0	No ben. prov.
Spain	2837	61	2.61	193	673	100.0	75.0	Yes
Ireland	2516	52	2.49	91	836	Cash limit	Cash limit	Yes
Singapore	2480	100	n.a.	271	1400	66.7	Lump sum	Yes
Greece	2380	65	1.70	158	499	Cash limit	60.0	Yes
Trinidad	2311	18	n.a.	218	2157	66.7	Lump sum	Yes
Venezuela	2047	74	1.74	339	866	66.7	66.7	No
Portugal	1827	26	1.22	169	851	33.0	66.7	No
Barbados	1617	4	n.a.	111	1500	75.0	75.0	No ben. prov.
Malta	1606	94	n.a.	96	988	Cash limit	Cash limit	No ben. prov.
Average	$2318	52.6	2.09 (6/11)	1/167.2	1/1407.3	66.85 (8/11)	73.9 (6/11)	3/11 No Charge

TABLE 18.2 (Contd.)

Country	Time limit on free med. services to workers	family allowances	Length (days) paid maternity leave	Maternity pay as % wage	Age of eligible old age pensions M	F	% of wage contr. to disab. pensions	% contr. to old age pension
Italy	None	Yes	217	80.0	60	55	0.15	6.65
Gabon	No ben. prov.	Yes	98	50.0	60	60	None	1.5
Spain	Yes	Yes	84	75.0	65	65	3.2	3-4.0
Ireland	None	Yes	84	Lump sum	70	70	None	Cash
Singapore	None	None	56	Cash limit	55	55	None	0-12.0
Greece	None	Yes	84	50.0	62	57	2.25-4.0	4.25
Trinidad	Yes	None	7	60.0	65	65	None	2.7
Venezuela	Yes	None	84	66.7	60	55	None	2-4.0
Portugal	Yes	Yes	60	100.0	65	62	None	5.5
Barbados	No ben. prov.	None	84	60.0	65	65	None	3.0
Malta	No ben. prov.	None	None spec.	None spec.	61	60	None	Cash
Average	No time limit 4/11	Yes 6/11	85.8 10/11	67.7 8/11	62.5	60.8	None	11/11 Contr. by workers

Sources for Tables 18.1 and 18.2:
1. GNP/capita figures from US Arms Control and Disarmament Agency, 1976.
2. Health and population figures, *US Statistical Yearbook*, 1976.
3. Welfare programme data from US Department of Health, Education and Welfare, *Social Security Programmes Throughout the World*, 1975.

of the 59 states, i.e. 79.7 per cent, of the comparison group. It was recognized, however, by all the socialist states. The lowest payable scale was 50 per cent of ordinary earnings for those workers with less than twelve months' prior employment – in Romania. This sum was paid for 112 days, 52 days before and 60 days after confinement. For Romanian workers employed for more than a year, 85 per cent of salary was the stipulated recompense. And for birth of a third child – regardless of work history – it was 94 per cent of the regular wage.

In contrast, one finds that the comparison group states included 10 which did not pay any maternity benefits to working mothers, and 2 which paid variable cash grants or lump sum payments rather than a fixed percentage of the wage. The 50 per cent minimum, which was, in fact, exceptional even in Romania, represented the norm for 6 comparison group states: Algeria, Costa Rica, Dominican Republic, Gabon, Ivory Coast, Morocco and Paraguay.

The proportion of the regular wage paid in maternity benefits among 47 comparison states was 65.3 per cent; this contrasted with 92.4 per cent among the Marxist–Leninist states.

Only 13 of the 49 comparison states (22 per cent) envisaged the payment of 100 per cent of salary to working mothers; but seven of the eleven socialist states (63.6 per cent) did so, while the remaining four (Albania, Czechoslovakia, Romania, USSR) provided minima of 75, 90, 85 and 66.7 per cent rates of compensation, respectively.

(2) *Leaves*. An even more extreme contrast is presented by the length of paid vacations given to working mothers. The shortest period among the Marxist states was in Cuba and Albania with a total of 84 days, 42 before and 42 after confinement. The longest was in Czechoslovakia with 182 days, 4 weeks before and 22 weeks after confinement. The shortest specified period in the comparison group was 7 days in Trinidad and Tobago, followed by 30 days in Tunisia, and 45 days in Taiwan. However, several countries, including Taiwan, Jamaica, Liberia, Malta and Syria, did not indicate any such leave periods. The average maternity leave among the eleven socialist states was 106.5 days, as compared with only 86.0 days in 47 comparison states where such a leave was actually granted and specified.

(f) *Old age pensions*: So far as retirement benefits were concerned, old age pensions were available to workers in all the socialist countries. The average age of eligibility was 60.8 years for men and 55.8 for women. On the other hand, 11 of 59 comparison states (18.6 per cent) did not provide old age pensions. Jordan, Malaysia, Singapore, Thailand, and Zambia, among others, paid lump sum benefits; Liberia had no general pension programme. The average age of eligibility in the 48 remaining comparison states was 60.3 years for men and 56.9 for women. On the whole, there-fore, eligibility was equally favourable for men as between the socialist states and the remainder of the comparison group. It was slightly more favourable in the Marxist–Leninist states for women.

Significantly, however, life expectancy at birth in the socialist states averaged approximately 69 years, with no state exceeding 71 and no state falling below 62 (PRC). On the other hand, the average life expectancy within the comparison group was 58.7 years, with a high of 72 years in Greece and a low of 41 in Nigeria.

The cash benefit provisions of old-age pensions were so complex in many countries that no percentage comparisons are feasible, or, at any rate, attempted in this chapter. While the basic principle of an old age pension for workers was universally accepted among the socialist countries but not among the comparison group, several comparison group countries provided inflation clauses in their old age pensions, generally lacking in the socialist systems. In at least a few cases, moreover, notably Uruguay, the maximum benefits appeared to exceed those available in any socialist state (Uruguay worker contributions, however, were also among the two or three highest in the world).

(g) *Worker contributions*. An issue of considerable importance to workers is what they must pay in order to earn their pension and welfare benefits. Save for Yugoslavia, workers in the socialist states did not pay either for disability pensions, temporary and permanent, or for sickness and maternity benefits. Among the socialist states, six of the eleven (Albania, Bulgaria, Cuba, Czechoslovakia, USSR, and PRC) did not exact any contributions from employees toward any of their pensions. For purposes of old age pensions, Poland collected between 1.2 and 1.3 per cent of the worker's wages; Hungary between 3 and 10 per cent; GDR 10 per cent; and Yugoslavia full cost up to 13 per cent of the wage. Romania collected 2 per cent.

Among the 42 comparison states which did offer workers medical services of any type, 19, i.e. 42.9 per cent, required worker contributions toward medical benefits, and these averaged 2.62 per cent of the workers' wages. Only 2 of the 59 comparison states (Guinea, Lebanon, i.e. 3.4 per cent of the group) paid an old age pension without requiring worker contributions, in contrast with 54.5 per cent of the Marxist–Leninist states. In 41 comparison states where such a percentage could be calculated, the averaged minimum worker contribution toward the old age pension was 3.8 per cent of the wage.

Conclusions

The findings of this chapter reflect not merely generally higher social welfare benefits among the socialist states – at generally lower direct cost to workers – but also more consistent, more homogeneous, levels of benefits among these states, as compared with their economic (GNP per capita) cohorts.

To begin with, this is illustrated most fundamentally by the acceptance of the pension principle among all the Marxist–Leninist states. Both in disability and old age cases, these states recognized a permanent social obligation to support the worker. This may be distinguished from a fairly prevalent practice in the comparison group of making various kinds of one-time grants to employees, whereupon they were presumably allowed to 'fend for themselves' by all sorts of private, family, or conceivably social charity arrangements. In some cases, comparison states had no compensation programmes at all. Altogether, 11 comparison group states offered no old age pensions, and 14 no permanent disability pensions to workers. In a few cases, as in Brazil, Cameroon and Gabon, very generous 100 per cent-of-wage disability pensions were paid.

With full allowance for the 'sharing of costs for some services' in some regions of socialist Yugoslavia, the eleven Marxist–Leninist states maintained a system of generally free and unlimited health care for injured and disabled workers which differed sharply from a veritable 'hodge-podge' of services, charges, and limitations found among the comparison states. In fact, only 10 of the 59 comparison states (16.9 per cent) adhered to the principle of free and unlimited medical care for disabled workers.

Likewise, all of the socialist states provided some form of family allowances. This policy, however, characterized fewer than half (47.6 per cent) of the comparison group countries. All of the Marxist–Leninist countries recognized the principle of regular maternity pay for workers, and set generally high standards of paid leave allowed and of the rate of remuneration. Many (10) comparison states did not even provide for any kind of maternity pay and the great majority that did provided distinctly shorter leaves and lower rates of pay. Above all, one finds great variability in maternity benefits within the comparison group: from a lump sum grant in Zambia to 100 per cent of regular pay in Argentina; from a 7 day leave in Trinidad and Tobago to a 217 day leave in Italy.

The principle of paying an old age pension to workers received wide acceptance within the comparison group, but even here, as noted earlier, several states (11) did not conform to it. Among those that did, qualifying conditions in terms of age closely approximated those in the socialist states. Life expectancy statistics, however, tended to undermine the value of such pensions in many countries, and again with greater variability in the comparison group than among the Marxist–Leninist states. Finally, with respect to worker costs in support of these various social welfare benefits, Yugoslavia, East Germany and to a lesser degree Hungary represented significant deviations from the pattern of the remaining 8 Marxist–Leninist regimes. That pattern was one of no cost, or very low cost, to the worker. In fact, however, even in this relatively most 'deviant' area of performance for the socialist states, the variation in costs was greater still within the comparison states ranging from nil in Guinea to 15 per cent in Uruguay. While a majority of Marxist–Leninist states exacted no contributions from employees, the overwhelming majority of the comparison states (all but two) did.

The above conclusions are both reinforced and illustrated by a comparison of Tables 18.1 and 18.2. Here we may compare the eleven Marxist–Leninist regimes not against all 59 comparison states but only against the eleven wealthiest ones among them. These eleven states actually had a somewhat higher average GNP per capita than the Marxist–Leninist states, and also a slightly higher ratio of urban to rural population. Yet, the 11 wealthiest comparison states clearly lagged behind the socialist countries in terms of most calculable average benefits, qualifying conditions, and costs to workers. Beyond the immediate subject of this chapter, what is suggested here is that the salience of politics for policy ought not to be underestimated (cf. Kautsky, 1968, p. 216, who argues that 'Communism' as a 'descriptive, analytical category . . . has become useless'. For further discussion, see Groth and Wade, 1973; Kushman *et al.*, 1980; and Groth and Hunt, 1985).

19

Does Socialism mean Greater Equality? A Comparison of East and West along Several Major Dimensions

JOHN M. ECHOLS III

If one word can be said to be associated with 'socialism', that word would most likely be 'equality' (Lukes, 1975, p. 74). This is not to say that socialism promises full equality. Even Marx's vision of communism does not foresee that result. All invidious distinctions would end, but complete leveling – in an age where each receives according to need – would be patently absurd. However, the promise of greater equality than one finds in, say, a capitalist order, is definitely present.

But what actually happens with respect to inequality in socialist societies? We know it is not by any means eradicated. Particularly since the publication of Milovan Djilas's *The New Class* (1957), study upon study has noted the persistence of significant inequalities and stratification in socialist societies (see, for instance, Lane, 1971; Parkin, 1971). But what about the comparative question? Are these inequalities at least significantly below those that pertain in societies not ruled by socialist administrations?

Scholars have begun to address this question as well. However, analysts have generally focused their attention on only one dimension of inequality – the distribution of well-being by class. There are other, perhaps equally important aspects of inequality (for example, racial/ethnic, regional, sexual, and urban/rural differences). In this chapter I examine those other aspects, and analyze the extent to which socialist administrations have treated various dimensions differently, promoting greater equality in some areas – i.e., class–than in others.

Reprinted with adaptations from the *American Journal of Political Science*, vol. 25, no. 1 (February 1981) with the permission of author's executor and publisher.

TABLE 19.1   *Income distribution by quintile, the United States and Czechoslovakia (percentages)*

	US 1929	US 1959	Czech. 1930	Czech. 1965
Lowest Fifth	5.4	4.0	2.5	6.3
Second Fifth	10.1	10.9	8.5	14.0
Third Fifth	14.4	17.0	16.0	19.7
Fourth Fifth	18.8	23.4	26.0	25.6
Highest Fifth	51.3	44.7	47.0	34.4

Sources: Kolko, 1964, p. 14; Krejci, 1972, p. 26.

In the extensive literature concerning the distribution of economic well-being by income or occupational class, scholars have concluded that socialist societies are more egalitarian than are Western democracies (see Wiles, 1974, 1975; Wiles and Markowski, 1971; Pryor, 1971, 1972; Chenery *et al.*, 1974, ch. 1; Schnitzer, 1974; and Krejci, 1976, ch. 2). The impact of a socialist regime can perhaps be best illustrated with prerevolutionary and postrevolutionary data. Table 19.1 presents data on income distribution by quintiles for the United States and Czechoslovakia; as is evident from the table, the Czechs were highly unequal in the 1930s, an approximate match for the United States. However, by 1965, they had made remarkable absolute and relative progress. The highest stratum has had its share reduced considerably, and the benefits of that redistribution have been spread out across the remaining strata.

Scholars explain these findings by stressing the impact of the takeover of power by a new elite committed ideologically to the reduction of inequalities. The economy is socialized, with the new leadership consolidating control over the important economic levers. Power and property are expropriated from the old owners and managers, and it is the new elite, not the old bourgeoisie, that sets the economic parameters – wages, prices, profit levels, taxes, bonuses, etc. – that determine the distribution of well-being in the society. The result is a redistribution of income and other benefits in favor of the lower classes. While a new elite, perhaps even a 'new class', is created in the process, with greater privileges in nearly every area of well-being (Matthews, 1978), the differences across income strata are generally less than what is found in comparable non-socialist systems.

There are similar differences in the distribution of powerful political positions in the Soviet Union and Eastern Europe. With respect to class, for instance, it is accepted by virtually every scholar that lower-class standing is not nearly the barrier to high political office in these countries that it is in the West (for example, see Nagle, 1977, pp. 157, 241; and Connor, 1979, pp. 165–7). Coming from a worker or peasant family, in fact, can occasionally be a boon in a socialist country. Although children of elite members are much more likely to get to the top than are children of peasants, the correlation is not nearly as strong as it is in the West. Thus, with respect to class inequalities, socialist administrations have tended to have their predicted impact. But what about the economic and political status of women, minorities, the rural sector, or different regions of the country? Have inequalities been reduced for them as well, or has the egalitarian thrust of a socialist regime only had an impact on the class dimension?

On the face of it, we would expect a similar impact in these other areas. Socialist literature argues emphatically that differences, for example, between the sexes or across nationalities would 'vanish still faster' under 'the supremacy of the proletariat' (Marx, 1954, p. 51; also see *Fundamentals of Marxism-Leninism*, 1963, p. 544; Mao, 1966, p. 297; Engels, 1978). As in the case of class, the argument is in large part that the revolution would usher into power a new group, representatives of 'the dictatorship of the proletariat'. We shall examine the extent to which such a comparative reduction in inequality has occurred. Each of the four other dimensions will be analyzed in turn, focusing first on economic, then on political inequality.

Women, work, and income – east and west

A socialist revolution, its leadership argues, puts 'an end to the inequality of women' (*Fundamentals of Marxism-Leninism*, 1963, p. 544). In some ways, that claim is justified: women's educational levels and participation in the work-force have advanced far beyond prerevolutionary levels and well past comparable figures in the West (this is one dimension where comparative work has been done – see Galenson, 1973, p. 85 and Wolchik, 1978, pp. 4–10).

However, while these longitudinal and cross-national patterns seem impressive, they do not result in any greater economic standing for women in the Soviet Union and Eastern Europe than we find in the West. The key indicator is earnings, and, as the data in Table 19.2 indicate, the ratio of female to male income is remarkably similar, East and West. In some Western nations (Britain and the United States, for example) women earn significantly less, but in others (Scandinavia) they earn more; overall, differences with socialist systems cannot be detected.

How can this be explained, given the higher levels of education and greater concentration of women in professional positions in Eastern Europe? With respect to education, women very often obtain jobs not commensurate with their qualifications. In addition, female students tend distinctly to be concentrated in certain fields, and upon graduation they are generally placed in 'female' sectors (which include many of the professions). These sectors are invariably less remunerative than other sectors of the economy (Chapman, 1977; Wolchik, 1978, pp. 11–14). Moreover,

TABLE 19.2   *Women's earnings as a percentage of men's, overall and for selected occupational categories, Eastern and Western Europe*

Country	Year	Percentages		
		All activities	Manual	Other
Belgium	1965	59	60	
Denmark	1965		67	
Unskilled workers	mid–1960s			82
France	1965	65	65	
Higher managerial	1964			64
West Germany	1965	60	63	
Higher managerial	1965			78
Netherlands	1965	60	61	
Norway	1965		70	
Manufacturing	1969			74
Sweden	1965		71	
	1968		79	
Switzerland	1964	63		
Salaried	1964			68
United Kingdom	1965	50	48	
Higher managerial	1960			56
Czechoslovakia	1966	66		
Skilled	1966			72
Hungary	1959	66	64	
Employees	1959			62
Managers, engineers, technicians	1959			75
Poland	1957–1962		62	
Non-manual	1957–1962			65
Soviet Union	1963	65		

Sources: United Nations, 1967, ch. 8, pp. 35, 36; ch. 5, pp. 25, 26; Galenson, 1973, pp. 55, 57, 77; Krejci, 1972, p. 65; Swafford, 1978, p. 660.

within both the feminized and non-feminized sectors, women are heavily concentrated at the bottom. For example, although women make up nearly 80 per cent of all practicing physicians in the Soviet Union, they are woefully under-represented at the top. In 1964, for example, there were only four women out of a membership of 104 in the very prestigious Academy of Medical Science. In other words, 4 per cent at the top of a profession that is 80 per cent female (Galenson, 1973, p. 93). Thus, even within feminized sectors, women earn much less, again around two-thirds of what men command (Wolchik, 1978, p. 13). In other sectors, the story is the same – women controlling around 3 to 5 per cent of the leading positions, also equivalent to corresponding Western figures (Wolchik, 1978, p. 14), but earning 60 to 70 per cent of the average wage for men (Table 19.2).

Thus, the economic status of women in the East does not differ significantly from that in the economic hierarchy. The overall gaps, in fact, are not even as different as we found for class inequalities. In terms of the most important indicators of status in the economy (and polity, as we will note in a later section), women have only achieved approximately what they 'enjoy' in the West. Thus, women do not have an equal status with the working class. Before we attempt to elaborate and explain this distinction and note its implications, let us examine the other dimensions.

Regional development

The Soviet Union is very proud of its record of development in Central Asia. In many ways, that pride is justified, as on numerous indicators the Soviet transformation of that area has been impressive (see, for instance, Nove and Newth, 1967). However, to note an obvious but important point, growth and equality are different issues. While Central Asia has been growing, so has the rest of the Soviet Union. As a result, large inequalities persist. Compared with the United States and Western Europe these inequalities do not present a progressive picture (Table 19.3).

Socialist nations have not provided greater regional economic equality than is evident in capitalist systems. What is more, the trends are not favorable for socialist economies; the explanation is not simply that we have picked unusual years, or that with time the socialist record will look comparatively better.

Indeed, the greatest impact of these socialist gains seems to have come in the early years of these regimes. In the Soviet Union and Poland, for

TABLE 19.3 *Coefficients of variation* * for regional per capita personal income, east and west*

Country	Year	CV	Country	Year	CV
United States	1957	0.23	Soviet Union	1958	0.24
	1967	0.17		1968	0.36
	1973	0.14		1972	0.28
Canada	1956	0.27	Poland	1956	0.23
	1972	0.20		1961	0.20
Australia	1956	0.08		1965	0.24
	1970	0.09	Yugoslavia[†]	1952	0.52
Japan	1958	0.27		1971	0.51
	1968	0.25			
West Germany	1960	0.14			
	1970	0.11			

* The coefficient of variation is the standard deviation over the mean.
† These data are for the six republics. If Serbia is divided into Serbia proper, Kosovo, and Vojvodina, the difference in the coefficients is imperceptible (no change for 1952; 53 for 1971).

Sources: Wiley, 1975; Kruczale, 1970, p. 126; Kuklinski, 1967, p. 54; Leszczycki, 1970, p. 22; Lang, 1975, p. 314; US Bureau of the Census, 1959, p. 311; 1969, p. 319; 1974, p. 730; Urquhart and Buckley, 1965, p. 134; Statistics Canada, 1973, p. 858; Archer, 1965, p. 40; Maxwell, 1971, p. 263; *Japanese Economic Yearbook*, 1963, p. 85; 1968, p. 286; *Statistiches Bundesamt*, 1966, p. 550; 1973, p. 526.

example, money was poured into the backward regions in the 1920s and 1950s, respectively (Sheehy, 1972, pp. 556–7). However, the redistribution ended, in part because of complaints from the better-off republics (Davies, 1958, p. 310). But the bigger reason seems to be concern over economic growth, which takes precedence over regional leveling (Kuklinski, 1970, p. 272). Leonid Brezhnev's argument that 'the task of equalizing – is basically resolved' (*Pravda*, 22 December 1972, p. 5) is thus remarkable since the Soviet Union, and other communist nations, are a long way from fulfilling that task. They are, in fact, even further away than are many Western nations.

Racial and ethnic inequalities

In the Soviet Union and Eastern Europe, racial and ethnic cleavages are closely tied to regional divisions, since most important minorities are territorially concentrated. The regional data just presented, then, suggest that inequalities across racial and ethnic groups are also severe. This is, in fact, the case. Indeed, the status of minorities under socialism seems quite comparable to the status of their counterparts in the West.

In order to demonstrate this, we need to uncover comparable cleavages – not an easy task. While it is not difficult, for instance, to define 'women' comparatively, it is harder to establish comparable systems of racial and ethnic cleavages, especially when there are so many to choose from. The solution offered here is to select what seem to be the most important cleavages in the Soviet Union and Eastern Europe, i.e., the ones most salient to the leadership. We will match patterns and trends of inequalities on these cleavages with comparable cleavages in the West, comparable in terms of their salience and intensity, and in terms of the size and positioning of the various groups in society.

The three that seem to be most important in Eastern Europe and the Soviet Union are (1) the division between Russians and Central Asians in the Soviet Union, (2) the multi-ethnic divisions in Yugoslavia, and (3) the Czech/Slovak split in Czechoslovakia. If these are not the most important, they are certainly close to it, and should provide reasonable test cases.

There are several important dimensions to the Central Asian-Russian cleavages: (1) the division is both racial and ethnic, i.e., it involves clear physical and cultural differences; (2) there are sharp religious and linguistic differences; (3) the proportion of Central Asians in the Soviet population is small (8 per cent) but growing; (4) Central Asians have their own territorial units; and (5) Central Asians are predominantly rural based.

The Western cleavage that matches this set of characteristics best is the Maori/European cleavage in New Zealand. While the Maori do not hold territorial units of their own, they are racially, culturally, and until re-

TABLE 19.4 *Racial income comparisons, the Soviet Union, United States, and New Zealand*

Country	Ratio	Year	Measure	Income ratio*
Soviet Union	Tadzhikstan/ RSFSR[†]	1958	% Disposable Income	0.61
		1964		0.55
		1969		0.51
	Turkmenistan/ RSFSR	1965	% National income (produced)	0.77
		1975		0.40
	Uzbekistan/RSFSR	1966	Gross domestic product	0.73
United States	Black/White	1959	Family income	0.52
		1970		0.61
		1975		0.62
		1973		0.56
New Zealand	Maori/European	1951	% Income median male income	0.78
		1961		0.81
		1971		0.86

* We are using ratios rather than absolute measures because the former are more directly and meaningfully comparable.

[†] Since regional data are being employed (those are all that are available), we are using only the three Central Asian republics that have a much smaller proportion of non-natives in order to reduce that intervening effect. In all cases, of course, the inequality it still understated, because the indigenous nationalities are worse off than the republic as a whole.

Sources: Holubnychy, 1968 (or derived from his measure, using various Soviet statistical yearbooks); Schroeder, 1973, p. 191; Radio Liberty, 1976, p. 2; Koropeckyj, 1975, p. 316; US Bureau of the Census, various years; Grove, 1978, p. 186.

cently, linguistically quite distinct. Their proportion of the population is both growing and equal to the share of the population held by Central Asians in the Soviet Union. Finally, they are rural based, relative to the dominant population, in proportions similar to the Central Asians in the Soviet Union.

We shall also look at the black/white cleavage in the United States. That cleavage lacks the religious and linguistic distinctiveness, as well as the territorial and greater rural concentration of the Central Asian case. However, these differences with the Soviet cleavage, which should make equalization easier in the United States, can be said to be counterbalanced by the tradition of slavery and higher visibility of the American cleavage. (Paul Hollander [1973, p. 345] makes these points in his argument that a comparison of the treatment of these groups is a legitimate exercise.)

In Table 19.4, we present various measures of income differences for the three sets of pairs, Russians and Central Asians, whites and blacks, and Europeans and Maoris. The data that are most clearly comparable are per capita income for the United States and per capita disposable income for the Soviet Union (presented for Tadzhikstan as an illustrative case).

The other data for the Soviet Union only serve to confirm the picture presented with the disposable income – Central Asians lag considerably behind Russians in income. Indeed, we should note that the differences in the Soviet Union are even more pronounced than these data show, because republic data include many non-Central Asians, who, on the whole, are much better off than the indigenous population. Thus, it seems fair to conclude that black/white and Maori/European income differences are no greater and, in the case of New Zealand, substantially smaller, than what we find across races in the Soviet Union. In addition, as is evident in Table 19.4, the Soviet differences are growing steadily worse (on this trend, also see Holubnychy, 1968, and Koropeckyj, 1975), a pattern that is not evident in the United States, at least until very recently, or New Zealand.

Turning to the Czechoslovak case, Canada and Great Britain provide the best comparative cases for the Czech/Slovak division; both Western nations also have significant, ethnically distinct minority groups (the French, the Welsh, and the Scots) that have been pushing hard for greater autonomy and more equal shares of the various pies. As the data in Table 19.5 demonstrate, these cleavages are similar with respect to income differences as well. In all three cases, the differences have been declining over the years. This trend (with a longer time-series) is more pronounced in Czechoslovakia, but the cross-sectional comparisons favor the West.

TABLE 19.5   *Ethnic inequalities in income, Czechoslovakia, Canada, and Great Britain*

Country	Groups	Year	Measure	Income ratio
Czechoslovakia	Slovakia/ Czech lands	1948	% Material national income ('produced')	0.60
		1968		0.80
Great Britain	Scotland/ England	1966	Gross domestic product	0.86
		1972		0.89
		1959	Net personal income	0.80
		1972		0.78
	Wales/England	1959		0.76
		1972		0.86
Canada	French/English	1961	Mean income of males	0.80
		1971		0.86
	Quebec/Canada	1956	Personal income	0.85
		1971		0.89

Sources: Krejci, 1972, p. 30; Central Statistical Office, 1965, p. 41; 1974, p. 136; 1975, pp. 25, 183; Grove, 1978, p. 186; Urquhart and Buckley, 1965, p. 134; Statistics Canada, 1973, pp. 209, 858.

The conclusion that can be drawn from these data, then, is that important differences across the three systems are not at all apparent.

The key characteristic of the divisions in Yugoslavia are (1) they are intensely felt, especially the Serb/Croat split; (2) they include cultural, religious, and linguistic differences; (3) they are generally territorially based, in the context of a federal system; (4) no one group holds a numerical majority; and (5) there are several groups involved.

There are two cases in the West, Belgium and Switzerland, that match, respectively, characteristics four and three (and these, it could be argued, are the most important ones). The Flemish/Walloon division in Belgium is, to say the least, intensely felt; it encompasses cultural, religious, and linguistic differences; it is territorially based in a federal system; and the population division is close enough to argue that one group is not, for practical purposes, numerically dominant. The major difference with Yugoslavia is that only two groups are involved. In that sense, though, it might be suggested that it matches the Serb/Croat division. The Swiss case also fails to match with respect to the number of groups involved (three – or four, if the Grisons are included – as opposed to Yugoslavia's eight). But the Swiss ethnic divisions are comparable to the Yugoslav case in several very important ways: they are intensely felt, territorially based, and encompass linguistic, cultural, and religious differences.

One reason Yugoslavia is so divided is the tremendous disparities in economic well-being across the ethnic regions. As the data in Table 19.6 illustrate, these disparities have not been declining; if anything, they have become worse, in large part because the government has failed to intervene significantly to attempt to assist the backward regions. The Swiss and Belgian cases show much greater equality than we find in Yugoslavia; leaving these gaps largely to the operation of the market has worked out well in the Western countries, but not in Yugoslavia. Whatever the cause for the progressive picture in Belgium and Switzerland, it is clear that Yugoslavia certainly shows no greater record of success in regional equalization than its two Western counterparts.

Thus, an examination of three of the most important ethnic and racial cleavages in Eastern Europe and the Soviet Union has turned up no case in which the patterns of inequality are substantially more progressive than what we find for comparable Western cases. As with the other dimensions, the socialist nations demonstrate no greater equalization than is evident in the West; in some instances, in fact, they seem to provide less. Our final dimension, however, will provide a break in this pattern.

Urban/rural differences

A perusal of the relevant literature in socialist countries suggests that, next to class inequality, the dimension of greatest concern to the leadership is

TABLE 19.6   *Ethnic inequalities in income, Yugoslavia, Switzerland, and Belgium*

Country	Groups	Year	Measure	Income ratio
Yugoslavia	Macedonia/ Yugoslavia	1952	% National income	0.64
		1971		0.64
	Montenegro/ Yugoslavia	1952		0.55
		1971		0.59
	Bosnia-Herc./ Yugoslavia	1952		0.76
		1971		0.66
	Kosovo/ Yugoslavia	1952		0.44
		1971		0.33
Switzerland	French/German Cantons	1966	% National income	1.18
	Ticino (Italian)/ German Cantons			0.95
Belgium	Flemish/ Walloons	1964	Revenue per inhabitant	0.95
		1974		1.03

Sources: Lang, 1975, p. 314; Gretler and Mandl, 1973, p. 151; Grove, 1978, p. 186.

the urban/rural division – the lesser status of the 'rural proletariat' (for example, see Schram, 1963, ch. 4). To what extent has that concern been translated into significant reductions in differences in well-being between city and countryside? The data in Tables 19.7 and 19.8 suggest that there has been substantial translation. Both cross-sectional and longitudinal comparisons point to a substantially more egalitarian distribution of earnings in socialist nations.

Inequality in the political sphere

Thus, we have found that there *is* differentiation across dimensions of economic inequality in comparison with Western patterns and trends. A significant cross-system distinction is only apparent with respect to class inequalities (with special emphasis on the urban working class, but also including the rural sectors). Further evidence for this differentiation by dimensions can be provided by analyzing the distribution of powerful political positions in the Soviet Union and Eastern Europe.

As noted in the introduction, working-class and peasant representation in the political elite is substantially greater in the socialist countries than in the West. Once again, however, this cross-system contrast disappears when we examine other cleavages. Women, for instance, or racial and

TABLE 19.7 *Earnings of male wage-earners in agriculture as a percentage of corresponding earnings in manufacturing (Western Europe)*

Country	1954 (%)	1964 (%)
Denmark	60	63
West Germany	67	75
Italy	60	57
Netherlands	88	88
Norway	71	68
Sweden	68	73
Switzerland	47	55
United Kingdom	69	66

Source: United Nations, 1967, ch. 5, p. 16.

TABLE 19.8 *Average monthly earnings in the state sector of agriculture as a percentage of average earnings in industry (Eastern Europe and the Soviet Union)*

Country	1950 (%)	1955 (%)	1964 (%)	1976 (%)
Bulgaria	78	78	85	95
Czechoslovakia	66	70	82	95
East Germany		78	87	94
Hungary	56	76	84	98
Poland	64	70	76	86
Soviet Union		61	70	79

Sources: United Nations, 1967, ch. 8, p. 29; *Soviet Ekonomicheskoi Vzaimopomoshchi*, 1977.

ethnic minorities, do not receive a higher share of important offices than their counterparts hold in the West.

With respect to sex, high politics in socialist countries is almost totally a man's world. In the early 1970s, only four of the countries of Eastern Europe and the Soviet Union had even one woman on their ruling Politburos (Jancar, 1974a, p. 231). The USSR has had only one in its history – Madame Furtseva, who was also the only female minister in recent times. Barbara Jancar (1971, p. 234) calculates that of 416 possible high government positions in the Soviet Union and Eastern Europe, only 13, or 3 per cent, are filled by women. Moreover, what women there are at the top (or any level, for that matter) are heavily concentrated in 'women's' fields such as culture and propaganda. Women are not found in charge of heavy industry.

This is not to say, however, that the communist record, dismal as it is, lags behind the West; we do every bit as poorly. Germany did not have its first female minister until 1965. The Swiss have barely given women the vote, much less high office. The point is that women do not do well politically in virtually any society. Robert Putnam, for example, examined

Western legislatures and socialist central committees, and found (with the significant exception of Scandinavia) remarkable similarities in female representation – between 5 and 10 per cent in virtually every case. His selection included only the Soviet Union and China for socialist states; however, data for central committees in Eastern Europe confirm the ubiquity of his findings (Wolchik 1978, p. 21). The females who are on the central committees, moreover, are much less likely than the men to be party members and government officials, they are more likely to be collective farmers, doctors, and teachers. These women, in addition, have a substantially higher turnover rate than men. Even if power did exist in these bodies, women are not around long enough to acquire any of it. Instead, their service is primarily symbolic.

We find the same comparative patterns with respect to minorities. There is little to choose, East and West, in terms of political representation for the sets of comparable cleavages we employed above for income comparisons. In two of our comparisons, the cleavages are generally accounted for in the leading political bodies of various countries, and socialist polities do not demonstrate any *greater* propensity for equality than their Western counterparts. The proportion of Slovaks, French, Welsh, and Scots in the national legislatures and cabinets (or their Czech equivalents), relative to their proportion in the population, are at least about equal. The same picture is evident for Yugoslavia, Switzerland, and Belgium. In fact, concern for fair representation (even over-representation) of the various minorities in all three of these societies is exceedingly strong (see, for example, Shoup, 1968; Girod, 1974; Bertsch, 1977; and Heisler, 1977).

Racial minorities in the Soviet Union, the United States, and New Zealand are under-represented in virtually all the important political bodies. In all three countries, although there seems to be a trend towards greater proportionality in the Soviet Union and the United States, the percentage of minority-held positions is still far below the percentage of minorities in the total population (see Table 19.9). Similarly small percentages make it to the top in the Soviet Union as well as the Western nations. In fact, in the middle 1960s, in a Soviet hierarchy of nearly 100 members constituting the Politburo, Secretariat and Council of Ministers, there was not a single Central Asian, even though they make up 8 per cent of the population. Of course, the picture in the West is not any better – only in the last ten to 15 years have blacks in the United States begun to receive any representation at the top. But *comparatively*, their status is no worse than that of Central Asians.

TABLE 19.9 *Minority representation in the Legislature, Cabinet, and Bureaucracy, the Soviet Union, United States, and New Zealand*

Country and group	Body	Year	Proportion, members to population
Soviet Union	Politburo and	1962	0
Central Asians*	Secretariat[†]	1976	0.46
	Central Committee[‡]	1956	0.81
		1972	0.67
	Communist Party	1973	0.58
	Council of Ministers	1966	0
United States	Cabinet	1964	0
Blacks			
		1976	1.51
	House of Representatives	1964	0.12
		1976	0.32
	Senate	1964	0
		1976	0.09
	Federal Bureaucracy 'Supergrades'	1974	0.17
New Zealand Maoris	Cabinet	1965	0
		1975	1.26
	Parliament	1965	0.63
		1975	0.63

* Central Asians include Kazakhs, Uzbeks, Tadjiks, Turkmeni, and Kirghiz.

[†] The Politburo and Secretariat, the two most powerful bodies, constitute the Soviet equivalent of the Western Cabinet. The data include full members only.

[‡] The Central Committee data include candidate members; that was the way they were reported.

Sources: Brzezinski and Huntington, 1963, p. 133; Duevel, 1976, p. 2; Donaldson and Waller, 1970, p. 34; Donaldson, 1972, p. 387; Rakowska-Harmstone, 1974, p. 5; *Congressional Quarterly Almanac*, selected years; Grove, 1978, p. 182; *Europa Yearbook*, 1976; Department of Statistics, 1966, 1976.

Are China and Cuba exceptions?

Thus far, only the Soviet Union and Eastern Europe have been used to exemplify socialism. But are there similar patterns and trends in Cuban and Chinese socialism?

Though the data are not as complete as for the Soviet and Eastern European cases, there does seem to be significantly greater equality in these countries with respect to class cleavages. Wage differentials, for example, have been reduced to levels generally below what is found in comparable, non-socialist societies (Whyte, 1975; Blecher, 1976; Mesa-Lago and Hernandez, 1976). On some other aspects as well, such as education and political representation, lower-class background is not nearly the barrier that it is in alternative systems (Whyte, 1975).

However, in the other areas of inequality, change is less evident. Chinese women have been freed of many legal restraints, educated, and brought into the labor force, but progress again stops well short of equality. Women are virtually invisible in the high positions of the economy. Indeed, in China, they hold far fewer top positions than they do even in the Soviet Union (Richman, 1969, pp. 302–5). Earnings data are scarce, but women in Chinese communes can only average two-thirds of male earnings; their scale is set at that level because, it is argued, they cannot 'work as hard' (Curtin, 1975, pp. 66–7).

In politics, the story is the same. Women currently constitute only 12.8 per cent of the Chinese Communist Party Central Committee (Seymour, 1976, p. 233; also see Chao, 1978, p. 169). In Cuba, even the largely symbolic National Assembly has only 22 per cent female representation (Mesa-Lago, 1978, pp. 80–1), and there were no women at all in 1977 on the Central Executive Committee of Ministerial Advisers (Dominguez, 1978). Even during the Chinese Cultural Revolution (when class differences were under sharp attack), one district singled out for special praise for its number of women in power had only 10 per cent female representation on its Revolutionary Committee (Curtin, 1975, p. 74). At the very top, women are rarely seen, and those that are are wives of prominent leaders.

Improvements in the status of minorities in these two countries also lags considerably behind progress on class cleavages. In Cuba, a great deal has been done with respect to discrimination and segregation, but not, to any substantial degree, political and economical inequality. Several commentators have noted the persistence – even at levels that held before the revolution – of sharp black/white differentials in the polity and the economy (Amara and Mesa-Lago, 1971, p. 351; Nicholson, 1974, p. 109; Dominguez, 1978, pp. 226ff). Even though, for example, blacks constitute between 30 and 40 per cent of the population, in the mid-1960s they did not hold either of the top two positions in any of Cuba's 17 ministries (Amaro and Mesa-Lago, 1971, p. 351). Further, their percentage of the 1965 Central Committee (9 per cent) was no higher than their share of the legislature in 1945 (Dominguez, 1978, p. 226).

In China, there have been programs and money directed explicitly at minority populations (Echols, 1975; Lardy, 1975). However, social and economic development gaps remain substantial and in some cases staggering, well above inequalities in other countries (Lardy, 1975; Lampton, 1978; Howe, 1978, p. 188). Moreover, political representation of minorities has proceeded at a very slow pace. Their numbers in important political bodies, relative to their share of the Chinese population, has only very recently begun to approach the low levels of power held by racial minorities in the West and the Soviet Union (Waller, 1973, pp. 174–5; Dreyer, 1976, pp. 233, 248).

Thus, what evidence we have suggests that it is, again, on the class dimension alone that significant effects appear. Improvements in the status of women and minorities, though clearly noticeable in many areas, especially in the early years of the new regime, have not received nearly the attention that class inequalities have (on this point, see also Radosh, 1976, pp. 96–101).

Summary and explanations of findings

Socialist revolutions (or takeovers), at least those led by undeniably Marxist-Leninist parties (Huntington, 1968, pp. 336ff), have as one major goal the beginnings, at least, of the eradication of invidious societal inequalities. In the early years of the new administrations, substantial progress is often made towards this end.

Yet across the initial wave of egalitarian transformation, important differences emerge. It becomes clear that not all cleavages receive equal treatment – some dimensions, to borrow from Orwell, walk on two legs. Specifically, it is *class* inequalities that are reduced to levels significantly below what we find in the West. There is greater opportunity to rise in the political sphere (again, see Connor, 1979) and significantly less inequality in income (for example, Wiles, 1974). However, progress on other inequalities – sex, racial, ethnic, regional – tends to be much less evident in comparative terms.

How do we explain this differentiation across dimensions? Why is class inequality the one area in which socialist administrations have made an important difference? Several possible explanations come to mind. While these help explain the general retention of inequalities in socialist societies, they do not fail in several respects to help us understand the *differential* treatment of the various dimensions.

First, there is the argument that more significant moves towards equality for women, or minorities, or regions are not possible until a higher level of development is attained. The reasoning, with respect to women and minorities at least, is that a certain level of 'development' (meaning education, experience in the work-force, etc.) is required before they can be moved into positions of equal standing with males from the dominant group. In other words, the contention is that leaders in these countries are doing all they can; it will simply require many more years before the final steps are taken.

There is a serious problem, however, with the 'level of development' argument, a problem illustrated by our comparative analysis of dimensions of inequality. If time and 'development' are required before women and minorities can move significantly closer to equality, why does the same constraint not hold for lower classes? Why have the latter managed to catch up faster? Or, if there is a conflict between growth and equality for women and minorities, why does the same conflict not hold as much for the lower classes? Indeed, many economists would suggest that sex and racial/ethnic discrimination may actually *hurt* economic growth because the pool for the top positions does not include all the best possible people (Okun, 1975, pp. 77ff). Conversely, reducing income differences across economic classes hurts growth, it is argued, because large differentials are supposedly needed to provide incentives for the best to work hard and seek to advance.

To summarize the point, growth and development explanations do not hold up in the face of the comparative analysis of dimensions of inequality. We still must explain, for example, why Brezhnev – who, as we noted above, explicitly rejected leveling in favor of growth – waged a war on poverty in the 1960s (Feiwel, 1972, pp. 599–607; Wiles, 1975, p. 34), and not on sexism or racism; we clearly need to look beyond development and growth considerations for understanding the patterns we have found.

A second possible explanation for these patterns involved what many scholars see as certain constants in the dynamics of a revolution. Revolutions have a substantial impact in the early years after takeover, but then the arteries begin to harden, the 'thermidor' appears, the revolution loses strength (for the latest version of this argument, see Kelley and Klein, 1977). One can, indeed, point to numerous examples in these countries of early egalitarian efforts that either culminated far short of equality, or were later rescinded:

(a) The radical egalitarian measures of the first months of the Bolshevik revolution, cut back sharply under War Communism;
(b) The liberation of women in the USSR in the 1920s and China in the 1950s has stalled in important ways ever since that period (Salaff and Merkle, 1973; Lapidus, 1977);
(c) The substantial redistribution of well-being in Cuba in the first years of the new regime, followed by more marginal adjustments and even retrenchment since then (Dominguez, 1978; Mesa-Lago, 1978);
(d) The remarkably large redistribution of funds for social and economic development to backward republics in the USSR in the 1920s and early 1930s, cut back after that and, for economic purposes at least, never resumed (Davies, 1958, p. 310; Sheehy, 1972, pp. 556–7);
(e) The well-publicized, national campaign in the 1960s against racial discrimination in Cuba, which contrasts with the relative silence on the subject today (Black, 1976, p. 104; Dominguez, 1978, pp. 225–7).

Reductions in inequality in socialist societies, then, seem to come primarily in the early years of the revolution. The processes of transformation that require decades in pluralist-capitalist systems are a matter of years under a socialist administration. However, the momentum needed to effect this remarkable transformation can only be sustained for a finite period, in part because the regimes turn to other, less revolutionary concerns (such as growth), and in part because a new elite is beginning to be locked into place, long before women and minorities have achieved an equal position.

The problem with this argument is much the same as the difficulty with the economic development explanation: it cannot encompass the differential treatment of the various inequalities. How do we explain the distinction between classes and the other dimensions? Why did early Czechoslovak efforts result in income inequalities substantially below those in the West, but leave sex differences about the same as in democracies? Or, after the period of transformation, why did Brezhnev begin a war on poverty and not on other inequalities? We still lack a major part of the picture.

Perhaps that part can be supplied by political factors, specifically decisions of the leadership of these various countries. This argument suggests we focus on Brezhnev and his cohorts in explaining the decision to attack poverty and not other areas of inequality. It further suggests that 'the political authorities can overtly and effectively change the class structure; . . . the privileges that are most essential for social status, including that of a high share in the national income, are conferred by a decision of the political authorities' (Ossowski, 1963, p. 184; also see Lenski, 1966, pp. 44–5; Dahrendorf, 1969, p. 38; and Runciman, 1974, p. 63). Thus, it is political choices that are the key. Indeed, this contention is to a large extent at the heart of the first two explanations – that political leadership chooses economic growth as its central priority and relegates equality to a lesser status; that the new political elite, once entrenched in power, ends the drive for equality in order to retain a significant share for itself. The argument with respect to differentiation across dimensions is that it is *conscious elite choices* that are involved in the greater emphasis on class equality.

This is much more compelling than the first two arguments. For support, we merely need to point to the Brezhnev example once more – programs are explicitly designed to reduce income inequalities by class but not other inequalities. More generally, if we agree with Ralf Dahrendorf (1969, p. 38) that 'the origin of inequality . . . is to be found in the existence in all human societies of norms of behavior to which sanctions are attached', and that elites determine these norms, then we must focus on the elites for explanations. It is certainly the case that the norms and concerns they establish vary in both their nature and intensity across dimensions. The working class in socialist countries stands out as the key element in society, the group to be most admired and rewarded. As David Lane has noted,

'The working class is given pride of place in the Soviet sociologists' description of the Soviet social structure. It is the creator, the builder of a new society of labour' (1971, p. 55). Of course, there is a vanguard to the workers' vanguard, which directs the latter in building that society. The working class does not rule, does not make the most money, and does not have the most prestige. However, Lane's point is valid in a relative sense. Relative to the working class in other countries, and relative to other elements in their own societies, the communist workers do have 'pride of place'. Women and minorities do not receive the same attention (for support for this point, see Jancar, 1974a, p. 236). Relatedly, we can revive the economic development argument, but with reference not to certain 'imperatives' of development, but rather to conscious choices about priorities. This line of reasoning is that economic growth is the chosen central priority in the development of socialism, and most dimensions of equality are subordinate to growth. As Brezhnev put it, the need is 'to approach economic questions first of all from the point of view of the interests of the state as a whole, the heightened effectiveness of the whole economy of the USSR' (*Pravda*, 22 December 1972, p. 5) or, to go back to Lenin, 'Our main concern must be the economic construction of the state' (quoted in Voznesensky, 1971, p. 6).

Socialist leaders, like their Western counterparts, thus perceive the existence of conflicts between equality and growth, and the latter generally takes precedence. Specifically, numerous scholars have argued that concerns for economic growth have led directly to a lesser status for women, minorities, and backward regions in these countries. Gail Lapidus argues, for instance, that 'the position of women in Soviet society has been shaped in fundamental ways by economic and political choices in which a concern for sexual equality has been negligible' (1977, p. 117; also see Wolchik, 1979; and Holubnychy, 1968).

Most dimensions of inequality are, then, subordinated to other concerns, while class inequality receives special attention. But why is *that* choice made? Why is class given differential treatment? The answer seems rooted in the ideology, the texts of Marx and Engels that guide these administrations. For Marx and Engels, and especially the former, class divisions are the primary concern (Marx, 1978). The other inequalities flow from the class structure. It follows that the first task in the creation of a just order is to abolish that structure and end class inequalities. Marx simply had little time for other cleavages, and that is readily evident in his writings. 'Just as Marx and Engels had no theoretical work on racism, . . . so did they lack a developed critique of sexism under capitalism' (Charrie Geuttel, cited in Meyer, 1977, pp. 95–6). Meyer calls that 'a bit harsh'; Middleton, however, makes much the same point (1974, pp. 185–6). Socialist leaders, in emphasizing the class dimension, are following ideological priorities emanating from Marx.

Thus, while numerous factors enter into the explanation for the continued retention of the entire region of inequalities in socialist societies, we can specify a smaller set of explanations behind the *differential* treatment of inequalities in these systems. The proximate cause is leadership choice, but underlying that 'choice' is the important predisposing factor of the ideology and its emphasis on class inequality.

Implications of the findings

What do these findings tell us generally about trends in, and explanations for, social inequalities? The findings from one dimension may not, one must stress, be at all applicable to another. This is especially important since most studies of inequality seem to focus on income distribution by class, which we have seen (at least for the comparative analysis in this study) is an unusual dimension. It is not possible to generalize to 'inequality' from the finding that socialist administrations are more egalitarian with respect to class.

As for explanations for inequality, these findings seem to support those analysts (Jackman, 1975; Wilensky, 1975) who have concluded that political variables, or even political-economic systems, have no discernible impact on social inequalities. The often remarkable similarities across two different political-economic orders in the status of women, minorities, and backward regions do, to an important extent, bolster that conclusion. However, in the explanation of those findings, the importance of political choice was emphasized. The leadership of socialist systems has demonstrated, for different dimensions at different times, what *could* be done, even in the face of often powerful constraints. Decisions were made in favor of greater equality, and then rescinded, or at least brought to a halt at certain points (and, as the class dimension illustrates, at different points). These are distinctly political choices, shaped by the structure of political-economic power and the prevailing political culture and ideology, and these decisions have produced both similar and distinctive patterns of inequality across different socio-economic systems.

Bibliography

The bibliography that follows is confined in principle to works cited in the previous chapters, other than references to newspapers and journals where full details are given in the original citation. A number of other works have been added for the sake of completeness.

Aimbetov, Aldan A. *et al.* (1967) *Problemy sovershenstvovaniya organizatsii i deyatel'nosti mestnykh sovetov* (Alma-Ata: Nauka).

Almond, Gabriel, A. (1966) 'Political Theory and Political Science', *American Political Science Review*, vol. 60, no. 4 (December) pp. 869–79.

Almond, Gabriel A. and G. Bingham Powell, Jr. (1966) *Comparative Politics: A Developmental Approach* (Boston: Little, Brown).

Amaro, Nelson and Carmelo Mesa-Lago (1971) 'Inequality and Classes', in Mesa-Lago (1971) pp. 341–74.

Andors, Stephen (1980) 'The Political and Organizational Implications of China's New Economic Policies, 1976–1979', *Bulletin of Concerned Asian Scholars*, vol. 12, no. 2 (April–June) pp. 44–57.

Apter, David E. (1965) *The Politics of Modernization* (Chiago: University of Chicago Press).

Archer, K. M. (1963) *Australian National Accounts: National Income and Expenditure, 1948/49–1962/63* (Canberra: Government Publishing Office).

Arendt, Hannah (1958) *The Origins of Totalitarianism* (London: Allen & Unwin).

Armstrong, John A. (1969) 'Sources of administrative behavior: some Soviet and West European comparisons', in Fleron, (1969).

———— (1978) *Ideology, Politics and Government in the Soviet Union*, 4th ed. (New York: Praeger).

Aspaturian, Vernon (1980) 'Political Participation in Eastern Europe: a Conceptual Critique'. Paper presented at the Second World Congress for Soviet and East European Studies, Garmisch, West Germany.

Atkinson, Dorothy *et al.* (eds) (1977) *Women in Russia* (Stanford, Calif.: Stanford University Press).

Azrael, Jeremy (1970) 'Decision-making in the USSR', in Richard P. Cornell (ed.), *The Soviet Political System: a Book of Readings* (Englewood Cliffs, NJ: Prentice-Hall).

Badina, Ovidiu and Catalin Mamali (1973) 'Adaptation of Youth to Production Tasks', in Badina and Mamali (eds), *Tineret Industrial* (Bucharest: Editura Academiei).

Bahry, Donna (1980) 'Measuring Communist Priorities: Budgets, Investments and the Problem of Equivalence', *Comparative Political Studies*, vol. 13, no. 3 (October) pp. 267–92.

Bandera, V. N. and Z. I. Melnyk (eds) (1973) *The Soviet Economy in Regional Perspective* (New York: Praeger).

Barnett, A. Doak (1967) *Cadres, Bureaucracy and Political Power in Communist China* (New York and London: Columbia University Press).

Barry, Donald D. *et al.* (eds) (1977–79). *Soviet Law after Stalin*, 3 vols (Leyden: Sijthoff).

Bauman, Zygmunt (1971) 'Twenty Years After: the Crisis in Soviet-type Systems', *Problems of Communism*, vol. 20, no. 6 (November–December) pp. 45–53.

_____ (1973) *Culture as Praxis* (London: Routledge).

_____ (1974) 'Officialdom and Class: Bases of Inequality in Socialist Society', in Parkin (1974), pp. 129–48.

Bentley, Arthur (1949) *The Process of Government* (Evanston, Ill.: Principia).

Berger, Suzanne (ed.) (1981) *Organizing Interests in Western Europe: Pluralism, Corporatism and the Transformation of Politics* (New York: Cambridge University Press).

Bergson, Abram (1974) 'Development Under Two Systems: Comparative Productivity Growth since 1950' in Morris Bornstein (ed.), *Comparative Economic Systems* (Homewood, Ill.: Dorsey Press).

Bertsch, Gary K. (1977) 'Ethnicity and Politics in Socialist Yugoslavia', *The Annals*, vol. 433 (September) pp. 88–99.

_____ (1982) *Power and Policy in Communist Systems*. New York: Wiley.

Bertsch, Gary K. and Ganschow, Thomas W. (eds) (1976) *Comparative Communism: The Soviet, Chinese, and Yugoslav Models* (San Francisco: W. H. Freeman).

Beskid, Lidia·(1979) 'Warunki zycia klasy robotniczej', in Wajda (1979).

_____ (1980) 'Potrzeby ludosci w swietle badan społecznych', *Nowe Drogi*, no. 6 (June).

Bezuglov, A. A. (1973) *Soviet Deputy – Legal Status* (Moscow: Progress).

_____ (1978) *Deputat v sovete v izbiratel'nom okruge* (Moscow: Yuridicheskaya literatura).

Bialer, Seweryn (1980) *Stalin's Successors*. New York: Cambridge University Press.

_____ (ed.) (1981) *The Domestic Context of Soviet Foreign Policy* (Boulder, Col.: Westview Press).

Biddulph, Howard (1983) 'Local Interest Articulation at CPSU Congresses', *World Politics*, vol. 36, no. 1 (October) pp. 28–52.

Bielasiak, Jack (1977) 'Policy Choices and Regional Equality at the Soviet Republic Level'. Paper presented at the American Political Science Association Convention, Washington DC.

_____ (1980a) 'Policy Choices and Regional Equality Among the Soviet Republics', *American Political Science Review*, vol. 74, no. 2 (June) pp. 394–405.

_____ (1980b) 'Polish Politics: the Permanence of Crisis'. Paper presented to the Annual Meeting of the American Political Science Association, Washington DC.

_____ (1981a) 'Workers and Mass Participation', in Triska and Gati (1981).

_____ (1981b) 'Recruitment Policy, Elite Integration and Political Stability in People's Poland', in Simon and Kanet (eds), 1981.

_____ (1982) 'Party Leadership and Mass Participation in Developed Socialism', in Seroka and Simon (eds), 1982.

_____ (1983) 'The Party: Permanent Crisis', in Brumberg (ed.), 1983.

_____ (1984) 'The Evolution of Crises in Poland', in Bielasiak and Simon, (eds), 1984.

Bielasiak, Jack and Maurice Simon (eds) (1984) *Polish Politics: Edge of the Abyss.* (New York: Praeger).
Bierzanek, Remogiosz and Andresej Gwizds (1967) 'Parliamentary Control over the Administration in Poland', *Polish Round Table*, pp. 146–69.
Bilandzic, Dusan (1978) *Historija SFRJ* (Zagreb: Skolska knjiga).
Black, Cyril (1966) *The Dynamics of Modernization* (New York: Harper & Row).
―――― (1980) 'Political Participation: From Estates to Interest Groups'. Paper presented at the American Historical Association, Washington DC.
―――― (1982) 'Organizational Participation in Imperial Russia and the Soviet Union'. Paper presented to the American Association for the Advancement of Slavic Studies, Washington DC.
Black, Cyril and John Burke (1983) 'Organizational Participation and Public Policy', *World Politics*, vol. 35, no. 3 (April) pp. 393–425.
Black, Jan Knippers (1976) *Area Handbook for China* (Washington DC: U.S. Government Publishing Office).
Blackwell, Robert E. (1973) 'The Soviet Political Elite: Alternative Recruitment at the Obkom Level', *Comparative Politics*, vol. 6, no. 1 (October) pp. 99–122.
Blazynski, George (1979) *Flashpoint Poland* (New York: Pergamon).
Blecher, Mark (1976) 'Income Distribution in Small Rural Chinese Communities', *China Quarterly*, no. 68 (December) pp. 797–816.
Blondel, Jean (1973) *Comparative Legislatures* (Englewood Cliffs, NJ: Prentice-Hall).
Bluszkowski, Jan (1979) 'Procesy ujednolicanja polozenia społecznego klasy robot-niczeji i inteligencji w społecnenstwie socjalistycznym', in Wajda (ed.) (1979).
Brezhnev, Leonid I. (1972) 'Otchetnyi doklad XXIV s''ezdu KPSS', in *Leninskim kursom: rechi i stat'i*, vol. 2 (Moscow: Politizdat).
―――― (1979) *Leninskim kursom: rechi i stat'i*, vol. 7 (Moscow: Izdatel'stvo politi-cheskoi literatury).
―――― (1981) *Leninskim kursom: rechi i stat'i*, vol. 8 (Moscow: Izdatel'stvo politi-cheskoi literatury).
Britain. An Official Handbook (1978) (London: HMSO).
Bromke, Adam (1972) 'Poland under Gierek: a New Political Style', *Problems of Communism*, vol. 21, no. 5 (September–October) pp. 1–19.
―――― (1981) 'Policy and Politics in Gierek's Poland', in Simon and Kanet (eds), 1981.
Brown, A. H. (1966) 'Pluralistic Trends in Czechoslovakia'. *Soviet Studies*, vol. 17, no. 4 (April) pp. 453–72.
―――― (1974) *Soviet Politics and Political Science* (London: Macmillan).
Brown, Archie, and Jack Gray (eds) (1979) *Political Culture and Political Change in Communist States*, 2nd ed. (London: Macmillan)
Brown, Archie and Michael Kaser (eds) (1975) *The Soviet Union since the Fall of Khrushchev* (London: Macmillan).
―――― (eds) (1982) *Soviet Policy for the 1980s* (London: Macmillan/St Antony's).
Brown, Bess (1979) 'Concerns of the Central Asian Republics Aired at USSR. Supreme Soviet'. Radio Liberty Research Report No. 378, 20 December.
Bruce, James and Robert Clawson (1977) 'A Zonal Analysis Model for Compara-tive Politics', *World Politics*, vol. 29, no. 2 (January) pp. 177–215.
Brumberg, Abraham (ed.) (1983) *Poland: Genesis of a Revolution* (New York: Vintage).
Brunner, Georg (1982) 'Recent Developments in the Soviet Concept of Human Rights', in Feldbrugge and Simons (1982).
Brzezinski, Zbigniew (1967) *Ideology and Power in Soviet Politics*, rev. ed. (New York: Praeger).

_____ (ed.) (1969) *Dilemmas of Change in Soviet Politics* (New York: Columbia University Press).

Brzezinski, Zbigniew and Samuel Huntington (1963) *Political Power: USA/USSR* (New York: Viking).

Bunce, Valerie (1976) 'Elite Succession, Policy Innovation and Petrification in Communist Systems: an Empirical Assessment', *Comparative Political Studies*, vol. 9, no. 1 (April) pp. 3–42.

_____ (1979) 'Leadership Succession and Policy Innovation in the Soviet Republics', *Comparative Politics*, vol. 11 no. 4 (July) pp, 379–402.

_____ (1981) *Do New Leaders Make a Difference? Executive Succession and Public Policy under Capitalism and Socialist* (Princeton, NJ: Princeton University Press).

Bunce, Valerie and John M. Echols (1975) 'Aggregate Data in the Study of Policy Change in Communist Systems'. Paper presented to the American Association for the Advancement of Slavic Studies Convention, Atlanta, Georgia.

_____ (1978) 'Power and Policy in Communist Systems: the Problem of Incrementalism', *Journal of Politics*, vol. 40, no. 4 (November) pp. 911–32.

_____ (1979) 'From Soviet Studies to Comparative Politics: the Unfinished Revolution', *Soviet Studies*, vol. 31, no. 1 (January) pp. 43–55.

_____ (1980) 'Soviet Politics in the Brezhnev Era: "Pluralism" or "Corporatism"?', in Kelley (1980) pp. 1–26.

Bunyan, James and H. H. Fisher (eds) (1934) *The Bolshevik Revolution 1917–1918: Documents and Materials* (Stanford, Calif.: Hoover War Library).

Burda, Andrzej (1975) *Sejm Polskiej Rzeczypospolitej Ludowej* (Warsaw: Ossolineum).

_____ (1978) *Parliament of the Polish People's Republic* (Warsaw: Ossolineum).

Burke, John P. (1982) *Organizational Participation and Public Policy: A Conference Report.* (Princeton, NJ: Center for International Studies, Memo no. 41).

Butler, David (ed.) (1959) *Elections Abroad* (London: Macmillan).

Campbell, Tom (1983) *The Left and Rights.* (London: Routledge).

Campeanu, Pavel (1978) 'The Evaluation of Current Events Information', *Viitorul Social*, no. 1.

_____ (1979) *Oamenii si televiziunea* (Bucharest: Editura Meridiane).

Carson, George B. (1956) *Electoral Practices in the USSR* (London: Atlantic Press).

Castles, Francis G. and R. D. McKinlay (1979) 'Public Welfare Provision, Scandinavia, and the Sheer Futility of the Sociological Approach to Politics', *British Journal of Political Science*, vol. 9, no. 2 (April) pp. 157–71.

Castro, Fidel (1963) 'El PURS, espina dorsal de la Revolucion', *Cuba socialista*, no. 19 (March) pp. 1–32.

_____ (1976) 'Report of the Central Committee of the Communist Party of Cuba to the First Congress', in *The First Congress of the Communist Party of Cuba* (Moscow: Progress).

_____ (1978) 'The Baraqua Protest took Place 100 Years Ago', *Granma Weekly Review*, 16 March, pp. 1–5.

Castro, Raul (1974) 'Speech to the delegates to People's Power in Matanzas', *Granma Weekly Review* 8 September.

_____ (1976) 'Opening speech', in *First Congress of the Communist Party of Cuba* (Moscow: Progress).

Ceausescu, Nicolae (1968–78) *Romania pe drumul construirii societati multilateral dezvoltate* (Bucharest: Editura Politica).

_____ (1969) *Raport la cel de-al X-lea Congres al Partidul Comunist Roman* (Bucharest: Editura Politica).

––––– (1972) *Raport la Conferinta Nationala a Partidului Comunist Roman* (Bucharest: Editura Politica).

Central Statistical Office. Various years. *Abstract of Regional Statistics*. (London: HMSO).

Chalidze, Valery (1974) *To Defend these Rights: Human Rights and the Soviet Union*. (New York: Random House).

Chang, Parris (1978) *Power and Policy in China* (University Park: Pennsylvannia State University Press).

Chao, Paul (1978) *Women under Communism* (Bayside, NY: General Hall).

Chapman, Dale (1977) 'A Note on the Ageing of the Politburo', *Soviet Studies*, vol. 29, no. 2 (April) pp. 296–305.

Chapman, Janet G. (1977) 'Equal Pay for Equal Work?', in Atkinson, *et al.*, (1977)

Chenery, Hollis *et al.* (1974) *Redistribution with Growth* (London: Oxford University Press).

Chernenko, K. U. (1981) *Human Rights in Soviet Society* (New York: International Publishers).

China Almanac (1980) (Beijing: China Encyclopedia Press).

Chkhikvadze, V. M. (1972) *The Soviet Form of Popular Government* (Moscow: Progress).

Chrypinski, Vicent D. (1965) 'Poland's Parliamentary Committees', *East Europe*, vol. 14, no. 1 (January) pp. 17–23.

––––– (1966) 'Legislative Committees in Polish Lawmaking', *Slavic Review*, vol. 25, no. 2 (June) pp. 247–58.

Churchward, Lloyd G. (1966) 'Soviet Local Government Today', *Soviet Studies*, vol. 17, no. 4 (April) pp. 431–52.

––––– (1975) *Contemporary Soviet Government*, 2nd ed. (London: Routledge).

Cihai (1978) *Cihai: zhengzhi jingjixue* [The Encyclopedia: Political Economics]. (Shanghai: Shanghai Cishu Chubanshe).

Clarke, Roger A. (1967) 'The Composition of the USSR Supreme Soviet, 1958–66', *Soviet Studies*, vol. 19, no. 1 (July) pp. 53–65.

Claude, Richard P. (1976) *Comparative Human Rights* (London and Baltimore: Johns Hopkins University Press).

Cnudde, Charles and Donald McCrone (1969) 'Party Competition and Welfare Policies in the American States', *American Political Science Review*, vol. 63, no. 3 (September) pp. 858–66.

Coates, Ken (1975) 'Civil Liberty and Socialism', in Pelikan (1975).

Cocks, Paul (1976) 'The Policy Process and Bureaucratic Politics', in Cocks *et al.* (1976).

Cocks, Paul *et al.* (eds) 1976. *The Dynamics of Soviet Politics* (Cambridge, Mass.: Harvard Univerity Press).

Cohen, Lenard J. (1977a) 'Conflict Management and Political Institutionalization in Socialist Yugoslavia: a Case Study of the Parliamentary System', in Eldridge, (ed.), 1977, pp. 122–65.

––––– (1977b) 'Political Participation, Competition, and Dissent in Yugoslavia', in Triska and Cocks (1977) pp. 178–216.

Cohen, Lenard J. and Jane P. Shapiro (eds) (1974) *Communist Systems in Comparative Perspective* (New York: Anchor).

Cohen, Stephen F. (1977) 'Bolshevism and Stalinism', in Tucker (1977).

––––– (1985) *Rethinking the Soviet Experience* (New York: Oxford University Press).

Colton, Timothy J. (1976) 'Military Councils and Military Politics in the Russian Civil War', *Canadian Slavonic Papers*, vol. 18, no. 1 (March) pp. 36–57.

_____ (1977) 'The Zhukov Affair Reconsidered', *Soviet Studies*, vol. 29, no. 2 (April) pp. 185–213.

_____ (1979) *Commissars, Commanders and Civilian Authority, The Structure of Soviet Military Politics* (Cambridge, Mass.: Harvard University Press).

Connor, Walter D. (1975) 'Generations and Politics in the USSR', *Problems of Communism*, vol. 24, no. 5 (September–October) pp. 20–31.

_____ (1977) 'Social Change and Stability in Eastern Europe', Problems of Communism, vol. 26, no. 6 (November–December) pp. 16–32.

_____ (1979) *Socialism, Politics, and Equality: Hierarchy and Change in Eastern Europe and the USSR*. New York: Columbia University Press).

_____ (1981) 'Mass Expectations and Regime Performance', in Bialer (1981).

Connor, Walter and Zvi Gitelman (eds) (1977) *Public Opinion in European Socialist Systems* (New York: Praeger).

Constitution of the People's Republic of China (1983) (Beijing: Foreign Languages Press).

Constitution of the Socialist Federal Republic of Yugoslavia (1976) (New York: Merrick).

Coombes, David and S. A. Walkland (eds) (1980) *Parliament and Economic Affairs in Britain, France, Italy and the Netherlands* (London: Heinemann).

Cranston, Maurice (1967) 'Human Rights, Real and Supposed', in Raphael (ed.), 1967.

'Cronica abreviada del Primer Congreso' (1976) *Verde Olivo*, no. 2, pp. 28–33.

Curtin, Kate (1975) *Women in China* (New York: Pathfinder).

Cutright, Phillips (1965) 'Political Structure, Economic Development and National Social Security Programs', *American Journal of Sociology* vol. 70, no. 5 (March) pp. 537–50.

Czabanski, Krzysztof (1981) 'Przywileje', *Tygodnik Solidarnosc*, 20 and 27 November.

Dahl, Robert A. (1980) 'Pluralism revisited', in Stanislaw Ehrlich and Graham Wootton (eds), *Three Faces of Pluralism* (Farnborough, Hants.: Gower).

Dahrendorf, Ralf (1969) 'On the Origin of Inequality Among Men', in Andre Beteille (ed.), *Social Inequality* (Baltimore: Penguin).

Dallin, Alexander and George Breslauer (1970) *Political Terror in Communist Systems* (Stanford, Calif.: Stanford University Press).

Damian, Liviu and E. Dobrescu (1974) 'New Housing Arrangements and the Improvement of Human Relations', *Viitorul Social*, no. 2.

Danecki, Jan (1978) 'Assumptions of Perspective Policy of Income Distribution in Poland', in Polish Sociological Association, *Social Structure* (Wroclaw: Ossolinskick) pp. 53–78.

Davies, R. W. (1958) *The Development of the Soviet Budgetary System* (London: Cambridge University Press).

Deber, R. B. (1980) 'Planning: Lessons from the USSR', *Policy Studies Journal*, vol. 9, no. 2 (November) pp. 286–93.

Dellenbrant, Jan Ake (1980) *Soviet Regional Policy* (Stockholm: Almqvist and Wiksell).

Denitch, Bogdan (1976) *The Legitimation of a Revolution: the Yugoslav Case*. (New Haven, Conn.: Yale University Press).

De Tocqueville, Alexis (1960) *Democracy in America* (ed.), (Phillips Bradley, 2 vols., vol. 1. New York: Knopf).

De Weydenthal, Jan (1979) *Poland: Communism Adrift*. The Washington Post Papers, vol. 1, no. 8 (Beverly Hills and London: Sage Publications).

Dienes, Leslie (1972) 'Regional Variations of Capital and Labor Productivity in

Soviet Industry', *Journal of Regional Science*, vol. 12, no. 3 (December) pp. 401–6.

Dinka, Frank and Max J. Skidmore (1973) 'The Functions of Communist One-party Elections: the Case of Czechoslovakia 1971', *Political Science Quarterly*, vol. 88, no. 3 (September) pp. 395–422.

'The Directions of the Operations of Solidarity in the Current Situation of the Country' (1981) *Głos Pracy*, 14 April; translated in Radio Free Europe, Background Report no. 210, 22 July.

Dittmer, Lowell (1974) *Liu Shao Ch'i and the Chinese Cultural Revolution* (Berkeley: University of California Press).

_____ (1978) 'Bases of Power in Chinese Politics', *World Politics*, vol. 21, no. 1 (October) pp. 26–60.

Djilas, Milovan (1957) *The New Class* (New York: Praeger).

Dobieszewski, Adolf (1977) *Organizacja polityczna społeczenstwa socjalistycznege w Polsce* (Warsaw: Ksiazka i wiedza).

Dodge, Norton (1977) 'Women in the Professions', in Atkinson *et al.* (1977).

Dominguez, Jorge I. (1978) *Cuba: Order and Revolution* (Cambridge, Mass.: Harvard University Press).

Dominion Bureau of Statistics (various years) *Canada Yearbook* (Ottawa: Queen's Printer).

Donaldson, Robert H. (1972) 'The 1971 Soviet Central Committee: an Assessment of the New Elite', *World Politics*, vol. 24, no. 3 (April) pp. 382–409.

Donaldson, Robert H. and Derek T. Waller (1970) *Status and Change in Revolutionary Elites: a Comparative Analysis of the 1956 Party Central Committees in China and the USSR* (Beverly Hills, Calif.: Sage Publications).

Drazkiewicz, Jerzy (1975) 'Udzial klasy robotniczej w aktywnosci społecznej', in Jan Malanowski (ed.), *Nierownosci społeczne w Polsce w swietle badan empiriycznych* (Warsaw).

Dreyer, June Teufel (1976) *China's Forty Millions* (Cambridge, Mass.: Harvard University Press).

Duevel, Christian (1976) 'The Newly Elevated Politburo and Secretariat', Radio Liberty Research Report, 20 July.

Dye, Thomas R. (1966) *Politics, Economics and the Public. Policy Outcomes in the American States*. (Chicago: Rand McNally).

Eberstadt, Nick (1979) 'Has China Failed?', *New York Review of Books*, vol. 26, no. 5, p. 33; no. 6, p. 41; no. 7, p. 39.

Echols, John M. III (1975) 'Politics, Budgets and Regional Equality in Communist and Capitalist Systems', *Comparative Political Studies*, vol. 8, no. 3 (October) pp. 259–92.

_____ (1976) 'Politics, Policy and Equality under Communism and Democracy', unpublished PhD thesis, University of Michigan.

_____ (1979) 'Fiscal Redistribution and Regional Equality in the Soviet Union', *Public Finance*, vol. 34, no. 3, pp. 357–74.

Eckstein, Otto (ed.) (1967) *Studies in the Economics of Income Maintenance* (Washington DC: Brookings).

Ehrlich, Stanislaw (1982) *Pluralism On and Off Course* (Oxford: Pergamon).

Eldridge, Albert F. (ed.) (1977) Legislatures in Plural Societies (Durham NC: Duke University Press).

Elling, Ray (1980) *Cross-National Studies of Health Systems* (New Brunswick: Transaction Books).

Ellman, Michael (1984) 'Full Employment: Lessons from State Socialism', in Michael Ellman, *Collectivisation, Convergence and Capitalism* (London: Academic Press).

Emmons, Terence (1983) *The Formation of Political Parties and the First National Elections in Russia* (Cambridge, Mass.: Harvard University Press).

Engels, Frederick (1978) *The Origin of the Family, Private Property and the State*, in Robert C. Tucker (ed.), *The Marx-Engels Reader* (New York: Norton).

Estatutos del Partido Comunista de Cuba (1976) (La Habana: Departamento de Orientacion Revolucionaria).

Evans, Alfred B. (1977) 'Developed Socialism in Soviet Ideology', *Soviet Studies*, vol. 29, no. 3 (July) pp. 409–28.

Ezhegodnik (various dates) *Ezhegodnik Bol'shoi Sovetskoi Entsiklopedii* (Moscow: Sovetskaya entsiklopediya).

Fainsod, Merle (1963 (rev. ed. 1965)) *How Russia is Ruled* (Cambridge, Mass.: Harvard University Press).

Falkenheim, Victor (Nd) *Citizens and Groups in Chinese Politics*. Manuscript.

Fallenbuchl, Zbigniew (1977) 'The Polish Economy in the 1970s', in U.S. Congress, Joint Economic Committee, *East European Economies Post-Helsinki* (Washington DC: U.S. Government Publishing Office).

Federani Statisticky Urad (1973) Statisticka rocenka CSSR, 1973 (Prague: SNTL).

Feiwel, George R. (1972) *The Soviet Quest for Economic Efficiency* (New York: Praeger).

Feldbrugge, F. J. M. (1975) *Samizdat and Political Dissent in the Soviet Union*. (Leyden: Sijthoff).

—— (ed.) (1979). *The Constitutions of the USSR and the Union Republics* (Alphen aan den Rijn: Sijthoff & Noordhoff).

Feldbrugge, F. J. M. and William B. Simons (eds) (1982) *Perspective on Soviet Law for the 1980s* (The Hague: Nijhoff).

'First regular session of the National Assembly of People's Power' (1977) (Havana).

Firuta, Argentina (1978) 'Changes in the Life Style of the Working Class', *Viitorul Social*, no. 1.

Fischer, George (1968) *The Soviet System and Modern Society* (New York: Atherton).

Fiszman, Joseph R. (1977) 'Educational Equality and Equality of Opportunity in Eastern Europe, with Special Focus on Poland', *Politics and Society*, vol. 7, no. 3 (September) pp. 297–329.

Flakierski, Henry (1981) 'Economic reform and income distribution in Poland: the negative evidence', *Cambridge Journal of Economics*, vol. 5, no. 2 (June) pp. 137–58.

Fleron, Frederic J. (1968) 'Soviet Area Studies and the Social Sciences: Some Methodological Problems in Communist Studies', *Soviet Studies*, vol. 19, no. 3 (January) pp. 313–39.

—— (ed.), (1969) *Communist Studies and the Social Sciences* (Chicago: Rand McNally).

—— (1971) 'Cooptation as a mechanism of adaptation to change: the Soviet political leadership', in Kanet, (ed.), 1971.

Fried, Robert C. (1966) *Comparative Political Institutions* (New York: Macmillan).

Friedgut, Theodore H. (1976) 'Interests and Groups in Soviet Policy-making: the MTS Reforms', *Soviet Studies*, vol. 28, no. 4 (October) pp. 524–47.

—— (1979) *Political Participation in the USSR* (Princeton, NJ: Princeton University Press).

Friedrich, Carl and Zbigniew K. Brzezinski (1965) *Totalitarian Dictatorship and Autocracy*, rev. ed. (Cambridge, Mass.: Harvard University Press).

Frunze, M. V. (1925) *Sobranie sochinenii*, vol. 1 (Moscow: Gosizdat).

Fry, Brian R. and Richard F. Winters (1970) 'The Politics of Redistribution', *American Political Science Review*, vol. 64, no. 2 (June) pp. 508–22.

Fuller, Elizabeth (1980) 'Georgian Officials Present Economic Demands at the USSR Supreme Soviet Session', Radio Liberty Research Report No. 410, 3 November.

Fundamentals of Marxism–Leninism (1963) (Moscow: Foreign Languages Publishing House).

Furtak, Robert K. (1974) 'Interessenpluralismus in den politischen Systemen Osteuropas', *Osteuropa*, vol. 24, no. 11–12 (November–December) pp. 779–92.

Gadomska, Magdalena (1981) 'Swiadomosc nierownosci', *Przeglad Technicny*, 24 May.

Gaidukov, D. A. (ed.) (1979) *Aktual'nye problemy gosudarstvovedeniya* (Moscow: Institut gosudarstva i prava AN SSSR).

Gajda, Stefan *et al.* (1979) 'Społeczno-polityczna i producyjna aktywnosc zalog Kluczowych zakladdow pracy' in Wajda (1979).

Galenson, Marjorie (1973) *Women and Work: An International Comparison* (Ithaca, NY: Cornell University).

Garaudy, Roger (1970) *Marxism in the Twentieth Century* (London: Collins).

Garson, G. David (1978) *Group Theories of Politics* (Beverly Hills and London: Sage).

Garthoff, Raymond L. (1975) 'SALT and the Soviet Military', *Problems of Communism*, vol. 24, no. 1 (January–February) pp. 21–37.

Gebert, S. (1976) 'Wspolna ordynacja wyborcza do Sejmu i rad narodnowych' *Panstwo i Prawo*, vol. 31, nos 1–2 (January–February) pp. 112–26.

Gebethner, Stanislaw (1976) *Ustroj polityczny Polskiej Rzeczypospolitej Ludowej.* (Warsaw: Krajowa agencja wydawnicza).

———— (1978) 'Ustroj Panstwowy PRL' in Zofia Lewandowska (ed.), *Polska kraj i ludzie* (Warsaw: Polska Agencja Interpress).

Gélard, Patrice (1975) *Les systèmes politiques des états socialistes*, 2 vols (Paris: Cujas).

Georgadze, M. P. (ed.) (1975) *Verkhovnyi Sovet SSSR* (Moscow: Izvestiya).

George, Vic and Nick Manning (1980) *Socialism, Social Welfare and the Soviet Union* (London: Routledge).

Gerskovic, Leon (1976) 'Istorijski razvoj drustveno-politickog sistema Jugoslavije', in Pasic and Spadjier (1976).

Gilejko, Lezlek (1979) 'Postawy społecznopolityczne robotniczej i ich unwarunkowania', in Wajda (1979).

Gilison, Jerome M. (1968) 'Soviet Elections as a Measure of Dissent: the Missing One Per Cent', *American Political Science Review*, vol. 62, no. 3 (September) pp. 814–23.

———— (1972) *British and Soviet Politics: Legitimacy and Convergence* (Baltimore and London: Johns Hopkins University Press).

Girod, Roger (1974) 'Switzerland: Geography of the Swiss Party System', in Kenneth McRae (ed.), *Consociational Democracy: Political Accommodation in Segmented Societies* (Toronto: McClelland & Stewart).

Gitelman, Zvi (1970) 'Power and Authority in Eastern Europe', in Johnson (ed.), 1970.

———— (1972) 'Beyond Leninism: Political Development in Eastern Europe', *Newsletter on Comparative Studies of Communism*, vol. 5, no. 3 (May) pp. 18–43.

Golan, Galia (1971) *The Czechoslovak Reform Movement* (Cambridge: Cambridge University Press).

Goldhammer, Herbert (1975) *The Soviet Soldier* (New York: Crane, Russak).

Goma, Paul (1979) Situation Report: Romania, Radio Free Europe, March.

Goodman, David S. G. (1980) 'The Provincial First Party Secretary in the People's

Republic of China, 1949–1978: a profile', *British Journal of Political Science*, vol. 10, no. 1 (January) pp. 39–74.

––––– (1981a) 'The Provincial Revolutionary Committee in the People's Republic of China, 1967–79: an Obituary', *China Quarterly*, no. 85 (March) pp. 49–79.

––––– (1981b) 'The Sixth Plenum of the 11th Central Committee of the Chinese Communist Party: Look Back in Anger?', *China Quarterly*, no. '87 (September) pp. 518–27.

––––– (1984) 'State Reforms in the People's Republic of China since 1976: a Historical Perspective', in Harding (ed.), 1984, pp. 277–98.

––––– (1985) 'The Chinese Political Order after Mao: 'Socialist Democracy' and the Exercise of State Power', *Political Studies*, vol. 33, no. 2 (June) pp. 218–35.

Gostkowski, Zygmunt (1959) 'Popular Interest in the Municipal Elections of Lodz, Poland', *Public Opinion Quarterly*, vol. 23, no. 3 (Fall) pp. 371–81.

––––– (1967) 'Analysis of the Panel Effect in the Study of an Election Campaign in Poland', *Polish Sociological Bulletin*, no. 1 (15) pp. 44–57.

Gray, Jack and Gordon White (eds) (1982) *China's New Development Strategy* (London: Academic Press).

Greenstein, Fred I. and Nelson W. Polsby (eds) (1975) *Handbook of Political Science*, 5 vols (Reading, Mass.: Addison-Wesley).

Greenstone, J. David. (1975) 'Group Theories', in Greenstein and Polsby (eds), 1975.

Gretler, Armin and Pierre-Emeric Mandl (1973) *Values, Trends, and Alternatives in Swiss Society* (New York: Praeger).

Gripp, Richard C. (1973) *The Political System of Communism* (London: Nelson).

Gross, Jan T. (1979) 'Thirty Years of Crisis Management in Poland', in Teresa Rakowska-Harmstone (ed.), *Perspectives for Change in Communist Societies* (Boulder, Col.: Westview Press).

Groth, Alexander J. (1971) *Comparative Politics: A Distributive Approach* (New York: Macmillan).

––––– (1982) 'Worker Welfare Systems in Marxist–Leninist States: a Comparative Analysis', *Coexistence*, vol. 19, no. 1 (April) pp. 33–50.

Groth, Alexander J. and William R. Hunt (1985) 'Marxist–Leninist Communication Systems in Comparative Perspective', *Coexistence*, vol. 22, no. 2 (July) pp. 123–38.

Groth, Alexander J. and L. L. Wade (1973) 'International Educational Policy Outcomes', in Sidjanski (1973).

Grove, D. John (1978) 'A Test of the Ethnic Equalization Hypothesis: a Cross-national Study', *Ethnic and Racial Studies*, vol. 1, no. 2 (April) pp. 175–95.

Gureyev, P. P. and P. I. Segudin (eds) (1977) *Legislation in the USSR* (Moscow: Progress).

Gustafson, Thane (1981) *Reform in Soviet Politics: Lessons of Recent Policies on Land and Water* (Cambridge: Cambridge University Press).

Habermas, Jurgen (1974) *Theory and Practice* (London: Heinemann).

Halperin, Morton (1974) *Bureaucratic Politics and Foreign Policy* (Washington DC: Brookings).

Hammer, Darrell P. (1971) 'The Dilemma of Party Growth', *Problems of Communism*, vol. 20, no. 4 (July–August) pp. 16–21.

––––– (1974) *USSR: The Politics of Oligarchy* (Hinsdale, Ill.: Dryden).

––––– (1979) 'Bureaucratic Pluralism'. Paper presented to the International Political Science Association Congress, Moscow.

Harasymiw, Bohdan (1969) '*Nomenklatura*: the Soviet Communist Party's leadership recruitment system', *Canadian Journal of Political Science*, vol. 2, no. 4 (December) pp. 493–512.

―――― (1977) 'Die sowjetische Nomenklatur', *Osteuropa*, vol. 27, nos 7 and 8 (July and August) pp. 583–98 and 665–81.

Harding, Neil (1981) 'What Does It Mean to Call a Regime Marxist?', in Szajkowski (1981).

―――― (ed.) (1984) *The State in Socialist Society* (London: Macmillan/St Antony's).

Hart, Armando (1966) 'Debemos elevar la organizacion del Partido a la altura de nuestra Revolucion', *Granma Weekly Review*, 19 September.

―――― (1969) 'Production's First Need is Technical and Cultural Improvement of Party Cadres and Members', *Granma Weekly Review*, 20 July.

Headey, Bruce (1974) *British Cabinet Ministers: The Roles of Politicians in Executive Office* (London: Allen & Unwin).

Heer, Nancy W. (1976) 'Political Leadership in Soviet Historiography: Cult or Collective?', in Cocks *et al.* (1976).

Heisler, Martin D. (1977) 'Managing ethnic conflict in Belgium', *The Annals*, vol. 433 (September) pp. 32–46.

Heller, Agnes (1979) 'The Declaration of Independence and the Principles of Socialism', *Social Praxis*, vol. 6, nos 1–2, pp. 109–12.

Herman, Valentine and Francoise Mandel (1976) *Parliaments of the World* (London: Macmillan).

Herspring, Dale R. and Ivan Volgyes (eds) (1978) *Civil–Military Relations in Communist Systems* (Boulder, Col.: Westview Press).

Hill, Ronald J. (1972) 'Continuity and Change in USSR Supreme Soviet Elections', *British Journal of Political Science*, vol. 2, no. 1 (January) pp. 47–67.

―――― (1973) 'Patterns of Deputy Selection to Local Soviets', *Soviet Studies*, vol. 25, no. 2 (October) pp. 196–212.

―――― (1976a) 'The CPSU in a Soviet Election Campaign', *Soviet Studies*, vol. 28, no. 4 (October) pp. 590–8.

―――― (1976b) 'Soviet Literature on Electoral Reform: a Review', *Government and Opposition*, vol. 11, no. 4 (autumn) pp. 481–95.

―――― (1980) *Soviet Politics, Political Science and Reform* (Oxford: Martin Robertson).

―――― (1983) 'The Development of Soviet Local Government since Stalin's Death', in Jacobs (1983) pp. 18–33.

Hill, Ronald J. and Peter Frank (1983) *The Soviet Communist Party*, 2nd ed. (London: Allen & Unwin).

Hirschman, Albert O. (1958) *The Strategy of Economic Development* (New Haven, Conn.: Yale University Press).

Hodnett, Grey and Val Ogareff (1973) *Leaders of the Soviet Republics, 1955–1972* (Canberra: Australian National University).

Hoffman, David and Norman Ward (1970) *Bilingualism and Biculturalism in the Canadian House of Commons* (Ottawa: Queen's Printer).

Hoffman, George W. and Fred W. Neal (1962) *Yugoslavia and the New Communism* (New York: Twentieth Century Fund).

Hoffmann, Erik P. and Robbin F. Laird (1982) *The Politics of Economic Modernization in the Soviet Union* (Ithaca, NY: Cornell University Press).

Hollander, Paul (1973) *Soviet and American Society: A Comparison* (New York: Oxford University Press).

Holt, Robert and John E. Turner (1966) *The Political Basis of Economic Development* (Princeton, NJ: Van Nostrand).

Holubnychy, Vsevolod (1968) 'Some Economic Aspects of Relations among the Soviet Republics', in Eric Goldhagen (ed.), *Ethnic Minorities in the Soviet Union* (New York: Praeger).

Hooson, David (1972) 'The Outlook for Regional Development in the Soviet Union'. *Slavic Review*, vol. 31, no. 3 (September) pp. 535–54.

Hough, Jerry F. (1969) *The Soviet Prefects: The Local Party Organs in Industrial Decision-Making* (Cambridge: Mass.: Harvard University Press).

_____ (1972) 'The Soviet System: Petrification or Pluralism?', *Problems of Communism*, vol. 21, no. 2 (March–April) pp. 25–45.

_____ (1973) 'The Bureaucratic Model and the Nature of the Soviet System', *Journal of Comparative Administration*, vol. 5, no. 2 (August) pp. 134–67.

_____ (1975) 'The Soviet Experience and the Measurement of Power', *Journal of Politics*, vol. 37, no. 3 (August) pp. 685–710.

_____ (1976) 'Political Participation in the Soviet Union', *Soviet Studies*, vol. 28, no. 1 (January) pp. 3–20.

_____ (1977) *The Soviet Union and Social Science Theory* (Cambridge, Mass.: Harvard University Press).

_____ (1979) (with Merle Fainsod). *How the Soviet Union is Governed* (Cambridge, Mass.: Harvard University Press).

_____ (1983) 'Pluralism, Corporatism and the Soviet Union', in Solomon (1983).

Howe, Christopher (1978) *China's Economy* (New York: Basic Books).

Huntington, Samuel P. (1968) *Political Order in Changing Societies* (New Haven, Conn.: Yale University Press).

Hutchings, Raymond (1983) *The Soviet Budget* (London: Macmillan).

'Information Biuletynu MKZ, NSZZ Solidarnosc' (1981) Lublin, 30 January.

'Integracion del Secretariado y de Comisiones de la Direccion Nacional de las ORI' (1962) *Cuba Socialista*, vol. 8 (April) pp. 136–7.

Ionescu, Ghita (1967) *The Politics of the European Communist States* (New York: Praeger).

_____ (1972) *Comparative Communist Politics* (London: Macmillan).

Ippolito, Dennis S. (1978) *The Budget and National Politics* (San Francisco: Freeman).

Itogi (1970) (published 1972–4) *Itogi Vsesoyuznoi perepisi naseleniya*, 7 vols (Moscow: Statistika).

Jackman, Robert (1975) *Politics and Social Equality: A Comparative Analysis* (New York: Wiley).

Jackson, Marvin (1981) 'Perspectives on Romania's Economic Development in the 1980s', in Nelson (1981b).

Jackson, Marvin and Stephen Happel (1977) 'Population Structure', in Klaus-Detlev Grothausen (ed.), *Rumanien* (Gottingen: Vandhoeck and Ruprecht).

Jacobs, Everett M. (1970) 'Soviet Local Elections: What They Are and What They Are Not', *Soviet Studies*, vol. 22, no. 1 (July) pp. 61–76.

_____ (ed.) (1983) *Soviet Local Politics and Government* (London: Allen & Unwin).

Jambrek, Peter (1975) *Development and Social Change in Yugoslavia* (Lexington: Heath).

James, Gwyn (1971) *Agricultural Policy in Wealthy Countries* (Sydney: Angus & Robertson).

Jancar, Barbara Wolfe (1971) *Czechoslovakia and the Absolute Monopoly of Power* (New York: Praeger).

_____ (1974a) 'Women under Communism', in Jane P. Jacquette (ed.), *Women in Politics* (New York: Wiley).

_____ (1974b) 'Women in Soviet Politics', in Henry Morton and Rudolf Tokes, (eds) (1974).

Janos, Andrew C. (1970) 'Group Politics in Communist Society: a Second Look at the Pluralistic Model', in Samuel P. Huntington and Clement H. Moore (eds), *Authoritarian Politics in Modern Society* (New York: Basic Books).

_____ (1976) 'Systemic Models and the Theory of Change in the Comparative Study of Communist Politics', in Andrew C. Janos (ed.), *Authoritarian Politics in Communist Europe* (Berkeley: Institute of International Studies, Research Series no. 28).

Japanese Economic Yearbook. Various years. Tokyo.

Jarosz, Zdzislaw and Wojciech Popkowski (1980) *Sejm PRL VII kadencji* (Warsaw: Ksiazka i wiedza).

Johnson, Chalmers (ed.) (1970) *Change in Communist Systems* (Stanford, Calif.: Stanford University Press).

Jowitt, Kenneth (1974) 'An Organizational Approach to the Study of Political Culture in Marxist–Leninist Regimes', *American Political Science Review*, vol. 68, no. 3 (September) pp. 1171–91.

_____ (1975) 'Inclusion and Mobilization in European Leninist Regimes', *World Politics*, vol. 28, no. 1 (October) pp. 69–96.

Kabaj, Mieczyslaw (1980) 'Efektynosc wzrostu plac', *Nowe Drogi*, no. 2, February, pp. 128–42.

Kadar, Janos (1971) *Nepszabag*, 19 February, as cited in Radio Free Europe: Hungarian Background Report, 25 February.

Kamenka, Eugene and Alice Ehr-Soon Tay (1978) *Human Rights* (London: Arnold).

_____ (1980) 'Human Rights in the Soviet Union', *World Review*, vol. 19, no. 2 (June).

Kanet, Roger (ed.) (1971) *The Behavioral Revolution in Communist Studies* (New York: Free Press).

Kantecki, Anton and Jolanta Supinska (1979) 'Społeczne problemy konsumpcji', in Antoni Rajkiewicz (ed.), *Polityka społeczna* (Warsaw: PWE).

Karatnycky, Adrian *et al.*, (eds) (1980) *Workers' Rights, East and West* (New Brunswick NJ: Transaction Books).

Kardelj, Edvard (1977) 'Revolutionaries in Their Visions and Realists in Respect of Possibilities', *Socialist Theory and Practice*, vol. 17, no. 5 (May) pp. 60–82.

_____ (1978) *Democracy and Socialism* (London: Summerfield).

Kassof, Allen (1969) 'The Administered Society: Totalitarianism Without Terror', in Fleron (1969).

Kautsky, John H. (1962) *Political Change in Underdeveloped Countries: Nationalism and Communism* (New York: Wiley).

_____ (1968) *Communism and the Politics of Development* (New York: Wiley).

_____ (1972) *The Political Consequences of Modernity* (New York: Wiley).

_____ (1973) 'Comparative Communism Versus Comparative Politics', *Studies in Comparative Communism*, vol. 6, nos 1–2 (spring–summer) pp. 135–70.

Kedzia, Zdzislaw (1975) *Parliament socjalistyczny* (Warsaw: Ksiazka i wiedza).

Kellas, James G. (1975) *The Scottish Political System* (London: Cambridge University Press).

Kelley, Donald R. (1972) 'Interest Groups in the USSR: the Impact of Political Sensitivity on Group Influence', *Journal of Politics*, vol. 34, no. 3 (August) pp. 860–88.

_____ (1974) 'Toward a Model of Soviet Decision-making: a Research Note', *American Political Science Review*, vol. 68, no. 2 (June) pp. 701–6.

_____ (1976) 'Environmental Policy-making in the USSR: the Role of Industrial and Environmental Pressure Groups', *Soviet Studies*, vol. 28, no. 4 (October) pp. 570–89.

——— (1977) 'Group and Specialist Influence in Soviet Politics: In Search of Theory', in Richard B. Remnek (ed.), *Social Scientists and Policy Making in the USSR* (New York: Praeger).

——— (1979) 'The Soviet Image of the Future', in Robert Wesson (ed.), *The Soviet Union: Problems and Prospects* (Stanford, Calif.: Hoover Institution Press).

——— (ed.) (1980) *Soviet Politics in the Brezhnev Era* (New York: Praeger).

Kelley, Jonathan and Herbert S. Klein (1977) 'Revolution and the Rebirth of Inequality: a Theory of Stratification in Postrevolutionary Society', *American Journal of Sociology*, vol. 83, no. 1 (July) pp. 78–99.

Khazikov, A. G. (ed.) (1964) *Sbornik normativnykh aktov po sovetskomu administrativnomu pravu* (Moscow: Vysshaya shkola).

Kim, A. I. (1965) *Sovetskoe izbiratel'noe pravo* (Moscow: Yuridicheskaya literatura).

King, Anthony (1973) 'Ideas, Institutions and the Policies of Government: a Comparative Analysis', *British Journal of Political Science*, vol. 3, nos 2 and 3 (July and October) pp. 293–313, 409–23.

Klokocka, Vladimir (1968) *Volby v pluralitnich demokraciich* (Prague: Svoboda).

Koff, Sondra Z. (1980–81) 'The Delivery of Health Care and Political Culture', *Policy Studies Journal*, vol. 9, no. 2 (November) pp. 294–300.

Kolakowski, Lezlek (1978) *Main Currents of Marxism*, 3 vols (Oxford: Oxford University Press).

——— (1983) 'Marxism and Human Rights', *Daedalus*, vol. 112, no. 4 (Fall) pp. 81–92.

Kolakowski, Lezlek and Stuart Hampshire (eds) (1975) *The Socialist Idea* (London: Weindenfeld & Nicolson).

Kolankiewicz, George (1982) 'The Politics of Socialist Renewal', in Jean Woodall, (ed.), *Policy and Politics in Contemporary Poland* (New York: St Martin's).

Kolko, Gabriel (1964) *Wealth and Power in America* (New York: Praeger).

Kolkowicz, Roman (1967) *The Soviet Military and the Communist Party* (Princeton, NJ: Princeton University Press).

Korbonski, Andrzej (1977) 'The "Change to Change" in Eastern Europe', in Triska and Cocks (1977).

Koropeckyj, I. S. (1975) 'National Income of the Soviet Union Republics in 1970: Revision and some Applications', in Z. M. Fallenbuchl (ed.), *Economic Development in the Soviet Union and Eastern Europe*, vol. 1 (New York: Praeger).

Kowalewski, David (1980) 'Human Rights Protest in the USSR: Statistical Trends for 1965–78', *Universal Human Rights*, vol. 2, no. 1, pp. 5–29.

Krejci, Jaroslav (1972) *Social Change and Stratification in Postwar Czechoslovakia* (New York: Columbia University Press).

——— (1976) *Social Structure in Divided Germany* (London: Croom Helm).

Krencik, Wieslaw. (1980) 'Tempo zrostu a rozpietosc plac', *Gospodarka Planowa*, no. 4 (April) pp. 202–11.

Kudryavtsev, V. (1978) 'The New Constitution and the Development of Socialist Law', in *The Development of Soviet Law and Jurisprudence* (Moscow: Academy of Sciences).

Kuklinski, Antoni R. (1967) 'Regional differentiation of the Polish National Economy', In *Proceedings of the First Scandinavian-Polish Regional Science Seminar* (Warsaw: PWN).

——— (1970) 'Regional Development, Regional Policies and Regional Planning', *Regional Studies*, vol. 4, no. 3 (October) pp. 269–78.

Kurczewski, Jacek (1981) 'W oczach opinii publicznej', *Kultura*, 21 March.

——— (1982) 'W oczach opinii publicznej', *Kultura*, 1 March.

Kurszala, Jerzy (1970) 'Differentiation of Subregions and the Possibility of their Economical Equalization', in *Proceedings of the Second Poland–Norden Regional Science Seminar* (Warsaw: PWN).

Kushman, John, Alexander J. Groth, and Robin Childs (1980) 'Political Systems and International Travel', *Social Science Quarterly*, vol. 60, no. 4 (March) pp. 605–16.

Kuznets, Simon (1968) *Toward a Theory of Economic Growth* (New York: Norton).

Laca, Ivan (1977) 'The League of Communists of Yugoslavia', *Yugoslav Survey*, vol. 18, no. 2.

Lampton, David (1977) *The Politics of Medicine in China: The Policy Process 1949–1977* (Boulder, Col.: Westview Press).

_____ (1978) 'Performance and the Chinese Political System: a Preliminary Assessment of Education and Health Policies', *China Quarterly*, no. 75 (September) pp. 509–39.

Lane, David (1971) *The End of Inequality?* (Harmondsworth: Penguin).

_____ (1974) 'Leninism as an Ideology of Socialist Development', in de Kadt, Ellen and Williams, Gavin (eds), *Sociology and Development* (London: Tavistock).

_____ (1976) *The Socialist Industrial State* (London: Allen & Unwin).

_____ (1981) *Leninism: A Sociological Interpretation*. (Cambridge: Cambridge University Press).

_____ (1982) *The End of Social Inequality? Class, Status and Power under State Socialism* (London: Allen & Unwin).

_____ (1985) *State and Politics in the USSR* (Oxford: Blackwell).

Lang, Nicholas R. (1975) 'The Dialectics of Decentralization: Economic Reforms and Regional Inequality in Yugoslavia', *World Politics*, vol. 27, no. 3 (April) pp. 309–35.

LaPalombara, Joseph (1968) 'Macro Theories and Micro Applications in Comparative Politics: a Widening Chasm', *Comparative Politics*, vol. 1, no. 1 (October) pp. 52–78.

_____ (1974) *Politics within Nations*. (Englewood Cliffs, NJ: Prentice-Hall).

_____ (1975) 'Monoliths or Plural Systems: Through Conceptual Lenses Darkly', *Studies in Comparative Communism*, vol. 8, no. 3 (autumn) pp. 305–32.

Lapidus, Gail W. (1975) 'Political Mobilization, Participation, and Leadership: Women in Soviet Politics', *Comparative Politics*, vol. 8, no. 1 (October) pp. 90–118.

_____ (1976) 'Socialism and Modernity: Education, Industrialization and Social Change in the USSR', in Cocks *et al.* (1976).

_____ (1977) 'Sexual Equality in Soviet Policy: a Developmental Perspective', in Atkinson *et al.* (1977).

Lardy, Nicholas (1975) 'Centralization and Decentralization in China's Fiscal Management', *China Quarterly*, no. 61 (March) pp. 25–60.

_____ (1978) *Economic Growth and Distribution in China* (Cambridge: Cambridge University Press).

Lazarcik, Gregor (1967) 'The Performance of Czechoslovak Agriculture since World War II', in Jerzy K. Karcz (ed.), *Soviet and East European Agriculture* (Berkeley: Univeristy of California Press).

Lazarev, B. M. (1971) 'Sotsial'nye interesy i kompetentsiya organov upravleniya', *Sovetskoe gosudarstvo i pravo*, no. 10, pp. 86–94.

Lazreg, Marina (1979) 'Human Rights, State and Ideology: an Historical Perspective', in Pollis and Schwab (1979).

Lees, John D. and Malcolm Shaw (eds) (1979) *Committees in Legislatures* (Oxford: Martin Robertson).

Leichter, Howard M. (1979) *A Comparative Approach to Policy Analysis: Health Care Policy in Four Nations* (Cambridge: Cambridge University Press).

Leifried, Stephen (1978) 'Public Assistance in the United States and the Federal Republic of Germany: does Social Democracy make a Difference?', *Comparative Politics*, vol. 11, no. 1 (October) pp. 59–76.

Lenin, V. I. (1932) *State and Revolution* (New York: International Publishers).

Lennon, Lotta (1971) 'Women in the USSR', *Problems of Communism*, vol. 20, no. 4 (July–August) pp. 47–58.

Lenski, Gerhard (1966) *Power and Privilege: A Theory of Social Stratification* (New York: McGraw-Hill).

LeoGrande, William M. (1978a) 'A Bureaucratic Approach to Civil-military Relations in Communist Systems: the Case of Cuba', in Herspring and Volgyes (1978).

_____ (1978b) *The Development of the Party System in Revolutionary Cuba* (Erie, Pa.: Northwestern Pennsylvania Institute for Latin American Studies).

_____ (1978c) 'Continuity and Change in the Cuban Political Elite', *Cuban Studies*, vol. 8, no. 2 (July) pp. 1–31.

_____ (1978d) 'Civil-military Relations in Cuba', *Studies in Comparative Communism*, vol. 11, no. 3 (autumn) pp. 278–91.

Leonhard, Wolfgang (1965) *The Kremlin since Stalin* (London: Oxford University Press).

Leszczycki, Stanislaw (1970) 'Spatial Macro Structure of Poland's National Economy between 1961–1965', in *Proceedings of the Second Polish-Norden Regional Science Seminar* (Warsaw: PWN).

Lewis, John W. (1968) 'Leader, Commissar, and Bureaucrat: the Chinese Political System in the Last days of the Revolution', in Ping-ti Ho and Tang Tsou, (eds) *China in Crisis* (Chicago: University of Chicago Press).

Lezenski, Cezary (1978) 'Political Geography: the Democratic Party', *Polish Perspectives*, vol. 21, no. 11 (November) pp. 42–6.

Lieberthal, Kenneth (1976) *A Research Guide to Central Party and Government Meetings in China, 1949–1975* (White Plains, NY: IASP).

_____ (1979) *Central Documents and Politburo Politics in China* (Ann Arbor: University of Michigan Center for Chinese Studies).

Lijphart, Arend (1971) 'Comparative Politics and the Comparative Method', *American Political Science Review*, vol. 64, no. 3 (September) pp. 682–93.

Linden, Carl (1966) *Khrushchev and the Soviet Leadership, 1957–1964* (Baltimore, Md.: Johns Hopkins University Press).

Linz, Juan (1975) 'Totalitarian and Authoritarian Regimes', in Greenstein and Polsby (1975).

Lipset, Seymour M. (1963) (rev. ed. 1981). *Political Man* (London: Heinemann).

Lipski, Witold (1978) 'Political Geography: the United Peasants' Party', *Polish Perspectives*, vol. 21, no. 7–8 (July–August) pp. 25–9.

Lisandru, N. (1973) 'Modernization and the Development of Domestic Commerce', *Probleme Economica*, January.

'List Komitetu Centralnego KPZR do Komitetu Centralnego PZPR' (1981) *Nowe Drogi*, July, pp. 29–32.

Little, D. Richard (1969) 'Communist Studies in a Comparative Framework: Some Unorthodox Proposals', in Fleron (1969).

_____ (1971) 'Legislative Authority in the Soviet Political System', *Slavic Review*, vol. 30, no. 1 (March) pp. 57–73.

—— (1972) 'Soviet Parliamentary Committees after Khrushchev', *Soviet Studies*, vol. 24, no. 1 (July) pp. 41–60.

—— (1976) 'Mass Political Participation in the United States and the USSR', *Comparative Political Studies*, vol. 8, no. 4 (January) pp. 437–60.

—— (1977) 'Weak Legislatures: Potential Power as an Empirical Construct', unpublished paper, San Diego State University, California.

Łodz Survey (1980) 'Survey of 1000 males in the City of Łodz' (Warsaw: University of Warsaw Institute of Sociology and Institute of Philosophy and Sociology of the Polish Academy of Sciences).

Long, E. Norton (1966) 'Open and Closed Systems', in R. Barry Farrell (ed.), *Approaches to Comparative and International Politics* (Evanston, Ill.: Aldine).

Lowenhardt, John (1981) *Decision Making in Soviet Politics* (London: Macmillan).

Lowenthal, Richard (1970) 'Development vs. Utopia in Communist Policy', in Johnson (1970).

—— (1974) 'On "Established" Communist Party Regimes', *Studies in Comparative Communism*, vol. 7, no. 4 (winter) pp. 335–58.

Lowit, Thomas (1979) 'Y a-t-il des états en Europe de l'Est?', *Revue Française de Sociologie*, vol. 20, no. 2 (June) pp. 431–66.

Lukes, Steven (1975) 'Socialism and Equality', in Kolakowski and Hampshire (1975).

—— (1981) 'The Illusory Rhetoric of Human Rights', *Times Higher Education Supplement*, 30 January.

Lutrzykowski, Alfred and Janusz Zemke (1980) 'PZPR, ZSL i SD w sistemie politycznym Polski Ludowej', *Studia Nauk Politycznych*, no. 2, pp. 11–37.

Luryi, Yuri I. (1982) 'Three Years of the New USSR Constitution: the Soviet Approach to Human Rights', in Feldbrugge and Simons (1982).

Macartney, Carlile A. and Alan W. Palmer (1962) *Independent Eastern Europe: a History* (London: Macmillan).

McAuley, Alastair (1979) *Economic Welfare in the Soviet Union* (London: Allen & Unwin).

McAuley, Mary (1977) *Politics and the Soviet Union* (Harmondsworth: Penguin).

—— (1980) 'Party Recruitment and the Nationalities in the USSR', *British Journal of Political Science*, vol. 10. no. 4 (October) pp. 461–87.

MacClosky, Herbert and John E. Turner (1960) *The Soviet Dictatorship* (New York: McGraw-Hill).

MacFarquhar, Roderick (1974) *The Origins of the Cultural Revolution. Vol. 1: Contradictions among the People, 1956–57* (London: Oxford University Press).

McGrath, Bill and Simon McInnis (1976) 'Better Fewer but Better: on Approaches to the Study of Soviet and East European Politics', *Canadian Slavonic Papers*, vol. 18, no. 3 (September) pp. 327–37.

Machado, Jose (1969) 'In the Face of all Difficulties we Will not Forget the Fundamental Factor', *Granma Weekly Review*, 29 June.

—— (1978) 'The Party Leadership has Confidence in the Work You Will be Doing', *Granma Weekly Review*, 8 October.

Madison, Bernice Q. (1968) *Social Welfare in the Soviet Union* (Stanford, Calif.: Stanford University Press).

Malanowski, Jan (1981) *Polscy robotnicy* (Warsaw: Ksiazka i wiedza).

Mao Tse-Tung (1966) *Quotations from Chairman Mao Tse-Tung* (Peking: Foreign Languages Press).

Marx, Karl (1954) *The Communist Manifesto* (Chicago: Regnery).

—— (1978) 'Critique of the Gotha Program', in Robert C. Tucker (ed.), *The Marx-Engels Reader* (New York: Norton).

Mason, David (1977) 'Elite Change and Policy in Communist Poland', unpublished PhD dissertation, Indiana University, Bloomington, Ind.

_____ (1982a) 'Membership of the Polish United Workers' Party', *The Polish Review*, vol. 27, nos 3–4, pp. 138–53.

_____ (1982b) 'Solidarity and Public Opinion'. Paper presented to the Annual Meeting of the American Association for the Advancement of Slavic Studies, Washington DC.

_____ (1983a) 'Solidarity, the Regime and the Public', *Soviet Studies*, vol. 34, no. 4 (October) pp. 533–45.

_____ (1983b) 'Policy Dilemmas and Political Unrest in Poland', *Journal of Politics*, vol. 45, no. 2 (May) pp. 397–421.

_____ (1984) 'Solidarity and Socialism', in Bielasiak and Simon (1984).

Matthews, Mervyn (1972) *Class and Society in Soviet Russia* (New York: Walker).

_____ (comp., 1974) *Soviet Government: A Selection of Official Documents on Internal Policy* (London: Cape).

_____ (1975) 'Top Incomes in the USSR: Towards a Definition of the Soviet Elite', *Survey*, vol. 21, no. 3 (summer) pp. 1–27.

_____ (1978) *Privilege in the Soviet Union* (London: Allen & Unwin).

Maxwell, James A. (1971) 'Revenue Sharing in Canada and Australia: some Implications for the United States', *National Tax Journal*, vol. 24 (June) pp. 251–65.

Medvedev, Roy A. (1975) *On Socialist Democracy* (London: Macmillan).

_____ (1979) *On Stalin and Stalinism* (Oxford: Oxford University Press).

Meissner, Boris and Georg Brunner (1975) *Gruppeninteressen und Entscheidungsprozesse in der Sowjetunion* (Cologne: Wissenschaft und Politik).

Merritt, Richard L. (1970) *Systematic Approaches to Comparative Politics* (Chicago: Rand McNally).

Mesa-Lago, Carmelo (ed.) (1971) *Revolutionary Change in Cuba* (Pittsburgh: University of Pittsburgh Press).

_____ (1978) *Cuba in the 1970s* (Albuqurque: University of New Mexico Press).

Mesa-Lago, Carmelo and Carl Beck (eds) (1975) *Comparative Socialist Systems. Essays on Politics and Economics* (Pittsburgh: University of Pittsburgh Press).

Mesa-Lago, Carmelo and Hernandez, Roberto E. (1976) 'Workers' Incomes in Socialist Cuba', in Alejandro Foxley (ed.), *Income Distribution in Latin America* (Cambridge: Cambridge University Press).

Meyer, Alfred G. (1965) *The Soviet Political System: An Interpretation* (New York: Random House).

_____ (1969) 'The Comparative Study of Communist Political Systems', in Fleron, (1969).

_____ (1972) 'Communist Revolutions and Cultural Change', *Studies in Comparative Communism*, vol. 5, no. 4 (winter) pp. 345–72.

_____ (1977) 'Marxism and the Women's Movement', in Atkinson *et al.* (1977).

Mezey, Michael L. (1979) *Comparative Legislatures* (Durham, NC: Duke University Press).

Middleton, Chris (1974) 'Sexual Inequality and Stratification Theory', in Frank Parkin (ed.), *The Social Analysis of Class Structure* (London: Tavistock).

Mihu, Achim and Voicu Lascus (1973) 'Which Careers are Preferred by Young Students?', *Era Socialista*, no. 7.

Milc, Stanislaw (1978) 'Political Geography: the Polish United Workers' Party', *Polish Perspectives*, vol. 21, no. 12 (December) pp. 22–6.

Milenkovitch, Deborah (1971) *Plan and Market in Yugoslav Economic Thought* (New Haven: Yale University Press).

Millar, James R. (1977) 'The Prospects for Soviet Agriculture', *Problems of Communism*, vol. 26, no. 3 (May–June) pp. 1–16.

Miller, John H. (1977) 'Cadres Policy in Nationality Areas', *Soviet Studies*, vol. 29, no. 1 (January) pp. 3–36.

—— (1982) 'The Communist Party: Trends and Problems', in Brown and Kaser (1982).

—— (1983) 'Nomenklatura: Check on Localism?', in Rigby and Harasymiw (1983).

Minagawa, Shugo (1975) 'The Functions of Supreme Soviet Organs', *Soviet Studies*, vol. 27, no. 1 (January) pp. 46–70.

—— (1979) 'Regional First Secretaries in Soviet Parliamentary Committees', *Soviet Union*, vol. 6, part 1, pp. 1–40.

Misztal, Barbara and Bronislaw Misztal (1982) 'Transformations of Political Elites in Poland'. Paper presented at the Annual Meeting of the Midwest Political Science Association, Milwaukee, Wisc.

Moore, Barrington (1967) *Social Origins of Dictartorship and Democracy* (London: Allen Lane).

Moraca, Pero *et al.* (1976) *Istorija Saveza komunista Jugoslavije* (Belgrade: Rad).

Morawski, Witold (1981) 'O zrodlach i naturze kryzsu 1980–1981 w Polsce', *Literatura*, 24 September.

Morton, Henry W. and Rudolf L. Tokes (eds) (1974) *Soviet Politics and Society in the 1970s* (New York: Free Press).

Moses, Joel (1974) *Regional Party Leadership and Policy-Making in the USSR* (New York: Praeger).

Mote, Max E. (1965) *Soviet Local and Republican Elections* (Stanford, Calif.: Hoover Institution).

Myrdal, Gunnar (1957) *Economic Theory and Underdeveloped Regions* (New York: Harper).

Nagle, John (1977) *Systems and Succession: The Social Bases of Elite Recruitment* (Austin, Texas: University of Texas Press).

Narkhoz (Various dates) *Narodnoe khozyaistvo SSSR v . . . godu. Statisticheskii ezhegodnik* (Moscow: Finansy i statistika).

Naselenie SSSR (1975) *Naselenie SSSR: statisticheskii sbornik* (Moscow: Statistika).

Neal, Fred W. (1958) *Titoism in Action. The Reforms in Yugoslavia after 1948* (Berkeley: University of California Press).

Nee, Victor and David Mozingo (eds) (1983) *State and Society in Contemporary China* (Ithaca: Cornell University Press).

Nelson, Daniel N. (1980a) 'Editor's Introduction: Communist Legislatures and Communist Politics', *Legislative Studies Quarterly*, vol. 5, no. 2 (May) pp. 161–73.

—— (1980b) *Democratic Centralism in Romania* (Boulder, Col.: East European Monographs).

—— (ed.) (1980c) *Local Politics in Communist Countries* (Lexington, Ky.: University of Kentucky Press).

—— (1981a) 'Vertical Integration and Political Control in Eastern Europe: the Polish and Romanian Cases', *Slavic Review*, vol. 40, no. 2 (June) pp. 210–27.

—— (ed.) (1981b) *Romania in the 1980s* (Boulder, Col.: Westview Press).

—— (1981c) 'Romania', in Welsh (1981).

—— (1981d) 'The Worker and Political Alienation in Communist Europe'. Paper presented to the Midwestern Political Science Association Meeting, Cincinnati, Ohio.

Nelson, Daniel N. and Stephen White (eds) (1982) *Communist Legislatures in Comparative Perspective* (London: Macmillan and New York: SUNY Press).

Nettl, John P. (1967) *Political Mobilisation* (London: Faber).

Nicholson, Joe (1974) *Inside Cuba* (New York: Sheed & Ward).

Nie, Norman, *et al.* (1969) 'Social Structure and Political Participation: Developmental Relationships', 2 parts. *American Political Science Review*, vol. 63, nos 2 and 3 (June and September) pp. 361–78 and 808–32.

Notle, Hans-Heinrich (1979) *Gruppeninteressen und Aussenpolitik: Die Sowjetunion in der Geschichte Internationaler Beziehungen* (Gottingen: Munster-Schmidt).

Nove, Alec (1975) 'Is There a Ruling Class in the USSR?', *Soviet Studies*, vol. 27, no. 4 (October) pp. 615–38.

—— (1977) *The Soviet Economic System* (London: Allen & Unwin).

Nove, Alec and J. A. Newth, (1967) *The Soviet Middle East* (New York: Praeger).

Nowak, Stefan (1979) 'System wartosci spoleczenstwa Polskiego', *Studia Socio-logiczne*, no. 4, pp. 155-73.

—— (1981) 'Values and Attitudes of the Polish People', *Scientific American*, no. 245 (July) pp. 45–53.

Nudnenko, L. A. (1975) 'Otchety deputatov Verkhovnogo Soveta SSSR pered izbiratelyami', *Vestnik MGU: pravo*, no. 4, pp. 42–8.

Oakley, Ann (1981) *Subject Women* (Oxford: Martin Robertson).

Odom, William (1973) 'The Soviet Military: the Party Connection', *Problems of Communism*, vol. 22, no. 5 (September–October) pp. 12–26.

—— (1976a) 'A Dissenting View on the Group Approach to Soviet Politics', *World Politics*, vol. 28, no. 4 (July) pp. 542–67.

—— (1976b) 'The "Militarization" of Soviety Society', *Problems of Communism*, vol. 25, no. 5 (September–October) pp. 34–51.

Oksenberg, Michel (1974) 'Methods of Communication within the Chinese Bureaucracy', *China Quarterly*, no. 57 (January–March) pp. 1–39.

Oksenberg, Michel and Richard Bush (1982) 'China's Political Evolution: 1972–82', *Problems of Communism*, vol. 31, no. 5 (September–October) pp. 1–19.

Okun, Arthur M. (1975) *Equality and Efficiency: The Big Trade-Off* (Washington DC: Brookings).

Oliver, James H. (1969) 'Citizen Demands and the Soviet Political System', *American Political Science Review*, vol. 63, no. 2 (June) pp. 465–75.

—— (1973) 'Turnover and Family Circles in Soviet Administration', *Slavic Review*, vol. 32, no. 3 (September) pp. 527–45.

Olson, David M. (1980) *The Legislative Process: A Comparative Approach* (New York: Harper & Row).

—— (1982) 'The Polish Sejm in Comparative Perspective: Dimensions of Analysis', *The Polish Roundtable* (Warsaw).

Osrodek Badania Opinii Publicznej i Studiow Programowych (1980, 1981) Survey no. 27 (189), December 1980; no. 1 (192), January 1981; no. 10 (20), March 1981.

Ossowski, Stanislaw (1963) *Class Structure in the Social Consciousness* (London: Routledge).

Ostrowski, Krzysztof (1979) 'Aktywnosc polityczna robotnikow', in Wajda (ed.) (1979).

Ostrowski, Krzysztof and Sufin, Zbigniew (1979) 'Aktywnosc spoleczne w swietle badan', *Nowe Drogi*, no. 11 (November) pp. 161–3.

Park, Hans S. (1980) 'Human Rights and Modernisation: a Dialectical Relationship?', *Universal Human Rights*, vol. 2, no. 1.

Parkin, Frank (1971) *Class Inequality and Political Order: Social Stratification in Communist and Capitalist Societies* (New York: Praeger).

―― (ed.) (1974) *The Social Analysis of Class Structure* (London: Tavistock).

―― (1979) *Marxism and Class Theory: A Bourgeois Critique*. (London: Tavistock).

Partiino-politicheskaya rabota v Sovetskikh vooruzhennykh silakh (1974) (Moscow: Voenizdat).

Pasic, Najdan (1976) 'Osnove karakteristike i pravci razvoya drustvenopolitickog sistema SFRJ', in Pasic and Spadjier (eds) (1976).

Pasic, Najdan and Balsa Spadjier (eds) (1976) *Drustveno Politicki Sistem SFRJ* (Belgrade: Radnicka stampa).

Patterson, Samuel C. and John C. Wahlke (1978) 'Trends and Prospects in Legislative Behavior Research', in Heinz Eulau and John C. Wahlke (eds), *The Politics of Representation* (Beverly Hills, Calif.: Sage Publications).

Pelczynski, Zbigniew (1959) 'Poland 1957', in Butler (1959).

Pelikan, Jiri (ed.) (1972) *The Secret Vysocany Congress* (London: Allen Lane).

―― (ed.) (1975) *Civil and Academic Freedom in the USSR and Eastern Europe* Nottingham, Eng.: Spokesman).

Pervan, Ralph (1978) *Tito and the Students* (Nedlands: University of Western Australia Press).

Petrescu, Ion (1977) *Psihosociologia Conducerii Colectiva a Intreprinderii Industriale* (Craiova: Scrisul Romanesc).

Peikalkiewicz, Jaroslav A. (1972) *Public Opinion Polling in Czechoslovakia 1968–69* (New York: Praeger).

Pirages, Dennis (1969) 'Socioeconomic Development and Political Access in the Communist Party States', in Jan Triska (ed.), *Communist Party States* (Indianapolis: Bobbs-Merrill).

Plataforma Programatica del Partido Comunista de Cuba (1976) (La Habana: Departamento de Orientacion Revolucionaria).

Pohorille, Maksymillian (1982) 'Question of Income Distribution in Poland', *Economic and Industrial Democracy*, vol. 3, pp. 159–76.

Polacy '80,'81 (1981, 1982) (Warsaw: Polska Akademia Nauk).

Poland (1978) *Constitution of the Polish People's Republic* (Warsaw: KAW).

Poland. Sejm. (1976a) *Informacja o dzialanosci Sejmu (VI kadencja, 1972–76)* (Warsaw).

―― (1976b) *Spis poslow na Sejm*. (Warsaw).

―― (1978/79) Unpublished file of legislative documents, Sejm Library.

Poland Today: The State of the Republic (1981) (White Plains, NY: M. E. Sharpe).

Polish United Workers' Party (1976) *For a Further Dynamic Development of Socialist Construction* (Warsaw: Polska Agencja Interpress).

―― (1980) *VIII Zjazd PZPR: Podstawowe dokumenty i materialy* (Warsaw: Ksiazka i wiedza).

Pollis, Adamantia and Peter Schwab (eds) (1979) *Human Rights: Cultural and Ideological Perspectives* (New York: Praeger).

Polonsky, Antony (1972) *Politics in Independent Poland* (Oxford: Clarendon Press).

Popkowski, Wojciech (1980) 'Niektore problemy działalnosci komisji Sejmu VII i VI kadencji ', *Panstwo i Prawo*, vol. 35 (February) pp. 37–51.

Popovic, Mirko (1978) 'Sitem socijalisticke samoupravne demokratije i uloga Saveza komunista Jugoslavije', in Roksandic (1978).

Powell, David and Paul Shoup (1970) 'The Emergence of Political Science in Communist Countries', *American Political Science Review*, vol. 64, no. 2 (June) pp. 572–88.

Pravda, Alex (1976) 'Gierek's Poland: Five Years On', *The World Today*, vol. 32, no. 7 (July) pp. 270–8.

—— (1982) 'Poland 1980: from "Premature Consumerism" to Labour Solidarity', *Soviet Studies*, vol. 34, no. 2 (April) pp. 167–99.

Preda, Micea and Ioan Vida (1975) 'Ethical, Political and Juridical Interferences at the Level of Individual Conscience', *Viitorul Social*, no. 2, pp. 322–30.

Pressman, Jeffrey and Aaron Wildavsky (1973) *Implementation* (Berkeley: University of California).

'Program NZSS Solidarnosci', (1981) *Tygodnik Solidarnosc*, 16 October.

Program of the Romanian Communist Party for the Building of the Multilaterally Developed Society (1975) (Bucharest: Agerpress).

Programme (1977) *Programme of the League of Communists of Yugoslavia* (Belgrade: Komunist).

Proiect-directivele Congresului al XII-lea al Partidului Comunist Roman cu privire la Devoltarea Economica-Sociala a Romaniei in Cincianul 1981–1985 si Orientarile de Perspectiva Pina in 1990 (1980) (Bucharest).

Protokoly Porozumien Gdansk, Szczecin, Jastrzebie i Status NSZZ "Solidarnosc" (1980) (Warsaw: KAW).

Pryor, Frederick L. (1968) *Public Expenditures in Communist and Capitalist Countries* (London: Allen & Unwin).

—— (1971) *Economic System and the Size Distribution of Income and Wealth* (Bloomington, Ind.: International Development Research Center, Indiana University).

—— (1972) 'The Distribution of Nonagricultural Labor Incomes in Communist and Capitalist Nations', *Slavic Review*, vol. 31, no. 3 (September) pp. 639–50.

Ptakowski, Jerzy (1965) 'Parliamentary Elections in Poland', *East Europe*, vol. 14, no. 8 (August) pp. 15–19.

Puklov, S. (1981) 'Otnoshenie Moskvichei k profsoyuzu *Solidarnost*', in Valery Chalidze (ed.), *SSSR: Vnutrennye protivorechiya* (New York: Chalidze Press).

Pusic, E. (1976) 'The Yugoslav System of Self-management', *Encyclopedia Moderna*, vol. 9, nos 32–35.

Putnam, Robert D. (1976) *The Comparative Study of Political Elites* (Englewood Cliffs NJ: Prentice-Hall).

Putnam, Ruth A. (1976) 'Rights of Persons and the Liberal Tradition', in Ted Honderich, (ed.), *Social Ends and Political Means* (London: Routledge).

Pye, Lucian (1980) *The Dynamics of Factions and Consensus in Chinese Politics* (Santa Monica: Rand Corporation).

—— (1981) *The Dynamics of Chinese Politics* (Cambridge, Mass: Oelgeschlager, Gunn and Haigh).

Radosh, Ronald (ed.) (1976) *The New Cuba: Paradoxes and Potentials* (New York: Morrow).

Radu-Radulescu, Nicolae (1977) *Forta de munca: stabilitate-mobilitate* (Bucharest; Editura Stintifica si).

Rakowska-Harmstone, Teresa (1974) 'The Dialectics of Nationalism in the USSR', *Problems of Communism*, vol. 23, no. 3 (May-June) pp. 1–22.

—— (1976) 'Toward a Theory of Soviet Leadership Maintenance', in Cocks *et al.* (1976).

Ranney, Austin (ed.) (1962) *Essays on the Behavioral Study of Politics* (Urbana, Ill.: University of Illinois Press).

Raphael, David D. (ed.) (1967) *Political Theory and the Rights of Man* (London: Macmillan).

Rashidov, Sh. R. (1971) In *Pravda vostoka*, 4 February.

Rausser, Vasile (1972) 'Romania's Economic Relations with the Developing Countries', *Revue Roumaine des Sciences Sociales: Série de Sciences Economiques*, vol. 16, no. 2.

Reddaway, Peter (1975) 'The Development of Opposition', in Brown and Kaser (1975), pp. 121–56.

_____ (1983) 'Dissent in the Soviet Union', *Problems of Communism*, vol. 32, no. 6 (November–December) pp. 1–15.

Ren-min Shou-ce (1979) (Peking: People's Daily Press).

'Resolucion del VIII pleno del Comite Central' (1979) *Bohemia*, 25 May, pp. 58–65.

Resolution (1981) *Resolution on CPC History (1949–81)* (Beijing: Foreign Languages Press).

Richman, Barry (1969) *Industrial Society in Communist China* (New York: Random House).

Rigby, T. H. (1968) *Communist Party Membership in the USSR, 1917–1967* (Princeton, NJ: Princeton University Press).

_____ (1969) 'Traditional, Market and Organisational Societies and the USSR', in Fleron (1969), pp. 170–87.

_____ (1972) 'The Soviet Politburo: a Comparative Profile, 1951–1971', *Soviet Studies*, vol. 24, no. 1 (July) pp. 3–23.

_____ (1976) 'Hough on Political Participation in the Soviet Union', *Soviet Studies*, vol. 28, no. 2 (April) pp. 257–61.

_____ (1980) 'A Conceptual Approach to Authority, Power and Policy in the Soviet Union', in T. H. Rigby *et al.* (eds), *Authority, Power and Policy in the USSR* (London: Macmillan).

_____ (1982) 'Political Legitimacy, Weber and Communist Mono-organisational Systems', in T. H. Rigby and Ferenc Feher (eds), *Political Legitimation in Communist Systems* (London: Macmillan).

Rigby, T. H. and Bogdan Harasymiw (eds) (1983) *Leadership Selection and Patron-Client Relations in the USSR and Yugoslavia* (London: Allen & Unwin).

Rimlinger, Gaston V. (1971) *Welfare Policy and Industrialization in Europe, America and Russia* (New York: Wiley).

Robinson, Ann (1978) *Parliament and Public Spending* (London: Heinemann).

Rocznik Polityczny i Gospodarczy (various years) (Warsaw: PWE).

Rocznik Statystyczny (various years) (Warsaw: Glowny Urzad Statystyczny).

Roksandic, Drago (ed.) (1978) *Savez Komunista Jugoslavije u razvoju socialistog samoupravljanja*, vol. 1 (Belgrade: Komunist).

Rothschild, Joseph (1974) *East Central Europe between the Two World Wars* (Seattle and London: University of Washington Press).

Rothstein, Andrew (ed.) (1923) *The Soviet Constitution* (London: Labour Publishing Co.)

Rovinsky, E. A. (ed.) (1978) *Sovetskoe finansovoe pravo* (Moscow: Yuridicheskaya literatura).

Ruble, Blair (1981) *Soviet Trade Unions: Their Development in the 1970s.* (Cambridge: Cambridge University Press).

Runciman, W. G. (1974) 'Towards a Theory of Social Stratification', in Parkin (ed) (1974).

Rusinow, Dennison (1977) *The Yugoslav Experiment 1948–1974* (London: Hurst).

Russett, Bruce M. (1967) 'Inequality and Instability: the Relation of Land Tenure to Politics', in Robert A. Dahl and Deane E. Neubauer (eds), *Readings in Modern Political Analysis* (Englewood Cliffs, NJ: Prentice-Hall).

_____ (1970) *What Price Vigilance? The Burdens of National Defense* (New Haven, Conn.: Yale University Press).

Sadowski, Michał (1978) 'Zycie społezno-politiczne', in Zofie Lewandowska (ed.), *Polska kraj i ludzie* (Warsaw: Polska Agencja Ludowej).

Saich, Tony (1984) 'Party-building since Mao: a Question of Style?', in Neville Maxwell and Bruce McFarlane (eds), *China's Changed Road to Development* (Oxford: Pergamon).

Sakwa, George and Martin Crouch (1978) 'Sejm Elections in Communist Poland: an Overview and a Reappraisal', *British Journal of Political Science*, vol. 8, no. 4 (October) pp. 403–24.

Salaff, Janet W. and Judith Merkle, (1973) 'Women and Revolutions: the Lessons of the Soviet Union and China', in Marilyn B. Young (ed.), *Women in China: Studies in Social Change and Feminism* (Ann Arbor: University of Michigan Center for Chinese Studies).

Salisbury, Robert, (1975) 'Interest Groups', in Greenstein and Polsby, (eds.) (1975).

Samoupravni (1978) *Samoupravni drustveno ekonomski razvoj Jugoslavije 1947–1977* (Belgrade: Savezni zavod za statistiku).

Sanford, George (1983) *Polish Communism in Crisis* (New York: St Martin's).

Sarapata, Adam (1979) 'Polish Automobile Workers and Automation', in Jan Forslin *et al.* (eds), *Automation and Industrial Workers*, vol. 1 (Oxford: Pergamon).

Sartori, Giovanni (1970) 'Concept Misinformation in Comparative Politics', *American Political Science Review*, vol. 64, no. 4 (December) pp. 1033–53.

Scase, Richard (1974). 'Conceptions of the Class Structure and Political Ideology', in Parkin (ed.) (1974).

Scharf, C. Bradley (1984) *Politics and Change in East Germany* (Boulder, Col.: Westview Press).

Schmitter, Philippe (1974) 'Still the Century of Corporatism?', *Review of Politics*, vol. 36, no. 1 (January) pp. 85–131.

_____ (1977) 'Modes of Interest Intermediation and Models of Societal Change in Western Europe', *Comparative Political Studies*, vol. 10, no. 1 (April) pp. 7–38.

Schram, Stuart R. (1963) *The Political Thought of Mao Tse-Tung* (New York: Praeger).

_____ (1969) 'The Party in Chinese Communist Ideology', *China Quarterly*, no. 38 (April–June) pp. 1–26.

_____ (1973) 'The Cultural Revolution in Historical Perspective', in Stuart R. Schram (ed.), *Authority, Participation and Cultural Change in China* (Cambridge: Cambridge University Press).

_____ (ed.) (1974) *Mao Tse-Tung Unrehearsed* (Harmondsworth: Penguin).

_____ (1981) 'To Utopia and Back: a Cycle in the History of the Chinese Communist Party', *China Quarterly*, no. 87 (September) pp. 407–39.

Schnitzer, Martin (1974) *Income Distribution. A Comparative Study of the United States, Sweden, West Germany, East Germany, the United Kingdom, and Japan* (New York: Praeger).

Schroeder, Gertrude (1973) 'Regional Differences in Incomes and Levels of Living in the USSR', in V. N. Bandera and Z. L. Melnyk (1973).

Schurmann, Franz (1966) (rev. ed. 1968) *Ideology and Organization in Communist China* (Berkeley: University of California Press).

Seroka, James H. (1979) 'Legislative Recruitment and Political Change in Yugoslavia', *Legislative Studies Quarterly*, vol. 4, no. 1 (February) pp. 105–19.

_____ (1982) 'The Limits of Aggregate Budgetary Analysis of Communist States: the Case of Yugoslavia', *Politics*, vol. 2, no. 1 (April) pp. 20–6.

Seroka, James H. and Maurice Simon (eds.) (1982) *Developed Socialism* (Boulder, Col.: Westview Press).
Seymour, James D. (1976) *China: The Politics of Revolutionary Reintegration* (New York: Crowell).
Sharlet, Robert (1978) *The New Soviet Constitution of 1977. Analysis and Text* (Brunswick, Ohio: King's Court Communications).
Shcherbitsky, V. V. (1971) In *Pravda Ukrainy*, 11 February.
Sheehy, Ann (1972) 'Some Aspects of Regional Development in Soviet Central Asia', *Slavic Review*, vol. 31, no. 3 (September) pp. 555–63.
Sheliag, V. V. *et al.* (1972) *Voennaya psikhologiya* (Moscow: Voenizdat).
Shermenev, M. K. (ed.) (1978) *Gosudarstvennyi byudzhet SSSR*, 2nd ed. (Moscow: Finansy).
Shibata, XXX Shingo (1975) 'Fundamental Human rights and Problems of Freedom', *Social Praxis*, vol. 3, nos 3–4, pp. 157–86.
Shibutani, Tamotsu and Kain M. Kwan (1965) *Ethnic Stratification* (New York: Macmillan).
Shitikov, A. P. (1979) 'Devyatyi sozyv', *Sovety narodnykh deputatov*, no. 2, pp. 16–25.
Shoup, Paul (1968) *Communism and the Yugoslav National Question* (New York: Columbia University Press).
_____ (1971) 'Comparing Communist Nations: Prospects for an Empirical Approach', in Kanet (ed.) (1971).
_____ (1975) 'Indicators of Socio-political-economic Development', in Mesa-Lago and Beck (1975).
Shtemenko, S. M. (1968) *General'nyi shtab v gody voiny*, vol. 1 (Moscow: Voenizdat).
Shtromas, Alexander (1979) 'Dissent and Political Change in the Soviet Union', *Studies in Comparative Communism*, vol. 12, nos 2–3 (Spring–Summer) pp. 212–44.
_____ (1981) *Political Change and Social Development: the Case of the Soviet Union* (Frankfurt/Main: Peter Lang).
Sidjanski, Dusan (ed.) (1973) *Political Decision-Making Processes* (Amsterdam: Elsevier).
Silver, Brian (1974a) 'Social Mobilization and the Russification of Soviet Nationalities', *American Political Science Review*, vol. 68, no. 1 (March) pp. 45–66.
_____ (1974b) 'Levels of Sociocultural Development among Soviet Nationalities: a Partial Test of the Equalization Hypothesis', *American Political Science Review*, vol. 68, no. 4 (December) pp. 1618–37.
Simon, Herbert (1976) *Administrative Behavior* (New York: Free Press).
Simon, Maurice D. (1980) 'A Window on Poland's Social Transformation', *Problems of Communism*, vol. 29, no. 2 (March–April) pp. 76–80.
Simon, Maurice D. and Roger E. Kanet (eds) (1981) *Background to Crisis: Policy and Politics in Gierek's Poland* (Boulder, Col.: Westview Press).
Simons, William B. (ed.) (1980) *The Constitutions of the Communist World* (Alphen aan den Rijn: Sijthoff and Noordhoff).
Simons, William B. and Stephen White (eds) (1984) *The Party Statutes of the Communist World* (The Hague: Martinus Nijhoff).
Singleton, Fred (1976) *Twentieth-Century Yugoslavia* (London: Macmillan).
_____ (1985) *A Short History of the Yugoslav Peoples* (Cambridge: Cambridge University Press).
Sirbu, Mariana (1977) 'Integration in Work and Political Participation in the Process of Developing Socialist Consciousness', in Constantin Potinga and

Vasile Popescu (eds), *Constiinta Socialista si participare sociala* (Bucharest: Editura Academiei).
Skilling, H. Gordon (1966a) *The Governments of Communist East Europe* (New York: Crowell).
_____ (1966b) 'Interest Groups and Communist Politics', *World Politics*, vol. 18, no. 3 (April) pp. 435–51.
_____ (1968) 'Background to the Study of Opposition in Communist Europe'. *Government and Opposition*, vol. 3, no. 3 (summer) pp. 294–324.
_____ (1970) 'Group Conflict and Political Change', in Johnson (1970).
_____ (1974) *Pressure Groups in der Sowjetunion* (Vienna: Europaverlag).
_____ (1976) *Czechoslovakia's Interrupted Revolution* (Princeton, NJ: Princeton University Press).
_____ (1980) 'Pluralism in Communist Societies: Straw Men and Red Herrings', *Studies in Comparative Communism*, vol. 13, no. 1 (Spring) pp. 82–8.
_____ (1981) *Charter 77 and Human Rights in Czechoslovakia* (London: Allen & Unwin).
Skilling, H. Gordon and Franklyn Griffiths (eds) (1971) *Interest Groups in Soviet Politics* (Princeton, NJ: Princeton University Press).
Smith, Gordon B. (1982) 'Development and Evolution of "Socialist Legality" in the Soviet Union', in Feldbrugge and Simons (1982).
Smith, Hedrick (1976) *The Russians* (New York: Quadrangle).
Smolar, Aleksander (1981) 'Dystribucja dobr spo\łecznych i rozklad systemu', *Aneks*, no. 26, pp. 24, 35.
Sobre los organos del poder popular (1976) (La Habana: Departamento de Orientacion Revolucionaria).
Sobre la vida interna del Partido (1976) In *Tesis y Resoluciones* (1976).
Sobre el pleno ejercicio de la igualdad de la mujer (1976) (La Habana: Departamento de Orientacion Revolucionaria).
Sokolewicz, Wojciech (1975) 'Changes in the Structure and Functions of the Polish Sejm', *East Central Europe*, vol. 11, no. 1 (January) pp. 78–91.
Sokolovsky, V. D. *et al.* (1968) *Voennaya strategiya* (Moscow: Voenizdat).
Solomon, Peter H. (1978) *Soviet Criminologists and Criminal Policy: Specialists in Policy Making* (New York: Columbia University Press).
Solomon, Susan G. (ed.) (1983) *Pluralism in the Soviet Union* (London: Macmillan).
Sontheimer, Kurt and Wilhelm Bleek (1975) *The Government and Politics of East Germany* (London: Hutchinson).
Soskic, Budislav (1978) 'Razvoj i sustina drustvene uloge Saveza Komunista Jugoslavije', in Roksandic (1978).
Soviet Ekonomicheskoi Vzaimopomoshchi (1977) *Statisticheskii ezhegodnik stranchlenov Soveta Ekonomicheskoi Vzaimopomoshchi* (Moscow: Statistika).
Spielman, Karl F. (1976) 'Defense Industrialists in the USSR', *Problems of Communism*, vol. 25, no. 5 (September–October) pp. 52–69.
Spielman, Richard (1982–3) 'Crisis in Poland', *Foreign Policy*, no. 49 (winter) pp. 20.
Staar, Richard F. (ed.) (1978) *Yearbook of International Communist Affairs 1978*, (Stanford, Calif.: Hoover Institution Press).
Stalin, I. V. (1949) *Sochineniya*, vol. 10 (Moscow: Gospolitizdat).
Staniszkis, Jadwiga (1979) 'On some Contradictions of Socialist Society: the Case of Poland', *Soviet Studies*, vol. 31, no. 2 (April) pp. 167–87.
_____ (1981) 'The Evolution of Working-class Protest in Poland', *Soviet Studies*, vol. 33, no. 2 (April) pp. 204–31.

Statistiches Bundesamt (Various years) *Statistiches Jahrbuch fur die Bundes-republik Deutschland* (Stuttgart: W. Kohlhammer).

Statisticki (1978) *Statisticki podaci o SKJ desetog i jedanaestog kongresa SKJ* (Belgrade; Komunist).

Statistics Canada (various years) *Canada Yearbook* (Ottawa: Information Canada).

Stefanowski, Roman (1977) 'Workers' Councils 1956–1977', Radio Free Europe, Background Report No. 160, 9 August.

—— (1982) *Poland: A Chronology of Events February–July 1981* (Munich: Radio Free Europe).

Stelmach, Waldemar (1979) 'Udziałrobotnikow w procesach zarzadonia socjalis-tycznymi zakładami pracy', in Wajda (1979).

Stewart, Philip (1969) 'Soviet Interest Groups and the Policy Process: the Repeal of Production Education', *World Politics*, vol. 22, no. (October) pp. 29–50.

Stewart, Philip *et al.* (1972) 'Political Mobility and the Soviet Political Process: a Partial Test of Two Models', *American Political Science Review*, vol. 66, no. 4 (December) pp. 1269–90.

Sufin, Zbigniew (ed.) (1981) *Diagnozy społeczne w okresie narastajacego kryszysu* (Warsaw: Institut Podstawowych Problemow Marksizmu-Leninizmu).

Sullivan, John C. (1972) 'A Note on Redistributive Politics', *American Political Science Review*, vol. 66, no. 4 (December) pp. 1301–5.

Suvar, Stipe (1976) In Pasic and Spadjier (1976).

Swafford, Michael (1978) 'Sex Differences in Soviet Earnings', *American Socio-logical Review*, vol. 43, no. 5 (October) pp. 657–73.

Swearer, Howard R. (1961) 'The Functions of Soviet Local Elections', *Midwest Journal of Political Science*, vol. 5, no. 2 (May) pp. 129–49.

Szajkowski, Bogdan (ed.) (1981) *Marxist Governments. A World Survey*, 3 vols (London: Macmillan).

—— (1982) *The Evolution of Marxist Regimes* (London: Butterworths).

—— (gen. ed.) (1985ff) *Marxist Regimes. Politics, Economics and Society*, 36 vols (London: Frances Pinter).

Szczypiorski, Andrej (1982) *The Polish Ordeal: The View from Within* (London: Croom Helm).

Szelenyi, Ivan (1978) 'Social Inequalities in State Socialist Redistributive Econ-omies', *International Journal of Comparative Sociology*, vol. 19, no. 1–2 (March –June) pp. 63–87.

Szubert, Wacław (1979) 'Przedmiot, geneza i zakres socjalistycznej polityki społecznej', in Antoni Rajkiewicz (ed.), *Polityka społeczna* (Warsaw: PWE).

Talbott, Strobe (ed.) (1976) *Khrushchev Remembers: The Last Testament* (New York: Bantam).

Tarkowski, Jacek (1983) 'Władze terenowe po reformie', in Jerzy Wiatr (ed.), *Władza lokalna u progu kryzysu* (Warsaw).

Taubman, William (1974) 'The Change to Change in Communist Systems: Modern-ization, Post-modernization and Soviet Politics', in Morton and Tokes (1974).

Teague, Elizabeth (1983) In Radio Liberty Research Report, RL 109/83.

Teiwes, Frederick (1979) *Politics and Purges in China. Rectification and the Decline of Party Norms, 1950–1965* (White Plains NY: M. E. Sharpe).

Terry, Sarah M. (1979) 'The Case for a "Group" Approach to Polish Politics: Comment', *Studies in Comparative Communism*, vol. 12, no. 1 (spring) pp. 28–34.

—— (1981) 'The Sejm as Symbol: Recent Polish Attitudes Toward Political Participation', in Simon and Kanet 1981.

Tesis y Resoluciones: Primer Congreso del Partido Comunista de Cuba (1976) (La Habana: Departamento de Orientacion Revolucionario).

Thornton, Richard (1972) 'The Structure of Communist Politics', *World Politics*, vol. 24, no. 4 (July) pp. 498–517.

Thurow, Lester C. (1975) 'Equity Concepts and the World of Work', *American Behavioral Scientist*, vol. 18, no. 3 (January–February) pp. 387–99.

Tismeau, Leonte and Zaharia Rolica (1977) *Present and Prospect in Romania's Social and Economic Development* (Bucharest: Meridiane).

Tokes, Rudolf L. (ed.) (1975) *Dissent in the USSR: Politics, Ideology and People* (Baltimore and London: Johns Hopkins University Press).

Toma, Peter A. and Ivan Volgyes (1977) *Politics in Hungary* (San Francisco: W. H. Freeman).

Toporkov, Stepan (1972) 'Worker is a Proud Title', *Izvestiya*, 12 December.

Touraine, Alain *et al.* (1983) *Solidarity: The Analysis of a Social Movement* (Cambridge: Cambridge University Press).

Triska, Jan and Charles Gati (eds) (1981) *Blue-Collar Workers in Eastern Europe* (London: Allen & Unwin).

Triska, Jan and Paul Johnson (eds) (1975) *Political Development and Political Change in Eastern Europe: A Comparative Study* (Denver, Col.: GSIS Monographs).

Triska, Jan and Paul Cocks (eds) (1977) *Political Development in Eastern Europe* (New York: Praeger).

Truman, David (1951) *The Governmental Process, Political Interests and Public Opinion* (New York: Knopf).

Tucker, Robert C. (1961) 'Towards a Comparative Politics of Movement-regimes', *American Political Science Review*, vol. 55, no. 2 (June) pp. 281–90.

—— (1973) 'Culture, Political Culture, and Communist Society', *Political Science Quarterly*, vol. 88, no. 2 (June) pp. 173–90.

—— (ed.) (1977) *Stalinism: Essays in Historical Interpretation* (New York: Norton).

Tymowski, Andrzej (1981) *The Strike in Gdansk, August 14–31, 1980* (New Haven, Conn: Don't Hold Back).

Uibopuu, Henn-Juri (1979) 'The Individual in Soviet Administrative Procedure', in Barry (1977–9) vol. 3.

Ulicki, Włodzimierz (1980) *Partia a Sejm w PRL* (Warsaw: Krajowa Agencja Wydawnicza).

Unger, Aryeh L. (1977) 'Soviet Communist Party Membership under Brezhnev: a Comment'. *Soviet Studies*, vol. 29, no. 2 (April) pp. 306–16.

—— (1981) *Constitutional Development in the USSR* (London: Methuen).

United Nations (1967) *Economic Survey of Europe in 1965*, Part 2 (Geneva: United Nations Economic Commission for Europe).

United States. Bureau of the Census (Various years) *Statistical Abstracts of the United States* (Washington DC: US Government Publishing Office).

—— Central Intelligence Agency. (1977) *Directory of Officials of the Polish People's Republic* (Washington DC: US Government Publishing Office).

—— Congress. *Country Reports* (1982) *Country Reports on Human Rights Practices for 1981*. (Washington, DC: US Government Publishing Office).

Urquhart, M. C. and A. H. Buckley (1965) *Historical Statistics of Canada* (Cambridge: Cambridge University Press).

Ustav (various dates) *Ustav Kommunisticheskoi Partii Sovetskogo Soyuza* (Moscow: Izdatel'stvo politicheskoi literatury).

Vali, F. A. (1962) *Rift and Revolt in Hungary*. (Cambridge, Mass.: Harvard University Press).

Vanneman, Peter (1977) *The Supreme Soviet: Politics and the Legislative Process in the Soviet Political System* (Durham NC: Duke University Press).

Vedomosti (various dates) *Vedomosti Verkhovnogo Soveta SSSR.* (Moscow: Izvestiya).

Von Beyme, Klaus (1982) *Economics and Politics within Socialist Systems* (New York: Praeger).

Voslensky, Michael (1984) *Nomenklatura. Anatomy of the Soviet Ruling Class* (London: Bodley Head).

Voznesensky, L. A. (1971) 'Ekonomika i politika, ikh vzaimodeistvie v sotsialisticheskom obshchestve', in *Voprosy ekonomicheskoi politiki KPSS na sovremennom etape* (Moscow: Politizdat).

Vucinich, Wayne S. (ed.) (1969) *Contemporary Yugoslavia. Twenty Years of the Yugoslav Experiment* (Berkeley: University of California Press).

Wagener, Hans-Jurgen (1973) 'Rules of Location and the Concept of Rationality: the Case of the USSR', in V. N. Bandera and Z. I. Melnyk (1973).

Wajda, Augustyn (ed.) (1979) *Klasa robotnicza w społeczenstwie socjalistycznym* (Warsaw: Ksiazka i wiedza).

Walker, R. L. (1980) 'PRC under Teng: Back to Leninist Organisation', *Issues and Studies*, vol. 16, no. 8 (August) pp. 12–25.

Waller, Derek J. (1973) 'The Chinese Communist Political Elite: Continuity and Innovation', in Carl Beck *et al.* (eds), *Comparative Communist Political Leadership* (New York: David McKay).

Waller, Michael (1979) 'Problems of Comparative Communism', *Studies in Comparative Communism*, vol. 12, no. 2–3 (summer–autumn) pp. 107–32.

—— (1981) *Democratic Centralism* (Manchester: Manchester University Press).

—— (1982) 'A Movement is a Movement', *Communist Affairs*, vol. 1, no. 1 (January) pp. 40–4.

Weintraub, Zissu (1973) 'Motivational Indicators for Professional Integration', in Badina and Mamali (1973).

Welsh, William. (1973) 'Introduction: the Comparative Study of Political Leadership in Communist Systems', in Carl Beck *et al.* (eds), *Comparative Communist Political Leadership* (New York: David McKay).

—— (ed.) (1981) *Survey Research and Public Attitudes in Eastern Europe and the Soviet Union* (New York: Praeger).

Whetten, Lawrence (1976) *Current Research in Comparative Communism: An Analysis and Bibliographic Guide to the Soviet System* (New York: Praeger).

White, Gordon (1982) 'The New Course in Chinese Development Strategy: Context, Problems and Prospects', in Gray and White (1982).

—— (1983) 'The Post-revolutionary Chinese State: Dictatorship, Democracy and the Distribution of Power', in Nee and Mozingo (1983) pp. 27–52.

White, Stephen (1979) *Political Culture and Soviet Politics* (London: Macmillan).

—— (1980) 'The USSR Supreme Soviet: a Development Perspective', *Legislative Studies Quarterly*, vol. 5, no. 2 (May) pp. 247–74.

—— (1982) 'The USSR Supreme Soviet: a Developmental Perspective', in Nelson and White (1982).

—— (1983a) 'Political Communications in the USSR: Letters to Party, State and the Press', *Political Studies*, vol. 31, no. 1 (January) pp. 43–60.

—— (1983b) 'What is a Communist System?', *Studies in Comparative Communism*, vol. 16, no. 4 (winter) pp. 247–63.

—— (Forthcoming) 'Noncompetitive Elections and National Politics: the USSR Supreme Soviet Elections of March 1984', *Electoral Studies*, vol. 4 no. 3 (1985).

White, Stephen, John Gardner and George Schopflin (1982) *Communist Political Systems: An Introduction* (London: Macmillan and New York: St. Martin's).

Whyte, Martin K. (1975) 'Inequality and Stratification in China', *China Quarterly*, no. 64 (December) pp. 684–711.

Wiatr, Jerzy (1959) 'Niekotore zagadnienia opinii publiczne w swietle Wyborow 1957 i 1958', *Studia socjologiczno-politiczyne*, no. 4, pp. 1–214.
_____ (1962) 'Elections and Voting Behavior in Poland', in Ranney (1962).
_____ (1978) *Essays in Political Sociology* (Warsaw: Ossolineum).
Wightman, Gordon and Archie Brown (1975) 'Changes in the Levels of Membership and National and Social Composition of the Communist Party of Czechoslovakia, 1945–73'. *Soviet Studies*, vol. 27, no. 3 (July) pp. 396–417.
Wilczynski, Jozef (1972) *Socialist Economic Development and Reform* (London: Macmillan).
Wildavsky, Aaron (1975) *Budgeting: A Comparative Theory of Budgetary Processes* (Boston: Little, Brown).
_____ (1979) *The Politics of the Budgetary Process*, 3rd ed. (Boston: Little, Brown).
Wilensky, Harold L. (1975) *The Welfare State and Equality. Structural and Ideological Roots of Public Expenditure* (Berkeley: University of California Press).
Wiles, Peter (1974) *Distribution of Income: East and West* (Amsterdam: North-Holland).
_____ (1975) 'Recent Data on Soviet Income Distribution', *Survey*, vol. 21, no. 3 (summer) pp. 28–41.
Wiles, Peter and Stefan Markowski (1971) 'Income Distribution Under Communism and Capitalism. Some Facts about Poland, the UK, the USA, and the USSR', *Soviet Studies*, vol. 22, nos 3 and 4 (January and April) pp. 344–69 and 487–511.
Willerton, J. P. (1979) 'Clientelism in the Soviet Union: an Initial Examination', *Studies in Comparative Communism*, vol. 12, nos 2–3 (summer–autumn) pp. 159–83.
Williams, Raymond (1975) 'You're a Marxist, Aren't You?', in Bhiku Parekh (ed.), *The Concept of Socialism* (London: Croom Helm).
Wolchik, Sharon (1978) 'Women's Equality in Communist and Capitalist Countries'. Paper presented at the American Political Science Association Convention, New York.
_____ (1979) 'The Status of Women in a Socialist Order: Czechoslovakia, 1948–1975', *Slavic Review*, vol. 38, no. 4 (December) pp. 583–602.
Woodall, Jean (1981) 'New Social Factors in the Unrest in Poland', *Government and Opposition*, vol. 16, no. 1 (winter) pp. 37–57.
Wortman, Richard (1980) 'The Autocracy and Interests, 1861–1905'. Paper presented to the American Historical Association Convention, Washington DC.
XXIII [etc.] *S"ezd KPSS* (various dates) (Moscow: Politizdat).
Yakir, P. I. and Yu. A. Geller (1963) *Komandarm Yakir* (Moscow: Voennoe izdatel'stvo).
Young, Graham (1980) 'Non-revolutionary Vanguard: the Transformation of the Chinese Communist Party', in Bill Brugger (ed.), *China since the Gang of Four* (London: Croom Helm).
Zabigailo, V. (1978) 'The Modern State: Growing Law-making Functions', in *The Development of Soviet Law and Jurisprudence* (Moscow: Progress).
Zakon SSSR o vyborakh (1978) *Zakon SSSR o vyborakh v Verkhovnyi Sovet SSSR* (Moscow: Yuridicheskaya literatura).
Zaninovich, M. George (1968) *The Development of Socialist Yugoslavia* (Baltimore: Johns Hopkins University Press).
Zasedaniya (various years) *Zasedaniya Verkhovnogo Soveta SSSR: stenograficheskii otchet* (Moscow: Izvestiya).
Zaslavsky, Victor and Robert Brym (1978) 'The functions of elections in the USSR', *Soviet Studies*, vol. 30, no. 3 (July) pp. 362–71.

_____ (1983) 'The Structure of Power and the Functions of Soviet Local Elections', in Jacobs (1983).

Zawadski, Sylwester (1976) 'Z doswiadczen Sejmu w okresie 30-lecie Polskiej Ludowej', *Studia Juridica*, vol. 4, pp. 9–26.

_____ (1980a) *Z teorii i praktyki demokracji socjalistycznej: wybor artykulow* (Warsaw: Ksizka i wiedza).

_____ (1980b) 'Demokracja socjalistyczna–cele, kierunki, zadania', *Nowe Drogi*, no. 4 (April) pp. 65–75.

_____ (1980c) 'Funcja kontrolna Sejmu PRL', *Ruch Prawniczy, Ekonomiczny i Socjologiczny*, vol. 42, no. 1, pp. 15–38.

_____ (1980d) 'Polish parliamentarismism', *Contemporary Poland*, vol. 14 (March) pp. 5–12.

Zimmerman, Hartmut (1978) 'The GDR in the 1970s', *Problems of Communism*, vol. 27, no. 2 (March–April) pp. 1–40.

Zinner, Paul E. (1963) *Communist Strategy and Tactics in Czechoslovakia 1918–48* (London: Pall Mall).

Zverev, A. G. (1973) *Zapiski ministra* (Moscow: Politizdat).

Zwick, Peter (1979) 'Ethnoregional socio-economic fragmentation and Soviet budgetary policy', *Soviet Studies*, vol. 31, no. 3 (July) pp. 380–400.

Index

411